KINGDOMS of ASIA the MIDDLE EAST and AFRICA

Other Books by Gene Gurney

AGRICULTURE CAREERS

THE AIR FORCE MUSEUM

AMERICAN HISTORY IN WAX MUSEUMS

AMERICANS INTO ORBIT

AMERICANS TO THE MOON

ARLINGTON NATIONAL CEMETERY

BEAUTIFUL WASHINGTON, D.C.

THE B-29 STORY

CHRONOLOGY OF WORLD AVIATION

COSMONAUTS IN ORBIT

EDUCATIONAL GUIDE TO U.S. SERVICE AND MARITIME ACADEMIES

FIVE DOWN AND GLORY

FLYING ACES OF WORLD WAR I

FLYING MINUTEMEN—THE STORY OF THE CIVIL AIR PATROL

GREAT AIR BATTLES

HANDBOOK FOR SUCCESSFUL FRANCHISING

HIGHER, FASTER AND FARTHER

HOW TO SAVE YOUR LIFE ON THE NATION'S HIGHWAYS AND BYWAYS

THE JEEP: IN PEACE AND WAR

JOURNEY OF THE GIANTS

KINGDOMS OF EUROPE

THE LIBRARY OF CONGRESS

MARYLAND

MONTICELLO

MOUNT VERNON

NORTH AND SOUTH KOREA

THE OFFICIAL WASHINGTON, D.C., DIRECTORY

THE PENTAGON

THE PICTORIAL HISTORY OF THE U.S. ARMY

PILOT'S HANDBOOK OF NAVIGATION

PILOT'S HANDBOOK OF WEATHER

THE P-38 LIGHTNING

ROCKET AND MISSILE TECHNOLOGY

THE SMITHSONIAN INSTITUTION

SPACE TECHNOLOGY SPINOFFS

TEST PILOTS

UNIDENTIFIED FLYING OBJECTS

THE UNITED STATES COAST GUARD

VIETNAM—THE WAR IN THE AIR

WALK IN SPACE - THE STORY OF PROJECT GEMINI

THE WAR IN THE AIR - WW II

WOMEN ON THE MARCH

KINGDOMS of ASIA the MIDDLE EAST and AFRICA

An Illustrated Encyclopedia of Ruling Monarchs from Ancient Times to the Present

Gene Gurney

Crown Publishers, Inc. • New York

Book design by Deborah and Richard Waxberg

Library of Congress Cataloging in Publication Data
Gurney, Gene.
Kingdoms of Asia, the Middle East, and Africa
1. Asia—Kings and rulers—Biography. 2. Near East—Kings and
rulers—Biography. 3. Africa—Kings and rulers—Biography. 4.
Asia—History. 5. Near East—History. 6. Africa—History. 7.
Monarchy—History. I. Title.
DS32.G87 1986 909'.09811 84-4270
ISBN 0-517-55256-6

10 9 8 7 6 5 4 3 2 1

First Edition

Contents

APPENDIX

Acknowledgments

The text for this book was mainly derived from three sources: the U.S. Army *Area Handbooks*, Francis R. Niglutsch's publications *The Story of the Greatest Nations*, and the U.S. Department of State's *Background Notes* publications on the countries of the world. The first, started by the War Department in World War II, were published by Alfred A. Knopf and served as a definitive study of the various foreign nations with which the United States was engaged in that war. Later, the research, writing, and publication was taken over for the Department of the Army by the Foreign Area Studies of the American University in Washington, D.C. The individual publications for the foreign countries were than called *Area Handbooks* and were made available to all armed forces and government personnel concerned with obtaining the best possible information about nations around the world. *The Story of the Greatest Nations* is probably the most comprehensive history about foreign nations ever written in the United States. (Additional important works I consulted were: Ridpath's *History of the World*, Henry Smith Williams's *Historians' History of the World*, and Henry Cabot Lodge's twenty-five volumes of *History of Nations*.) The third primary source was the U.S. State Department's *Background Notes*, which are published—and updated frequently—as a political science and historical aid for its personnel around the world.

The lists of the four thousand some royal sovereigns covered in this book were compiled from various sources, mainly, *Kings, Rulers and Statesmen* by L. F. Egan, *Rulers and Governments of the World* by Bertold Spuler, and Burke's *Royal Families of the World*. Where my lists differ from these are in the spellings, dates, and so forth, where the individual country's embassy, or government's historical records showed better evidence of the information.

For the photographs and illustrations, I have special thanks for the many sources who helped me acquire the "pictures" for the book. Bibliothèque Nationale, Paris, has, in my estimation, the greatest collection of royalty illustrations in the entire world. Also, the special collections at the New York Public Library, Cleveland Public Library, George Mason University, Fairfax, Virginia, and the Newark (New Jersey) Public Library are quite extensive: my thanks to all. The next category would be the individual foreign embassies in Washington, D.C., who were an endless source for acquiring from their countries, all of the information and photographs that I needed to write and illustrate this book. And, last but not least, the United Nations Information Service-Photo Section in New York City and the White House Public Affairs Office.

I welcome any comments or questions and hope to incorporate them into the next edition of the book, as I have with the *Kingdoms of Europe*.

Gene Gurney
Wash., D.C. 20044-7206

KINGDOMS of ASIA the MIDDLE EAST and AFRICA

I

The Dynasties and Kingdom of Egypt

The history of Egypt is marked by a sharp distinction between rulers and ruled that prevailed from the time of the Egyptian pharaoh-gods through the entire span of foreign domination up to the 1952 revolution which ended Egypt's monarchism (King Farouk I).

The constriction of the Nile River and its delta between sea and desert brought about in ancient times a homogeneous Egyptian people characterized by the hard-working, impoverished, apolitical agricultural peasant, or *fellah*. Location of the country at the land and sea junction of three continents facilitated eras of outward expansion and also foreign incursion. Despite conquests by foreign powers, the influence of Islam commencing in the seventh century A.D., the three-century reign of the Ottoman Turks, and the European influence of the nineteenth century, the Egpytian people retained their ethnic homogeneity.

As a unified state, Egypt has endured more than five thousand years; in fact, archaeological evidence indicates information of even earlier spans. Conscious of their nation's uninterrupted identity, modern Egyptian leaders have called upon the people to take pride in their heritage and in their claim as descendants of mankind's earliest civilized community. (The Arabic word for "Egypt" is *misr,* which means "to civilize, to become a populated area.")

Foreign control of Egypt commenced in 525 B.C. with the Persian conquest and continued almost uninterrupted for about twenty-five hundred years. From the last Egyptian pharaoh, or king, to Mohammed Naguib in 1952, no native Egyptian was head of state.

From the most ancient times, religion was a major influence in the lives of the Egyptians. In the pharaonic period the vast array of nature and animal gods reflected the close relationship of the people with the Nile. Society was devoted to the service of the pharaoh, who "owned" the country and was regarded as a god. He held absolute authority. Strong concepts of spirit life and immortality prevailed.

Christianity was accepted by about two-thirds of the population during the first six centuries of the Christian

The official portrait of King Farouk I

A 1949 postage stamp commemorating the centenary of the death of Mohammed Ali.

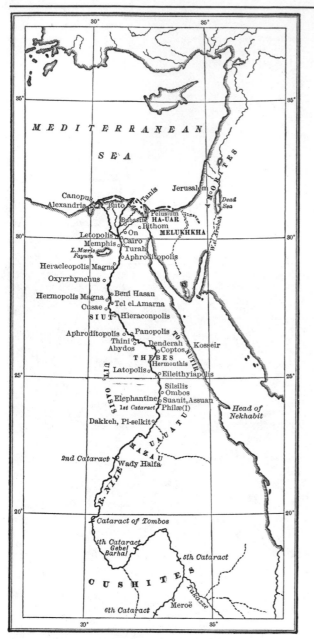

Ancient and modern Egyptian cities are depicted on this map.

reinforced by the old pharaonic religion. This fatalistic outlook is embodied in the Arabic expression *"In Sha' Allah"* (If it be God's will).

In attempting to build a new Egypt, the government of the Republic established by the Revolutionary Command Council, which seized power on July 23, 1952, was confronted with the background of these persistent factors in the nation's history. The magnitude of the task that the new government set by its broad objectives of modernization and industrialization was such as to require a transformation of the society.

ORIGINS OF THE PEOPLE

Archaeological findings show that primitive people lived along the Nile River long before the dynastic history of the pharaoh began. Where they came from is not certain. Authorities regard multiple places of origin as more probable, with the Nile Valley, in the prehistoric era, receiving numerous accretions of people of varying culture and life patterns.

Similarly, northern Sinai provided a route for incoming peoples from Asia, in particular from Mesopotamia and the intermediate region that became known as Syria and Palestine. In Upper Egypt predynastic peoples from farther south were of Nubian African stock.

By 6000 B.C. the Nile Valley was the scene of a Neolithic, or New Stone Age, culture marked by the characteristic elements of settled village life: pottery, agriculture, and raising domestic animals. Mediterranean and Nubian African sources were fused to form the distinctive Egyptian type as seen at the start of the historic era. The Egyptian peasant of modern times is anthropologically recognizable as a descendant of the farmers who paid grain tax to the pharaohs. Later elements—the Asian Hyksos, Assyrians, Ethiopians, Alexandrine Greeks, Romans, Byzantines, Arabs, Turks, Albanians, Circassians, French, and British—left their impression on the nation's history. However, coming as conquerors or members of privileged groups, they remained ethnically separate from the native Egyptians whom they ruled.

How have we come to know Egyptian history? Herodotus the Greek went to Egypt about the year 418 B.C. and the Egyptian priests laughed at him because his nation "had no history,"—that is, its history only extended back in a rather hazy fashion some seven centuries. So Herodotus sat himself down at the feet of these men, who filled him full of their own history; and he wrote it all down. What was true and what was false the priests themselves probably did not know.

Only one writer added much to Herodotus. This was Manetho, an Egyptian priest of the third century B.C. He wrote a history of Egypt, but only a few fragments have been preserved. So at the beginning of the nineteenth century little of ancient Egypt was known beyond the writings of Herodotus. The land itself was covered with stone carv-

Era, but after the Arab conquest in the seventh century most of the people yielded to Islam. Among the *fellahin* substantial traces of the animistic spirits lore and supernatural beliefs were carried over into Islam, which became a stabilizing, conservative influence.

Until the second half of the twentieth century, society was characterized by a political, economic, and cultural gap between rulers and ruled. In the Pharaonic era the *fellahin* were an important part of the social order. They appear to have accepted the ruler's role as having been ordained by the gods, but, at least their rulers during this era were Egyptians. Political communication and mutual responsiveness did not exist between the elite and the *fellahin*. The *fellah* was not led to expect more from life than had traditionally been his lot. This essential conservatism was

ings, hieroglyphics meant to tell its story; but little of it could be read by scholars.

ANCIENT EGYPT: THE PHARAOHS

By 3500 B.C. the many separate tribes living in the Nile Valley had coalesced into the kingdoms of Upper and Lower Egypt, ruled by predynastic kings.

About 3200 B.C., Upper and Lower Egypt were united under the ruler Menes, or Mena, as recorded in the fifth century B.C. by Herodotus. Menes has been identified as a king of Upper Egypt, recorded elsewhere under another name—Narmer—whose seat was at Nekhen, or Hierakonpolis, on the Nile about eighty miles south of Qena. After bringing the northern kingdom under his control, Menes ruled from Memphis, about fifteen miles south of modern Cairo, where the capital remained throughout the Old Kingdom period. Menes' rule was the first of the thirty-one pharaonic dynasties in Egyptian history. It is worth noting that the word *pharaoh* did not refer to a single person, but was applied to each ruler, no matter what his name, thus the basis for the word *king*.

For centuries, learned men considered Menes an imaginary ruler. His name was thought to be an eponym: the people of Memphis, having no record of who built their city, invented a builder from the city's name and declared it to be the work of a king named Menes, or Memphes. However, the learned men of old were wrong, for in 1897, the tomb of Menes was found, with many interesting relics of Menes and his descendants. He is the most ancient man whose name has come down to us from his own time. The name of the first created man seems to have been long forgotten; and then God told it again as a special revelation to Moses, about the year 1500 B.C. It was probably earlier than 5000 B.C. that this man Menes lived. His name stands today, carved in the rock as he ordered it.

Napoleon Bonaparte led an expedition into Egypt in 1798. In August 1799, while digging the foundations of a fort near the Rosetta section of the mouth of the Nile, one of his engineering officers came upon a stone tablet some three feet by two feet on which was an inscription in three different alphabets. The bottom inscription was in Greek, so it was easy to translate. It was found to be an ordinance of the priests ordering certain honors to an Egyptian sovereign on the occasion of his coronation, 196 B.C. It commanded that the three decrees should be inscribed in the sacred letters—hieroglyphics, in the letters of the country, or demotic, and in Greek letters. This was for the convenience of the mixed population.

Obviously, the Rosetta stone was a valuable find for scholars who, after a time, succeeded in unraveling the alphabet of the hieroglyphics. This allowed the carvings to be understood, which threw a flood of light on the ancient history of Egypt.

The mace head of King Scorpion, First Dynasty. The pharaoh is wearing the Northern Crown, which depicts his victory over the North. He is seen here, hoe in hand, directing the construction of canals and dikes around the Nile. The king wanted to be known for his early efforts in controlling the Nile for cultivation.

Left: *Ip (the Scorpion) is considered by the expert historians to be the earliest ruler of the First Dynasty in Egypt, 3400–3200 B.C.* Center: *His successor, Narmer, was a warrior who is known to have defeated the Libyans. These two kings, along with Aha Men,* right, *brought a united Egypt out of the upper and lower Nile separate territories and probably in combination became the traditional first king—Menes.*

The palette of ruler Narmer, First Dynasty

A statuette of King Menes
of the First Dynasty

An Egyptian princess hunting on the Nile in the days when the royal
families gave the leadership to the people and the women were considered
equals in all endeavors except combat

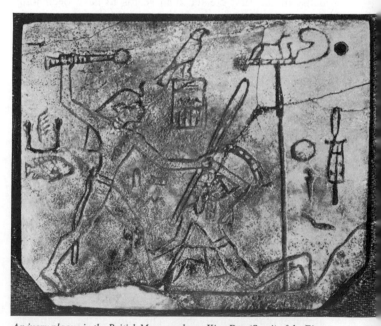

An ivory plaque in the British Museum shows King Den (Senti) of the First
Dynasty, smiting a Libyan with his mace. This is one of a group of tablets
that shows the beginning of historical records in Egypt.

Ten of the more famous Egyptian rulers are illustrated here in the various headdress crowns of the period. Left column, top to bottom: *Aahmes Nefertari (New Kingdom), Ptolemy IX, Euergetas II, Amenhotep III, and Seti I (Sethos).* Center, top: *Thotmes I.* Center, middle: *Rameses III.* Right columns, top to bottom: *Aksinoe II, Philadelphus, Cleopatra II, and Mutemua.*

The one major problem with Egyptian history is that the Egyptians have had no regular system of chronology. They did not date all of their history from one great event, as we do from the birth of Christ. Rather, each new king, apparently in compliment to himself, began counting again, and events were dated according to the year of the king's reign. Although a fairly complete list of Egyptian kings exists, it is no easy matter to determine the dates of their reigns. For example, Herodotus, adding the years of all previous reigns, placed Menes in the year 12,000 B.C., while another writer placed Menes at 16,492 B.C. The fragments of Manetho, and later the hieroglyphics themselves, indicate that these dates were absurd. But even recently scientists have disagreed to the extent of over three thousand years: one authority placed Menes' date at 5702 B.C., while another put it at 2691. Also, many of the kings—even whole families of them—appear to have been contemporaneous. A father would associate his son with him on the throne, or one family might rule in Memphis while another was ruling at Thebes. Within the last decade, 2700 B.C. has been abandoned as obviously far too late a date; and now, with the discovery of the tomb of the old king, we are inclined to place him not far from 3200 B.C. We can be reasonably certain that 3400 to 3200 B.C. is not too ancient a period for the establishment of his empire. These are the dates historians at the National Egyptian Museum in Cairo use—3400 to 3200.

Menes appears to have been a hereditary king of the district around Abydos in Upper Egypt. But he was not buried there, his tomb being on the edge of the desert twenty miles beyond Thebes, at the southern boundary of his dominion. The tomb is not at all like the stone sepulchers of the later kings. Wall after wall of brick was built around and above Menes' body.

Menes was a great builder; but, even before he'd managed to get the area he wanted for his capital, he'd erected a huge dam that changed the entire course of the lower Nile. Its old channel can still be traced, close under the western cliffs of the valley, some miles from where it now flows. Menes reigned for sixty-two years, and then fell, it is recorded, in combat with a hippopotamus. Whether the hippopotamus is to be taken literally is debatable, for the

The Egyptians in battle with the Ethiopians about 700 B.C.

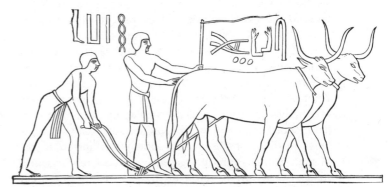

Egyptians plowing along the Nile, from a bas-relief of the Memphite Dynasty period

The Rosetta stone on display in the British Museum in London

A close-up of the Rosetta tablet

hippopotamus was the Egyptian symbol for a foreign foe. Perhaps Menes died, not in sports activity or hunting, but in defending the empire he had created.

Athothis, the second king of this dynasty, who is believed to have built the citadel and palace of Memphis, was a physician. Fragments of a work on anatomy by him have been uncovered. Little is known of the third king, Kenkenes, but the first famine in Egyptian history happened during the reign of Uenestes, the fourth king, to whom belongs the glory of building, at Kochome, the first pyramid.

Undoubtedly, the most brilliant era in the history of Egypt was that of the building of the pyramids. The government was consolidated and powerful. The population had so increased by that time that the lives of thousands of workmen were risked during the Nile flooding to fulfill the building dreams of the ruler. On the plateau west of Memphis nearly seventy of these fantastic monuments were erected. The three most famous—because of their enormous size—are known as the pyramids of Gizeh.

The greatest of all, the Great Pyramid, is the pyramid of Khufu, founder of the Fourth Dynasty. The pyramid was originally 480 feet high, but the weathering away of its apex has reduced it some 30 feet. Each side of the base is 764 feet long, and the vast pile contains about 90 million cubic feet of masonry, covering thirteen acres. The Great Pyramid stands exactly on the thirtieth parallel of latitude, and the four sides face the cardinal points of the compass with geometric accuracy. On the north side, in the very middle,

52 feet above the original ground level, a door is cut, opening a passage 3 feet wide and 4 feet high. This leads downward to a burial chamber hewn in the rock of the foundation, 100 feet below the ground level of the base. This chamber is located directly under the apex of the pyramid and precisely 600 feet below. Two other burial chambers lie directly above it. Within each grave the stone coffin of the king was placed. On the walls above each grave the story of the king's life was carved. The door of the passage was sealed with a stone and the name of the dead monarch was added to the list of the gods of the time.

The pyramids form one of the Seven Wonders of the World, and how they were built is a problem that even in these modern days it is hard to solve. There is no machine or apparatus in existence today powerful enough to raise those colossal-sized stones to their correct places in the monument. It has been suggested that they were molded in their position by chemical means from the sands of the desert, but the marks of the machinery used in building the pyramids are still distinctly visible. It is calculated that 360,000 men were employed for twenty years in building the Great Pyramid.

The second pyramid resembles in form and interior the largest. It was originally 457 feet in height, while the third,

The Egyptian ancient alphabet. For some two thousand years the Egyptian language was a dead language in the fullest sense of the term, and the records, locked imperishably in the hieroglyphics, seemed likely to hold their mysterious secret from the prying minds of all generations of men. But then, in the early days of the nineteenth century, the key was unexpectedly found, to the delight of the scholarly world. This came about through a study of the famous Rosetta stone, an Egyptian monument now preserved in the British Museum. On this stone three sets of inscriptions are recorded. The upper one, occupying about a fourth of the surface, is a pictured scroll, made up of chains of those strange outlines of serpents, hawks, lions, and so on, which are recognized, even by the least initiated, as hieroglyphics. The middle inscription, made up of lines, angles, and half-pictures, one might suppose to be a sort of abbreviated or shorthand hieroglyphic. It is called the enchorial or demotic character. The third, or lower, inscription is manifestly Greek. It is now known that these three inscriptions are renderings of the same message, and that this message is a "decree of the Priests of Memphis conferring divine honors on Ptolemy V, Epiphanes, King of Egypt, 195 B.C.

"This stone was found by the French in 1798 among the ruins of Fort St. Julian, near the Rosetta mouth of the Nile. It passed into the hands of the British by the treaty of Alexandria, and was deposited in the British Museum in the year 1801."

The value of the Rosetta stone depended on the fact that it gave promise, even when originally inspected, of furnishing a key to the centuries-old mystery of the hieroglyphics. For two thousand years the secret of these strange markings had been forgotten. Nowhere in the world—quite as little in Egypt as elsewhere—had anyone the slightest clue to their meaning; there were even those who doubted whether these droll picturings really had any specific meaning, questioning whether they were not merely vague symbols of esoteric religious import and nothing more. And it was the Rosetta stone that gave the answer to these doubters, and restored to the world a lost language and a forgotten literature.

Zeser, the son of Khasekhemui Besh who founded the Third Dynasty, is considered by authorities to be one of the most important Egyptian kings. An indication of his stature is the fact that he built the first pyramid (at Sakkara).

An		Mu		Am			
Âu		Na		Ar			
'Au		Na		As			
Ba		Nu		Âk			
Ba		Pa		Hk			
Bu		Pu		Rn			
Fi		Ra		Hr			
Zi		Ru		Km			
Ha		Sa		Kr			
Ha		Su		Mh			
H'a		Su		Mr			
Nu		Su		Nfr			
Iu		Ta		Nn			
Iu		Tu		Pr			
Iu		Ua		Sb			
I		Ui		Sb			
I		Ui		Ts			
Ka		Kh'a		Uh			
Ka		Khi		Ur			
Ka		Shâ		Shm			
K'u		Sha		Sh'n			
Ma		Shi		Sh'b			
Ma		Shu		Kh'pr			
Ma				Khu			

Two of the three famous pyramids of Gizeh and the Sphinx near Cairo. The pyramid, left, was the burial place of King Khafre and, right, that of King Khufu. The head of the Sphinx represents King Khafre. Both were of the Fourth Dynasty.

King Khafre, Fourth Dynasty. A sphinx statue of the king, who was the builder of the second pyramid of Gizeh, was found in the temple in front of his pyramid. Perched behind his head is the god Horus protecting the king with his wings.

Little is known of King Khufu and King Khafre, but historians calculate that from the size and magnificence of their tombs they were of wealthy, war-free dynasties and that they were absolute monarchs.

Khufu constructing, along with his multitude of workers, his pyramid

The great king Menkure, seen here with his wife, for whom the third pyramid at Gizeh was built. The smallness of it suggests that the wealth of the pharaohs was running out.

but 233 feet high, was built by a fourth or fifth king of the Fourth Dynasty. With this dynasty authentic Egyptian history began. Its kings were distinguished for military achievements and architectural grandeur. Khufu, the first of them, conquered Ethiopia, while Khafre built the Sphinx, which stands north of the second pyramid of Gizeh. It is hewn out of solid rock, has the body of a crouching lion and the head of a man, capped and bearded. It is 190 feet in length, and between the paws, extended forward for fifty feet, is a monumental stone with the name of Khafre carved on it. The width of the shoulders is 36 feet and the head from top to chin is 28½ feet.

The closing years of the Fourth Dynasty showed a decline in the political power of Egypt, and the Fifth Dynasty, composed of nine reigns, gave little to the world that is worthy of record. The kings of the Sixth Dynasty belonged to a family from a small island in the Nile known as Elephantis, in Upper Egypt. This epoch saw the beginning of foreign wars of conquest and the decline of art. The Egyptian dominion was carried far into the Syrian and Arabian deserts and Nubia was conquered. The most won-

A sphinx (human head and lion's body) represents King Amenemhet III, the great successor to Sesostris III. He was as prominent in peace as Sesostris III was in war. He was buried in a temple in Hawara (the Labyrinth). This statue was later moved by the Hyksos kings to their capital at Tanis (Twelfth Dynasty).

derful and almost incredible statement regarding the Sixth Dynasty is that King Pepi II, ascending the throne at the age of six, held it for *ninety-five years!* During that marvelous reign Egyptian conquests and Egyptian dominion were extended to the Red Sea and the cataracts of the Nile. The king founded in Middle Egypt the "City of Pepi," whose site has been lost, and built one of the great pyramids of Sakkara for his tomb.

Under his successor, his son Meren-Ra II, Ethiopia became a tributary province, and the copper mines of Arabia and of the peninsula of Sinai were opened and developed. Then several rulers followed of whom little is known, but Manetho states that Dynasties Seven and Eight belonged to the Memphian line, while the following two were in a Heracleopolitan family, some of whom were probably contemporaneous in Upper and Middle Egypt. Little is known of the dynasties between the Eighth and Twelfth.

The Twelfth Dynasty, extending from 2000 to 1788 B.C., was introduced by Amenemhet I, during whose reign Egyptian dominion extended from the Red Sea to the western desert. This was a memorable period in the history of the country. Many canals were constructed for irrigation, and the civil administration of the various governors improved, while sculpture, architecture, and the building of monumental tombs were extensively revived.

Under Sesostris I, the next king, Egypt attained a glory and magnificence unequaled since the downfall of the Fourth Dynasty. Sesostris' two successors followed his policy, and the next king, Sesostris III, had the most glorious reign of all. The boundary was fixed beyond the second Nile cataract, where forts and outposts were built and stone tablets set up defining the limits of the kingdom. The engineering works were extraordinary. Through the hills the engineers constructed a canal which led the waters of the Nile into the valley of Fayum, where the supply from the annual inundation formed an artificial lake. Thus by the distribution of the water, which was well stocked with fish, a large area of country was turned into a luxuriant garden.

But most amazing of all was the national temple known as the Labyrinth, erected near the entrance of the canal into the lake. Herodotus, who examined it, was astounded and declared that all the temples of the Greeks put together did not equal it in cost and splendor. It contained twelve roofed courts joining one another, with opposite entrances, six facing the north and six the south, the whole being enclosed by an immense wall. One-half the temple was above and one-half below ground, and each division contained fifteen hundred apartments. Those below ground were the sepulchers of the kings and the halls of the sacred crocodiles.

Herodotus was allowed to visit the aboveground apartments but not the subterranean ones. Regarding the former he said: "I pronounce them among the grandest efforts of human industry and art."

The Thirteenth Dynasty included sixty Diospolite kings who are said to have reigned 453 years. The Fourteenth numbered seventy-six Xoite kings with reigns extending over 184 years; but of these Xoites many appear to have

The statue of King Sesostris I, Twelfth Dynasty, found in the burial temple of his pyramid at Lisht

been mere puppets, ruling under the Hyksos, or Shepherd kings, who now invaded the land.

These Diospolite, Xoite, and Shepherd kings continued to rule through the Thirteenth, Fourteenth, Fifteenth, Sixteenth, and Seventeenth dynasties, from 1788 to 1580 B.C. The Hyksos are supposed to have been a nomadic race from either Arabia or Syria who invaded Lower Egypt, where they destroyed the native monarchy of Memphis and then conquered the Theban Kingdom of Upper Egypt. Their dominion was completely established by 1580 B.C., and was followed by the darkest period in Egyptian history. It was during the reign of the Shepherd kings that Abraham visited Egypt, and they were still reigning when Jacob and his sons settled in the country more than two hundred years later. It is indeed this fact that somewhat accounts for Joseph's rise to power. The king who so welcomed and honored him was, like himself, a stranger and a Semite.

There were many rebellions during the reign of the Shepherd kings, but all were put down until finally a revolt broke out in the district of Thebes, where, through the skill of the native leaders and the bravery of the insurgents, the Shepherds were decisively beaten and compelled to concentrate at Avaris. Being besieged there, they finally agreed to withdraw with their flocks and herds and leave the country forever.

The Shepherds having been expelled, the Theban house

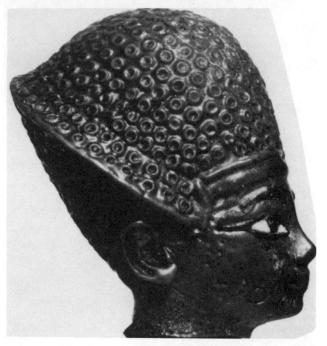

This head of Amenhotep III reveals the abstract art form used by the kings to create the illusion that the pharaoh was really a god and did not have human appearance.

became the dominant power in Egypt, and the Eighteenth Dynasty began about 1580 B.C. Here an impressive biblical truth must be remembered: the head of this Eighteenth Dynasty is believed to have been that pharaoh "who knew not Joseph," and the Exodus of the Israelites from Egypt is supposed to have taken place about 1491 B.C., perhaps during the reign of Thotmes III or Amenhotep II, the pharaoh who, while pursuing the Israelites into the Red Sea, was drowned with all his horsemen.

Under the Eighteenth Dynasty and those dynasties immediately following, Upper and Lower Egypt were once more united under one crown; the ruined temples were restored, the military spirit kindled anew, and the surrounding nations brought under Egyptian dominion. Egypt became a single great centralized power. The splendid temple-palaces of Thebes were built. Ethiopia, Arabia, and Syria were invaded, the Euphrates was crossed, and a part of Mesopotamia added to the empire.

Thotmes III, the greatest of the rulers of the Eighteenth Dynasty, has been called the Alexander of Egypt. He overran the whole of the civilized world, as it was known at that time. The kings of Babylon and Assyria were his vassals.

Amenhotep III was brought up in the state religion of the god of Thebes called Amun. He built his palace on the west bank of the Nile, and set up a private worship of the Aten, or Solar Disk, a cult which had been in existence for at least a century previously. In his later years he saw, and apparently feared, the ever-growing power of the priesthood. (Some one hundred eighty years after his death, the priests actually seized the throne of Egypt from the later Ramessides of the Twentieth Dynasty.)

Amenhotep I of the early Eighteenth Dynasty re-created an image with the people that the pharaoh was a god. This lasted until the end of the reign of Amenhotep III.

Thotmes II was an illegitimate son of Thotmes I by a slave of the name Aset and as a minor, Queen Hatshepsut married him off to one of her daughters, Hatshepsitu II, and ruled for him. This was the pattern more often than not in those early Egyptian times. Thotmes III, however, was legitimate.

The head of a statue of King Thotmes III, Eighteenth Dynasty (Cairo Museum). He was the husband of Hatshepsut, the first queen of Egypt, and for some time was a joint ruler with her half-brother. After her death he came out of the background and became one of the greatest conquerors in history, and is called by historians the Napoleon of Egypt.

own name he changed to Akhenaten, which signifies "he who is devoted to the Aten."

Early in his reign, Akhenaten constructed a temple at Karnak to honor himself. After the sixth year of his reign, Akhenaten founded a new capital, which he called Akhetaten, or "the horizon of the Aten." This is now called el-Amarna and consists of an immense series of ruins on the east bank opposite the community of Deir Mawas in Middle Egypt. At el-Amarna, Akhenaten constructed a series of palaces and temples which he decorated profusely. He also had tombs hewn in the rock, made for the royal family and for his nobles.

Akhenaten's wife, Nefertete, whose name signifies "the beautiful one has come," entered into her husband's religion, but later they seem to have quarreled, and at one period in the history of the new capital, Akhenaten and Sakere, his elder and favorite son-in-law, lived in one quarter of the town, while Nefertete and Tutankhamun, also a son-in-law, lived in another. Nefertete's name was subsequently erased from her monuments.

Of the parentage of Nefertete, Sakere, and Tutankhamun, nothing has been established definitely, but there is a possibility that all three were children of Amenhotep III by

King Amenhotep IV (Akhenaten), Eighteenth Dynasty, was the pharaoh who was a religious fanatic and who attempted to combine all the gods into one. He adored his wife, Queen Nefertete, and had statues of her everywhere during his reign.

Amenhotep III, son of Thotmes IV by a Mesopotamian (Mitanni) mother, married a girl of noble, but not royal parentage—the famous Queen Tyi. She was the daughter of Yuyu and Thuyu. By Tyi, Amenhotep III had a son, Amenhotep IV, a king about whom much controversy raged. His reliefs and statues show him to have been physically very abnormal. He entered fanatically into the worship of the Aten and he carried his hatred of the god Amun to such an extent, that on becoming king he shut down the worship of Amun throughout the land and erased the god's name wherever his agents could find it in temples, private tombs, and chapels, even in the second *cartouche* (a French word for an ornamental tablet with an inscription that usually consisted of names of the royal family and were sometimes engraved on the king's ring) of his father's name. His

Sitamun, who was of royal birth, and whom Amenhotep is known to have married in addition to Tyi. The historical documentation at this time is very sketchy on kings at the end of the Eighteenth Dynasty.

The history of the country during Akhenaten's heresy was not a happy one. The king, occupied with religious quibblings and domestic differences, could not be made to realize the fact that Egypt's possessions in Palestine and Syria were being lost, although Queen Tyi is known to have paid one visit at least to the new capital, very likely to warn her son of what was going on.

The gradual collapse of Egypt's Asiatic Empire is proved by what are now known as the Tall-el-Amarna tablets, which were reports to Egypt from Asia, written in cuneiform on clay, a selection of which are on view in the Cairo Museum. Those addressed to Akhenaten by his viceroys frequently call for help, and state that the writers can no longer hold out for long against Egypt's enemies.

Sakere is believed to have been a coregent with Akhenaten and he appears to have left el-Amarna for Thebes, possibly to attempt some kind of reconciliation with the priesthood of Amun. His body was found in a cache in the Royal Valley at Thebes, with some funerary equipment, prepared apparently by Akhenaten for Tyi. However, noth-

Queen Tyi, the wife of Amenhotep III and the mother of King Akhernaten

ing is known of the death of Akhenaten, nor where either he or Tyi was buried.

THE TOMB OF TUT

The history of the young King Tutankhamun and the contents of his tomb have been of great interest to the modern world. In the records of the ancient Egyptians all mention of the history of what is now called the Heresy Period of the Eighteenth Dynasty was expunged after its conclusion, but it can now be deduced as a result of findings in King Tut's tomb.

His name was changed to Tutankhamun from Tutankhaton, which signifies "the living image of Amun" in place of a similar laudatory phrase of the Aten. As stated on the walls of his tomb, he was buried by his successor, Ay, his Grand Vizier, who married Tutankhamun's widow, Ankhesenamun.

It is practically certain that the tomb which contained Tutankhamun's body and treasures was not made for him. To begin with, it is different in general shape from all others of his period in the Royal Valley. Among other strong indications to the same effect is the fact that the great

Queen Nefertete, wife of Amenhotep IV and mother-in-law of the now-famous King Tutankhamun. This is the most widely reproduced Egyptian statue. The original shown here is in the Berlin Museum.

Three stamps commemorating the fiftieth anniversary of the discovery in 1922 by Howard Carter and Lord Carnarvon of the tomb of Tutankhamun

A photograph by the author of the site and entrance to King Tutankhamun's tomb

A close-up of the panel on the royal chair. The background is of heavy sheet gold, the garments of silver, the flesh tones are done in a reddish glass, and the ornamental details are made of stones shaped from brightly colored glass. The king is on his throne and the queen is adjusting his collar and administering perfume to him.

A solid gold mask of Tutankhamun found in the tomb among the many treasures

One of the treasures of the 1922 find of King Tutankhamun's tomb is this chair, which shows the king and his young queen, Ankhesenamun, on the front panel of the back.

shrines were actually oriented in the reverse sense from the indications left in ink by joiners on their panels. From the evidence on the ancient wine jars, Tutankhamun reigned nine years, that is, until he was eighteen years old, which was proved when his mummy was examined. During that period, he and his advisers would be expected to have found ample time to make a full-sized royal tomb of more or less standard pattern, since quartzite colossi were made for his mortuary temple. It is likely that the Tomb of Ay in the Western Valley at Thebes, was begun and perhaps partly completed for Tutankhamun, and that Ay, on Tutankhamun's possibly unexpected death, buried him in an unoccupied tomb in the Royal Valley. We can only conjecture that this tomb may have been made for Ay himself, since very great, nonroyal personages were sometimes permitted burial there during the Eighteenth Dynasty. Be this as it may, Ay, on becoming king, took Tutankhamun's tomb in the Western Valley for himself.

Tutankhamun, at about nine years of age, succeeded Sakere (who appears to have died about the same time as Akhenaten—1358 B.C.) and returned, either voluntarily or by compulsion, to Thebes and to the worship of Amun. Tutankhamun reigned from 1358 to 1353 B.C. and was succeeded by King Ay and Queen Eye, who coruled Egypt for eighteen years and closed out the Eighteenth Dynasty.

The statue of Horemheb, commander in chief of King Tutankhamun's armies and later king of Egypt, himself

King Tutankhamun on his throne giving an audience to the governor of Ethiopia. Note the cartouches by the king's head. They describe him, as "the King of Upper Egypt and King of Lower Egypt, the god Re for all beings" and "Tuet-anch-Amun, the Lord of Hermonthis, the son of Re, who [like God] lives forever like Re."

Seti I was a very religious ruler. Here he is seen offering wine to the chief god, Osiris. Behind Osiris is the great god Isis, the divine mother, and behind her, Horus, the son of Osiris and Isis.

King Horemheb was the founder of the Nineteenth Dynasty. He is seen here being carried by his soldiers.

THE NEW EMPIRE

Ancient Egypt reached the peak of its power, wealth, and territorial extent in the period called the New Empire (from 1580 to 1090 B.C., under the Eighteenth, Nineteenth, and Twentieth dynasties. The first pharaoh of the Eighteenth Dynasty drove the remnants of the Hyksos out of the northeastern delta area and pursued them across the Sinai Peninsula. Subsequently, Nubia was reconquered, the government was reorganized, and the country became a military state. Administration was centralized in the hands of the pharaoh and his chief minister, and no trace remained of the feudal decentralization of the Middle Kingdom. Through the intensive campaigns of Pharaoh Thotmes III, the regions later to be known in history as Palestine, Syria, and the northern Euphrates area in Mesopotamia were brought within the boundaries of the New Empire.

FROM THE FIRST RAMESES TO THE CONQUEST BY THE GREEKS

The first Rameses was an insignificant ruler, of whom little is known. He appointed his son coregent, or joint ruler with him, and after several raids into Nubia, he died, having reigned only two years. Among the mummies found at Der-el-Bahari, some time ago, was one that was identified as that of Rameses I. His only importance lies in that he began the line of rulers in the Nineteenth Dynasty under whom Egypt became so prosperous and powerful.

With Seti I opened the reign of one of the most illustrious and warlike monarchs of Egypt. He speedily became involved in a series of important wars, one of which was notable because it resulted in the capture of Saluma, or Salem, which afterward became the city of Jerusalem. He was a man of great military ability, and was so successful that he compelled Syria to sue for peace and strengthened his hold on the province by marrying a princess of that nation. He gave much attention to maritime affairs, and it is said that a powerful fleet of his swept up and down the Mediterranean. There has been too much praise, however, given to this ruler, for it is impossible that all of the triumphs placed to his credit could have been gained by any man in a single lifetime. This unquestionably great ruler, who was vain to the last degree, resorted to a trick by which to add to his glory. Many famous buildings, built by his predecessors, had the names of the builders inscribed upon them. Seti caused these to be obliterated and his own placed in their stead. But it remains true that his empire was extended northward to the shores of the Caspian Sea; southward beyond the second Nile cataract; westward to the interior of the desert; and it included Arabia to the east.

This ruler devoted most of his architectural activity to the city of Thebes, where he built upon the temple of Amun-Ra at Karnak, and began the splendid hypostyle which was completed by his son and successor. He restored two funereal temples and left his kingdom to his son, who is known in history as Rameses II.

This king was perhaps the most illustrious of all the rulers of Egypt, and was surnamed the Great. When only ten years old he accompanied his father in many of his campaigns, and upon succeeding to the throne was fired with the ambition to become the conqueror of the world. The Greeks named him Sesostris and saw in him the representative of the highest possible Egyptian greatness. Their accounts of his marvelous exploits, however, have greatly overestimated them. His principal campaigns were in Ethiopia, Syria, and Arabia, and it is probable that he pushed his conquests as far as Mesopotamia and ruled the larger part of western Asia. His greatest battle was at Kaddish, the capital city of the Hittites. On his monuments he is very fond of referring to his personal prowess in this great battle. Charging at the head of his forces he alone, with his chariot and lions, succeeded in breaking through the Hittite line. The rest of the Egyptians were driven back, and the king remained alone in a position of great peril.

It is interesting to step back through the centuries and read Rameses' own boastful account of the matter, as scholars have translated it. "I became like the god Mentu. I hurled the dart with my right hand; I fought with my left hand. . . . I had come upon two thousand teams of horses; I was in the midst of them, but they were dashed in pieces before my steeds. Not one of them raised his hand to fight; their courage was sunken in their breasts; their limbs gave way. . . . I made them fall into the water like crocodiles; they tumbled down on their faces one after another. I killed them at my pleasure." The inscription runs on as far again in the same strain. It is the tone of all the monuments. These old Egyptian kings were in no way bashful about telling their exploits.

That is one thing which makes it so difficult to get at the facts of ancient history. The Hittites certainly were defeated in this battle, but the act of Rameses in building an immense wall from Pelusium to Heliopolis to protect his eastern frontier does not look like the work of a resistless con-

The victorious King Seti I going into battle. Above him are the three divinities who protect him in combat: Horus as a hawk; Horus as the Solar Disk; and the goddess of the south as a vulture. And behind Seti is the fan-bearer, the symbol (hieroglyph) for life.

A black granite statue of Rameses II in the Turin Museum shows the king when he first took the throne.

The Greek historians reported that Rameses II was the greatest of all kings of ancient Egypt. But modern research has shown that in fact he did not conquer the world as he had planned. The deciphering of the inscriptions on the Beirut rocks at Tanis, in the Ramesseum at Karnak, and in the Nubia temple built by Rameses II, himself, contain verification that he was limited in his conquests to Ethiopia, Syria, and Arabia. He had to build a great wall from Pelusium to Heliopolis to protect his interests. He started at the age of ten and ruled sixty-six years, all of them involved in battle.

Rameses II in personal battle with the lions of Kaddish

Rameses the Great was succeeded in 1232 B.C. by King Merneptah, who reigned for twenty-years. Historians generally accept the premise that he was the pharaoh of the Exodus of Israel. The story of this remarkable event begins with the call of Abraham from his home in Ur, near the Euphrates, to his promised abode in Canaan. Here his descendants multiplied to the fifth generation, when Jacob, the grandson of Abraham, with his children and grandchildren to the number of about seventy, "went down into Egypt." For a famine had arisen in Canaan, and Jacob dispatched his sons to the Egyptian granaries to purchase supplies. Joseph, one of the sons of Jacob, had previously been sold by his brothers into bondage, and had come to fill an important position in the government of Egypt; and thus it happened that the wicked clansmen were brought face to face with the injured brother, who, instead of punishing, forgave them, and sent for the aged father and his household.

Rameses II is accompanied by eight of his sons in this attack on a Syrian fortress.

queror, and the cutting of a system of canals from Memphis downward was probably meant to obstruct the advance of his enemies.

His works in architecture were sufficient to make the name of Rameses immortal. He completed the famous Hall of Columns, begun by his father at Karnak, and the temple of Amenhotep III at Luxor.

The two colossi of Rameses, and one of the two obelisks of red granite which he placed in front of Amenhotep's grand temple, are still standing with the inscription as sharp and distinct as on the day it was graven in the flinty stone. The other obelisk is in the Place de la Concorde in Paris.

Rameses died in the sixty-eighth year of his reign, and was succeeded by his fourteenth son, Merneptah, who made Memphis his capital. As an evidence of the uncertainty of historical records, it may be stated that a good many writers claim that this ruler was the pharaoh of the Exodus, who was drowned in the Red Sea.

When Merneptah came to the throne, Egypt was at peace with the world, and, unless we accept the Exodus as taking place during his reign, it was uneventful. Under his son Seti II there was disorder and rebellion. Seti was credited with numerous victories, but it was probably done by flatterers, for no authentic records of such triumphs have been preserved. After his death came a period of anarchy, during which several usurpers reigned for a brief while, until at last Setnakht succeeded in restoring order and founded the Twentieth Dynasty.

All the kings of this dynasty, after Setnakht, are known as Rameses, the first one being III, while the last was XII. Rameses III subdued a rebellion in Ethiopia and won a number of naval battles on the Mediterranean. He, like so many of his predecessors, was a great builder, and his name is found in all parts of Egypt connected with temples and

Four statues were erected at the rock temples of Abu-Simbel in Egyptian Nubia. Each is seventy-five feet tall. The one on the left is of Rameses II. It bears a strong resemblance to the face of his mummy. The statues were built in his time and have been looking down on the Nile for these last 3,300 years.

other monuments, his chief attention having been given to the delta, and to the district about Thebes where he built his famous temple of Amun. With this dynasty ended the period known as the New Empire, and the years of decline began. This dynasty had seen Egypt as the first power of the then-known world, but the dry rot was gnawing at the root, and was not to cease until the passing centuries saw the once-mighty kingdom among the weakest and most insignificant of nations.

The priests had been steadily gaining power, and they now secured the throne, under the name of the Tanite kings, and held it for one hundred and thirty years, or, according to some writers, for one hundred and fifty years. Then followed the Bubastite or Twenty-second Dynasty, believed to have descended from the foreign settlers in Bubastis, now known as Tel-Bustak, on the Peludiac Nile, about seventy miles from the mouth.

We now reach secure ground, for it is covered by Hebrew history. Shashank, founder of the Bubastite dynasty, was Shishak of the Old Testament, who captured Jerusalem about 972 B.C. If you will read the first ten verses of the twelfth chapter of 2 Chronicles, you will find the account of this event, which is also related by the historian Josephus, while the name of the king with a record of his achieve-ments is inscribed on the pylon of the Great Temple of Karnak. It is believed that his successor was Zerah of the Bible (Osorthern or Osorkon), who suffered defeat at Mareshah, from Asa, king of Judah, as related in 2 Kings 18:4 and 2 Chron. 16:8,9.

The Twenty-third Dynasty was also Tanite, and Egypt declined more rapidly than ever. At the close of the Twen-ty-fourth Dynasty it was conquered by Ethiopia, its last monarch, Bokenranef, being taken prisoner and burned alive. Shabaka, founder of the Twenty-fifth or Ethiopian Dynasty, may have been the So of the Hebrew records, with

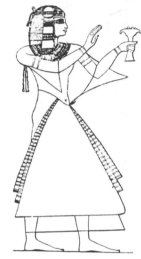

*Prince Mentuherchopshef,
son of Rameses III*

Statue and Temple of Rameses III at Karnak in Egypt. He was the last of the great sovereigns of Egypt. His idol was his namesake Rameses the Great and he tried to equal his conquests. He defeated the Bedouins and had conquered Libya when Egypt was attacked by the nations of Asia Minor in a confederation that swept down across Syria into the Nile Valley looking for the riches of the fertile land. Rameses III met them and at the head of his soldiers shouted time and again, "I, the King Rameses, I have acted like a hero, who knows his valor and who stretches his arm over his people in the day of the struggle. Those who have violated frontiers will no longer cultivate the land, the time for their souls to pass on into eternity is fixed." The Asia Minor confederation was annihilated.

The mummy of Rameses III

whom Hosea, king of Israel, formed an alliance. His successor, Taharka, was Tirhakah, king of Ethiopia, the enemy of Assyria and Sennacherib, an account of whom is given in the book of Isaiah 27:9. How our interest deepens and intensifies when we find ourselves reading history that is also given in the Bible!

There was much trouble and warring after the death of Taharka, a sure indication of the rapid decay of the empire. Twelve kings probably reigned at the same time in different parts of the country. Each had his own province, and they united only to repel foreign invasion. This was about seven centuries before the birth of Christ. Where there were so many pulling in different ways, they were easily overthrown by one of their own number, Psamtek I, aided by Greek and Phoenician mercenaries, and he formed the Twenty-sixth Dynasty. During his reign of more than fifty years, he united Egypt into a compact kingdom and introduced a number of important reforms. One of his changes, however, was scarcely for the better. He built new and more gorgeous temples for the successive bulls in which the god Apis was supposed to be living. He made the worship of these bulls the main part of the religious ceremony of the nation, having grand processions and feasts in their honor.

His successor, Necho II (Nekas or Nechao), was Pharaoh Necho of the Bible (2 Kings 23:29–34). He was a ruler of ability, and during his reign of sixteen years he carried on a war against the Babylonian Empire, defeated its ally, Josiah, king of Judah, entered Jerusalem in triumph, and placed Eliakim, younger brother of Jehoahaz, on the throne. He invaded Assyria and for four years had a series of continued victories. Then he was defeated on the banks of the Euphrates by Nebuchadnezzar and driven back into Egypt. It is said that by his command a Phoenician fleet attempted the circumnavigation of Africa, and he began the cutting of a canal between the Red Sea and the Nile.

During the reign of his successor, Psamtek II, Egyptian supremacy was restored over Ethiopia. Disasters overtook the kingdom under Uahibra, Pharaoh Hophra of Scripture. Nebuchadnezzar invaded Lower Egypt and the Greeks swarmed into western Egypt, where the king was defeated.

We now reach another momentous era in the history of Egypt. It was 525 B.C. and Cambyses II was king of Persia, which had grown into a powerful and mighty nation. Previous to this time, Aahmes, king of Egypt, had formed an alliance with King Croesus of Lydia and King Nabunaid of Babylon, who were bitter enemies of Persia. The alliance was for protection against the growing power of Persia, but it gave Cambyses the excuse he needed to march against Egypt.

This campaign promised to be of the most trying nature. Along the eastern frontier extended the Syrian desert, which was so difficult to cross that Aahmes did not believe there was any danger to him in such an attempt. He therefore brought his forces together at Pelusium, confident that he would gain an easy victory over the invaders, who after

Cambyses II, king of Persia, conquered Egypt in 525 B.C. in a decisive battle at Pelusium. He was a first-class barbarian who showed his savage nature by destroying the Egyptian idols. At the festival of the reincarnation of Apis, he personally slew the new bull. As seen in this illustration, Cambyses collected all of the sacred cats of Pelusium and galloped by the main gate of the city flinging the cats high in the air to their death.

crossing the desert would be so worn out that they must fall easy victims to his warriors. Cambyses understood the difficulties before him, and collected an immense fleet to attack Pelusium by sea while his army assailed it by land. But on the eve of starting an astounding piece of good fortune befell him.

Phanes, one of the best officers in the Egyptian army, was aggrieved over his treatment by Aahmes, and so angered that he set out to join the Persian monarch. Suspecting his purpose, Aahmes sent his favorite eunuch in pursuit, and he overtook Phanes on the road; but the latter eluded him and reached the Persian camp, where he received a warm welcome from Cambyses.

It was a sad day for Aahmes when he offended his young officer, for he not only revealed all the secrets of his former master, but showed his enemies the way to cross the desert with little difficulty. As a first step, envoys were sent to the bedouin sheiks or chiefs, who were given bounteous presents, and in return they made treaties by which they promised to furnish the expedition with camels and water, and to guide them by the shortest and best route to Pelusium.

In the interval Aahmes died, so that it was his son Psamtek III, a young and inexperienced leader, who met the Persians at Pelusium. After a prolonged and furious battle the Egyptians were totally defeated. Psamtek fled to Memphis and a ship was sent there to demand the submission of the city. This ship contained only two hundred men, and its errand being known, it should have been safe against attack; but when it entered the harbor it was boarded by an overwhelming number of men, who killed everyone on board and burned the vessel.

Cambyses punished this perfidy tenfold. He laid siege to Memphis, took it, and executed two thousand of the sons of the most respected citizens, among them the son of the king, whose daughter and a number of leading young women were sold into slavery. Cambyses intended, however, to make Psamtek governor of Egypt, but he was detected in a conspiracy against the Persian, who permitted him to take poison as the best way out of his trouble. He may be considered the last of the pharaohs, for the Persian hosts now tramped unopposed over Egypt. The New Empire, once the pride of the world, was blotted out in darkness, and the Land of the Pharaohs became a Persian province.

The Twenty-seventh Dynasty thus founded by Cambyses consisted of six kings whose joint reigns lasted from 525 to 424 B.C. Having been so successful, Cambyses II determined to conquer the rest of Africa. He planned three expeditions. The first was against Carthage, but it had to be abandoned because the Phoenicians, who composed most of the fleet, refused to make war against Carthage, and since they were volunteers, Cambyses did not dare to use severe measures against them.

The second expedition was directed against the oasis of Amon, and a force of fifty thousand men left Thebes and started across the desert of Sahara, but were never heard of again. It is probable that all perished in one of those terrific sandstorms that sweep over that flaming desert.

The third expedition was against Ethiopia and, in the main, was successful, but on the return of the army, which numbered 150,000 men, nearly all perished in a sandstorm. Nevertheless, Egypt was thoroughly subdued and held with a firm hand.

Cambyses was subject to epileptic fits, and he now became insane and committed many sacrileges that grievously offended the Egyptians, his own country suffering almost as much from his wild doings. He killed his brother, and has been accused of many unnatural crimes. He wounded himself, it is thought accidentally, and died therefrom in the year 522 B.C.

Darius became king of Persia and was confronted by many revolts, but Egypt remained loyal. He visited the country in 517 B.C., and by his course won the goodwill of the people. He founded a city named for himself near the route of the canal he'd completed from the Nile to the Red Sea, and then, for some unknown reason, caused half of it to be destroyed. The most important act of his reign was the erection of Egypt, including Libya, Barca, and Cyrene, into the sixth satrapy, which was required to pay an annual tax amounting to $826,000.

Xerxes became king of Persia in 486 B.C. and found the Egyptians in revolt. He reconquered them and appointed his own brother satrap of the country.

As we shall learn in the history of Persia, Xerxes was assassinated in 465 B.C. and was succeeded by Artaxerxes in 465 B.C., who found a formidable rebellion confronting him in Egypt, where the Greeks gave assistance to his enemies. He suffered a number of defeats, but was successful in the end, and induced the Athenians to withdraw their support of the Egyptians. After a time, tranquillity was established, but in the middle part of the reign of Darius II

Alexander the Great

the Egyptians succeeded in gaining their independence under the leadership of Amyrtaeus, the Greek, who reigned from 414 to 408 B.C. He was deposed, and in his place Nepherites lasted from 408 to 386 B.C. Nepherites II succeeded his father, but was slain by his soldiers in 386 B.C.

The Thirtieth Dynasty began in 378 B.C., with Nectanebos I on the throne. He was the greatest king of the period, and under him, Egypt once more assumed an important rank among nations, defying Persia and making her influence felt in Asia. Many extensive and costly campaigns were set on foot against Egypt, but when Artaxerxes died all had resulted in dismal failure.

Nectanebos II ascended the Egyptian throne in 361 B.C. and was the last native pharaoh. He abandoned the attempts to conquer Phoenicia and Syria and confined himself within the boundaries of Egypt, probably because of the internal troubles. Persia pushed her conquests in different directions and finally attacked Egypt. Her forces suffered severe losses in the desert, but, with their Greek allies, laid siege to Pelusium. The Thebans made the first attack, but the battle, which lasted far into the night, ended without advantage to either side. The Egyptians, however, lacked a good general and, after more severe fighting, retreated to Memphis.

The invaders now marched through the delta, promising pardon to all who would submit, and threatening with the sword those who continued resistance. It may be said that the Egyptian and Greek garrisons (for there were Greeks on both sides) fell over each other in their haste to submit. So it came about that Egypt, after an independence of sixty-five years, became again a Persian province.

Egypt remained passive and tranquil throughout the terrific war between Alexander the Great and Persia, even though hardly a Persian garrison was left in the country. When the power of Persia was shattered, Egypt did not strike a blow for her freedom, though she did strike hard at the robber bands which terrorized many parts of the country.

Having captured Tyre and Gaza, Alexander was determined to take Egypt. Pelusium surrendered without resistance. Alexander garrisoned the city and sent his fleet up the Nile to Memphis. He entered the city not as a conqueror, but as a pharaoh, reverently observing all the ancient religious ceremonies. Sacrifices were offered to the gods, athletic games and prize contests in arts were instituted in which many of the Greek masters took part. This conduct was in such contrast to that of previous Persian rulers that the Egyptians were captivated and hailed him as their best friend.

Passing down the Nile from Memphis, Alexander went to sea from Canopus, and landing at the outlet of Lake Mareotis, near the site of Rakote, he was impressed by the splendid harbor facilities offered by the place. He determined to found a city there which would bear his name. Thus the important metropolis Alexandria came into existence. It soon became the intellectual exchange between the nations of the Occident and the Orient, and the mother of a new civilization. Leaving a portion of his army in Egypt, Alexander left the country in 332 B.C. and never returned. When he died his body was brought to Alexandria for interment where it rests today.

EGYPT UNDER GREEK AND ROMAN RULE

Alexander died in 323 B.C., and almost immediately the vast empire created by his genius crumbled to pieces, as a house does when the foundations are swept away. His chief captains divided his vast possessions among themselves, and it came about that Egypt fell to the share of Ptolemy Lagos, or Soter, the first of the Greek sovereigns. He was an able ruler and added more "leaven" to the Egyptian lump, until, had you been unfamiliar with its history, you would have suspected that the country had always been a part of Greece. He changed the names of many of the leading cities, dethroned the abstract religion and supplanted it with a singular compound of the two systems, while science and learning found a congenial home in the

A cameo of the Greek conqueror, King Ptolemy II, Philadelphus (285–247 B.C.), with Arsinoe, daughter of Lysimachus

court of the Ptolemies. Alexandria drew within its walls the learning of the age; the unsurpassed Alexandrian Library was founded by Ptolemy Philadelphus, who encouraged the Septuagint version of the Hebrew Bible and patronized the labors of the historians and learned men. The delta became a scene of bustling activity like an American city, for commerce was rapidly developed and nearly all Europe eagerly sought the corn, linen, and papyrus of Egypt; the products of Libya; and the apparently exhaustless treasures of the East.

The third Ptolemy was Euergetes, who, through a Syrian war, extended his conquests to Babylon and Susa and swept the shores of the Mediterranean with his fleets. He added to the volumes in the Alexandrian Library, and did his utmost to aid in the material and intellectual prosperity of his people.

The fatal defect of every monarchical system is that, while some rulers may be of the highest virtue and ability, there are sure to be others whose reigns are a deadly blight to their subjects. Untold evil is done and the hands on the dial of progress are turned back for generations. The turn of Egypt came when Epiphanes, the fifth Ptolemy, became king. He was a bloated wretch, incapable of giving his country even a pretense of good government. After inflicting disaster and evil, he was poisoned when preparing to set out on a military expedition.

During his reign, Rome began to show her hand in Egyptian affairs, and Ptolemy VI, Philometor, was a nominee of the Roman Senate. He was a good and wise ruler, but his successor, Euergetes II, was one of the most loathsome miscreants who'd ever lived. He had a sister, Cleopatra, who had also been the sister of her (dead) husband. Euergetes II married her and, on the day he did so, murdered her infant son. He afterward divorced Cleopatra and married her daughter by her first husband, thereby making Cleopatra his mother-in-law. This was too much for his subjects, who rebelled and placed Cleopatra on the throne. In revenge he murdered a son who had been born to them, and sent the youth's head to her as a present.

One must not confuse this Cleopatra with the one more famous in history, for that individual did not come upon the stage until a hundred years later. Moreover, it has been stated by some that the term "sister," as used among the Egyptians, did not always imply the close relationship which we today understand by the term.

Several successors are not worth noting, but coming down to the time of Ptolemy XII, who became king in 51 B.C., we reach the period of the dazzling Egyptian Cleopatra, whose luminous beauty and marvelous fascination completely turned the heads of men whose ambition and mental genius, it would be supposed, would have lifted them above any temptation in that direction.

Ptolemy XIII placed the guardianship of Egypt in the Roman Senate. His daughter Cleopatra and his son Ptolemy XIV were nominated as successors to the throne. She was seventeen and he ten years old, and their joint authority was cemented by the marriage of the brother and sister. The particulars of the romantic tragedy that follows will be found in our history of Rome. The ministers of Ptolemy excluded Cleopatra from her share in the sovereignty, when fortunately for the deposed queen a new actor came upon the stage in the person of the great Julius Caesar.

Probably having unbounded faith in her power of fascination, Cleopatra sought and obtained entrance to the presence of the illustrious Roman leader. Her confidence was warranted, for she completely bewitched Caesar, who, as might have been supposed, made a fool of himself.

Won by her smiles, he became her champion. He captured Pelusium, the key to the Nile, and crossing that river at the head of the delta, routed the army of Ptolemy, who, while fleeing, was drowned. Caesar's success being complete, the Alexandrians submitted and, with a Roman garrison in the capital, they acknowledged Cleopatra as the queen of Egypt.

One of the strangest stories of history tells how after the death of Caesar she threw a spell over Mark Antony, who lavished princely fortunes upon her and their children. Then, forgetting honor and everything in his infatuation, he met his death through her treachery when she and her fleet deserted him in the critical hour, when the prize for which he was about to contend was the dominion of the world. Later, she exerted her subtle fascinations upon Augustus, the conqueror of Antony, but in vain. Finally, when told she must take her place in the procession that was to celebrate a Roman triumph, she committed suicide, in the year 30 B.C.

It is uncertain in what manner Cleopatra died, for there were no marks of violence on her person, and her face and body showed none of the effects produced by poison that has been swallowed. The general belief is that she obtained a venomous asp, which was brought to her in a basket of figs. This may or may not be true, and it is of little moment either way. Doubtless she was the possessor of a certain style of barbarian beauty which would have awakened no admiration in modern days, but she was one of the most vicious and abandoned of her sex, of whom it could be truthfully said that the world was well rid of her.

Egypt no longer bore the semblance of independence. It became a part of the Roman Empire, governed by a prefect appointed by Caesar and responsible directly to him. It was divided into Upper Egypt, with Thebes the capital; Middle Egypt, with Heptanomis the capital; and Lower Egypt, with Alexandria the capital. Each of these divisions was subdivided into what were termed nomes, and these again into toparchies. Strong military forces were stationed in different parts, and Egypt formed one of the numerous members of the mighty empire of the Romans, who developed the resources of the country until it became the granary of the empire.

But the natives had not given up the hope of freedom. The first formidable revolt was by the soldiery, who, after a resistance lasting from A.D. 171 to 175, were brought under

Julius Caesar

Cleopatra the Great, an ambitious young woman who did everything in her rare intellectual powers and with her physical prowess—said to be matched in history only by that of Catherine the Great of Russia—to save Egypt from the control of either Latin Rome or Greek Alexandria

Mark Antony as he appeared on a coin of the times

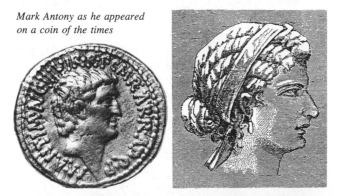

submission, and imperial authority was fully reestablished. Eighteen years later, Pescennius Niger declared himself emperor, but in 196 was defeated and killed. Some time later the Egyptians were allowed representatives in the Roman Senate, and the worship of Isis, which had long existed in the Roman cities, was publicly sanctioned.

Zenobia, the famous empress of Palmyra, conquered the land in A.D. 269, but she had hardly occupied it when she herself was conquered by Aurelian, the Roman emperor. Immediately afterward her friend Firmus, a leading merchant of Egypt, raised the standard of revolt, and went so far as to don the imperial purple at Alexandria, issue edicts, coin money, and equip an army which Aurelian scattered like so much chaff. Firmus was made prisoner and tortured to death.

Cleopatra, on September 2, 31 B.C., in the sea battle of Actium in which she and her husband Mark Antony fought off the Greeks. But at the height of battle she turned and fled with her sixty galleys and the enemy went on to conquer her land. During a land battle that followed. Mark Antony committed suicide when he was wrongly led to believe that Cleopatra was dead.

Cleopatra committed suicide because she could not endure the ordeal of living in a conquered Egypt. She is depicted here on her deathbed.

Napoleon Bonaparte, after his invasion of Egypt in 1788, did his very best to please the Shaykhs of Al-Ahzar. Right: He is shown here in a Muslim costume greeting a Shaykh.

Now came troublous times to the Land of the Pharaohs, and the Roman legions were kept busy in putting down rebellions. Then the religious factions harried one another with a fierceness always seen in such wars. But Christianity had taken root and was aggressive against paganism. Christian monks made their homes in Upper Egypt, and their bishops held sway in Alexandria, where the battle royal was fought between the two faiths. Finally, in A.D. 389, Theodosius I forbade by decree the worship of idols and ordered the temples to be closed. Such of the magnificent buildings as were not changed to Christian churches were stripped of their decorations or suffered to fall into decay. The pagans defended their property with fanatical desperation, but were assailed with equal fury, and in the struggle the great Alexandrian Library was pillaged, perhaps destroyed. Its mines of treasures could never be replaced.

Through the third century A.D. the decay of the Roman Empire was more and more manifest in Egypt. The Roman bureaucracy became overcentralized and ill-managed. A renaissance of imperial authority and effectiveness, however, took place with the emperor Diocletian, during whose reign, beginning in A.D. 284, the division of the Roman Empire into two separate entities called the Eastern Roman Empire (or Byzantine Empire) and the Western Roman Empire, was later included in what became known as the Holy Roman Empire. Egypt continued as a province of the Eastern Roman Empire, which had its capital at Byzantium (later, Constantinople; today, Istanbul).

Diocletian inaugurated drastic political and fiscal reforms, greatly simplifying imperial administration. Seeing in Christianity a threat to the Roman state religion, he launched a violent persecution of Christians, which fell on the Coptic church in Egypt with greater severity than any persecutions it was to know under the Muslims. The sectarian doctrinal divisions of the Egyptian church came to the fore as a central factor in Egyptian history during the Byzantine period, for Egyptian opposition to the imperial rule was often expressed in religious terms. When Constantinople, the eastern capital, was heretical, Egypt rallied to Roman Catholicism; when the capital was Catholic, Egypt fell into heresy.

By the seventh century evidence of the retreat of Hellenism could be seen in the declining use of the Greek language. Coptic was again coming to the fore, with even church dignitaries losing the ability to communicate in Greek, although the old Egyptian language was preserved in writing largely by use of Greek characters. At the same time, the Eastern Empire came under heavy assault from the north and east. In A.D. 616 the Persians again conquered Egypt, but their triumph there was short-lived, lasting only ten years. The end of Byzantine rule, after the Persian withdrawal, came suddenly, with the appearance of an Arab army in A.D. 640 on the historic north Sinai invasion route at Pelusium (at the site of present-day Tell al-Farama, about fifteen miles east of the Suez Canal).

ISLAM AND
THE ARAB CALIPHATE

Mohammed, the Prophet of the Islamic faith, died in A.D. 632 at Medina on the west coast of the Arabian Peninsula. After his death, his Muslim followers quickly confirmed control in Arabia and launched an Islamic wave of expansion northward out of the peninsula and spreading east and west. Syria had fallen to the Arab conquerors in A.D. 636, but the Byzantine authorities failed to anticipate an attack on Egypt by putting the Sinai approaches in a state of defense. In A.D. 639 the Arabian general Amr ibn al-As secured from Umar, the second caliph of Islam (the spiritual and temporal ruler of the Muslims), tentative permission to invade Egypt. The resulting invasion was overwhelmingly successful, and in September 642 the Byzantine Empire's army in Egypt sailed out of the harbor of Alexandria. Political absorption of the country by the Arabs then proceeded with extreme rapidity. After nearly one thousand years of Greek, Roman, and Byzantine rule from across the Mediterranean, the northern influence subsided, and Egypt was again oriented eastward.

The first Arab commander, Amr ibn al-As, established the Arab capital at al-Fustat, immediately south of modern Cairo at a site called Babylon by the Byzantines but more recently sometimes called Old Cairo, where it remained from 641 to 968. From the time of Amr to 968, Egypt was ruled by a sequence of 111 governors assigned by the Arab caliphates in the successive six dynastic periods. Throughout, Arab rule was characterized by a lack of economic and fiscal planning and by intense suspicion on the part of the caliph that his governor in Egypt might gain too much power or popularity. Along with the spread of Islam, Arab policy changed from one of mere occupation to one of colonization, and the Arabic language was made that of official transactions in 706.

The Arab caliphs Umar (634–44), Uthman (644–56), and Ali (656–61) were followed, after the great schism of Islam into Sunni and Shia branches during Ali's reign, by the Umayyad caliphate, which ruled Egypt from Damascus from 661 to the end of the eastern Umayyad Dynasty in 750. This line was succeeded by the Abbassides, whose capital was at Baghdad, from 750 to 1258, but ruling in Egypt only

to 868. An unsuccessful Coptic and Arab-Muslim revolt in Egypt in 831 was followed by Abbaside assignment of the province as a fief to non-Arabs residing in Baghdad who governed through slave mercenaries of Turkish, Kurdish, Circassian, Mongol, or other northern origin. Collectively, these military slave-rulers were known as *Mamluks* (Arabic for "owned"), thus introducing this class into the Egyptian society.

In 868 a Turkish officer named Ahmad ibn Tulum, on the governor's staff in Egypt, seized power and established the Tulunid succession lasting until 905. Weak control then reverted to the Abbassides in Baghdad for thirty years, to be succeeded by another Turkish adventurer line, called the Ikhshidid Dynasty, from 935 to 969, when it succumbed to the Fatimid power from the west. As the rule of the Abbassides had waned, a Shiite Islamic leader claiming descent from Fatima, daughter of the Prophet Mohammed, established in North Africa a rival power and caliphate in 909 that, at its greatest extent, was to include North Africa, Egypt, Palestine, Syria, and the Hejaz region of western Arabia. After the Fatimid forces in 969 destroyed the remnants of Ikhshidid rule in Egypt, they established their capital at modern Cairo and developed the city. Among the early Fatimid accomplishments was the founding of al-Azhar University in the tenth century.

Like preceding dynasties, the Fatimid's power waned, and its last days witnessed the Christian Crusaders' invasion of Syria and Palestine. The nephew of the last Fatimid vizier (senior minister) was a Kurdish officer of Sunni Islamic faith named Salah al-Din Yusuf ibn Ayyub, better known to history as Saladin. Appointed as Fatimid vizier in 1169, Saladin restored Egypt to the Sunni religion in 1171—an act welcomed by the Egyptian Muslim people at large, who had always been Sunni and had never truly accepted the Shiite tenets of the Fatimids.

Saladin became the independent ruler of Egypt in 1174. He consolidated his temporal control there and also in Palestine and Syria, but acknowledged the religious suzerainty of the Sunni Abbasside caliph in Baghdad. Saladin defeated the Crusaders, retook Jerusalem, and ultimately reduced the Crusader holdings to a small entity of modern Lebanon. Saladin, greatest of the Islamic war leaders who ruled Egypt, died in Damascus in 1193. His descendants and relatives continued as the Ayyubid Dynasty in Egypt until 1260.

THE MAMLUKS AND THE
OTTOMAN CALIPHATE TO 1800

The last years of the Ayyubid caliphate in Egypt were featured by instability, intrigue, and the emergent power of the Mamluk officers associated with the court in Cairo. Mamluk sultans ruled in Egypt and parts of Syria from 1257 to 1382 in a line known as the Bahris. Baibars, the first of the line, in an attempt to legitimize his regime, brought to

Cairo in 1261 a refugee scion of the Islamic caliphs of Baghdad (where the last of the Abbasside rule had been wiped out by the Mongols in 1268), and there maintained the caliphal succession. After 1382 the Bahri Mamluks gave way to a similar line called the Burjis, who maintained themselves precariously in power until 1517.

The vigor of the central Mamluk sultans gradually declined, and the power of provincial governors grew. Under these conditions, Egypt fell before the assault of the Ottoman Turkish sultan Selim I (also known as Selim the Grim) in 1517. The Turks seized the Islamic caliphal descendant and carried him off to Constantinople, after which the Turkish sultans assumed the title of caliph. Selim I incorporated the country into the Ottoman caliphate, which lasted (in Egypt) to 1914. Tuman Bey, last of the Mamluk sultans, had resisted to the end but was caught and hanged.

Egypt again was reduced in status from an independent state to a province. The Turkish sultans continued the commercial relations with Europe established by the Mamluks and confirmed the "capitulations" already held by the French and English. This was a system of extraterritoriality under which nations of these countries enjoyed the protection of their own law, administered by their consuls, rather than being subject to the *sharia* or Islamic law. These privileges had been granted, not by force, but as concessions of condescension to unenlightened foreign commercial agents. In later centuries, however, these privileges were to prove a major source of contention between Egypt and the European powers.

As a *pashaliq* of the Ottoman Turkish Empire (the area under the jurisdiction of a Turkish pasha, or viceroy), the country was divided into twelve *sanjaos* (Turkish for provinces). Each of the twelve was placed under one of the Mamluks from the previous regime. These Mamluks surrounded themselves with the usual following of slave warriors. In the roughly two hundred and eighty years of direct Turkish rule, at least one hundred pashas succeeded each other. As time went on, the control of the pashas became ever more shadowy, the army became more undisciplined and violent, and the Mamluk beys (governors of districts or minor provinces) again emerged as the real authorities in the land.

Mamluk power reached its peak in 1769, when a Circassian Mamluk named Ali Bey became powerful enough to expel the pasha and declare Egypt's independence. Ali Bey went on to conquer Syria and Arabia, but he was soon betrayed to the Sublime Porte (the Turkish caliphate), whose suzerainty was restored by 1773. Turkish vulnerability had nevertheless been revealed by Ali Bey's brief career. The struggles among the Mamluk beys for control of Egypt continued until a new conqueror, Napoleon Bonaparte, appeared on the delta and set the country upon a new course of history.

The brief but dramatic sojourn in Egypt, from 1798 to 1801, of Napoleon's army accompanied by a retinue of French scientists, initiated the tradition in modern Egypt of strong attachment to French culture. More significant, the Napoleonic adventure accented the importance of Egypt as a vital communications link with India and the Far East. The whole Middle Eastern area, with Egypt as an important focus, was hurled into the vortex of European power-politics and diplomacy, and influence from the north again came to the fore.

Although Ottoman rule before Napoleon lasted almost three centuries, the Turks made little real internal impression or change in Egypt. In contrast to the Arab conquerors of the seventh century who imposed their language and religion on Coptic Egypt, the Ottoman Turks, although of the same religion as the Muslim Egyptians, never implanted the Turkish language outside a small official and social arena. The populace regarded the Ottomans and Mamluks as aliens; the Ottomans looked down on the native Arabic-speaking people as fit only to be ruled. To all of them, the French were total aliens. Napoleon's attempts to identify himself with Islam were not accepted, but French learning and science did arouse considerable interest among Muslim scholars.

The French fleet had been destroyed in 1798 by British Admiral Horatio Nelson at Abu Qir Bay (some twenty miles east of Alexandria); Napoleon personally left Egypt on August 22, 1799; and combined British and Turkish military operations forced withdrawal of the last French forces by October 1801. A noteworthy result of the French occupation was the publication in Paris after 1809 of the results of the scientific and scholarly research performed. This work, called the *Description de l'Egypte*, was an encyclopedia of the country. It aroused serious interest in

The famous Mohammed Ali, the great pasha, began his reign of the country in 1805, which is a landmark date in Egyptian modern history— the beginning of their independence. He reigned until 1849.

Europe in Egypt's ancient past, inspiring the intensive study of Egyptology and Islam.

MOHAMMED ALI AND THE NINETEENTH CENTURY

At the turn of the nineteenth century Egypt was pushed into the modern era by the developing power of industrial Europe. In Egypt itself, however, the principal agent of the changes that followed was an officer named Mohammed Ali. With the Albanian contingent of the Turkish forces, he had assisted in driving out the French. Mohammed Ali was born in 1769 at Kavala, in modern Greece, and his national extraction has been a matter of some speculation. Although traditionally he was regarded as an Albanian, his parents, according to more recent historians, appear to have been Turkish. After a period of chaos subsequent to the French withdrawal in 1801, the Sublime Porte designated Mohammed Ali as pasha of Egypt in 1805, and from that time until his death in 1849 his story is virtually that of Egypt. He was an enthusiastic importer of European culture and techniques, but his political methods were those of the authoritarian past. A dynamic economic innovator, he cast European techniques into a framework of nationalization and state organization that was unfamiliar to the Europe of his time and completely novel in the Arab world.

By a policy of confiscation, he became the sole proprietor of land; through a system of monopolies, he became Egypt's exclusive manufacturer and contractor. Armed with such power, he achieved an economic transformation, particularly in the building of canals for irrigation and transportation, in the promotion of scientific agriculture, and in the introduction of cotton cultivation in the Nile Delta. No less energetic in the sphere of education, he fostered training in engineering and medicine, brought in academicians and physicians from Europe, sent students abroad to learn needed skills, and imported educational and military training missions for the edification of Egyptians at home.

Mohammed Ali devoted much attention to the construction of an Egyptian army and navy. One of his early steps in this area was to crush the Mamluks who, under the Ottoman caliphate, had been confirmed in the power they had usurped during the Arabian period. On March 1, 1811, on the eve of the departure of an Egyptian force for Arabia, the Mamluk beys were invited to a reception, the main feature of which was an ambush prepared by their host from which only one escaped. Mohammed summoned the leaders to come to Cairo to consult with him about a campaign into Arabia. Donning their gayest uniforms and mounting their best horses, this body of the finest cavalry in the world rode to the city, where they were warmly welcomed by the pasha, who invited them to parade in the courts of the citadel. With no thought of treachery, they rode within the lofty walls and the portcullis dropped behind them. Then

they saw that they had been caught in a trap and turned to retreat.

But there was no way by which to retreat. Barred doors and windows and blank, gloomy walls frowned on every side, with thousands of muskets leveled from all directions. At a signal these flamed out with a thunderous crash, and men and horses tumbled writhing to the earth. Seeing there was no escape, some folded their arms and calmly awaited death with turbaned heads bowed and their dusky lips murmuring in prayer. Others dashed here and there, madly waving their swords, vainly seeking a foe, and cursing those who had thus basely betrayed them. But the rattling of musketry continued and the horses and riders continued to fall until only one man—Emim Bey—was left alive. And then took place what looked like a miracle. He drove his spurs into the bleeding flanks of his steed, which leaped over a pile of his dead and dying comrades, and with a tremendous bound landed upon the battlements, amid a shower of bullets; then the frenzied animal sprang outward and went down, crushed and dying; the bullets whistled around him, but Emim tore himself free and ran with the

The 1811 massacre of the Mamluks

The escape of Emim Bey

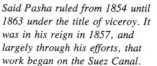
Said Pasha ruled from 1854 until 1863 under the title of viceroy. It was in his reign in 1857, and largely through his efforts, that work began on the Suez Canal.

Ferdinand Count de Lesseps, the builder of the Suez Canal

Khedive Ismail Pasha ruled from 1863 to 1879.

speed of a deer until he reached the sanctuary of a mosque, from which he finally escaped into the desert. The massacre in Cairo set off a general killing throughout Egypt, and the Mamluk power was conclusively broken.

Between 1811 and 1818 Mohammed Ali pursued a war in Arabia, supporting the sultan by suppression of the revolt of the Wahabi, an ultraconservative Islamic sect. In 1820 his armies began an invasion of the eastern Sudan. This was the beginning of a movement that was to occupy his successors and constitute a principal problem in later Anglo-Egyptian relations. Another military venture in the late 1820s found the Egyptian pasha assisting the Turkish sultan in the repression of Greek independence. This resulted in Turkey and Egypt being forced off the eastern Mediterranean by the destruction at Navarino (off the southern coast of Greece) of their combined naval strength.

Mohammed Ali's fourth and most important foreign venture was a war against the Sublime Porte itself, the occasion for which was the sultan's refusal to honor his commitment to give Syria and Morea (Peloponnesus) to Mohammed Ali in return for assistance in repressing the Greek rebellion. The Egyptian forces came within sight of Constantinople, but the great powers (France, Great Britain, Austria, Russia, and Prussia), committed to the preservation of Turkey and fearing a threat to their lines of communication to the east, forced Mohammed Ali to withdraw his troops to Egypt. The one tangible benefit to Mohammed Ali from the adventure was a decree of the Sublime Porte making the *pashaliq* of Egypt hereditary in his family and another decree granting him the government of the Sudan.

The great pasha's immediate successors, Abbas I (1849–54), Said (1854–63), and Ismail (1863–79), were less capable than he. Abbas I has been described as a reactionary, and Said as a jovial, gargantuan sybarite. In 1856 the latter granted to the French promoter Ferdinand de Lesseps a concession for construction of the present-day Suez Canal, begun in 1859 although not opened until 1869. Said, however, initiated unwise major expenditures and personal extravagances that, enlarged under Ismail, finally brought a

Ismail Pasha, the grandson of Mohammed Ali, in his military uniform on a stamp issued in 1945 commemorating the fiftieth anniversary of his death (1895)

The Suez Canal was opened in 1869 with Khedive Ismail Pasha presiding. Among foreign royalty present was Empress Eugenie.

Mohammed Tewfik Pasha ruled from 1879 to 1892 as the khedive. He was a feeble ruler compared to Ismail Pasha, and the people soon rebelled against him and his encouragement of the financial investment of foreign countries.

bankrupt Egypt under British control in the latter part of the nineteenth century.

Ismail's financial irresponsibility invited the subordination of the country to the interests of the great powers, and this fact was not offset by his being granted in 1867 the title khedive of Egypt ("khedive" was applied to Turkish viceroys in Egypt from 1867 to 1914). England, under Prime Minister Benjamin Disraeli, was able to purchase in 1875 Egypt's shares in the Suez Canal Company. This made the British government the largest single shareholder, the balance of the stock being held by various French owners. In 1876 Ismail was forced to accept a French-British debt commission to manage a receivership for Egypt's fiscal affairs and to run the economy of the country. Ismail sought by turns to place responsibility for the financial impasse on others and to placate local and foreign opinion by accepting constitutional limitation upon khedive authority. Finally, his policy became too sinuous for the Dual Control (Great Britain and France), and in 1879 he was forced to abdicate in favor of his son Tewfik and to go into exile at Constantinople, where he died in 1895.

There was an army officers' mutiny in 1879 and continuing unrest. Lieutenant Colonel Ah-mad Arabi, the head of the revolt and the first Egyptian leader in modern times to come from a fellah background, is regarded as the first hero of modern Egyptian nationalism. Civilian political elements and Arabi's Nationalist officers' movement exerted such pressure on the khedive as to cause him to form in 1882 a new and liberalized government with Arabi as minister of war, and it appeared that a settlement between the khedive and the Nationalists might be reached.

The Nationalist movement, however, could not be contained by Tewfik, and the international control was threatened. Great Britain and France supported the khedive and sent naval forces to Alexandria in May of 1882. In June rioting in the city resulted in the death of fifty Christians, and on July 11 the British fleet bombarded Alexandria. The British government decided to suppress the revolt in the interior and invited France and Italy to join in the operation. Both declined and, from that time forward, did not figure in the intervention. A British expeditionary force was landed

at Ismailia and, on September 13, 1882, decisively defeated Arabi in the battle at Tell al-Kabir (about twenty-eight miles west of Ismailia). Arabi surrendered soon afterward in Cairo. The khedive, who had taken refuge under British protection in Alexandria, returned to the capital, and a cabinet acceptable to Great Britain was formed. British occupation of Egypt and virtual inclusion of the country within the British Empire began at that time.

Arabi was tried and convicted. British influence prevented his execution by the khedive, and he was banished with some of his supporters to Ceylon, from which he was permitted to return, almost forgotten, in 1899. His Nationalist revolt had failed, but for a time he had been to all classes of native Egyptian society, including the fellahin, a symbol of protest against foreign control of any kind.

THE BRITISH PRESENCE AND MODERN NATIONALISM

Lord Frederick Dufferin, British ambassador in Constantinople and a noted diplomat, was sent to Egypt soon after Arabi's defeat to survey the governmental situation and devise policy guidance for the British occupation administration. His findings and recommendations were contained in a thorough report published in March 1883. As a result, an Egyptian governmental system was devised to establish the form and limits of governmental authority. This plan was embodied in the Organic Law of May 1, 1883, and provision was made for an elective structure of government under the khedive, which it was hoped might stimulate the development of democratic political processes.

Subsequent to Lord Dufferin's mission, the record of the British occupation is, in effect, the story of three outstanding proconsuls of the empire. These, each of whom bore the title of British agent and consul general, were: Sir Evelyn Baring, later the Lord Cromer, from 1883 to his retirement in 1907; Sir J. Eldon Gorst, from 1907 until his death in 1911; and Lord Horatio Kitchener, from 1911 until 1914. During their tenure, it was the British Agency, and not the khedive's palace, that was the real locus of authority. An Egyptian ministry functioned under the khedive, whose decrees were ostensibly the principal governmental decisions, but the basic policy was British. Khedive Tewfik died in 1892 and was succeeded by his son, Abbas Hilmi, also known as Abbas II, who aspired to rid himself of British control.

Sir J. Eldon Gorst, an experienced Arabist and a milder personality than the redoubtable Lord Cromer, continued public improvements in Egypt and sponsored governmental reforms. Egyptian Nationalists, however, instead of cultivating Gorst as an ally, rejected his overtures. Similarly, he failed to gain the confidence of his more intransigent British colleagues in Egypt and was caught in the middle. In 1910 Egyptian premier Butrus Ghali, a Copt, introduced a bill in the usually compliant legislative assem-

The palace of Khedive Mohammed Tewfik Pasha

Ah-mad Arabi is considered by Egyptians as the "first hero of modern nationalism."

The Arab revolution of 1881–82. This stamp depicts Ah-mad Arabi speaking to the khedive at the time of the revolution.

bly for extension of the Suez Canal Company's concession beyond the terminal time of ninety-nine years. The assembly rejected the measure, and two days later, on February 10, Ghali was assassinated—an act that temporarily alienated the Coptic community from the Nationalist movement. In 1911, upon Gorst's death, the British government determined to replace him with a more forceful personality. Lord Kitchener was designated and vigorously continued Gorst's reform projects while maintaining strict law and order. He largely ignored the khedive Abbas Hilmi, who had quarreled both with the Nationalists and legislative assembly and had become politically isolated.

The outbreak of World War I in 1914 focused attention on the strategic importance of Egypt and the Suez Canal to the British lifeline to the east. Khedive Abbas Hilmi was in

Ahmed Fuad I (1868–1936), king of Egypt, born in Gizeh. In 1914, when Turkey, nominally Egypt's suzerain, entered the war on the side of Germany, the British officially seized Egypt, which it had controlled in actuality for many years. Fuad's brother was made sultan and in 1917 Fuad succeeded to the throne. In 1922 he became first king of modern Egypt. His reign was one of conflict between the British and the Egyptian Wafdist Nationalists, with Fuad in the bad graces of both sides. He abrogated the constitution in 1928 and attempted autocratic rule, but he was finally forced, in 1935, to restore the constitution of 1923. A stamp was issued, April 28, 1944, commemorating the eighth anniversary of his death in 1936, when he was succeeded by his son, Farouk I.

Turkey at the time. Upon Turkey's alignment with the Central Powers and the adherence of Abbas to the Turkish cause, Great Britain forbade Abbas to return and, on December 18, 1914, declared a formal protectorate over Egypt that lasted until 1922. Lord Kitchener, the last British agent, was in England at the outbreak of the war. He was made secretary of state for war and did not return. His successor in Cairo, the first high commissioner for Egypt, was Sir Frederick McMahon. The nominal rule of the Ottoman caliphate was ended. The title of khedive was abolished, and Abbas's uncle, Hussein Kemal, succeeded to the throne with the title of sultan of Egypt. Upon his death in 1917, he was succeeded by his brother, Prince Ahmed Fuad.

Egyptian nationalism was relatively quiescent in the early phases of the war, but by 1917, when the Allied victory began to be visible and after President Woodrow Wilson's pronouncement of the principle of national self-determination, demands for Egyptian independence and for representation at the peace conferences multiplied. The British government sent a special mission to Egypt under the leadership of Lord Alfred Milner in December 1919.

After its investigation the mission proposed the renunciation of the protectorate, a declaration of Egyptian independence, and a treaty of alliance. In tacit recognition of the declaration, Prince Fuad assumed the title of king on March 15, 1922. Egypt was thus independent, at least by formal pronouncement of the British government.

An Egyptian constitution was promulgated on April 19, 1923. It made no claim to Egyptian sovereignty over the Sudan, and this issue was held over for subsequent adjustment between the British and Egyptian governments. In September 1923 the Nationalist leader Saad Zaghlul returned from exile. His party, the Wafd, won a sweeping success in the elections of January 1924. Zaghlul went to London to negotiate with the British, but negotiations with the Labour government foundered over the issue of the

Prince Farouk on his seventh birthday, February 11, 1927

On January 20, 1938, King Farouk married Miss Farida Zulficar in the Kourbeh Palace in Cairo. King Farouk was crowned king on April 28, 1936 upon his father's death and was, later, invested again on his eighteenth birthday. He was well educated, speaking English, French, and Arabic fluently, and, of note, he was the chief of the Boy Scouts in Egypt for many years.

Sudan, and Zaghlul returned to Egypt, having failed in his mission.

Sporadic rioting occurred in the months after Zaghlul's return. The British governor-general of Sudan and commander in chief of the Anglo-Egyptian army, Sir Lee Stack, was assassinated in Cairo on November 19, 1924. The crime climaxed a series of murders of British subjects beginning in 1920. Through Lord Allenby, the British demanded and got compensation, concessions, and removal of all Egyptians from the Sudan. Allenby continued as high commissioner until 1925, after the trial and conviction of persons implicated in Sir Lee Stack's murder. He left the post in May of that year. Meanwhile, Zaghlul, who was under the pressure of bad relations with the palace, had resigned in 1924. He had succeeded in initiating a modicum of parliamentary government in Egypt and in transforming the Wafd into the dominating political force in the country. Upon his death in 1927, Zaghlul was succeeded by Mustafa Nahas, who remained a dominant figure in Egyptian politics until the 1952 revolution.

In the political situation that prevailed from 1924 to 1936, the year of the death of King Fuad (succeeded by his son, King Farouk), three forces competed with one another: the Wafd, the king, and British power. The first two were agreed upon one thing: the desire for real independence from Great Britain. On other grounds they were at odds, with the Wafd working to curtail the royal prerogative and the king striving to prevent the Wafd from forming governments that might carry out the popular Wafd program. In the course of the struggle, the constitution of 1923 was suspended in 1928, restored in 1929, replaced in 1930 by a modification favoring royal authority, and restored again in 1935. During part of this period Mustafa Nahas led the Wafd in extraparliamentary opposition to the government of Ismail Sidgi.

A constructive development of this period was the successful negotiation leading to agreement with Great Britain. The Italian invasion of Ethiopia had underscored the vulnerability of an Egypt unsupported by Great Britain. The king worked for and produced a united front and restored the constitution as a bid to the Wafd. In May 1936 the Wafd won in the elections, and Nahas led a delegation, representing several parties, in negotiations with Great Britain. Agreement was reached in August 1936.

By the terms of this Anglo-Egyptian Treaty of 1936, the occupation of Egypt was terminated. Great Britain retained the right to maintain troops for twenty years along the Suez Canal and the right to have the Royal Air Force fly over Egyptian soil for training purposes. In the event of war, the treaty provided for large-scale mutual assistance. Moreover, it was agreed that the alliance would be extended after 1956. It was stipulated that the Sudan would continue to be ruled under the Sudan Condominium Treaty of 1899 with the proviso that Egyptian troops would be readmitted into the Sudanese military forces. Great Britain undertook to sponsor Egyptian membership in the League of Nations, and Egypt gained admission in 1937.

Prince Farouk at the age of thirteen with three of his four sisters. Left to right: Princess Faiza (born November 8, 1923), Prince Farouk, Princess Faika, (born June 8, 1926), and Princess Fawziya (born November 5, 1921). Princess Fathiya, not present, was born on December 17, 1930.

With the outbreak of World War II in 1939, the war clauses of the 1936 treaty, rather than those relating to Egypt's independence, were applied. It was not until 1947 that British troops finally left Upper and Lower Egypt. During half of that time they were present on a war footing, with Egypt functioning as a base of Allied operations. On British advice, Egypt declared its neutrality but provided more assistance to the Allied cause than was stipulated by the treaty.

The war deepened the cleavages of Egyptian politics. The young King Farouk early showed his independence by refusing to accede to Wafd demands for dismissal of the Saadist leader, Ali Maher, as chief of the royal cabinet. Farouk's temperament came into conflict with the dictatorial nature of Nahas, and the critical issue between them became the attitude toward the war. In this conflict the king came to symbolize what was suspected to be a pro-Nazi attitude, whereas Nahas and the Wafd represented a pro-Allied position. The king was forced by an ultimatum from the British ambassador Lord Killearn and by a show of British military strength before the palace on February 2, 1942, to appoint Nahas as prime minister.

Throughout the critical phases of the war, especially in North Africa, Egypt, under Wafdist leadership, supported the Allied cause. As the war progressed, however, the Wafdist tendency toward corruption, second thoughts on its involvement in the British humiliation of the king, and a disastrous malarial epidemic in Upper Egypt created a situation in which it was possible for the king to dismiss Nahas. This he did in October 1944, in spite of Nahas's successful efforts toward creating the League of Arab States (Arab League), which was to be established on March 22, 1945, in Cairo by Egypt, Iraq, Lebanon, Syria, Saudi Arabia, and Transjordan. (Yemen, the seventh founding state, signed the pact on May 10, 1945.)

Nationalist feeling became more and more inflamed during this period. Anomalously, the Wafd, once again in opposition, began to exploit this feeling, which had been intensified by inflation and the Wafd's own record of misgovernment. The Egyptian government under Ahmad Maher nevertheless declared war against the Axis powers on February 24, 1945, with British approval, in order to be able to participate in the peace settlements. On the same day Ahmad Maher was assassinated by an Egyptian Fascist earlier released from internment. The declaration of war, which made Egypt an outright ally of Great Britain, was necessary in order to serve Egyptian Nationalist interests in the international arena. Egypt became a member of the United Nations (UN) on October 24, 1945.

But the main stumbling block was the Sudan issue. The Egyptian objective, as it had always been since the time of the pharaohs, was to incorporate the Sudan into Egypt and, thus, ensure exclusive control of the Nile and its valley. Great Britain, as always, was committed to an independent posture in the Sudan, and its intention to accord self-government there aroused bitter Egyptian opposition, in-

Iran's crown prince, Reza Pahlevi, married Princess Fawzia, the eigh-teen-year-old sister of King Farouk at the Abdin Palace in Cairo. Left to right: *Queen Farida, King Farouk, Princess Fawzia, Crown Prince Reza, and the Queen Mother Nazli of Egypt.*

cluding inconclusive submission of the problem to the United Nations.

Attention was diverted from the Sudan, however, by events in Palestine, where Great Britain formally ter-minated its mandate on May 15, 1948. On the night of May 14–15, the Israeli Proclamation of Independence was an-nounced by David Ben-Gurion and Zionist representatives at Tel Aviv. At about the same time, the Egyptian prime minister Mahmud Fahmi Nakrashi broadcast an announce-ment that Egyptian forces had entered Palestine to restore order and suppress the "terrorist Zionist gangs." In the Palestine War of 1948 that followed, Egyptian and other Arab forces were defeated by the Israelis. An Egyptian-Israeli armistice agreement arranged through UN mediation was signed on February 24, 1949, leaving the coastal area of Palestine known as the Gaza Strip under Egyptian ad-ministration.

A stamp honors Prince Farouk on his ninth birthday, 1929.

King Farouk on his twenty-fifth birthday, 1945

This stamp commemorates the first wedding of King Farouk I (with Queen Farida Zulficar), January 20, 1938.

A special issue of a stamp commemorating the second marriage of King Farouk I (with Narriman Sadek), May 6, 1951

King Farouk I consulting with President Franklin D. Roosevelt, president of the United States, aboard an American warship during World War II

Other political parties accused Nahas of setting up a dictatorship. Possibly to divert attention outward, Nahas asked Parliament to abrogate the Anglo-Egyptian Treaty of 1936 and to proclaim Farouk king of the Sudan.

Great Britain categorically rejected this line of action;

A May 28, 1946 set of stamps was issued to commemorate the Arab League Congress held in Cairo that year. The attending dignitaries are (top to bottom): King Farouk, with the Royal Palace in the background; Prince Abdullah of Yemen; President Bechara el Khoury, Lebanon; King ibn Saud (Abd-al-Azis III) of Saudi Arabia; King Faisal II of Iraq; Amir Abdullah ibn al-Hussein of Jordan; and President Shukri el Kouatly, Syria.

In Egypt popular reaction had blamed Egyptian defeats on corruption and incompetence of the government and the populace increasingly supported the Muslim Brotherhood. In Cairo the chief of police was assassinated on December 8, 1948. Prime Minister Nakrashi ordered the brotherhood dissolved; however, he was assassinated himself on December 28. King Farouk replaced him with Ibrahim Abdul Hadi. Hassan al-Banna, founder and leader of the Muslim Brotherhood, was assassinated on February 13, 1949.

After the election of January 3, 1950, the Wafd party returned to power, with Mustafa Nahas as prime minister.

King Farouk seated on his throne in typical attire while making public announcements or attending to various matters of protocol.

Lieutenant Colonel Gamal Abdul Nasser, the operational head of the Free Officers who seized control of Egypt in the 1952 Revolution, eventually became president in 1956. On July 27, 1956, he seized control of the Suez Canal in retaliation for the withdrawal by Western interests of financial support from the Aswan Dam project. He declared that the revenue from the Canal would be used to finance the Aswan project. Nasser, an antiroyalist, is reported to have plotted for the assassination of Middle East rulers of kingdoms.

guerrilla warfare broke out between Egyptians and British in the canal area; British forces seized a police barracks at Ismailia. Anti-Western rioting broke out in Cairo on January 26, 1952, with extensive damage and loss of life. King Farouk dismissed Nahas as prime minister but the political situation had become so chaotic that neither the authority of the king nor of the government was secure. One of the contributing sources of discontent and embarrassment to many Egyptians at this time, and for some years previously, was the sybaritic extravagance of Farouk and his court. Public disorders continued and, in the months from February to late July 1952, Egypt had five governments, all of which failed to stabilize the situation while the conduct of public affairs floundered in a political vacuum.

THE 1952 REVOLUTION

King Farouk and his security police had been aware of the existence of a disaffected group of army officers even before the Palestine War of 1948, but they had never been able to discover its leaders or the details of its organization. The Free Officers, headed by Lieutenant Colonel Gamal Abdul Nasser, moved on the night of July 22–23, 1952, and seized control of Cairo, and shortly afterward the whole country, in a virtually bloodless coup d'etat.

Major General Mohammed Naguib, a popular senior Egyptian officer of Egyptian-Sudanese descent, who had fought well in Palestine and been seriously wounded, was called upon to become president of the Revolutionary Command Council. General Naguib had been associated with

the Free Officers since December 1951, although not actively so. Too well-known to avoid discovery, he was not made privy to the secret organization and did not participate in the planning or the execution of the army revolt. Naguib was fifty-one years old. The average age of the eleven other members of the Revolutionary Command Council was only thirty-three. They were: Gamal Abdul Nasser, Abdul Hakim Amer, Abdul Latif Baghdadi, Zakariya Muhieddin, Anwar el-Sadat, Gamal Salem, Salah Salem, Husayn al-Shafi, Kamal Husayn, Hasan Ibrahim, and Khalid Muhieddin. The first eight graduated from the Military Academy in Cairo in 1938, the next two in 1939, and Khalid Muhieddin in 1940.

The Revolutionary Command Council was conscious of the possibility that British troops from the Canal Zone might be directed to save King Farouk, as they had intervened to save the khedive Tewfik in 1882. The Egyptian officers' group acted swiftly. Ali Maher, a respected neutral political figure who had held the office before, was designated as prime minister to form a new government. On July 26 King Farouk, who was in Alexandria when the coup occurred, abdicated in favor of his infant son as King Ahmed Fuad II with a council of regency. But it was not to be! The dynastic rule of Mohammed Ali's line ended with the abdication.

Farouk and his family, including his son Ahmed Fuad, were allowed to leave Egypt the same day for Italy, unharmed, on his yacht, the *Mahroussa*. The events of July 22–26, 1952, known as the 1952 revolution, constituted a turning point in the history of the Middle East.

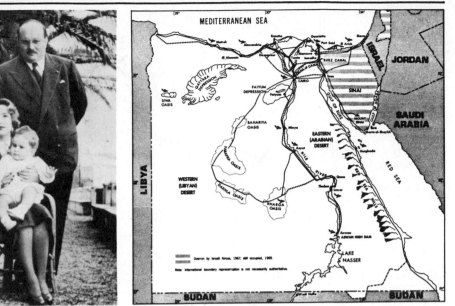

King Farouk with Queen Narriman and their infant son, the young king, Fuad II, in exile in 1952

Egypt in 1980

THE ROYAL SOVEREIGNS OF THE DYNASTIES AND KINGDOM OF EGYPT

(Egyptian names with Greek or biblical versions in parentheses)

PREDYNASTY KINGS

Ro (South Egypt)
Tiu (North Egypt)
Thesh (North Egypt)
Heskin (North Egypt)
Uaznar (North Egpyt)
The Scorpion (Ip)
Narmer
Aha Men

FIRST DYNASTY (THINITE)
3400–3200 B.C.

Menes (Mena)
Athothis
Kenkenes
Uenestes
Zer Atoti (Khent)
Za (Zet, Ata)
Den (Senti)
Enzib Merpeba
Semerkhet Hui (Shemsu)
Ka Sen

SECOND DYNASTY (THINITE)
3200–2980 B.C.

Aksinoe
Hotep-Sekhemui
Raneb Kakau
Neneter
Perenamaat
Peribsen
Senedi
Neferka-Ra
Neferka-Sokari
Huzefa

THIRD DYNASTY (MEMPHITE)
2980–2900 B.C.

Khasekhemui Besh (Bebi)
Zeser (Tcheser, Zoser)
Sanekht
Zeserteti
Sezes
Neferka-Huni
Sneferu

FOURTH DYNASTY (MEMPHITE)
2900–2750 B.C.

2900–2898 Sharu
2898–2875 Khufu (Cheops)
2875–2867 Razedef
2867–2811 Khafre (Chephren)
2811–2788 Menkure (Mycerinus)
2788–2755 Shepsekaf and others
2755–2750 Thamphthis

FIFTH DYNASTY (MEMPHITE)
2750–2625 B.C.

2750–2743 Userkaf
2743–2731 Sahu-Ra
2731–2730 Neferirika-Ra
2730–2723 Shepseska-Ra
2723–2722 Khanefer-Ra
2722–2691 Ne-User-Ra (User-er-Ra)
2691–2683 Menkau-Heru
2683–2655 Dedka-Ra Isesi
2655–2625 Unis

SIXTH DYNASTY (MEMPHITE)
2625–2431 B.C.

2625–2611 Teti
2611–2595 Userka-Ra Ati
2595–2542 Pepi I
2542–2538 Meren-Ra I
2538–2444 Pepi II
2444–2443 Meren-Ra II
2443–2437 Neterka-Ra
2437–2431 Menka-Ra

SEVENTH AND EIGHTH DYNASTIES (MEMPHITE)
2431–2405 B.C.

Period of anarchy.

NINTH AND TENTH DYNASTIES (HERACEOPOLITAN)
2405–2152 B.C.

Period of invasion, multirule.

ELEVENTH DYNASTY (THEBAN)
2152–2000 B.C.

2152–2150 King Intef I
    (Horus Wahenskh)
2150–2090 King Intef II
    (Horus Nakhtneb-Tepnefer)
2090–2085 King Intef III
2085–2065 King Mentuhotep I
    (Horus Sehekhibtone)
2065–2060 King Mentuhotep II
    (Nibhepetre)
2060–2015 King Mentuhotep III
    (Nibtonere)
2015–2005 King Mentuhotep IV
    (Nibhepetre)
2005–2000 King Mentuhotep V
    (Senekhkere)

TWELFTH DYNASTY (THEBAN)
2000–1788 B.C.

2000–1970 Amenemhet I
1970–1935 Sesostris I
    (Senusret, Usertesen)
1935–1904 Amenemhet II
1906–1887 Sesostris II
1887–1849 Sesostris III
1849–1801 Amenemhet III
1801–1792 Amenemhet IV
1792–1788 Queen Sebekneferu-Ra

THIRTEENTH, FOURTEENTH, FIFTEENTH, AND SIXTEENTH DYNASTIES
HYKSOS OR "SHEPHERD KINGS" DYNASTY
1788–1635 B.C.

SEVENTEENTH DYNASTY (THEBAN)
1635–1580 B.C.

1635–1615 Sekenen-Ra I
1615–1605 Sekenen-Ra II
1605–1591 Sekenen-Ra III
1591–1581 Uazkheperfa-Kamose
1581–1580 Senekhten-Ra

NEW KINGDOM

EIGHTEENTH DYNASTY (DIOSPOLITE)
1580–1350 B.C.

1580–1557 King Ahmose I
    (Amasis)
1557–1541 King Amenhotep I
1541–1505 King Thotmes I
    (Tuthmosis)
1505–1501 King Thotmes II
1501–1501 King Mutemua
1501–1498 Queen Hatshepsut
    (co-ruler), daughter of Thotmes II
1501–1447 King Thotmes III
    (co-ruler), brother of Hatshepsut
1447–1420 King Amenhotep II
1420–1411 King Thotmes IV
1411–1375 King Amenhotep III
1375–1358 King Amenhotep IV
    (Akhenaten)
1358–1358 King Sakere
1358–1353 King Tutankhamun
1358–1350 King Ay (Ai)

NINETEENTH DYNASTY (DIOSPOLITE)
1350–1205 B.C.

1350–1315 King Horemheb (Harmhab)
1315–1314 King Rameses I
1314–1292 King Seti I (Sethos)
1292–1225 King Rameses II (Sesostris)
1225–1215 King Merneptah
1215–1215 King Amenmeses
1215–1209 King Siptak (Saptah)
1209–1205 Seti II

TWENTIETH DYNASTY (DIOSPOLITE)
1205–1085 B.C.

1205–1200 Anarchy and Reign
    of Syrian Usurper
1200–1198 King Setnakht
1198–1167 King Rameses III
1167–1161 King Rameses IV
1161–1157 King Rameses V
1157–1142 King Rameses VI, VII, VIII
1142–1123 King Rameses IX
1123–1121 King Rameses X
1121–1118 King Rameses XI
1118–1085 King Rameses XII

TWENTY-FIRST DYNASTY (TANITE)
1085–950 B.C.

1090–1085 King Nesubenebded/King Hrihor
1085–1067 King Pesibkhenno I
1067–1026 King Paynozem I
1026– 976 King Amenemopet
 976– 958 King Siamon
 958– 950 King Pesibkhenno II

TWENTY-SECOND DYNASTY (BUBASTITE DYNASTY)
950–730 B.C.

950–929 King Shashank
          (Shishak, Sheshonk)
929–895 King Osorkon I (Osorthern)
895–870 King Takelot I
870–847 King Osorkon II
847–877 King Sheshonk II
          (co-regency)
860–823 King Takelot II
          (Iuput) (co-regency)
823–772 King Sheshonk III
772–782 King Pemou (Pamai)
782–745 King Sheshonk IV
745–730 King Osorkon IV

TWENTY-THIRD DYNASTY (TANITE)
PRIEST KINGS OF THEBES
860–742 B.C.

860–838 King Harsiesi
838–815 King Pedubaste
          (Peta-bast)
815–780 King Takeleth II
780–750 King Osorkon III
750–745 King Takeleth III
          (co-regent 757)
745–742 King Rudament
          (co-regent 750)

TWENTY-FOURTH DYNASTY (SAITE)
730–712 B.C.

730–715 King Tafhekht
715–712 King Uahkere Bokenranef (Bocchoris)

TWENTY-FIFTH DYNASTY (ETHIOPIAN)
751–656 B.C.

751–751 King Kashla
751–716 King Piankhy
716–701 King Shabaka (Sabacon, So)
700–689 King Shabataka
689–664 King Taharka (Tirhakah, Tarkus)
664–653 King Tanutamen

Fall of Memphis to Esarhaddon of Assyria, 671 B.C.

Fall of Thebes to Ashurbanipal of Assyria, 663 B.C.

(Cecho I—Assyrian Reign 670–663)

TWENTY-SIXTH DYNASTY (SAITE)
663–525 B.C.

663–609 King Psamtek I
          (Psammetichos)
609–593 King Necho II
          (Nechon, Nekas, Nechao)
593–588 King Psamtek II
          (Psammetichos)
588–569 King Uahibra
          (Hophra, Apries)
569–526 King Aahmes II
          (Amasis, Ahmosi)
526–525 King Psamtek III
          (Psammetichos)

TWENTY-SEVENTH DYNASTY
525–404 B.C.

Ruled by Persian kings.

558–529 King Cyrus II,
          "the Great"
529–522 King Cambyses II
522–486 King Darius I
486–465 King Xerxes I
465–425 King Artaxerxes I
425–424 Xerxes II
424–414 King Darius II,
          Nothus
414–408 King Amyrtaeus

TWENTY-EIGHTH AND TWENTY-NINTH DYNASTIES
404–378 B.C.
408–386 King Nepherites I
386–386 King Nepherites II

THIRTIETH DYNASTY
378–341 B.C.
386–361 King Nectanebos I
386–361 King Artaxerxes II
361–338 King Nectanebos II
361–338 King Artaxerxes III,
          Ochus
338–336 King Arses I
336–330 King Darius III

The last Egyptian king was Nectanebos II.

Ruled by Persians in 340 B.C.

THIRTY-FIRST DYNASTY
340–332 B.C.

Kings Arses I and Darius III ruled.

THIRTY-SECOND DYNASTY
(THE PTOLEMIES—THE GREEK PERIOD)
332–30 B.C.

332–323 Alexander the Great
323–285 King Ptolemy I (Soter, Lagos)
285–247 King Ptolemy II (Philadelphus)
247–221 King Ptolemy III (Euergetes)
221–203 King Ptolemy IV (Philopator)
203–180 King Ptolemy V (Epiphanes)
180–144 King Ptolemy VI (Philometor)
144–117 King Ptolemy VII (Euergetes II)
117–108 King Ptolemy VIII (Lathyrus)
108– 89 King Ptolemy IX (Alexander I)
 88– 80 King Ptolemy VIII
 81– 80 Queen Berenice
 81– 80 King Ptolemy X, Alexander II
 81– 44 King Ptolemy XI, Auletes
 44– 30 Queen Cleopatra VII (co-ruler)
 44– 30 King Ptolemy XIV (Cesarion)
 51– 47 King Ptolemy XII
 47– 44 King Ptolemy XIII

ROMAN RULE
30 B.C.–A.D. 324

COPTIC (EAST ROMAN) RULE
A.D. 324–640

Arab Empire conquest of Egypt, A.D. 640–1517.

Ottoman Empire conquest of Egypt, 1517, which lasted until 1805, when Turkish control began.

Reign	Title	Name	Birth	Death	Relationship
1805–1849	Viceroy	Mohammed Ali	1769	1849	
1849–1854	Viceroy	Abbas I	1813	1854	Son of Mohammed Ali
1854–1863	Viceroy	Said Pasha	1823	1863	Grandson of Mohammed Ali
1863–1879	Khedive	Ismail Pasha	1830	1895	Grandson of Mohammed Ali
1879–1892	Khedive	Mohammed Tewfik Pasha	1853	1892	Son of Ismail Pasha
1892–1914	Khedive	Abbas II Hilmi	1874	1944	Son of Tewfik Pasha
Egypt was under British rule from 1882–1922.					
1914–1917	Sultan	Hussein Kemal	1854	1917	Son of Ismail Pasha
1917–1922	Sultan	Ahmed Fuad Pasha			
1922–1936	King	Ahmed Fuad (Fuad I)			
1936–1952	King	Farouk	1920	1965	Son of Fuad I
1952–1953	King	Ahmed II	1951	—	Son of Farouk

2

The Empire of Ethiopia

The founders of the original Ethiopian city-states probably arrived from the Arabian Peninsula in the first half of the first millennium B.C., mixed with the local Cushitic peoples, and developed their states into the kingdom of Axum, which remained powerful for many centuries. In the fourth century A.D. its rulers and, gradually, its people were converted to Christianity, an event of enormous importance in later Ethiopian history. Their religious faith, linked to the belief in the divinely ordained position of the emperor, gave a common purpose to the people of Axum and their descendants. Its strength was continually tested after the seventh and particularly after the tenth century, by which time Ethiopia had become a Christian island in a Muslim sea. The rise of a hostile Islam around it led to the severing of ties, until then relatively strong, to the outside world and imposed an isolation from foreign influences that lasted into the twentieth century.

During the interim Ethiopia developed and preserved cultural, religious, artistic, and political forms distinct from European and Middle Eastern Christian societies. In the early sixteenth century, however, Muslim forces ravaged almost the entire country, destroying much of the existing artistic and architectural heritage of the country's ancient culture. Until that point its cultural achievements had remained on a par with those of much of Europe.

The Muslim incursion led to a tentative renewal of ties to the Christian world with the arrival, also in the early sixteenth century, of Portuguese diplomatic and military missions seeking joint action against the Muslim forces. These ties were aborted shortly thereafter, however, by religious conflicts between Western Christianity, in the form of the Roman Catholicism brought by the Portuguese, and the traditional forms of the Ethiopian Orthodox church. These conflicts disappointed the Ethiopians, who had long hoped for renewed ties to the Christian world, and left the country with a profound distrust of Europeans.

These internal and external conflicts weakened the position of the emperor in the seventeenth century, and for the first time feudal political arrangements invaded on the imperial power. For one hundred fifty years the emperors

A modern map of Ethiopia

remained weak, sometimes being little more than puppets for powerful regional rulers although still respected as the divinely ordained holders of the throne. In the mid-nineteenth century came a resurgence of their power, first under the usurper Emperor Theodore and later, after his defeat by British forces supported by Ethiopian regional leaders, by his legitimate successors of the Tigre and Shoa royal lines.

The emperors after Theodore were occupied by efforts to ensure the dominance of the imperial power, at first over the regional lords and then over peripheral territories. In the later expansion the control of the Amhara-Tigre was extended over nearly all the territories populated by non-Christian, often Muslim, peoples to the south and east of the Amhara-Tigre highland plateau.

This expansion was carried out in the face of European efforts to extend colonial control over these same or adjacent areas and brought the country into direct contact with the modern world. These later emperors therefore became modernists in varying degrees, adopting first the arms and then the administrative structures they saw as advantageous. Their ability to acquire modern arms and make effective use of them was demonstrated to the outside world at the crucial battle of Adowa in 1896 when Ethiopian forces crushed the Italian colonial advance.

The last emperor of Ethiopia, Haile Selassie, came to power as regent for the empress Zauditu in 1916. He had become coruler by 1928 and was crowned emperor, after Zauditu's death, in 1930. During the period until the Italian invasion of the country in 1935, he was the champion of modernist forces while still retaining the position and methods of the traditional ruler. The country fell under Italian rule for five years between 1936 and 1941, during which time modernization was carried a step further through the creation by the Italians of a road infrastructure and other public works. The Ethiopians strongly resisted the Italian conquest and rule and took advantage of British support against the Fascist power after the outbreak of World War II to regain control for themselves in 1941.

The postwar era has been characterized by slow but continuing modernization and the establishment of Ethiopia, or its emperor, as a significant voice in international affairs, particularly within the newly developing states of Africa. The 1960s were marked by the development of a generation of younger men with modern education who demanded a faster pace in the country's efforts to move forward into the modern world technologically and socially, although most of them wished to sacrifice as little as possible of the country's ancient traditions in doing so.

ORIGINS
AND THE EARLY PERIOD

The precise nature of the early origins of Ethiopian peoples is still a matter of conjecture. The first important source of pressure and influence in that part of Africa was probably the kingdom of Cush or Meroe, a strong contender with Egypt for control of the upper Nile. Its kings ruled Egypt from 751 to 656 B.C. and dominated an area reaching from the Mediterranean south through what is now the Republic of Sudan, portions of Ethiopia, and perhaps even Uganda.

The name Ethiopia was sometimes-applied to them, but the term *Ethiopian,* probably first used by Homer or Herodotus, meant all the lands inhabited by black men. The origins of Ethiopia itself, however, are found in the kingdom of Axum and the city-states that preceded it which may date from as early as the tenth century B.C., in what is now the area occupied by the Tigre people.

In this early period direct relationships between Ethiopia and Egypt were maintained by way of the Nile and its tributaries and, more important, by sea. A relationship also was maintained between southern Arabia and the Horn of Africa and Ethiopia. A significant two-way movement of peoples took place from a very early time.

It is accepted as historical fact in the Revised Constitution of 1955 and by the average Christian Ethiopian that the imperial dynasty of the country began with Menelik I, the son of Makeda, the queen of Saba (Sheba), and King Solomon. The ruling emperor continued to be referred to as a member of the Solomonic dynastic line, which is presumed to have exercised sovereign power with minor interruptions since its inception in the tenth century B.C. The same Ethiopian traditions form a basis for the religious nature of the state. According to that tradition, Menelik I, then a young man, was sent on a lengthy visit to his father, Solomon. On his departure he stole the Ark of the Covenant and, accompanied by Israelite noble youths to serve the country as priests, transported it to his Ethiopian homeland.

From the *Kebra Negast* (Glory of Kings), a chronicle considered a very important document by Ethiopians, the people conclude that Menelik I and his successors are descendants of holy men, since Solomon was one of a series through whose bodies had passed a "pearl" first placed by God in Adam and intended finally, having entered the body of Hannah, to be the essence of her daughter, the Virgin Mary. Christ being the Son of God and Menelik a kinsman of Christ, the kings of Ethiopia, as descendants of Menelik, were considered to be of a divine line.

THE EARLY KINGDOM: AXUM

Axum was the creation of a relatively small number of Semitic invaders from southern Arabia, who arrived between 1000 and 400 B.C. and combined with, and provided leadership for, earlier Cushitic-speaking inhabitants. The mixed population, forebears of the Tigrinya-speaking peoples of Tigre and Eritrea provinces, slowly built a novel and distinctive civilization and founded the Axumite Kingdom. The Amharas descend from members of this population who moved south and mixed with more southerly Cushitic inhabitants.

Ezana, the greatest Ethiopian king of the Axumite period, reigned in the fourth century A.D. According to most sources, he made Geez the official language, with its own script, which refined the Sabean system of Arabic, and he extended Axum's power in all directions. Most important, he was converted to Christianity, which became the official religion of the country and the accepted religion of most of the people and bound the Ethiopian state together for sixteen centuries. The country had already come into contact with the Byzantine Empire and undertook, at the request of its Roman emperor, a special mission to protect and extend Christianity in eastern Africa. Byzantium considered the Axumite-Ethiopian Kingdom an acceptable outpost of Christianity despite the Ethiopian church's fealty to the Coptic Church of Egypt, which both Greek and Roman churches regarded as heretical because of its adherence to the Monophysite doctrine—that is, that Christ had only one nature, divine, rather than a human and a divine nature in one being, as the larger churches maintain.

Until the rise of Islam in the seventh century A.D., Axum

played a significant political role in southern Arabia. At its fullest extension, between the fourth and seventh centuries, its sovereignty was acknowledged from Meroe in the Nile Valley to Mecca in Arabia.

THE PRESSURE OF ISLAM

The spread of Islam cut off the Axumite-Ethiopian Kingdom from Byzantium. At first, before the followers of the Prophet Muhammad achieved acceptance in Arabia, some of them found refuge with the Ethiopian king. As time passed and the Islamic star rose, the Ethiopians gained a reputation for benevolence toward the Arabs. This benevolence helped preserve the central territories from the conquests by which Arabs spread Islam throughout North Africa and the Middle East, but it did not prevent the isolation of the country from the rest of the Christian world for nearly six hundred years and from its Muslim neighbors as well.

The decline in Ethiopian fortunes appears to have halted for a time by the early tenth century. The Red Sea littoral was partly reoccupied, and contacts were reestablished with southern Arabia. At the end of the tenth century, however, the Cushitic-speaking Agau people, in some versions said to be the *Falasha,* the so-called Black Jews, which are still numerous, rebelled and succeeded in defeating the Christian forces, sacking Axum. The Agau were subdued only after the arrival from Alexandria of a new and vigorous archbishop *(abune)* who was able not only to stimulate Christianity to a renewed life but also to begin a national moral and political revival.

In 1137 a new force appeared in Christian Ethiopia in the form of an Agau (Cushitic) Dynasty, known as the Zagwe. The Zagwe, who came from the Lasta mountains, occupied the throne for one hundred thirty-three years. Claiming descent from Moses rather than Solomon, they have been viewed by later generations as usurpers, nonrepresentative of legitimate tradition. Nevertheless, one of the Zagwe kings, Lalibela, had a distinguished reign, made notable particularly by his construction of the remarkable solid stone churches at the town of Lalibela. He and three other Zagwe rulers have been canonized by the Ethiopian Orthodox church.

THE MIDDLE PERIOD

The year 1270 saw the end of the Agau Dynasty and the reestablishment by force of a Solomonic line. Tekla Haimanot, a saint of the church and the founder of the monastery of Debra Libanos, is credited in Ethiopian sources with having effected the restoration of the Solomonic line. Ethiopian contact increased not only with the Levant and the Middle East in general but also with Europe.

The first emperor of the restored Solomonic line was Yekuno Amalak. The political and geographic center of the state became the Amhara region. The ruler's main aim became the consolidation of control over the high plateau and the gradual weakening and destruction of the encircling power of Muslim states, initially that of Yfat, which threatened the heart of Shoa. The Ethiopians then carried out continuous military activity; they also continued the literary renaissance begun under the Zagwe Dynasty and the religious development that led to a complete merger of the church with the state.

The next monarch of importance was Amba Sion, the grandson of Yekuno Amalak who, in the early part of the fourteenth century, rose to heights as a military leader, reformer, and administrator. Having taken Gojam, Damot, and Begemder, he was able finally to turn his attention to the problem of the encroachments of the Muslim states. During his reign the long contest was begun with the sultanate of Adal in the Danakil-Somali region. His initial successes, giving him complete command of the highlands and enhancing the advantages of his central position, were victories over Yfat and Hadya. These extensions of the emperor's power were accompanied by the spreading of Christianity to such an extent that Amba Sion has been named a saint in the Ethiopian Orthodox church.

Zara Yakob (1434–68) is judged by some to have been the greatest Ethiopian ruler since Ezana of Axum and without peer until the time of Menelik II and Haile Selassie. His military accomplishments were substantial, especially his defeat of the Sidamo peoples in the Dowar region. More remarkable, however, were his achievements in the spheres of administrative and church reform. It is asserted that, having written or inspired others to write some of the fundamental texts of the state church, he was primarily responsible for the present organization and doctrine of the Ethiopian Orthodox church. He began the struggle of the monarchy to limit, if not destroy, the increasing power of the great regional *rases* (princes or dukes). The achievements of Zara Yakob, however, were weakened by a lessening of central control under his successors.

ORGANIZATION OF THE STATE

During the Middle Ages the power of the *Negusa Nagast,* or "king of kings," was unlimited in theory and often in fact. The imperial government rested immediately and directly upon his ability to retain the obedience of the governors or kings of the provinces. The apparatus itself was relatively simple. The agencies of direction, except for the judiciary, were primarily provincial. When the military had to be used, it was under central control but was composed of provincial levies or troops who lived off the country or were supported by the provincial governments contributing them. The result was that the expenses borne by the imperial administration were very small and substantially exceeded by the contributions and tribute provided by the provinces.

The writ of the emperor did not depend fundamentally upon force but, rather, upon the obedience rendered to a monarch ordained by God to rule the country. Forces supplied by subordinates were the major determinants of the scope and extent of power, but at the center was an idea rather than a physical force.

The state during this period was at once unitary and imperial. No powers were reserved to the local provincial or regional authorities. In theory, the emperor could decree, modify, or seek any political condition he desired. In fact, however, special interests were recognized and established in particular areas with which the monarch would hesitate to interfere, especially the areas of longest standing Amhara-Tigre control. The emperor, whose capital moved with him as he continually changed the location of his court, was surrounded by ceremony and protocol, which accented his sacred descent and legitimacy. He lived in a suclusion that shielded him, except on rare occasions during the year, from the gaze of all but his pages and a few of the highest state officials. Even the nobility had no access to his person.

The monarch's judicial function was of paramount importance. The administration of justice was centralized as a means of expressing the imperial will, conditioned by a known body of customary law, which in the later years was formally based on a code, the *Fetha Nagast* (Law of Kings), drawn up in Egypt in the twelfth century. Judges appointed by the emperor were attached to the administration of every provincial governor and every *ras*. They not only heard cases but also determined when cases could be referred to the governor or sent on appeal to the central government.

All male members of the royal family who might challenge the emperor were kept, together with their families, on *ambas* (flat-topped mountains), impregnable against attack and from which they generally could not escape for the remainder of their lives. All others were forbidden access to the place of confinement except at the risk of severe punishment. Those imprisoned were well provided for. With minor intervals, the practice was continued from the time of Yekuno Amalak until well into the eighteenth century. In the nineteenth and twentieth centuries the practice of exile to *ambas* was applied to other important figures.

THE MUSLIM ASSAULT

The pressure of Muslim aggression and encirclement was the most important problem facing the Ethiopian rulers and people from a very early period after the appearance of Islam and has persisted in a different context down to the early 1970s. Islam achieved its greatest success in Ethiopia during the reign of Lebna Dengel (1508–40).

In the second half of the fifteenth century the depredations of forces from Adal led by Mahfuz, the sultan of Zeila on the Somali coast, began to increase in number and significance. In 1516, when the Muslim forces began to move in strength against Ethiopian territories, the emperor achieved a major success by ambushing them and killing all who were not driven into retreat, including Mahfuz. This victory was followed up by an Ethiopian incursion of re-

prisal into Adal, which coincided with a Portuguese attack upon Zeila and appeared to the new emperor to complete the destruction of Muslim power in the region.

With the Ottoman conquest of Egypt and Arabia in the same period, the political patterns in the Red Sea area became much more seriously altered against Ethiopian interests. Local Muslim forces were enabled to procure firearms as well as to add well-disciplined troops for employment against their Christian neighbors.

After disturbances and confusion in Adal, during which its capital was removed to Harar, a new Muslim religious and military leader brought all Muslim territories in Ethiopia under his control. Ahmed Ibrahim el-Ghaz or, as the Christians called him, Ahmed Grañ (the Left-Handed), took the title of *imam* (politicoreligious leader) and set about creating a formidable military organization of the Danakil and Somali forces who were motivated by the spirit of religious war and an appetite for plunder. These forces were bolstered with a company of Turkish riflemen. Beginning in 1528, he defeated Lebna Dengel's forces in successive battles and devastated almost the entire Ethiopian plateau.

The result was chaos in traditional Ethiopia, involving not only the destruction of religious institutions and the large-scale conversion of the people to Islam but also the loss of the bulk of great works of historic and artistic value of the earlier Ethiopian civilization. A great deal of the country's intellectual heritage was permanently lost. The Muslims experienced their most determined opposition in Tigre, which was, however, not sufficient to prevent the emperor's becoming a fugitive. At this point Lebna Dengel enlisted Portuguese military aid from India, which eventually turned the tide of Muslim expansion.

RENEWAL OF CONTACT WITH THE CHRISTIAN WORLD

The neighboring Christian states of the Nile had been snuffed out by Egyptian Muslims in the fourteenth and fifteenth centuries, but limited contact with the Western, or Christian, world had been continued through the Egyptian Coptic church.

A further and more direct contact with the Western world was maintained through the Ethiopian Orthodox church's community at Jerusalem and the visits of pilgrims to the Holy Land. Ethiopian monks from the Jerusalem community attended the church council called by the Roman pope in 1441 in an effort to unite the Eastern and Western churches at Florence. The Westerners, who had learned of the Ethiopians through these monks and pilgrims, were attracted to them by two factors. First, Ethiopia was identified with the long-sought land of the legendary Christian priest-king, Prester John. Second, the Ethiopians were viewed as a potentially valuable ally in the then still vital war against the Islamic forces that continued to threaten southern Europe until after the Turkish defeat at the Battle of Lepanto in 1571.

After a raid on Suez, four hundred men under Christovao da Gama landed at Massawa and moved southward to join Emperor Claudius, who had succeeded Lebna Dengel. Two battles were fought with the forces of Ahmed Grañ. The Portuguese forces remained intact, and the Muslim leader retreated only to be reinforced by a larger troop of Turkish riflemen from Yemen. In the next battle over half the Portuguese were killed, including da Gama. The remaining men rallied, however, along with Ethiopian forces, on an *amba* that had previously been occupied by da Gama and, after making their own gun powder from local supplies of sulfur and saltpeter, attacked Ahmed Grañ near Lake Tana. Taken by surprise, his troops were routed and dispersed, and he himself was killed.

The surviving Portuguese, under the orders of the Portuguese king, remained in Ethiopia and were assimilated into the population. Future Muslim attacks were minor, and the Muslim threat tapered off. Near the close of the reign of Claudius, however, the Turks conquered Massawa, and the presence of a garrison there prevented any further hope of Ethiopian access to overseas assistance.

Portuguese Roman Catholic missionaries began to arrive in 1554 in the wake of the closer ties between two countries. Efforts made to induce the Ethiopian Orthodox church to reject its Monophysite beliefs and to accept the leadership of Rome continued for nearly a century and engendered great bitterness within the empire as pro- and anti-Catholic parties strove for control of the state. At least two of the emperors in this period were converted to Catholicism but, after a particularly bloody battle between adherents of the two faiths, the second of the Catholic emperors, Susenyos, abdicated in favor of his son Basilides (or Fasiladas) in 1632 in order to spare the country any further bloodshed. The expulsion of the Jesuits and, later, all Catholic missionaries followed.

ISOLATION AND DECLINE OF IMPERIAL POWER

Emperor Basilides, in the mid-seventeenth century, kept out disruptive influences of the foreign Christians, dealt with the Muslims, and brought many of the weakened Muslim states along the borders under Ethiopian control. He revived the practice of confining members of the royal family on a remote mountaintop to lessen the challenges to his rule and is remembered for his reconstruction of the cathedral at Axum.

A most significant move was the establishment of a permanent capital at Gondar, selected because of the beauty of the site. This ended the tradition of a traveling capital that had allowed the emperor to maintain personal contact with the various regions and to exert direct influence over his subordinates. The dynasty lost power rapidly after settling at remote Gondar, and its rulers began to be identified with one group of regional leaders against which the other regions or kingdoms could align themselves.

It became possible for the first time for local leaders to seek independent authority as permanent rulers of particular areas, no longer subject to removal at the emperor's whim. Feudalism in Ethiopia began only at this point late in the country's history. Most of the succeeding emperors until 1855 were but pawns in the struggles for power of local leaders. They retained their titles of emperor (king of kings) but were without the real power they had once held through the common acceptance of their divinely provided right to rule.

Nevertheless, some emperors of the period were effective leaders. Iyasu I (the Great), in the late seventeenth century, was a military leader of stature and an effective administrative reformer. The imperial authority over the church was strengthened, and relaxation of the xenophobic policy of the two previous rulers resulted in some renewed contacts with western Europeans.

The elevation to the throne of Justus (Yost'os), *ras* of Tigre, early in the eighteenth century, set aside the Solomonic line. Even though placed in power by the nobles, he could not remove the effects of jealousy among them, and the people could not be brought to view him as a legitimate king of kings. An uprising of the army after his death prevented the enthronement of his son and returned the throne to members of the legitimate line.

Under Iyasu II (the Little) the Solomonic line fell into decline. To revive his reputation, Iyasu II undertook a war against the kingdom of Sennar, between Ethiopia and Nubia, and lost an army. His prestige was overshadowed by that of Ras Mikael Suhul of Tigre, where an independent, self-contained power arose.

After the death of Iyasu II, a period of Galla supremacy began that further alienated the Amhara-Tigre peoples and stimulated internal division. After a series of domestic conflicts, the reign of Tekla Haimanot began a period of disintegration known as the Age of the Judges and comparable to the Dark Ages of Europe, which lasted until after the mid-nineteenth century. Warfare in this period was constant, and much of the country, particularly in the north, was frequently devastated.

During the most confused period, around 1800, there were as many as six rival emperors. The foremost chiefs were: Sahle Selassie of Shoa, a ruler of great ability and an ancestor of Emperor Haile Selassie; Ras Ali of Begemder; Ras Wube of Tigre; and Ras Hailu of Gojam. The first half of the nineteenth century was dominated by the division among these four men, which produced a general civil war. Finally, the rulers of Gondar and Gojam were killed, and two contenders were left. In the meantime, however, another figure appeared on the scene in the person of Kassa, later the Emperor Theodore II (Tewodros). Kassa became the instrument of political coordination; with his advent, the making of the modern empire of Ethiopia was begun.

Kassa was born in 1818 of a father who was a local chief but who claimed descent from the queen of Saba (Sheba). Kassa was educated in a monastery on Lake Tana, where he acquired a strong devotion to the cause of Ethiopian Christianity. Later, he gained a reputation for preying on traveling Muslim traders. He also defeated Muslim forces in the Sudan. After an attempt by the queen mother of Gondar to suppress him failed, Ras Ali, then effectively the ruler of Gondar, recognized Kassa's jurisdiction over the territories he controlled and gave him his own daughter as a wife. During the civil war that followed, Kassa established control over Gondar and Gojam. By 1854 he emerged as the strongest leader in the country. Having routed and slain Ras Ali of Gondar, he attacked Wube of Tigre, who had proclaimed himself king of kings.

Three days after defeating the forces of Tigre and making Wube a prisoner, he was crowned emperor. In return he promised to expel Roman Catholic missionaries from the country. He took the name Theodore in recognition of a prophecy promising an Emperor Theodore who would come as a national savior. He deposed John III, the last of the shadow emperors at Gondar, and transferred the capital to the fortress of Magdala, a more central position in the Amhara highlands.

THEODORE II (1855–68)

Theodore II halted and reversed the decline of imperial power and reestablished, even though imperfectly, the ideal as well as the reality of central government. During his reign the country was forced to begin adjustment to the new external forces from Europe and Egypt. The end of the second long period of Ethiopian isolation, brought about by conditions beyond Ethiopian control, demanded the reshaping of an Ethiopian political unity able to meet the external challenge.

The most important accomplishments of the period include the beginning of the campaigns against the Galla and the reunification of Shoa, Gojam, Amhara, Begemder and, eventually, Tigre under central imperial control. In the process Theodore brought the crown prince of Shoa (later to become Emperor Menelik II) to Magdala as a captive.

The emperor's actions in favor of modernization and centralization as well as his personality, which was by all accounts erratic, soon generated opposition that he was never able to suppress completely. His enemies labeled him insane. During his reign European powers involved themselves in internal Ethiopian affairs. For example, Negusie, a Tigre chieftain, rose to power in that province and became powerful enough to serve as a champion of French interests in the hinterland of the Eritrean coast. The British chose to support Theodore, who was finally able to defeat the Tigrean leader at the cost of many lives in the province.

After 1860 his power began to wane. His actions became so extreme that most groups in the country became alienated, and even his hold on his military forces was weakened. His reaction to his declining fortunes was to initiate a great slaughter of his enemies. When a new British representative, Captain Peter Cameron, arrived in 1862 to replace W. C. Plowden, the recently murdered British

consul and friend of the emperor, the extent of the chaotic situation was revealed by the emperor's announcement that fifteen hundred men of the tribe responsible for Plowden's death had to be executed.

The denouement of Theodore's reign arose from his reaction to the failure of the British Foreign Office to reply to a letter from the emperor requesting an exchange of embassies that the British knew would result in Ethiopian efforts to get British support against Turkey and Egypt. When in 1864 he discovered that the British consistently failed to reply, he reacted by imprisoning the European diplomatic community, including Captain Cameron, and many other Europeans in his fortress at Magdala. Attempts to explain his action have varied: Theodore took this step because he considered Great Britain's failure to reply as an insult to Ethiopian sovereignty, or he felt that his action would force the British to treat his request seriously, or he had become mentally deranged and suspected the Europeans of complicity in an Egyptian plot against him.

Emperor Theodore on his throne at play with his pet lions. He frequently gave audiences to visiting dignitaries in this manner.

Emperor Theodore, whose powerful and clever rule as a leader and a warrior brought together the independent territories of Ethiopia under one monarch, was to quickly find that while he could deal with barbarians, he had trouble with the outside civilized elements. Here he is seen threatening a British missionary. The emperor committed suicide in 1868 after a reign of thirteen years.

When Theodore refused a British request to release the prisoners, they replied by sending a military expedition from India under Sir Robert Napier.

The Napier expedition was viewed in its day as an extraordinary military, engineering, and logistical feat, but the Ethiopians themselves provided the Napier forces with their greatest advantage since many supported the efforts to bring down the emperor. The emperor's forces were routed in a battle at Aroge on April 10, 1868. Theodore retired to Magdala, where he later committed suicide after releasing his prisoners to Napier as the British forces took the fortress. Napier returned to the coast, taking with him, among other spoils, the *Kebra Negast*.

JOHN IV (1871–89)

About the time Theodore began his hostile encounters with the British, Prince Menelik of Shoa escaped from his confinement and returned to Shoa, where he proclaimed himself king. The continuity of the Shoan Dynasty, which traced itself back through King Haile Malakot, father of Menelik, and King Sahle Selassie, his predecessor, to the Emperor Lebna Dengel of the Solomonic line, was thus assured. After the suicide of Theodore, however, four years of civil strife took place among rival chiefs, in which the main contention was between Gobayze, ruler of Lasta, and Kassai, *ras* of Tigre. Kassai was victorious in the struggle and was crowned king of kings in 1872 under the name of John IV.

Like Theodore, John was an ardent devotee of Ethiopian Christianity but without most of the intemperate proclivities of his predecessor. After his rise to power, two main figures dominated the Ethiopian scene: the emperor and Menelik of Shoa. John came to power by struggling against opposing factions in the north. Menelik consolidated himself in Shoa and spread his rule among the Galla to the south and west. He garrisoned Shoan forces among them and received military and financial support from them. His conquests were facilitated by his acquisition of firearms from European sources. In 1882 the two came to an agreement by which Menelik was assigned a free hand to the southern part of the empire. The emperor's concordat with the Shoan king was strengthened by the provision for his son's marriage to Zauditu, daughter of Menelik.

This agreement, made because of John's fear of Menelik's growing power, seemed to amount only to a truce in the long-standing conflict between Tigre and Shoa, but was given stability by John's constant preoccupation with external enemies and pressures. In many of John's external struggles Menelik did not support him; indeed, he negotiated with the emperor's enemies and continued to consolidate Shoan authority in order to strengthen his position.

John first had to meet attacks in 1875 from Egypt. The Egyptians drove in from three points. A force moved in from Tadjoura on the Gulf of Tadjoura opposite Djibouti; it was annihilated by Danakil tribesmen. Other Egyptians set out from Zeila to the south and occupied Harar, where they

remained for ten years, long after the Egyptian cause had been lost. Another and more ambitious attack launched from Massawa was defeated by Tigrean arms, and the Egyptian forces were almost completely destroyed. A fourth Egyptian army was dispatched but encountered a united Ethiopia and was decisively defeated in 1876 southwest of Massawa near Gura.

Italy was the next source of danger. The Italian government took over Assab in Eritrea from an Italian shipping company that had purchased it from a local ruler some years before. Italy's main interest was not the port but the exploitation of the back country; in the process of exploitation, it entered into a relationship with Menelik. The main Italian drive was begun in 1885 and was based on Massawa, which Italy had occupied. With British encouragement, from this port the Italians began the penetration of the Eritrean hinterland. After a drastic defeat in 1887 at Dogali at the hands of the governor of Eritrea, they sent a stronger force to the area.

John was unable to give his attention to this threat because of difficulties to the west in Gondar (Begemder) and Gojam. In 1887 followers of the Sudanese Muslim movement, known as Mahdists, led by a self-proclaimed *mahdi* (messiah), spilled over from the Sudan into Ethiopia and laid waste parts of the country. The emperor viewed it as his main duty to retaliate against these forces. He met them in the battle of Matamma on the border. What initially appeared to be a victory was turned into a defeat by John's being killed in battle, for with his death the Ethiopian forces lost their fighting spirit. Just before his death John designated his illegitimate son, Ras Mangasha of Tigre, as his successor but without effect as Menelik was successful in his efforts to claim the throne.

Menelik now stood out as the dominant personage in Ethiopia, recognized as such by all except John's son and Ras Allula, governor of Eritrea. During a temporary period of confusion, the Italians advanced farther into the hinterland from Massawa and established their foothold in Eritrea, from which Menelik was not able to displace them. From this time until after World War II, Ethiopia lost its maritime frontier and was forced to accept the presence of an ambitious European power on its borders.

MENELIK II (1889–13)

Emperor Menelik II was the chief creator of the modern Ethiopian Empire. He was a ruler of great foresight, political acumen, and personality. He is remembered as one of the three or four greatest leaders in the country's history.

The emperor's first important act was the signing of the Treaty of Ucciale with Italy in May 1889. Ostensibly, the most important part of the treaty was a provision with respect to the handling of Ethiopia's foreign relations, a point about which the Italian and the Amharic versions were in conflict. According to the unsigned Italian version, the Ethiopian government was required to act through the Italian government in dealing with any other foreign states,

Emperor Menelik II
(reigned 1889–1913)

A 1964 stamp issue of famous Ethiopian queens: Sheba, 990; Helen, 1500; Seble Wongel, 1530; Mentiwab, 1730; and Taitu, 1890, the consort of Menelik II

ries. In 1890 Eritrea was declared by Italy to be its colony.

With the elevation of Menelik to the imperial throne, Shoan interests had already begun to overshadow those of Tigre. His decision in 1893 to maintain his capital near Entoto, newly named Addis Ababa (New Flower), confirmed the southern orientation of the empire. Menelik was in effect creating a new Ethiopian empire with its center farther south and its expansionist ambitions so directed.

Throughout the 1890s, except for a short period during the conflict with Italy, Ras Mangasha of Tigre, Menelik's rival for the throne, alternated submission to Menelik and accommodation to the Italians, with the purpose of getting their support against Menelik, even at the sacrifice of Tigrean territorial interests and political prestige. This continued until his defeat in 1898 by the emperor's forces under Ras Makonnen, which brought the province effectively under imperial authority.

Menelik signified his rejection of the Italian version of the Treaty of Ucciale by carrying on diplomatic relations with other states, including the reception of French and Russian missions. He refused Italian protests and showed increasing displeasure with the buildup of Italian power and organization in Eritrea. Although accepting an Italian gift of 2 million cartridges, he paid off the Italian loan in full and, in 1893, formally denounced the treaty.

Italian-Ethiopian relations reached a low point in 1895 when Ras Mangasha, having recognized the diminishing returns of his alliance with the Italians, came to the support of Menelik. The emperor was able to galvanize popular support in the country by the issuance of a proclamation defining the external threat to the country.

War broke out in November 1895. After suffering the defeat of his advance forces in a series of minor battles, including one at Macalle, the Italian commander in Eritrea, General Baratieri, decided to attack Adowa, the capital of Tigre. Possessing inadequate intelligence information and sketch maps of the area, the Italian forces were completely routed in the ensuing three-day battle that resulted in eight thousand Italians and four thousand native Eritrean troops killed and many prisoners. Only the decision of Menelik not to pursue his victory by cutting off the Italian retreat prevented the capture, if not the destruction, of all the remaining Italian forces.

This great victory brought the Ethiopian Empire new prestige and standing that forced the world to recognize the fact that an important independent African state had demonstrated its right to sovereignty. The Treaty of Peace, besides confirming the annulment of the Treaty of Ucciale, asserted the full independence of the empire.

In 1893 and 1894 Ethiopian forces completed the conquest of the Kambatta and Wolamo regions north of Lake Abaya (Margherita). In 1896 and 1897 Fitawrari Habata Giorgis began the conquest of Borana on the Kenya border and, on his return, after a vigorous campaign, completed the conquest of Kaffa. Tribes in surrounding areas were subdued in 1898. Ras Gobana completed the conquest of

thus making Ethiopia in effect an Italian protectorate. In the Ethiopian text it was stated that the emperor might avail himself at his own option of the assistance of the Italian government in dealing with other powers. Disagreements concerning the proper language led to Menelik's denunciation of the treaty and a steady worsening of relations with Italy.

In the meantime, however, the Italians, laboring under the illusion that they possessed a protectorate over the country, made a 4-million-lira loan to Menelik with the customs duties of Harar to secure the loan. In addition, and even more important for Menelik's internal strength, they made him a present of twenty-eight cannons and thirty-eight thousand rifles, which he had cleverly requested.

The other terms of the treaty reflected the internal politics of the country in that it indicated a willingness to sacrifice Tigrean interests in the Eritrean region, particularly on the Red Sea littoral and its hinterland, areas that, in Tigrean eyes, had always formed part of the main Ethiopian territo-

Beni Sciangul, the land of the *shankella* (blacks), in 1898; and in the same year a joint Franco-Ethiopian expedition penetrated the Sudan for the purpose of joining up with a French force at Fashoda, reaching the banks of the White Nile. Fitawrari Habata Giorgis, about the same time penetrated the Ogaden where, between 1900 and 1904, the emperor's forces combined with the British to fight the Somali leader Mohammed Abdulla Hassan, often called the Mad Mullah, who for twenty years kept much of the Horn of Africa in a state of rebellion.

From 1897 to 1908 the emperor and the foreign powers made a series of agreements fixing Ethiopia's territorial limits very much as they were to remain, except for the boundary with Italian Somaliland, upon which no agreement could be reached.

After the emperor had a stroke in May 1906, the strength of his personal control seemed to weaken. British, French, and Italian apprehensions concerning the future encouraged these in which it would be appropriate to establish separate spheres of interest within Ethiopia. In the treaty, Great Britain, France, and Italy agreed that in dealing with future developments they would act together to protect their respective spheres of influence. In the same year, 1906, Ras Makonnen and Ras Mangasha, the foremost aspirants to the throne, died, but the emperor made clear that he would not recognize any agreement among outside powers affecting Ethiopia that implied a limitation of the country's sovereignty.

Apparently recognizing that his strength was ebbing, in late 1907 Menelik set up a Council of Ministers to aid him in the management of the government. Shortly thereafter, in June 1908, he designated his nephew, Lij Yasu, son of Ras Mikael of Wallo, as his successor before a gathering of *rases*. In late 1908 another stroke completely immobilized him, and he appointed Ras Tasamma as regent and formalized the designation of his successor.

These developments ushered in a decade of political chaos. The great nobles, some with foreign financial support, engaged in determined intrigues anticipating a time of troubles as well as of opportunity upon Menelik's death. Taitu, the empress, heavily involved in court politics on behalf of her northern friends, contributed to political disorder by her attempts to concentrate power in her own hands and those of members of her family. By 1910 her efforts in support of her daughter Zauditu and against Lij Yasu had been thwarted by the Shoan nobles, and she withdrew from political activity.

Three years of total disorganization followed. Many of Menelik's achievements were dissipated, but some remained—the postal service, the electrical and telephone systems, and the beginnings of health measures, especially vaccination.

MENELIK TO HAILE SELASSIE

The last two years of Menelik's reign, after the death of the regent Ras Tasamma, found Lij Yasu acting under the

Council of Ministers but with much real power in the hands of his father, Ras Mikael. By the time of the emperor's death in December 1913, the confusion had increased. The emperor-designate weakened his position in the conflict by his close ties to the Muslim supporters of his father, a convert who had been forced to accept Christianity, and Lij Yasu's enemies accused him of renouncing Christianity. He thus lost the support of the powerful Ethiopian Orthodox church.

When Lij Yasu was reported to have proclaimed his descent from Mohammed rather than Solomon and embarked upon a course of Islamizing his personal life, accepted Islamic state symbols, and declared the religious subjection of Ethiopia to the *khalifa* (caliph) in Turkey, all

The Italian emissaries arranging peace terms with Emperor Menelik II

Queen Taitu with her attendants

the opposing forces saw a clear challenge. The emperor had in fact ranged Muslim-Galla influences against the country's traditional ruling groups.

When Lij Yasu went to Jijiga in 1916 to gather Muslim supporters and troops to aid him, the Shoan nobility marched into Addis Ababa, declared their desire to be released from their oath to him, and proclaimed Zauditu, daughter of Menelik, empress, and Ras Tafari Makonnen, later to become Emperor Haile Selassie, regent and heir presumptive. The *abune* confirmed these decisions and excommunicated Lij Yasu who, after a brief, largely bloodless military campaign fled into the Danakil region.

The empress was crowned on February 11, 1917. Ras Wolde Giorgis was proclaimed *negus* (king) in view of the youth of Ras Tafari, who was not yet twenty-five years old, but he did not become the third member of the triumvirate that now figured at the center of the political stage. Fitawrari Habata Giorgis, the minister of war, by virtue of his power and prestige, played that role. In the new situation Tafari represented modernist influences, the empress a vague and uncertain middle ground, and the war minister, along with the *abune*, the forces of tradition.

The forces of Negus Mikael of Wallo, Gallo father of Lij Yasu, had to be crushed before the new order could be stabilized. Even afterward the former emperor's presence continued to be a political problem providing a potential rallying point of dissident factions, particularly in the north where civil strife broke out, in some cases involving the declaration of rebel governments. Some of the chief personages of the country, such as Ras Gugsa Wolle of Begemder (whom Zauditu was required to divorce), Ras Hailu Balaw of Gojam, and Dejazmach Balcha of Sidamo, were unreliable as supporters of the government. The tensions were somewhat eased in 1921, however, by the capture of Lij Yasu. Zauditu kept him imprisoned in Shoa until 1932.

The balance of the government was stabilized until the death of Fitawrari Habata Giorgis in 1926. Thereafter, Ras Tafari entered into determined contest with Zauditu and proved to be more than a match for her. He was able to gather quickly a more effective military force than any rival, actual or potential. Moreover, he brought about the expulsion of a chief opponent, the *ichege*, ranking leader of the Ethiopian Orthodox church. Thus fortified, he was able to counterbalance the threat of Ras Kassa of Tigre, who had been called upon by the empress for help, and to bring Dejazmach Balcha of Sidamo under control. In 1928, when his power had been amply demonstrated, Ras Tafari at last was crowned negus.

Before his victory against Zauditu, Ras Tafari had concretely revealed his modernist inclinations. He had been able to accomplish his purposes in foreign relations because of the preoccupation of his competitors with domestic problems and because of his own great capacity to outwait his opponents. His first moves in the realm of foreign affairs consisted of increasing personal contacts abroad. He visited Aden in 1923 and Europe in 1925; from Great Britain he

Regent Ras Tafari is honored on two 1919 stamps.

Two 1919 stamps depict Empress Zauditu.

1928 stamps honor the co-rulers Emperor Ras Tafari and Empress Zauditu.

brought back Theodore's crown, taken by Napier from Magdala in 1867.

After an abortive move to achieve membership in the League of Nations in 1919, blocked because of the existence of slavery in the country, he clearly saw the need of meeting international standards in this regard. In 1923 he and the empress established the death penalty for the buying and selling of slaves, and in the same year Ethiopia was unanimously voted league membership. Continuing to seek international approval of the country's internal conditions, the government enacted laws in 1924 making provision for the freeing of slaves and their offspring. In 1926 Ethiopia signed the International Slavery Convention of the league aimed at abolishing slavery in any form.

Membership in the league quickly proved to be of value. In 1925 Great Britain and Italy came to an agreement in an exchange of notes setting forth their separate spheres of interest within Ethiopia. Ras Tafari immediately dispatched protests to the two governments and referred the matter to the league. Full use of league machinery was not required, since both powers backed away from the implications of their settlement and stipulated that they had not intended to limit Ethiopia's sovereignty. This victory for Ethiopian diplomacy had the effect, however, of leading Ras Tafari to think, erroneously, that the league would be effective in most other situations.

With his establishment as negus and his achievement of the highest authority, Ras Tafari embarked upon a program of modernization that required the opening of the country to Western influences. The chief immediate expression of this policy was the signing in 1928 of a twenty-year Treaty of Friendship with Italy.

Negotiations with other outside powers had bearing upon internal Ethiopian affairs. In 1930 negotiations were begun for the establishment of a state bank. The negus brought about the appointment of a new head of the state church, Abuna Kerlos, and indicated his interest in the management of church affairs. In the same year he signed the Arms Traffic Act with Great Britain, France, and Italy, by which unauthorized persons were denied the right to import arms, but the government was acknowledged to have the right to procure arms for defense against external aggression and for the maintenance of internal order. He thus retained access to the arms he required to maintain Ethiopia's internal and external security while preventing rival forces within the country from gaining arms. The result was confirmation of his paramount authority.

The coronation in 1930 of Ras Tafari in Addis Ababa as Emperor Haile Selassie I marked the beginning of a new period of effective central government. With power no longer even formally divided in the central government, the great *rases* were forced either to render the emperor obedience or engage in treasonable opposition to him.

The emperor promulgated a new constitution on July 16, 1931, and said that he wanted it to provide means of allowing more Ethiopians to share the responsibilities of government. But the most substantial changes consisted of gradual replacement of the traditional provincial rulers by appointees loyal to the new regime and in most cases having sufficient experience to have some understanding of the working of a modern state. By 1934, reliable provincial rulers were established throughout the traditional territories of Shoa, Gojam, and Amhara and south in Kaffa and Sidamo. Other peoples, however, remained almost outside the control of the imperial government. The successful strengthening of imperial powers had been demonstrated in 1932, when a revolt led by Ras Hailu Balaw of Gojam in support of Lij Yasu, who had escaped, was quickly suppressed and a new nontraditional governor put in his place. Thereafter the only traditional leader remaining to symbolize the longstanding Amharic-Tigre divergence and the possibility of overtly challenging central rule was the *ras* of Tigre.

Haile Selassie continued to oversee and direct all details of government, and the members of his new Parliament,

Haile Selassie (1891–1975), emperor of Ethiopia. He was the grandson of Menelik II and was known as Ras Tafari before he came to the throne. He led a revolt against Lij Yasu, successor of Menelik, placed Menelik's daughter Judith on the throne, and acted as her regent until her death in 1930, when he assumed the title of emperor.

Ras Tafari when he was ten years old. He is seen here with his father, Ras Makonnen.

The royal coat of arms

Emperor Haile Selassie during the coronation ceremony. He is seen here holding the scepter and orb.

For the coronation of Haile Selassie, a coach built for the German emperors in the nineteenth century was purchased by the Ethiopian government for the occasion. It is seen here in front of St. George's Church during the coronation ceremony in 1930.

Emperor Haile Selassie on his throne on a 1956 stamp commemorating the twenty-fifth anniversary of the promulgation of the first constitution

handpicked by authorities under his supervision in the provinces, did little of importance beyond discussing the legislative proposals put before them. Enactment of the laws was completely determined by the emperor's will. Nevertheless, the emperor was sincerely interested in modernization and in adopting new principles of government. His habit of personally directing the details of government was to some degree a brake on the forces for change and seriously hampered decision making on lower levels, but he viewed himself as a father and therefore overseer of a people just barely breaking away from the traditionalist mold. His desire to accelerate the spread of knowledge of more modern administration was shown by his creation of three model provinces with civil services created by the imperial administration.

THE ITALO-ETHIOPIAN WAR

Ethiopia was the victim of Italian aggression in 1935. The charges made by the Italian government that Ethiopia had failed to fulfill treaty obligations or control border tribes in raids across frontiers did not hide its intention, which fast matured in 1935, to round out its East African possessions by taking over Ethiopia by military force.

The decision was influenced by developing European international policies. The Italian hope had been that Ethiopia might become an Italian protectorate, be thus removed from the sphere of any other power, and afford Italy special political, economic, and social advantages. As late as September 29, 1934, Rome reaffirmed the 1928 Treaty of Friendship with Ethiopia, but the climate of international affairs at the time provided Italy with assurance that aggression could be undertaken with impunity. The Italian Fascist government, determined to create a *casus belli,* deliberately exploited the minor provocations that arose in its relations with Ethiopia.

The League of Nations addressed itself to the problems of deteriorating relations between Italy and Ethiopia only after a prolonged delay, which convinced the Italians that they would be allowed to accomplish their purposes without hindrance.

In August 1935 the British and the French proposed that the signatories of the 1906 Tripartite Treaty collaborate for the purpose of assisting in the modernization and reorganization of Ethiopian internal affairs subject to the consent of Ethiopia. The Italians flatly refused, even

though Ethiopia had concurred in the proposal, since they hoped to gain control of the entire territory.

By this time the efforts of the League had failed. At a meeting of the council of the League of Nations on September 4, 1935, the Italian representative made it plain that Italy considered Ethiopia to be an enemy and unworthy of equal treatment in the League. This was the final expression of a decision calling for an immediate attack on Ethiopia and a major Italian intrusion in East Africa. The buildup of Italian military strength had begun early in the year. In the war that began with an Italian invasion on October 3, 1935, and lasted seven months, Ethiopia was outmatched in armament, a development aided by the major powers, which applied an arms embargo equally to both powers, an act of major disadvantage to Ethiopia.

Despite the valiant defense efforts by the majority of the Ethiopian peoples, the fall of 1935 and the winter of 1935–36 saw a decline in Ethiopian fortunes on the northern front

After he had been defeated by the Italians in 1936 and had gone into exile first to Palestine and then to England, Emperor Selassie delivered a stirring speech before the League of Nations Assembly at Geneva on June 30, 1936, but it fell on the deaf ears of the world's representatives.

Emperor Selassie with his daughter and two sons in 1936

Emperor Selassie discusses the progress of the war with President Franklin D. Roosevelt aboard the U.S.S. Quincy *off Egypt in February 1945.*

and in Hararge. After the defection of part of the Tigre forces led by Leul-Ras Seyoum Mangasha and of the Galla in some areas, as well as the Fascists' heavy use of poison gas, the Ethiopians were defeated in an attack on the main Italian force at Maichew on March 31, 1936. By mid-April 1936 Italian forces had reached Lake Tana in the north and Harar in the south. On May 2 Haile Selassie left for Djibouti and exile. The Italian forces entered Addis Ababa on May 5. Four days later Italy announced the formal annexation of the country.

On June 30, 1936, the Emperor made a powerful and dignified speech before the League of Nations in which he called upon that body to uphold "the value of promises made to small states that their integrity and their independence shall be respected and assured."

By June 1940, when the Italians declared war against France, the Allies—with the emperor's participation and that of Ethiopian forces inside and outside the country— were in a position to prepare a campaign of dislodgment of the Italians from their East African possession, now made vulnerable by British command of the sea-lanes.

THE WAR OF RESTORATION, 1940–41

Upon the Italian declaration of war, the emperor proceeded

to Khartoum where he established closer liaison with both the British headquarters and Ethiopian resistance forces. On May 5, 1941, he reentered Addis Ababa, five years to the day after the Italian occupation of the capital. From the capital the emperor could gather control in his own hands. Continuing operations resulted in the surrender of the duke of Aosta and his forces at Amba Alage on May 18. By January 1942 the Italians in Gondar had surrendered to the British and Ethiopian forces.

THE POSTWAR ERA: RECONSTRUCTION AND DEVELOPMENT

An agreement signed with the British government on December 19, 1944, placed the two countries on a plane of complete equality by revising the wartime agreements. British administration in the Haud area was continued into the 1950s, and the complete formal readmission of Ethiopia to sovereignty was acknowledged and accepted. The association with the British had been constructive, if not always happy, since the Ethiopians, wary of the close ties Great Britain had established, suspected that the British intended to serve their own interests at the expense of Ethiopia.

The reformed imperial administration of the country

involved the supplanting of the old nobility as representatives of the emperor in the provinces by administrators with more modern training and experience.

In July 1948 the Ethiopian Orthodox church began steps, completed by 1956, by which it obtained independence from the long domination of the Coptic patriarchs of Egypt. The emperor obtained the agreement of the patriarch of Alexandria to appoint an Ethiopian *abune,* so that for the first time in the sixteen centuries of Ethiopian Christianity an Ethiopian, rather than an Egyptian, sat at the head of the national church. This appointment was followed by the creation of sufficient new bishoprics to allow the Ethiopians to elect their own patriarch. The postwar years also saw a change in the relationship between church and state; the vast church lands came under tax legislation, and the clergy lost the right to try their fellows for civil offenses in their own courts.

Motivated by the memory of the failure of the League of Nations in which he had placed such hopes in 1935, Emperor Haile Selassie reacted to the first postwar challenge to the United Nations by dispatching a considerable force to serve with the United Nations troops in Korea.

THE ERITREAN FEDERATION

The most significant change in the composition of the Ethiopian state in the twentieth century was brought about by the addition of Eritrea to its territories in 1952 in accordance with a decision of the United Nations General Assembly. The acquisition of the former Italian colony, which had been administered by Great Britain after 1941, restored a maritime frontier to the empire for the first time since the triumph of Islam over the African shore of the Red Sea in the tenth century A.D. It also brought under the control of the empire an entity with a more advanced political structure and society.

Emperor Selassie and Queen Elizabeth II photographed during the emperor's state visit to Great Britain in October 1954

Emperor Haile Selassie I, right, *on a state visit in 1954 to the United Nations Headquarters in New York City. The emperor is seen chatting here with the UN secretary-general, Dag Hammarskjöld.*

After seizing Eritrea from the Italians, the British established a military administration to rule it until the final disposition of the Italian colonial empire was decided upon by the Allied powers, a duty later relegated to the United Nations.

The United Nations General Assembly provided that Eritrea would be linked to the Ethiopian Empire through a loose federal structure under the sovereignty of the emperor but with a form and organization of internal self-government of its own. Finally, the Eritrean Parliament dissolved itself, and the territory became a regular province of the empire in November 1962.

CONSTITUTIONAL DEVELOPMENT

In the 1940s and as late as 1951, traditional—regional and feudal—forces continued to oppose imperial control. By the late 1950s these same traditional forces saw Emperor Haile Selassie as their main prop against the modernizing elements that would bring about a revolution unfavorable to their interests. The younger modernizing leaders were the sons of the traditional elite. They had obtained a knowledge of the outside world, often through an education overseas. They had become alienated by their inability under existing leadership to initate and implement the reforms necessary to bring their country's development into line with that in the rest of Africa. They had lost contact even with the progressive elements of the existing leadership with whom the emperor had most often aligned himself.

The desire to satisfy these younger critics led the emperor to adopt a reformed constitution in 1955, as well as a new legal code and the country's first national development plan. But, despite these constitutional changes, the emperor remained the pinnacle of the state in law as well as supreme in fact. Not until the late 1960s did meaningful devolution of his personal concentration of power to the handpicked cabinet occur.

THE 1960 COUP

The most dramatic political event of the postwar era was an attempted coup on December 13 and 14, 1960. The coup was staged while the emperor was in Brazil on the most distant of his numerous state visits overseas. The coup's leaders were a small segment of the modernist elements of the country's younger and more educated elite, backed by a four thousand-man force of the Imperial Bodyguard, whose commander, Brigadier General Mengitsu Neway, was one of the chief plotters. The other major leaders were his brother, Germame, a United States-educated Pan-Africanist intellectual; the head of the national police; and the head of the emperor's intelligence service. Until the coup all, except Germame, were closely tied to the emperor.

The coup was initially successful in the capital as the rebels seized the crown prince at gunpoint and, by a subterfuge, captured more than twenty of the cabinet ministers and other important government leaders. The support of the Imperial Bodyguard, an elite military unit, was obtained without informing the men or even a majority of the officers of the purpose of their actions. The proclaimed intent of the coup leaders was the establishment of a government that would improve the economic, social, and political position of the masses of the population by ending the rule of the aristocracy and by land reform.

The initial success of the coup leaders was not followed up. The other military forces, particularly the army's First Division, headquartered at Addis Ababa, and the air force at Debre Zeyt thirty miles to the south, refused to support them; the units loyal to the emperor treated with the rebels at first in the hope of avoiding bloodshed but moved superior forces against them. The revolt had been completely crushed by the time the emperor arrived in the city on December 17.

Just before their final defeat, however, the rebel leaders had assassinated nearly all their captives in the imperial palace's Green Salon. The crown prince and Leul-Ras Imru, both of whom had been forced to cooperate with the rebels, were spared. Nearly all of the rebel leaders were killed in the battle or by pursuing forces, or they committed suicide to avoid capture. None escaped, and only four were taken captive. Three of these were executed after public trials—General Neway for treason and rebellion, and the other two for the murders in the Green Salon. Their trials were noted for their fairness by the International Commission of Jurists, and the emperor showed considerable moderation in his treatment of the lesser guilty parties. He extended a mass pardon to the students of Addis Ababa's colleges who, although not actively involved in the coup itself, had come out publicly in support of the coup's leaders on its second day.

The emperor's photograph appeared on many of his country's stamps. Second from bottom: *commemorating the state visit of the shah of Iran to Ethiopia on June 3, 1968.*

A tired-looking Emperor Haile Selassie I conferring with Secretary-General U Thant at United Nations Headquarters in New York City in 1970.

Emperor Selassie inspects the honor guard aboard the U.S.S. Waddell, *a guided missile destroyer, during Ethiopian Navy Days in March 1972.*

THE 1960s, 1970s
AND THE FINAL REVOLUTION

Heavy losses to both traditional and modernist elites resulted from the attempted coup. Those who succeeded to the leadership then found more opportunity for reform within the system than had previously existed, partly because of the loss of the most conservative traditional leaders and partly because of the emperor's renewed support for evolutionary change. The modernists, for a number of reasons, became less interested in seeking sudden change through coup or revolution: the emperor's own reforms had begun to answer some of what they saw as the need for change; they also assumed that a time for change would

come with the death of the emperor, already in his seventies. In addition, many of the younger African states whose modern governmental forms they had admired and envied in 1960 succumbed to chaos or military rule without effectively carrying out the social reforms that were the aims of Ethiopia's modernists. They also observed from the military coups that occurred elsewhere that coups in their own country would probably have similar results, as Ethiopia had the largest and strongest army in black Africa.

But, in the face of widespread famine, inflation, and unemployment, the armed forces, in September 1974, brought about a coup and suspended the Parliament and the constitution. Haile Selassie was placed under house arrest. A Provisional Military Government (PMG) was formed by the Armed Forces Coordinating Committee known as the Derg, a small group of anonymous members who engineered the revolution. In November 1974 the PMG was replaced by the Provisional Military Administrative Council (PMAC) chaired by the head of state, Brigadier General Teferi Benti. The PMG eventually came under Soviet Communist influence.

The royal reign and regime was abolished in March 1975, and the emperor died while still in captivity in August of that year. In September 1977 twenty members of the late Haile Selassie's royal family, which had been in house arrest in Addis Ababa, escaped to Sweden. The members included four princes and six princesses, all between ten and twenty years of age.

A 1961 stamp was issued to commemorate Emperor Haile Selassie I and Empress Zanditu.

THE ROYAL SOVEREIGNS OF THE EMPIRE OF ETHIOPIA

Reign	Title	Ruler	Birth	Death	Relationship
Prior to 1855 Ethiopia was divided into separate city-states.					
1855–1868	Emperor	Theodore (Kassa) (Tewodros)	1818	1868	
1868–1871	Ethiopia was involved in civil war.				
1871–1889	King	John IV (Kassai)	1832	1889	
1889–1913	Emperor	Menelik II	1844	1913	Son of king of Shoa
1913–1916	Emperor	Lij Yasu	1896	1935	Nephew of Menelik II
1916–1930	Empress	Zauditu (Waizeri)	1876	1930	Daughter of Menelik II
1916–1928	Regent	Ras Tafari	1891	1975	Grandson of Menelik II; son of Ras Makonnen
1928–1930	Coruler	Ras Tafari			
1930–1975	Emperor	Haile Selassie I (Ras Tafari)			

The Ancient Kingdoms of Israel
3

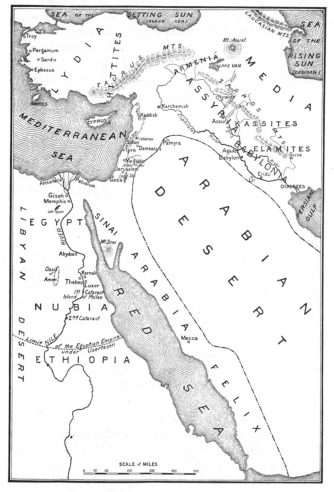

The birthplace of civilization

The state of Israel and its associations with the Jewish people have a long and complex history, much of it interwoven with that of the people in other countries, particularly with the Arabs of Egypt, Ethiopia, Syria, and Jordan.

The earliest settlers with whom modern Israel identifies itself culturally and historically were from a Mesopotamian Semitic stock who established themselves in Canaan, later known as Palestine. After several generations, they became known as Jews. Over the centuries, interspersed with varying periods of Jewish independence, the land was ruled by foreign conquerors, and the people were subjected to deportation, exile, and dispersion. Consequently, sizable groups established communities in various countries throughout the world, particularly in Europe and around the Mediterranean.

Wherever they went, the Jewish people retained significant historical, cultural, and religious traditions, which contributed to a strong sense of common identity and to hopes for eventual return to the land of ancient Israel.

The people and the government manifest a lively interest in Israel's antiquity and its history throughout the ages. In discussing modern issues and events, frequent references to the historic past serve to link it with the present and to draw benefits from its lessons.

JEWISH ORIGINS
AND ANCIENT ISRAEL

Establishing modern Israel's concept of a connection with the past, the Proclamation of Independence of May 14, 1948, declares at the start:

"In the land of Israel the Jewish people came into being. In this land was shaped their spiritual, religious, and national character. Here they lived in sovereign independence. Here they create a culture of national and universal import, and gave to the world the eternal Book of Books."

Occupation of the region west of the Jordan Rift, known in ancient times as Canaan, later both as Israel and Palestine, extends back to the Paleolithic era. Neanderthal remains from at least one hundred thousand years ago have been identified. The Jews of ancient Israel appear to have derived from an early Mesopotamian Semitic line, part of the population movements of the Middle Bronze Age from east and north into the previously settled, Egyptian-dominated area of Canaan. These migrations are not precisely dated, but are believed to have occurred in the twentieth and nineteenth centuries B.C. In biblical narratives the line of Jewish patriarchs headed by Abraham appears, vague in history but clear in cultural memory, and continues down through Moses, the Exodus from Egypt, and the Hebrew return to Canaan.

In this account Abraham led his family from Ur in Chaldaea, southern Mesopotamia, through Syria and southwest into Canaan. Here Abraham made the first Hebrew lodgment and received the divine covenant (Gen. 12:7): "Unto thy seed will I give this land." In return, Abraham was to serve only this single God of the covenant, and the rite of circumcision was instituted as the token of the contract. Later, possibly during the Hyksos invasions of Egypt in the late eighteenth century B.C., some of Abraham's Hebrew descendants migrated to Egypt, where they remained, according to tradition, for four hundred years. After the Hyksos were expelled, about 1570 B.C., the Hebrews fell under Egyptian bondage, which lasted until the Exodus under Moses. This movement back to Canaan, the Promised Land, may have occurred in the thirteenth century B.C., during the reign of Pharaoh Rameses II, circa 1304–1237 B.C. The central hero is Moses, traditionally portrayed in the dual role of leader and priest-prophet, maker of the nation and organizer of the Hebrew religion. During years of nomadic adversity in the Sinai wilderness, the Ten Commandments were written and Mosaic law was formed. Religious scholars believe that God kept them in the wilderness to remove the "slave" generation from their heritage to better equip them for the future struggle.

Joshua, successor of Moses, led the people of Israel as they entered Canaan. The Canaanites were still in the land, and on the coast were the Philistines, from whom the word Palestine is derived. During the thirteenth to eleventh centuries B.C., the Hebrew tribal peoples experienced only a loose political cohesion, usually for military purposes in times of stress, under a succession of tribal leaders known as judges. The Philistine and Canaanite peoples fought, lived with, and received tribute from or paid tribute to the Hebrews in fluctuating, uneasy accommodation. During this time, Jewish principles stressed unity of people and religion, rejected other gods (the idol worship and orgiastic rites of the Canaanite Baal cult), and maintained the ancient claim to the land. When times were good, the people tended to backslide and accommodate despite the denunciations of ancient prophets. In danger and bad times, the stern disciplines of their own Jewish law were reasserted for unity, self-preservation, and advancement.

History becomes more precise with establishment of the kingdom of Israel under Saul, in 1020 B.C. David, the Psalmist king (circa 1000–961 B.C.) conquered Jerusalem and established his capital there. Under Solomon his son (961–922 B.C.), the first temple was built and ancient Israel reached its zenith. After Solomon, the kingdom split in two: Israel, to the north, had its capital at Samaria, near modern Nabulus, thirty miles north of Jerusalem, and encompassed ten of the old twelve tribes; Judah, to the south, had its capital still at Jerusalem and encompassed the remaining two tribes. In 722 B.C. the northern kingdom fell to the Assyrian conqueror, Shalmaneser V (726–722 B.C.), whose successor Sargon deported its Jews in vast numbers and replaced them with people from Mesopotamia in an apparent effort to eliminate the Jews by exile and diffusion. The southern kingdom of Judah, although tributary to Assyria, preserved a shaky political independence until the Assyrian empire broke up before the growing power of Babylon.

In July 587 B.C. Jerusalem was burned, and the walls and temple destroyed. The last king of Judah and thousands of selected Jews were carried off to captivity in Babylon by Nebuchadnezzar II (also known as Nebuchadrezzar II). Many of the remaining Jews migrated to Egypt. Among those in Babylon, some adapted themselves to the new surroundings and lost their identity, as did the northern Jews whom Sargon had deported more than a century earlier. A hard core in Babylon maintained the unity of people and religion; from these and later dispersions derived the Jewish communities of Mesopotamia, which remained to modern times.

Babylon, in its turn, fell before Cyrus II of Persia in 539 B.C. The liberal Cyrus, memorialized by the Hebrew prophet Isaiah, allowed voluntary return of the Jewish exiles to

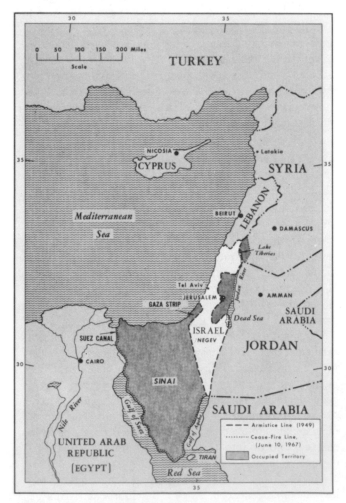

The geographical position of Israel in the eastern Mediterranean

Young David slays Goliath and becomes a national hero who would eventually be a challenge to King Saul.

the ancestral land beginning in 538 B.C. and the temple was rebuilt at Jerusalem in the years 520–515 B.C. There followed a period of Jewish theocratic unity, with local autonomy under Persian suzerainty, until Alexander's conquest of the area in 333 B.C. With Alexander came the Greek language, literature, and ways of life. In Jerusalem, as elsewhere, Hellenistic tendencies gained a footing among the Jews in contention, like the earlier Canaanite Baal deviations, with Orthodox Jewish tenets. After Alexander's death in 323 B.C., his Eastern Empire fell to rival Greek generals and became divided between the Ptolemies of Egypt and the Seleucids of Syria.

Judaea (formerly Judah) was at the strategic crossroads and was caught between Egypt and Syria. Ptolemaic overlordship was succeeded by Seleucid control in 198 B.C. In time, the practice of Jewish customs and religion was harshly repressed as constituting a source of disaffection and rebellion. After an interval of ineffectual passive resistance, the Jewish Revolt of the Maccabees broke out in 168 B.C. at the instigation of an aged priest named Mattathias and under the dynamic leadership of Judas Maccabeus, his son. His victories over the Syrians led to rededication of the temple in Jerusalem in December 165 B.C., an event since celebrated annually by Jews as the Feast of Rededication (Hanukkah). Judas fell in battle in 161 B.C., but the revolt continued under his brothers Jonathan (161–143 B.C.) and Simon (143–135 B.C.), the latter of whom was recognized

The Prophet Samuel anoints (pours the oil on the head of) Saul, carrying out God's desire to make him the first king of Israel.

David holding the head of Goliath (by the artist Caravaggio)

as high priest and ruler of Judaea in 143 B.C. Jewish independence was thus reestablished, and the four identities—land, people, political sovereignty, and religion—were restored.

Under the Hasmonean (Maccabean) line that followed, Judaea became in extent and power comparable to the ancient Davidic dominion. Rulers, however became corrupt and oppressive. Internal political and religious discord ran high, especially between the Pharisees, fundamental interpreters of the Jewish law and tradition, and the Sadducee faction, supporters of imperialistic royal policies. In 64 B.C. dynastic contenders for the throne appealed for support to Pompey, who was then establishing Roman power in Asia Minor. In the next year Roman legions seized Jerusalem with much carnage, and Pompey installed one of the contenders for the throne as high priest, but without the title of king. Eighty years of independent Jewish sovereignty ended, and the period of Roman dominion began.

Eventually King Saul became jealous of David and at Bethlehem the "Lord said to Samuel, 'Arise, anoint him, for this is he' " and the Prophet anointed him king.

ROME AND BYZANTIUM
IN PALESTINE

In the subsequent period of Roman wars, the half-Jew Herod was confirmed by the Roman Senate as king of Judaea in 39 B.C. and reigned from 37 B.C. until his death in 4 B.C. Nominally independent, Judaea was actually a client state of Rome, and the land was formally annexed in A.D. 6 as part of the province of Syria. Among the Jews in Jerusalem, two councils, called Sanhedrins, developed. The political Sanhedrin was composed primarily of the Sadducee aristocracy and was charged by the Roman procurator with overwatching and reporting on civil order, specifically in matters involving imperial directives. The religious Sanhedrin of the Pharisees was concerned with the Jewish religious law and doctrine, which the Romans disregarded as long as civil order was not threatened. Foremost among the Pharisee leaders of the time were the noted teachers Hillel and Shammai. The era of Christianity began under the governorship of Pontius Pilate, who was Roman procurator of Judaea from A.D. 26 to 36.

Chafing under foreign rule, the Jewish nationalist movement of the fanatical sect known as Zealots seriously challenged Roman control in a rebellion that broke out in A.D. 66.

David continues in the court of Saul. Here he is seen playing the harp before Saul.

King Saul, finally mentally deranged, flings a javelin at David while he plays.

King Saul is defeated by the Philistines in battle and falls on his sword to end his life and throne.

THE DESTRUCTION OF JERUSALEM

The government of the country of Palestine had undergone many changes since it was first conquered by the Romans under Pompey. Julius Caesar had cultivated the favor of the inhabitants, and M. Antonius had conferred the sovereignty of Judea upon Herod. Augustus confirmed the independence of the Jews under this prince, whom they cherished as a native ruler. At his death in 4 B.C., his ample dominions were divided among his four children, of whom

David is formally made king at Hebron.

King David leading the procession of the Ark of the Covenant, containing the two tablets of Moses' Ten Commandments, into Jerusalem (by the artist Pesselino)

The rule of King Solomon depicted in a fresco in the Basilica of St. Paul in Rome

King David in later life (by the artist Witz)

King David tells Solomon that he shall be the next king.

The Encounter of King Solomon with the Queen of Sheba *by the artist della Francesco*

King Jeroboam I, the first king of the Northern Kingdom of Israel, appears for a formal occasion in his royal dress.

King Rehoboam, the first king of the Southern Kingdom of Judah, is seen here consulting with the "old men" of his empire.

Archelaus occupied Jerusalem and Judaea. But this prince fell into disfavor with the emperor; his kingdom was taken from him and annexed as a dependency to the Roman province of Syria. Herod Agrippa, grandson of the Great Herod, was allowed by the favor of Caligula and afterward of Claudius, to reunite the whole of his grandfather's possessions under his own scepter; but on his death, A.D. 44, the territory was again divided, some portions being given to his brother and afterward to his son Agrippa, who held his government in Chalcis, on the borders of Ituraea. Judaea was reinstituted by the empire. Caesarea, on the coast of the Mediterranean, was established as the residence of the procurator of Judaea, who was content for the most part to avoid all collision with the prejudices of the Jews at the national capital of Jerusalem. The Jews were at this period in a state of political effervescence. One leader had risen who, under the title of Jesus Christ, had engaged their religious sympathies and excited their hopes, by an appeal to prophecies and traditions that pointed to an impending revolution, and the reestablishment of the kingdom of David. Caligula had wantonly trampled on the national prejudices and had required the priests to place a statue of himself in the great Temple of Jerusalem. Petitions against this act of desecration had been addressed to him, but without effect, and it was only by the politic delay of the procurator and the timely death of the emperor himself that a general outbreak was averted. Claudius was not indisposed to humor these religious scruples, and the oppressions and cruelties exercised by his officers were probably unauthorized by him; but doubtless it was most difficult for any governor on the spot to maintain the peace among a population ever excitable, and ever disposed—not at Jerusalem only, but at Rome and Alexandria, and wherever they were gathered together in considerable numbers—to quarrel among themselves and with all the

King Ahab, king of the Northern Kingdom of Israel from 869 to 850 B.C., did not believe the Prophet Micaiah's prediction and died in battle trying to recover a city from the Syrians.

When King Joash (Jehoash), who was king of the Northern Kingdom of Israel from 801 to 786 B.C., visited the Prophet Elisha on his deathbed, he was told to shoot an arrow out of the window and it would be a symbol of his victory over the Syrians, and the release of the children of Israel would follow.

King Hezekiah ruled the Southern Kingdom of Judah from 715 to 687 B.C. Here he is seen showing his treasury to visiting royalty.

King Hezekiah in sackcloth pleading with the Lord to forgive him for seeking worldly gains.

foreigners around them. At last, under the harsher government of Nero, the spirit of disaffection came to a head. The Jews broke out in a general rebellion. The procurators exercised great severities, and those were avenged by great losses. It had become necessary to make a strong effort once and for all, and extinguish forever, at whatever cost, the national aspirations of an unfortunate people. The spirit of the Jews was, indeed, very different from that of the Gauls or the Britons; the influence of their priests was far more powerful than that of the Druids. Their religion, their polity, and their national character were all far more integrated with everyday life. And the resistance they showed their conquerors was more persistent than resistance shown in other counties.

The Sanhedrin, or national Senate, cast the procurator and the king Agrippa equally aside, and assumed the conduct of this national revolt. They divided the country into seven military governments. The command in Galilee, the outpost of Palestine against Syria, was confided to Josephus, who, also, has recorded the history of the Jewish war. His defense of Galilee, however able it may have been, was graced by few successes. Vespasian was the captain to whom the conduct of the war was entrusted by Nero. We are told, indeed, that Josephus held Iotapata for forty-seven days, and Vespasian was himself wounded in the final assault. Josephus was captured by the Romans.

The tactics of Vespasian were slow and cautious. The reduction of Iotapata, in Galilee, was followed by the surrender of Tiberias and the storm of Tarichea, when the Jews were made fully aware of the remorseless cruelty with which they would be treated. The campaign of the year following was conducted on the same principle. Vespasian refrained from a direct attack upon Jerusalem, but reduced and ravaged all the country around. During the heat of the struggle for the succession in Rome these operations were relaxed. Titus, his son, was sent to Antioch to confer with Mucianus on the measures it might be expedient to take, and the right moment for striking for the empire. His interests were diligently served by Tiberius Alexander,

who commanded in Egypt, and by Agrippa, king of Chalcis.

From that time Vespasian ceased to direct the affairs of Palestine, which he committed to Titus. In the year 70 Titus moved with all the forces he could command against Jerusalem itself. He united four legions in this service, together with twenty cohorts of auxiliaries and the troops maintained by various dependent sovereigns. The whole amounted to eighty thousand men. To these the Jews opposed, from behind their defenses, twenty-four thousand trained soldiers, and these too were supported by a multitude of irregular combatants. The defenses of Jerusalem were remarkably strong; but the defenders must have been fatally impeded by the crowd of worshipers, computed at some hundreds of thousands, who had collected within the walls for the celebration of the Passover and were now unable to escape from them.

But it was by the dissension of the Jewish factions themselves, more than by any natural obstructions, that the defense was impeded, and finally frustrated. The reduction of Galilee and Samaria had driven crowds of reckless swordsmen into the city. The Zealots, under their leader Eleazar, filled the streets with tumult and disorder, seized the persons of the chiefs of the nobility and priesthood, and urged the mob to massacre them. When the better sort of people, under Ananus the high priest, rallied in self-defense, their opponents seized the temple and established themselves in its strong enclosure. The Zealots invited assistance from beyond the walls. Ananus and his friends were speedily overpowered, and the extreme party, pledged against all compromise with Rome, reigned in Jerusalem. Jehovah, they proclaimed, had manifestly declared himself on their side. The furious fanaticism of the Jewish people, at least within the walls of their sacred city, was excited to the utmost. But the armies of Titus closed around the devoted city.

The Zealots themselves, at the moment of their victory, were split into three factions. Eleazar, at the head of the residents in Jerusalem, held his strong position in the inner enclosure of the temple; John of Giscala, who led a less violent party, was lodged in the outer precincts; Simon Bargiora entered the city with a third army and became responsible for defense of the the ramparts. Eleazar was assassinated, and the defense of the temple fortress fell to John.

Titus advanced from the north and planted his camp on the ridge of Scopus. He first encountered an outer wall which crowned the eminences around the city. The Jews made a spirited defense, and inflicted great loss upon their assailants. But the Romans, proceeding methodically with the means and implements of modern warfare, succeeded in making a breach in these ramparts. They blockaded the narrower enclosure which was now before them, but they did not cease from constant attacks upon the second wall. In the first instance Titus had attempted conciliation and sent Josephus to the gates with the offer of honorable terms. The enthusiasts in the city had driven away his envoy with arrows. He repeated his offers, but with no better success. Then at last he determined to proceed to extremities. Famine began to prevail among the Jews.

The fortress of Antonia was destroyed, and the temple close at hand lay exposed to the assailants. The struggle still continued desperately, and the Romans suffered many reverses. At last the temple was no longer tenable. John and Simon, united together, withdrew into the upper city on Zion, breaking down the causeway which connected it with the temple. The temple itself was stormed and entered. Titus would have saved the Holy of Holies from general destruction, but a soldier wantonly set fire to the inner doors, and the whole of the sacred edifice was soon consumed in uncontrollable flames. Behind the walls of the upper city the last remnant of the nation stood hopelessly at bay. Once more Titus sent Josephus to parley with them; again the renegade was dismissed with imprecations. Then he came forward himself to the chasm of the broken bridge and conferred, but still in vain, with the leaders of the people. He had shown more clemency than perhaps any Roman chief before him; but his patience was now exhausted, and he vowed to effect the entire destruction of the city. The demolition was carried out to that end. The remnant were captured and sold, with many thousands of their countrymen, into slavery. John and Simon concealed

The speech of Titus to the Romans before the final assault on the walls of Jerusalem: "Let my first argument to move you be taken from what probably some would think a reason to dissuade you. I mean the constancy and patience of these Jews, even under their ill successes; for it is unbecoming you, who are Romans and my soldiers, who have in peace been taught how to make wars, and who have also been used to conquer in those wars, to be inferior to Jews, either in action of the hand, or in courage of the soul, and this especially when you are at the conclusion of your victory, and are assisted by God himself. . . . This discourse have I made, upon the supposition that those who at first attempt to go upon this wall must need be killed in the attempt, though still men of true courage have a chance to escape even in the most hazardous undertakings. . . . As for the man who first mounts the wall, I should blush for shame if I did not make him to be envied of others, by those rewards I would bestow upon him. If such a one escape with his life, he shall have the command of others that are now but his equals; although it be true also that the greatest rewards will accrue to such as die in the attempt."

themselves in the subterranean galleries of the rock on which Jerusalem is founded. They attempted to work themselves a passage into the country beyond the walls. Their supplies fell short, they were compelled to issue forth and were caught and recognized. John was given life imprisonment; Simon was reserved to be an ornament of the imperator's triumph. The Jews still maintained themselves for a moment in the fortresses of Machaerus and Massada. But the final result was no longer doubtful, nor was the presence of Titus himself any further required for completing the subjugation of the country. He hastened to Rome, and threw himself into the arms of his father, whose jealousy might have been excited by the title of imperator which the soldiers had fastened upon him. But Vespasian was a man of sense and feeling, and the confidence between the father and son was never shaken. The destruction of Jerusalem, the subjugation of Palestine, resulted in the glory and the aggrandizement of both.

During the siege of Jerusalem, Rabbi Yohannan ben Zakki received Vespasian's permission to withdraw to the small Jewish school at the town of Jabneh on the coastal plain, about fifteen miles southwest of present-day Tel Aviv. There an academic Sanhedrin was set up that soon established itself as the central religious authority, with jurisdiction recognized by Jews in Palestine and beyond. Roman rule, nevertheless, continued. The emperor Hadrian (117–138) endeavoring to establish cultural uniformity, issued several repressive edicts, including one against circumcision. These sparked the significant Bar Kochba-Rabbi Akiba revolt of 132–135, which was crushed by Severus, the Roman commander. Hadrian then suppressed the Sanhedrin, closed the center at Jabneh, and prohibited both the study of the Jewish Scripture (the Torah) and the observance of the Jewish pattern of life derived from it.

Judaea became Syria Palestina, Jerusalem was renamed Aelia Capitolina, and Jews were forbidden to come within sight of the city. Once a year, on the anniversary of the destruction of the temple, controlled entry was permitted, allowing Jews to mourn at a remaining fragment on the temple site which became known as the Wailing Wall. With these repressions by Hadrian, the political history of the Jewish state in antiquity ended. Jews were again dispersed throughout the known world. This movement became known as the *Diaspora,* literally the "Dispersion," a term applied collectively and referring in general to Jews living outside Palestine. Since 1948 it has referred to those living outside the state of Israel. By the end of the second century A.D., Jewish life in Palestine was on the verge of extinction, and a long period of exile had begun.

DISPERSION

During the centuries of dispersion the Jews had no separate sovereignty and were largely excluded from the land of ancient Israel. The identity, however, of people and religion was maintained not only by choice, but also by

The coronation of King Baldwin I, the first ruler of Jerusalem (A.D. 1100) (by the artist Dandolo). He was the first formal protector of the Holy Sepulcher during the Crusades.

The Church of the Holy Sepulcher. In recent centuries it has been in a state of disrepair.

try of residence and despite their contributions to science, art, industry, and government, they remained aliens.

MODERN ZIONISM

Creation of the modern state of Israel in 1948 was the culmination of fifty years of effort by the World Zionist Organization, the first significant outside impetus being given by the endorsement of a Jewish National Home in Palestine by Great Britain's Balfour Declaration in 1917. During the late nineteenth and early twentieth centuries, the groundwork had been laid by the establishment of social welfare and economic institutions to enable and maintain Jewish immigration to Palestine. As a result, the small country has absorbed many people with a wide variety of languages and backgrounds.

Understanding of the new state is facilitated by knowledge of the origins and historical vicissitudes of the Jewish people, their strong cultural identification with the land of ancient Israel, the emergence of the Zionist movement and associated events of World War I, the experiences under the British Palestine Mandate (1923–48), as well as the major events subsequently influencing the development of the state. The Nazi Holocaust which caused the death of over six million central European Jews provided the most compelling force for the creation of the state of Israel as a homeland for the Jewish people.

Principal holy places in the vicinity of the walled city of Jerusalem

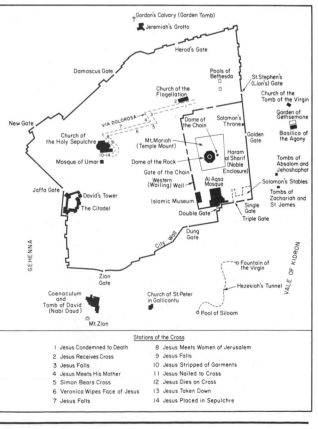

enforcement. The ghetto of the Christian and Muslim worlds has been described by Jewish historians as both a prison and a spiritual fortress. Even in western Europe at the close of the nineteenth century, it seemed to many Jews that, despite efforts to identify themselves with their coun-

THE ROYAL SOVEREIGNS OF THE ANCIENT KINGDOMS OF ISRAEL

Note: Chronology of the kings of Israel and Judah is based upon two widely accepted systems of chronology developed by authorities W. F. Albright and E. R. Thiele. The dates of Thiele's system are enclosed within parentheses wherever his dates differ from Albright's. The length of King Saul's, David's, and Solomon's reigns is not clearly known.	**UNITED MONARCHY**

Reign	Ruler
1020–1000 B.C.	King Saul
1000–961(965)	King David
961(965)–921(931)	King Solomon

DIVIDED MONARCHY
NORTHERN KINGDOM OF ISRAEL

Reign	Title	Ruler	Reign	Title	Ruler
931–922 B.C.	King	Jeroboam I	815–814	King	Jehoahaz
910–901	King	Nadab	801–798	King	Joash (Jehoash) (son of Jehoahaz)
909–900	King	Baasha			
886–877	King	Elah	786–782	King	Jeroboam II
885–876	King	Zimri	753–746	King	Zechariah
885–876	King	Tibni	752–745	King	Shallum
885–880	King	Omri	752–745	King	Menachem
874–869	King	Ahab	742–738	King	Pekahiah
853–850	King	Ahaziah	740–737	King	Pekah
850–843	King	Jehoram	732–732	King	Hoshea
844–842	King	Jehu ben-Nimshi			

SOUTHERN KINGDOM OF JUDAH

Reign	Title	Ruler	Reign	Title	Ruler
931–922 B.C.	King	Reho-boam	783–767	King	Uzziah
			742–740	King	Jotham
915–913	King	Abijah	740–732	King	Ahaz
913–911	King	Asa	715–687	King	Hezekiah
873–870	King	Jehoshap	687–686	King	Manasseh
870–848	King	Jehosha-phat	642–640	King	Amon
			640–609	King	Josiah
848–841	King	Jehoram	609	King	Jehoahaz
842–841	King	Ahaziah	609–598	King	Jehoiakim
842–837	Queen	Athaliah	598	King	Jehoia-chim
837–791	King	Joash			
800–796	King	Amaziah	597–587	King	Zedekiah

RULERS OF ISRAEL DURING NEW TESTAMENT

Reign	Herodian Rulers
37–4 B.C.	Herod
4 B.C.–A.D. 6	Archelaus
4 B.C.–A.D. 39	Herod Antipas
4 B.C.–A.D. 34	Philip
A.D. 37–44	Herod Agrippa I
A.D. 53–100	Herod Agrippa II

PROCURATORS OF JUDEA

Reign	Ruler
A.D. 6–8	Coponius
9–12	M. Ambivius
12–15	Annius Rufus
15–26	Valerius Gratus
26–36	Pontius Pilate
37–37	Marullus
37–41	Herennius Capito

PROCURATORS OF PALESTINE

Reign	Ruler
A.D. 44–46	Cuspius Fadus
46–48	Tiberius Alexander
48–52	Ventidius Cumanus
52–60	M. Antonius Felix
60–62	Porcius Festus
62–64	Clodius Albinus
64–66	Gessius Florus

KINGS OF JERUSALEM

Reign	Title	Ruler	Reign	Title	Ruler
A.D. 1099–1100	Protector of the Holy Sepulchre	Godfrey of Bouillon	1174–1185	King	Baldwin IV
			1185–1186	King	Baldwin V
			1186–1192	King	Guy of Lusignan
1100–1118	King	Baldwin I	1192–1197	King	Henry of Champagne
1118–1131	King	Baldwin II	1197–1205	King	Amalric II of Cyprus
1131–1143	King	Fulk of Anjou	1205–1229	King	John of Brienne
1143–1162	King	Baldwin III	1229–1244	King	Frederick II
1162–1174	King	Amalric I			

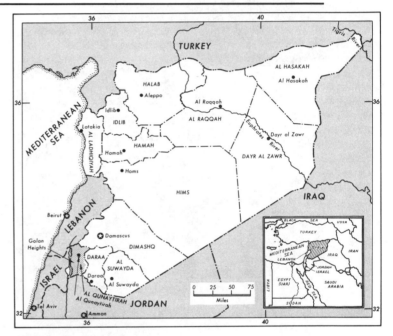

4
The Kingdoms
and Caliphates of Syria

Syria is at once an ancient and a new nation. Although full independence was secured from the French only after World War II, the capital city, Damascus, is one of the oldest continuously inhabited cities in the world. The area now known as Syria was occupied by Canaanites, Phoenicians, Hebrews, Aramaeans, Assyrians, Babylonians, Persians, Greeks, Romans, Nabataeans, and Byzantines, and each in turn left an imprint on the physical and social landscape. It was the advent of Arab Muslim rule in A.D. 636, however, that provided the two major themes of Syrian history: the Islamic religion and the world community of Arabs.

Because most Syrians are Arabs and because most Arabs are Muslims, the history of Syria is interwoven with the history of Islam and the history of the Arabs. Traditionally, Muslims view history as an integral part of religion—the life of Islamic society is the fulfillment, under divine guidance, of man's purpose on earth. The days before the appearance of Mohammed were "the period of ignorance" *(al-jahiliyyah),* during which man believed in pagan gods and idols, and Jews and Christians strayed far from the paths properly pointed out to them by their prophets. It was to steer man from this depravity that God renewed his message through the Prophet.

According to traditionalist Muslims, the greatest period of Islamic history was the time of the brief rule of Mohammed and the first four caliphs, when man presumably behaved as God commanded and established a society on earth unequaled before or after. Religion and state were one; Muslims ruled Muslims according to Muslim law. The succeeding Umayyad and Abbasside caliphates were extensions of this first period and proved the military and intellectual might of Muslims. Muslims sincerely believe that man can achieve the perfect society on earth—an Islamic society. History is the working out of this society, which one day will again be as it was during the first days of Islam. The date for such development is in the hands of the omnipotent God.

To these Muslims, their society declined because of the interference of non-Muslim foreigners. First came the

Map of modern-day Syria

Crusaders, whom the Syrians brand as the initiators of Western imperialism. To them, the evil of the Crusaders is matched by the virtue of those who rose to fight them, such as Saladin (Salah al-Din Yusaf ibn). The era of rule by non-Muslims, they believe were evil days during which Muslims were forced to live in ungodly ways. Indeed, only when Muslims rule Muslims according to the Quran (Koran) will Syrian society ever reach fulfillment.

The purely Arab view of Syrian history, which many Muslims share with many Christians, denies that the greatness of the Arab past was a purely Islamic manifestation. The history of the Arabs began before the coming of Mohammed, and what Arabs achieved during the Umayyad and Abbasside empires was evidence not only of the rich inheritance from Greek and Roman days, but of the vitality of Arab culture. Its decline was the fault of Western imperialism.

Most Syrian attitudes toward history lie between these

King Tutankhamun (1358–53 B.C.) attempted to renew Egyptian authority over general area of Palestine and Syria.

Alexander the Great

The Prophet Mohammed (570–632) was the founder of Islam.

Mohammed explaining the Koran to his followers at Medina

two extremes, but there is an increasing tendency to emphasize the Arab over the purely Islamic view. Most Syrian Muslim leaders remain religiously Muslim but subordinate religion to the demands of an Arab nationalism that they feel cannot succeed as a purely Islamic phenomenon.

Syria's history since independence has been dominated by four overriding issues. First is the deeply felt desire among Syrian Arabs—Christian and Muslim alike—to achieve some kind of unity with the other Arabic-speaking peoples of the Middle East. The Arab unity that the Syrians feel their ancestors had under the Umayyads is a unity they want again in some form. Second is a desire for economic and social prosperity. Third is a universal dislike of Israel, which they feel was forcibly imposed into their midst by the West and exists as a threat to Arab unity.

The fourth issue is the political role of the military. Between independence and mid-1971, there were ten successful coups and perhaps as many unsuccessful coup attempts. In many respects, this is a continuation of the role of the military as it existed in the early Islamic dynasties, when the support of the military was the *sine qua non* of succession to the caliphal throne.

ANCIENT SYRIA

From at least the earliest period of recorded history, Syria has been inhabited by a largely Semitic population that has been reinforced by successive waves of invasion by other Semitic peoples. The Canaanites and the related Phoenicians entered the area in the third millennium B.C. and the Hebrews and Aramaeans, in the second. Around 1700 B.C. the Amorites ruled most of Syria from their flourishing city of Mari, whose excavated remains have yielded much important historical data. During the same period, Phoenician city-states flourished along the coast. A tablet inscribed with the world's first alphabet, invented by the Phoenicians, was found a few miles north of Latakia.

In about 1600 B.C. Egypt invaded and conquered Phoenicia and Palestine, and under Thotmes III all of Syria came under Egyptian suzerainty. During the fifteenth and fourteenth centuries B.C. the area was in political upheaval, Hittites invading from the north and the growing Assyrian Kingdom pressing from the east. At the same time, the Aramaeans, a Semitic people from northern Arabia, were establishing principalities over northern and central Syria and a great part of Mesopotamia. By the end of the eleventh century B.C. the Aramaeans had established their principal kingdom at what is now Damascus and in subsequent centuries made it a great capital. They built a giant temple to their god, Baal-Hadad, in Damascus and a great fortress in Aleppo. Their greatest achievement, however, was to promote a general use of the alphabet in both public and private business. According to some sources, it was from the name that the Aramaeans gave to the dialect spoken in the vicinity of Damascus—Syriac—that Syrians derived their name; other experts suggest that the name is of Greek origin.

After many wars, the Assyrians, sometimes in alliance with the Hebrews, finally conquered the Aramaeans around 700 B.C. Assyrian rule lasted about a century until Nebuchadnezzar, the Babylonian, marched to the Oronte valley and defeated the Assyrians at Riblah, south of Homs. His successors ruled over Syria for half a century.

Semitic rule of Syria ended with the coming of the Persians, who established their headquarters in Damascus. The Persians were conquered by Alexander the Great in 333 B.C. near present-day Iskenderun, which he named Alexandretta. During the Hellenistic period, Greek culture flourished in the coastal cities and in the Hawran, a fertile plain in southwest Syria. Upon Alexander's death, one of his generals, Seleucus, founded a monarchy, which his descendants referred to as the kingdom of Syria. Seleucus named many cities after his mother, Laodicea; the greatest became Latakia, Syria's major port.

Replacing the Greeks and the Seleucids, Roman emperors inherited already thriving cities—Damascus, Tudmur (once called Palmyra), and Busra al-Sham in the fertile Hawran. Under the emperor Hadrian Syria was prosperous; its cities, major trading centers; the Hawran, a well-watered breadbasket. After making a survey of the country, the Romans established a tax system—based on the potential harvest of farmlands—that remained the key to Syria's land tax structure until 1945. On the site of the ancient Aramaean temple to Baal-Hadad in Damascus, the Romans built a great temple to Jupiter. They left in Syria some of the grandest ruins in the world as well as aqueducts, wells, and roads that were still in use in modern times.

Neither the Seleucids nor the Romans ruled without conflict with native princes. The Seleucids had to deal with powerful Arab peoples called Nabataeans, who had established an empire at Petra in what is present-day Jordan and at Busra al-Sham in the Hawran. Nabataean monuments are among the world's most impressive pre-Christian antiquities. The Romans had to face the Palmyrenes, who had built a city more magnificent even than Damascus, Palmyra, on the Tudmur oasis, the principal stop on the caravan route from Homs to the Euphrates.

By the time the Romans came, the Syrians had developed irrigation techniques, the alphabet, and astronomy. In A.D. 324 the emperor Constantine moved his capital from Rome to Byzantium, eventually renaming it Constantinople (modern Istanbul). From there the Byzantines ruled Syria, separating it into two provinces: Syria Prima, with Antioch as its capital and Aleppo its major city; and Syria Secunda, frequently ruled from Hamah. Syria Secunda was divided into two districts: Phoenicia Prima, with Tyre as its capital; and Phoenicia Secunda, ruled from Damascus. Most of Phoenicia Prima is now the Republic of Lebanon.

The Byzantine heritage remains in Syria's Christian sects and great monastic ruins. In the fourth century A.D. the Roman emperor Theodosius destroyed the temple to Jupiter in Damascus and built a cathedral in honor of John the Baptist. The huge monastery at Dayr Siman near Aleppo,

Seleucus I Nicator, one of Alexander's top generals, took command after Alexander's untimely death and then created the Kingdom of Syria, naming himself its first king.

The rulers of the Empire of Seleucid from 301 to 64 B.C. The dynasty and empire of the Seleucid was founded by Seleucus I about 301 B.C. Under the rule of his three successors, Antiochus I, II, and Seleucus II, who waged the three Syrian wars, the empire fared badly. Seleucus III reigned for three turbulent years but his brother Antiochus III, the Great restored the empire to its original importance. Both he and his son, Antiochus IV, however, had to submit to Rome. Alexander Balas, an upstart king, who wasn't in the line of succession, was ousted by Demetrius II, and he in turn was driven out by Diodotus Tryphon. Antiochus VIII and IX, and the latter's son, all in turn married, Cleopatra Selene. Tigranes the Great, king of Armenia, conquered Syria before the final capitulation by Rome.

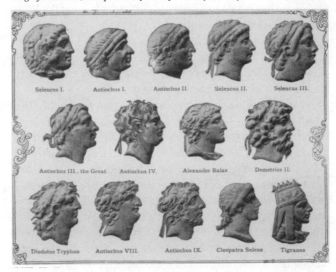

erected by Simeon Stylites in the fifth century, was the greatest Christian monument built before the tenth century.

The ruling families of Syria during this period were the Ghassanids, Christian Arabs loyal to Byzantium, from whom many Syrians now trace descent.

KINGDOM OF GHASSAN

In spite of the best efforts of generations of distinguished Arabists, the history of the Arabs before Islam remains obscure. But thanks to a new commitment to archeological reclamation in countries like Saudi Arabia, Yemen, and Oman, it is likely that such knowledge will expand dramatically in the coming years.

Paradoxically, far less is known about the three centuries immediately preceding the *hijra* of the Prophet Mohammed in 622—his migration with his followers from Makkah (Mecca) to Medina—than about other, even more remote eras in the history of the Arabs. The ancient Sabeans of South Arabia, the Nabatean Kingdom with its capital at rose-red Petra, and the Palmyrene Kingdom of Odenathus and Zenobia are much better documented—and consequently more familiar to us—than such later Arab states as the Lakhmid state at Hira, the central Arabian confederation of Kinda, or—a vital force in the sixth-century rivalry between Sassanid Persia and Byzantium—Ghassan. Yet even for that legend-enshrouded age, literary sources, when used judiciously and with extreme care, can shed light on a few key figures—such as al-Harith ibn Jabala of the Ghassan tribal confederation.

The Ghassanids were an Arab dynasty whose members belonged to a clan of the South Arabian tribe of Azd, believed to have arrived in the Syrian desert about A.D. 250–300 and, about the year 500, to have become the dominant confederation in the desert east of the Jordan and southeast of Damascus. Scholars admit, however, that any attempt to reconstruct Ghassanid history rests on exceedingly shaky ground until we reach the year 529, when al-Harith ibn Jabala succeeded his father as head of the Bani Ghassan tribal confederation.

For the historian, perhaps the most frustrating problem in studying the Ghassanids is the relative lateness of the Arabic sources. The stirring odes of the pre-Islamic Arab poets overflow with references to Ghassan. Three of the most famous poets, Labid ibn-Rabi'a—"the man with the crooked staff"—Nabigha al-Dhubyani, and Hassan ibn-Thabit, were associated with Ghassan by virtue of either kinship or official Ghassanid patronage. But the poetry of "the days of anarchy or the days of ignorance"—as Muslims call the pre-Islamic era—was handed down orally and was not committed to writing until the eighth, ninth, and tenth centuries. Moreover, many of the poems eventually underwent considerable revision. Coupled with the obvious fact that poets everywhere are creative artists and not academic historians, this makes it almost impossible for mod-

Seleucus I Nicator, the first king of Syria in the Seleucid Dynasty. The king is seen, right, in this painting with his son Antiochus I Soter, who succeeded him in 281 B.C. when he was assassinated. Far left is King Antiochus's wife, Stratomice.

King al-Harith slew his enemy king, al-Mundhir, at the famous battle of "The Day of Halima" in A.D. 554.

ern scholars to extract reliable historical data from the polished lyrics of the pre-Islamic bards.

The key Arab and Persian historians wrote long after Ghassan had ceased to exist, and though each used the written and oral sources available, their results sometimes differ radically. Abu al-Fida, for example, lists thirty-one kings of Ghassan, whereas the scrupulously critical tenth-century historian al-Mas'udi, writing almost four centuries earlier, knows of only eleven.

Fortunately, the modern historian's task is not hopeless. In many respects, in fact, it is easier than that faced by al-Mas'udi and Abu al-Fida. Written sources contemporary with the Ghassanids—in some cases even contemporary with the reign of al-Harith ibn Jabala—have survived in Greek and Syriac manuscripts, in Epigraphic South Arabian, and in documents in Ethiopic, Coptic, Armenian, and Georgian. They do help elucidate the history of the sixth-century Arabs.

From the standpoint of world history, the dominant motif of the sixth century was the epic rivalry between Byzantium and Sassanid Persia—and Ghassan played a pivotal part in that ongoing conflict. In fact, it is in its role as a Byzantine-sponsored buffer state that Ghassan definitely enters the clear light of history. This was in or around 529, when the Byzantine emperor Justinian appointed al-Harith ibn Jabala leader of the Arabs of the Syrian desert and authorized him to use the title of king—which may imply that the Ghassanid chiefs normally did not use the title.

The investiture of al-Harith ibn Jabala was Justinian's countermove in the endless political and military chess match with the Persian emperor Chosroes Anushirvan, who for years had subsidized another Arab dynasty—the Lakhmids of Hira, in southern Mesopotamia—as *its* buffer state in the struggle with the Byzantines. Justinian hoped that al-Harith would neutralize the formidable Lakhmids, who had already mounted a series of spectacular raids into Byzantine territory on behalf of the Persians.

As it turned out, al-Harith was capable of the task. The first Ghassanid ruler to mold the Arabs of what are now Syria and Jordan into a cohesive tribal confederation, the dynamic and charismatic al-Harith, as the sixth-century Syrian churchman John of Ephesus put it, "was held in . . . awe and terror by all the nomad tribes of Syria . . ."

As a result of Justinian's move, the history of the northern pre-Islamic Arabs was dominated—from 529 to 554—by the wars of al-Harith and al-Mundhir, the also-remarkable leader of the Lakhmids. Sometimes their battles were part of the larger Perso-Byzantine conflict, but just as often, al-Harith and al-Mundhir carried on a private struggle of their own, one that looms large in Arabic literature.

During this period, Byzantium and Persia were stalemated in the Middle East. Each of the Arab buffer states was a pivotal factor in the regional defense system of an empire.

The final encounter between al-Harith and al-Mundhir has gone down in Arab tradition as "The Day of Halima." The battle, which took place in northern Syria in 554, resulted in al-Mundhir's death and a decisive victory for Ghassan. Here is the account of the ninth-century Baghdadi historian, Ibn Qutaiba.

> When al-Mundhir ibn Má al-Samá marched against him with an army of 1,000,000 strong, al-Harith sent only 100 men to meet him—among them the poet Labid, who was then a youth—ostensibly to make peace. They surrounded al-Mundhir's tent and slew the king and his companions, then they took horse, and some escaped, while others were slain. The Ghassanid cavalry attacked the army of al-Mundhir and put them to flight. King al-Harith had a daughter named Halima, who perfumed

the top 100 champions on that day and clad them in shrouds of white linen to make them ready for burial in the event they were killed.

The strife between Ghassanids and Lakhmids did not abate after al-Mundhir's death, any more than did the Perso-Byzantine wars, but, with his rival out of the picture, al-Harith ibn Jabala of Ghassan became the preeminent figure.

Unfortunately, little is known about the Ghassanid society, in al-Harith's time, or for that matter, in any other time, since most of the clans and tribes were nomadic, with no permanent capital other than an encampment at Jabiya, south of Damascus.

Unlike many pre-Islamic Arab tribes, the Ghassanids were not pagans but Monophysite Christians—members of what later came to be called the Syrian-Jacobite church. It was, in fact, through the personal intervention of al-Harith ibn Jabala that Ya'qub Bar-Addai, better known as Jacob Baradai (whence the term "Jacobite"), was consecrated bishop of Edessa for the provinces of Syria and Mesopotamia, in 543. The rigidly monotheistic doctrine of Syrian Christianity probably helped to prepare the Arabs of Ghassan for the revelation of Islam, whose Prophet Mohammed was born very soon after al-Harith ibn Jabala's death in 569.

In November, in the year 563, al-Harith and the emperor Justinian held a summit meeting in Constantinople, at which al-Harith was to tell Justinian which of his sons

Byzantine emperor Justinian appointed al-Harith ibn Jabala as leader of the Arabs of the Syrian desert and authorized him to use the title of king of Ghassan.

would succeed him. And though the Ghassanid king was the head of what we would today call a client state, he and the emperor met on an equal footing—as comrades in arms—discussing matters of earthshaking and less-than-earthshaking importance.

We know that they covered the crucial question of al-Harith's successor—it was to be his capable son, al-Mundhir ibn al-Harith.

Perhaps, also, they chatted about Justinian's late wife, the empress Theodora, whom al-Harith had met in Constantinople some twenty years earlier, and with whom he had arranged the consecration of Ya'qub Bar-Addai. A meeting in Constantinople between a Byzantine emperor and a pre-Islamic Arab king is truly a stimulant to the active historical imagination.

Unfortunately, the skimpy records from contemporary historians preclude our saying anything about al-Harith's appearance, the size of his entourage, or the impression he made upon Justinian and his courtiers. We can suppose that al-Harith's arrival in the Byzantine capital caused quite a stir among the citizenry.

We do know that al-Harith ibn Jabala has a role in Byzantine history, in Syrian and Jordanian history, and in Christian ecclesiastical history. Above all, however, he is a protagonist of Arab history. He stands as one of the towering figures of the pre-Islamic era, right alongside Odenathus and Zenobia of Palmyra, al-Mundhir ibn Má al-Samá of Hira, and the celebrated poets of Ukaz. Under his stalwart leadership, a significant portion of the Arabs were successfully united, prefiguring, in a secular sense, the more complete unification of the Arabs that was to take place only a few decades later, under the Prophet Mohammed and the early caliphs of Islam.

MUSLIM EMPIRES

During the first decades of the seventh century, a merchant from Mecca called Mohammed converted many of his fellow Arabs to a new religion known as Islam. By A.D. 629 the religious fervor, desire for booty, and pressures of an expanding population impelled these Muslim Arab tribes to invade lands to the north of the Arabian Peninsula. The lands that they invaded they called *al-Sham* (the north), and Arabs have known Syria as Sham ever since. To most Arabs, Syrians are *shammis*. In A.D. 635 Damascus surrendered to the great Muslim general, Khalid ibn al-Walid. Undermined by Persian incursions, religious schisms, and rebellions in the provinces, especially among the Ghassanids in Syria, Byzantium could offer little resistance to Islam.

In succeeding centuries Muslims extended and consolidated their rule in many areas, and by 1200 they controlled lands from the Atlantic to the Bay of Bengal, from central Russia to the Gulf of Aden. Wherever they went they built mosques, tombs, and forts. The ruins of such structures are widely found in Syria.

Mohammed made Medina his first capital, and it was here that he died. Leadership of the faithful fell to Abu Bakr (A.D. 632–34) Mohammed's father-in-law. Umar followed him (634–44) and organized the government of captured provinces. The third caliph, leader of the Muslims, was Uthman (644–56), under whose administration the compilation of the Quran was accomplished. Among the aspirants to the caliphate was Ali, Mohammed's cousin and son-in-law, whose supporters felt that only he should be the Prophet's successor. Upon the murder of Uthman, Ali became caliph (656–61). After a civil war with other aspirants to the caliphate, Ali moved his capital to Mesopotamia and was later assassinated at al-Kufah (Kafa). Ali's early followers established the first of Islam's dissident sects, the Shiites (from the words *shiat* Ali, "party of Ali"). Those who had accepted the successions remained the orthodox of Islam; they were called Sunnis—from the word *sunna* (the traditions that developed around Mohammed's life, sometimes referred to as the way of the Prophet), which they accept.

UMAYYAD CALIPHATE

After Ali's murder, Muawiyah—the governor of Syria during the early Arab conquests, a kinsman of Uthman, and a member of the Umayyad branch of the Quraysh lineage—proclaimed himself caliph and established his capital in Damascus. From there he conquered Muslim enemies to the east, south, and west and fought the Christians in the north. Later Umayyad caliphs sent Muslim armies into Russia and India, and an Umayyad prince built a kingdom in Spain in 755. Damascus achieved a glory unrivaled since the ancient Aramaeans. A symbol of that glory was the great mosque built by Walid I (705–15) from the Cathedral of Saint John. It stands in the heart of the Syrian capital.

The Umayyad Muslims established a military government in Syria and used the country primarily as a base of operations. They lived aloof from the people and at first made little effort to convert the Christians to Islam. They subjected non-Muslims to tribute and kept them disarmed, whereas Muslims paid no tribute and bore arms. Non-Muslims were not allowed to bear witness against Muslims and were required to distinguish themselves by their clothing. The Umayyads administered the lands in the manner of the Byzantines, giving complete authority to provincial governors.

In the application of laws the Umayyads followed the traditions set by the Hellenistic monarchies and the Roman Empire. The conqueror's law—in this case, Muslim law *(sharia)*—applied only to those of the same faith or nationality as the conquerors. Civil law for non-Muslims was the law of their particular *milla*, also called *millet* (separate religious community); the religious leaders administered the laws of the *milla*. The system was to prevail throughout Islam and has survived in Syrian legal codes.

During the eighty-nine years of Umayyad rule (661–750), most Syrians adopted Islam, and the Arabic language replaced Aramaic. The Umayyads organized the postal and fiscal systems, minted coins, built hospitals, and constructed underground canals to bring water to the towns. The country prospered both economically and intellectually. Trade from Syrian ports boomed, and educated Jews and Christians, many of them Greek, found employment in the caliphal courts, where they studied and practiced medicine, alchemy, and philosophy.

Under later dissolute caliphs the Umayyad Dynasty began to decline. Because of pressure to convert to Islam, Christians rebelled or fled, and at the same time Muslims in the east became powerful through Persian backing and pressed against Umayyad borders. By 750 the Abbassides had conquered the Umayyads and established the caliphate in Baghdad. Syria became a province of an empire later to be noted for its own intellectual achievements.

OTHER CALIPHATES AND KINGDOMS

Abbasside rule over Syria, however, was precarious and often challenged by independent Muslim princes. The greatest of these was Abu Ali Hasan, who founded a kingdom known as the Hamdani. A Shiite, he established his capital at Aleppo, and the Abbassides recognized him as *Saif al-Dawlah* (sword of the state). The Hamdanid Dynasty ruled throughout the tenth century and became famous for its achievements in science and letters. In Europe it was known for its persistent attacks against Byzantium. The Hamdanid Kingdom fell in 1094 to Muslim Seljuk Turks from the northeast.

During the same period the Fatimids established themselves in Egypt and drove north against Syria. Persecution of non-Muslims reached its height as the Fatimid caliphs, especially under Abu Ali Mansur al-Hakim (996–1021), destroyed churches and drove Christians into the mountains. Hakim claimed to be divine, and it was in the secluded valleys of Mount Hermon in Syria that his followers found tribesmen to adopt his religion. These people were the ancestors of the present-day Druzes.

Muslim expansion throughout the world and Muslim rule of holy places claimed by the Christians roused Europe, and in the twelfth century waves of Crusaders poured into the

Saladin (Salah al-Din al-Ayyubi) was Islam's greatest leader against the Franks.

Middle East. Following the path of Alexander the Great, they swept down the coast of Syria; along their route they built forts *(kraks)*, such as Hisn al-Akrad, between Homs and Tripoli.

The greatest of all Muslim leaders in the days of the Crusades was a Kurd named Saladin (Salah al-Din Yusuf ibn Ayyub), born in Mesopotamia but raised in Baalbek, Syria. A religious as well as a military leader, he defeated the Fatimids in Egypt, seized temporal leadership while acknowledging the spiritual suzerainty of the Sunni caliph in Baghdad, and united Islam against Christianity. Saladin inflicted Islam's mightiest blows against the Franks (Crusaders), raised Muslim pride and self-respect, and founded the Ayyubid Dynasty, which governed Egypt until 1260. During his lifetime he created harmony among Muslims in the Middle East and gained a position of affection and honor among them that remains strong to the present day.

Saladin's death in 1193 brought this unity to an end. His Ayyubid successors quarreled among themselves, and Syria broke into small dynasties centered in Aleppo, Hamah, Homs, and Damascus. By the fourteenth century, after repelling repeated invasions from the north by the Mongols who had sacked Aleppo and Damascus, the Mamluk sultans of Egypt, successors to the Ayyubids, ruled from the Nile to the Euphrates. Their great citadels and monuments still stand. In 1516 the Ottoman sultan in Turkey defeated the Mamluks at Aleppo and made Syria a province of a new Muslim empire.

OTTOMAN EMPIRE

The Ottomans were nomadic Muslim Turks from central Asia who had been converted long before by Umayyad conquerors. Led by Uthman, they founded a principality in 1300 amid the ruins of the Mongol-wrecked Seljuk Empire in northwest Turkey. Fifty years later Uthman's successors invaded Europe. They conquered Constantinople in 1453 and in the sixteenth century conquered all of the Middle East. From 1300 to 1918, when the empire fell, thirty-six sultans, all descendants of Uthman, ruled most of the Muslim world. Europeans referred to the Ottoman throne as the Sublime Porte, a name derived from a gate of the sultan's palace in Constantinople.

The Ottomans ruled Syria through pashas, who governed

Caliph Abul-Abbas greets a foreign dignitary to his throne. The Caliph, who ruled from 750 to 754, was the founder of the Abbassid Dynasty.

Egypt occupied Syria from 1831 to 1839. Ibrahim Pasha, the son of the Egyptian ruler, was their overseer in Syria.

with unlimited authority over the land under their control though responsible ultimately to the Sublime Porte. The pashas were both administrative and military leaders. So long as they collected their taxes, maintained order, and ruled an area not of immediate military importance, the Sublime Porte left them alone. In turn, the pashas ruled through smaller administrative districts headed either by a subordinate Turk or a loyal Arab. Occasionally, as in Lebanon, the Arab subordinate maintained his position more through his own power than through loyalty. Throughout Ottoman rule, governors and governed remained strangers except among those wealthier Syrians who entered government service or studied in Turkish universities.

Ottoman administration often followed patterns set by previous rulers. Each religious minority—Shiite Muslim, Greek Orthodox, Maronite, Armenian, and Jewish—constituted a *milla*. The religious heads of each community administered all personal law and had certain civil functions as well.

Syria had known economic prosperity in the past but did not know it again under the Ottomans. At times attempts were made to rebuild the country, but on the whole Syria remained poor. The population decreased by nearly 30 percent, and hundreds of villages virtually disappeared into the desert. At the end of the eighteenth century, only one-eighth of the villages formerly on the tax register of the Aleppo *pashaliq* (domain of a pasha) were still inhabited. Only the area now known as Lebanon achieved economic progress, resulting largely from the relatively independent rule of the Druze amirs.

With the traders from the West came missionaries, teachers, scientists, and tourists whose governments began to clamor for certain rights. France demanded the right to protect the Christians, and in 1535 Sultan Suleyman I granted France several "capitulations"—extraterritorial rights that developed later into political semiautonomy not only for the French but also for the Christians protected by them. The British acquired similar rights in 1580 and established the Levant Company in Aleppo. By the end of the eighteenth century the Russians claimed protective rights over the Greek Orthodox.

The strength of the Ottoman Empire began to show signs of decline in the eighteenth century. By the nineteenth century European powers had started to take advantage of Ottoman weakness through both military and political penetration, including Napoleon's invasion of Egypt, subsequent British intervention, and French occupation of Lebanon. Economic development of Syria through the use of European capital—for example, the railways, built largely with French money—brought further incursions.

Western penetration became decidedly political after the Druze uprising in the Syrian province of Lebanon in 1860. The revolt began in the north as a Maronite Christian peasant uprising against Christian landlords. As the revolt moved southward to the territories where the landlords were Druzes, the conflagration acquired an intersectarian character, and the Druzes massacred some ten thousand Maronites. France sent in troops and removed them a year later only after the European powers had forced the Sublime Porte to grant new laws for Lebanon. By the Statute of 1861, Lebanon was for the first time officially detached from Syria, and its administration came increasingly under the control of France.

Because of European pressure, as well as the discontent of the Syrian people, the Ottoman sultans made some reforms during the nineteenth century. The Egyptian occupation of Syria from 1831 to 1839 under the nominal authority of the sultan brought a centralized government, judicial reform, and regular taxation. But Ibrahim Pasha, son of the Egyptian ruler, became unpopular with the landowners because of the limitations he placed on their influence and with the peasants because of the conscription and taxation he imposed. He was eventually driven from Syria by the sultan's forces. The subsequent reforms of Turkish sultan Mahmud II and his son were more theoretical than real and were counteracted by reactionary forces inside the state as well as by the inertia of Ottoman officials. Reforms proved somewhat more successful with the Kurds and Turkomans in the north and with the Alawites around Latakia but were unsuccessful with the Druzes of the Jabal Druze, a rugged mountainous area in southwest Syria, who managed to retain their administrative and judicial autonomy and exemption from military service.

Although further reform attempts generally failed, the results of the more successful still exist. Among them are colonization of Syria's frontiers; suppression of tribal raiding; opening of new lands to cultivation; and the start toward settling bedouin tribes. Attempts to register all the land failed, however, because of the peasants' fear of taxation and conscription.

Sultan Abdul Hamid II (1876–1909), sometimes known as Abdul Hamid the Damned, acquired a reputation as the

A history of the royalty of Syria would be lacking if a mention were not made of Abd-el-Kader, who was the sultan of Algeria and later retired to Damascus. He is honored on a Syrian stamp as a great Arab leader. He fought the French in Algeria and North Africa. After being captured by the French, he and his family were exiled to France in 1848. (He had been the sultan of Algeria since 1832.) The French government kept him, his family and his top military staff imprisoned in the Chateau d'Amboise on the Loire, the old palace of King Louis XI, until he was freed by the prince president, Louis Napoleon in 1852. Abd-el-Kader, his family, and his close followers, then went to Damascus to live out their lives. He died there in 1883. In the expanse of his final thirty years of life, there is little recorded, except for his sheltering of 1,500 foreign Christians, mainly diplomats and their families, during the infamous massacre of 1860 when an uprising of the natives, backed by the government, resulted in over 10,000 Christians being killed throughout Syria.

most oppressive Ottoman sultan in modern history. Opponents died quickly; taxes became heavy. Abdul Hamid tried to obtain the loyalty of his Muslim subjects by preaching pan-Islamic ideas and completing in 1908 the Hejaz Railway between Constantinople and Medina. The sultan's cruelty—he was also known as The Butcher in Syria—and increasing Western cultural influence set the stage for the last act of Ottoman rule and the first act of Arab nationalism; World War I brought the climax.

WORLD WAR I AND ARAB NATIONALISM

The period from the outbreak of World War I in 1914 to the granting of France's mandate over Syria by the League of Nations in 1922 was marked by a complicated sequence of events and power politics during which Syrians achieved a brief moment of independence. Revolt against the Turks had been a goal for some Syrians for more than two decades. Syrian intellectuals, many of them graduates of European and European- or American-run universities, were urging the study of Arab history, literature, and language. Groups of Syrians publicly demanded decentralization of Ottoman administration and administrative reform. As Ottoman governors, such as Jamal Pasha, suppressed them, the Syrians went underground and demanded complete Arab independence. One of the first secret groups to form was al-Jamiyyah al-Arabiyah al-Fatah, of which Prince Faisal, son of Sharif Hussein of Mecca, was a member. Another group was al-Ahd (the Covenant), a secret association of Arab army officers.

The outbreak of World War I and Turkey's alignment with Germany impelled Jamal Pasha to tighten his control over Syria. Attacking insurgents ruthlessly, he arrested al-Fatah members. On the morning of May 6, 1915, twenty-one Arabs were hanged in the city squares of Damascus and Beirut. Martyrs' Day is now a national holiday in Syria.

Events leading up to Syria's momentary independence began in the Arabian Peninsula. The British—anxious for Arab support against the Ottomans in the war and desirous of strengthening their position vis-à-vis the French in the determination of the Middle East's future—asked Sharif Hussein ibn-Ali of Mecca, leader of the Hashemite family and an Ottoman appointee over the Hejaz, to lead the Arabs in revolt. In return the British gave certain assurances, which Hussein interpreted as an endorsement of his kingship of the Arab world. From the Arab nationalists in Damascus came pleas for the Hashemites to assume the leadership. Hussein ibn-Ali accepted, and on June 5, 1916, the Hejazi tribesmen, led by Hussein's sons and later advised by British officers such as T. E. Lawrence, rose against the Turks. In October 1918 Prince Faisal entered Damascus as a popular hero.

Prince Faisal, as military governor, assumed immediate control of all Syria except the areas along the Mediterranean coast where French troops were garrisoned. In July 1919 he convened the General Syrian Congress, which declared Syria sovereign and free. In March 1920 the congress proclaimed Faisal king of Syria.

Faisal and his Syrian supporters began reconstructing Syria. They established Arabic as the official language and proceeded to have school texts translated from Turkish. They reopened schools and started new ones, including the Faculty of Law at the Syrian University and the Arab Academy in Damascus. Also, Faisal appointed a committee to begin drawing up a constitution.

In the areas still held by the French, Syrians continued to revolt. In the Jabal al-Nusayriyah around Latakia in the northwest, Salah al-Ali led an uprising against French troops in May 1919. Along the Turkish border the nationalist leader Ibrahim Hananu started another rebellion in July 1919. The French defeated the attempts but not before both men had acquired a permanent place in Syrian history as heroes.

Three forces worked against Arab nationalism and Faisal's budding Arab monarchy. One was Britain's earlier interest in keeping eastern Mesopotamia under control, both to counter Russian influence in the north and to protect oil interests in the area. The second was Zionism and the Jewish interest in Palestine. Although Great Britain had promised the Arabs independence, in the Balfour Declaration of 1917 it had also promised Zionists a "national home" in Palestine. The two promises subsequently proved to be in direct conflict. The third force was France's determination to remain a power in the Middle East. Earlier in the war the French, British, Italians, and Czarist Russians had met secretly to decide the fate of the Arab lands. In the Sykes-Picot Agreement of May 16, 1916, signed only six months after the British vaguely promised Hussein an Arab kingdom, Britain and France agreed to give the French paramount influence in Syria; the British were to have predominance in what became Transjordan and Iraq.

At the Versailles Peace Conference, Woodrow Wilson asked that the Arab claims to independence be given consideration, and Faisal was invited to present the Arab cause. His pleas were unavailing, as was a report recommending Syrian independence under Faisal or a United States mandate over the country. Disappointed by his failure at Versailles, Faisal returned to Damascus and declared Syria free and independent.

France and Great Britain refused to recognize Syria's independence, and the Supreme Allied Council, meeting in San Remo, Italy, in April 1920, partitioned the Arab world into mandates, following the earlier Sykes-Picot Agreement. Syria became a French mandate, and French soldiers began marching from Beirut to Damascus. Arab resistance was crushed, and on July 25, 1920, the French marched into Damascus. Faisal fled to Europe and did not return to the Middle East until he was made king of Iraq in 1921. Abdullah was recognized by the British as the amir of the region that became known as Transjordan. The boundaries of these states were thus drawn by the European Allies after World War I. Syria, eventually, gained its independence. But, the experiences with France and Great Britain left a strong bitterness against the West and a deep-seated determination to reunite Arabs into one state.

AFTER INDEPENDENCE

The legacy of ancient Syria, the Arab Empire, Ottoman rule, and the French Mandate left the people of Syria with diverse loyalties toward both their own nation and their neighbors. During the period Syria's leaders—though often competing with each other for personal power—were generally united in their single goal of freedom from French rule. Conflicts between diverse groups were postponed, and Syrian unity became important as Syrians sought independence.

With the departure of the French, unity among the leaders disappeared. Aleppines contested with Damascenes for dominance in commercial and political life; the Druzes pledged allegiance to Druzes, the Kurds to Kurds, and tribal peoples to tribal institutions. Alawites, poorest yet largest of the minorities, felt outside the sphere of Sunni Muslim control and tried to rebel. Rural leaders contended with urban leaders; the progressive, increasingly secularized younger generation vied with the older, religious-minded leaders. Politicians differed over the kind of government Syria should have—monarchy or republic, parliamentary or presidential democracy.

Although most leaders agreed that the Syria they inherited was merely a part of a larger Arab nation, they disagreed on the form it should take. Trade-minded Aleppines felt close to Iraq and the Hashimites, as did some of the older leaders who had joined Faisal in 1918. Young, educated Damascenes rejected the Hashimites, whom they felt were backed by the British. The cultural heritage of France and the American ideals of democracy induced many Syrians to look westward for friendship. Others looked north to the Soviet Union, which had no apparent record of intrigue in the Arab world but was more than willing to begin. Such diversity was not conducive to unity.

THE ROYAL SOVEREIGNS OF THE KINGDOMS AND CALIPHATES OF SYRIA

Reign	Title	Ruler	Reign	Title	Ruler
333–323 B.C.		Alexander the Great	744–744	Caliph	Yazid III
323–301	King	Antigonus I	744–744	Caliph	Ibrahim
SELEUCID DYNASTY			744–750	Caliph	Marwan II
301–281 B.C.	King	Seleucus I Nicator	**THE ABBASSID CALIPHATE**		
281–261	King	Antiochus I Soter	750–754	Caliph	Abul-Abbas
261–246	King	Antiochus II Theos	754–775	Caliph	Abu-djafar El-mansur
246–226	King	Seleucus II	775–785	Caliph	Mohammed al-Mahdi
226–223	King	Seleucus III	785–786	Caliph	Musa al-hadi
223–187	King	Antiochus III, the Great	786–809	Caliph	Harun al-Rashid
187–176	King	Seleucus IV	809–813	Caliph	Mohammed al-Amin
175–164	King	Antiochus IV Epiphanes	813–833	Caliph	Abdullah-al-Mamun
164–162	King	Antiochus V Eupator	833–842	Caliph	El-mutasim-billah
162–150	King	Demetrius I Soter	842–847	Caliph	Harum al-Wathik-billah
150–145	King	Alexander Balas	847–861	Caliph	Djafar al-Mutawakkil
145–138	King	Demetrius II Nicator	861–862	Caliph	Mohammed al-Muntasir-billah
138–129	King	Antiochus VII	862–866	Caliph	Ahmed al-Mustain-billah
129–125	King	Demetrius II	866–869	Caliph	Mohammed al-Mustain-billah
125–96	King	Antiochus VIII	869–870	Caliph	Mohammed al-Muhtadi-billah
96–95	King	Antiochus IX	870–892	Caliph	Ahmed al-Mutamid alallah
95–94	King	Antiochus X	892–902	Caliph	Ahmed al-Mutamid-billah
95–88	King	Demetrius III	902–908	Caliph	Ali al-Muktafi-billah
69–64	King	Antiochus XIII	908–932	Caliph	Djafar al-Muktadir-billah
64—Syria became a Roman province.			932–934	Caliph	Mohammed al-Kahir-billah
THE SYRIAN CALIPHATES			934–940	Caliph	Ahmed ar-radi-billah
A.D. 622–632		Mohammed	940–944	Caliph	Ibrahim al-Muttaki-billah
632–634	Caliph	Abu Bekr	944–946	Caliph	Al-Mustakfi-billah
634–644	Caliph	Omari	946–974	Caliph	Al-Muti
644–656	Caliph	Othman bin Afan	974–991	Caliph	Al-Tai li-amrillah
656–661	Caliph	Ali	991–1031	Caliph	Al-Kadir-billah
			1031–1075	Caliph	Al-Ka-im
THE UMAYYAD CALIPHATE			1075–1094	Caliph	Al-Muktadi
661–680	Caliph	Muawiyah	1094–1118	Caliph	Al-Mustazhi-billah
680–683	Caliph	Yazid I	1118–1135	Caliph	Al-Mustarshir-billah
683–684	Caliph	Muawiyah II	1135–1136	Caliph	Al-Raschid
684–685	Caliph	Marwan I	1136–1160	Caliph	Al-Muktafi
685–705	Caliph	Abd al-Melik	1160–1170	Caliph	Al-Muktanijd-billah
705–715	Caliph	Walid I	1170–1180	Caliph	Al-Mustadi
715–717	Caliph	Suleiman	1180–1225	Caliph	Al-Nasir
717–720	Caliph	Omar II	1225–1226	Caliph	Al-Zahir
720–724	Caliph	Yazid II	1226–1242	Caliph	Al-Munstansir
724–743	Caliph	Hisham I	1242–1258	Caliph	Al-Mustasin-billah
743–744	Caliph	Walid II	1258—Mongol invasion began		

The Hashemite Kingdom of Jordan

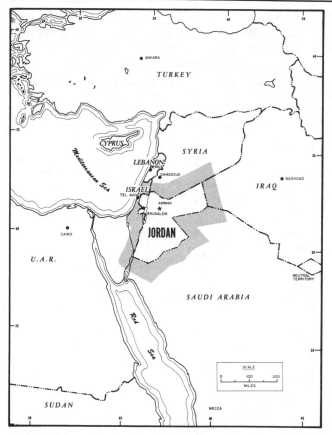

Jordan and its position in the Middle East

Jordan's central location as a trade crossroads and buffer between the settled region of the Mediterranean littoral west of the Jordan River and the desert to the east contributed significantly to the country's experience in ancient and more recent times. Until 1921, however, Jordan's history was that of a vaguely defined territory without a separate existence. Its earlier history, closely associated with the religions of Judaism, Christianity, and Islam, is therefore included in that of the surrounding states and contending empires of which it often formed a part.

By the time of the Ottoman Turkish Conquest of 1517, three general geographic regions had developed distinct

emphases and loyalties that continued to be identifiable in modern times: the villagers and town dwellers of Palestine, west of the Jordan River; the scattered villagers and tribesmen of northern Jordan, who tended to associate themselves with Syria; and the tribesmen of southern Jordan, who identified themselves with the deserts of the Arabian Peninsula to the south. Although most of them were Muslim Arabs, the integration of these somewhat differing backgrounds and regional orientations presented problems for the later Jordanian ruling monarchy in establishing the cohesion and identity of the state.

Late in the nineteenth century, two political nationalist movements developed that were to affect the history of Jordan profoundly: Arab nationalism, articulated first in Lebanon and Syria; and Zionism, of European Jewish origin. Arising separately, these movements at length converged in Palestine and proved to be irreconcilable.

The state of Jordan first emerged immediately after World War I when Great Britain divided into two parts the mandate for Palestine that it had received from the League of Nations. The Arab amirate of Transjordan was then established in the portion east of the Jordan River, within boundaries much the same as those of the East Bank of Jordan in 1973. Great Britain supported as ruler the Hashemite prince (later king), Abdullah ibn al-Hussein (also Husayn), one of the principal figures of the British-aided Arab revolt against the Turks in World War I. West of the Jordan River, direct British administration was set up in Palestine, and within this administration the Jewish national home promised by Great Britain to the Zionist organization in 1917 was implemented.

After a United Nations (UN) resolution of 1947 had endorsed the formation of separate Arab and Jewish states in Palestine, Great Britain gave up the League of Nations mandate on May 14, 1948, and at the same time the establishment of the state of Israel was proclaimed. Transjordan's Arab Legion then joined with forces of several other Arab states in the unsuccessful 1948–49 war against Israel. The end of these hostilities left Transjordan in control of the old portion of the city of Jerusalem and part of Palestine and with a trebled population, one-third of whom were refugees. The country's name was changed to the Hashemite Kingdom of Jordan, and in 1950 the holdings on the West Bank were annexed. The West Bank was lost to Israeli control in the Arab-Israeli War of 1967.

Since 1950 perhaps the chief characteristic of the kingdom has been political and economic stability under severe stress. Among the major factors responsible for Jordan's survival were the legacy of the period of British aid and guidance from 1921 to 1958, the United States programs of extensive economic and military aid after 1957, and the leadership and personality first of King Abdullah and then of his grandson, King Hussein I (Hussein ibn Talal).

EARLY HISTORY

THE JORDAN AREA
AND ANCIENT ISRAEL

The region east of the Jordan River constituting the present-day state of Jordan was an important transit or connecting area in the great land bridge between Africa and Southwest Asia—composed of the northern reaches of the Arabian Peninsula, Palestine, Syria, and Mesopotamia—that is often referred to as the Fertile Crescent. At various times, in whole or in part, the area of Jordan was held by contending, successive empires to the east and west, by small local kingdoms, and by ancient Israel at its height. The principal centers of history affecting the country were located in the more populous coastal lands west of the Jordan River, the Egyptian empires on the Nile, the rival eastern empires of Mesopotamia and Persia, and the Arabian Peninsula on the south.

About 2000 B.C. large numbers of Semitic peoples known as Amorites, apparently from northern Syria, moved southeast into Mesopotamia and also southwest into the land of the Jordan River, called Canaan. By about 1500 B.C. the dominant population element on both sides of the Jordan River was Semitic.

About 1500 B.C. both Hittite marauders from Anatolia (Turkey) and Semitic people, called Habiru by the Egyptians, from northern Syria began to intrude upon Canaan. The Habiru have been identified also as early Hebrews. On the larger stage, the Egyptian and Hittite empires in 1280 B.C. entered into a treaty by which northern Syria was allocated to the Hittites, but southern Syria and the whole area of Canaan ostensibly remained under Egypt.

During the struggle between Egypt and the Hittites, Hebrew infiltration continued. The exodus of the Israelites from Egypt under Moses occurred about 1300 B.C., and the main phase of the Israelite conquest of Canaan under Joshua began apparently during the years 1250 to 1225 B.C. Only a few decades later another invasion of Canaan began, by Mediterranean sea people, possibly from Crete, called Philistines. From them the area designation Palestine is

Official portrait of King Hussein for the Silver Jubilee (twenty-five years) of his reign

derived; the modern Arabic word *Falastin* preserves the name intact.

The ancient kingdom of Israel was established about 1020 B.C. with the war leader Saul as first king. In the time of David, Saul's successor, the Israelite people were firmly united, the native Canaanites were subdued, and the Philistines were finally driven back into coastal enclaves between present-day Gaza and Tel Aviv. David expanded the realm well beyond the old tribal allocations made to the twelve tribes of Israel (three of which lay east of the Jordan River), and scholars have estimated that the population of the expanded realm contained more non-Israelites than Israelites. At its maximum extent, David's kingdom has been estimated to have stretched from the upper Euphrates River south to the Gulf of Aqaba. Amman was held briefly under David but broke away again after his death.

Under David's son and successor, Solomon, ancient Israel reached its peak of cultural splendor and influence, but after Solomon's death the realm split into two kingdoms: Israel, north of Jerusalem, and Judah, encompassing much of the former southern and western holdings, including Edom, that lay south of the Dead Sea. The balance of the territory that became Jordan in modern times included the desert areas where bedouin tribal life prevailed, the Semitic kingdom of Ammon, and some of land claimed by the Aramaic kingdom of Damascus.

EGYPT, ASSYRIA, BABYLONIA,
AND PERSIA

As the Egyptian power declined, the Assyrian Empire rose among the Semitic peoples of the upper Tigris River region. In the early eighth century B.C. the capital of the northern Hebrew kingdom of Israel fell to the Assyrian king. The southern kingdom of Judah, although tributary to Assyria, preserved a shaky political independence for another one hundred fifty years. The rest of the area, including Jordan, was divided into provinces and ruled under Assyrian governors.

Assyria declined when confronted with the insurgent neo-Babylonian power of southern Mesopotamia. Nineveh, the Assyrian capital, fell in 612 B.C., and Babylon became supreme in the area, also defeating Egypt to the west. The kingdom of Judah was ended when Emperor Nebuchadnezzar II (605–562 B.C.) seized and destroyed Jerusalem in 586 B.C. Babylon, in its turn, was overthrown by the new imperial surge of the Persians under Cyrus II in 539 B.C.

GREECE, ROME, AND BYZANTIUM

Alexander the Great of Macedon and his highly trained Greek army crossed the Dardanelles into Asia in 334 B.C. and, administering a crushing defeat to Persian forces, by 332 established Greek dominance in Egypt, Syria, Jordan, Palestine, and to areas east of them. After his death in 323 the empire became divided among his governors-general who, in Egypt, became the Ptolemaic line of pharaohs and, in greater Syria, the line of Seleucid kings. The city of Amman, in modern Jordan, was renamed Philadelphia during the Greek era.

The lands east and west of the Jordan River were thus caught again between rival realms. Both the Jews in Palestine and the Nabataeans east of the Dead Sea took advantage of the contention between the Ptolemaic and Seleucid empires. The Seleucid Empire, having successfully displaced Ptolemaic efforts to absorb Palestine by 198 B.C., launched repressive measures against Jewish customs and religion. In 168 the Jewish revolt of the Maccabees erupted. The victories of Judas Maccabeus over the Seleucid Syrians were continued by his brothers, and in 143 a Jewish independent kingdom was reestablished under the line known as the Hasmoneans. This kingdom quickly expanded east of the Jordan but did not last long.

Rival claimants to the Hasmonean throne appealed for support in 64 B.C. to Pompey, the Roman commander who was then implanting Roman rule in Asia Minor, and in the following year the Roman legions seized Jerusalem. Petra, the Nabataean Arab Kingdom that rose in southern Jordan after 800 B.C., was also taken. The period of Roman dominion began, followed soon by the start of the Christian Era in Jerusalem, and was maintained despite revolts from A.D. 66 to 70 and from A.D. 132 to 135. After the 132–35 revolt, the Roman emperor Hadrian renamed the area Syria Palestina, renamed Jerusalem Aelia Capitolina, and dispersed the Jews. The Jews in the Palestine area, after these major repressions and dispersions, dwindled rapidly and, although a few remained, were not again to be a majority in the area for seventeen centuries.

By the Edict of Milan in A.D. 313 the Roman emperor Constantine permitted Christianity to develop as a recognized and tolerated religion. Constantine shifted his capital to Byzantium on the Bosporus Straits in 324, renaming the site Constantinople. The holiest Christian place, however, was Jerusalem. In the de facto partition of the Roman Empire in 395, the Jordanian area, along with most of the rest of the Middle East and North Africa remained under the eastern portion—the empire of Byzantium, which was ruled from Constantinople. The ruling families of Syria during this period were the Ghassanids, Christian Arabs

loyal to Byzantium. They only intermittently controlled areas of Jordan south of Amman and were often in confrontation with the Arabs to the south, thus illustrating the rough differentiation between Syrian, or northern Arabs and those having closest roots with the Arabian Peninsula to the south. This differentiation even then was not new in history and has continued to manifest itself in modern times.

By the seventh century A.D. Petra had gone deeply into decline. Byzantium and Persia fought a series of wars in the sixth and seventh centuries that devastated much of the central Middle East, and Persian forces were briefly in control of parts of Palestine and Jordan. The Persians were finally driven back in 927. The Christianized society in greater Syria and elsewhere in the empire, however, had become divided by war and by the doctrinal disputes of the early Christian church. It was at this time that a weakened Byzantium was hit by the new thrust of Islam surging out of the south, where religious ideology now formed a focus for the economic and population pressures in the Arabian Peninsula.

ISLAMIC CONQUEST AND ARAB RULE

By the time of his death in 632 the Prophet Mohammed had brought most of the tribes of the Arabian Peninsula under the banner of the new monotheistic religion of Islam (submission), uniting the individual, state, and society under the universalism of the all-powerful will of God. Adherents of Islam, called Muslims, collectively formed the Dar al-Islam (House of Islam). By the middle of the seventh century Mohammed's successors carried the conquests of Islam north and east from the Arabian Peninsula and also westward into North Africa. Although most of the population west and east of the Jordan became Islamized, the small Jewish remnant in Palestine and the larger Christian groups on both banks preserved their identity.

After Mohammed's death at Medina, he was succeeded as spiritual and temporal head of all Muslims by his father-in-law, Abu Bakr, who ruled from 632 to 634. The occupant of this highest Islamic office became known as caliph, from the Arabic word for successor or deputy. Later the designation Commander of the Faithful was also used. Under Umar, who ruled from 634 to 644, external conquests were undertaken, and the government of conquered areas was organized. In 636 an Arab general crushed the Byzantine army at the Battle of Yarmuk River. Syria, Jordan, and Palestine were thus brought securely under Arab Muslim rule. Jerusalem itself was occupied by Umar in 638.

The scripture of Islam, or Quran (Koran), was compiled during the rule of the third caliph, Uthman. Uthman was assassinated and was succeeded by the Prophet Mohammed's cousin and son-in-law, Ali—the last of the four

;o-called orthodox caliphs. After a civil war among Muslim factions, Ali moved his capital to Mesopotamia, where he was assassinated in 661. Thus began the great schism in Islam between the Shia, or supporters of Ali and his descendants as the true successors to the caliphate, and the Sunni, or those regarding themselves as orthodox followers of the Quran, who supported consensual succession. The Arab Muslims of Palestine and Jordan became and remained predominantly Sunni.

After Ali's murder his chief rival, Muawiyah, the Arab governor of Syria, proclaimed himself caliph and established his capital in Damascus. As Philip K. Hitti has written, Muawiyah initiated "a brand new style of the caliphate—monarchical, worldly, and anchored in Syria."

The Umayyad caliphs administered their territories much as the Byzantines and earlier empires had done—by the traditional mode of pyramidal, military-executive government with absolute and final authority held by the caliph, assisted by a few ministers, but with extensive power delegated to provincial governors general. The conqueror's law—in this case, the *sharia,* or Muslim law—applied only to those of the same faith as the conquerors. This system was to prevail throughout the world of Islam and survives in modified form in the legal system of present-day Jordan.

The Umayyad Dynasty was overthrown in 750 by a rival Sunni faction, the Abbassides, who moved the capital to Baghdad. The Jordan area was remote from the center of power; it declined economically, retaining its bedouin tribal way of life. The Jordanian area continued under Baghdad until the accession of the Shia Fatimid Dynasty in Egypt in 969. After 1071 the Fatimids were displaced briefly by the Seljuk Turks.

Muslim expansionism and Muslim rule of the holy places in Jerusalem and Palestine at last aroused western Europe and, late in the eleventh century, waves of Crusaders poured into the Middle East. The devastation of this invasion, mounted in the name of God as were the earlier Islamic and the ancient Israelite conquests, reached a climax in 1099 when the Crusaders took Jerusalem. Subsequently, the Latin Kingdom of Jerusalem was established and expanded east of the Jordan River, where the province of Outre Jourdain (Beyond Jordan) was formed. This may have been the first use of a form of the later term Transjordan, meaning the desert region east of the river and away from the more developed and populated coastal zone of Palestine.

In the mid-twelfth century the grand vizier of the Fatimid Dynasty in Cairo was a Sunni scholar and soldier of Kurdish extraction named Salah al-Din Yusuf ibn Ayyub, better known to Western history as Saladin. Saladin became independent ruler of Egypt in 1174 and soon directed his forces against the Crusaders in Palestine and Syria. At the decisive Battle of Hattin on the west shore of Lake Tiberias (Sea of Galilee), Saladin destroyed the Crusaders' army on July 4, 1187, and retook Jerusalem soon aferward. Further campaigns reduced the Crusader domain to a small entity in what is now northern Lebanon, where the tiny state endured tenuously until 1291.

Saladin died at Damascus in 1193. His Ayyubid successors as sultans of Egypt and the revived empire quarreled among themselves, however, and the Syrian region broke up into small conflicting princedoms. The Ayyubid line was succeeded in 1260 by the Mamluk warlord sultans of Egypt. The Mamluks, after finally repelling successive Mongol invasions from the north and east, by the late fourteenth century held sway from the Nile to the Euphrates. Their power, weakened in internal factionalism, then declined, and Mamluk rule was confronted by the new power in the Middle East—the Ottoman Turks.

OTTOMAN TURKISH CONQUEST AND RULE

By the end of 1517 Syria, Jordan, Palestine, and Egypt had fallen to the Ottoman Turkish dominion. The stagnation into which Jordan and other Arab lands fell during the four centuries of Ottoman control left them out of phase with Europe and significantly affected their later history when independence was attained and nationalist self-development was attempted.

Led by an early succession of able sultans, the Ottoman Turkish Dynasty had effectively defeated Byzantium and in 1453 ended that ancient regime by seizing Constantinople, which they renamed Istanbul and made their capital. Subsequent conquest spread the Ottoman domain rapidly over Anatolia and the Arab lands to the east, south, and west as far as Morocco and northwest into Europe as far as the walls of Vienna. The apogee of Ottoman power is usually considered to have been the reign of Sultan Suleyman I (reigned 1520–66), known to the West as Suleyman the Magnificent. Thereafter the empire began its decline.

The Ottomans ruled their domains through the traditional military-imperial system of viceroyalties, or governorates, each called a *vilayet* and headed by a pasha, or governor-general, who ruled with complete authority in the name and at the pleasure of the sultan at Istanbul. Palestine, west of the Jordan River, became part of the *vilayet* of Beirut; and Jordan, east of the river, was part of the *vilayet* of Syria, of which Damascus was the capital.

In Jordan Egyptian influence briefly displaced Turkish influence from about 1831 to 1839 during the insurgence of the pasha of Egypt, Mohammed Ali, against the sultan. Egypt withdrew, however, under pressure of Great Britain and Russia, and Turkish governors returned. In 1900 the Turks, with German assistance, began construction of the Hejaz Railway, which by 1908 linked Damascus in Syria with the holy city of Medina in the Arabian Peninsula. The original purpose was twofold: to transport Muslim pilgrims to the Medina-Mecca pilgrimage sites and to enable better strategic control of the distant Arabian Peninsula. To protect the railway, as they had earlier endeavored to protect the caravan route, the Turks subsidized rival Arab tribal shaykhs along the way.

The Ottoman regime and its governors followed traditional patterns in employing the *millet* system of ruling minority religious communities. The Turkish codification of the Islamic *sharia* was utilized in towns and cities; in the desert, the less formal tribal customary law was followed. Maintaining order, however, was not necessarily easy. Although the Turks were Muslims and the sultan in Istanbul was the caliph, the Turks were non-Arab, foreign oppressors in Jordan. The individualistic, fiercely independent bedouins revolted against them when good opportunities arose. Serious uprisings occurred in the nineteenth century, in 1905, and again in 1910 and were put down by Turkish garrisons with some difficulty.

WORLD WAR I:
ARABISM, ZIONISM, REVOLT,
AND THE MANDATE

In the last two decades of the nineteenth century two separate movements developed that were to have continuing effects of the first magnitude not only for Jordan and Palestine but for all of the Middle East and North Africa. One was the Arab revival—first clearly identifiable in Syria and Lebanon. The other was Zionism—the Jewish revival rising in Europe, led by east European Jews, and articulating a quest for Jewish communal survival and identity in political terms.

Commencing about the same time, the two movements developed separately. Both were and became increasingly ultranationalistic and had other general resemblances—chiefly, the aim in each case of uniting in independence dispersed oppressed peoples considered to have elements of commonality in culture, religion, language, and history. Both movements, however, were highly individual; their bases of objectives, attitudes, and action were different. They were to converge and confront each other finally in the geographical region of Palestine where, it was initially thought, they could develop in mutual accommodation. As history to the present has shown, they were, in fact, to prove incompatible.

In Beirut, by 1875, a small number of Lebanese and Syrian intellectuals, both Christian and Muslim in composition and acclimated to Western thought by European-style education, were urging the study of Arab history, literature, and language to revive the Arab identity. By means of pamphlets and posters secretly printed and disseminated, they attempted to expose the oppressions of Ottoman rule and to arouse Arab consciousness in the interest of autonomy or even independence. The idea of independence was expressed in context of a unity of "the Arab nation" as a whole. Because of tight Turkish security, this group atrophied after 1880.

During this time, but quite separately, a new spirit of

Jewish identity was seeking expression in Europe. By 1890 the Odessa-based Society of Lovers of Zion was encouraging the movement of small bands of immigrants to Palestine. This effort met with constant difficulty from the Turkish governors and was not particularly successful. The missing dynamism for European Jewish nationalism was supplied by Theodor Herzl, an Austrian Jew and a well-known journalist in Vienna, who was dispatched by his newspaper to Paris in 1894 to cover the treason trial of a French army officer of Jewish faith, Captain Alfred Dreyfus.

Herzl saw the problem primarily as a political-national question of international scope. Encouraged by the backing of eastern European Jewish intellectuals, Herzl convened the First Zionist Congress at Basel, Switzerland, in August 1897. This body then founded the World Zionist Organization (WZO), with the stated aim "to create for the Jewish people a home in Palestine secured by public law."

In 1907 WZO set up an office in Palestine at Jaffa (Yafo), near which the Jewish city of Tel Aviv was founded in 1909. The small Jewish settlements, which became known as *kibbutzim,* evolved a distinctive system of communal living, and Jewish schools, press, and labor movements came into existence.

Meanwhile, in Istanbul the Young Turk nationalist revolution initiated by the army-based Committee of Union and Progress had forced Sultan Abdul Hamid II, on July 24, 1908, to restore the Constitution of 1876 and later, in April 1909, had deposed him in favor of his aged brother, Mehmed V. These developments generated an initial wave of good feeling in the empire and aroused the hopes and expectations of its various nationalities.

After 1909, however, it soon became clear to Arabs and Zionists alike that the new Turkish nationalism was bent on increasingly centralized and intensified turkification of the Ottoman domains rather than the granting of local autonomies, to say nothing of independence. Arab opposition to the new Turkish despotism arose in two separate arenas. One developed among Arab intellectuals of Beirut and

Sharif Husein ibn Ali of Mecca, king of Hejaz, great-grandfather of King Hussein

King Abdullah ibn al-Hussein on 1947 and 1949 stamps.

A 1963 stamp issued to commemorate the Arab Renaissance Day, June 10, 1916. Husein ibn-Ali (left) and King Hussein.

Damascus who enunciated the ideas of a new Arab nationalism but who at first sought autonomy within rather than secession from the Ottoman Empire. The second, more traditional in form, emerged among the remote desert tribes of Jordan and Arabia, who were politically inarticulate but resentful of any kind of outside control.

The Arab committees and clubs of Lebanon and Syria that had emerged in the first flush of optimism in 1908 were forced into clandestine political conspiracy in the form of secret societies, especially the Young Arab Society (al-Jamiyyah al-Arabiyah al-Fatah). The objectives became independence for all Arab societies, not only from Turkey but any foreign control.

The link between the urban Arab societies and the tribesmen in the desert was Hussein ibn-Ali al-Hashimi, the grand sharif and amir of Mecca, the custodian of the Muslim holy places of Mecca and Medina and the Hejaz region of western Arabia. Hussein, head of the Hashemite branch of the Quraysh, the tribe of the Prophet Mohammed, was himself a descendant of the Prophet (hence, by Muslim usage, a sharif, or noble). He had four sons, the middle two of whom, Abdullah and Faisal, were to become major figures in Middle Eastern events during and after World War I.

Hussein and his sons had received Turkish as well as Arabic (but not Western) education and from time to time had spent enforced years of restraint in Istanbul. Sharif Hussein had been appointed prince of Mecca in 1908 because the Turks thought he would be a quieting influence, but once in office he did not prove to be as tractable as the Istanbul government had expected.

Both Abdullah, later king of Jordan and grandfather of King Hussein I of Jordan, and Faisal, later king of Syria (1919–20) and of Iraq (1921–33), were by 1915 associated secretly with the Arab nationalist societies of Syria and Lebanon, and it was partly through the sons' efforts that Sharif Hussein accepted from the northern societies what was called the Damascus Protocol as a basis for his later negotiations with the British. In return the northern societies accepted the Hashemites as leaders and spokesmen.

The first of the major events leading to the Arab uprising occurred with the visit of Abdullah in February 1914 to Lord Horatio Kitchener, the British agent and consul general at Cairo. Abdullah inquired about the possibility of British support if his father should raise a revolt against the Turks. Kitchener's reply was noncommittal, as Turkey was not then allied with Germany and World War I had not begun. The war broke out in August, however, and by early November Turkey was aligned with Germany and Austria-Hungary and at war with Great Britain, France, and Russia. Great Britain declared Egypt a protectorate and assigned Sir Henry McMahon as first British high commissioner; Kitchener was made British secretary of state for war and, in the changed circumstances, sought Arab support against Turkey. In Cairo McMahon conducted an extensive correspondence with Hussein between July 1915 and January 1916.

In a letter to McMahon in July 1915 Hussein specified an area for Arab independence under the "Sharifian Arab Government" consisting of the Arabian Peninsula (except Aden) and the Fertile Crescent of Palestine, Lebanon, Syria, and Iraq. In his reply of October 24, 1915, McMahon, on behalf of the British government, declared British support for postwar Arab independence, subject to certain reservations and exclusions of territory. As with the later Balfour Declaration, the exact meaning was not clear, although Arab spokesmen since then have usually maintained that Palestine was within the pledged area of independence. In any case, on June 5, 1916, Hussein launched the Arab Revolt against Turkey and in October proclaimed himself king of the Arabs. Supplies and money were provided by Great Britain for the tribal forces led by Abdullah and Faisal and various prominent shaykhs. British army technicians and advisers were also detailed from Cairo to assist the Arab irregular forces. Of these advisers, T. E. Lawrence (Lawrence of Arabia) was to become the best known.

Meanwhile, on May 16, 1916, the British and French governments concluded the secret Sykes-Picot Agreement. This undertaking, although allowing for a postwar Arab state on the Arabian Peninsula and an ill-defined plan for an international arrangement over Jerusalem and part of Palestine, divided the rest of the Ottoman domains in the Fertile Crescent between the two powers.

However, in the meantime, Allied military operations were progressing favorably. Al-Aqaba was taken by Faisal's Arabs in July 1917, and Jerusalem fell to Field Marshall Edmund Allenby on December 9, 1917. Turkish forces remaining in Syria were subsequently defeated by the British and Arabs after hard fighting, and Faisal entered Damascus in triumph on October 1, 1918. The armistice with Turkey was concluded on October 31, 1918.

Faisal, as chief Arab delegate to the Paris Peace Conference convened in 1919, was a dramatic and eloquent advocate but could not prevail against the European power interests. He met with Chaim Weizmann, representing WZO, on January 3, 1919, and signed an agreement pledging the two parties to mutual cooperation. Faisal, however, wrote on the document that his signature was dependent upon fulfillment of Allied wartime pledges regarding Arab independence. Because these pledges were never fulfilled to Arab satisfaction, Arab leaders and spokesmen have consistently held the Faisal-Weizmann agreement to be invalid.

From the Paris Peace Conference and the subconference of San Remo emerged the League of Nations Covenant and the mandate allocations making Great Britain the mandatory power for Palestine and Iraq and granting France the mandate for Syria and Lebanon. The mandate's terms called upon the mandatory power to "secure establishment of the Jewish national home." Hussein, Abdullah, Faisal, and other Arab spokesmen opposed the mandate's terms because the League of Nations Covenant had endorsed the Wilsonian principle of self-determination of peoples and thereby, they maintained, logically and necessarily supported the cause of the majority—namely, the Arabs—in Palestine.

To British authority, pressed with heavy responsibilities and commitments after World War I, the objective of mandate administration was a peaceful accommodation in and development of Palestine by Arabs and Jews under British control. To Hussein, cooperation with the Zionists had meant no more than providing within his intended Arab kingdom a refuge for Jews. To the leaders of WZO, the recognition in the mandate was simply a welcome first step on the way to attainment of a separate Jewish national state.

Meanwhile, in Damascus Faisal had convened the General Syrian Congress in July 1919 and proclaimed Syria sovereign and independent. In March 1920 this congress reaffirmed the independence of both Syria and Iraq, and it declared Faisal king of Syria and Abdullah king of Iraq. In April, however, the San Remo conference carved out the mandates, and soon French troops began moving from Beirut into Syria. The French took Damascus on July 25, 1920. Faisal, thus deposed, fled to Europe and remained there until installed by the British as king of Iraq in 1921.

At the time of Faisal's ouster, his brother Abdullah was in what is now Jordan endeavoring to organize a countereffort against the French. It then became clear to Abdullah and the British that Abdullah was acceptable as ruler to the bedouin tribes east of the Jordan, including the locally powerful Bani Sakhr. Palestine had not been specifically defined. After the British and French had agreed, under the Sykes-Picot guidelines, as to what constituted Lebanon, Syria, and Iraq, what was left over, by elimination, was the mandate of Palestine. This included, in effect, the territory of pre–June 1967 Jordan and Israel.

In March 1921 Winston Churchill, then colonial secretary, convened a high-level British policy council in Cairo. As a result of its deliberations, Great Britain divided the

Palestine mandate along the Jordan River–al-Aqaba line. The eastern portion, or Transjordan, was to have an Arab administration, under British guidance, with Abdullah as amir. He was recognized as de facto ruler in April 1921. A British memorandum in September 1922 excluded Transjordan from the zone of the Jewish national home. This division was aimed, as was British support of Faisal in Iraq, at satisfying wartime pledges to the Arabs. It was in this manner that what in 1973 was known as the East Bank of Jordan first came into being.

TRANSJORDAN AND MANDATED PALESTINE: 1921–39

The new entity of Transjordan at its inception in 1921 contained not more than four hundred thousand inhabitants.

Abdullah ruled directly with a small executive council, much in the traditional manner. British colonial administration concerned itself mainly with defense, financial, and foreign policy and left internal political affairs to Abdullah. Defense was assigned to the British Royal Air Force. After a visit to London by Abdullah, Great Britain on May 15, 1923, recognized Transjordan as a national entity en route to independence with Great Britain in a special advisory and tutelary role.

From 1925 to 1939 Transjordan as a desert realm under the British aegis progressed slowly toward independence and modernization. Roads, communications, education, and other public services had slow but steady development, although not in as great degree as occurred in the more wealthy, populated, and accessible area of Palestine, where British administration was direct.

A further step in the direction of full self-government was taken in February 1928 when Great Britain and Transjordan executed a new treaty that relaxed British controls. A constitution was promulgated in April 1928, and in April 1929 the Legislative Council, replacing the old Executive Council, was installed. In January 1934 a new agreement with Great Britain allowed Abdullah to set up consular representation in Arab countries, and in May 1939 the Legislative Council was converted to a regular cabinet, or Council of Ministers.

In contrast with the comparative tranquillity and localism of Transjordan, the years after World War I were full of disturbance west of the Jordan River in British mandated Palestine. Royal commissions of 1929 and 1930, dispatched after outbreaks of violence in Palestine, recognized, as did later bodies, that the basic problem lay in the opposed positions of Zionism and Arab nationalism.

The rapid growth of anti-Semitism in Nazi Germany after 1933 augmented Jewish movement, legal or underground, to Palestine. Palestinian Arabs were disturbed at the increase in Jewish immigration and land acquisition. However the British government maintained the concept of peaceful accommodation between Jews and Arabs and called for a conference in March 1938 in London between the Jewish Agency and Arab representatives from Palestine and adjoining Arab states.

The conference failed to reach agreement, and the result was complicated by the fact that the Arab representatives refused, as they have since consistently done in comparable circumstances, to negotiate directly and openly with the Jewish Agency or, after 1948, with Israeli government representatives. On May 27, 1939, a British White Paper was issued that extended British rule for ten years, limited Jewish immigration and land purchases in Palestine, and projected a Palestinian government at the end of the ten-year period subject to Jewish-Arab accommodation. This White Paper met a mixed Arab reception, being rejected by the Palestinian Arab Higher Committee. The Jewish Agency rejected it as a total repudiation of the Balfour Declaration and mandate obligations.

*King Abdullah,
king of Jordan (1946–51)*

THE ESTABLISHMENT OF ISRAEL

During 1943 and 1944 Abdullah and his representatives had taken part in the inter-Arab preliminary discussions that resulted in the formation of the League of Arab States, or Arab League. Association with this cause identified Egypt with Arabism, an inclusion not previously clearly established. The Arab League was an outgrowth of older Arab nationalist visions of some kind of Fertile Crescent unity in the broad area covering Palestine, Lebanon, Syria, Transjordan, and Iraq. Abdullah's concept of a Greater Syria under a Hashemite monarchy was familiar by this time and was opposed by new nationalists in Syria, by the Saudi Arabians, by the Zionists, and by France. In the end the Arab League became simply an association of sovereign states without real central unity or power. The league charter was signed at Cairo on March 22, 1945, by Syria, Egypt, Iraq, Lebanon, Saudi Arabia, and Transjordan, and the imam of Yemen signed on May 10.

On March 22, 1946, Transjordan and Great Britain entered into the Treaty of London, under which another major step was taken toward full sovereignty of the Arab state. Transjordan was proclaimed a kingdom on May 25 with Abdullah as king, and a new constitution replaced the obsolete document of 1928. Abdullah signed treaties of friendship and cooperation with Turkey and Iraq in 1947. His application for membership in the United Nations, however, was disapproved by a veto of the Soviet Union on grounds that the country was not fully independent. Also, Transjordan was not diplomatically recognized by the United States until January 31, 1949. A further treaty with Great Britain was executed in March 1948, under which all restrictions on sovereignty were removed except minimal considerations relating to defense and to British base and transit rights in Transjordan.

In Great Britain the Labour party came to power in July 1945, and Ernest Bevin, as new secretary of state for foreign affairs and in implementation of the 1939 White Paper, limited Jewish immigration to Palestine. These actions in the postwar atmosphere inflamed Zionists and the Jewish Agency, and Palestine in effect became an armed camp. The Jewish Resistance Movement was formed in an attempt to unite or at least to coordinate the disparate Hagana, Irgun, and Stern paramilitary Jewish groups. Reprisals and counterreprisals between Jews and the authorities and between Arabs and the mandate authorities continued. The Palestinian Arab Higher Committee reappeared to oppose renewals of immigration.

The British in early 1947 decided to place the problem of Palestine before the United Nations (UN) and on May 15, 1947, a special session of the UN General Assembly established the United Nations Special Committee on Palestine (UNSCOPS). On August 31 UNSCOPS issued a report supporting a geographically complex system of partition into separate Arab and Jewish states, a special international status for Jerusalem, and an economic union linking the three members. Supported by both the United States and the Soviet Union, this plan was adopted by the UN General Assembly on November 29, 1947.

On the next day the Arab Higher Committee totally rejected the plan and called for a general strike in Palestine; violence between Arabs and Jews mounted. The Zionist General Council stated willingness in principle to accept partition. The Arab League Council, meeting in December 1947, stated it would take whatever measures were required to prevent implementation of the UN resolution. Amid increasing conflict, representatives of the United Nations Implementation Commission were unable to function. In January 1948 Great Britain announced its intention to relinquish the mandate and to withdraw from Palestine on May 15, 1948, and it did so at that time.

Almost simultaneously forces of Egypt, Transjordan, Iraq, Syria, and Lebanon, with Saudi Arabian and Yemeni increments, advanced into Palestine. Arab units, except for the British-raised Arab Legion of Transjordan, were largely ill trained and had had little experience. Israeli forces, usually operating from interior lines of communication, included an estimated twenty thousand to twenty-five thousand European World War II veterans. The Arabs gained some initial success, but their advances were stemmed. By January 1949 the part of Palestine remaining in Arab hands was limited to that held by the Transjordan Arab Legion at the cessation of hostilities. Other Arab forces had been defeated or neutralized. This area was subsequently annexed by Jordan and commonly referred to as the West Bank. Abdullah had been particularly insistent that the Arab Legion must hold the part of the old city of Jerusalem containing the main Muslim holy places, and this had been accomplished.

On May 29, 1948, the UN Security Council established the Truce Commission, headed by a Swedish diplomat, Folke Bernadotte, who was assassinated in Jerusalem by the Irgun on September 17, 1948. He was succeeded by an American, Ralph Bunche. This commission, which later evolved into the United Nations Truce Supervision Organization—Palestine (UNTSOP), attempted to devise new plans of settlement and arranged the truces of June 11 to July 8 and July 19 to October 14, 1948. Armistice talks were initiated with Egypt in January 1949, and an armistice agreement between Israel and Egypt was established on February 24; similar agreements were concluded with Lebanon on March 23, with Transjordan on April 3, and with Syria on July 20. Iraq did not enter into an armistice agreement but withdrew its forces.

STABILITY AND ISOLATION IN KING ABDULLAH'S LAST YEARS

Transjordan, one of the smallest of the Arab states and least blessed with natural resources, had done much of the fighting and had ended the war of 1948 in control of the only substantial part of Palestine remaining in Arab hands. This irregularly shaped area, which became commonly referred to as the West Bank, covered about 2,165 square miles.

In December 1948 Abdullah declared himself king of Palestine, and in April 1949 he changed his country's name to Jordan. In April 1950 elections were held in both banks that were considered favorable by Abdullah, and on April 25, 1950, he formally annexed the West Bank to Jordan. This important step was immediately recognized and endorsed by Great Britain and was regarded by Abdullah as an act of responsibility on the part of Jordan. Within the Arab League, however, it was not generally approved, and monarchies and radical spokesmen alike condemned the move as a furtherance of Hashemite dynastic ambitions.

In 1951, faced with greater and more immediate problems and vulnerability than any other state in confronting Israel, Abdullah continued to search for a long-term, peaceful solution. Jordan alone of the Arab host countries extended full citizenship rights to the refugees. For security reasons, Abdullah did not favor the immediate internationalization of Jerusalem. In all these positions, he was opposed in the Arab League, finding support only from Hashemite kinsmen in Iraq. Radical Socialist-nationalist propaganda, especially in Egypt and Syria, denounced him as a reactionary, medieval monarch and a tool of British colonial imperialism.

The Arab League debates after the Jordanian annexation of the West Bank were inconclusive, and Abdullah continued to set his own course. The East Bank during the period from early 1949 to early 1950 was relatively free from internal disturbance. The residual special relationship with Great Britain continued. Although not yet a member of the UN, Jordan supported the UN action in Korea and entered into an economic developmental aid agreement (under President Harry S. Truman's Point Four program) with the United States in March 1951.

THE ASSASSINATION OF ABDULLAH, REIGN OF TALAL, AND ACCESSION OF HUSSEIN

On July 20, 1951, King Abdullah was assassinated as he entered the al-Aqsa Mosque in Jerusalem for Friday prayers. His grandson, the sixteen-year-old prince Hussein, was at his side. Before he was killed by the king's guard, the assassin also fired at Hussein. The assassin was a Palestinian reportedly hired by relatives of Haj Amin al-Husseini, a former mufti of Jerusalem, who was a bitter enemy of Abdullah.

Although many radical Palestinians blamed Abdullah for the reverses of 1948, there was no organized political follow-up after the murder of the king. Public disturbances were minor, order was quickly established by the Arab Legion, and a confused calm prevailed. The main political question was the succession to the throne.

Abdullah's son, Prince Naif, acted temporarily as regent, and some support existed for him to become king. The older son, Prince Talal, was in Switzerland receiving treatment for mental illness but reportedly had made much progress. It was widely believed that Abdullah would have favored Talal in order that the succession might then pass more easily to the young Hussein, Talal's son.

Accordingly, the government invited Talal to return and assume the throne, and he did so on September 6, 1951. During Talal's short reign he supported and promulgated a new constitution in January 1952, which still remains as the basic instrument. Talal showed an inclination to improve relations with other Arab states, and Jordan in early 1952 joined the Arab League's Collective Security Pact, which Abdullah had rejected. Talal was popular among the people of the East Bank, who were not aware of his periodic seizures of mental illness. These increased in frequency and became clearly identified as schizophrenia.

On August 11, 1952, the prime minister presented to a secret session of the Jordanian legislature a report by three Jordanian Arab doctors and a recommendation that Talal be

The young prince Hussein with his grandfather, King Abdullah. King Hussein was but sixteen years of age when his grandfather was assassinated in Jerusalem in 1951. Young Hussein was beside him when the bullets struck. One bullet even glanced off a medal on his chest. This traumatic beginning in the world of politics, which would have terrified or at least discouraged an ordinary man, only seems to have strengthened Hussein and to have readied him to meet the harsh realities of the power struggles in the Middle East.

King Talal, father of King Hussein

Prince Hussein, age seventeen, proclaimed king of the Hashemite Kingdom of Jordan, August 11, 1952

asked to abdicate in favor of Hussein. The legislature so decreed, and the abdication order was taken to Talal. He received it without surprise and acceded to it with dignity. He retired briefly to Cairo and then to a villa near Istanbul, where he lived quietly under medical attention until his death on July 8, 1972.

Hussein, who had been attending a private school in England, returned immediately to Jordan. Because he was under eighteen years of age, he could not, under the constitution, be crowned, and a regency council was therefore formed. Hussein decided to continue his education during the interim before he could come to the throne by attending the British Royal Military Academy at Sandhurst. After about six months, having attained eighteen years by the Muslim calendar, he returned to Jordan and, accompanied by much public ceremony, formally took the constitutional oath as king on May 2, 1952.

EARLY REIGN AND SURVIVAL OF KING HUSSEIN I

When King Hussein I came to the throne, the chief influences that had thus far guided him were the example and teachings of his grandfather, the shocking experience of his grandfather's assassination, and his own education in conservative English schools. Hussein's own views, policies, and mode of operation were not yet firmly established. As king he had extensive legal powers. Although Jordan had

The king, next to his cousin and close friend, King Faisal of Iraq (who was executed in a coup in Iraq in 1958); Prince Mohammed, and front, Princess Basma and Prince Hassan

President Nasser of Egypt comes to visit the king during the Jordanian crisis with the Palestinians.

King Hussein on one of his many visits to army bases in the kingdom

The king with a trusted friend, Jordanian general Ali Abu Nuwar, who plotted the overthrow and death of King Hussein

The Family Album. The infant crown prince Hussein with his parents King Talal and Queen Zein

become a constitutional monarchy, the constitution itself allowed the king to dismiss the National Assembly and to appoint the prime minister and other ministers at will. In addition, he enjoyed the traditional support of the East Bank Jordanian bedouin tribes. The Arab Legion, paid for by a British subsidy, was composed mostly of intensely loyal bedouin and British military officers.

Severe problems confronted the new king. Two-thirds of the citizens were Palestinians, whereas the government elite were most East Bank Jordanians, more conservative and traditional than the Palestinians whose spokesmen often reflected the new trend in radical Arab nationalism. In Cairo in July 1952 the successful coup d'etat of the Egyptian Free Officers movement headed by Gamal Abdul Nasser had overthrown the monarchy and established a republic. This example and the image of Nasser as the new champion of Arabism were, even by mid-1953, highly regarded by many Palestinians. Generally, and especially among the refugees, Great Britain, the United States, and the Hashemites were blamed by the Palestinians for their misfortunes.

Problems were magnified by the intensification during

1953 of border incidents with Israel that escalated in a succession of reprisals and counterreprisals between Palestinian infiltrators and Israeli forces. The Arab Legion endeavored to secure the armistice line and prevent infiltration, but its numbers were inadequate to provide complete and continuous coverage by day and night. Israeli forces during this time adopted the technique of massive retaliation that thereafter characterized their reaction pattern.

In May 1953 Hussein designated as prime minister Fawzi al-Mulqi, the former Jordanian ambassador to Great Britain and a liberal in comparison with Tewfik Abul Huda, whom he succeeded. By May 1954, however, internal tensions caused the Mulqi government to resign. Abul Huda returned to office, and his government was confirmed by the elections of October 16, 1954. Abul Huda's government was replaced in May 1955 by a new cabinet headed by Said al-Mufti. Relations with Saudi Arabia were somewhat improved by an exchange of state visits by King Hussein and King Saud; also in 1955 Jordan was admitted to the UN.

The pattern of Western cold war alliances was extended on February 24, 1955, when Turkey and Iraq, later joined by Great Britain, Iran, and Pakistan, signed the United States–supported Baghdad Pact, which ultimately became the Central Treaty Organization (CENTO). Early in December 1955 the chief of the British general staff visited Amman to discuss conditions and terms under which Jordan might join the Baghdad Pact. The purpose of his visit was generally known, and radical Arab nationalist propaganda, especially from Palestinians and Radio Cairo, raised a storm of protest denouncing the pact and the monarchy as "tools of Western imperialism" and a "sellout to the Jews" and making other inflammatory charges.

The Mufti government resigned in disarray on December 13, and Hussein called upon a young former cabinet minister, Hazza al-Majali, to form a new government. Al-Majali was from a distinguished family of tribal shaykhs long predominant in the Karak region of south-central Jordan. He was known to be pro-Western, and after forming his cabinet, he stated without equivocation that he intended to take Jordan into the Baghdad Pact. Three days of mass demonstrations and rioting, raised by the political opposition, then followed in Amman.

The Arab Legion contained the mobs with minimal firing and casualties. Under this pressure, several of al-Majali's

The queen mother Zein in a recent photograph

ministers resigned, and he then recommended a caretaker government. The mob dispersed, and Ibrahim Hashim became a prime minister on December 20, 1955, followed by a regularized government under Samir Rifai on January 9, 1956. Order was restored. Jordan did not sign the Baghdad Pact but found itself again isolated in the Arab world.

On March 1, 1956, Hussein dismissed Lieutenant General Sir John Bagot Glubb as commander of the Arab Legion, thus precipitating a diplomatic crisis that threatened to isolate Hussein from his principal ally, Great Britain. Some observers held that Hussein was advised to take this step as an act of defiance against Great Britain and of identification with the new Arab nationalism personified by Egypt's Nasser. Hussein stated that the decision was his alone, that he had found himself for some time in disagreement with Glubb over military organization and planning, and that the British government ought not to identify this personal action as an official cause.

In May 1956 Hussein designated a young officer named Ali Abu Nuwar as major general and commander of the Arab Legion. The name of the force was, then, officially changed to the Jordan Arab Army. Abu Nuwar was an advocate of Arab nationalism and elimination of foreign controls in the army and government. As chief of general staff, Abu Nuwar began his attempts to deanglicize the army and to break the tight pattern of its control by officers and men of Transjordanian bedouin origin.

Border incidents with Israel were a continuing source of anxiety in 1956, and events reached a climax on October 10. At that time, in reprisal for a guerrilla attack on two farmers, an Israeli task group, supported by air and artillery, attacked the West Bank village of Qalqilyah, killing forty-eight. The Palestinians clamored for war, and in this atmosphere of crisis Jordanian politics took its brief venture into anti-Western radical nationalism.

In the parliamentary elections of October 21, 1956, the National Socialist party received the most votes, and its leader, Suleiman Nabulsi, was designated by Hussein as prime minister. When Israel attacked Egypt in the Sinai Peninsula starting October 29, 1956, and the British and French invaded Port Said on November 5, Nabulsi suddenly became indecisive. Hussein, however, proposed that Jordan attack Israel at once but was urged personally by Nasser not to do so because Jordan's forces would be wasted in an action that by then was already lost. Jordan, as a result, did not become engaged in the brief Second Arab-Israeli War (1956). By early 1957, largely because of diplomatic pressures from both the United States and the Soviet Union, the Israeli, British, and French forces had been withdrawn from the Sinai. British participation in this attack made it politically imperative that Jordan end its special relationship under the 1948 treaty.

Hussein attended a conference with King Saud, President Nasser, and Syrian leaders at Cairo, January 18 and 19, 1957. Under the Arab Solidarity Agreement emanating from this conference, Saudi Arabia, Egypt, and Syria un-

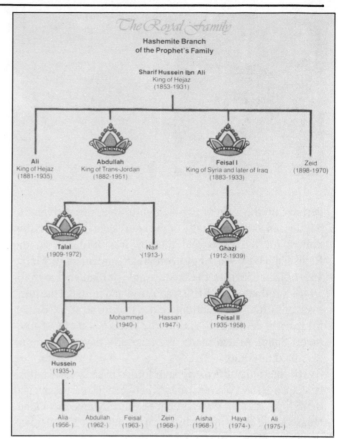

The royal Hashemite branch of the Prophet Mohammed family

King Hussein's son, Prince Abdullah, posing with his sister, Princess Aliya, left, and aunt, Princess Basma, right.

The king, the proud father with his sons, Prince Abdullah, left, and Prince Faisal, in London, 1970

King Hussein's twin daughters, Zein and Aisha, 1970

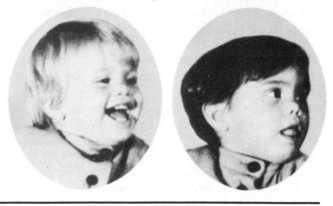

To Princess Haya the king is simply her "daddy."

dertook, in the ratio of two-to-two-to-one, respectively, to pay Jordan a total annually of the equivalent of 35.8 million dollars for ten years and thereby free Jordan from the British subsidy. An Anglo-Jordanian agreement of March 13, 1957, abrogated the basic Anglo-Jordanian Treaty of 1948, terminated the British subsidy, and initiated the turnover of British installations and withdrawal of all British troops still in Jordan. As for the Arab Solidarity Agreement, Saudi Arabia made one quarterly payment; no one else paid anything.

The internal political scene in Jordan in early 1957 quickly shaped up as a power struggle between the monarchy and the Egypt-oriented government of Prime Minister Nabulsi. Hussein and the conservatives suspected that Nabulsi was maneuvering to disestablish the monarchy. Also, Nabulsi began negotiations aimed at opening diplomatic relations with the Soviet Union and securing Soviet arms aid. After the Egyptian-Soviet arms deal of 1955, the Soviet Union had increasingly supported the Arab cause against Israel and had begun by this means the establishment of a position of influence in the Middle East.

Hussein saw hopes of support in the Eisenhower Doctrine enunciated in January 1957 by the United States president as an offer of military and economic aid to those governments requesting help to save themselves from communism. Nabulsi rejected this doctrine. Political tension and Hussein's suspicions increased, and on April 10, 1957, exercising his constitutional prerogative, Hussein demanded the resignation of the Nabulsi government. On April 13 General Abu Nuwar made a statement to Said al-Mufti, who was attempting to form a caretaker government, that was capable of being interpreted as an ultimatum that any new cabinet be approved by Abu Nuwar and the army officers of his staff aligned with him.

There followed a sequence of dramatic events that day and night that became known as the Zarqa affair. The public, sensing the explosive political atmosphere, had become restive in Amman. This was even more true of a large concentration of troops at the main army base at al-Zarqa, where rumors spread that the king was dead; taking Abu Nuwar with him, Hussein set off for al-Zarqa. En route he met several truckloads of troops who were overjoyed at seeing Hussein alive and who demanded the head of Abu Nuwar. At Abu Nuwar's request, the king sent

him back to the safety of the royal palace and continued to al-Zarqa. There he spent several hours amid wildly enthusiastic demonstrations of loyalty to the throne and returned to Amman after reassuring and quieting the troops.

On the next day Hussein allowed Abu Nuwar to leave the country. He fled first to Syria, then to Egypt. Hussein appointed General Ali Hiyari, Abu Nuwar's cousin, as chief of general staff. On April 19 Hiyari followed his cousin in fleeing to Syria, and Hussein designated as his top commander a tough bedouin officer, Habis al-Majali. During the balance of the month several cabinet crises occurred, as the remnants of the Nabulsi faction fought a rearguard action and external propaganda against Hussein continued. Ibrahim Hashim, however, successfully formed a government, and all political party activity was outlawed.

Hussein had won; what had counted was the loyalty of the combat units of the army, and that loyalty clearly belonged to him. Hussein unequivocally placed his country on the side of the West in the great power global confrontation and sought a new principal source of aid—the United States.

CRISIS AND REALIGNMENT WITH WESTERN AID

The United States replaced Great Britain as the major source of foreign aid, but under the Eisenhower Doctrine, rather than by bilateral treaty or alliance mechanisms. Existing economic aid programs were expanded, and military aid was initiated. An airlift arriving at Amman on September 9, 1957, brought a substantial amount of military equipment and was followed soon by shipments to al-Aqaba.

In seeking a viable, long-term arrangement for political stability in face of the hostile Nasser-style revolutionary nationalism then prevalent in the Middle East, Jordan turned to neighboring Iraq. Iraq, far larger than Jordan and more populous, was also far wealthier in oil and other resources. It had usually supported Jordan in Arab councils, although without deep involvement since the 1948 war. Its conservative government had taken Iraq into the Baghdad Pact in 1954 to ensure continued Western support against the Soviet Union or, more particularly, against radical Arab movements.

On February 1, 1958, the announcement by Egypt and Syria of the integration of their two countries to form the United Arab Republic (UAR) was greeted with high enthusiasm by the new nationalist advocates of unity in the Arab world, but it made the situation of conservative or moderate regimes more perilous. The initial phase of Jordanian-Iraqi negotiation was quickly concluded, and on February 14, 1958, a proclamation was issued in Amman by Hussein and King Faisal II, Hussein's cousin, joining the Hashemite kingdoms of Iraq and Jordan in a federation to be called the Arab Union. Faisal was to be head of state; and Hussein, deputy head of state. Baghdad and Amman were to alter-

Crown Prince Hassan   *The king's brother, Mohammed*

nate every six months as the capital. In May, Samir Rifai became prime minister of Jordan; his predecessor, Hashim, became prime minister in the new union.

Meanwhile, a severe political crisis had developed in Lebanon in connection with the presidential election. The incumbent government faction, conventional and Western-oriented, was opposed by another faction of subversive and strongly pro-Nasser orientation supported from Syria. Civil disorders and violence mounted in May 1958. The Syrian Region of the UAR closed the Syria-Jordan border. In Lebanon full-scale civil war was averted, but the situation became so incendiary that the government requested United States assistance, and United States forces began landing at Beirut on July 15, 1958. An Iraqi motorized brigade, under the command of Brigadier Abdul Karim Qassim, seized control of Baghdad on July 14, 1958. King Faisal and the rest of the Iraqi royal family were seized and immediately shot to death. The Jordanian leaders Hashim and Suleiman Tuqan, who were in Baghdad at the time of the coup, were seized by the mob and killed.

Hussein, enraged with shock and grief, at first wished to throw the Jordan Arab Army into Iraq to avenge Faisal and restore the Arab Union but, advised by his chief civilian ministers, decided against this course. In Iraq the army and police supported the coup, and Qassim became president-dictator, taking Iraq out of the Arab Union and the Baghdad Pact.

Jordan was cut off as it had never been before: The Syrian and Iraqi borders were closed, and to the west lay Israel, whose intentions in this crisis were unknown but whose military capabilities were well known. Hussein appealed to both the United States and Great Britain. An emergency airlift of petroleum by the United States Air Force was instituted, and on July 17, 1958, British troops began to be airlanded at Amman. Ironically, these flights came in over Israel, since overflight clearances for alternate routes over Arab countries could not be secured in time.

The political atmosphere in Jordan after the coup in Iraq appeared for some weeks highly combustible, but the government, operating within a pattern of partial martial law, endured; the airlift continued, the British brigade was reinforced, the loyalty of the army remained unimpeached, and

the Israeli frontier, after one incident in early June, continued to be quiet. During October a United States military aid was planned. By early November the British brigade was withdrawn; a British military advisory mission, however, remained with the Jordan army and air force.

On November 10, 1958, Hussein considered it safe to leave Jordan for Europe for a brief rest and took off in a small commercial aircraft marked with the Jordanian royal insignia. Over Syria he was first ordered by Damascus radio to land and then attacked by two Syrian MIG-17s that

King Hussein's first marriage was in 1954 to a Jordanian woman of Hashemite blood named Dina, who bore him one child, a daughter, Aliya.

His second marriage was in 1961 to Toni Gardiner, who then became Queen Muna.

The king with the late queen Alya and their children in an official portrait. This photograph was taken shortly before the queen died in a helicopter accident on February 9, 1977.

The crown prince in the role of the proper schoolboy at Harrow in England.

Young Hussein received his military schooling at Sandhurst in England.

King Faisal of Iraq and King Saud of Saudi Arabia visit King Hussein to give him counsel in a crisis.

Dag Hammarskjöld, secretary-general of the United Nations, also visits with the king in Jordan during the period of conflict with the Palestinian problem.

attempted, although without firing, to force him down. Taking evasive action at low altitudes, Hussein and the copilot returned the aircraft successfully to Jordanian airspace and to Amman. Wild enthusiasm and rejoicing, especially among the Jordanian military forces, immediately broke out because of the king's escape. On the following day morale was further boosted by the arrival of the first two of six transonic British fighter aircraft provided by United States offshore procurement for the Jordan air force. These two incidents, the king's escape and the delivery of the Hawker Hunters, taken against the background of United States and British aid, did much to relieve the high tension of the previous six months.

On May 6, 1959, Rifai turned over the prime ministership to Hazza al-Majali, an act leaving no doubt as to where Jordan's orientation lay. United States aid of all kinds amounted to more than 50 million dollars annually. The rebuilt port of al-Aqaba, with twelve new oil storage tanks, new berthing facilities, and a new phosphate loading plant, was opened. Diplomatic relations were resumed in August 1959 with the UAR, and border incidents with Israel were less frequent than the low-level subversive infiltration attempts intercepted from Syria. Hussein visited King Saud in February 1960, and relations with Saudi Arabia began to improve.

The two-year period of relative tranquillity was broken on August 29, 1960, when Prime Minister al-Majali was assassinated by a time-bomb charge concealed in his desk. Twelve people were killed, and some fifty were injured by this bomb and another that exploded about twenty minutes later. Again, as at the time of Abdullah's assassination, no organized political follow-up appeared. Curfew was declared, and bedouin troops moved into Amman. Some analysts speculated that the conspirators expected the assassination to generate a public uprising. Precisely the opposite occurred, however, as Hussein quickly formed a new government with his chief aide, Bahjat al-Talhouni, as prime minister. The assassination plot was traced to Syria and further identified with Cairo. Four suspects were caught, convicted, and hanged. The army was, for a time, concentrated near the Syrian border. The threat of Israel remained, however, so Hussein, at a late moment, decided not to invade Syria.

The al-Majali tragedy proved to be an external rather than an internal crisis. Domestic calm prevailed, extending to the general acceptance of Hussein's marriage to Antoinette Gardiner on May 25, 1961. (Hussein had been first married on April 19, 1955, to Sharifa Dina Abdul Hamid al-Aun of Cairo. This marriage, after the birth in 1956 of a daughter, was dissolved in 1957.) Antoinette Gardiner, upon conversion to Islam and marriage to the king, became Princess Muna. Four children were born to this union: Prince Abdullah (1962); Prince Faisal (1963); and the twin princesses, Zein and Aisha (1968). Abdullah was technically crown prince until April 1965, when the king, by constitutional processes, shifted the designation to his own

King Hussein, on an official visit to the United Nations Headquarters in New York City in 1964, is seen here with U.N. Secretary-General U Thant.

In the middle of a national emergency the king is out of the country; returning to lead his troops, he is met with great rejoicing.

The king in New York City, in a press conference before testifying before the UN in 1967. The young king emerged as a leader of some reknown after settling his country's problems between anti-Hussein Palestinians and pro-Hussein Jordanians.

A favorite pose of the king's—on military maneuvers

younger brother, Prince Hasan. The king's marriage to Princess Muna was dissolved on December 21, 1972. On December 26, 1972, Hussein married Alya Tuqan, of a prominent Palestinian family, and she became Queen Alya. The queen died in a helicopter accident on February 9, 1977. The king's next marriage was to Lisa Halaby, an American, on June 15, 1978. She became Queen Noor.

DEVELOPMENT AND DISASTER: 1962–67

In January 1962 Wasfi al-Tal became prime minister, and in December 1962 the resumption of limited political party activity in Jordan was permitted. Samir Rifai, succeeding Tal in March 1963, was able to remain in office only about one month. A caretaker government under the king's great uncle, Sharif Hussein ibn Nasir, was confirmed in office after new elections in July 1963, and the year closed in a conciliatory atmosphere at home and abroad. Diplomatic relations had been opened for the first time with the Soviet Union in August 1963, but Soviet offers of military equipment were not accepted.

By early 1964 Arab governments and Palestinian spokesmen had become seriously alarmed at the intention stated by Israel in 1963 to draw water from Lake Tiberias in order to irrigate the Negev Desert in southern Israel. President Nasser thereupon invited the Arab heads of state to attend a summit conference in Cairo in January 1964. From his new

A souvenir sheet stamp issued to commemorate the first anniversary of the visit of Pope Paul VI to the Holy Land, on May 1, 1964. Pope Paul VI (left), the Dome of the Rock, and King Hussein.

A 1966 stamp issued to honor King Hussein

position of strength, both internally and externally in the Arab world, Hussein promptly accepted the invitation and took the occasion to resume diplomatic relations with the UAR. (Technically, despite the Syrian secession of September 28, 1961, Egypt retained the name United Arab Republic until September 2, 1971, when it again became the Arab Republic of Egypt.)

At the conference the principal issue was the Jordan waters question. Israel, with its pipeline nearing completion, had announced the intention to take from Lake Tiberias quantities of water approximating the allocations of the 1954–55 Johnston plan. The conference, despite Syria's militant rhetoric, excluded war with Israel, at least for the time being, because of the absence of unified Arab political and military systems.

Instead, three alternative courses of action were approved: the diversion of the tributary sources of the Jordan River north of Lake Tiberias in Lebanon and Syria; the establishment of the United Arab Command under an Egyptian commander; and the formation of the new Palestine Liberation Organization (PLO), to be headed by a former Jerusalem lawyer, Ahmad Shukairy, as the recognized focus for Palestinian expression and resistance against Israel. The Cairo Conference of January 1964 ended in a euphoric atmosphere of goodwill and brotherhood.

Talhouni succeeded Nasir as Jordanian prime minister in July 1964, pledging his government to implement the spirit of the Cairo Conference "according to the king's instructions." The revived Jordan-UAR friendship was cultivated; Jordan entered the Arab Common Market in August 1964, and in September Hussein attended the second Arab summit at Alexandria. In May 1965 Jordan, along with nine other Arab states, broke off relations with the Federal Republic of Germany (West Germany) because of its recognition of Israel. Jordan and Saudi Arabia on August 9, 1965, signed an important agreement defining for the first time the boundary between the two countries. By this agreement Jordan gave up some territory in the southeast but was able to gain an extension of about twelve miles down the gulf from the crowded port of al-Aqaba.

Shukairy, famous for the often hysterical violence of his political rhetoric, was to play a role in Palestinian history somewhat analogous to that of the old mufti, Haj Amin al-Husseini, one of the principal architects of the Arab disasters of 1948 and 1949. Shukairy organized the PLO at a conference in Jerusalem on May 28, 1964. The PLO objective, according to the Palestine National Charter produced at the conference, was the liberation of Palestine in cooperation with all Arab states but without interfering in their internal affairs or claiming sovereignty on the West Bank. Almost from the start, trouble developed with Hussein's government and was apparent in February 1965 when the king called on Tal to become prime minister again. The rift between the PLO and the government was far advanced by the time of the third Arab summit in September 1965.

Essentially, conflict arose because the PLO, despite its stated intentions to the contrary, attempted to assume governmental functions, such as taxing Palestinians and distributing arms to the villagers, acts that infringed on Jordanian sovereignty. In December 1964, with Syrian assistance, the guerrilla organization called al-Fatah was formed in Damascus under the leadership of a Palestinian refugee, Yasir Arafat. Al-Fatah and PLO raids and sabotage were carried out against Israel without clearance from either the United Arab Command or the Jordanian military. Jordanian policy since 1949 had been and continued to be one of avoiding border incidents and terrorism that would generate

On a 1977 trip to Disney World in Florida, the king rides a merry-go-round with one of his daughters. King Hussein also enjoys racing GoKarts with his family.

Here he is giving the queen a start in a GoKart race.

Each year, King Hussein personally bestows the degrees to the University of Jordan graduates.

reprisal and possibly an untimely war. State policy and the guerrilla policy were thus at odds as to the mode and timing of operations.

Al-Fatah attacks, although planned in Syria, were most often launched in Israel by infiltration through Lebanon or Jordan. Israeli reprisals against selected Jordanian West Bank villages became increasingly severe and frequent from May 1965 onward. Syrian policy and propaganda became increasingly extremist, and in July 1966, when Hussein cut off Jordanian official endorsement and support for the PLO, both that organization and the Syrian government openly turned against him with all the devices of propaganda at their disposal.

In reprisal for the terrorist attacks by the guerrillas Israel, on November 13, 1966, destroyed the Jordanian village of al-Samu with an attack by a reinforced brigade. Political pressure against Hussein mounted, however, along with clashes and incidents on the Syria-Jordan border; and after the uneasy winter of 1966 Hussein again designated Nasir as head of another interim government. After general elections on April 23 the moderate Saad Juma became Jordanian prime minister. In mid-May the UAR commenced on extensive military buildup in the Sinai Peninsula in response to Syrian allegations that it was in imminent danger of invasion by strong Israeli forces grouped in attack posture. The UAR declared a state of emergency on May 16 and on May 18 demanded removal of the United Nations Emergency Force from the Sinai. This demand was acceded to by United Nations Secretary General U Thant and immediately carried out.

On May 22, 1967, President Nasser announced that the Strait of Tiran, at the entrance to the Gulf of Aqaba, would be closed to Israeli shipping, and Israel immediately declared this action to be a cause of war. Hussein quickly decided that it would not again be possible, as in 1956, for Jordan to stay out of the conflict. He got in touch with Nasser, proceeded to Cairo, and on May 30, 1967, un-

hesitatingly signed a military alliance with the UAR.

The tempo of scattered firing along the Arab-Israeli borders increased. On the morning of June 5, 1967, declaring itself surrounded and with danger of attack increasing daily, Israel launched a massive air assault that effectively eliminated UAR, Jordanian, Syrian, and Iraqi air forces on the ground. Israeli follow-up ground attacks successively engaged and routed the UAR army in the Sinai, defeated the Jordanians on the West Bank, and finally overpowered the southwestern Syrian defenses. By June 11 a cease-fire had been established, and Israel was in possession of, among other areas, Jordan's West Bank, including all of Jerusalem.

Of all the Arab states Jordan, which could least afford it, lost most in the war. Government figures list 6,094 killed or missing. The best one-third of its agricultural land and its main tourist centers were lost. Jerusalem was wholly in Israeli hands; the Israeli parliament legislated the annexation of the old city on June 27, 1967. (The United States did not recognize this annexation.) During the short war more than 200,000 refugees—many of whom had first been refugees from the 1948–49 war—fled from the West Bank to the East Bank.

THE PROBLEM
OF THE HOLY PLACES

The West Bank, occupied by Israeli forces since the Arab-Israeli War of 1967, contains numerous sites sacred to three major world religions, jurisdiction over and administration of which have created sensitive and difficult problems, particularly in the international arena. Although numerous sites associated with biblical figures sacred to Jews or Muslims or both, as well as numerous places associated with incidents in the life of Jesus, are scattered throughout the Israeli-occupied Territory, a truly astonishing concentration of holy places lies within or near the walled city of Jerusalem.

As the locale of the last days of Jesus, the ancient capital of the Jewish Kingdom, and the scene of the Prophet's nocturnal ascent to heaven, the city is without peer in Christianity and Judaism and is the third holiest city in Islam. Possession of Jerusalem has therefore been a major source of contention. Proclaimed an international city under the 1947 armistice, it came under Jordanian domination in 1948. During the twenty years until it fell to the Israelis in 1967, several ancient synagogues were destroyed, and Jewish religious pilgrimage was not allowed. During Israeli tenure Muslim religious observances have been permitted, but a number of Muslim mosques have reportedly been destroyed, and the number of Muslim pilgrims has understandably diminished drastically.

The sensibilities of the three faiths particularly converge on Mount Moriah, or Temple Mount. Here, on a flat rock face, is the legendary spot where Abraham offered to sacrifice his son, Ishmael according to Islam, or Isaac according to Judaism. On this site later stood the Temple of Solomon and then the Temple of Herod, the ritual center of Judaism in biblical days. The latter was the temple in which Jesus preached and from which he drove the moneychangers. Later still, the sacred rock was covered by a massive Muslim shrine, the Dome of the Rock which, along with the al-Aqsa Mosque, occupies the *Haram al-Sharif,* or "Noble Enclosure." Arson by an Australian religious fanatic severely damaged the al-Aqsa Mosque in 1969, to the extreme consternation and shock of the world's Muslim community. The wall enclosing the Haram al-Sharif rests in part on several courses of ancient stone that are the sole remnants of the Temple of Solomon. Thus, a portion of it is the Western (Wailing) Wall, the most sacred place of Judaism.

Other locations sacred to more than one faith include the tombs of various prophets and biblical figures, such as the Tomb of David, known to Muslims as Nabi Daud, which lies close to the Coenaculum, the traditional site of Jesus' Last Supper. As a result of this extraordinary juxtaposition and intermingling of shrines, administration has been quite complex. In general, each faith administers its own holy places. A number of Christian churches, including various Catholic, Orthodox, and Protestant groups, contribute to the maintenance of various shrines. Nevertheless, animosities are difficult to avoid. For example, various Christian denominations have competed over a number of years for prerogatives in such places as the Church of the Holy Sepulchre, traditional site of Jesus' tomb.

Because of the deep and ancient attachment to it by three great faiths, Jerusalem cannot be considered as merely contested territory. Its symbolic importance is probably as great as that of any city in the world, and the extraordinary tenacity with which the faithful of each of the faiths cling to their memories of it removes it from the realm of ordinary international discourse.

POSTWAR SURVIVAL AND THE GUERRILLA CRISIS

In the wake of the war Hussein and his government were confronted with the critical problems of a shattered economy, the welfare and management of the refugees, the need for external aid and readjustments in international relations, the requirement for a rapid rebuilding of the Jordanian army and replacement of its losses, and the loss of the West Bank to Israel. Internally, however, the major problem was the continuing confrontation with the Palestinian guerrilla organizations—also known as commandos, or *fedayeen.*

The Arab heads of state met at Khartoum at the end of August 1967. The conference, generally considered to represent the views of Arab moderates, reached four major decisions: oil production, suspended by the oil states during the war to be resumed; continued nonrecognition of a nonnegotiation with Israel, individually or collectively;

King Hussein at prayers, with his two brothers

continued closure of the Suez Canal and the elimination of all foreign military bases in Arab territory; and provision of financial subsidy aid to the UAR and Jordan by the oil-rich states of Saudi Arabia, Libya, and Kuwait. The total annual subsidy, promised for the indefinite future, amounted to the sterling equivalent of 378 million dollars, of which Jordan was to receive about 112 million dollars. Donor states at first regularly paid their shares in quarterly installments, but Libya and Kuwait withdrew their support to Jordan during the 1970–71 war between the Jordan government and the guerrillas.

In addition to the Khartoum subsidies, Jordan also received grants from the shaykhdoms of Abu Dhabi and Qatar and a special grant of 42 million dollars from Saudi Arabia for arms purchases. Great Britain provided an emergency loan to cushion the immediate effects of the June 1967 war and later extended further long-term credits. West Germany, with whom Jordan had resumed relations, also extended certain development loans. Although the direct United States subsidy had been terminated, substantial long-term loans were extended to Jordan for emergency relief, development, and military assistance, and in February 1968 United States arms shipments to Jordan were resumed. By such means and its own meager resources, Jordan averted financial disaster.

On November 22, 1967, after months of diplomatic wrangling, the UN Security Council adopted Resolution 242 as a guidline for the settlement of the 1967 war. The principal provisions of this resolution proclaimed the inadmissibility of territorial acquisition by war and called for withdrawal of Israeli forces from areas occupied in the 1967 war; termination of all states of belligerency; acknowledgement of the sovereignty of all states in the area within secure and recognized boundaries; freedom of navigation on all international waterways in the area; a just settlement of the refugee problem; and the designation of a special UN representative as a contact between the states concerned.

In time Jordan, the UAR, and Israel accepted this resolution in general but with distinctly varying policy interpretations. Hussein rested his case for a settlement of the 1967 war squarely on this resolution, such settlement not implying an overall solution to the general Arab-Israeli problem. In the six years after 1967 both Jordanian and

Egyptian policies at length admitted to at least a de facto recognition of Israel, but the question of the Israeli attitude toward the occupied territories, the procedural complexities of negotiation, and the implacable opposition to negotiated settlement by the radical Palestinians and other Arab nationalists in Syria, Libya, and elsewhere prevented it.

Hostilities with Israel did not end with the cease-fire on June 11, 1967. On the Jordanian front the guerrilla organizations, especially al-Fatah, became increasingly active after June 1967 and attempted to employ the methods of the so-called wars of national liberation in the style of the Provisional Revolutionary Government of South Vietnam (Viet Cong) and within a doctrinal framework of ill-digested Maoism.

The irregular forces of the PLO had played little part in the war. After the Arab failures in conventional warfare against Israel, however, the seemingly cheap and effective methodology of guerrilla war was seized upon by Palestinian nationalists as the new instrument through which Israel could be defeated. In December 1967 Shukairy was replaced as head of the PLO by Yahya Hammouda. Hammouda was succeeded in February 1969 by Arafat, who continued also as head of al-Fatah and its action arm, al-Asifah. By early 1970 at least seven fedayeen organizations became identified in Jordan. Other than al-Fatah, the most important was the Popular Front for the Liberation of Palestine (PFLP), led by George Habbash. Although the PLO sought to integrate these various bands and announcements were made from time to time that this had occurred, they were never effectively united.

At first by genuine inclination and then by political necessity, Hussein sought accommodation with the guerrillas and provided training sites and assistance. In Jordan's internal politics, however, the main issue from mid 1967 to mid 1971 was the struggle for political control between the government and the guerrilla organizations. The guerrillas, based in the refugee camps, gradually became virtually a state within a state; money and arms, from both the Arab states and private individuals, were easily secured.

As the guerrilla effort mounted, Israel retaliated quickly and with increasing effectiveness. In March 1968 an Israeli brigade attacked the Jordanian village of Karameh, said to be the guerrilla capital. Damage was inflicted, but the Israeli force was driven back with substantial loss by the fedayeen and the Jordan army. This action was cited as a great fedayeen victory.

Israel launched further heavy attacks at Irbid in June 1968 and at al-Salt in August. The constricted area and generally open terrain of the West Bank did not provide the kind of concealment and refuge featured in classic guerrilla operations, and the Palestinian population failed to provide the universal "friendly sea" of Mao Tse-tung's doctrine in which the guerrilla could "swim like a fish." The guerrillas' main activities in Jordan increasingly appeared to turn away from fighting Israel and to be directed instead to the overthrow of Hussein.

A major guerrilla-government confrontation occurred in November 1968 when the government sought to disarm the refugee camps, but civil war was averted by a compromise that favored the Palestinians. In June 1969, in another major reprisal aimed at forcing Jordan to curb the guerrillas, Israeli forces blew up key sections of the East Ghor irrigation canal, previously damaged in the 1967 war. Severe confrontations between the Jordan army and the guerrillas occurred again in February and June 1970, including several assassination attempts against Hussein, but were settled by further concessions to the guerrillas and the removal of antifedayeen officers from top army commands. The guerrillas were at the height of their political power in Jordan, but the army and the tribal shaykhs of south Jordan, held in check only by Hussein's word, were increasingly restive.

Fighting between army and guerrilla forces broke out late in August 1970. At the end of the first week in September, the PFLP hijacked three European airliners and forced them to land at a Jordanian desert field. The passengers were held hostage for the release of certain guerrillas, and the aircraft were blown up. All hostages were eventually released, most of them by mid-September.

Hussein's patience was exhausted. On September 16 he formed a military cabinet, recalled Field Marshall Habis al-Majali as army commander, and gave the order to suppress the guerrillas. On September 17 Jordan armor and infantry units attacked the guerrilla strongholds in Amman. Within three days the guerrillas were defeated in Amman, although not totally driven out. Fighting in Amman was heavy, with much destruction and loss of life. The number of those killed on all sides has been responsibly estimated at up to thirty-five hundred, although guerrilla propaganda then and later cited much higher figures.

Meanwhile, on September 19 a force of at least two hundred Syrian tanks invaded northern Jordan to assist the guerrillas. The Syrian invasion force was fully withdrawn by September 25 after suffering at least 50 percent tank losses from Jordanian armor and air strikes and from logistical problems. Syria was at the same time influenced by the possibility of Israeli intervention, by diplomatic pressure and possible intervention by the United States, and by separate diplomatic pressures from the Soviet Union.

With the Syrian invasion thrown back and the guerrillas mostly driven from Amman, Hussein and his government once more had survived. Assassination attempts against Hussein again had failed. The crisis of 1970 was regarded, however, as having been the most serious of the many threats to the government during its history.

On September 26, 1970, Hussein restored a civilian cabinet with Ahmad Tuqan as prime minister, and on September 27 the king proceeded to Cairo to attend a summit conference hastily summoned by Nasser to reestablish inter-Arab peace. At the urging of Nasser and other Arab heads of state, Hussein and Arafat entered into a new agreement to keep the peace and maintain the identity of both the Jordan government and the guerrilla movements. The Tunisian premier, Bahi Ladgham, undertook to head a commission to oversee implementation of the agreement.

Hussein and Arafat signed a further agreement in Amman on October 13, 1970, that appeared highly favorable to the guerrillas. In practice, however, the Jordanian army and security forces quietly began the steady reassertion of Jordanian law and sovereignty. Guerrilla refusals to comply were cited as violations of the agreement, and arrests were made. At the end of October Hussein again called on Tal to become prime minister. By early 1971 the systematic, piecemeal mop-up of the guerrillas had proceeded so far as to cause Ladgham to suspend efforts to enforce the Cairo agreement. Syria, the UAR, Algeria, and Libya all denounced Jordan verbally. In Syria, however, a more pragmatic wing of the Baath Party had come to power in November 1970, and by early April 1971, as the last of the guerrillas were forced from Amman, the Syrian party press suddenly changed its line by calling upon the fedayeen to become realistic. On June 5, however, al-Fatah and six other remnant bands called for a new effort to overthrow Hussein.

On July 13, 1971, Jordanian army forces launched a coordinated attack on the last guerrilla redoubt in the area and seized it by July 18. All bases were destroyed, and all the bands in Jordan were broken up. About twenty-five hundred prisoners were taken. The contest for political control in Jordan between the government and the guerrillas of 1967 to 1971 was finished. King Hussein and his government were again firmly in control of the country.

Principal political events in the period 1972–76 include the announcement by King Hussein in March 1972 of his United Arab Kingdom plan, a proposal for a federal Jordan in which the Palestinians would enjoy a large measure of autonomy in the West Bank wing of the kingdom. The plan would be implemented following Israeli withdrawal from the West Bank.

Following the October 1974 Arab summit conference (at Rabat, at which King Hussein acquiesced in a general Arab decision to recognize the PLO as the sole legitimate representative of the Palestinians), the Jordanian government was obliged to reassess its traditional role as spokesman for Palestinians residing on the West Bank. King Hussein dissolved Parliament and appointed a new Senate in which the percentage of Palestinians was reduced from 50 percent to 20 percent, and a new cabinet was formed with fewer Palestinians represented.

STRUCTURE AND FUNCTION OF NATIONAL GOVERNMENT

THE KING

Jordan is a constitutional monarchy based on the constitution promulgated on January 8, 1952. Executive power is vested in the king and the cabinet. The monarch appoints the prime minister and appoints or dismisses members of the cabinet at the recommendation of the prime minister. The king also appoints the members of the Senate, designates its president, and is empowered to dissolve the House of Representatives. The king signs and promulgates laws and holds veto power that can only be overridden by a two-thirds vote of each house. He may issue royal decrees (*iradah*) but only with the consent of the prime minister and four members of the cabinet. The king appoints and may dismiss all judges by decree, approves amendments to the constitution, declares war, and commands the armed forces. Cabinet decisions, court judgments, and the national currency are issued in his name, and he is immune from all liability for his acts.

Because of the critical importance of the monarchical institution, the constitution makes careful provision for royal succession. Basically, the throne "devolves by inheritance in the dynasty of King Abdullah ibn al-Hussein in direct line through his male heirs," but exceptions to the procedure of primogeniture are possible. Succession flows from the eldest son but, should a reigning king die without a direct male heir, the deceased king's eldest brother would have first claim, followed by the claim of the eldest son of the eldest brother. Should there be no suitable direct heir, the National Assembly would select a new king "from among the descendants of the founder of the Arab Revolt, the late King Hussein ibn-Ali." The constitution also states that a successor to the throne must "be sane, a Muslim, the son of Muslim parents, and born of a lawful wife."

A reigning monarch may alter the succession, however, by means of a royal decree. In 1965 Hussein used this method to exclude from the line of succession his two sons by his Muslim, but English, second wife (Princess Muna). He also issued a royal decree that excluded from succession his next younger brother, Mohammed, and designated a second brother, Hassan, as crown prince and heir apparent.

King Hussein has met repeatedly with world leaders, including U.S. president Ronald Reagan and the Palestine Liberation Organization (PLO) chairman, Yassir Arafat, in attempts to bring peace to the Middle East area of conflict among the countries of Jordan, Israel, Lebanon, Iraq, Iran,

The official photographs of the king and queen

and Syria. In that period of time Israel invaded Lebanon and drove out the PLO and arranged for its members to be dispersed to various countries, including Jordan.

King Hussein believes that Jordan's principal security interests are based in acquiring the military resources necessary to compete with Israel and to defend itself against future war.

The king and queen of Jordan arrive for a formal dinner at the White House, November 2, 1981, during a state visit to the U.S. Left to right: King Hussein, First Lady Nancy Reagan, Queen Noor, and President Ronald Reagan. (Official White House photograph by Mary Anne Fackelman)

The king and his bride on June 17, 1980, visit the White House in Washington, D.C. as the guests of President Jimmy Carter and First Lady Rosalynn Carter. Here the four of them pose on the balcony of the White House.

The guests, the king and queen, at a state dinner that night in the White House.

President Reagan (right) *with King Hussein during the monarch's visit on May 29, 1985.* Official White House photograph by Pete Souza

THE ROYAL SOVEREIGNS OF THE HASHEMITE KINGDOM OF JORDAN

Reign	Title	Ruler
1921–1946	Amir	Abdullah ibn al-Hussein
1946—Hashemite kingdom of Jordan created		
1946–1951	King	Abdullah ibn al-Hussein
1951–1952	King	Talal ibn Abdullah
1952–	King	Hussein ibn Talal

6
The Kingdom of Saudi Arabia

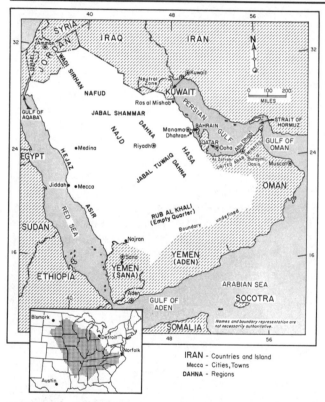

The Kingdom of Saudi Arabia

IRAN - Countries and Island
Mecca - Cities, Towns
DAHNA - Regions

The position of Saudi Arabia as the world's largest oil exporter makes its internal changes of critical interest to the rest of the world. But the assassination of King Faisal ibn Abd al-Azis al-Saud on March 25, 1975, aroused little consternation in either the Arab or the Western worlds as to the future stability of the young nation. The kingdom of Saudi Arabia did not always have such an optimistic future. In the days before the discovery of oil its future was of concern only to those nations that had territorial interests in the immediate area and to Muslims who wished to make the pilgrimage to Mecca in relative safety.

Faisal's father, ibn Saud (Abd al-Azis III), established the state through a combination of tribal conquest and diplomatic maneuvering over a period of twenty-five years, and in 1932 he proclaimed the creation of the kingdom of Saudi Arabia. Saudi Arabia was named after the House of Saud (al-Saud) and was ruled by its first two monarchs as if it were a tribal confederation. Ibn Saud was a political and religious leader of some genius, but the administrative complexities that accompanied the discovery of oil, the introduction of various aspects of Western technology, and the sudden acquisition of considerable wealth made the last years of his reign very difficult.

His successor was ibn Saud I (Abd al-Azis IV). When in 1964 Faisal ascended the throne, he faced the onerous task of transforming the nearly bankrupt nation with a legacy of tribal attitudes and methods into a modern state while placating the opposing forces of religious conservatism and modernization. By the year of his death Faisal had managed to take steps to ensure that the vastly increased wealth of his country would be directed toward long-term industrial and social welfare programs that would eventually benefit all sectors of the society and would secure Saudi Arabia as a permanent and important power in the Arab world and in the international community. Faisal accomplished this without seriously offending tribal sensitivities and at the same time retained the traditional religious base of his family's power and the conservative orientation of the society.

Although Saudi Arabia was founded in the twentieth century, its heritage was thirteen hundred years old, and its methods, those of the nomadic bedouin, were even more ancient. In the eighteenth century a local leader in the Najd, the Saudi homeland in north-central Arabia, Mohammed ibn Saud, had aligned himself with a local religious leader, Mohammed ibn Abd al-Wahhab, who wished to revive the spirit and practices of Islam as it was in the seventh century A.D. Saud and al-Wahhab acting together offered conversion or the sword, basically the same method used by Mohammed, the Prophet of Islam, in his conquest of Arabia. Intermarriage cemented the Saud-al-Wahhab alliance, and a series of descendants kept the movement alive, however feebly, until ibn Saud (Abd al-Azis) decisively established his rule in the twentieth century. David Hogarth, a British specialist on Arabia, predicted in 1925 that ibn Saud's domination outside the Najd would probably not last more than a decade and certainly would not survive his death. Although ibn Saud was a sagacious ruler, Hogarth's prophecy almost certainly would have come true were it not for the discovery of oil a decade later.

Western powers have only had economic reasons to be interested in Saudi Arabia since the 1930s, but to the world's Muslims the area has always been important because their two holiest cities are located there: Mecca, the city that holds its most important shrine, the Kaabah; and Medina, the city where the Prophet established his first community and laid the foundation of the Islamic nation.

PRE-ISLAMIC ARABIA

THE CIVILIZATIONS OF PREHISTORIC ARABIA

Archaeological investigations of pre-Islamic Arabia are still in an embryonic state, and the results are hypothetical and controversial at best. Through the middle of the twentieth century few people had the physical endurance or the survival techniques crucial to investigate the area. Scarcity of water, the difficulties of desert transport, and until the 1940s hostile tribes made systematic research a heroic undertaking. Further, little was known about present-day Arabia beyond its coastal settlements. Initial archaeological discoveries were often the accidental finds of explorers anxious to investigate this isolated land and map its interior.

The first three known Arabian civilizations were coastal settlements. The oldest evidence of civilized man in northern Arabia is artifacts found sixty miles to the north of Dhahran on the coast of the Persian Gulf. Dated to 5000 B.C. they are identical to those of the al-Ubaid culture of Mesopotamia, the first people to cultivate and settle the Fertile Crescent and the ancestors of the Sumerians, the first known people to develop a high culture. If al-Ubaid culture originated in Mesopotamia, then civilization reached Arabia from the north. If, however, Arabia was the parent site, then the first known agriculturists in the Middle East were migrants from Arabia. This would substantiate the Sumerian myth that agriculture had been brought to Mesopotamia by a fisherman from the Persian Gulf.

From about 4000 to 2000 B.C. the civilization called Dilmun dominated two hundred fifty miles of the eastern coast of Arabia from present-day Kuwait to Bahrain and extended sixty miles into the interior to the oasis of Hufuf. At its zenith in 2000 B.C. Dilmun controlled the route to the Indies and was the trading link between the civilizations of the Indus Valley and those of Mesopotamia. The Mesopotamians regarded Dilmun as a holy place and its people as extraordinarily blessed. At Oman and Abu Dhabi remains of another civilization were found that might be related to Dilmun.

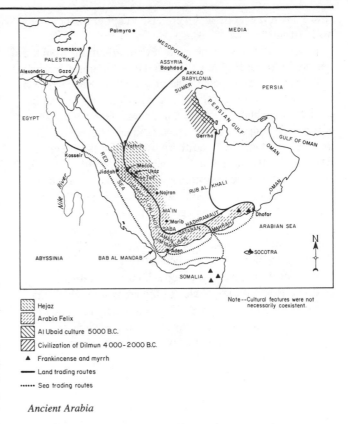

Hejaz
Arabia Felix
Al Ubaid culture 5000 B.C.
Civilization of Dilmun 4000-2000 B.C.
▲ Frankincense and myrrh
— Land trading routes
······ Sea trading routes

Note--Cultural features were not necessarily coexistent.

Ancient Arabia

Arabia was only sparsely peopled in the interior. Until about 3000 B.C. inland Arabia was sufficiently verdant to support both cereal agriculturists and herding peoples in the north and hunting and gathering societies in the south. As climatic conditions changed and the desert slowly encroached upon land that formerly had supported both animal and human life, the inhabitants were faced with three choices: to cling to the inland oases, to move to the coasts, or to leave Arabia entirely. Those who made the third choice and migrated to the north, northeast, and southwest are the only ones who left a historical record.

THE MIGRATIONS

In the middle of the fourth millennium B.C. a pattern emerged that proved disastrous to the material advancement of the peninsula but that benefited the rest of the world immeasurably. Approximately every thousand years either because of population pressures caused by inadequate food and resources or because they were following wild herds, major migrations of Semitic-speaking people from the Arabian Peninsula insinuated themselves into the more hospitable lands around them. In about 3500 B.C. two parallel migrations occurred: one by the western route northward to the Sinai Peninsula and into Egypt, where the immigrants mixed with the indigenous people to produce the historical Egyptians; the other by the eastern route to Sumer where they amalgamated and became known as Babylonians. The Egyptians made important innovations in irrigation, mathematics, and architecture and developed the world's first solar calendar. The Babylonians developed the world's first known law code and were also adept at mathematics and astronomy.

In about 2500 B.C. there were further migrations from the peninsula to the Fertile Crescent. These migrants merged with the indigenous people and became the Canaanites and the Phoenicians (collectively, the Amorites). Both peoples devised alphabetical scripts; the Phoenicians developed a commercial empire based on navigational routes that linked the Mediterranean with northern Europe for the first time. Between 1500 and 1200 B.C. some migrants settled in Syria and were among the ancestors of the Aramaeans, or modern Syrians. The others settled in southern Syria and Palestine and were among the forebears of the Hebrews. The Aramaeans provided some of the biblical authors their language, which was also to be the language of Christ. The Hebrews developed ethical monotheism.

Each of these groups merged with and absorbed certain characteristics of the peoples of the areas into which they moved, but they retained Semitic languages. Few, however, were able to withstand the eventual invasions of other non-Semitic peoples and the eventual adulteration of their culture.

ARABIA FELIX

If Arabia seemed virtually resourceless to its inhabitants, other more technologically advanced peoples found it very alluring. Sometime in the third millennium B.C. peoples of Mesopotamia and Egypt discovered that the area of southern Arabia uniquely possessed two highly desirable gum resins: frankincense and myrrh. Egyptian records survive detailing expeditions to Punt (Somalia and the Bab al-Mandab) to collect the resins that were grown only in Dhofar and its colonies of Somalia and the island of Socotra.

Frankincense, an essential element in certain pagan rituals, was burned as an offering to the gods. It was used lavishly in cremation services and, in Egypt, for embalming. For the funeral of Nero's wife an entire year's harvest was reputedly consumed. Myrrh was the foundation of many cosmetics and perfumes and was also used medicinally. Although myrrh was always expensive, the demand far exceeded the supply, so that workers were minutely examined upon leaving the harvesting much as they are in diamond fields.

For almost two millennia foreigners dominated and controlled this trade until descendants of Arabian migrants, attracted by the products from southern Arabia, returned from eastern Jordan and southern Iraq to their ancestral homeland. These colonists from the Fertile Crescent had benefited from the diaspora of their ancestors into Mesopotamia. They were familiar with the institutions of urban life and brought with them irrigation techniques, metallurgical and ceramic skills, an alphabetic script, a complex religion, and a developed art. They arrived in southern Arabia in two waves: one before 1500 B.C. and one at about 1200 B.C.

The immigrants possessed a common culture, and the kingdoms of Saba (Sheba), Qataban, Hadhramaut, Ma'in, Himyar, and Ausan—the area known as Arabia Felix—were formed into a confederation of states during the first millennium B.C. Each kingdom enjoyed periods of prosperity and prominence. Although internecine warfare was rife, apparently they felt secure enough from outside forces, because of their relative inaccessibility, to have unfortified towns. They shared a common religious system based on an astral triad and initially were ruled by a *makkarib* similar to the Mesopotamian priest-king.

Eventually this position became secularized. Under the *malik* (king) were prominent *gayls* (chieftains) who controlled the *ash'b* (sedentary tribal units). Unlike the northern tribes, whose allegiance was based on blood ties, those of the *ash'b* were commercial and labor oriented.

In the fourth century A.D. the civilization of Arabia Felix began a slow but inevitable decline. The southern Arabian monopoly was challenged, and indigenous people of the caravan cities and distribution points began to assert their own control over trade tolls. In the third century B.C. the Ptolemaic merchant marine had reopened the Nile-Red Sea Canal and actively had begun to compete for trade. When the Romans captured Egypt in the middle of the first century B.C., they continued and intensified this competition. Petra, Palmyra, and northwest Mesopotamia incorporated into the Roman Empire. A matter of even greater significance occurred early in the Roman period when Greek shippers plotted the vagaries of the monsoon winds and successfully traveled to India and back to Alexandria, discovering in the process that many of the products thought to be of Arabian origin were in fact from other lands.

The core of the market, which was frankincense and myrrh, was retained by Arabia until the demand eventually evaporated when Christianity was made the religion of the Roman Empire by edict in A.D. 325 and cremations and pagan rituals, in which large amounts of frankincense were used, were banned. This edict created further difficulties when Christian missionaries entered Arabia in 356. Judaism was well established in the south by that time, brought to Arabia Felix by refugees after the destruction of Jerusalem by Titus in A.D. 70. The Jews quickly made converts there because the Arabians' traditional enemies, Byzantium and Abyssinia, were Christian countries. By the fourth century there were numerous Judaized Aramaeans and Arabians. For example, the last Himyarite king was a Jew.

Religious rivalry led to hostility and eventually to a massacre of Christians at Najran. The Christians sought help from Constantinople, which in turn requested the Abyssinians—their Christian allies closest to Arabia—to intervene. In A.D. 570 an Abyssinian protectorate was established in southern Arabia, but the protectorate was replaced in 575 by a Persian satrapy. Persian help had been requested by Jewish and pagan Arabians who regarded a Zoroastrian presence less of a threat than a Christian one. When the Persian satrap embraced Islam in 628, thereby opening the area to influence from the north Arabians, Arabia Felix became effectively absorbed into their cultural orbit.

MOHAMMED AND THE CONQUEST OF ISLAM

A combination of outstanding qualities was to be found in Mohammed, the Prophet of Islam, who was born in 570 into the prosperous Quraysh tribe. His own position within the tribe was not an especially happy one. Orphaned at the age of six, he was raised by his grandfather and after his death by an uncle, Abu Talib. As a youth he accompanied his uncle on caravans to Syria and became practiced in trade. At twenty-five he married a wealthy widow of his tribe, the forty-year-old Khadijah. He worked with her in the trading business, and this auspicious change of luck gave him the leisure to contemplate his life and that of his fellow Meccans. Perhaps his own impoverished beginnings made him sensitive to the moral malaise of Mecca. When nomads adapted to a sedentary commercial life, tribal solidarity was weakened, and strong members gave little protection to the weak and poor members of their tribe. Widows, who were always numerous, were often forced into prostitution instead of remarrying into the tribe or being supported by it. Wealth had made the tribes less generous than they had been when poor, and there were no urban institutions to replace humane tribal mores.

About 610, when he was nearly forty, Mohammed began to seclude himself in a cave outside Mecca and one evening there received the first of a series of divine revelations from the angel Gabriel. After a period of self-doubt he began preaching the messages he received first to his extended family and then to his tribe. Initially his message was relatively innocuous: there was only one God, who had created all things, and there was a day of judgment after which all men would be assigned to paradise or to hell. Exclusive of his wife and a few friends he was generally scoffed at as a harmless but unbalanced religious enthusiast.

Gradually his approach changed from *rasul* (prophet) to *nadhir* (warner). The punishment of evildoers and those who refused his message was painted more luridly, and the uproar he was raising became serious enough for members

Mohammed the Prophet

The angel Gabriel appears to the Prophet Mohammed in this popular Persian painting.

of his tribe to oppose him firmly. Abu Sufyan, who represented the Umayyad—the most influential branch of the Quraysh—began to harass Mohammed and his converts because of the danger to Meccan economic life that Mohammed gospel posed. Income from the pilgrimage to the many gods of the Kaabah was secondary only to the profits of trade. If monotheism became prevalent, who would make the pilgrimage? Trade itself would be disrupted if faith, as Mohammed suggested, replaced blood as a social bond because the administration of trading interests was regulated through tribal leaders and was organized according to the geographical position of clans. Although generosity was a tribal value, what would be the results if the poor believed Mohammed's teaching that they had a right to partake of the wealth around them?

The Quraysh had good cause for anxiety. Exclusive of converts within Mohammed's clan, the Hashim, the first Muslims were those dissatisfied with the status quo either because of tribal laws inappropriate in an urban setting or because of the intensely competitive commercialism in Mecca. Younger brothers and younger sons of merchants were in a reduced state because of tribal primogeniture. Foreigners and outlawed tribesmen who did not have clan protection were in an extremely vulnerable situation since there were no civic protective institutions. Tribesmen whose clans were not in the first order of economic importance resented the monopolistic practices of the wealthier clans. As his father's posthumous child, Mohammed too had been hurt by tribal laws because he had not been able to inherit. The Hashim was a weak clan, and Mohammed had felt the indignities of a low position.

Pressure was placed on Mohammed's uncle, Abu Talib, to excommunicate him from the clan. Although Abu Talib had not converted, as a member of the Hashim he was eager to support any movement that might dilute the power of the wealthier clans, and he knew that if he excommunicated his nephew, he would be delivering him up to certain death. When this approach failed, the Prophet's clan was blacklisted from business or social relations with the other Quraysh. Prevented in Mecca, Mohammed tried to win converts in Taif but was rejected and physically ousted from there; he campaigned among the various tribes at the Ukaz fair of 620.

The only major tribe to show interest at the fair was one from Yathrib. After a series of conferences between Mohammed and the tribe's leaders, Mohammed and his converts were invited to live in Yathrib. The tribal leaders thought Mohammed might be able to mediate among them and to settle some long-standing blood debts. The *hijra* to Yathrib was a well-planned quiet migration of two hundred people who left in small groups. It was a very dangerous undertaking since their clans could not protect them once they left the city. Sixteen years later the caliph Umar designated July 16, 622, when Mohammed left Mecca, as the starting point of the Muslim calendar and era.

In Yathrib, whose name would be changed to Medina—the city of the prophet—Mohammed was welcomed as a powerful shaykh. In this new security he was able to assess his position, stabilize his leadership, and make practical political plans for Islam's infant *umma* (community of believers), who were the nucleus of the Islamic state. The most pressing problem was economic support for the *muhajirun* (emigrants). They were boarding with Medinese *ansar* (supporters), but in two years their assets were depleted. Using the device most familiar to them they began to raid and plunder the caravans. Not only did raiding not provide economic relief, but it also damaged the Meccans who controlled the trade. Early raids were unsuccessful because Mohammed's Medinese opponents alerted the Meccans. The first successful raid was accomplished by guile during the month of holy truce—when guards were fewer—by twelve men operating under sealed orders. Although reactions were mixed because the holy truce had been violated and because of fear of blood vengeance, Mohammed continued to organize raids.

A plan was devised to strike at the caravan of Mohammed's major antagonist, Abu Sufyan. Abu Sufyan had received intelligence that there might be trouble and had secured nine hundred reinforcements from Mecca. Eighty-five miles south of Medina at Badr the three hundred Muslims attacked. The overconfident Meccans were vanquished, and Islam was established as a militant polity. A year later Abu Sufyan defeated the Muslims at Uhud, but Islamic warriors already had won a reputation as highly disciplined warriors who were contemptuous of death. Under the banner of Islam, raiding and warring were legitimized as *jihad,* or holy war. Warriors could not lose: if they died, they went to a sensual and verdant paradise; if they were victorious, they received plunder. Encouraged by their victory at Uhud the Meccans, allied with bedouin and Abyssinian mercenaries, besieged Medina with a force of ten thousand. The Muslims had only a third of that number and, preferring military innovation to foolhardiness, dug a trench around the city. There had been only twenty Muslim

casualties when the Meccans departed a month later in disgust at the shamefulness of the Muslims in avoiding open combat.

The fact that half of the major tribes of Medina were Jewish had an important effect on the early development of Islam. Mohammed had apparently hoped that by incorporating Judaistic elements into Islamic practice the Jews might recognize him at least as a prophet to the Arabs and possibly might view Islam as the fulfillment of their religion, as Mohammed believed it was. When the Jews made it clear that they could not consider a non-Jew a prophet, Jewish-Muslim relations deteriorated. Islam became more exclusively Arabian and more specifically bedouin in its orientation; the *qibla* (direction of prayer) was changed from Jerusalem to Mecca; a *muadhdhin* called people to prayer, as opposed to the trumpet and gong; and *dhimmis* (people of the Book)—Christians, Jews, and Zoroastrians—were accused of having obstructed the divine plan.

Within Medina religious differences were fed by political rivalries. Abd Allah ibn Ubayy, the potential prince of Medina, had strong support in several Jewish clans. If Mohammed's hegemony increased, any influence to be gained by supporting Ubayy would be threatened. Mohammed, knowing that the Meccans would try an all-out offensive after their defeat at Badr, tried to weed out his enemies and spies in Medina and strengthen his political hold there by increasing allegiance to his cause.

A squabble between Muslims and a Jewish clan was taken up by Mohammed, who besieged the clan and finally expelled them from Medina. During the battle at Uhud a Jewish contingent under Ubayy had abruptly left the Muslim side, which no doubt contributed to the Muslim defeat. In 625 the Jewish clan that controlled the date palms was expelled. At the siege of Medina the remaining Jewish group leagued with the Meccans and planned a rear assault as soon as the forces at the front were engaged. After the siege the Muslims attacked the clan, which had returned to their fortified mud enclave. The women and children were sold, and all the men were killed. Exiled Jewish clans of the earlier disturbances had fled to the Khaybar Oasis to the north. When the Muslims captured Khaybar and exacted as tribute a percentage of agricultural production, all Jewish resistance in the Hejaz was effectively quelled.

The unsuccessful siege of Medina proved to be a greater victory than Badr in winning Meccans to the Islamic side. Meccan trade to the north had been virtually destroyed by Muslim raids, and now Meccan prestige was weakened when they could not dislodge Mohammed with a force three times as large as his. Muslim forces continued to harass any caravans foolish enough to venture out of Mecca, but on the whole, Mohammed, aware of his superior position, initiated a policy of conciliation toward the Meccans, preferring to have a team of astute businessmen with excellent administrative abilities on his side than a conquered and dead city.

The Great Mosque of Medina, one of the holiest shrines of the Islamic world, where the tomb of Prophet Mohammed is located

In the town of Mecca, at about the age of forty Mohammed began to have revelations. He became convinced that God had chosen him to perfect the religion earlier revealed to Abraham, the prophets of Israel and Jesus. Among his initial converts were his wife, his first cousin 'Ali (later also his son-in-law), and another kinsman Abu Bakr (later also one of his fathers-in-law), a leader among Quraysh. Other leaders of Qurayish were jealous and suspicious of Mohammed's teachings.

Mohammed continued to make converts, mostly among poor people and slaves. The hostility against him twice grew to a point where he advised his followers to take refuge in Christian Abyssinia. At length his enemies plotted to murder him; but he was forewarned, and 'Ali, his cousin, heroically lay in Mohammed's bed feigning sleep when the would-be murderers arrived. Meanwhile Mohammed, accompanied by Abu Bakr, fled to a nearby mountain cave, and after two nights continued on to Medina, then known as Yathrib. The way had been prepared in the previous year by a compact between the Prophet and leaders of Medina.

The year of this transfer to Medina, the hijra (commonly written Hegira), was later taken as Anno Hegirae or A.H. 1 of the Muslim calendar (A.D. 622). At that time Mohammed was fifty-one.

Mohammed's teachings were widely accepted in his new home except by local Judaized Arabs. The new faith began to spread also to other parts of Arabia. The people of Mecca, however, remained hostile, and a number of battles were fought before they came to terms. In 629 Mohammed returned to Mecca as its master. By the time he died, in 632, large numbers of people in all parts of Arabia had embraced the faith of Islam.

Late in life Mohammed began thinking of extending his work beyond the borders of Arabia, and his followers proceeded to put this idea into effect. After quelling some rebellious elements in the country, including

eastern Arabia, they started forth with an army of from 3,000 to 4,000 men on campaigns that were to lead to extensive conquests. As the movement gathered momentum, the numbers were swelled from newly converted populations outside Arabia.

Abu Bakr, the devoted companion of Mohammed, succeeded to the leadership of Islam and became the first caliph (khalifa or successor). Khalid ibn al-Walid was one of his most brilliant generals, and ranks among the foremost military men of history. Under Khalid's leadership the Muslim armies struck east toward Sassanide Persia and north toward the Eastern Roman or Byzantine province of Syria. Wherever the armies encountered resistance they offered three alternatives: embrace the religion of the true God, or surrender and pay tribute, or war.

The Dome of the Rock ("the Mosque of Omar") in Jerusalem where the spirit of the Prophet Mohammed left the imprint of his foot as he ascended into heaven

In 630 the city submitted to Mohammed. Meccan contingents were critical in subduing other tribes of the Hejaz. Many outlying tribes rushed to pledge allegiance or make treaties of various kinds. Acceptance of Islam became a requisite to alliance with the Muslims. The political result was that a federation of tribes was formed with Mecca functioning as the area of central authority.

When Mohammed died in 632, the Hejaz, the Najd, and areas on the southern and eastern shores of the Arabian Peninsula were under Islamic rule. Immediately after his death, the wars of ridda (apostasy) began. Southern tribes were reluctant to pay zakat (annual alms tax) to Medina and resented the rising power of the Hejaz, and many powerful tribes reverted to their previous situation. Exclusive of

Hejazi and Najdi tribes, for the most part only weak ones remained Muslim. Religious conversion of tribes outside the Hejaz had been nominal, and Islam had not become an integral part of tribal life during Mohammed's short ministry. Powerful peninsular tribes joined after the conquest showed signs of success. Mohammed had unified the tribes, but expansion with its economic benefits was necessary to keep their energies directed away from each other.

After Mohammed's death his followers compiled those of his words regarded as coming directly and literally from God into the Quran (Koran), the holy scripture of Islam; others of his sayings and teachings and the precedents of his personal behavior, recalled by those who had known him during his lifetime, became the hadith. Together they form the Sunna, a comprehensive guide to the spiritual, ethical, and social life of the orthodox Muslim.

Islam means submission (to God), and one who submits is a Muslim. Mohammed is the "seal of the prophets"; his revelation is said to complete for all time the series of biblical revelations received by the Jews and the Christians. God is believed to have remained one and the same throughout time, but men had strayed from his true teachings until set aright by Mohammed. True monotheists who preceded Islam are known in Quranic tradition as Hanifs; prophets and sages of the biblical tradition, such as Abraham, Moses, and Jesus (known in Arabic as Ibrahim, Musa, and Isa), are recognized as inspired vehicles of God's will. Islam, however, reveres as sacred only the message and rejects Christianity's deification of the messenger. It accepts the concepts of guardian angels, the Day of Judgment (last day), general resurrection, heaven and hell, and the eternal life of the soul.

Finally, all Muslims at least once in their lifetime should, if possible, make a trip to the holy city of Mecca to participate in special rites held there during the twelfth month of the lunar calendar. The Prophet instituted this requirement, modifying pre-Islamic custom to emphasize sites associated with Allah and Abraham, founder of monotheism and father of the northern Arabs through his son Ishmael (Ismail). In Islamic belief Abraham offered to sacrifice Ishmael, son of the servant woman Hagar, rather than Isaac, son of Sarah, as described in the Bible.

The *jihad*—the permanent struggle for the triumph of the law of God on earth—is an additional general duty of all Muslims. In addition to specific duties Islam imposes a code of ethical conduct encouraging generosity, fairness, honesty, and respect and forbidding adultery, gambling, usury, and the consumption of carrion, blood, pork, and alcohol.

A Muslim stands in a personal relationship to God; there is neither intermediary nor clergy in orthodox Islam. Those who lead prayers, preach sermons, and interpret the law do so by virtue of their superior knowledge and scholarship rather than because of any special powers or prerogatives conferred by ordination.

During his lifetime Mohammed held both spiritual and temporal leadership of the Muslim community; he established the concept of Islam as a total and all-encompassing way of life for man and society. Islam teaches that Allah revealed to Mohammed the immutable principles governing decent behavior; it is therefore incumbent on the individual to live in the manner prescribed by revealed law and on the community to perfect human society on earth according to the holy injunctions. Islam traditionally recognized no distinction between religion and state; religious and secular life merged, as did religious and secular law. Mohammed, however, left no mechanism for selection of subsequent leaders.

After Mohammed's death in 632 the leaders of the Muslim community consensually chose Abu Bakr, the father of the Prophet's favorite living wife, Aisha, and one of his earliest followers, to succeed him. At that time some persons favored Ali, who, besides being a member of the Hashemite lineage, was the Prophet's cousin and the husband of his favorite daughter, Fatima. Ali and Fatima, parents of the Prophet's grandsons, believed the leadership of Islam belonged to them by inheritance. Ali and his supporters (called the Shiat Ali, or party of Ali) eventually recognized the community's choice but only after Fatima's death. The next two caliphs (from *khalifa*, "successor")— Umar, who succeeded in 634, and Uthman, who took power in 646—enjoyed the recognition of the entire community.

Dissatisfaction with the rule of Uthman began to mount in various parts of the Islamic empire, however. For example, the codification of the Quran, which took place under Uthman, hurt the interests of the professional Quran reciters. Some, such as those at Kufa in present-day Iraq, refused to go along with this reform. Others accused Uthman of nepotism. Though himself an early Muslim, Uthman came from the Banu Umayyah lineage of the Quraysh, whose members had been Mohammed's main detractors in Mecca.

Ali, his claim to the caliphate frustrated, became a perfect focus for dissatisfaction. In 656 disgruntled soldiers killed Uthman. After the ensuing five years of civil war, known in Islamic history as *fitnah* (trials), the caliphate finally devolved on Ali. But Aisha, who had long been a bitter foe of Fatima and Ali, objected, demanding that Uthman's killing be avenged and his killers punished by the Hashemites. She helped rally opposition to Ali's caliphate.

The killers insisted that Uthman, by ruling unjustly, had relinquished his right to be caliph and deserved to die. Ali, whose political position depended on their action and their support, was forced to side with them. From his capital at Kufa he refused to reprimand the killers.

At this point Muawiyah, the governor of Syria and a member of the Banu Umayyah, refused to recognize Ali's authority and called for revenge for his murdered kinsman, Uthman. Ali attacked, but the battle of Siffin was inconclusive. Muawiyah's soldiers advanced with copies of the Quran on their spears, thus calling symbolically for God to decide or for the question to be submitted to arbitration. Ali agreed to this settlement.

Some of Ali's supporters, however, rejected the notion that the caliph, the Prophet's successor and head of the community, should submit to the authority of others. By so doing, they reasoned, he effectively relinquished his authority as caliph. They argued that, according to Quranic teaching, rebels must be brought to obedience by force; arbitrating the dispute with the rebellious Muawiyah was therefore wrong. They further argued that the question of Uthman's right to rule had been settled by war during the *fitnah*. When Ali insisted on his course, this group, which came to be known as the *Kharajites* (those who seceded), withdrew to Harura near Kufa and chose their own leader.

The arbitration went against Ali in 658. He refused to accept the decision but did not renounce the principle of arbitration. At this point the Kharajites became convinced that personal interest, not principle, motivated Ali. His support dwindled among all elements of his followers, and he tried unsuccessfully to attack Syria. Muawiyah gained in battle. Ali also engaged in numerous battles with the Kharajites, including the massacre at Nahrawan in which most of them were killed. In revenge for the slaying of his wifes' family in these raids, the Kharajite Abd al-Rahman ibn Muljam al-Muradi murdered Ali in 661.

Ali's death ended the last of the so-called four orthodox caliphates, and the period when the entire community of Islam recognized a single head. Muawiyah then proclaimed himself caliph from Damascus. The *shiat* Ali, however, refused to recognize Muawiyah or the Umayyad line. They withdrew and in the first great schism of Islam proclaimed Hassan, Ali's son, the caliph. Hassan, however, eventually relinquished his claim in favor of Muawiyah and went to live in Medina, supported by wealth apparently supplied by Muawiyah.

The claims of the Alid line and its supporters did not end here, however. In 680 Yazid succeeded to the caliphate while his father, Muawiyah, was still alive. Ali's younger son, Husain, refused to recognize the succession and revolted at Kufa. He was unable to gain widespread support, however, and was killed, along with a small band of his soldiers, at Karbala in present-day Iraq in 680. To the Shiites Husain then became a martyred hero, the tragic reminder of the lost glories of the Alid line, and the repository of the Prophet's family's special claim of presumptive right to the caliphate. The political victor of this second period of *fitnah* was Marwar of the Umayyad line, but Husain's death aroused increased interest among his supporters, enhanced by feelings of guilt and remorse and a desire for revenge.

Although they did not gain political preeminence in the world Muslim community, supporters of the Alid cause became if anything more fervent in their beliefs. As they had since the earliest days of the caliphate, Ali and his family served as a lightning rod for discontent. With continued conquests the number of Muslims from non-Arab cultural backgrounds grew. It was inevitable that their religious values, quite foreign to the austere faith born in the Arabian desert, should demand some outlet.

The Shiites founded their objections to the Umayyad and later non-Shiite caliphs on the notion that members of the House of Mohammed, through Ali, were most appropriate successors to his position as both political leader and, more important, imam or prayer leader. Many believed that Ali, as a close associate, early had a special insight into the Prophet's teachings and habits. In addition many felt that he deserved the post because of his personal merits and, indeed, that the Prophet had expressed a wish that Ali succeed him. In time these views became transformed for many Shiites into an almost mystical reverence for the spiritual superiority of Ali's line. Some Shiites also believe that Mohammed had left a written will naming Ali as his successor but that it had been destroyed by Ali's enemies, who then usurped leadership.

The early political rivalry remained active as well. Shiism eventually gained political dominance in Iraq and Persia (present-day Iran), as well as in Yemen. Shiites are also numerous in Syria and Lebanon and constitute about half the Muslim population of Bahrain.

THE HOUSE OF SAUD

WAHHABI ISLAM

Islam was still strong in the Hejaz but weak or nonexistent elsewhere in Arabia. Animistic practices had been resumed in the interior and integrated into Islamic rituals. Although developed by desert people, Islamic tenets and values needed an urban setting in order to flourish. Islam presumed a settled life or at least access to one. The Najd, although perforce inhabited mostly by tribes on the move, did possess some settlements where rudiments of Islam were taught. Uyaynah, not far from the main Saudi settlement at Dariyah, was one of these. In 1703 Mohammed ibn Abd al-Wahhab, a religious prodigy, was born in Uyaynah into the Banu Sinan tribe. His religious enthusiasm was encouraged by his family, who were experts in Islamic law, and they sent him to study at a number of Islamic cities noted for theological learning.

Apparently al-Wahhab's enthusiasm early progressed to fanaticism because he was expelled from Basra for his extreme criticism of local religious practices. He preached a return to the orthodox practices of Mohammed's day and particularly condemned any devotion that detracted from the oneness of God. His interpretation of Islam was primarily based on the works of the strict Hanbali scholar Taki al-Din Ahmad ibn Taimiya.

His reception at home in Uyaynah was as cool as the Prophet's had been in Mecca. Finally at the instigation of the Bani Khalid, who were Shiites, he was expelled from his village in 1744. He eventually sought physical protection at Dariyah with Mohammed ibn Saud, who was im-

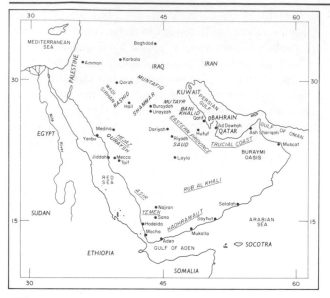

HEJAZ   - Regions
RED SEA - Geographical Features
SAUD   - Tribes
Mecca   - Cities, Towns
IRAN   - Countries and Island

Nineteenth-century Arabia

The front entrance to the Great Mosque in Mecca (Makkah)

pressed with Wahhab's views and became his ally. Together they planned a jihad to purify and, in the process, conquer Arabia. A procedure that had been successful in the seventh century might work again. A series of intermarriages, the most important being Saud's marriage to al-Wahhab's daughter, cemented the relationship.

By the time of Mohammed ibn Saud's death in 1765 most of the Najd was Wahhabi. Al-Wahhab renewed the alliance with the dead shaykh's son, Abdul Azis (1766–1803), and together they took the city of Riyadh. Expansion out of the Najd was blocked in all directions by enemies who felt less threatened by the religious doctrine than by the political manifestation that accompanied it. To the east the powerful Bani Khalid harried the Wahhabis with unremitting raids. To the southwest the sharifians banned any Wahhabis in the holy cities. Farther to the southwest the Ismailis—Shiites like the Bani Khalid—began to invade the Najd. From the north Muntafiqis, an Iraqi tribal confederation, attacked. Many Muntafiqis, however, converted and joined the Najdi forces.

By the time of Al-Wahhab's death in 1792 Wahhabis had established suzerainty south to the Rub al-Khali (Empty Quarter). Gradually the south and east accepted the movement, and Hasa (particularly the oases of Qatif and Hufuf) was compelled by the sword. In 1801 Karbala, a Shiite holy city in present-day Iraq, was attacked, the tomb of Hussein stripped of its jeweled encasing, and the surrounding area looted. When Abdul Azis died in 1803, the march between the Najd and the Hejaz was more Wahhabi than sharifian, and Wahhabis were firmly established at the Buraymi oasis.

Control of the Hejaz was of paramount importance to secure the newly conquered area. Mecca was taken in 1801 and Medina in 1805, and both cities were cleansed of

Nineteenth-century view of Mecca (Makkah) with the Great Mosque in the foreground

anything perceived as a religious infraction. Hookahs and tombs of saints were attacked with similar ferocity. Sharif Ghalib was authorized to continue administering the area, and Saud (1803–14) attempted to sort out the chaos of the conquest by standardizing governmental procedures in the widely scattered territories. *Sharia* (the sacred Islamic law) was reintroduced where necessary and safeguarded by *qadis* in villages and *qadis* and muftis in towns and cities. Tribal feuds were regulated by mediators of the central Wahhabi authority. The area was pacified under the watchful eyes of district governors and deputies stationed in moated forts outside captured towns.

NINETEENTH-CENTURY ARABIA

The government of the Ottoman Empire in Constantinople, although uneasy about the Saudi movement, had largely ignored requests from the pasha in Baghdad to put down the insurrection, underestimating its importance. The loss of the holy cities, destructive of both prestige and income, made a reprisal imperative. The Ottoman government asked its viceroy in Cairo, the formidable Mohammed Ali, to crush the upstarts. The viceroy's son, Tusun, led the first advance in 1816. Modern weapons at first proved ineffectual against tribal tactics in the desert, although Mecca and Medina were taken. Mohammed Ali, surprised at the Saudi military competence, assumed command. In the end the Saudi defeat came from within. Abd-Allah (1814–18) retreated to Dariyah after his father Saud's death in 1814. Ibrahim, another of Mohammed Ali's sons, battered the town until it fell. Dariyah was razed, and Abd-Allah paid with his head in Constantinople for his cowardice.

The Saudi clan was not deterred. Abd-Allah's uncle, Turki ibn Abd-Allah (1818–34), organized troops to oust the Egyptians who had occupied the Najd. Settling in Riyadh after the destruction of Dariyah and establishing Riyadh as the Saudi capital, he harassed the Egyptian garrison to the point of mutiny, causing them to be transferred to the Hejaz. Turki protected the integrity of Saudi-Wahhabi rule and warned oppressive governers that they would be dealt with severely if they forgot that the establishment of true Islamic rule was the reason for the movement, not political oppression of subject peoples. Successive exploitation and occupation of Arabia by foreigners had made Turki sensitive to the fact that justice alone could legitimize this conquest in the name of religion. Wahhabism had become a nationalistic movement, though the concept had not been articulated by its leaders.

Once again internal dissension ravaged the movement when Turki was assassinated in 1834 by a rival within the family. Turki's son, Faisal (1834–38 and 1843–65), quickly picked up the reins of government. Faisal was as intelligent as his father, but internal problems diluted his potency against foreign powers. The rulers in Qatar and Bahrain, sensing the Saudi family troubles, revolted as did the ferocious Bani Khalid of Hasa. In 1834 Mohammed Ali, having broken with the Ottomans, decided to bring

Arabia into his own sphere of influence and brought forth a rival claimant to Saudi leadership as his wedge. Khalid ibn Saud (1840–41), Faisal's cousin, had been imprisoned in Egypt since Abd-Allah's capture two decades before. Faisal now became Cairo's token Saudi prisoner. Egyptian forces occupied the Najd and Hasa and directed the activities of their vassal, Khalid.

Mohammed Ali had overextended himself in many areas. The British rebuffed him in Yemen, and this reversal, compounded with the difficulty of securing the Arabian interior, caused him to quit the field in 1840. In 1843 Faisal escaped from Egypt and resumed the position of leader. The present-day Saudi family proudly refers to itself as the House of Faisal-House of Saud, for more reasons than ancestry. Faisal endeavored like his father, Turki, to restore order to the land and like his grandson, Abd al-Azis, was tough enough to curb the excesses of the bedouin. Pilgrimages could be made in safety, and agricultural and mercantile pursuits were encouraged. Faisal, perhaps because he was so conscientious himself, overestimated the selfless altruism of his sons. To the present day, effective Saudi rule is based on two determinants: first the family must be kept in order, and then the tribes.

In two decades the stability and tribal cohesion built up by Faisal were destroyed through civil wars between two of Faisal's sons, Abd Allah (1865–71 and 1875–89) and Saud (1871–75). By 1871 Saud was established in power at the cost of anarchy throughout the territory. Famine was rife, and even weak tribes became uncontrollable. The Ottomans, who had repossessed the Hejaz after Mohammed Ali's death in 1849, sniffed carrion and easily occupied Hasa and imprisoned Abd Allah, who foolishly had sought support from them. Abd Allah escaped from prison and gained power again for a period of several months, after

Imam (Chief) Abd-Allah ruled from 1814 to 1818.

This is the only known photograph of the large mosque of Hakam which encloses the Kaabah, the chief goal of the Moslem pilgrimage.

which power was returned to Saud. At Saud's death in 1875 Abd-al-Rahman (1875 and 1889–91), the younger brother of Saud and Abd Allah, announced his accession. Abd Allah regained power after one year and ruled until his death in 1889 when Abd-al-Rahman once again assumed leadership.

The Saudi preoccupation with the warring sons and brothers had distracted them to the point that they were unprepared to withstand the growing power of the Rashidis, who had been established by the Sauds in Hail to govern the northern province of Jabal Shammar. Mohammed ibn Rashid, an able administrator and general, had much of the Najd under his control when Faisal's youngest son, Abd-al-Rahman, was finally forced out of Riyadh. Exiled, he eventually settled in Kuwait with his family, among whom was his eleven-year-old son, Abd-al-Azis, founder of the modern state of Saudi Arabia. Rashid was succeeded by a son of greater vision and lesser administrative abilities; his harsh rule alienated tribes in his domain and facilitated the eventual reconquest.

In the nineteenth century in addition to the dynamics of tribal rivalries and occupation by foreign Muslim powers, Western interest in Arabia quickened because of the British desire to safeguard its Indian trade by retaining control over Arabian ports and coastal areas. French interest was aroused by French mercenaries who had fought with Mohammed Ali, and by the 1850s both France and Great Britain had consulates in Jiddah. Through the nineteenth century the British had been reluctant to interfere in land-ward political affairs. Arabia had already benefited from British interest in the Middle East when British forces stymied Mohammed Ali's activities in Yemen. A plethora of British protectorate treaties limited the future expansion of the Saudis into south Arabia. Such British alliances were actually advantageous to the Saudis because they prevented Saudi forces from dissipating their strength, although they never perceived them as such.

All political power rests ultimately with the king, who is responsible for protecting the institutions of Islam and the interests of the Islamic community, for defending the state, and for furthering the interests of the nation. Other sources of political influence are based on affiliation with the king's office and those around him.

THE REIGN OF ABD AL-AZIS (1902–53)

In 1902, at the age of twenty-one, Abd al-Azis ibn Abd al-Rahman, called by his tribesmen the patronymic ibn Saud, recaptured Riyadh with a force of less than fifty men in a dramatic dawn raid. Abd-al-Rahman, aware that his son would be a more effective leader, quickly abdicated his title of amir in favor of his son but retained the title of *imam*, which ceased to be used after his death because his son preferred secular titles. His leadership legitimized, ibn Saud engaged in successful battles with the Rashidis and their Turkish allies from Hasa and reestablished Saudi rule in the Najd. Ibn Saud was forced to acknowledge Ottoman suzerainty of the area, however, because Husein, a Hashemite installed as sharif of Mecca by the Ottomans in 1908, had captured one of ibn Saud's brothers and was holding him hostage. As soon as the boy was released, Ottoman control of the Najd was extinguished. By 1913 the Turks were eliminated in Hasa, and the territory from Kuwait to Qatar was under Saudi control.

Abd-al-Rahman had a short rule in 1902.

King Abd-al-Azis III, ibn Saud. The creation of the United Kingdom of Saudi Arabia can be said to have started one evening in 1901, when Abd-al-Azis set out from Kuwait with forty gallant comrades toward Riyadh. Before leaving for his appointment with destiny, he told his father: "You will either see me victorious or not at all."

On January 15, 1902, Ab-al-Azis scored the promised resounding victory and captured Riyadh. The retaking of this great city marks the turning point in Saudi Arabia's modern history, while the unification of the kingdom itself is an outstanding chapter in Arab history.

After over a thousand years of strife and disunity in the Arabian Peninsula, King Abd-al-Azis finally managed to create a single nation and homeland, proceeding step by step to achieve what has been described as the greatest accomplishment of any single man in this era.

THE CREATION OF THE IKHWAN AL-MUSLIMIN (MUSLIM BRETHREN)

Ibn Saud realized very early that allegiance to the House of Saud as a secular power was not sufficient to retain volatile and fickle tribesmen. The suprastructure needed was supplied in a revival of Wahhabism in which ibn Saud was an ardent believer. Bedouins, forced by nature to be ascetic, responded eagerly to imposing asceticism on others. A *hijra* (agricultural oasis settlement; pl., *hujar*) had the triple purpose of breaking down tribal allegiance (by settling a variety of tribesmen in each settlement), inculcating the tribesmen thoroughly with Wahhabi precepts, and providing reserves of ready warriors.

By 1912 there were eleven thousand Ikhwan al-Muslimin, the term used for both the settlers and the organization, settled on oases. In 1916 all bedouin tribes were ordered to join the Ikhwan and pay *zakat*. Tribal shaykhs were required to attend the school of Islamic law and religion at the mosque in Riyadh and were encouraged to remain in the town and become part of ibn Saud's court. By depriving the Ikhwan of a resident tribal leader, Ibn Saud hoped to transfer all such allegiance to himself, his movement, and the House of Saud.

WORLD WAR I

Alliances of some Arabian power groups with the Ottomans and of some with the British ultimately favored the full conquest of Arabia by the Sauds. The Rashidis allied themselves with the Ottomans, and Sharif Hussein ibn-Ali, wishing to be recognized as an independent sovereign, allied himself with the British. The British, aware of but consistently underestimating ibn Saud's growing power, attempted to enlist him in the general Arab revolt against the Ottomans. This would have meant subordinating himself to Husein, which ibn Saud admantly refused to do, and would have weakened his forces, which were as yet unready for a major foray in the Hejaz against the Ottomans. A series of negotiations between the British and ibn Saud culminated in 1916; the British recognized ibn Saud as amir of the Najd and Hasa and gave him a subsidy both to encourage his efforts against the Rashidis and to discourage an all-out offensive against Husein.

In 1916 Husein with the assistance of T. E. Lawrence ousted the Turks from the Hejaz, unwittingly smoothing the way for his enemy ibn Saud. Bolstered by Ikhwan forces, by 1917 Saudi control was extended to the outskirts of Hail, the Rashidi capital. Ibn Saud refrained from attacking the Hejaz and contented himself with consolidating the surrounding areas.

THE TAKING OF THE HEJAZ

After World War I, as a result of British and French support, Husein's sons, Abdullah and Faisal, were established as kings of Transjordan and Iraq. When Abdullah and Faisal began to negotiate with the Rashidis, ibn Saud was

The sharif of Mecca, King Husein, as he appeared during his reign as king of Hejaz (1916–1924)

As the sharif of Mecca appeared in later life

King ibn Saud with his son Saud, the future king

forced to take decisive action to avoid being encircled by Hashemite powers. In 1921 the Ikhwan seized Hail, and ibn Saud married the widow of Saud ibn Rashid, who had been murdered a year before by a cousin. He adopted her children, made peace with her relatives, and thus forestalled any further Rashidi alliance that would be conflict with his own.

A series of successful Ikhwan border raids on Transjordan encouraged Ikhwan forces to invade the interior without orders. They seized the caravan city of Jawf and massacred the inhabitants of Turayf but were finally driven south by British Royal Air Force bombers.

Ibn Saud proceeded to negotiate with the British resident minister in Iraq, Sir Percy Cox, over disputed frontiers with Iraq and Kuwait. Borders were fixed, and neutral zones, the cause of much friction in the future, were agreed on.

Ibn Saud could now concentrate his efforts on the Hejaz where Husein, a self-proclaimed king, was making himself generally unpopular by levying exorbitant taxes on the citizenry but allowing a decline of public services. The Ikhwan, obsessed with desire for the Hejaz because the holy cities were there, grew impatient and unruly. In 1924 they carried out a massacre at Taif, after which the citizens of Jiddah, not given to senseless heroics, surrendered. Ibn Saud carefully marshaled his forces for the decisive attack on the Hejaz and had one of his sons, the amir Faisal, conquer Asir as a precaution. Husein, in an attempt to gain prestige, declared himself caliph of all Muslims. Aware that after this outrage the Ikhwan could no longer be restrained, ibn Saud led them in battle. Mecca and Medina fell without massacre; the Ikhwan were content to destroy and plunder all religious manifestations deviant to their belief. The most zealous Ikhwan were quickly ordered to remote areas in the interior, and in 1926 ibn Saud was proclaimed king of the Hejaz.

The British wished to support ibn Saud, but first disagreements over frontiers shared by the Saudis and British allies and protégés had to be settled. A series of negotiations between ibn Saud and Sir Gilbert Clayton was finalized in the Treaty of Jiddah in 1927, which recognized ibn Saud's authority from the gulf to the Red Sea and set limits on his expansion. In the same year ibn Saud was crowned king of the Hejaz and Najd and its dependencies.

Frontier agreements were complicated by the ever-eager Ikhwan, who were unenthusiastic about agricultural pursuits and refused to be dissuaded from raiding Iraq. Additionally, Ikhwan extremists were discontent with the introduction of such modern devices as motor vehicles, aircraft, telephones, and telegraph. The denouement came with an Ikhwan revolt and the crushing of dissident Ikhwan at the battle of Sibila in 1929. After a period of consolidation, in 1932 ibn Saud proclaimed that the realm was to be called the Kingdom of Saudi Arabia, this establishing in no uncertain terms that in the Saudi-Wahhabi affiliation the secular arm would predominate.

TOWARD A MODERN STATE

Ibn Saud was aware that the legitimacy of his rule was based on the Wahhabi interpretation of Islam and that his role, as perceived by the *ulama* (religious scholars) was to preserve a divine nomocracy in Arabia. At the same time he had become familiar enough with the great powers to realize that a continuation of extremist religious policy would hinder the introduction of modern technology. If Arabia wished to survive, it had to modernize or face the consequence of the eternal Arabian cycle of tribal upheavals and conquest by foreign powers. The urbanized Hejazi, for example, viewed the Saudi force as another group of foreign invaders and certainly not the most sophisticated they had experienced.

Within the Hejaz ibn Saud began to walk his diplomatic tightrope between the forces of modernization and religious conservatism. In 1929 the Committee for Encouragement of Virtue and Discouragement of Vice, based on long-standing Wahhabi practice, was formed to eradicate religious sloth and such spiritually dangerous practices as smoking, drinking alcohol, and singing. At the same time, the Organic Instructions of the Hejaz were formulated, which guaranteed existing governmental institutions. The

1926 legislation established the important principle that secular law could supplement and complement the sacred sharia. Ibn Saud called a pan-Islamic conference in Mecca in 1929 to regulate pilgrimage affairs. This was an important bit of public relations to assure other Arab leaders that the holy cities were not in the hands of wild and uncouth tribesmen.

GOVERNMENT

Power had two fonts: the secular political power of ibn Saud and the religious authority of the ulama, the *mutawwiun* (missionaries), and ibn Saud. On the secular level ibn Saud began the formation of his first formal governmental system in the Hejaz. Major cities were administered by local and experienced administrators, but the most senior officials were Najdi.

The country as a whole fell into four divisions: the Najd was ruled by the crown prince, Saud; the Hejaz by Amir Faisal with the special rank of viceroy; Hasa by Abdullah ibn Jiluwi; and Asir by Amir Turki. These last two positions indicate ibn Saud's keen understanding of tribal politics and his cleverness in dealing with them. Jiluwi was a cousin and a long-time intimate and colleague, but he was also a powerful potential rival. Amir Turki was a nephew and a member of the still-powerful Sudairi clan. Ibn Saud's dedication to the extinction of tribal rivalries was so fervent that he personally entered into over twenty dynastic marriages.

Ministers of foreign affairs and finance were appointed in 1931 and 1932 respectively, a minister of defense in 1944, and a minister of interior affairs in 1951. In October 1953, shortly before his death, ibn Saud appointed the Council of Ministers under the leadership of the prime minister, Crown Prince Saud. Existing departments were made ministries, and new ones were created. The head of each ministry was a member of the council. The council had neither legislative nor executive authority. It made recommendations to the king, who alone had the power to enact law. Most of the ministries were originally established in

King Saud cuts a ribbon opening a new school in 1957. He was known for his great interest in improving the education of his subjects.

Here, left to right, *the two princes, Amir Faisal and Amir Khalid, are with the librarian of Congress, Archibald MacLeish, examining an ancient scroll containing the official genealogy of the Prophet Mohammed, through his favorite daughter, Fatima, and continuing through her husband Ali to as late as the year 1798 (twenty-six generations). This important legal and religious document is substantiated by fourteen seals, the first of which is Mohammed's.*

Two Saudian princes, future kings, visit San Francisco in 1943. Left to right: *Amir Faisal and Amir Khalid.*

the Hejaz but during the mid-1950s were transferred to Riyadh, establishing without question the location of the heart of the kingdom. The earlier ministerial experience within the Hejaz helped bring about the cultural integration of that area with the Najd.

Aware of the need for a modern military force, ibn Saud brought in advisers from various Arab countries. Because he feared political control by outsiders and also reactions from religious leaders, he tended to rely heavily on support from his sons and a peninsular Arabian, Shaykh Abdullah Sulaiman, who became minister of finance.

The system was patrimonial, but Arabians were most familiar with this kind of rule. Ibn Saud's tact, personal charm, sense of justice, and deep concern for his people mitigated the effects of his absolute monarchy. He functioned as a tribal leader and held a *majlis* every week when any citizen could approach him for help. When it became clear that great distances prohibited certain citizens from coming directly to him for assistance, he responded with a curious mixture of tribal and modern ingenuity. Instead of delegating authority, which might seem a logical solution, he expanded the postal service and telegraph systems so that citizens could continue to reach him directly. He was infuriated when he found that messages were being censored or kept from him entirely and commanded severe penalties for the offenders.

The holding of the *majlis,* an ancient tribal custom, was not altogether an altruistic device. Bedouin shaykhs perceiving him as first among equals expected him to listen to their counsel and display in their meetings tribal leadership

values developed almost a millennium before. In the old days generosity meant the sharing of one's food with the wayfarer; in the new kingdom of Saudi Arabia it meant job patronage and large sums of cash. A value necessary for survival in the desert was inappropriate in this new setting and brought the kingdom to the verge of economic ruin.

FISCAL POLICY

Almost in desperation for funds and going against the nearly xenophobic feelings of the ulama, the king in 1923 granted the first oil exploration rights to a British firm. Additional exploration rights were granted to secure more funds, and among these grants was one in 1933 to the Standard Oil Company of California. After the discovery of large oil fields in the Japal Dhahran region, the Arabian American Oil Company (Aramco) was formed. Largely because of World War II, development of the fields was relatively slow, and the annual oil revenues received by the king did not exceed 4 million dollars until after 1944. By 1948 the kingdom's annual revenue was about 85 million dollars and because of oil increased geometrically each year thereafter.

Internal development proceeded slowly. Social services were initiated, experimental agricultural projects were set up, the nation began to acquire the paraphernalia of a modern state, and new industries in addition to the ever-burgeoning oil companies were begun. But ibn Saud was "the state"; and as his health declined, his tribal methods of ruling proved inadequate to control a nation of vast wealth. Millions of riyals were wasted in graft, corruption, and conspicuous consumption by certain members of the royal family.

SOCIAL CLIMATE

By the time of ibn Saud's death in 1953 the only contented people in the kingdom seemed to be the more grasping members of the royal family and the foreigners who were cashing in on oil and on sales to the government and the royal family. For ibn Saud money had only been something to spend. In 1930 he nonchalantly and arbitrarily had chosen the rate at which his new nickel coins would be exchanged for a riyal. The king became less placid, though no more able, as his lack of administrative abilities became evident even to himself. H. St. John Philby, certainly his most loyal non-Arab friend, wrote in 1934: "Things at present are in a frightful muddle and everyone seems to be robbing the King and the government just as fast as they can and the King is helping them splendidly."

Members of the royal family who had been educated abroad returned shocked and disgusted at the waste and at the slow pace of change. To the religious leaders change was happening all too fast, and modernization and the presence of foreigners were having precisely the effect they had predicted. The effect was most noticeable among the royal family where religious laws could not reach.

Saudi workers at Aramco viewing the educational, health, and recreational facilities made available for American and other foreign workers resented religious leaders who would not permit them access to the Aramco facilities and the fact that their government did not provide similar benefits for them. Economic discontent culminated in a strike of Aramco workers in 1953. Based on the report of a royal commission that investigated the strike, the leading spokesmen of the workers were jailed and unionization forbidden.

THE "INTERLUDE" OF SAUD

All of the problems of ibn Saud's reign but few of his personal qualities were bequeathed to his son and successor, ibn Saud I (Abd-al-Azis IV) (1953–64). Ibn Saud I's first administrative assignment in the new kingdom had been the governorship of the Najd, and this may have

contributed to his disastrous rule as king. Governorship of the Najd did not require learning new ways to approach the problems of governing. Ibn Saud I relied on his father's charismatic leadership and cash to maintain tribal loyalty in the Najd and relaxed to enjoy the fruits of royal privilege and royal income.

Not having the qualities expected of tribal leaders, yet knowing no alternative, upon his accession to kingship ibn Saud I secluded himself from the citizen body and relied heavily on his advisers, many of whom, including native Saudis, were concerned only with the personal acquisition of wealth and power. Ibn Saud I paid huge sums to maintain tribal acquiescence to his rule in return for recruits for an immense palace guard, the White Army. Revenues could not match Ibn Saud I's expenditures for the tribes, subsidies to the revolutionary movement in Algeria, and his personal

King ibn Saud confers with President Franklin D. Roosevelt aboard the USS Quincy *off Egypt in early 1945.*

King ibn Saud with Winston Churchill in 1945

Ibn Saud I (Abd-al-Azis IV) ruled from 1953 to 1964.

During their 1943 visit to the United States, the Saudi princes visited the Library of Congress in Washington, D.C. They are seen here on either side of the librarian of Congress on the veranda of the Library. Left to right: Amir Faisal, Librarian Archibald MacLeish, and Amir Khalid.

King ibn Saud I as he appeared in earlier years

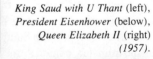

King Saud visits with President Dwight D. Eisenhower in Washington, D.C. while visiting in the United States in 1957.

King Saud with U Thant (left), President Eisenhower (below), Queen Elizabeth II (right) (1957).

follies. By 1958 the riyal had to be devalued nearly 80 percent, despite annual oil revenues in excess of 300 million dollars.

Dissatisfaction came from many sources, chief of which were a few of the more liberal princes and the sons of the rising middle class educated abroad. The rising discontent found an outlet in the nation's first daily newspaper published in 1953. Ibn Saud I's first response to the dissatisfaction was to issue a *fatwa* (royal decree) in April 1955 requiring the return of all precollege Saudis being educated abroad. Refusal would incur loss of citizenship. In an effort to discourage the formation of critical attitudes, college students abroad were forbidden to major in law, political science, or related areas. In 1956 native Aramco workers called a strike. The strike featured nationalistic and anti-imperialistic slogans. Ibn Saud I issued a *fatwa* in June 1956 forbidding further strikes under penalty of dismissal.

There were some positive accomplishments. In 1954 ministries of commerce and industry and of health were created largely at the instigation of Crown Prince Faisal.

In foreign relations ibn Saud I followed the inclinations of his father and promoted Arab unity by demanding the liberation of Palestine in cooperation with Gamal Abdul Nasser of Egypt. Saudi Arabia's ties with Egypt had been strengthened by a mutual defense pact in October 1955. Together Nasser and Saud assisted in financing an effort to discourage Jordan from joining the Western-sponsored Baghdad Pact. When the French, British, and Israeli forces invaded Egypt in 1956 as a result of Nasser's nationalization of the Suez Canal, Saud granted the equivalent of 10 million dollars to Egypt, severed diplomatic relations with Great Britain and France, and placed an embargo on oil shipments to both countries. American-Saudi relations also declined during the early years of ibn Saud I's reign.

A major reorientation of Saudi policy began in 1957 after ibn Saud I's successful visit to the United States. In a conference with President Dwight D. Eisenhower, ibn Saud I gave support to the Eisenhower Doctrine and agreed to a five-year renewal of the lease of the Dhahran Air Base.

But as Western relations improved, those with Egypt worsened. Egypt and Saudi Arabia had been drawn together because of their mutual interest in securing Arab independence from non-Arab foreign intervention. Beyond that point all similarity of objectives vanished. Nasser had deposed a king in Egypt and was encouraging revolutionary attitudes in other Arab countries. His notions of Arab unity and economic socialism were abhorrent to ibn Saud I and to many Saudis who wished to preserve an independent and capitalistically oriented kingdom. Further, the Egyptians trafficked with the Soviet Union, from whom the Saudis had declined an arms offer and to whom they denied diplomatic recognition because of their hatred of communism. The presence of large numbers of Egyptian military attachés and teachers in Saudi Arabia caused fear among the Saudis that, at the very least, unacceptable views would circulate. Saudi officials were aghast when Syria and Egypt

merged in 1958 to form the United Arab Republic. Yet the shock generated by news of the union paled before the subsequent disclosures of an alleged conspiracy by ibn Saud I to subvert the venture and to assassinate Nasser. The embarrassed senior members of the House of Saud urged ibn Saud I to relinquish power to Faisal.

On March 24, 1958, ibn Saud I issued a *fatwa* giving Faisal executive powers in foreign and internal affairs, including fiscal planning. By 1959 as a result of Faisal's initiation of an austerity program, which included a reduction of subsidies to the royal family, the budget had been balanced, currency stabilized, and embarrassing national debts resolved. Faisal increased the powers of the Council of Ministers and assumed a neutral position in Arab politics.

The reductions in the royal household budget incensed ibn Saud I and his circle; and a dispute, arising out of ibn Saud I's desire to give full control of a Hejaz oil refinery to one of his sons, made Faisal's position increasingly precarious. In January 1961 Faisal and his Council of Ministers tendered their resignations.

Ibn Saud I assumed the post of prime minister and made another brother, the progressive amir Talal, minister of finance and economy. A new cabinet was formed composed of many Western-educated commoners. There was much talk of innovative governmental moves, but none materialized. Talal, concluding that ibn Saud I had misrepresented his intentions to engage his support, departed for Cairo, taking several air force officers and their planes with him. Ibn Saud I reacted passionately and accused Nasser of being an ally of the Zionists and of trying to destroy Islam. When civil war broke out in Yemen in September 1962 and Egyptian forces arrived to support the revolutionaries against the Saudis who supported the overthrown royalist government, the destruction of the Saudi monarchy seemed a distinct possibility.

Faisal had been restored as deputy prime minister and foreign minister in March 1962 to substitute for Saud, who was in the United States for medical treatment. In October 1962 Faisal was urged by the ulama and many princes to accept the kingship, but he declined, citing his promise to his father to support ibn Saud I. Instead Faisal again became prime minister, named Amir Khalid deputy prime minister, and formed a government from among his supporters. He took command of the armed forces and quickly restored their loyalty and morale.

Consultations between Faisal and President John F. Kennedy led to promises of United States support of Faisal's plans for reform and of Saudi Arabia's territorial integrity. Diplomatic relations were reestablished with Great Britain and France, and debts to them were repaid.

Faisal's projects and the budgetary allowance necessary to modernize the armed forces meant that the king's personal income had to be cut. In March 1964 a *fatwa* endorsed by the royal family and the ulama reduced ibn Saud I's powers and his personal budget. The White Army was placed under the Ministry of Defense and Aviation, and the royal court was abolished. The response from ibn Saud I, who had been on an extended and expensive tour of Europe with a large entourage, was outrage. Ibn Saud I tried to garner support for a return to power, but the royal family and ulama held firm. On November 2, 1964, the ulama issued a final *fatwa* on the matter. Ibn Saud I was deposed, and Faisal was declared king. This decision terminated almost a decade of external and internal pressure to depose ibn Saud I and assert the power and integrity of conservative forces within the Saudi family.

THE REIGN OF FAISAL

Faisal ibn Abd al-Azis (1964-75) was the first king of Saudi Arabia to comprehend the enormity of the task of modernization and to accept total responsibility for achieving it. His first two official acts were protective, directed toward securing the nation from potential internal and external threats that could thwart development. In the first month of his reign, Amir Khalid ibn Abd al-Azis, a half-brother, was designated crown prince, thus ensuring that the succession would not be disturbed by the kind of family power politics that had nearly destroyed Saudi hegemony in the past.

Faisal reorganized the Central Planning Organization to develop priorities for economic development. The result was that oil revenues were spent on investments designed to stimulate growth.

Continually troubled by the spread of revolutionary ideas generated by foreign Arab leaders, especially by Nasser, Faisal called an Islamic summit conference in 1965 to reaffirm Islamic principles against the rising tide of modern ideologies. During 1965 Faisal traveled to Turkey, Pakistan, Iran, Morocco, and Tunisia—countries with close ties to the West—to interest other leaders in the conference. Nasser denounced Faisal's conference proposal, which Nasser referred to as the Islamic Pact, as a political maneuver aimed at uniting "reactionary" Muslim states against the modern and necessary forces of revolutionary socialism. Faisal continually insisted that his only aim was to encourage Muslim countries to assist and support one another.

Both Faisal's and Nasser's assessments of the situation were correct. Saudi Arabia had emerged in the 1960s having the revenues usually associated with nations that had undergone a sophisticated developmental process over a period of centuries. Yet Saudi Arabia remained a model of the medieval Islamic state, and Faisal had internalized the attitudes proper to a ruler of such a state. He understood his primary role, enunciated a millennium before, as protecting and securing the Dar al-Islam (territory under Islamic rule) and the well-being of the Muslim community *(umma)*. His duties also included safeguarding and supporting the *sharia* (body of Islamic law) within his land. Finally, he was to be a benevolent ruler who would strive to increase the well-

King Faisal visits with President Lyndon B. Johnson at the White House in Washington, D.C. in June 1966.

King Faisal ibn Abd-al-Azis ruled from 1964 to 1975.

being of his subjects without placing them in moral danger.

Faisal's dedication to these ideals had its roots in his upbringing in the house of his maternal grandfather, a direct descendant of Abd al-Wahhab, the eighteenth-century initiator of the revival of religious orthodoxy in Arabia. Faisal was raised in a spartan atmosphere, unlike that of most of his half-brothers, and was encouraged by his mother to develop values consonant with tribal leadership. Faisal's religious idealism did not diminish his secular effectiveness. For him political functioning was a religious act that demanded thoughtfulness, dignity, and integrity. Respect for Faisal increased in the Arab world based on the remarkable changes within Saudi Arabia, Faisal's excellent management of the holy cities, his reputation as a stalwart enemy of Zionism, and his rapidly increasing financial power.

Under Faisal's reign a massive educational program was initiated. Expenditures for education increased to an annual level of approximately 10 percent of the overall budget. Vocational training centers and institutes of higher education were built in addition to the more than one hundred twenty-five elementary and secondary schools built annually. Women's demands, increasingly vocalized, led to the establishment of elementary schools for girls. These were placed under religious control to pacify the many (including members of the royal household) who were opposed to education for women.

Health centers multiplied, and at least one was among the best in the world. Faisal instituted many qualitative changes in the governmental structure, but it remained highly centralized and basically autocratic.

In 1965 border delineations with Qatar were also agreed upon. The Continental Shelf Agreement with Iran in October of 1968 established the separate rights of Iran and Saudi Arabia within the Persian Gulf (called the Arabian Gulf in Saudi Arabia), and an agreement was reached to discourage foreign intervention there. Faisal greeted with seeming equanimity the new government formed in July 1970 in Oman by the son of the deposed sultan but tightened Saudi Arabia's security in the area. The formation of the United Arab Emirates did not receive official recognition until the settlement of the long-standing Buraymi Oasis dispute.

Saudi Arabia's largest problem within the peninsula remained the settlement of the Yemen crisis. In August 1965 Faisal and Nasser agreed at Jiddah to an immediate ceasefire, the termination of Saudi Arabian aid to the royalists, and the withdrawal of Egyptian forces. In 1965 at Harad in Yemen, Saudi Arabia and Egypt sponsored a meeting of Yemenite representatives from the opposing sides. The conference became deadlocked, and hostilities resumed after the promised Egyptian troop withdrawals did not materialize. Egyptian aircraft bombed royalist installations and towns in southern Saudi Arabia. Saudi Arabia responded by closing its two Egyptian banks, an action countered by Egypt's sequestration of all Saudi Arabian property holdings in Egypt.

Ibn Saud I, then residing in Egypt, made a personal gift of one million dollars to the Republic of Yemen and made broadcasts from Sana, Yemen's capital and from Cairo, stating his intention to return to rule "to save the people and land of Saudi Arabia." A series of terrorist bomb attacks against residences of the royal family and American and British personnel led to the arrests of a group including seventeen Yemenis accused of the sabotage. They were found guilty and were publicly beheaded in accordance with the law. Egyptian and Saudi disagreements over the area were not resolved until the Khartoum Conference of August 1967.

In the aftermath of the June 1967 war between Israel and various Arab states, the disputes between Arab states had to take a secondary position to what the Arabs called the "alien threat." Faisal's pan-Islamic pronouncements, vague in the first two years of his reign, took concrete form after the June 1967 war when an Islamic nation, Jordan, received a direct threat to its existence and that "infidel power," Israel, seized and retained Jerusalem, the third holiest city of Islam.

At the Khartoum Conference Saudi Arabia, Libya and Kuwait agreed to set up a fund equivalent to 378 million dollars to be distributed among countries that had suffered from the 1967 war. The Saudi contribution would be 140 million dollars. Jordan and Egypt were both in desperate financial positions. The monies were intended not only to ease this situation but also to buttress their political bargaining power. Egypt could no longer continue expensive commitments to the war in Yemen, and Nasser and Faisal agreed to a compromise proposed by Sudan for financial and economic pullouts in Yemen. Military aggression against Israel was not mentioned, but the conferees agreed neither to recognize nor to make peace with Israel and to continue to work for the rights of the Palestinians.

Saudi Arabian oil revenues continued to multiply. In addition to the 25 percent increase in production in 1971, gains resulted from the raising of posted prices by the Organization of Petroleum Exporting Countries (OPEC) at the Tehran meeting in February 1971. At the Beirut meeting of OPEC in March 1972 the idea of gradual nationalization of oil companies had been introduced.

Faisal, having increased his economic power, in July 1973 threatened to reduce oil deliveries if the United States did not seek to equalize its treatment of Egypt and Israel. The threat was realized during the October 1973 war between Israel and three Arab states when the Organization of Arab Petroleum Exporting Countires (OAPEC) imposed a general rise in oil prices and an oil embargo on major oil consumers who were either supporters of Israel or allies of its supporters. The embargo was a political protest aimed at securing Israeli withdrawal from occupied Arab territory and recognition of the rights of the Palestinian people.

At an Arab conference held at Algiers in November 1973 Saudi Arabia agreed with all the participants except the representative of Jordan to recognize the Palestine Liberation Organization (PLO) as the legitimate representative of the Palestinian people. Jordan's King Hussein refused to participate but was encouraged by Faisal to attend the follow-up conference in October 1974 in Rabat. At this meeting Hussein gave his reluctant agreement to the proposal that the PLO should be the negotiators with Israel over the establishment of a Palestinian entity in the territory newly occupied by Israel. In return Saudi Arabia promised Hussein 300 million dollars a year for the next four years.

Faisal's preoccupation with the Arab-Israeli conflict and the rash of revolutionary regimes near Saudi territory made him slow his pace in the development of domestic programs. Faisal's failing health, overwork, and age began to tell in his assessment of national priorities. His character and judgment, however, never failed him, and those he chose—men like amir Sultan, amir Fahd, and Shaykh Admad Zaki Yamani—carried out many of his plans after his assassination on March 25, 1975. The circumstances of Faisal's death were ironic. He was shot by a nephew, a member of the royal family whose dynasty Faisal worked so diligently to secure. The assassination occurred at a *majlis,* which Faisal had insisted on retaining.

GOVERNMENT AND POLITICS

The dynasty of the House of Saud (al-Saud) was in a stronger position in early 1976 than ever before in its history. King Khalid ibn Abd al-Azis, the new monarch, was adhering to the policies that his half-brother, King Faisal ibn Abd al-Azis, had formulated before his assassination. The primary emphasis of those policies was to promote modernization of the country without losing the many traditions incorporated in its Islamic society.

The monarchy itself is not hereditary. It is limited by the dictates of the *sharia* and designation to the throne is made by the royal family's choice, sanctioned by the ulama. This designation rests upon a consensus of support from a wide base of established Islamic traditions. Specific groups in the society must make up part of the consensus that offers legitimacy to the king: the royal family, the principal tribal leaders, the Council of Ministers, the Consultative Council, the ulama, and the armed forces. King Khalid appeared to be in full command of the loyalty of all these elements. Amir Fahd ibn Abd al-Azis, half-brother of King Khalid, formally received this consensus to perform the duties of crown prince, as in the case of the selection of the king. This occurred within hours after the death of King Faisal. In the event of the king's demise, a consensus would again be sought to confirm Fahd's success.

In the national society the integration of religion, state, and social forms continued to prevail, and the king's position continued to be the focus of all lines of power. Following traditional practices he is the head of state, the shaykh of shaykhs in the ancient pattern of Arabian social structure, the supreme religious leader, and the commander in chief of the armed forces.

King Khalid, in addition to being head of state and prime minister, is working executive head of the government.

Since the formal establishment of the kingdom of Saudi Arabia in 1932, successive kings have developed a central government to assist them in running the country.

ROYAL FAMILY, RELIGION, AND POLITICS

HOUSE OF SAUD

The political development of Saudi Arabia has been centered in the position and growth of a tribal family that had built a dynasty comparable with few others. From the meager beginnings of the Saud family, many generations ago, have emerged a country named after them and a royal family with five thousand or more living members. The descendants of a man who ruled only an Arabian city-state in the eighteenth century formed a nation-state of vast influence in the world—the kingdom of Saudi Arabia.

It was not until the mid-nineteenth century, however, that events took place that produced the predominance of the lineage of the present members of the royal family. These events concerned the bitter internal dissension that followed the assassination of Turki ibn Abd Allah (ruled

1818–34) by a family member. The members of one branch of the family, the sons of Saud ibn Abd al-Azis (ruled 1803–14), pitted themselves against Turki's sons, Faisal and Jiluwi, in a battle to determine who would rule the family. Eventually Faisal, assisted by his brother and Abd Allah ibn Thunayyan (from a third branch of the family), gained undisputed control as ruler and became the most successful leader of the family until the time of his grandson, Abd al-Azis ibn Abd-al-Rahman, in the early twentieth century.

Until that time the Saud Dynasty had two well-defined links to the past—the lineages of its founder, Mohammed ibn Saud, and that of Mohammed ibn Abd al-Wahhab, the religious leader responsible for the branch of Islam called Wahhabism. As the twentieth century began, there were three surviving branches—al-Abd Allah, al-Faisal, and al-Jiluwi—but only the al-Faisal could be noted as an important lineage.

Much confusion followed the death of Faisal in 1865, and his successor, Abd-al-Rahman (ruled 1875, 1889–91), was forced into exile in Kuwait from 1891 through 1902. This period, however, produced an important link between the Saud Dynasty and the ruling family of Kuwait, al-Sabbah. Abd-al-Rahman's son, Abd-al-Azis, who became the first king of Saudi Arabia, was only eleven years old when his father took him into exile.

Another change in the nature of the Saud Dynasty was in the notion of legitimacy that its rule was based on. Each head of the dynasty had held the title of imam, which had passed to the family after the death of al-Wahhab. Although ibn Saud was the paramount political leader after 1902, his father, Abd-al-Rahman, remained head of the dynasty and retained the title of imam until his death in 1928. The formal use of the title of imam ended with his death. Ibn Saud assumed the title of sultan in 1921 when he achieved complete victory over the Rashidis, and six years later he gave up this title to become king of the Najd and the Hejaz, forming the basis for a united kingdom under his rule within five years.

By 1932, when the kingdom was established, ibn Saud, assisted by his sons and numerous tribal leaders, had established his rule over most of the territory of present-day Saudi Arabia. He lived for twenty-one years after the creation of the kingdom and during this period personally managed most of the affairs of the country.

A prototype of a ministerial system did appear, however, as ibn Saud brought members of the royal family, leaders of the tribal families, and some non-Saudi Arabs into his Consultative Council as advisers, a body with an ancient tradition in Islamic history. This action was followed by the appointment of amir Faisal as minister of foreign affairs in 1931, and this in turn led to the creation of Saudi Arabia's first Council of Ministers in 1931. The designation of his eldest son, Saud, as crown prince in 1933 seemed to complete his plan for political stability. As ibn Saud became gradually weakened by advanced age, however, he recognized the need for a more fully developed political administration and became concerned over Saud's leadership potential. The new country would have to spend ten troubled years, however, before ibn Saud's fears were allayed.

SUCCESSION TO THE THRONE

Although Saud was personally chosen by his father to succeed him, many influential groups within and surrounding the royal family also had to take active roles. Precedents were set for a committee of senior amirs—from ibn Saud's brothers and sons—to sanction Saud's succession. He received formal support from many other members of the royal family, the senior ulama, and numerous tribal leaders. This affirmation of allegiance to a king was established as a prerequisite before he could begin his rule, as was a new king's pledge to defend the country, its religion, and its people. In effect these procedures have become a bilateral oath between the king and the ruled that if broken could bring about the deposition of the king.

If the king is deposed, the determination of his successor can be somewhat difficult. The process of succession is not based on primogeniture—the tradition in most monarchies of choosing the eldest son of the preceding ruler. Arabic traditions of succession generally dictate that the most able member of the family should be the successor, even if he is not the next oldest son.

Providing for effective succession has been limited to only three actual experiences for the royal family. The first two successions—Saud (ibn Saud I) and Faisal—were determined by ibn Saud before his death; only the succession of the king, Khalid, offers an example that could be seen as a test of the system. There are precedents to be considered in choosing a successor, and these begin with the choice of crown prince.

The country's first crown prince, Saud, was named not in the tradition of the most able but rather in an attempt by ibn Saud to create a formal process of succession, possibly based on the British system, with which he was familiar. He named his eldest surviving son crown prince and later, having second thoughts about the choice he had made, decided to establish formally a Council of Ministers of which Faisal, whom he considered his most able son, was designated prime minister in addition to being crown prince when Saud succeeded to the throne. In taking such a step ibn Saud probably intended Faisal to head the government and be responsible for all decisions during the period Saud reigned. Saud became king as ibn Saud I one month later, when his father died suddenly.

The country's first approach to dealing with succession was not entirely effective. In fact it put into office a man who was obviously unable to cope with the assigned duties and was eventually deposed. The fact that the system was still flexible enough to include the tradition of replacing a ruler who had lost consensus in favor of a family member who had gained it may indicate the present method's potential for handling crises of legitimacy.

For many reasons ibn Saud I did not maintain his original consensus for very long. Before he began his reign, many had opposed him, feeling that Faisal was the obvious choice to succeed his father. During ibn Saud I's eleven-year reign Faisal was idle until 1958 when except for a brief period he was, as his father had intended, head of the government and ruled with an authority that formerly had been reserved to the king. In late March 1964 Faisal had the king accept a decision by the royal family and the ulama that reduced ibn Saud I's powers even further. The king's royal guard was removed from his personal command and placed under the Ministry of Defense and Aviation, the royal court was abolished, and the king's income was cut in half and that of the royal family reduced sharply. From then on Faisal was in complete control of the government, and seven months later the royal family deposed ibn Saud I and proclaimed Faisal king. After the consolidation of power and authority in the monarch the divisions in the royal family were healed. This ended the attempt to formulate a primogeniture system of succession; instead there was a return to the traditional process that determines a successor by his known ability to lead and receive consensus.

Mohammed, the next oldest son of ibn Saud after Faisal, was not named crown prince by Faisal; rather, after consulting many influential groups and the committee of senior amirs, Faisal chose Khalid as the most desirable. Mohammed, as a member of the amir group, disqualified himself, establishing yet another precedent in the process of succession.

Although many observers became skeptical over this return to a traditional way of doing things, the succession of Khalid to the throne abated their fears. Within hours of Faisal's assassination on March 25, 1975, a committee of senior amirs met and left intact Faisal's plan for succession, naming Khalid king and Fahd crown prince. Renewing the precedent set by Mohammed, Nasir and Saad, both older half-brothers of Fahd, disqualified themselves. The decisions were made and announced very quickly, without the dissension among branches of the royal family that many people had feared.

The successors of ibn Saud have thus far been chosen from his surviving sons. It is probably safe to say that future kings will also be chosen from the descendants of ibn Saud, if not from his many sons then from his grandsons. There are many influential amirs, however, descendants of ibn Saud's brothers or cousins, who should not be completely discounted.

The most obvious source of future leaders is the "nephews," grandsons of ibn Saud. Many of these amirs were among the first to receive an education in the United States or Western Europe, and they have returned to play important roles in the government. For the most part they include Faisal's sons and the sons of the so-called Sudairi Seven, one of whom was Crown Prince Fahd, and exclude numerous other grandsons who have failed to become educated or contribute to the family.

Because ibn Saud's mother was a Sudairi, all of his descendants have and will continue to have connections with that family. The strongest inroads into the royal family were made by another daughter of the Sudairi family, who gave birth to seven sons by ibn Saud, all of whom have gained prominent positions as the Sudairi Seven.

The mother of the two eldest surviving sons of ibn Saud also had Sudairi connections through her father. Her first son, Mohammed ibn Abd al-Azis, is a member of the committee of senior amirs, and her second son was King Khalid.

A phenomenon that has been a tradition in the Saud Dynasty is the intermarriage of cousins, either cousins within the royal family or those already related by marriage to the royal family. A typical example of this is Saud ibn Faisal. He was born of Faisal's marriage to a woman of the Thunayyan family who was related to the royal family through ibn Saud's great-uncle Abd-Allah. Saud ibn Faisal married a daughter of King ibn Saud I, who had Sudairi connections through her father, the son of ibn Saud's first wife and a member of the Sudairi family. Therefore Saud ibn Faisal's children will have strong connections within both the Sudairi and Jiluwi families and, through their grandfather Faisal, with the al-ash Shaykh family.

The consolidation of influence and power by intermarriage, however, is only one method that the royal family of Khalid's generation has continued to use. Beginning with his generation, and certainly an important aspect in the next, are the younger amirs who have chosen to seek success in nongovernmental roles. In 1976 more than ever before, royal amirs pursued careers in business, technological fields, and the professions.

DECISION-MAKING IN SAUDI ARABIA

Although by the mid-1980s the political system in Saudi Arabia was becoming increasingly complex because of the country's attempt to develop rapidly, the procedures for making decisions remained much as they were during ibn Saud's reign. Policy was determined in the final analysis by one person, the king; its formulation depended on few other individuals. Many Saudis might be involved in formulating any single decision, but it was still the king who decided what that policy should be.

Since the legitimacy and therefore the authority of the office of the king was based on his ability to maintain a consensus among numerous factions within the country, his power was not truly absolute. This need for consensus has been a traditional feature in maintaining leadership in the Saud Dynasty and is well documented.

KING KHALID (1975–1982)

In March 1975, King Faisal was assassinated by a discontented and unstable young relative, who was subsequently executed after an extensive investigation concluded that the assassination was the act of one individual. King Faisal was succeeded by Crown Prince Khalid as king, and Prince Fahd was named crown prince and first deputy prime minister. The transition went smoothly. King Khalid empowered Crown Prince Fahd to oversee many aspects of the government's international and domestic affairs. Economic development continued under the rule of King Khalid.

With the assassination of Faisal and the efficient succession of Khalid, the process of decision-making appeared to take on some new features. Khalid clearly remained the king, the chief of state, the head of government, and the commander in chief of all military forces, but he delegated to Crown Prince Fahd considerable authority to oversee most day-to-day affairs.

Prince Sultan Salman Abdel Aziz Saud, a nephew of King Fahd was a crew member on NASA's Shuttle flight 51-G, which was in space from June 17 to June 25, 1985. (The prince is shown in this photograph of the 51-G crew, standing fourth from the left.)

During a visit to the United States, King Fahd dined with President Ronald Reagan and the First Lady, Nancy Reagan, on February 11, 1985. They are seen here at the entrance of the White House. Official White House photograph by Mary Anne Fackelman.

At the end of Khalid's first year as king, foreign observers were convinced that all prominent and influential members of the royal family were unreservedly committed to a continuation of the system of which Khalid as king was the public symbol, that is, the dominance of the House of Saud. In the opinion of those observers the several discernible groups within the royal family not only posed no threat to the unity of the House of Saud but actually strengthened the family, and there was no public evidence of dissension within the family.

The most prominent group of senior family members was that headed by Crown Prince Fahd, whose full brothers Sultan, Turki, and Naif respectively held the positions of minister of defense and aviation, vice minister of defense and aviation, and minister of interior. Amir Abd Allah, the National Guard commander, was sometimes described as the focal point of another center of influence and as one of the more important links of the House of Saud to the noble bedouin tribes.

KING FAHD (1982–)

King Khalid died of a heart attack, at age sixty-nine, on June 13, 1982, at his mountain retreat in Taif. He was succeeded by his half-brother, Crown Prince Fahd, who also became the prime minister as was the portfolio with King Khalid. Prince Abdullah, a half-brother of both King Khalid and King Fahd, was chosen as crown prince and first deputy prime minister. Defense Minister Prince Sultan, a full brother of King Khalid, became the second prime minister. Also, on June 13, King Khalid was buried in a simple funeral ceremony in a cemetery outside the capital city of Riyadh. Again the transition was smooth, and King Fahd has emphasized the continuity of Saudi policy.

THE ROYAL SOVEREIGNS OF THE KINGDOM OF SAUDI ARABIA

WAHHABI DYNASTY

Reign	Title	Ruler	Reign	Title	Ruler
1753–1766		Mohammed ibn Saud	1932–1953	King of Saudi Arabia	ibn Saud (Abd-al-Azis III)
1766–1803		Abdul Azis ibn Saud			
1803–1814		Saud the Great	1953–1964	King of Saudi Arabia	ibn Saud I (Abd-al-Azis IV)
1814–1818		Abd-Allah			
1818–1834		Turki	1964–1975	King of Saudi Arabia	Faisal
1834–1865		Faisal			
1865–1897	—Rivalry among Faisal's sons dissipates power of Saudi state; Mohammed ibn Rashid, ruler of Shamman tribes, drives Abd-al-Rahman (Faisal's son, father of ibn Saud) from Riyadh. Mohammed ibn Rashid dies.		1975–1982	King of Saudi Arabia	Khalid
			1982–	King of Saudi Arabia	Fahd
1902–1902	Sultan of Nejd	Abd-al-Rahman			
1902–1926	Sultan of Nejd	ibn Saud (Abd-al-Azis III)		**HEJAZ (HIJAZ)**	
			1916—Proclaimed an independent kingdom		
1926–1932	Sultan of Nejd and King of Hejaz	ibn Saud (Abd-al-Azis III)	1916–1924	King	Husein ibn-Ali

SAUDI ARABIA, SIMPLIFIED GENEALOGY OF HOUSE OF SAUD WITH ORDER AND DURATION OF RULE, 1976

Note: Numerous brothers of rulers have been omitted, including thirty-four brothers of King Khalid. Numbers indicate order of rule, and dates indicate period of rule.

7
The Persian Gulf Shaikdoms of Kuwait, Bahrain, Qatar, the United Arab Emirates, and the Sultanate of Oman

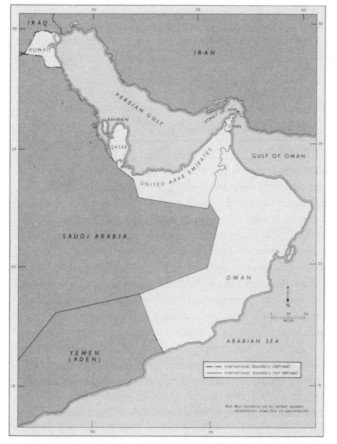

The Persian Gulf States of Kuwait, Bahrain, Qatar, the United Arab Emirates, and Oman

The Persian gulf-state thalassocracies differed from those of other cultures in that political rule did not derive from an originally oligarchic settled merchant class with a long history of urban living and urban institutions. The orientation of the gulf city-states was based on the traditional political model of the desert Arabs. Usually the dominant tribe in the area produced the city's rulers; the shaikh who ruled the tribe was the town's leader and its most affluent merchant. The shaikh's main objects were to secure peaceful internal conditions so that trading would not be dis-

rupted and to secure profits sufficient to maintain his own position. The ruler's income was derived from licenses for trade and pearl fishing, customs duties, and the taxation on such commodities as date palms, all of which were secondary in importance to the profits he made as a result of his own commercial transactions. The shaikh secured his political primacy by payments to his military forces, usually fellow tribesmen; tribute to larger and potentially troublemaking neighboring states; and a variety of subsidies to those in a position to challenge his authority. As has been the case for much of the gulf's modern history, the total income of a city was the shaikh's personal purse to dispense privately or in the public interest according to his discretion. The shaikh would attempt to placate nomadic tribes close to the city and to guarantee their cooperation, that is, to encourage their hiring for seasonal activities in the city in order to discourage them from making sporadic attacks on townspeople.

The urban institutions that existed were not the result of the ruler's initiation but were those ordained by *sharia*, Islamic law. Because of the comprehensive nature of *sharia*, certain protections and rights were available to the citizens, as were certain restrictions.

Because rule was based on the patriarchal desert model, however, the fortunes of a city depended greatly on the strength and astuteness of its ruler. When gulf trade experienced moments of decline, competition between cities was sufficiently fierce to provoke intertribal and intercity violence that usually took the form of piracy on the sea and produced internal confusion at home. If a weak ruler succeeded a strong one, he was soon overthrown; rapid changes in the ruling family were the norm.

There is evidence that, before human beings had migrated to the European geographic area, indigenous traders of the western coast of the gulf were enriching the first civilizations of the Fertile Crescent both commercially and culturally. Despite periods of decline such trade appears to have continued for millennia. Gulf trade was active during the ancient period but extraordinarily so by medieval times. In the ninth century A.D. gulf traders were traveling to

China and returning up gulf waters to Basrah, facilitating the exchange of ideas and goods among the great civilizations of the time. The peoples of the gulf coast, unlike the inhabitants of the interior of the Arabian Peninsula, had always been exposed to outside influences.

One persistent factor in gulf history is the constant rivalry between merchant states and the desire for hegemony. Another factor, destined to be more fatal to gulf trade, was the interest in the area by outsiders—Europeans, Ottoman Turks, the Wahhabis of central Arabia, and the Egyptians. After the entrance of the Europeans but before European power reached its apogee in the gulf, Hormuz, located near the Persian coast, was for a time the foremost trading center in the world. A popular Arab and Persian saying is, "If the world were a ring, Hormuz would be its jewel."

Largely because of events in Europe, the British were able to outstay the Dutch and slowly but effectively build up power in the area. Tribal animosities and rivalries and mutual piracy among gulf states served British interests, and by means of a series of exclusive treaties the British eventually pacified the gulf. In the early years of the nineteenth century new gulf powers, particularly the states of Kuwait and Bahrain, were emerging and achieving great wealth through trade. Because the states had few natural resources besides pearls and date palms, maritime activity was not only the easiest way for Arab gulf states to achieve wealth but also virtually the only way they could survive. A dramatic change in living conditions occurred, therefore, when European steamships and the associated technology began to appear in the gulf in the 1860s. Fossilized into their political positions and isolated from much foreign influence

by British protectorate treaties, the Arab gulf states went into a certain decline and were revived only with the discovery of oil.

Oil and the change in British priorities, particularly after World War II, altered the situation. The discovery of oil and the practical utilization of wealth accruing from it were initially slow processes. The Arab gulf has never been a monolith, and the individual states moved at different rates depending on custom and income. A curious reversal had taken place. Oman, Ras al-Khaymah, and Sharjah, once the most powerful and oldest established of the gulf states, became the poorest.

Once the states realized their affluent position and what it could do, the traditional welfare system built into the tribal order served them well. None of the "welfare" states emerging in the modern gulf was socialistic; yet all that had oil money were extravagant, by any standards, in spending for the benefit of their citizens. This was not an idea introduced by the West; it was rather an expansion of the tribal belief, reinforced by Islam, that no chieftain is rich if a member of his clan is poor.

PRE-ISLAMIC INTERNAL HISTORY

There is very little definite or reliable information about the gulf area from the period of the decline of the great ancient peoples until the advent of Islam. Some scanty information exists for Oman because it was the most developed area of the gulf littoral at the time. In the second century A.D. the al-Azd tribe migrated to Oman. Future imams and sultans claimed descent from the tribe and usually took "al-Azdi" as the final part of their titles. The al-Julanda were rulers of Oman at the time of the Azdite invasion and were vassals of the Persians. The al-Azd, a numerous force, ousted the Persians for a brief period. In a short time, however, the al-Julanda ruled again from the coast in cooperation with the Persians, while the al-Azd moved beyond the mountains, thus creating an internal division in the country.

Also in the second or third century there was a major migration to Tuam (Buraymi Oasis) of two Adnani tribes, the Bani Said and the Bani Abd al-Qais. The latter provided the ruling family for Qais, a major medieval gulf port.

Among the many self-proclaimed prophets who appeared after the beginning of the Islamic conquest of the peninsula was Dhut Taj Lakit ibn Malik al-Azd of Oman. Abu Bakr, the first orthodox caliph, appointed three generals to suppress the growing revolt led by Dhut. The al-Azd of Sohar and Dibbah (tribesmen of the rebellious Dhut) and the Bani Abd al-Qais fought with the generals, and a Muslim victory was achieved. The battle became known as the Day of Dibbah and became a symbol for the defeat of paganism by Islam.

The conquest of the Arabian Peninsula was the most protracted and difficult of all the Muslim conquests. In addition the Qahtanis of Oman and the mixed tribes of the

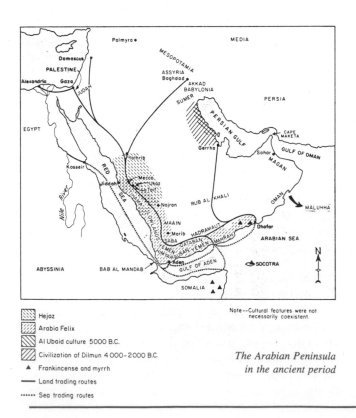

Hejaz

Arabia Felix

Al Ubaid culture 5000 B.C.

Civilization of Dilmun 4000–2000 B.C.

▲ Frankincense and myrrh

— Land trading routes

······ Sea trading routes

Note––Cultural features were not necessarily coexistent.

The Arabian Peninsula in the ancient period

gulf resented the rising power of the Hejaz. Except for Hejazi and Najdi tribes, for the most part only weak ones remained with Islam. Religious conversion of tribes outside the Hejaz had been nominal except for parts of Oman, and Islam had not become an integral part of tribal life during Mohammed's short ministry. Abu Bakr had to subdue much of Arabia before the conquest of the north began. Mohammed subdued the tribes.

It is perhaps typical of the traditional factionalism of the Arabian Peninsula that all three Islamic sects have significant numbers of adherents there, all settled by the eighth century. Because provisions had not been made for the temporal successor of Mohammed, three sects quickly emerged: the Sunni, the *shiat* Ali (Shias), and the Kharajites. Gulf areas north of Oman adhered to Sunni or orthodox Islam, which holds that the caliph (the successor) be a member of the Quraysh, the tribe of the Prophet Mohammed. Shias believe that only a descendant of the Prophet through the union of his daughter and only issue, Fatima, with his cousin Ali can be the successor. The Shias call the successor an *imam* (literally, he who sets an example). The Kharajites believe that any Muslim who meets standards of probity can be imam and that he must be elected to the position.

THE GULF DURING THE MEDIEVAL PERIOD

Arabia had become unified, but ironically it had to be virtually emptied to ensure unification. As in the great migrations of the past, Arabia in the immediate post-Mohammed period once again fed its people into the surrounding areas. Peasants were easier to control than refractory tribes, and the social structure and the agricultural assets of the conquered land outside the peninsula encouraged permanent settlements that were necessary in any case to secure Islamic rule. Thus Islamic politics moved from Arabia to Damascus and, in the period between the ministry of Mohammed and the discovery of oil, Arabia became an economic backwater except for trade on the gulf, which increased for the Arabs as the Muslim conquest expanded. Nevertheless, because Arabia was considered the homeland of the Arabs and because Mecca and Medina—Islam's holiest cities—were there, it could not be ignored. Pilgrims who made the hajj had to be afforded some protection. Furthermore, control of the holy cities gave a ruler instant prestige. The political unit that kept the Hejaz secure was usually Egyptian based, and Egypt was also the source of much of the Hejazi food supply. Islamic rulers in Damascus paid off religious leaders in Arabia who might cause trouble. Arabia became a frontier zone from which political rivals emerged. During the various struggles for religious and political supremacy in Damascus and later in Baghdad, Mecca and Medina became sites for the opposition, and both cities were virtually destroyed in the tumult that ensued. For the most part social organization in Arabia continued as it had been before Mohammed's unification.

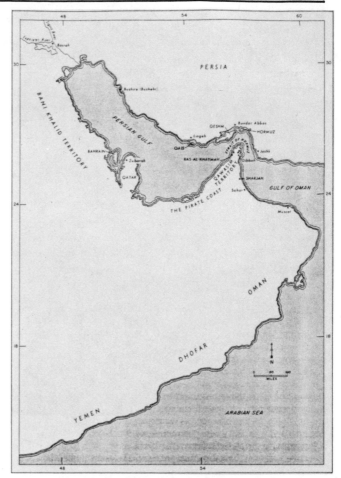

The Persian Gulf in the medieval period

During the centuries between the Islamic conquest of the gulf area and the founding of the modern polities in the eighteenth century, the focus of political activity was coastal.

The golden age of gulf shipping began in the eighth century with the establishment of the Abbasside caliphate (750-1258) in Baghdad. The general economic revival in the Middle East and Europe during the eighth century and the unification of China under the Tang Dynasty during the previous century were chiefly responsible for the acceleration of trade. But the gulf was particularly favored, over the Red Sea for instance, because of Baghdad's position due north of the gulf.

By the eleventh century the rise of the Fatimid caliphate in Egypt had siphoned off much of the gulf trade and redirected it through the Red Sea. In the late thirteenth century Hormuz became the chief center; it remained so until 1507, when it was destroyed by the Portuguese.

During the period of Hormuz's floruit, Sohar and Muscat in Oman prospered greatly from their strategic position on the Gulf of Oman near the entrance to the Persian Gulf. During the post-Islamic period, even though the main trading cities were on the Persian coast, Arabs were usually the town's rulers. When there was a strong and well-organized

Kuwait

The most influential tribe of the Utub were the al-Sabbah, but they were not the only Utub to settle Kuwait. The al-Khalifah and al-Jalahima were the next in importance; at least seven other families or clans emigrated there, though not simultaneously. The exact date of the Utbi settlement is unknown. It was certainly early in the eighteenth century but perhaps later than 1716, since neither the al-Sabbah nor the al-Khalifah were clan chiefs at the time. Until 1752 the al-Sabbah exerted mild internal leadership with the blessing of the shaikh of the Bani Khalid, Sulaiman al-Hamud. At Sulaiman's death, Sabbah ibn Jabir, ancestor of the present-day ruling house, was elected as the first recorded Utbi shaikh. There is much discussion about the reason Sabbah is remembered as the first of the Utbi shaikhs, since desert Arabs are particularly gifted at remembering genealogy and can usually trace a line for many generations.

In 1766 an Utbi settlement was established by the al-Khalifah at the short-lived city of Zubarah in Qatar. At the time of the al-Khalifah settlement on Qatar, nearby Bahrain was under the suzerainty of Shaikh Nasr al-Madhkur, an Omani Arab who ruled from Bushire on the Persian coast. Hostilities between Bushire and the Utbi-held areas led to attacks by Nasr on Zubarah in 1778 and 1782. In retaliation a joint attack by the al-Sabbah and al-Khalifah netted them Bahrain in 1783, a capture that obliterated Persian influence from the Utbi sphere of influence and gave the Utub access to the richest pearl beds of the gulf while providing a midway point for their increasing mercantile activities.

Kuwait's second ruler, Abd Allah al-Sabbah, succeeded his father in 1762. Abd Allah's long and prosperous reign, which lasted until his death in 1812, set patterns for Kuwait's future political and social development that prevailed until the exploitation of oil and in some cases after it. Neither the Ottomans in Iraq nor the Persians were strong enough to interfere with Kuwait's rising mercantile power in the eighteenth and the early part of the nineteenth centuries. Shaikh Mubarak al-Sabbah al-Sabiah (reigned 1896-1915) had the prescience to realize that the Ottomans would soon be a substantial threat to his shaykhdom and so in 1899 signed an agreement with the British whereby Great Britain assumed responsibility for Kuwait's foreign affairs and for its protection from foreign powers, in exchange for which Mubarak agreed to have no direct relations with foreign powers and not to cede them any land by sale or lease. Until 1946 there were no changes of substance in the agreement.

Bahrain already had an extensive and turbulent history by the time it was captured by the Utub from Kuwait and Zubarah. The al-Khalifah initially ruled Bahrain from Zubarah but established themselves permanently in Bahrain between 1796 and 1798.

In the late eighteenth and early nineteenth centuries it appeared that every power in the gulf was claiming Bahrain. Ruled first by the Bani Abd al-Qais and then successively by the Umayyads, Abbassides, Persians, Portuguese, and southern Omani Arabs, there were many to

Persian government, they paid tribute; otherwise they ruled quite independently.

THE FOUNDING OF THE MODERN GULF STATES IN THE EIGHTEENTH AND NINETEENTH CENTURIES

KUWAIT AND BAHRAIN

While the British were relocating their trading posts and solidifying their relationship with Persia, the gulf Arabs were involved in a highly turbulent period of mass migrations to the north and central parts of the gulf, local wars, and civil war in Oman. An unusually long drought that began in 1722 and the accompanying famine in the Alflaj region of Najd in central Arabia precipitated a major migration of Arab tribes of the Adnani-Anayzah confederation, including the Utub (adjective, Utbi), to the north coastal lands of the gulf. The area was under the domination of the Bani Khalid, whose suzerainty extended from Basrah in the north inland to the eastern part of Najd and south beyond al-Hasa to Qatar.

The Utub were well received, and they settled at a small town they began to call Kuwait, the diminutive of the Arabic *kut,* a fortress built near water.

dispute al-Khalifah claims. Claims were confused because of changing nomenclature. Until early in the sixteenth century Bahrain was a geographic entity that included not only the present-day archipelago but also the Arab gulf coast from Basrah to the Strait of Hormuz.

Because of the repeated acts of piracy by the Qawasim (adjective, Qasimi), which encouraged other Arab shaikhdoms to join the fray, the British made a concerted attack (their third) against Ras al-Khaymah, the headquarters of the Qawasim, in 1819. In 1820 Bahrain signed the General Treaty of Peace with the British, agreeing not to engage in piracy unless they were in a declared state of war. The treaty set the precedent for other states to sign, states that were inclusively referred to as the Trucial Coast until their independence in 1971.

Ottoman involvement in the Arabian Peninsula, usually nominal and concentrated in the Hejaz, became more intense when the Sublime Porte (the government of the Ottoman Empire), fearing the growing strength of the Wahhabi incursions, dispatched its vassal, Mohammed Ali Pasha of Egypt, to subdue the Wahhabis in the eastern part of the peninsula. As the Ottomans increased their activity in the area, they again put forth claims to Bahrain, in 1870 and 1874. Ottoman suzerainty in the gulf could only mean a diminution of British power there. For the benefit of both British and Bahraini interests, treaties were signed in 1880 and 1892. Shaikh Isa bin Ali al-Khalifah agreed, in a treaty similar to that which Britain had signed with Kuwait, not to dispose of Bahraini holdings without British consent and not to establish relationships with foreign powers without British agreement. Acting for the Bahrainis, in 1913 the British signed a convention with the Ottomans ensuring Bahrain's independence as a sovereign state. In 1916 a British agreement with Abd al-Azis, future king of Saudi Arabia, ensured that he would not attempt to conquer Bahrain.

KUWAIT

Although the title of amir was formally sanctioned in 1961

Amir Shaikh Abdullah ruled Kuwait from 1950 to 1965 and during that time was responsible for the gradual modernization of the country.

The amir of Kuwait, His Highness Shaykh Sabbah al-Salim al-Sabbah, and at his right is the crown prince and prime minister, His Highness Shaykh Jabir al-Ahmad al-Jabir al-Sabbah.

The amir of Kuwait entertaining his guest, the shaykh of Qatar on a visit to the Seif Royal Palace

The Clock Tower of the Seif Palace, the official residence of the amir

when the country became fully independent from the United Kingdom, the al-Sabbah Dynasty had maintained continuous rule within the country since 1756.

The monarchy in Kuwait is based on the concept of a traditional hereditary amirate. Succession must be accomplished by the selection of a shaikh from the descendants of the seventh ruler of Kuwait, Shaikh Mubarak al-Sabbah al-Sabiah. Rule is limited by the dictates of *sharia*—the sacred body of Islamic law—and, in choosing a successor to the amir, the nominee of the amir must be approved by a majority vote of the National Assembly. In 1966 the Assembly approved the choice by amir Sabbah al-Salim al-Sabbah of Shaikh Jabir al-Ahmad al-Jabir al-Sabbah.

The foremost groups that must be accommodated in carrying out the decision-making process are the royal family, the principal tribal leaders, the important merchant families, the *ulama* (religious scholars), and the senior military officers. Amir Sabbah appeared to enjoy the loyalty of all these elements. The prestige and power of the al-Sabbah family line depended not only on the family's noble lineage but also—and perhaps of greater significance—on the fact that from the outset the revenues from oil production have been paid to the head of the family.

In the early twentieth century events took place that produced the predominance of the lineage of the present leaders of the royal family. Two sons of Mubarak, Jabir II (reigned 1915–17) and Salim (reigned 1917–21), dominated the affairs of the royal family as well as the domestic affairs of the country. From their relatively stable positions of influence and power within the al-Sabbah family they created a situation in which their successors could be chosen only from among their descendants. Although Mubarak had other sons, it seemed unlikely that a ruler would be chosen from their descendants.

The royal family of Kuwait is based on these two sons of Mubarak, and the two important branches of the family derive their names from them: the al-Jabir branch and the al-Salim branch. Salim's successor in 1921 was Jabir's son Ahmad, and the intention of the family from that time forward has been to alternate the rule between the two branches. This is what occurred when Salim's son Abdullah succeeded Ahmad in 1950. These two branches of the royal family are sometimes referred to as "the cousins," and politics in Kuwait revolves around their activities.

When Abdullah al-Salim al-Sabbah (also known as Abdullah III) began his rule in 1950, the country had begun to realize an extended period of prosperity through increasing oil revenues, and his attempts to modernize the country eventually led to the renegotiation of Kuwait's protectorate treaty with the United Kingdom. By 1961 oil revenues almost thirty times greater than they had been in 1950, the basis for modern governmental and legal systems laid by Abdullah, and a public welfare system based on the British model all provided the foundation for a smooth transition to full independence and further modernization of the country under the guidance of the al-Sabbah family.

FULL INDEPENDENCE AND THE REIGN OF AMIR ABDULLAH

The first eleven years of Shaikh Abdullah's reign witnessed a gradual process of growth and modernization, highlighted by rapid progress in the fields of education and social welfare. The amir intended to promote parliamentary development by way of constitutional rule by the monarchy.

On August 26, 1961, Amir Abdullah ordered the election of a twenty-member constituent assembly to draft the country's first permanent constitution. This group completed its work within a year; and on November 11, 1962, the amir promulgated the final document.

KUWAIT UNDER AMIR SABBAH (1965–)

Abdullah died on November 24, 1965, and was succeeded by his brother, Shaikh Sabbah. The alternation of successive rulers between the two major branches of the family was broken. Sabbah, the twelfth ruler of Kuwait, was seen as a compromise choice within the family, however, because he was older and was highly respected by the traditional groups in Kuwait. The transition of authority was quickly accomplished, and the al-Jabir branch of the family was placated by the choice of Shaikh Jabir al-Ahmad al-Jabir al-Sabbah as the country's new prime minister.

In early 1966 Amir Sabbah chose Jabir to be his heir apparent, and in May 1966 the nomination received unanimous approval in the Assembly. This action completed the process of succession.

The first major challenge to the new government occurred during the June 1967 war when labor unions went on strike, accusing the government of not supporting the Arab states and the Palestinians. The crisis was soon resolved, however, when Kuwait took a leadership role at the League of Arab States (Arab League) Summit Conference, held in Khartoum in August and September 1967. Kuwait offered financial assistance to those Arab states involved in the war (called the confrontation or front-line states) to promote economic recovery. The royal family had been a strong supporter of the Palestinian groups and, from 1967 into the mid-1970s, contributed massive amounts of aid to their efforts.

Although the regime was striving to maintain cordial relations with Western nations, during the June 1967 war Kuwait joined the other Arab oil-producing states in stopping the flow of oil to the West. Shortly thereafter, however, the British announced their intention to withdraw from the gulf-states by the end of 1971 and specifically noted that the Kuwaiti-British agreement would end on May 13, 1971.

During the October 1973 war Kuwait's leaders acted to prevent criticism by the Assembly of nonsupport of the Arab side in the war. Kuwaiti troops fought on the Suez Canal battlefront against Israel, and Amir Sabbah called for an emergency meeting of the Organization of Arab Petroleum Exporting Countries (OAPEC) to determine a united policy for the use of the "oil weapon" against Western states supporting Israel.

Although in early 1974 a participation agreement with Britain for a 60 percent share in ownership of the oil-producing companies met opposition in the Assembly by those who demanded "100 percent of the oil or nothing," the fact that the 60 percent share gave the state controlling interest convinced enough deputies, and the agreement was ratified in May 1974. In December 1975 Kuwait became the sole owner of the Kuwait Oil Company (KOC).

Amir Sabbah dissolved the Assembly by decree on August 29, 1976, ending the fourteen years of parliamentary experimentation in Kuwait.

The amir's actions, which included suspending a number of constitutional articles and clamping down on the press, were not within the authority reserved to him in the 1962 constitution. His actions, however, were reportedly received with enthusiasm by many Kuwaitis, and many of the traditional leaders thought them long overdue. Stating that the measures were only "a pause for reflection on our path to democracy."

Amir Sabbah also decreed on August 29 that the prime minister and the Council of Ministers would resign immediately and that Shaikh Jabir should form a new government with additional authority to carry out the legislative functions of the state. On September 6, 1976, Shaikh Jabir announced the formation of a new cabinet that included seven members of the royal family out of a total of eighteen—an increase of three new ministerial posts. One of the newly created posts, Ministry of Legal and Legislative Affairs, was filled by Shaikh Salman ibn Duaij Sabbah. This ministry was seen by observers as the governmental organ responsible for the legislative functions of the dissolved Assembly.

The amir's government is in complete control of the country's foreign and domestic affairs. Amendments were proposed by a constitutional committee, and reports indicated that elections for a new assembly might be called. Attempts were being considered to placate the non-Kuwaiti community by extending the right to become a Kuwaiti citizen to more persons and increasing the community's participation in the welfare system. The future direction of political development in Kuwait seemed unclear, but most observers believed that the country would retain a constitutional, parliamentary monarchy and begin another phase of governmental experimentation.

GOVERNMENT STRUCTURE

The office of the amir of Kuwait, as established by a decree when the country became fully independent in 1961 and as defined by the constitution, dominates government. Ministries and civil servants are placed under a rigid system of central control directed by the amir and his heir apparent, who is also the country's prime minister. On January 1, 1978, Amir Sabbah, head of state was succeeded by Shaikh Jabir, the heir apparent.

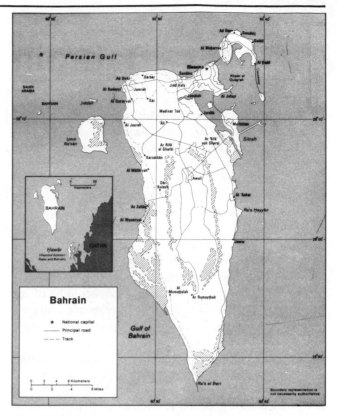

Map of Bahrain

His Highness Shaykh Sulman bin Hamed al-Khalifah ruled Bahrain from 1942 to 1961.

The crown prince, His Excellency Shaykh Isa bin Sulman al-Khalifah, became the ruler of Bahrain in 1961.

BAHRAIN

The country's ruler in 1985 was Shaikh Isa bin Sulman al-Khalifah, who had become the head of the al-Khalifah family on the death of his father, Shaikh Sulman bin Hamed al-Khalifah, in 1961. Shaikh Isa, who was born in 1933, was the tenth al-Khalifah ruler of the Bahrain archipelago; when Bahrain secured its independence from British protection and suzerainty on August 14, 1971, Isa became the first amir of Bahrain.

In late 1985 the al-Khalifah continued to dominate the government and the society. Isa's brother, Shaikh Khalifah bin Sulman al-Khalifah, was prime minister and head of government; Isa's eldest son, Shaikh Hamed bin Isa al-Khalifah, was defense minister and heir apparent. Seven other members of the royal family served in the fifteen-member cabinet.

The paramount family among the noble bedouin tribes from the interior of the Arabian Peninsula who in 1783 expelled the Persians from the islands, the al-Khalifah by the late nineteenth century had adopted a form of hereditary succession. Unlike most Arab monarchies, which select the heir apparent from among several able males within the royal family, the al-Khalifah succession is based on primogeniture. Since the rule of Shaikh Ali bin Khalifah al-Khalifah (1868–69) each ruler has been succeeded by his eldest son. A royal decree based on the consensus of the family leaders could designate someone other than the eldest son as the heir apparent, but learned foreign observers believed that the person designated would be of the ruler's immediate family, probably a brother or another son of the ruler. The 1973 constitution specifies that future rulers must be from the lineage of Amir Isa.

The political stability and relative economic prosperity of the royal family and Bahrain were fixed by the three men who ruled from 1869 to 1961: Shaikh Isa bin Ali al-Khalifah (1869–1932), his son Shaikh Hamed (1932-42), and his grandson Shaikh Sulman (1942–61), the father of Amir Isa. During this period the various shaikhs signed treaties of protection with Great Britain, granted oil concessions to foreign companies, and laid the groundwork for the government that was formed after independence. Bahrain was the first Arab state to benefit from the discovery of oil (1932), the first to institute general and free education and public health services (1925), and the first to experience serious domestic unrest (in the 1950s). By the mid-1970s Bahrain had peaked as an oil producer, and its relatively small production was expected to decline sharply during the 1980s. Its economic future and hence its ability to sustain a variety of social welfare programs depend on a continued expansion of refining and shipping capacities and of Bahrain's role as an entrepôt and financial commercial center.

QATAR

The withdrawal of the al-Khalifah from Zubarah to Bahrain decreased their power in Qatar, although the al-Khalifah returned for a short period in the nineteenth century and always kept close contact with Qatar. The most important clan in Qatar before the advent of the al-Khalifah were the al-Thani, descendants from Thani ibn Muhammad ibn Thamir ibn Ali of the Bani Tamim, a large Adnani clan. Tradition holds that ancestors of the al-Thani migrated from Najd and settled chiefly in eastern Qatar at the Jibrin Oasis late in the seventeenth century. They eventually moved to Doha (al-Dawhah), the present-day capital. Apparently the

al-Thani were subject to the al-Khalifah until Muhammad bin Thani, shaikh of Doha, began to seek autonomy from them. The al-Thani were, however, powerless against the al-Khalifah until Ottoman influence increased in the eastern gulf. The Ottomans were not concerned with direct rule of the states, realizing that such an attempt would net them little, but they did wish to establish a nominal suzerainty because of the strategic military position of states along gulf waters.

In 1872 the al-Thani became independent of the al-Khalifah when Shaikh Muhammad bin Thani became a *qaim-maqam* (Ottoman provincial ruler). Muhammad was succeeded by his son Qasim (reigned 1876-1913), who had a great vision for Qatar's future and for a time became very influential in the peninsula. Qasim's son Abd Allah (reigned 1913-49) attempted to continue the peninsular policies of his father and also remained under the tutelary direction of the Ottomans, but in 1916 he signed a treaty with Great Britain that was virtually identical with those signed by Kuwait and Bahrain.

MODERN QATAR

The approximately three hundred adult males of the al-Thani ruling family continue to dominate the Qatari society. The broader al-Thani tribe was estimated to number twenty thousand, perhaps more than half of the indigenous Qatari population. Qataris were bedouin from Najd in the interior of the Arabian Peninsula who came to the Qatar Peninsula in search of forage for their animals. Some continued their nomadic existence; others settled around wells to cultivate date palms and other crops, and some took up fishing. Doha (al-Dawhah) became a small trading center but did not develop the entrepôt business and the importance of such gulf ports as Bahrain, Dubai, and Kuwait City.

The discovery of oil in 1940 and the beginning of its commercial exploitation in 1949 doomed the traditional pattern of existence. The oil industry, unhampered by local constraints, developed much faster than the rest of the economy. Wage scales were set in other countries, not locally. Higher pay in the oil fields and subsequently in trade, construction, and government employment attracted workers from lower paying traditional pursuits in Qatar and from other countries. The economy was rapidly restructured, and economic growth was paced primarily by the flow of oil revenues.

By 1976 oil revenues made the country one of the world's richest in per capita terms, but income distribution was far from equal. There were extremes of poverty and wealth. The government's social welfare programs provided free schooling, free health care, and subsidized food, utilities, and housing that eased the lot of the poorest, although citizens fared better than expatriates.

In a 1916 treaty with Great Britain, Qatar agreed not to enter into any relations with foreign governments without British consent. In return Great Britain agreed to protect

Qatar in its geographical setting in the Arabian gulf

Shaykh Khalifah (right) *during a visit to Kuwait in 1953 to meet with Shaikh Abdullah.*

His Highness Shaykh Khalifah bin Ahmad al-Thani, the amir of Qatar

His Highness Shaykh Ahmad bin Khalifah al-Thani, the heir apparent (crown prince), is the minister of defense and commander in chief of the armed forces of Qatar.

The amir appears on many commemorative stamps of his country.

Qatar from all attacks from the sea and to offer its good offices for negotiations in the event Qatar was attacked by land. Technically the 1916 treaty and a subsequent one signed between the two countries in 1934 pertained only to foreign relations. In fact Great Britain exercised considerable influence over Qatar's internal politics.

In 1968 Great Britain announced its intention of withdrawing from military commitments east of Suez, including those in force with Qatar, by 1971. Anticipating the country's complete independence, the ruler of Qatar issued a written provisional constitution in April 1970. The constitution, which in late 1976 remained in force though still provisional, included provisions for modern state administration in the form of a governmental ministry system, which reduced and consolidated the more than thirty departments into ten ministries. The constitution also provides for a very limited extension of political participation and decision-making. In the realm of foreign relations the constitution committed Qatar to joining Bahrain and the Trucial Coast states in forming the proposed Federation of the Arab Amirates. The original federation became a moot issue when, in large part because of mutual rivalries and suspicions, Bahrain and Qatar decided not to join. In August 1971 Bahrain proclaimed its independence; Qatar followed suit on September 1. The Trucial Coast states eventually united to form the seven-member United Arab Emirates (UAE).

THE RULING FAMILY AND THE SUCCESSION OF SHAIKH KHALIFAH BIN HAMAD AL-THANI

In the mid-1980s the al-Thani ruling family comprised three main branches: the Bani Hamad, headed by Khalifah bin Hamad al-Thani (reigned 1972–); the Bani Ali, headed by Ahmad bin Ali al-Thani (reigned 1960-72); and the Bani Khalid, headed by Nasir bin Khalid al-Thani (the minister of commerce and economics in 1976).

Ahmad had succeeded his father, Ali bin Abdullah al-Thani (reigned 1949–60), as Qatar's ruler, but neither had any particular interest in supervising daily government. Thus somewhat by default those duties had been assumed, beginning in the 1950s, by Ahmad's cousin Khalifah, the heir apparent and deputy ruler. By 1971 Khalifah not only had served as prime minister but also had headed the ministries or departments of foreign affairs, finance and petroleum, education and culture, and police and internal security.

On February 22, 1972, with the support of the al-Thani family, Khalifah assumed power as ruler of Qatar. Western sources frequently refer to the event as an overthrow, a takeover, even a bloodless coup d'etat. The Qataris, at least officially, regarded Khalifah's assumption of full power as a simple succession. This was because the al-Thani family notables had declared Khalifah the heir apparent on October 24, 1960, and it was their consensus that Ahmad should be replaced.

The reasons for the transfer of power are not entirely clear. Khalifah has reportedly stated that his assumption of power was intended "to remove the elements which tried to hinder [Qatar's] progress and modernization." Khalifah has consistently attempted to lead and control the process of modernization caused by the petroleum industry boom and the concomitant influx of foreigners and foreign ideas so that traditional mores and values based on Islam could be preserved. Khalifah and other family notables were known to have been troubled by financial excesses on the part of many members of the al-Thani family. Ahmad was reported to have drawn one-fourth, and the entire al-Thani family together between one-third and one-half, of Qatar's oil revenues in 1971. The new ruler severely limited the family's financial privileges soon after taking power.

GOVERNMENT PROCESS AND CONSTITUTION

Qatar is governed by a regime that generally resembles a traditional monarchy. Because of the modernization process it probably is in some stage of transition, but to what is not yet clear. Qatar is a unitary state; it has no subnational political units possessing inherent authority. Municipal councils (in Doha, al-Wakrah, al-Khawr, Thakhira, al-Rayyan, and Umm Salal), however, plan their own development programs while remaining directly responsible to the Ministry of Municipal Affairs. Sovereignty is, according to the constitution, vested in the state, but to all intents and purposes it is vested in the head of state, or ruler. Although the ruler is supreme in relation to any other individual or institution, his rule is not in practice absolute.

Rule of Qatar is hereditary within the al-Thani family, but it is not automatically passed from father to son. Instead the ruler is designated by the consensus of family notables. Once a ruler loses that consensus, he will be replaced, as was illustrated in the transfer of power from Ahmad to Khalifah. A Qatari ruler is also guided, and to some degree constrained, by the ethics of Islam—particularly by the strictures of Wahhabi Islam—which emphasize fairness, honesty, generosity, and mutual respect. Islamic religious and ethical values are applicable both to the ruler's personal life and to his conduct of the amirship. Thus the ruler must retain the support of the religious community.

The state political organs include the ruler, the Council of Ministers, and the advisory council. The ruler makes all major executive decisions and legislates by decree. The 1970 constitution institutionalized the executive-legislative process, in effect formalizing the supremacy of the ruler. The more important of the ruler's duties enumerated in the constitution include convening the Council of Ministers, ratifying and promulgating laws and decrees, commanding and supervising the armed forces, appointing and dismissing senior civil servants and military officers (by decree), and reducing or waiving state penalties (also by decree). Finally, the constitution provides that the ruler possesses "any other powers with which he is vested under this provisional constitution or with which he may be vested under the law." This means, in short, that the ruler may extend or modify his own powers by personal decree.

The constitution also provided for a deputy ruler, who was to assume the post of prime minister. The prime minister was to formulate government programs and exercise final supervisory control over the financial and administrative affairs of government. Although Khalifah was the heir apparent and the prime minister concurrently, the constitution did not specify that the post of prime minister must be held by the heir apparent. As of March 1981 no heir apparent to Khalifah (who was born in 1932) had been designated. Khalifah retained the post of prime minister when he became ruler.

Qatar sends students abroad for university education and, when they return, they are able to fill many of the higher administrative posts. Having been exposed to relatively liberal ideas and philosophies, returning university-educated students might become dysfunctional in the Qatari system because of impatience with the rigid, albeit paternalistic, rule of Khalifah and the al-Thani family notables.

A major demonstration, culminating in a general strike, occurred in April 1963. The incident began with an altercation between one of Ahmad's nephews and a crowd that was celebrating the proposed union of Egypt, Syria, and Iraq. A national unity front was formed and made several demands, which included restricting royal privilege, ending employment of foreigners by the state bureaucracy, establishing social welfare facilities, legalizing labor unions, and instituting municipal councils composed at least partly of elected members. The demonstrations were centered in al-Khawr, which some al-Thani family members reportedly wanted attacked by army artillery. Ahmad and Khalifah prevented such a reaction but also refused to accede to the demands. The incident involved discontent with, or resistance to, the primacy of the ruling family not by the masses but by non-al-Thani village elites (many of whom were employed by the oil companies). To what extent this element of the Qatari population constituted a threat to the al-Thani regime after several years of relatively enlightened rule by Khalifah was unknown.

The president of the United Arab Emirates and ruler of Abu Dhabi, Shaykh Zayid bin Sultan al-Nuhayan.

Political parties and labor unions were prohibited in Qatar in 1976, although workers' committees, which attempted to settle grievances by means short of collective bargaining, were permitted. Most Qatari citizens were apparently satisfied with the social welfare programs of the ruler and had few grievances.

At least two revolutionary groups, the National Liberation Front of Qatar and the Organization for the National Struggle of Qatar, were reported to be operating in Qatar. Observers have also noted that the pan-Arab, nationalist, and Socialist (but anti-Communist) Baath party had an organized branch in Qatar as late as 1975, but their impact appeared to be insignificant. However, so long as there is a gap between the living standard of the minority of indigenous citizens and the majority of expatriate workers, and particularly if that gap continues to widen, the workers will probably provide the most fertile ground for internal radical ideological threats to the established regime.

UNITED ARAB EMIRATES

Between the mid-seventeenth and mid-eighteenth centuries Portugal, which had been the dominant European commercial and naval power in the Persian Gulf area since about 1500, was displaced by Great Britain as part of the surge of expansionism in which the British established their empire in India. In the gulf region British interests were primarily commercial and strategic—trade and naval stations for security of the sea route to India. The coast of the United Arab Emirates (UAE), for about two hundred miles along the Persian Gulf from the town of Abu Dhabi northeast to the tip of the peninsula jutting into the Strait of Hormuz, was known as the Pirate Coast, harassed both by European and by seafaring Arab marauders. With the rise of the Islamic Wahhabi movement in the Arabian Peninsula in the early nineteenth century, Arab seaborne depredations increased. In response Great Britain conducted punitive operations in 1806, in 1809 and, notably, in 1818. A treaty for suppression of piracy and the slave trade was concluded in 1820 between Great Britain and the Arab tribal shaikhs, and for a time a strong British naval squadron was based at Ras al-Khaymah. Intertribal sea and land raiding again broke out, however, and Great Britain in 1835 negotiated a successful and lasting maritime truce with the shaikhs,

who, in the further agreements of 1839 and 1847, undertook to prohibit slave traffic in their vessels and agreed to British enforcement of this prohibition.

This long series of treaties and agreements climaxed in May 1853 in the Treaty of Maritime Peace in Perpetuity between Great Britain and the Arab tribal rulers of what then became known as the Trucial Coast or the Trucial Oman. By consensus—the traditional, usually difficult, but most effective and necessary mode of joint action among the Arabs—the shaikhs, unable to trust one of themselves, entrusted an outsider, Great Britain, to supervise and enforce this maritime peace and to adjudicate alleged violations. Great Britain, in turn, undertook to perform this enforcement and to secure the Trucial Coast shaikhdoms against external attacks. Great Britain refrained from outright seizure or colonization of the inhospitable coast and from interference in the internal affairs and disputes of the shaikhs ashore. By the late nineteenth century, however, when France, Germany, and Russia began showing interest in the gulf area, the British imperial preeminence effectively established by the treaty of 1853 was strengthened further by identical, separate treaties between Great Britain and each of the Trucial Coast rulers. These prohibited the sale or disposal of any territories to any party except Great Britain and in effect gave the British control of the foreign relations of these states.

British control of the Persian Gulf in World War II was of major strategic importance to the Allied powers, although bases and stations in the Trucial Coast states had only a supporting role to the large Allied logistical installations at Abadan and other Iranian ports on the opposite side of the gulf. After the war Great Britain maintained a joint task force in the Trucial Coast area in continuation of its earlier obligations, which were unchanged. As part of the postwar adjustment period, however, and with a view to an eventual federation or union of the small shaikhdoms, Great Britain in 1951 set up the Trucial States Council of the seven rulers to meet at least twice annually under the chairmanship of the British political agent at Dubai.

As a result of changes in policy the British government in early 1968 announced that it would withdraw its force and terminate its special positions and obligations in the gulf by the end of 1971; in fact it did so. Representatives of Bahrain, Qatar, and the seven Trucial Coast states met in February 1968 and on March 30 announced the provisional formation of the Federation of the Arab Amirates. This arrangement did not last long, however, because of various boundary disputes, old dynastic quarrels, and inability to agree on details of precedence and organization. Bahrain and Qatar chose to remain separate and independent. Six of the shaikhdoms formed the UAE and adopted its provisional constitution on December 2, 1971; the seventh, Ras al-Khaymah, acceded to the union in February 1972. (Although the name of the new country is usually given as United Arab Emirates, the member units are referred to here as amirates or as shaikhdoms.)

THE FRAMEWORK
FOR THE FEDERATION

The first written constitution ever for any of the Trucial Coast states was signed on July 18, 1971, by Abu Dhabi, Dubai, Sharjah, Ajman, Umm al-Qaywayn, and Fujayrah. It marked the inauguration of a constitutional experiment on December 2, 1971, when an independent federation, the United Arab Emirates (UAE), was proclaimed established under the Provisional Constitution of the UAE. Ras al-Khaymah, the seventh member of the UAE, joined the federation on February 1, 1972.

The provisional charter, which was valid for five years, was to have been superseded by a permanent constitution in December 1976. On November 28, 1976, however, the rulers of the seven shaikhdoms formally extended the provisional constitution for another five years, mainly because many of the existing constitutional provisions had yet to be put fully into effect. For these shaikhdoms constitutional government was still a revolutionary concept, the acceptance of which for practical application was believed possible only through a long period of transition.

The constitutional framework provides for the separation of powers into the executive, legislative, and judicial branches. Additionally it separates legislative and executive powers into federal and local jurisdictions. Certain powers are expressly reserved for the central government, residual powers being exercisable by the individual shaikhdoms.

The separation of powers remained nominal in that the Supreme Council of Rulers—the Supreme Council for short—continued to function as the highest federal authority in executive and legislative capacities. Narrowly the executive branch consists of the Supreme Council, the Council of Ministers (the cabinet), and the presidency. The council is composed of the rulers of the seven amirates. The Chairman of the Supreme Council is automatically the president of the UAE and the head of state. The council elects from among its members a chairman and vice-chairman, who serve for a term of five years. Its responsibilities include formulation of general policy; ratification of federal laws and decrees, including those relating to annual budget and fiscal matters; ratification of international treaties and agreements; and assent to the appointment of the

Oman has been a traditional shipping and trading partner with the United States. In 1840 King Said ibn Sultan sent Ahmad ibn Na'man to New York City in a show of friendship.

prime minister and Supreme Court judges.

The rulers make decisions by a simple majority except on substantive issues; in that case a majority of five, including the votes of Abu Dhabi and Dubai, is mandatory. This requirement is in deference to the weighty role that the richest amirates were expected to play in the federation.

As it entered the 1980s, the UAE was on a steady course toward the goal of federalization. The amalgam envisioned in the provisional constitution was far from a reality. Admittedly much still remained to be done in removing obstacles in the way of a full-fledged union, but there were no immediate signs to bear out the gloomy prognostications at the time of the UAE's birth.

Challenges facing the UAE were formidable, however. The long tradition of rivalry and suspicion among the amirates was not expected to disappear overnight. The old tribal independence often slowed the efforts of federalists to organize an effective central authority. Although they acknowledged the importance of unity for common good, some of the rulers were disinclined to hasten the process of federalization, mindful that a strong central government in areas where they had retained autonomy would mean a loss of their power and prestige. Thus during the first several years of the UAE many rulers went through the motions of cooperation. There were some token achievements, but they fell far short of what UAE president Shaikh Zayid bin Sultan al-Nuhayan had hoped to accomplish.

It came as no surprise when in August 1976 Shaikh Zayid, the amir of Abu Dhabi and the principal architect of the UAE federation, expressed his intention to step down from the presidency when his five-year term ended on December 2, 1976. He was believed to have been very disappointed at the lack of necessary support from his fellow amirs on several issues.

Among the thorny issues was federal funding. Most rulers were reluctant to contribute "a specified proportion of their annual revenues" to the federal budget as they had originally agreed to do when they signed the provisional constitution. In 1972 Abu Dhabi, by far the richest of the amirates, was to underwrite 85 percent of the UAE's initial budget, and the other six amirates were to share the remainder. As it turned out, however, Abu Dhabi had to pay it all. The pattern was repeated in subsequent years, Abu Dhabi contributing close to 95 percent of the federal budget.

It had become obvious that the transition from tribal shaikhdoms to a federation could not be compressed into a period of only a few years. The constitutional order as envisaged in 1971 was not beyond the realm of possibility to the rulers of the Supreme Council. Realistically, however, they decided to opt for continuity rather than face the uncertainty of any drastic political innovation. Thus the rulers shelved the draft of a permanent constitution, which had been completed by mid-1976 after a year-long effort by a constitutional committee. If approved the draft would have gone into effect in December 1976, but the rulers apparently had many reservations. First and foremost they were reported to have strenuously objected to a provision that would have required individual amirates to contribute 50 percent of their respective revenues to federal funding. Moreover the draft document was believed to have substantially strengthened federal authority over other matters, Abu Dhabi being almost alone in supporting the adoption of the draft.

Nonetheless the rulers were apprehensive about the future of the fledgling federation, especially in light of Shaikh Zayid's threat to resign. His departure would have cast shadows over the politics of federation building because of Abu Dhabi's pivotal role in the evolution of the UAE.

Although Shaikh Zayid was unquestionably first among equals, he was by no means an autocratic or authoritarian chief executive. As far as could be determined, the decision-making within the Supreme Council was through consultation and consensus. Islamic concepts of brotherhood, equality, and self-reliance as tempered by bedouin tribal customs continued to influence the way decisions were made and then translated into policies and actions. In the case of serious disagreements over important policy matters, delay or compromise rather than confrontation was sought. The pattern of consensus politics was evidently occasioned by mutual concern that adversary relationships would undermine the fragile union.

POLITICAL PROCESS

In the Islamic political culture as influenced by bedouin tribal customs—of which the amirates of the UAE remain an integral part—politics and government were inseparable and continued to be so into the 1980s without any appreciable modification. These functions were the exclusive preserve of the tribal ruling families. The power to regulate the lives of pastoral nomads in the desert was perceived principally in terms of the paramount shaikh and the web of personal relations he maintained within his kinship group. Loyalty and obedience were focused on the patriarch of the ruling household less as the head of a formal administrative structure with fixed territorial boundaries than as the paternalistic guardian, protector, and adjudicator. The ruler was the epitome of authority, personifying the unity of religious and political authority. This Islamic, bedouin cultural heritage inhibited the rise of any notion that worldly affairs could be separate from religious faith, the latter being the sole source and repository of all authority. Politics and government, viewed as the ruler's prerogatives, could be neither differentiated nor delegated. The concept of a territorially bounded state or of a formal administrative structure was still embryonic.

The hold of tradition was still pronounced in the society of the amirates. It resulted at least in part from the long isolation of the Trucial Coast states from the societies and peoples of different cultures. Even during the more than a century of British hegemony in the area, the traditional way of life went on unruffled. Under special treaty relationships with the British, tribal shaikhs ruled their fiefdoms according to their personal predilections, a function of the British policy of noninterference in the internal affairs of the shaikhdoms. For their part, the paternalistic tribal chiefs pledged not to deal with any foreign power other than the political agents of the United Kingdom. These special ties enabled the British to enjoy dominant influence in the Trucial Coast to the exclusion of other foreign powers, namely, Russia, France, and Germany. The British protection ensured the continuance of political stability in the area, shielding the shaikhdoms not only from foreign encroachments but from the turbulence of changes and revolutionary fermentations that affected other parts of the region in the post-World War II era. The sociopolitical institutions of the Trucial Coast states remained all but frozen in their feudal ways through much of the 1970s.

In early 1976 President Shaikh Zayid stated that the UAE would need a transitional period before any parliamentary election was allowed. He did not specify how long this transition would last, nor did he elaborate on the mechanics of election. In any case the process of defining issues and channeling popular demands independently of the shaikhs was still alien to the society. The constitutional guarantee for political freedoms was academic. There was as yet no political party, either under official sponsorship or in opposition, anywhere in the amirates.

The only potential source of demand for change from below was the growing number of intellectuals and professionals who were educated abroad and politically sophisticated. But it appeared unlikely that they would become activist for any antiestablishment cause, individually or collectively. For one thing almost all of these individuals were gainfully employed as advisers and technocrats at the federal and amirate levels. For another many were foreign nationals who were recruited for temporary service and whose contracts were extended on the basis of technical merit and performance. Their activities were monitored closely by the UAE authorities.

The power structures were preempted by the hereditary ruling families—the central political and economic institutions—in all amirates. The members of these extended families or clans held nearly all important levers of power, and only rarely were members of nonruling tribes allowed access to power—and then only to the periphery of the power structure. At the center of power hierarchy was the paramount shaikh of the ruling household, whose preeminence was buttressed by the legitimacy of lineage and reinforced by such leadership qualities as courage, prudence, wisdom, wealth, benevolence, and fairness. Family unity was always important in preserving power but equally critical was the effectiveness of rulership, because in the tribal political culture the shaikh was accountable for his mandate to results as measured by peace within a given shaikhdom and material well-being among the influential members of the shaikh's immediate clan.

The transfer of power would generally take place within the ruling family. In order to forestall a palace coup or internecine violence, the ruling shaikh would appoint a son as heir apparent after consulting his family elders. The heir apparent might double as deputy ruler if he was over eighteen years of age. Otherwise a deputy ruler would usually be named from among the ruler's brothers.

The development of Abu Dhabi was portended by the discovery of oil in 1960, but it was not until after Shaikh Zayid's accession to rulership in August 1966 that the amirate witnessed a rapid increase in the number of government departments. At the time the UAE was formed, Abu Dhabi already had ministries responsible for such functions as finance, defense, education, public health, public works, police, communications, petroleum, electricity and water, and justice. These formal bodies scarcely affected Shaikh Zayid's personal authority inasmuch as they were placed mostly under the charge of members of his dynasty. Besides, the shaikh had his own personal advisory cabinet, *diwan,* whose small membership was answerable to him. These advisory members were chosen by the ruler from among the elders of the ruling family, influential tribal leaders, and prominent commoner families.

Political power resided in the al-Nuhayan family clan, a subtribe of the Bani Yas tribal confederation, which traced its origins to Liwa and became dominant settlers in the oasis region of Liwa, in the town of Abu Dhabi, and in the al-Ayn section of the Buraymi Oasis region. The richest of all tribal families, the al-Nuhayan had some thirty shaikhs, the most prominent and powerful being Shaikh Zayid, who before his assumption of rulership in 1966 had been governor of Eastern Province.

Among the influential figures assisting Shaikh Zayid were his sons, Khalifah and Sultan, the former being heir apparent, deputy ruler, and the federal deputy prime minister; and several nephews, sons of the late Shaikh Shakhbut. The balance of power or harmony within the al-Nuhayan remained essential to the political stability of the amirate. If the traditional pattern of succession politics held, a descendant of the Khalifah line might someday advance "his own right or that of his son to the rulership" of Abu Dhabi.

Political dominance was maintained partly by cultivating the support and allegiance of other leading, albeit nonruling, tribes. Among these tribes were the more than ten other subtribes of the Bani Yas; the Manasir tribe, traditionally influential in the interior of the western region of the amirate; the Dhawahir, in the al-Ayn area of Eastern Province; and the Awamir, in an area west of the Buraymi Oasis and south of al-Dafrah (Dafir). In addition the Suwaydis, Utaybahs, Habrushis, and al-Kindis were among the distinguished commoner families whose importance was considerable because of their commercial acumen, professional and managerial talents, and bureaucratic experience. Shaikh Rashid bin Said al-Maktum ruled, in an informal yet effective manner with as few administrative or regulatory strings as possible to ensure Dubai's thriving free enterprise system.

Shaikh Rashid presided over a power structure in which his immediate household—the al-Maktum—was the dominant force, controlling key political and commercial interests in several government departments, the Dubai Municipal Council, and such successful enterprises as the Dubai Electricity Company and the Dubai State Telephone System. The ruler was ably assisted by a number of expatriate advisers and personally maintained close touch with key non-Arab and British members of business and banking communities.

Among Shaikh Rashid's more influential supporters were his three sons: Shaikh Maktum bin Rashid al-Maktum, heir apparent and the federal prime minister; Shaikh Hamdan bin Rashid al-Maktum, the federal minister of finance and industry; and Shaikh Muhammad bin Rashid al-Maktum, the federal minister of defense.

Sharjah, which had three enclaves on the eastern coast of the Gulf of Oman and claimed sovereignty over two islands near the Strait of Hormuz, had a fairly elaborate administrative system combining traditional and modern features. Shaikh Sultan bin Muhammad al-Qasimi, the supreme ruler, attended to affairs of the shaikhdom personally through his *diwan* and also by holding a daily *majlis,* an informal audience. In addition, Shaikh Sultan presided over a number of departments whose operations were centrally coordinated by the municipality of Sharjah, which had a commendable managerial record dating back to the 1920s. As in the other amirates, key administrative positions were entrusted to members of the ruling dynasty.

In 1976 Sharjah was the seat of the Union Defense Force Headquarters; before 1971 British army and air bases and the headquarters of the Trucial Oman Scouts were located there. The presence of British residents in Sharjah influenced the development of a modern court system. Apart from the traditional *sharia* court, there was a separate court for civil and criminal matters involving non-Muslim foreigners. Sharjah's real progress came in 1974 when oil began to be produced for export.

The power group of Sharjah is the al-Qasimi tribe, whose three collateral branches accounted for most of the important figures. Among the influential supporters of Shaikh Sultan were Shaikh Saqr bin Muhammad al-Qasimi (deputy ruler) and Shaikh Abd al-Azis of the Muhammad line; Shaikh Khalid, Shaikh Muhammad, Shaikh Ahmad bin Rashid al-Mu alla of the Majid line. These shaikhs depended on the al-Madfa and the Taryam, two of the most prominent commoner families, for much of the administrative and managerial expertise as well as on a sizable number of expatriates including British, Egyptians, and Americans.

In the years after his accession to rulership in 1972 Shaikh Sultan, who at that time was the federal minister of education and was personally close to Shaikh Zayid of Abu Dhabi, actively supported the cause of the UAE federation. In 1975 he was the first amirate ruler to adopt the UAE flag in place of Sharjah's, and he handed over his militia, police, and courts to the federal jurisdiction. Relations with adjoining Dubai had been more competitive than cooperative, but they were expected to improve substantially.

Ras al-Khaymah, despite its reputation as the breadbasket of the UAE, was hampered in its socioeconomic development because of its limited internal revenues.

The two principal governing institutions were the al-Qasimi ruling family, which belonged to the same Qasimi tribe as ruled Sharjah, and the municipality of Ras al-Khaymah. The ruling dynasty had two competing collateral branches, the Muhammad line, headed by Shaikh Saqr bin Muhammad al-Qasimi, who was the ruler of the amirate; and the Sultan line, whose Shaikh Sultan had reigned from 1921 to 1948.

Shaikh Saqr's heir apparent and deputy ruler was his son, Shaikh Khalid, who was educated in the United States. Some of the prominent Ras al-Khaymah family members active at one time or another in federal government service were Shaikh Abd Allah bin Humaid al-Qasimi; Shaikh Abd al-Malik al-Qasimi; Said Ahmad Ghubash; Said bin Abd Allah bin Sulman; and Saif bin Ghubash.

The al-Qasimi shaikhs of Ras al-Khaymah, like some of their cousins in Sharjah, take pride in their former imperial dominance in the Trucial Coast, which often was fittingly called the Qasimi coast. The Qasimi's fortune sank precipitously after the British invasion of Ras al-Khaymah in 1819. In the years after 1971 the al-Qasimi of Ras al-Khaymah were known to wish for a bigger share of power at the federal level. Their feeling was sustained in part by their claim that Ras al-Khaymah had more indigenous Arabs than any other amirate and hence was entitled to a rightful place commensurate with tradition and contemporary numerical status. Predictably, Arab-centered sentiments tended to run deeper in Ras al-Khaymah than in other parts of the federation and yet were so diffuse that they failed to manifest themselves in any form or direction. The notable exception was Iran, which won the enmity of many Ras al-Khaymans by seizing control of the two Tunb Islands in the Strait of Hormuz in 1971. The islands, historically claimed by Ras al-Khaymah, remained a source of strain between the UAE and Iran. Ras al-Khaymah's refusal to join the UAE in 1971 stemmed in part from its unhappiness over the reluctance of the British and other amirates to support unequivocally Ras al-Khaymah's case against the Iranian occupation.

Ajman, Umm al-Qaywayn, and Fujayrah—the smallest and poorest shaikhdoms—depended heavily on federal subsidies. They were sometimes likened to village-states or described as being under one-man rule in that their administrative functions were exercised by the rulers' kinsmen and a few expatriate advisers. Reform was still in a nascent stage if undertaken at all; where it was initiated, it was prompted mainly by the need for coordination with the federal authorities responsible for development projects.

Administration in Ajman and Fujayrah was complicated somewhat because these amirates had enclaves scattered inside the territories of other amirates. These enclaves contained "a village here, a date palm oasis there, or a well or a grazing area," to which their rulers claimed "the right to collect the zakat, or Islamic tax, from various nomadic tribes" migrating between two or more amirates.

Information was scarce about the internal structures of the ruling families in the three amirates. Ajman was ruled by the Nuaimi family, which Shaikh Rashid bin Humaid al-Nuaimi headed from 1928 onward, the longest rulership in the UAE. The dominant tribe in Umm al-Qaywayn was the al-Mualla under the chieftainship of Shaikh Ahmad bin Rashid al-Mualla; because of his advanced age, Crown Prince Humaid was taking an active role in both federal and amirate affairs. Fujayrah was ruled by the youthful and well-educated Shaikh Hamad bin Muhammad al-Sharqi who presided over the dominant al-Sharqi tribe.

OMAN

The Sultanate of Oman continues to function as an absolute monarchy. Its ruler, Sultan Qaboos ibn Said, was the fourteenth ruler of the al-Bu Said dynasty, which had established its power in the country in the mid-eighteenth century. November 18, 1970, marks the National Day of

Oman

Sultan ibn Ahmad was the king of Oman from 1792 to 1804.

Oman. National Day commemorates the anniversary of the country under its new name, the Sultanate of Oman, and the accession to rule of Sultan Qaboos. It is indicative of the focus of the new government that National Day does not fall on the anniversary of the coup d'etat that occurred on July 23, 1970, in which Qaboos deposed his father and seized power, but rather on his birthday, thus underlining Qaboos's central and absolute authority and the mirrored association of him with the state.

Oman has no constitution, legislature, political parties, or elected assemblies on the federal level; nor is there suffrage. The sultan serves as his own prime minister, minister of defense, and minister of foreign affairs. He is also commander in chief of the armed forces and the Royal Oman Police, is the only source of new legislation, and embodies in his person the highest judicial power.

HISTORICAL BACKGROUND

In addition to the central subject of independence, defense and security concerns in Oman have historically involved the closely related matters of Muslim religious doctrine, intertribal warfare, personal power struggles, foreign influence and intervention and, in the 1960s and 1970s, protracted attempts by Marxist-oriented, radical Arab nationalist factions to overthrow the traditionalist monarchy through an externally assisted guerrilla war. The historical interplay of these factors has governed the political life of the country, its socioeconomic development, and the evolution of its military and security forces, supported since 1964 by modest oil revenues.

The Arab tribes of the Omani region, having been converted to Islam by the mid-seventh century A.D., fell under the rule of the Umayyad caliphal dynasty in Damascus. At about the same time the schismatic Kharajite movement (or Kharajite heresy) appeared in Iraq, North Africa, and elsewhere as an outgrowth of the dynastic warfare and theological contentions of early Islam. This belief held as its main tenet that the office of caliph, or earthly successor to the Prophet Mohammed as ruler of the Muslims, should be filled by consensual choice and should not pass in hereditary line or be limited to one family or tribe, or even necessarily to Arabs. The Kharajite movement soon became fragmented into numerous subsects, one of which was headed by the Iraqi theologian Abd Allah ibn Ibad al-Murri al-Tamimi and whose members became known as the Ibadis. Fleeing from suppression by the Umayyads, the Ibadis from Iraq made common cause with Omani tribes

who were also resisting the Damascus caliphate. The Ibadi brand of Islam thereafter became entrenched in Oman, becoming in effect the Omani ideology.

When the Abbasside faction of Sunni Islam overthrew the Umayyads and set up their capital at Baghdad in the mid-eighth century, the Omani tribes successfully withstood Abbasside attempts to establish permanent sovereignty throughout Oman. In consonance with Ibadi practice the tribes elected an imam in 749, who is often regarded as the first Omani ruler after the coming of Islam. Although subject temporarily to invasions by several external powers, including Iran, Oman generally maintained independence and attained substantial maritime power until 1507, when Portugal seized control of the coastline. In 1650 an Omani faction defeated the Portuguese forces in the region. Independence is generally reckoned from that date, making Oman the longest continuously independent Arab state in modern times.

In the Omani renaissance and resurgence after 1650 the imams extended their maritime conquests to the East African coast, incorporating Mogadiscio, Mombasa, and Zanzibar into the empire. During the first half of the eighteenth century, however, civil war between rival contenders for the office of imam shook the country. Although one of the unsuccessful contenders was supported by an Iranian military force, the victor was Ahmad ibn Said, who was duly elected imam in 1741 and became the founder of the al-bu Said Dynasty, which has ruled continuously since then in part or all of Oman. At about this time the head of the al-bu Said family began to be known as the sultan, although he frequently was also the imam. Another period of prosperity followed, and in 1786 the capital was moved from Nizwa and Rustaq to the principal Omani port city of Muscat. This move led to later political differentiations between the interior areas and the coast, and these differentiations became further identified with religious and tribal contentions and renewed contests for power.

In historical perspective possibly the most important long-term development contributing to the stability and continuance in power of the al-bu Said sultanate began in the nineteenth century, when Oman and Great Britain commenced a special relationship that continued thereafter and remained strong going into the 1980s. Treaties of friendship between Oman and Great Britain were negotiated in 1798 and 1800, and a full exchange of consular relations followed in 1839. Although treaty relations were established with other states outside the Middle East (for example, with the United States in 1833), the most consistent and influential connection has been with Great Britain. It cannot be neatly described in conventional foreign relations terms, but it illustrates the British capability of long-term, workable improvisation according to time and place.

In contrast to the Persian Gulf shaikhdoms, Egypt, Jordan, and other areas in the Middle East, Oman has not been in a colonial, protectorate, or mandated arrangement with

Sultan Qaboos appears in formal and informal dress on these Oman postage stamps.

Great Britain. Formal relations have rested on the treaties of friendship, commerce, and navigation of 1891, 1939, and 1951, and British military presence and assistance have never been based on treaty obligations. Nevertheless Great Britain from time to time has had regular British units, naval bases, and air stations in Oman; the last such base was closed in March 1977.

The British presence as political and military advisers and as active members of the Omani military forces has been distinctive. The arrangements have been ad hoc agreements implemented by contracted or attached (seconded) individual British military personnel, provision of training and equipment, and the stationing of small forces in Oman. Consequently the principal characteristics of the regular Omani military and security forces in uniforms, organization, equipment, and training became British (or adaptations of British usages) and continued to be so into the 1980s. Informed observers maintain that the British connection is still the "key to the sultan's survival."

During the reign of Said ibn Sultan al-bu Said (1804-56) the Omani domains attained their greatest extent—Dhofar province being added in 1826. Said had a strong navy of fifteen Western-style warships, including a seventy-four-gun ship of the line. In Oman Said could call on perhaps five thousand men from tribal levies, and he had a mercenary regular force of about one thousand five hundred. The practice of using regular forces of mercenaries thus has long-standing customary sanction in Oman. At Said's death the empire was divided between two of his sons, one becoming sultan of Zanzibar and the other of Oman. This major historical development and the sharp reduction—brought about through British influence—of the slave and arms trade through Muscat reduced Omani revenues and the economy in the second half of the nineteenth century and caused unrest. Two major insurrections occurred and many minor disturbances. Owing to British assistance and the traditional rivalry between the Ghafiri and Hinawi tribal confederations of the interior, the al-bu Saids maintained a precarious authority. The Hinawis of the southeast were strict, conservative Ibadis. The Ghafiris of the northwest

were also Ibadis but slightly more receptive to outside influences. When these groups temporarily united, however, the sultanate probably could not have survived without British help.

Over the years the conservative tribesmen of the interior had grown progressively disaffected from the al-bu Saids, who had established hereditary rule contrary to Ibadi traditions and had moved the capital. To protest against the growing secularization of what had once been a largely religious office, the tribesmen resorted in the late eighteenth century to electing another imam. This led to a situation that lasted for roughly one hundred and fifty years in which there was an imam of Oman and a sultan of Muscat and Oman. Sometimes, as for example between 1868 and 1873, the sultan was also acknowledged as the imam; sometimes there was no imam at all. Throughout this period and later it was the sultan in Muscat who was recognized by the major maritime powers: Great Britain, France, and the United States.

In 1913 Sultan Faisal ibn Turki al-bu Said died and was succeeded by his son, Taimur ibn Faisal al-bu Said. A different imam was elected in the interior, however, and there was a general rising of tribes from both federations

Sultan Qaboos is a very popular ruler with the people of Oman. He frequently makes public visits.

against Sultan Taimur. The tribesmen regarded the sultan's cooperation with Great Britain to restrict the arms traffic in Oman as subservience to Great Britain. Encouraged by propaganda emanating from Berlin and Istanbul, the tribesmen besieged Muscat in 1915 only to be routed by a British force. Eventually in 1920 the sultan and the tribes reached accommodation through the Treaty of Sib. In this agreement the sultan recognized the elected imam's spiritual authority and also allowed him temporal authority over those tribesmen who accepted his jurisdiction. The sultan did not relinquish his claim to full sovereignty.

Although the Treaty of Sib had left many fundamental questions unanswered, it endured unbroken for thirty-four years. Imam Muhammad Abd Allah al-Khalili was an archconservative, Ibadi to the core, firmly committed to Omani particularism, and was as hostile to foreign incursion as were the al-bu Said sultans. When Saudi Arabia seized the Buraymi Oasis in 1952, the imam supported efforts to oust the Saudis and provided Omani tribesmen to the sultan's army.

Imam Muhammad died in May 1954. In the election that followed the winner was Ghalib bin Ali of the Hina tribe of the Hinawi federation. His success was possible with the support of Sulyman bin Himyar, chief of the powerful Bani Riyam tribe and strongest figure in the Ghafiri federation, and Sahib bin Issa of the southern district of Sharqiyya. These three leaders commanded enough support across the tribal spectrum to establish a formidable grip over the interior. Encouraged by foreign assistance, Ghalib, through his brother, Talib bin Ali, applied to the League of Arab States (Arab League) for full membership for Oman. The new imam's application for membership in the Arab League in 1955 reopened the whole question of the Treaty of Sib, particularly in regard to the autonomy or independence of the imam in the conduct of foreign relations.

By 1955 Sultan Said ibn Taimur al-bu Said, who had become sultan in 1932, became convinced that his regime was threatened by a Saudi-backed coalition and that Imam Ghalib had, by his representations to the Arab League, violated the Treaty of Sib. In 1954 the sultan's forces occupied the town of Ibri, isolating the imam at his base in the interior from the Saudi-controlled Buraymi Oasis. In the meantime Said's army had been reorganized into four task forces, each of about battalion size, under British command: the Dhofar Force at Salalah; the Muscat and Oman Field Force at the oil camp of Petroleum Development (Oman) (PDO) near Fahud; the Batinah Force at the coastal town of Sohar; and the Muscat Levies, garrisoned near the capital.

From the advance base at Ibri the Muscat and Oman Field Force moved rapidly against Nizwa and occupied it on December 15, 1955, in an almost bloodless coup de main. Two days later the Batinah Force stormed Rustaq, which fell after determined resistance by the imam's brother, Talib. The civil war appeared over, and the sultan embarked on an unprecedented six hundred-mile truck trip

Sultan Taimur ibn Faisal ruled Oman from 1913 to 1932.

King Taimur on horseback. All of the ruling sultans were expert horsemen.

from Salalah to Nizwa. At Nizwa the sultan allowed Ghalib to retire to his village and accepted a pledge of fealty from Sulyman. The annexation of the interior was justified on the grounds that the imam had violated the Treaty of Sib and had collaborated with Saudi Arabia.

The sultan's triumphant entry into Nizwa in 1955 ended only the first phase of the civil war. The imam's brother, Talib, who had escaped to Saudi Arabia and thence to Cairo, where he had operated a publicity office for the imamate, returned to Oman in June 1957. Aided by an arms flow from abroad, Talib raised the tribes again, asserting the imam's authority in the interior. Sultan Said immediately requested British aid. Nizwa and most of inner Oman were reoccupied in September 1957. The imam, Talib, and Sulyman retreated to Sulyman's mountain stronghold at the summit of the Jabal Akhdar (Green Mountain); desultory fighting continued until early 1959, when the sultan's troops and three hundred British regulars attacked the stronghold, bringing the war to its conclusion. Although Ghalib, Talib, and Sulyman escaped to Saudi Arabia, the sultan's authority was recognized throughout Oman. He promptly decreed the Treaty of Sib terminated and the office of the interior imam abolished.

Sporadic acts of terrorism continued for several years, but the sultan's security forces gradually extirpated the imam's political apparatus. In the international arena, however, the imam's cause continued to find some support for various, often seemingly incongruous reasons. In October 1960 ten Arab countries succeeded in placing the "Question of Oman" on the agenda of the General Assembly of the United Nations, but a draft resolution calling for the imamate's independence did not secure the necessary majority in December 1961. A United Nations Commission of Inquiry visited Oman in the spring of 1963. The commission's report refuted the imam's charges of oppressive government and strong public feeling against the sultan. The case was reopened at intervals until October 1971, when Oman was finally admitted to full membership in the United Nations (UN).

SULTAN SAID IBN TAIMUR

The twentieth century did not appear to herald great change for Oman until 1932, when Sultan Taimur ibn Faisal abdicated in favor of his son, Said ibn Taimur. Secularists judged that the direction in which Said moved the sultanate was backward; although he clashed with the Ibadites of the interior, he was basically of their conservative mind. Geographical particularism made it impossible for him to be elected imam by the Ibadites of the interior, but the office of sultan under him became a very close approximation of the imamate. Ibadite restrictions were firmly enforced. Alcohol, tobacco, dancing, singing, and films were strictly prohibited. Women were forbidden to appear unveiled in public and were denied access even to religious schools.

It is not entirely clear what Said's motivation was. Certainly he did everything in his power to isolate his country from outside influence or even intercourse with foreigners with few minor exceptions: a few British were employed where absolutely necessary in the government and armed forces, and American missionaries ran the country's two hospitals. Entrance visas were denied to virtually all. The few exceptions were made mostly to employees of a British-operated oil firm. The sultan talked a great deal with his British contacts about moderation but increasingly moved away from it. Ultimately he discouraged trade except that necessary to sustain the country at barely subsistence level.

Although the sultan was unwanted in the interior, he nevertheless decided that Muscat was too close to foreign influence and so moved his capital to Salalah in Dhofar province. Relatively speaking, Said trusted the British more than any other foreigners and also realized the need for military leaders. He therefore permitted his only son, Qaboos ibn Said, to attend Sandhurst. When Qaboos completed his education and returned home, however, he was promptly placed under house arrest.

A new imam was elected in the interior in 1954, and he and his supporters attempted unsuccessfully to gain recognition for Oman as an independent state in the League of Arab States (Arab League). Between 1954 and 1959 forces of the sultan and the imam were in a state of constant warfare until the British, at Said's request, helped put down the revolt in 1959. The imam took sanctuary in Saudi Arabia, which had supported him just as the Wahhabis had consistently supported imams against Omani sultans.

Despite Said's paranoia and the enforced isolation of his subjects, modern ideas were spreading, particularly among the young, from the unlikely source of Saudi Arabia. On July 24, 1970, a bloodless coup by the liberals, led by the sultan's son, Qaboos, ousted Said and exiled him to England, where he died in 1972. In 1976 Omanis said, "Before Qaboos, nothing." Certainly this sums up the reign of his father and Oman's position when it finally entered the twentieth century in the 1970s.

Oman had a new ruler when it was granted full membership in the UN. Despite the cajoling of the British, Sultan Said had not diminished his isolationist stance, nor had he mitigated his savage and tyrannous practices. In the second week of June 1970 there was an outbreak of guerrilla activity in the interior of Oman, and Shell Oil pressed the British government for some action to ameliorate the rapidly deteriorating situation. On June 20 there was a change of government in Great Britain, and in July the coup d'etat in Oman occurred.

The events of the month before the coup have not been made available to the public. The British government noted that the sultan's son Qaboos, with the aid of loyal Dhofaris, had peacefully deposed the sultan on July 23 and then had him flown into exile in England. Qaboos, Said's only son, had been under house arrest since 1966, when he had returned from military training in Great Britain. Great Britain recognized Qaboos as sultan on July 29, and the British Foreign Office denied any knowledge of the coup or complicity in it. Observers noted that it would be highly improbable that such an event could have occurred without British knowledge and at the very least their tacit approval, because British officers held all the key positions in the armed forces.

GOVERNMENT AND POLITICS

Sultan Qaboos was born on November 18, 1939, in Salalah, the capital of Dhofar province, where his father had isolated himself. His mother is a Qara, a tribe of non-Arab ethnic origins, and Qaboos was his parents' only issue. He was sent to Sandhurst for training and served for a time in the British army of the Rhine.

Qaboos did not marry until March 1976. He had rejected the bride chosen for him by his father and married Kamilla, the daughter of his only surviving uncle, Tariq ibn Taimur al-bu Said. Foreign observers speculate that he may have postponed marriage well beyond the average age in order to devote himself fully to the consolidation of his political position. He may, of course, only have been waiting for Kamilla to complete her education abroad.

Qaboos is thought of by many foreign observers as an enigmatic ruler. Although he governs as an absolute monarch—his rule being more absolute than any other of the traditional rulers of the Arabian Peninsula—he is at the same time an extremely progressive social developer. Foreign observers believe that Qaboos is aware that he must develop the country as quickly as possible. In 1976 it was estimated that Oman could expect only ten more years of relatively small oil revenues. To this end Qaboos relies on the advice of international specialists and on former Omani expatriates who were educated abroad in places ranging from Western Europe to the Soviet Union. The sultan's policy of staffing the civil service and the armed forces with Omanis (a policy known as Omanization) was being implemented in the mid-1970s without waiting for the young to complete higher education and without waiting for the slow social evolution that might in several generations place women in the working force.

The sultan's political goals appeared to be to detribalize the society, break down regionalism, allow no threats to his political autonomy, and pacify Dhofar province completely. Qaboos was aware of the desire among the progressives in his country to have a more modern political form but responded by saying, "A parliament whose members we will choose can be created; we can create a phony parliament to give the impression of a semblance of democracy in our country. All this is possible, but does it correspond to the aim for which a parliament is supposed to exist? We need more time to reach this stage."

GOVERNMENT STRUCTURE AT THE NATIONAL LEVEL

Although Sultan Qaboos is the head of state and source of all authority, there are sixteen ministers who are appointed by him to be responsible for various governmental functions. In addition to the ministers the sultan had a council of advisers. The two most influential advisers were the sultan's uncle, Tariq, and Sayyid Thuwayyni ibn Shihab, the sultan's cousin. Sayyid Thuwayyni was also *wali* (governor) of the capital area and was acting sultan during Qaboos's absences from the country.

Qaboos's most pressing concern after his assumption of power was to gain support for his coup and to bring peace to Dhofar province. The establishment of the ministerial cabinet was therefore a lengthy and careful process. One of Qaboos's first political acts was to call Tariq out of exile and appoint him prime minister on August 9, 1970. Tariq enjoyed great popularity among the people because he was the only member of the royal family to have fought against

During a visit to Jordan, Sultan Qaboos reviews the troops with King Hussein.

His Majesty Sultan Qaboos with King Khalid of Saudi Arabia on a visit to that country for discussions of international importance on the oil question in the Middle East.

the imamic insurgency in the 1950s. He was known and respected more than the young sultan who, because of the house arrest imposed upon him by his father, had seldom been seen by the people. However, soon after his return Tariq became a controversial figure. He wished the country to have a formal written constitution, and he hoped that in time Oman would become a republic. He believed the institution of the sultanate to be anachronistic and intrinsically ill designed to serve Oman's entry into the modern world. On January 1, 1972, Tariq resigned his post, and his duties as prime minister were assumed by the sultan.

SUCCESSION, ROYAL FAMILY, AND TRIBES

The sultan has no brothers and as of late 1976 no successor had been designated. The succession issue was a matter of considerable discussion in the sultanate until March 1976, when Sultan Qaboos married his first cousin, Kamilla. Kamilla was twenty years old at the time of her marriage and had been educated in Geneva. The marriage is a politically astute one, primarily because Tariq, Kamilla's father, is second only to the sultan in the respect he commands

His Majesty Sultan Qaboos ibn Said, the ruler of Oman. He ascended the throne in 1970.

Sultan Qaboos was a close personal friend of the shah of Iran.

President Ronald Reagan and the First Lady Nancy Reagan greet Sultan Qaboos as he arrives at the White House.

Sultan Qaboos has a formal meeting with President Reagan.

Muhammad, *tamimah* of the al-Hirth, one of the most powerful tribes in the country. Qaboos's father hoped to buttress his political position by forming an alliance with a tribe that could call up large numbers of military reserves. Although tribal support remained necessary in 1976 because virtually the entire population continued to be tribally oriented, the sophisticated military machine developed by the sultan made such marriage alliances less necessary. Further, the sultan does not appear to wish to recognize one tribe over another or in fact even to suggest that the tribes have some de facto power that must be recognized.

Within the royal family, the clan of the al-bu Said, sultan's relatives, do not have the political clout enjoyed by many of the royalty of the Arabian Peninsula. The sultan's two chief advisers were relatives; in addition to them there were five other relatives in cabinet positions. Members of the royal family are frequently given in the press with the title Sayyid before their names. This is meant as a token of respect and does not have the usual connotation of the title—a descendant of the family of the Prophet Mohammed. In 1976 there were approximately ten *walis* who were related, some quite distantly, to the sultan.

The al-Hirth supported the followers of the imam in the 1950s and 1960s, however; this prompted Sultan Said to propose an alliance by marriage to prevent such allegiances in the future. The al-Hirth were reportedly displeased that their shaikh's daughter was not accepted by Sultan Qaboos, a matter that amounts to a violation of contract. The geographic proximity of this tribe to the Muscat municipality and its lack of sympathy with the office of sultan made it clear that its power had to be broken.

Other tribal groups that have less than harmonious relations with the central government are the Shihuh and the Habus of the Musandam Peninsula (Ras Musandam). These tribes have close ties with the amirates of Ras al-Khaymah and Fujayrah of the United Arab Emirates. In 1975 some of the Shihuh and Habus accepted an offer of citizenship from Ras al-Khaymah. Despite the sultan's efforts to develop the long-neglected Musandam area, he cannot match the kinds of goods and services available to the citizens of the UAE. The acceptance of citizenship was particularly unnerving to the central government because supplies and recruits for the Dhofar insurgency were known to have come from the Musandam area.

The three most powerful tribes of Dhofar province were those involved in the rebellion. They present special difficulties to the central government. The Mahrah and the al-Kathir share the cultural and social orientation of the tribes of the Hadramaut in Yemen (Aden). Until the rebellion they had very little interaction or involvement with the rest of Omani society. The Qara, who have distinguished themselves by their indefatigable warriors, are not of Arab origin. Their language differs from that spoken in Oman and, despite the fact that the sultan's mother is from that tribe, it will undoubtedly be a long and arduous process to integrate them into Omani society.

among the people and because, in the absence of a son by Qaboos, Tariq would be the most likely candidate for the throne. If Kamilla and Qaboos produce a son, any reservations some of the population may have about the absolute authority possessed by the sultan may diminish. Since Kamilla is the daughter of the sultan's father's brother, she is Qaboos' *bint amm* (daughter of father's brother). Such a marriage is the most highly regarded contract in the Middle East and therefore has great appeal to the traditionalists. Because Kamilla is Western educated, the progressives are also pleased.

Qaboos's father had arranged a marriage for him in April 1970, three months before the coup d'etat. The prospective bride was the uneducated daughter of Shaikh Ahmad bin

THE ROYAL SOVEREIGNS OF THE PERSIAN GULF SHAIKHDOMS OF KUWAIT, BAHRAIN, QATAR, THE UNITED ARAB EMIRATES, AND THE SULTANATE OF OMAN

Reign	Title	Ruler

SOVEREIGNS OF KUWAIT

Reign	Title	Ruler
1915–1917	Amir	Shaikh Jabir II
1917–1921	Amir	Shaikh Salim
1921–1950	Amir	Shaikh Ahmad
1950–1965	Amir	Shaikh Abdullah al-Salim al-Sabbah, (Abdullah III)
1965–1977	Amir	Sabbah al-Salim al-Sabbah
1978–	Amir	Jabir al-Ahmad al-Jabir al-Sabbah

SOVEREIGNS OF BAHRAIN

Reign	Title	Ruler
1861—British Protectorate		
1942–1961	Shaikh	Sulman bin Hamed al-Khalifah
1961–	Shaikh	Isa bin Sulman al-Khalifah

SOVEREIGNS OF QATAR

Reign	Title	Ruler
1949–1960	Shaikh	Ali bin Abdullah al-Thani
1960–1972	Shaikh	Ahmad bin Ali al-Thani
1972–	Shaikh	Khalifah bin Hamad al-Thani

SOVEREIGNS OF THE UNITED ARAB EMIRATES

In 1968 the government of the United Kingdom announced a policy decision, reaffirmed in March 1971, to end the treaty relationships with the Gulf shaikhdoms. The seven Trucial Shaikhdoms joined the other two states (Bahrain and Qatar) under British protection in an effort to form a union of Arab emirates. By mid-1971, however, the nine shaikhdoms still had not been able to agree on terms of union, and the termination date of the British treaty relationship was approaching (end of 1971). Bahrain became independent in August and Qatar became independent in September 1971. The British protective treaty with the Trucial Shaikhdoms ended on December 1, and they became fully independent. On December 2, 1971, six of them entered into a union called the United Arab Emirates. The seventh, Ras al-Khayimah, joined the union in early 1972.

PRINCIPAL GOVERNMENT OFFICIALS

Supreme Council
President, Ruler of Abu Dhabi—Shaikh Zayid bin Sultan al-Nuhayan
Vice President and Prime Minister, Ruler of Dubai—Shaikh Rashid bin Said al-Maktum
Ruler of Sharjah—Shaikh Sultan bin Muhammad al-Qasimi
Ruler of Ajman—Shaikh Rashid bin Humaid al-Nuaimi
Ruler of Umm al-Qaiwain—Shaikh Ahmad bin Rashid al-Mualla
Ruler of Ras al-Khaymah—Shaikh Saqr bin Muhammad al-Qasimi
Ruler of Fujayrah—Shaikh Hamad bin Muhammad al-Sharqi

SOVEREIGNS OF OMAN

Reign	Title	Ruler	Reign	Title	Ruler
	Imam		1500–1529	King (Sultan)	Muhammad ibn Ismail
751–	King (Sultan)	Julanda ibn Mas'ud	1529–1560	King (Sultan)	Barakat ibn Muhammad
–801	King (Sultan)	Muhammad ibn Affan	1560–1624	King (Sultan)	Abdulla ibn Muhammad
801–807	King (Sultan)	Warith ibn Kaab			
807–824	King (Sultan)	Ghassan ibn Abdulla			
824–840	King (Sultan)	Abdul Malik ibn Hamad	**THE YA'RUBA DYNASTY**		
840–851	King (Sultan)	al-Muhanna ibn Jaifar	1624–1649	King (Sultan)	Nasir ibn Murshid
851–886	King (Sultan)	al-Salt ibn Malik	1649–1688	King (Sultan)	Sultan ibn Saif (I)
886–890	King (Sultan)	Rashid ibn al-Nadhr	1688–1711	King (Sultan)	Bil'arub ibn Sultan
890–897	King (Sultan)	Azzan ibn Tamim	1711–1711	King (Sultan)	Saif ibn Sultan (I)
897–898	King (Sultan)	Muhammad ibn al-Hassan	1711–1718	King (Sultan)	Sultan ibn Saif (II)
898–899	King (Sultan)	Azzan ibn al-Hizr	1718–1718	King (Sultan)	Saif ibn Sultan (II)
899–900	King (Sultan)	Abdulla ibn Muhammad	1718–1721	King (Sultan)	Muhanna ibn Sultan
900–900	King (Sultan)	al-Salt ibn al Qasim	1721–1722	King (Sultan)	Ya'rub ibn Bil'arub
900–904	King (Sultan)	Hassan ibn Said	1722–1724	King (Sultan)	Saif ibn Sultan (II) (restored)
904–912	King (Sultan)	al-Hawari ibn Matraf	1724–1728	King (Sultan)	Muhammad ibn Nasir
912–	King (Sultan)	Omar ibn Muhammad	1728–1738	King (Sultan)	Saif ibn Sultan (II) (restored)
?	King (Sultan)	Muhammad ibn Yazid	1738–1741	King (Sultan)	Sultan ibn Murshid
–939	King (Sultan)	Mullah al-Bahari			
939–	King (Sultan)	Said ibn Abdulla			
–1009	Sultan	Rashid ibn Walid	**THE AL BU SAID DYNASTY ELECTED KINGS (SULTANS)**		
1009–1053	Sultan	al-Khalil ibn Shadzan	1741–1775	King (Sultan)	Ahmad ibn Said
1053–1053	Sultan	Rashid ibn Said	1775–1779	King (Sultan)	Said ibn Ahmad
1053–1054	Sultan	Hafs ibn Rashid			
1054–1054	Sultan	Rashid ibn Ali			
1054–	Sultan	ibn Jabir Musa	**SAYYIDS AND SULTANS**		
			1779–1792	King (Sultan)	Hamad ibn Said (Regent)
NABHAN PERIOD			1792–1804	King (Sultan)	Sultan ibn Ahmad
1106–	King (Malik)	Malik ibn Ali	1804–1856	King (Sultan)	Said ibn Sultan
1154–	King (Malik)	al-Fallah ibn al-Muhsin	1856–1866	King (Sultan)	Thuwaini ibn Said
		Arar ibn Fallah	1866–1868	King (Sultan)	Salim ibn Thuwaini
		Mudhaffar ibn Sulaiman	1868–1870	King (Sultan)	Azzan ibn Qais
1406–		Makhzum ibn al-Fallah	1870–1888	King (Sultan)	Turki ibn Said
1435–1451	King (Sultan)	Abu'l Hassan	1888–1913	King (Sultan)	Faisal ibn Turki
1451–1490	King (Sultan)	Omar ibn al-Khattab	1913–1932	King (Sultan)	Taimur ibn Faisal
1490–1500	King (Sultan)	Omar al-Sharif	1932–1970	King (Sultan)	Sir Said ibn Taimur
–1500	King (Sultan)	Ahmad ibn Muhammad	1970–	King (Sultan)	Qaboos (Quabus) ibn Said

8
The Kingdoms of Iraq

The map of Iraq

Iraq, a republic since the coup d'etat of 1958 which ended the reign of King Faisal II, became a sovereign, independent state in 1932. The history of the land and its people, however, dates back almost five thousand years to the time when the fertile area between the Tigris and Euphrates Rivers was known as Mesopotamia (meaning between rivers) and its inhabitants then called Sumerians, probably because the delta region of the two rivers was then called Sumer. Until World War I, the country was generally known in the West as Mesopotamia.

Geographically, the Mesopotamian region has been open to incursions from all sides. The deserts to the south and west harbored mounted nomads, and the passes to the north and east provided entry corridors from those directions. Numerous foreign conquerors came and went, each contributing to the physical mixture and cultural diversity of the area.

The most significant historical and cultural change occurred in the seventh century, when the Arab conquest brought Islam to the land, overlaying and reworking all that had gone before. It almost completely obliterated any conscious memory among the people of their ancient ways. The Arabs brought not only a new set of rulers but also their language, religion, and certain patterns of living which have characterized the country ever since. The conquerors also gave the country its modern name, *Iraq,* meaning basically "to sweat" or "to take root."

Despite the destruction wrought by the Mongols in the thirteenth century and the stultifying centuries of Turkish rule that followed, the past has continued to express itself in subtle details of social life and outlook which still distinguish the Arabized Iraqi majority on the Mesopotamian plain from Arab populations elsewhere in the Middle East. There are aspects of community life in Iraq and a characteristic approach to the problems of government, technology, and economic organization which in degree or kind set off the country from its neighbors, with whom the majority of its people share common Muslim traditions and faith as well as Arabic speech.

Iraq identifies itself as a bearer of the Arab tradition because of its thirteen centuries of participation in the Muslim Arab world. For most Iraqis not the grandeur of ancient Sumer or Babylon, but the magnificence of the medieval Abbasside Dynasty (750–1258) represents the zenith of the country's past achievement and nurtures a historical awareness that greatness is possible again in a revived and united Arab world. This outlook, more pan-Arab than nationalist in its implications, is being modified toward a more specific sense of Iraqi identity in the course of the country's experience as an independent nation while under the influence of the government's efforts to stress Iraq's inheritance of ancient civilization.

For the great majority of the people, Iraq's recent past is seen as a struggle for national freedom—first against the Ottomans (Turks), later against the British, and finally against "Western imperialism" and what is regarded as its "enemy", Israel.

The native heroes vary with the ethnic and religious affiliation of the viewer, but for the most part the people share the common dislike of all non-Arabs. History thus becomes an active factor in the contemporary Iraqi scene and an instrument available to political contenders. The anti-Western sentiments aroused during and since the British mandate worked to the disadvantage of the Hashemite monarchy (1921–58) and its supporters seeking to maintain an alignment with the West. Since the overthrow of the kingdom in the coup of 1958, nonalignment in world affairs, though erratic, has become an important concern of successive governments.

ANCIENT HISTORY

SUMER, AKKAD, BABYLON, AND ASSYRIA

Almost three thousand years before Christ, Sumerian kings, who were contemporary with the pharaohs of the earliest Egyptian dynasties (3100-2270 B.C.), developed what is often called the first civilization. It is not certain where they came from nor when they entered the area. It is clear, however, that they were preceded by numerous other peoples who had contributed to the social and political complexity of the region.

The Sumerians lived under a federation of city-states, devised the oldest form of writing based on pictorial as well as phonetic signs, used copper for tools and weapons, made highly polished painted pottery, and developed elaborate irrigation and water-control systems. So important were these irrigation works to survival and prosperity that even in wartime contestants took pains to avoid their destruction.

The Sumerian dynasties ended probably about 2800 B.C. when they were conquered by the Akkadians under Sargon, the founder of the Akkadian Kingdom. A Semitic people from the west and northwest, the Akkadians had entered in numbers sufficient to give their name to the territory surrounding what is now Baghdad. Despite their worship of the sun, they treated the agrarian religions of the conquered places with respect, placing their earth-gods into a kind of pantheon protected by a new and larger political order. The Akkadians and the Sumerians, in effect, combined their forces, and Sargon's military movements and exploits were extended to the Mediterranean and into Asia Minor.

After Sargon's death the empire slowly fell before the onslaughts of tribesmen from the north. Power was revived briefly with its center in the city of Erech (modern Warka) and later in that of Ur (now Makayyar), but it was, in turn, gradually weakened by the attack of Elamites, Semitic-speaking people from Elam in what is now the southwestern part of Iran.

The Sumerian-Akkadians were finally subjugated by the Semitic-speaking Amorites, probably from Syria. By 2000 B.C. the Amorites established a new state with its capital at Babylon on the southern Euphrates. Babylonian authority

Assur-nadir-ahe,
the first king of Assyria

Sargon, king of Assyria from
722 to 705 B.C., as depicted in
a Phrygian tributary from the
palace of Sargon

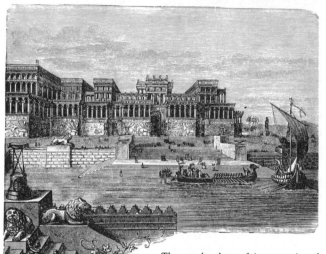

The royal palace of Assur-nasir-pal,
the ninth king of Assyria

King Shalmaneser II receiving tribute
from King Jehu, king of Israel

The inner court of the palace of King Sargon

was extended over southern Mesopotamia by Hammurabi (1947-05 B.C.), the sixth of his line of Amoritic rulers. One of the great kings of antiquity, Hammurabi is remembered not only as conqueror but also as a lawgiver. The code of laws he collected dealt with land tenure, rent, the position of women, marriage, divorce, inheritance, functions of money, contracts, control of public order, administration of justice, wages, and labor conditions.

Around 1500 B.C. the Kassites, a people speaking Elamitic (one of a group of languages related to modern Georgian) overthrew the Babylonian Dynasty and ruled the region until about 1170 B.C. The Kassite domination was supplanted by the Assyrians, a race of warriors from the north containing a mixture of Semites with non-Semitic tribes. The Assyrians were renowned not only for their military innovations and ruthless proficiency in war but also for their contributions in the spheres of administration, architecture, sculpture, and literature.

One of the Assyrian rulers of note was Tiglath-Pileser II (745–27 B.C.), who developed an important political idea—the maintenance of a permanent military force or standing army under the control of a permanent bureaucracy. He raised the Assyrian Empire, with its capital at Nineveh on the Tigris opposite present-day Mosul, to its pinnacle of power (even Egypt was required to recognize Assyrian supremacy), but the system he inaugurated eventually alienated subject peoples, who were driven to hatred and desperation by the severity of Assyrian methods. Revolt followed revolt; Egypt and Syria were lost; eventually, in 612 B.C. Scythians from the north destroyed Nineveh, and Assyrian power became a historic memory. Iraq's present-day Nestorian Christian minority calls itself Assyrian and claims ethnic descent from the peoples of this ancient empire.

This tablet dug up in 1934 at King Sargon II's palace at Khorsabad tells of the succession of ninety-five Assyrian kings from 2400 to 746 B.C.

King Assurbanipal (668–626 B.C.) killing a wounded lion.

Babylon rose again as the center of a New Babylonian Empire, also called the Chaldean Empire (625–538 B.C.). Favored by its geographical position, Babylon, after being rebuilt as one of the greatest cities of its day, became a center of trade and arts, but this glory also passed when it fell to the Persians under Cyrus the Great (559–529 B.C.) of the Achaemenid Empire (ca.650–328 B.C.).

PERSIAN AND GREEK INTRUSIONS

Mesopotamia, so long a seat of Semitic power, then came under an Indo-European-speaking people. It remained a province of the Achaemenid Empire for nearly one hundred and fifty years until subjugated by Alexander the Great around 331 B.C. Upon his death at Babylon in 323 B.C., the Greek power began to decline in the hands of his successors. Seleucus, one of Alexander's generals, became ruler of Mesopotamia and Persia, then known as the kingdom of the Seleucids, which had its power center at Seleucia on the Tigris south of modern Baghdad. Although his successors continued to spread Hellenistic civilization, by 200 B.C. the Seleucid power had shrunk to the confines of Mesopotamia and Syria.

The Seleucids were challenged by new powers to the north, the Parthian Persians who were by then in control of all Persia, and increasingly by the rapidly rising new power in the west, the Romans. Subduing Mesopotamia in 138 B.C., the Parthians thereafter had to contest with the Romans for supremacy over the region for nearly eight hundred years, until the coming of the Arabs. The Parthians were pushed aside in A.D. 226 by a new Persian power, the Sassanid Empire (A.D. 226–641), which in its hostility to the Romans and to Christianity, their favorite religion, gradually revived Zoroastrianism, the dominant religion in Persia since the sixth century B.C. As a result, the Sassanid efforts to consolidate power were aided by the powerful Zoroastrian priests, but by the mid-seventh century inconclusive struggles between Sassanids and the Romans left both of them exhausted and vulnerable.

ARAB CONQUEST AND THE COMING OF ISLAM

The process of detaching Iraq from the declining Sassanid power began during the brief reign of Abu Bakr (632–34), first caliph (spiritual and temporal ruler) and successor to Mohammed (570–632), founder of Islam. The many Arabs, mostly Christian, who were living under the Persian

The Assyrian Empire

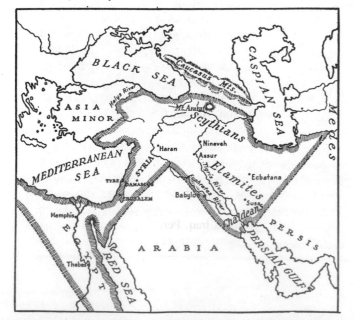

The great king Hammurabi was an early king of Babylonia. He is seen here on his throne talking to his "spiritual" advisers.

This is a stele of King Nebuchadnezzar I of Babylonia who ruled from 1146 to 1123 B.C. On it he describes his military campaign against the king of Elam (southwestern Persia).

King Asshur-Emid-Ilin, also known under his Greek name of Saracus, was the last of the Assyrian kings. Here he is pondering his fate as King Cvaxares of Medes conquers Assyria. In the final moments Saracus made a funeral pyre of himself and his family in the palace courtyard.

King Nebuchadnezzar of Babylonia points his finger at Zedekiah, the last king of Judah. Nebuchadnezzar destroyed Jerusalem and punished Zedekiah for rebelling by putting out his eyes, killing his sons, and taking him captive to Babylonia along with the people of Judah.

rule in lower Mesopotamia, at first supported their Persian masters against the Muslim invaders but slowly transferred their allegiance. By 637 Mesopotamia was completely subjugated by the second caliph, Umar (634–644), in a decisive battle at al-Qadisiyah (sometimes called Kadisiya), a locality on the Euphrates south of Baghdad. The religion and, only somewhat more slowly, the language of the victors were accepted by the majority of the population, which since has been Muslim and counted itself Arab.

The Iraqis, whose culture was more advanced than that of the victors themselves, however, did not passively accept the culture brought by the newcomers. Rather, Iraqi culture predominated so thoroughly that the Muslim Arab golden age that followed was centered in Iraq, not in the Arabian Peninsula, and it was the Muslim Arabs rather than the old population of Mesopotamia that may be said to have been culturally absorbed.

As the Islamic empire grew, the center of power shifted from Arabia northward to Syria and Iraq. In this process new divisions and conflicts were added to traditional Arab intertribal and interfactional strife; longstanding regional conflicts reasserted themselves in the new empire. From the beginning, Muslim Arab egalitarianism before Allah, or God, was perpetuated, but neither then nor since has the Arab ideal of political union among all Arabic-speaking peoples become a lasting reality. Down to the present time the world has witnessed a continual alternation in the Arab world between movements toward unity and countermovements toward schism.

After the stabilization of Muslim power in the territories which included present-day Iraq, Iran, Syria, and Egypt, the problem of the succession to the caliphate became pressing. In 661 Ali, the fourth caliph (656-61), with his center of power in Iraq, was murdered by his adversaries. Ali's son, Hassan, though proclaimed caliph, had to abdicate in the face of superior forces advancing under Muawiyah, who became the first of the Umayyad caliphs (661–750) ruling from Damascus in Syria. The last trace of armed resistance to the new Umayyad Dynasty was eliminated in 680 when Ali's second son, Husain, was killed in a battle.

Meanwhile, in opposition to the Umayyad Dynasty, supporters of Ali and his descendants founded a political organization called the *shiat* Ali, or "the party (partisans) of Ali." Centered in Iraq, this movement drew its initial members almost exclusively from among the Arabs involved in the succession struggles but gradually gained support from large numbers of disaffected Muslim converts in Iraq and Persia who had been treated as second-class Muslims by the Arab aristocracy in Damascus. The early political conflicts soon hardened into the first major religious schism in the Muslim world—the rival Shia and Sunni branches. Both Ali and Husain became Syria martyrs; Najaf, Ali's burial place some ninety miles south of Baghdad, and Karbala, fifty-five miles southwest of Baghdad, where Husain died, became holy places of pilgrimage as important to the Shiites as Mecca is to the Sunnites.

The Muslim Empire achieved its greatest political expansion under the Umayyads. From southern France, where it existed only fleetingly, its domains included the Iberian Peninsula, the whole of North Africa, including Egypt, the Mediterranean islands, the Arabian Peninsula, Asia Minor, the Fertile Crescent, Persia with its boundaries pushed eastward to the Amu Darya, Afghanistan, temporary possessions in India and the western-most portion of China.

Umayyad power waned in the early eighth century because of the age-old Arab difficulties of feud and schism within the ruling aristocracy. The dynasty was also being challenged by the dissident Shiites and other sectarian forces which questioned the legitimacy of the Umayyad caliphate. In 750 it was supplanted by the Abbasside rebels, Arab Sunnites who were most active in Persia but also had the support of Iraqi Shiites.

THE ABBASSIDE CALIPHATE (750–1258)

The Abbassides claimed their descent from al-Abbas (566–652), an uncle of Mohammed and, despite Shiite opposition, they asserted themselves as legitimate heirs of the Prophet. Under the Abbassides, Baghdad became the center of power where Arab and Persian cultures mingled to produce a blaze of philosophical, scientific, and literary glory remembered throughout the Arab world and by Iraqis in particular as the pinnacle of the Islamic past.

A cosmopolitan center of the medieval world, Baghdad had the advantages of an adequate water supply, river communications, and freedom from malaria. Although it was built entirely with the needs of political administration in mind, its population grew rapidly as it gained importance as a social, political, and trade center and by 800 it had become the second largest city in the Mediterranean world, next only to Constantinople (now Istanbul).

The greatest caliphs of the period combined outstanding administrative and intellectual capacities with unrelenting cruelty. Their ruthlessness is less significant as a personal trait than as evidence of the substitution, perhaps under Persian influence, of the caliph as absolute autocrat for the traditional Arab notion of the leader chosen by a council of his peers and answerable solely to the council. The Abbasside cultural renaissance roughly spanned the reigns of the first seven rulers of the dynasty (750-842). Of the seven, three achieved lasting fame: Mansur (754-75), Harun al-Rashid (786-806), and Mamun (813–33). These sovereigns had in common great administrative and political ability, both of which were vital in keeping under control the factional strife. The situation in Iraq with its Sunni dynasty and large Shia population was especially volatile, and it required all the guile and sternness of the Abbassides to stay in power. The Abbasside caliphs had to contend with continual Shia revolts in Iraq, Persia, and Arabia.

The Abbasside caliphate did not end abruptly but fell into

a long decline under the stresses of regional, ethnic, and religious differences. In areas under a relatively weak control, local forces revolted and gained autonomy as early as 756 when Spain broke away. Morocco followed in 788, Tunisia in 800, and Egypt in 868. The Abbasside decay was prompted by the Sunni-Shia split which had weakened the effectiveness of Islam as a single unifying force and as a sanction for a single political authority.

Although the intermingling of various linguistic and cultural groups contributed greatly to the enrichment of Islamic civilization, it was also a source of tensions. Not only was there the cleavage between the Arabs and Persians, but the growing prominence of the Turks in military and political affairs gave cause for discontent and rivalry in court. The Turks came as a stream of slaves brought in year by year to man the caliphs' imperial guard and fill the ranks of the regular military forces as mercenaries.

Excelling in combat, Turkish officers rose rapidly to high positions and began to replace the Arabs around the seat of power. This trend was quickened after the rule of Caliph Mutasim (833-42) whose mother was a Turkish slave. By the tenth century the Turkish commanders—no longer checked by their Persian rivals in court—were able to bring the caliphs under their effective control. Consequently, the political power of the caliphate was separated from its religious functions—functions which had heretofore been combined in the person of the caliph.

There was no disposition, however, to dispense with the office of the caliphate, since the sanction of the incumbent continued to be important as a symbol for legitimizing claims to authority. Thus, even the strong-handed Persian Buwayhid family of the Shia branch which ruled Iraq for a century (945–1055) retained the caliph as a shadowy symbol of spiritual authority. Until terminated in Iraq by the Mongols in 1258, the Abbasside caliphs continued to be treated with deference but only as nominal sovereigns. After 1258 the Abbassides fled to Cairo, where they continued to exercise, under Egyptian protection, the spiritual authority of the caliphate.

The highpoints of the Muslim renaissance in Iraq occurred during the reign of Harun al-Rashid, marked by its material splendor, and that of his son Mamun, which saw the greatest intellectual advances. In Mamun's time some of the great Islamic poetry was written. Under his successors, impressive advances were also made in mathematics, physics, astronomy, and geography. Historical and religious scholarship also prospered, and the compilation and further creation of Arabian tales began. In addition, the Abbasside caliphs sought to preserve the unity of Islamic thought by encouraging the use of Arabic as the common medium of expression for all peoples in the empire.

At the top of the Abbasside society was the caliph, the head of a theocratic state. He was assisted by the vizier, often the power behind the throne. Under them were a number of ministers and senior military officers presiding over a salaried bureaucracy and standing army. Learned men were highly honored in and outside the court for their literary pursuits. Artists, merchants, farmers, herdsmen, and slaves comprised the remainder of social groups, but there were relatively few rigid social barriers among them. Slavery existed, but little stigma was attached to it.

In the first half of the thirteenth century the Mongols had reached the lower edges of what is now Soviet Russia in Europe. In 1256 under Hulagu, a grandson of Genghis Khan (1162–1227), the Mongols sacked Baghdad. The material and artistic production of centuries was swept away. Iraq itself was laid waste, a tragedy from which the country recovered only in the twentieth century; the canal system, upon which the prosperity of the land depended, fell into ruin.

The Mongol overlords yielded to the Islamic culture of their subject peoples, but their rule remained alien to the end. Another wave of Mongols under Tamerlane (Timur Lenk) (1369–1405) further ravaged Baghdad in 1393, but he was no more successful than his predecessors in stabilizing the vast Mongol Empire. New local dynasties and additional Mongol groups rose to power in quick succession.

In Iraq, political chaos, economic depression, and social disintegration immediately followed the Mongolian invasions. Baghdad, so long a center of trade, rapidly lost its commercial importance. A major preoccupation of the governmental authorities has been to keep the peace in order to maintain the agricultural production essential to the whole economy. As central controls weakened, nomadic tribes encroached on the settled areas.

The first outside force to take advantage of these conditions was Ismail Shah (1499–1523), the founder of the Persian Safavid Dynasty (1499–1736) and self-proclaimed leader of all Shiites. In 1509 he conquered Iraq and in doing so came into conflict with the Ottomans (Turks) of the Sunni order, who had their capital at Istanbul. Persian rule ended in 1534 when Baghdad was captured by Suleyman the Magnificent (reigned 1520-66). Earlier in 1517 the Ottomans had taken Cairo, ending the reign of the last of the Abbasside caliphs, and thereafter Ottoman sultans claimed the title of caliph. Istanbul became the center of Islam, and Iraq was left to decay. Except for an interlude of Persian Safavid control in the seventeenth century (1623–38), Iraq remained under Ottoman rule until 1918.

THE OTTOMAN PERIOD (1534-1918)

Divided into the three provinces (*vilayet*) of Baghdad, Mosul, and Basrah, Iraq was administered by appointed governors (pasha) answerable directly to the sultan-caliph in Istanbul. As the eastern frontier outpost of the empire, it was subjected to recurrent forays by Shiite Persian powers and by tribes in Kurdistan as well as by the rebellious local chieftains of the predominantly Shia southern Iraq. A tenuous peace was maintained with the intractable tribes largely by leaving them alone. For more than a century, beginning in the early eighteenth century, the waning Ottoman sultan-caliphate could exercise its authority minimally by confirming as governors the strongest among the local chieftains in Iraq. Not until around 1830 did the Ottomans reassert absolute power under the strong leadership of Sultan Mahmud II (1808–39).

From 1831 until World War I the Ottoman rulers sought sporadically to modernize their administration, frequently with the help of European advisers, largely to revive national powers in face of various expansionist threats from Russia and Europe. The Ottoman sultans, gradually enforcing their right to appoint administrators and station troops, turned their attention to many semi-independent pashas. Finally they tried to extend government to the heretofore autonomous tribes, including those in Kurdistan. By selling land to the local rulers and encouraging them to accept government positions, it was hoped that the nomadic tribes could be forced to settle and to accept the government's right to tax and to conscript. Considerable unrest followed these efforts.

After the turn of the century, the Germans and the British became the primary contenders for influence in Iraq. Because of the British obstruction, for example, German plans to make Kuwait the terminus of the Berlin-Baghdad-Basra Railway were abandoned in June 1914. On another occasion the British combined with the shaikh of Kuwait, King Ibn Saud of Arabia, and a semi-independent local Iraqi ruling group to prevent a reassertion of the pro-German Ottoman power in the lower delta area around Basra.

THE TWENTIETH CENTURY

WORLD WAR I

In November 1914 the Ottoman Empire, allied with Germany, was at war with Great Britain, Russia, and France. The British dispatched an expeditionary force from India to Basra to protect their oil interests in adjacent Iran. The first major British advance under General Charles Townshend was stopped in 1915 below Baghdad at Kut on the Tigris by Turkish troops under the command of a German general, and the Anglo-Indian forces were captured. Aroused, the British decided upon a major engagement in Iraq; by March 1917 new forces led by General Stanley Maude seized Baghdad. In November 1918 the British ended the Ottoman rule in Iraq by occupying the remainder of the country to the Anatolian highlands north of Mosul, where Arabic speech is replaced by Turkish speech.

Upon capturing Baghdad, Maude proclaimed that Great Britain intended to return to Iraq some control of its own affairs, stressing that this step would pave the way for ending the subjection to alien rulers which the country had known since the Mongol conquest. The proclamation was in keeping with the encouragement the British had given to Arab nationalists, such as Jafar al-Askari, Nuri al-Said, and

Jamil al-Midfai, who sought emancipation from Ottoman rule. Although these nationalists had supported the Allied powers in expectation of the defeat of the Ottoman regime, the local population for the most part had shown only minimal interest in the struggle against the Turks.

During the war the course of events in Iraq was influenced greatly by the Hashemite family (descendants of the Prophet Mohammed) of Husein ibn-Ali, sharif of Mecca. Aspiring to the establishment of an independent Arab kingdom, Husein in October 1915 had secured Great Britain's conditional assurances of support for his cause in return for Arab support against Turkey. Refusing to rally to the Ottoman sultan-caliph's call for a holy war against the Allies, Husein in June 1916 led the revolt of the Arabs, marching northward in conjunction with the British into Transjordan (Jordan), Palestine, and Syria.

Anticipating the fulfillment of Allied pledges, Husein's son, Prince Faisal, then head of a new Arab regime set up in Damascus with British support, and later to become modern Iraq's first king, arrived in Paris in 1919 as chief spokesman of the Arab cause. Much to his disappointment, Faisal found Allied powers less than enthusiastic about Arab independence and contemplating the notion of a mandate for the ex-Ottoman territories.

THE BRITISH MANDATE

The fate of Iraq and other Arab territories was formally decided in April 1920 at San Remo, Italy, where a conference of Allied powers placed Iraq and Palestine under the British mandate and Syria under French mandate. Faisal, who had been proclaimed king of Syria by a Syrian national congress in Damascus in March 1920, was ejected from Syria by the French in July 1920; the British then invited him to London as a token of their regard.

The most troublesome issue confronting the British was the growing evidence of Iraqi nationalist discontent. Arab and Iraqi nationalism, directed initially against the Turks in the beginning of the twentieth century, became increasingly anti-European after World War I. In July 1920 an anti-British revolt broke out in southern Iraq among many tribes which had for centuries jealously guarded their political autonomy. The insurrection spread over one-third of the countryside which had been already aroused by the efficient British tax collection methods. For three months the country was in a state of anarchy; order was restored only with difficulty by British forces which had to call upon reinforcements from India.

This episode, known to Iraqis as the national war of liberation, gave dramatic evidence of Arab dissatisfaction with foreign rule. Nevertheless, at no time did the revolt show coordination or general direction; throughout, many outstanding local shaikhs and urban figures remained aloof from the insurrection; the Iraqi police and security forces were notably loyal to the British authorities.

The British military authorities accepted the revolt as an object lesson. Civil disturbances had cost much loss of life

The official portrait of King Faisal I in civilian dress. He was proclaimed king in August 23, 1921 and died on September 8, 1933.

King Faisal I reigned from 1921 to 1933.

and inordinately large sums of money, prompting the British people to demand the reduction of commitments in Iraq. In October 1920 the military regime was replaced by a provisional Arab government to be assisted by British advisers and answerable to the supreme authority of the high commissioner for Iraq, Sir Percy Cox. The new administration was to serve as a channel of communication between the British and the restive population, to give opportunity for Iraqi leaders to come forward, and to prepare the way for eventual self-government. After a canvass of various influential personalities for the official chief of state, the British persuaded Prince Faisal, the deposed king of Syria, to ascend the throne.

Prince Faisal of the Hashemite family traced his descent from Mohammed, and his ancestors had held political authority around the holy cities of Arabia. Hence he was endowed with traditional Arab standards of political legitimacy which he could invoke to install himself as the monarch of Iraq. Moreover, his achievements as a leader in the Arab emancipation movement made him an acceptable candidate to many Iraqis who were deeply concerned with the development of a national government, especially to the former Iraqi officers in the Ottoman army who had supported the 1916 revolt against the Turks. His candidacy, however, was sponsored by the British to repay Hashemite assistance in World War I and to assure future cooperation between Iraq and Great Britain. A referendum of Iraqi notables, tribal chiefs, and townsmen produced an almost unanimous return favoring the selection of Faisal. On August 23, 1921, he was proclaimed king of Iraq.

The British sought to cope with the growing nationalist demands for immediate and outright independence by concluding a compromise treaty with Iraq in October 1922. Intended to soften the mandate relationship, the treaty gave Iraq limited control in the spheres of both foreign and domestic affairs but retained Britain's ultimate mandatory power. Attempts to modify the 1922 treaty followed in 1923, 1926, and 1927; as a result, the British in December

1927 pledged to conditionally support Iraq's admission to the League of Nations in 1932.

A notable step toward independence was the British decision in September 1929 to terminate the mandate, support unconditionally the admission of Iraq into the league, and to open negotiations with the Iraqi government toward a treaty of alliance defining future relations between the two countries. This move was precipitated by the coming to power of the Labour party in London. This change of regime was paralleled by the emergence of a liberal nationalist government in Baghdad under Nuri al-Said, who the British authorities believed was capable of leading the country to self-rule.

A new pact called the Anglo-Iraqi treaty was signed in June 1930, providing for the establishment of a "close alliance" and for "full and frank consultation between them in all matters of foreign policy" and mutual assistance in case of war. Iraq granted to the British use of air bases at Basra and at Habbaniyah and the right to move troops across the country. To be of twenty-five years duration, the treaty was to come into force upon Iraq's admission to the League of Nations.

King Ghazi ruled Iraq from 1933 to 1939.

King Faisal II, although eligible for the throne from the death of his father in 1939, continued his education abroad. After graduating from Harrow in England in 1952, he returned to Iraq. This photograph shows him on his return. Great crowds greeted him upon his return to assume the crown and leadership of Iraq.

INDEPENDENCE

Iraq became a sovereign, independent state on October 3, 1932, when it was admitted to the league. The British mandate was automatically terminated. The independent government possessed adequate financial means to cope with many of its internal problems because of its growing oil revenues; oil had been discovered at Naft Khaneh (about ninety miles northeast of Baghdad) in 1923 and at Kirkuk in 1927. By 1930 oil products were being exported.

Among the problems confronting the government were the deep-seated Shia-Sunni conflicts. The Sunnites, favored by the Turks during Ottoman rule, had had more administrative experience than their adversaries. The Shiites, at the time constituting 50 percent or more of the population and being very conscious of the presence in Iraq of so many Sunni holy places, began to fear the possibility of complete Sunni domination in the government. On the other hand, some of the old-fashioned Sunnites felt that Faisal's 1916 revolt against the Ottoman sultan-caliph had been an impious act and were indisposed to give full support to the new monarch. In addition, many non-Arab groups, such as the Jews and Kurds, resented the accession of an Arab dynasty.

In Iraq Kurdish opposition to British encroachments upon their traditional autonomy erupted into anti-British and anti-Iraqi revolts in 1922–24. Their hostility increased after 1925 when the League of Nations awarded Mosul, to which Turkey laid claim, to Iraq; despite their traditional suspicion of all outsiders, many of the Kurds in the Mosul region appeared to have favored Turkish rather than Iraqi rule.

These problems were compounded by the death of King Faisal I in September 1933. His departure meant the loss of the main stabilizing personality in politics and the one figure with sufficient prestige to draw the politicians together around a concept of national interest and to balance nationalist and British pressures within the framework of the Anglo-Iraqi alliance. His son and successor, Ghazi, was a strong Arab nationalist, but he was inexperienced and

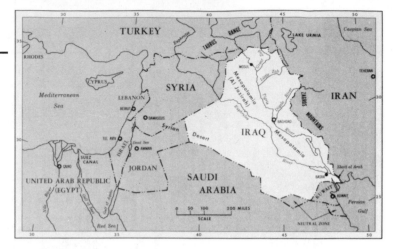

The position of Iraq in southwest Asia

unable to control the increasing factionalism stemming from tribal and communal tensions and the clamor of voices against Great Britain's dominant influence in Iraqi affairs.

The first military involvement occurred in October 1936 when a coup d'etat was executed by an alliance of the army, representing idealistic nationalism, and by a reformist political group, known as the Ahali (People) which advocated socialism and democracy. The incumbent government of Prime Minister General Yasin al-Hashimi was forced from office, and King Ghazi, a helpless bystander, was put in a position of having to sanction a regime coming to power by unconstitutional means. In the course of the coup, Minister of Defense General Jafar al-Askari, a highly regarded older statesman, a leading pro-British figure and founder of the Iraqi army, was assassinated.

After King Ghazi's death in 1939, the crown passed to his four-year-old son, Faisal II, and the royal authority devolved upon the regent, Abdul Illah, who was the young king's uncle and crown prince.

WORLD WAR II AND POSTWAR IRAQ

When World War II broke out in September 1939, Prime Minister Nuri al-Said severed diplomatic relations with Germany under the Anglo-Iraqi treaty of 1930. Rashid Ali al-Gailani was ostensibly neutral, but his sympathies lay with the Germans. By March 1940, when he replaced Nuri al-Said as prime minister (March 1940-January 1941), he had gradually gathered the support of anglophobes in general as well as ultranationalists impressed by Fascist ideology. Despite the opposition of the British and of Nuri al-Said and the regent, he sought to maintain friendly contacts with the Axis powers. He further antagonized the British by returning to power in April 1941 through a coup and by attempting to modify the Anglo-Iraqi treaty terms of 1930 governing wartime conditions.

The British retaliated by landing forces at Basra in late April 1941, and they justified their action under the 1930 pact. Many Iraqis, still in the flush of their recently won independence, regarded the move as an attempt to restore British rule. They rallied to the support of the Iraqi army, which received a token amount of aid from the Axis. By late

King Ghazi was but twenty-one when he accepted the throne in 1933.

King Faisal II as he appeared early in his reign

The official portrait of King Faisal II

King Faisal II reading the statement of accession

On his 1952 visit to the United States, the king toured the Library of Congress in Washington, D.C. He is seen here examining a document with Senator Theodore Francis Green, left, of Rhode Island, the then chairman of the Congressional Joint Committee on the Library.

The king and the crown prince were close friends. They are seen here leaving a state luncheon in Baghdad. They were both executed in the coup d'etat of July 14, 1958.

The official portrait of the crown prince Abdul Ilah

May, however, the uprising had been suppressed, and Rashid Ali and his associates had fled the country. Succeeding governments cooperated with the Allies. In January 1943, Iraq declared war on the Axis under the 1930 pact.

In March 1945 Iraq became a founding member of the Arab League (Iraq, Egypt, Jordan, Lebanon, Saudi Arabia, Syria, and Yemen) which was designed to promote "cooperation in economic, cultural, social, and other matters" in a loose framework of Arab unity. It also joined the United Nations in December 1945.

Although the country opposed the creation of Israel in 1948, its external orientation was strongly pro-Western in postwar years. In April 1954 the nation accepted United States military assistance, and in January 1955 the government of Prime Minister Nuri al-Said suspended diplomatic relations with the Soviet Union. In addition, in February 1955 Iraq signed a mutual defense treaty with Turkey (better known as the Baghdad Pact) to which Great Britain, Pakistan, and Iran acceded during the year. Iraq's pro-Western policy culminated in the formation of the Arab Federation (Iraq and Jordan) on February 14, 1958, as a counterweight to the avowed neutralist but anti-Western United Arab Republic (Egypt and Syria) that had been formed earlier on February 1, 1958.

Though not always prime minister, Nuri al-Said was consistently recognized as the ultimate arbiter in the affairs of state and, together with Crown Prince Abdul Illah, personified the government. Men who entered political life after 1946, however, found Nuri al-Said and the crown prince out of sympathy with their liberal, reformist sentiments. Prince Abdul Illah's regency was terminated on May 2, 1953, when King Faisal II mounted the throne at the age of eighteen.

THE 1958 REVOLUTION AND END OF THE MONARCHY

The kingdom of the Hashemite family was overthrown on July 14, 1958, in a swift coup executed by a group of army officers under Brigadier Abdul Karim Qasim and Colonel Abdul Salam Arif. According to later statements by Qasim, he had planned such a move for many years. The coup, or "revolution" as the Iraqis have called it since, met virtually no armed opposition. King Faisal II and Crown Prince Abdul Illah as well as other members of the royal family were executed. The following day Nuri al-Said was also killed after attempting to escape disguised as a veiled woman.

The proclamation of the revolution brought crowds of people into the Baghdad streets cheering the deaths of two "strong men," Nuri al-Said and Abdul Illah. The young king's death appears to have been regretted for he was regarded as a helpless bystander in the intrigues of Iraqi politics, but he was not mourned.

The leaders of the new regime, who declared their nation a republic, envisioned an Iraq reformed, egalitarian, democratic, united in spirit with the Arab world and committed to a foreign policy of nonalignment. Qasim declared his determination to resist all foreign ideologies—"Communist, American, British, or Fascist." Amnesty was declared for political prisoners, and exiled opponents of the old regime were invited to return home, but the government dealt severely with more than one hundred leading supporters of the ousted regime. In March 1959 Iraq announced its withdrawal from the Baghdad Pact.

The Qasim government was troubled, however, by divisive rivalry within its ranks and by serious internal threats to its own survival. Many people inside and outside the government became disillusioned with Qasim's inability to consolidate authority and bring about any improvement in either political life or material prosperity. Growing disenchantment with Qasim's "personal dictatorship" and mounting pan-Arab sentiments culminated in the overthrow of the regime on February 8, 1963. Qasim was executed on the following day.

THE ROYAL SOVEREIGNS OF THE KINGDOMS OF IRAQ

(Iraq geographically corresponds to ancient Babylonia and Assyria.)

SOVEREIGNS OF BABYLONIA

Reign	Title	Ruler
FIRST DYNASTY		
2049–2036 B.C.	King	Sumuabi
2035–2000	King	Sumu-la-ilu
1967–1948	King	Sin-muballit
1947–1905	King	Hammurabi
1904–1867	King	Samsu-iluna
1866–1839	King	Abeshuh
1838–1802	King	Ammi-ditana
1801–1781	King	Ammi-zaduga
1780–1750	King	Samsuditana
KASSITE DYNASTY		
1521–1503 B.C.	King	Burnaburiash I
1502–1484	King	Kashtiliash II
1483–1465	King	Agum III
1445–1427	King	Karaindash
1344–1320	King	Kurigalza III
1319–1294	King	Nazimaruttash II
1293–1277	King	Kadashman-Turgu
1276–1271	King	Kadashman-Enlil II
1270–1263	King	Kudur-Enlil
1262–1250	King	Sagarakti-Suriash
1249–1242	King	Kastiash III
1232–1203	King	Adad-shum-nasir
1202–1188	King	Melishipah II
1187–1175	King	Merodach-baladan I
1174–	King	Zabada-sum-iddin
1173–1171	King	Enlil-nadin-ahe

SOVEREIGNS OF ASSYRIA

Reign	Title	Ruler
1410–1393 B.C.	King	Assur-nadir-ahe
1392–1381	King	Enib-Adad
1380–1341	King	Assur-yuballidh
1340–1326	King	Enlil-nirari
1325–1311	King	Arik-den-ili
1310–1281	King	Adadnirari I
1280–1261	King	Shalmaneser II
1260–1232	King	Tukulti-Ninurta
1231–1214	King	Assur-nasir-pal I
1213–1208	King	Assur-nirari III
1207–1203	King	Bel-Kudur-Uzur
1202–1176	King	Nin-Pala-Zira
1175–1141	King	Assur-Dayan I
1140–1138	King	Ninurta-tutulti-Assur
1137–1128	King	Mutaccil-Nebo
1127–1116	King	Assur-res-isi
1115–1103	King	Tiglath-Pileser I
1102–1093	King	Ninurta-apal-ekur II
1092–1076	King	Assur-Bil-Kala I
1075–1069	King	Enlil-rabi
1061–1056	King	Enriba-Adad
1055–1050	King	Shamshi-Adad IV
1049–1031	King	Assurnasirpal I
1030–1019	King	Shalmaneser II
1018–1013	King	Assur-nirari IV
1012–995	King	Assur-rabi II

ELAMITE DYNASTY

Reign	Title	Ruler
1170–1153 B.C.	King	Merodash-shapik-zer
1152–1147	King	Ninurta-nadin-shumi
1146–1123	King	Nebuchadnezzar
1122–1117	King	Enlil-nadin-apli
1116–1101	King	Merodach-nadin-ahe
1100–1092	King	Itti-Marduk-balatu
1091–1084	King	Merodach-shapik-zer-mati
1083–1062	King	Adad-apal-iddin
990–995	King	Nabo-mukin-apli
954–	King	Ninurta-kudur-usur
953–942	King	Marbiti-ahe-iddin
941–901	King	Samas-mudaminiq
900–886	King	Nabo-shum-ukin
885–852	King	Nabo-apal-iddin
851–828	King	Merodach-zakir-shum
827–815	King	Merodach-balatsuiqbi
814–811	King	Bau-ahe-iddin
802–763	King	Eriba-Marduk
747–734	King	Nabonassar
734–733	King	Nadinu
732–730	King	Ukin-zer
729–728	King	Tiglathpileser III
727–723	King	Shalmaneser V
722–710	King	Merodach-baladan III
710–705	King	Sargon II
705–682	King	Sennacherib

NEW BABYLONIAN EMPIRE

Reign	Title	Ruler
625–605 B.C.	King	Nabopolassar
605–562	King	Nebuchadnezzar II
562–560	King	Evil-Merodach
559–556	King	Nergal-shar-usur
556–539	King	Nabonidus
539–538	King	Balshazzar

Reign	Title	Ruler
994–967	King	Assur-res-isi II
956–930	King	Tiglath-Pileser II
930–911	King	Asshur-Dayan II
911–889	King	Adadnirari II (Vul-Lush II)
889–883	King	Tukulti-Ninurta II
883–858	King	Assur-nasir-pal II
858–823	King	Shalmaneser III
824–812	King	Shamshi-Adad V
810–781	King	Adadnirari III (Vul-Lush III)
781–771	King	Shalmaneser IV
771–753	King	Assur-Dayan III
753–745	King	Assur-Lush
745–727	King	Tiglath-Pileser III
727–722	King	Shalmaneser V
722–705	King	Sargon
705–681	King	Sennacherib
681–668	King	Esaraddon
668–626	King	Assur-Bani-Pal
626–625	King	Assur-Emid-Ilin (Saracus)

SOVEREIGNS OF IRAQ

Reign	Title	Ruler
1921–1933	King	Faisal I
1933–1939	King	Ghazi
1939–1958	King	Faisal II
1958—Iraq becomes a republic.		

9
The Dynasties of Iran (Persia)

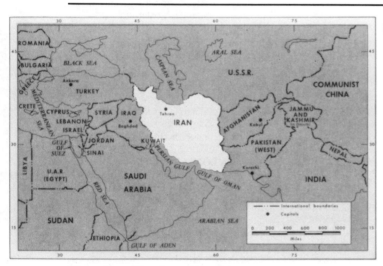
The position of Iran in southwest Asia

The country's national history goes back some twenty-five hundred years to the consolidated empire of the Indo-European Medes and Persians, who, in their southwestward migratory invasions, displaced and absorbed earlier native peoples. In the succeeding centuries the land was often subjected to foreign conquests as well as rule by native dynasties, and there developed a characteristic of national flexibility through which the people learned to absorb or adapt to external influences while retaining their own identity. Times of foreign domination were often overlooked in folklore and the common concepts of history, other than to acknowledge changes adopted from abroad. For example, most Iranians follow the religion of Islam but resent the historical period of political control by the Arabs who brought Islam to Iran in the seventh century A.D. Similarly, the technology of Europe was welcomed in the nineteenth and twentieth centuries but not the outside economic and political controls that sometimes came with it.

Major interaction with modern European systems and states began under the Kajar Dynasty, which ruled in Iran from 1795 to 1925. The introduction of European influence in the nineteenth century was followed by the rise of mod-ern Iranian nationalism and by constitutionalism early in the twentieth century. The first foreign oil concession was secured by a British firm in 1901, and oil was actually discovered in 1908. Great Britain and the Soviet Union, the principal contenders for economic and political power and influence, were challenged by Germany for eminence in Iran before and during the World War I period.

Riza Pahlevi, who succeeded the last of the Kajar shahs and founded the Pahlevi Dynasty in 1925, established a strong central government and strove for economic and industrial modernization while rejecting foreign domination. Between the two world wars the United States developed increased connections with Iran, but the principal foreign influences continued to be Great Britain and the Soviet Union, contending against each other and against the recurring challenge of Germany. When British and Soviet forces invaded and occupied Iran in 1941, Riza Pahlevi abdicated in protest, and (the late) Mohammed Riza Pahlevi, his son, commenced his reign on September 16, 1941, and ruled until January 1979 when he departed the country and its pressures for a "vacation."

ANCIENT PERSIA

Toward the end of the second millennium B.C., horseriding tribes speaking Indo-European languages began moving southward out of the Eurasian steppes in present-day southern Soviet Union territory. One branch of these Aryan peoples, the Hindus, moved southeast into the Indus Valley, while others distributed themselves on the plateau to the south and southwest of the Elburz Mountains, naming their new homeland Iran. Prevented from advancing farther westward by Assyria, Babylonia, and Elam, two separate groups of Iranians settled in the western sections of the Iranian plateau: the Medes in the area of modern East and West Azerbaijan provinces and the Persians in the area of modern Fars province. These vigorous peoples gradually intermarried with and displaced the older inhabitants of the Zagros Mountains.

154

During the seventh century B.C. the Medes, who had formerly lived in small feudal communities, were united into a nation-state with a capital at Ecbatana (modern Hamadan). This new state built up its military strength until 612 B.C., when Cyaxeres, king of the Medes, in league with Babylonia, destroyed the Assyrian capital of Nineveh. During this period the religious reformer Zoroaster (ca. 630-550 B.C.), also known as Zarathustra, in contrast to the polytheistic nature worship common among the Iranian tribes, introduced a new religious faith based on one god, already widely known to the people, named Ahura Mazda, as the only true god. This faith, which became known as Zoroastrianism, spread widely in Iran.

ACHAEMENID EMPIRE (CA. 650–328 B.C.)

In 559 B.C., under the leadership of Cyrus I, known as Cyrus the Great, of the Achaemenid Dynasty, the Persians, who had been held tributary to the Medes, asserted their independence and extended their rule from Persia through Media. Uniting the Medes and Persians into a single nation, Cyrus overthrew Babylonia in 539 B.C. and conquered several minor kingdoms to reach the Aegean coast of Asia Minor and the Mediterranean coast of Syria. He then turned his attention eastward and extended his domains to the Oxus River and the Hindu Kush in modern Afghanistan, creating the most extensive empire the world had ever known by the time of his death in 529 B.C.

In 522 B.C. Darius I, later known as Darius the Great, took the throne, suppressed invading nomads from north of the Caucasus, and extended the empire. His dominions stretched from Libya, Egypt, and Greek Thrace to the Indus River in modern Pakistan and included the ceremonial capital city built at Persepolis, near modern Shiraz. Like Cyrus, however, he continued to rule his empire from Susa, the ancient capital of the Elamites, during the winter and from Ecbatana, the capital of the Medes at the site of modern Hamadan, in the summer.

The early Achaemenids were known for their tolerance toward their subject peoples; they frequently adopted the titles of former rulers in such lands as Babylonia and Egypt. They permitted a variety of religions to flourish in the empire. Cyrus the Great after 539 B.C. had allowed the Jews to return to Jerusalem from their captivity in Mesopotamia under the Babylonians.

Darius divided the empire into twenty provinces, each ruled over by a *satrap*, who was usually a scion of a noble Persian family. Satraps were virtually autonomous and were not troubled by the central government unless they failed to produce the yearly tribute or attempted to stage a revolt against the Shahanshah. Darius also built and maintained an excellent system of roads and established an extensive intelligence network.

The economy of the Achaemenid Empire was based on agriculture, and the king saw to it that elaborate irrigation systems were created and maintained to support the agriculture. A bimetallic system of gold and silver coinage was

Bas-relief of Cyrus the Great. Military genius and concern for human rights were his attributes. This statue suggests he was a divine being.

The late shah of Iran placing a wreath before the tomb of Cyrus the Great at Pasagadae, the old Persian capital (1973)

When the humanitarian Cyrus the Great conquered Babylon, he decreed that the Jews be restored to the land King Nebuchadnezzar had taken from them and that their treasures (gold and silver vessels amongst others) be restored to them. In this painting by Doré, the scene of the restoration of the treasures is re-created.

A seal of Darius I preserved in the British Museum shows the king hunting lions among the palm trees.

Darius the Great, king of Persia, ruled from 522 to 486 B.C.

Three stamps issued in 1948. Top to bottom: the Palace of Darius the Great, the Tomb of Cyrus the Great at Pasargadae, and of King Darius on his throne.

A 1915 stamp issued to commemorate the coronation of Shah Ahmed, on his throne

In A.D. 226, Ardashir I, the grandson of a Persian chief named Sassan, created a throne for himself as "King of Kings" of Persia. The Sassanid Dynasty founded by him lasted until 641.

Xerxes I having a discussion with the god Ahura-Mazda in this crypt carving

The death of Darius in battle in 486 B.C.

The rock tomb of Darius near Persepolis

adopted and further served to foster trade. The central government was supported by a fixed money tax plus a contribution in goods from each province except Persis, from which the ruling Persian aristocracy came.

GRECO-PERSIAN PERIOD (330–250 B.C.)

In 499 B.C., while Darius I was still king, the Greek colonies in Asia Minor rebelled against Persian rule. The revolts were crushed, but a punitive expedition sent against Athens in 490 B.C. was turned back by the Athenians at the Battle of Marathon. The tolerance that Achaemenid kings had displayed in ruling their vast empire was gradually abandoned

as revolts increased in the parts of the empire farthest from the central province. Xerxes I succeeded his father, Darius I, in 486 B.C. and spent the first few years of his reign putting down minor revolts in Egypt and Babylon. In 481 B.C. Xerxes set out to conquer the Greek Peloponnesus peninsula but, after initial success at Thermopylae, was defeated at Salamis and again at Plataea. After the death of Xerxes' successor, Artaxerxes I, in 425 B.C., the Persian court disintegrated into contending factions.

By the end of the fifth century B.C., the Greek city-states also were so torn by civil wars that general peace prevailed between Greece and Persia, although both played active roles in one another's domestic politics. Persian kings sometimes intervened in the rivalries between Sparta and Athens, and Greek merchants played an important part in the schemes of many members of the Persian royal family to wrest the throne from rival Achaemenids.

Darius III (336–330 B.C.) ascended to the Achaemenid throne in the same year that Philip of Macdeon, who had put an end to the internecine wars in Greece, was succeeded by his son, Alexander the Great. By 334 B.C. Alexander had established his authority over the Greeks and had begun to advance into Asia Minor. Persian forces of the time were unable to stem the Greek advance. Alexander, after first conquering Egypt, turned northeastward to occupy Babylon, Susa, Persepolis, and Ecbatana. In 330 B.C. Darius III was put to death by his own subjects, thus ending the Achaemenid Dynasty. It took Alexander two years to occupy the eastern provinces, which had managed to discard Persian rule during the decline of the empire; he then advanced into India until a revolt among his soldiers forced him to return to Babylon, where he died in 323 B.C.

Alexander, after establishing himself as king of Persia, adopted the dress and ceremonial of the Persian court and was accepted as the legitimate head of the empire. His marriage to a Bactrian chieftain's daughter and other attempts, such as the mass marriage at Susa of ten thousand Macedonian veterans with Persian women, to blend Greek and Iranian cultures met with some success, primarily because the two civilizations had long been in commercial and cultural contact with one another. During and immediately after his conquest, a large influx of Greek immigrants entered the former Achaemenid territories and established new cities along the great trade routes from Greece to India.

PARTHIAN KINGDOM
(CA. 250 B.C.–A.D. 226)

After Alexander's death, his empire gradually split into minor kingdoms under native rulers, while his chief lieute-nants fought for the right to rule the entire territory. Around 312 B.C. Seleucus, one of Alexander's commanders, managed to establish his authority over most of the eastern part of the empire, which his successors, known as Seleucids, held for over two hundred years. In the middle of the third century B.C., however, a dynasty called the Arsacids—after their first king, Arsaces—was established in Parthia, in the modern province of Khorasan. The area of Mesopotamia in modern Iraq became the center of their power, but their kingdom is usually known to historians as the Parthian Kingdom. The Arsacids and their followers, like the earlier Medes or Persians, were not native to the area but apparently first were nomads from east of the Caspian Sea. They replaced the authority of the Seleucids in Media, Persia (area of the modern province of Fars), and much of Mesopotamia during the rule of their great king, Mithridates I (174-136 B.C.). Other Seleucid domains were gradually reduced by both Romans and the Arsacids until 63 B.C., when the Roman general Pompey deposed the last Seleucid and extended Rome's boundaries as far as the Parthian holdings.

When this historic contact took place, the scene was set for the revival of the conflict between East and West that was to dominate Middle Eastern affairs for the next seven hundred years.

The reign of the Arsacids over the Parthian Kingdom, lasting almost five centuries, is not noted in history for intellectual or artistic achievement. Arsacid kings built their winter capital, Ctesiphon, in Mesopotamia, about twenty miles southeast of modern Baghdad; in summer they traveled between Ecbatana, the old Medean capital at the site of modern Hamadan, and Hecatompylos in Parthia—the latter place being some one hundred sixty miles northeast of Tehran. Noble families, almost completely autonomous in their own small provinces, were the real powers in the kingdom.

The official religion of the Parthian Empire was a cor-

The young Riza Shah at Persepolis with his father, the shah of Iran, examining the inscriptions on Darius the Great's tomb

King Arsaces I, the monarch who founded the Arsacid Dynasty in 250 B.C.

A silver dish from the third century shows the Iranian monarch Hormisdas I hunting lions. The shah ruled from 272 to 273.

rupted form of Zoroastrianism with a substantial mixture of animistic beliefs. The Greek language was utilized in official documents, and Greek coinage was used throughout the empire.

SASSANID EMPIRE (A.D. 226-641)

Artabanus IV, the last Arsacid king, fought a successful defensive war against the Roman legions in A.D. 217 and held his western frontier. In A.D. 226, however, he was overthrown from within by his vassal, Ardashir, founder of the Sassanid Dynasty. The Sassanids came from Persis (the modern province of Fars); but their power was centered, as had been that of the Arsacids, in Mesopotamia.

The new dynasty turned with renewed vigor on the traditional enemy, Rome, and intermittent fighting was resumed. When the Roman emperor Constantine proclaimed Christianity as the religion of Rome in A.D. 323, historic hostilities between East and West assumed a religious aspect. While they were fighting Rome in the west, the Sassanids also struggled to protect their eastern provinces from incursions by nomads such as the Huns. Baranes V (Bahram Gor), one of the Sassanids' most famous kings, drove the Huns eastward and back across the Oxus River in A.D. 425. For several generations after the victory, however, Sassanid monarchs were preoccupied with the threat from the northeast.

The Sassanids, who claimed descent from the Achaemenids, set out to eliminate all Hellenistic influences. The Persian language of the Sassanids, written in an ideographic system called Pahlevi, became the first Persian tongue to be used as the official language in Iran.

During the Sassanid period, factional intrigue continued to characterize the processes of succession to the throne; nevertheless, the authority of the central government was strengthened. One of the most famous of Sassanid kings, Chosroes I (Khosrow), who ruled from 531 to 578, carried out significant administrative reforms. He was also known as *Anushirvan,* or "he of the immortal spirit." Under his direction a survey of Persia was made, and a fixed tax was determined, based on land unit area. Because of this change from the tradition of taking a percentage of the crop from each village, the peasants were encouraged to try to increase the yield of the land.

Chosroes I fostered agriculture in other ways, such as reclaiming wastelands, improving the irrigation system, and maintaining the safety of the highways. The economy of Iran prospered during this period, which also saw a revival of art and literature, and in modern times the era of the Sassanid kings is regarded as the golden age in Iranian history. Chosroes I, like other Sassanid shahs, was almost constantly at war with Rome on the west or invaders from the east. Peripheral boundaries varied from time to time, but the integrity of Iran was preserved.

Under Chosroes II, who reigned from 591 to 628, the Sassanian royal court of Iran attained an unprecedented level of splendor and wealth. Military victories carried Persian rule briefly to Syria, Jerusalem, and Egypt, only to be followed by successive defeats at the hands of a revived Roman Empire under Emperor Heraclius. The Sassanid Dynasty then declined in Iran and ended with the assassination of the last Sassanid king, Yazdegerd III, in 641 after severe military defeats in battles against the new Arab invaders.

MEDIEVAL CONQUEST AND RECONSTITUTION

MUSLIM CONQUEST

While the empires of Iran and Byzantium—the Con-

Alexander the Great charging the entourage of the Persian king in a mosaic of the Battle of Issus. This famous treasure is partially destroyed but the upper body of Alexander can be seen on the left. Alexander the Great ruled Persia from 331 to 323 B.C.

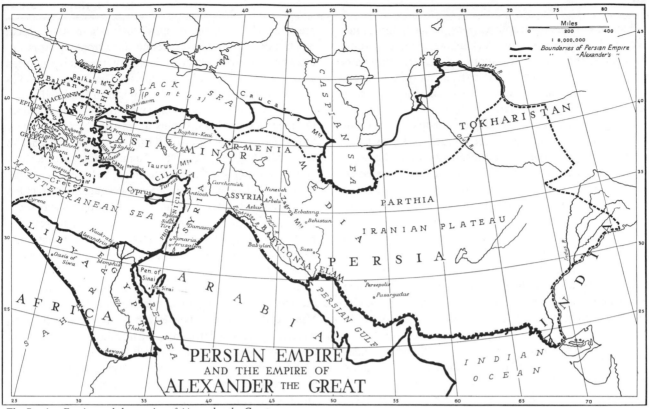

The Persian Empire and the empire of Alexander the Great

stantinople-based successor to the Roman Empire in the East—were expending their energies in battle against one another during the first part of the seventh century A.D., a new religious force grew up in the western part of the Arabian Peninsula. By the time of his death in A.D. 632, the Prophet Mohammed and his followers had united most of the important Arab tribes under the banner of Islam. In 633 Abu Bakr, the first caliph of Islam, successor to the Prophet Mohammed, was strong enough to attack simultaneously both the Byzantine and Persian empires.

After capturing Damascus and defeating the Byzantine army in 635, the Arab Muslims marched against and defeated the Iranian Sassanid forces; in 637 they occupied the capital of the Sassanid Empire at Ctesiphon and renamed it Madain. A few Iranian governors tried unsuccessfully to halt the Arab advance eastward, but the Muslims had reached the Oxus River by 650, and all the former Sassanid domains came under Arab administration.

Chosroes II in this relief shows the king to be an aggressive warrior, in evidence that he conquered Asia Minor, Syria, Palestine, and Egypt. His rule was from A.D. 591 to 628.

By the middle of the seventh century, the period of the Arabs' most dramatic expansion was ended, and the subsequent history of Islam centered on struggles for political power and religious orthodoxy. The murder of Uthman, the third caliph, in 656 sparked a civil war; its effects permanently divided Islam into separate factions. Ali, the cousin and son-in-law of the Prophet, became the fourth caliph in the succession recognized by Sunni Islam, but he was murdered in 661. In that year Muawiyah, the leader of a faction opposed to the caliphate of Ali, was able to assume the title of caliph. He established the Umayyad Dynasty with its capital in Damascus, and factionalism spread throughout the Islamic world.

Since this period an important Muslim segment, the Shiites, has believed that only Ali or a member of his house could have been a true caliph. Shia beliefs eventually came to predominate in Iran, the only Islamic country in which Shiites constitute a majority. They also gained a substantial number of adherents in Iraq, Yemen, and Syria. The majority of Muslims, however, belong to the Sunni branch of Islam, regarding themselves as preceptually correct and coming from those who supported the caliphal succession as it occurred. Since the original split, basic questions of theology and practice have widened the gap between the two branches.

Under the Sunni Umayyad caliphs, the former Sassanid Empire was divided into provinces, but administration was left in the hands of Iranian officials. Arabic replaced Persian as the official language; the educated Iranians, however, became conversant in both tongues, which led eventually to the Arabicization of the Persian language. The Arabs never attempted seriously to colonize the easternmost parts of their empire, but they did settle in the southwestern corner of Khuzistan, where the principal group of Arabs can be found in modern Iran.

During the first half of the eighth century, several unsuccessful insurrections were mounted against the Umayyad caliphs. Many of the rebels fled into Khorasan, which became a refuge for various factions of discontented Muslims. These groups were susceptible to the propaganda activities of a faction supporting the descendants of al-Abbas, an uncle of the Prophet Mohammed, as claimants to the caliphate in opposition to the Umayyads. In 747 an Iranian leader named Abu Muslim al-Khorasani gathered the Khorasan dissidents into an army. After a series of skillful political and military campaigns, he defeated the Umayyad forces, occupied Iraq, and established Abdul Abbas as caliph in 750, thus commencing the Abbasside Dynasty.

The Abbassides built a new capital at Baghdad. Under their rule, Iranians who had participated in the revolt gained great influence and paved the way for the spread of Islam throughout the Iranian population. During the next century, as the Abbasside caliphs adopted the pomp and pageantry of the earlier Persian dynasties, their power declined. Administrative functions were largely exercised through an appointed grand vizier (chief minister), chosen from outside the Abbasside family to prevent him legally from usurping the title of caliph.

As the power of the Abbassides waned, small principalities began asserting their independence in the provinces. Among these, the Safavid people in the region of Sistan (in the southeast near the boundary with modern Pakistan) are regarded by Iranians as the first native dynasty to assert its independence from Arab rule. Old Iranian noble families, as well as energetic adventurers, established their rule over small states in the eastern part of modern Iran, in Afghanistan, and in southern Russia. Some of these rulers began their careers as governors appointed from Baghdad; most were recent converts to Islam; and all sought legitimization by obtaining titles from the caliph. Generally, however, they paid only lip service to the ruling Abbasside, who was gradually reduced to a religious authority without political power.

Ever since Achaemenid times, Turkic-speaking tribesmen had been moving out of central Asia into Transoxiana (modern Soviet Turkistan). These nomadic peoples were noted for their skills in warfare, and in the early ninth century many Turks were brought into Baghdad to serve as warrior slaves (*mamluks*) of the caliph. Within a few years these slave troops had established themselves as the real power behind the throne in Baghdad, regularly deposed Abbasside caliphs, and brought new Abbassides to power in palace revolts. The independent Iranian princes ruling northeast of Baghdad failed to take heed of the lesson

presented them by the caliphs' fate. These rulers spent much time and energy protecting their frontiers from encroachments by Turkish raiders, but they too imported Turkic slaves into their own courts. The imported slaves gradually assumed control as they had in Baghdad.

For a time these Turkic rulers were successful in defending their new-settled domains against the attacks of their fellow Turks, who were still living a nomadic existence to the north. In 1037, however, Tughrul Beg succeeded in uniting warring Turkic tribal factions, founded the Seljuk Dynasty, and turned his military prowess against the settled Turks then ruling in Khorasan. After fighting his way south through various principalities, Tughrul Beg's forces took Baghdad in 1055. Later the Seljuks pushed westward into Asia Minor, which had until then been held as undisputed territory by the Byzantine Empire.

In 1072 the Seljuks controlled an area running from Mecca and Medina in Arabia north to include much of Asia Minor and east to the Oxus River. Unlike the Arabs, who had largely refrained from moving into the Iranian plateaus, the Turks migrated en masse into Iran, settling primarily in the northernmost provinces, intermarrying freely with Iranians, and thereby radically changing the ethnic composition in those provinces.

For the next fifty years Baghdad once more became the most important city in the Muslim world. Under the enlightened rule of certain Iranian grand viziers, such as Nizam al-Mulk, to whom the Turks left all administrative details, a university was founded in Baghdad, and there gathered some of the finest scholars in the world, such as Abu Hamid Ghazali and Omar Khayyam.

INVASIONS OF THE MONGOLS AND TAMERLANE

With the death of the powerful Turkic sultan, Malik Shah, in 1092, petty family rivalries divided the Seljuk domain into minor kingdoms, and the scene was set for the entry of the next conquerors from the northeast. The Mongols, like the Turks before them, were Asians speaking a Ural-Altaic language, but they lacked the civilizing influences of long contact with the Islamic world. Early in the thirteenth century the Mongol leader Genghis Khan led his nomadic horde against the weakened Islamic Empire. Moving westward, the Mongols devastated all the cities of northern Iran, as far west as modern East and West Azerbaijan provinces, before their leader's death in 1227. In 1251, Hulagu, grandson of Genghis, retraced his predecessor's steps westward across the country. He turned southward and seized Baghdad in 1258, capturing and putting to death the last of the Abbasside caliphs.

Hulagu's descendants, known to history as the Ilkhan Dynasty, were nominally subordinate to the Mongol great khan of China but actually governed their territories as autonomous provinces until their demise in 1335. They fought their way farther west but were finally checked in Syria by an expanding Egypt. Forced to return to the wasted plain of Mesopotamia and the Iranian plateau, the Ilkhans found their eastern domains threatened by incursions from other Mongol tribes seeking to follow the path of Genghis Khan.

In 1295 a Muslim convert and great-grandson of Hulagu Khan, Ghazan Khan, became ruler at Tabriz. He began the difficult task of reestablishing order in Iran and Mesopotamia and renewing old trade routes in order to assist the faltering economy. His reforms, other than the reestablishment of Islam, did not long outlast him, however; the Ilkhan family soon began quarreling over the line of succession, and various puppet kings were crowned by warring Mongol generals. Once more the country fell into anarchy.

In the latter part of the fourteenth century, new groups of Turkic tribesmen, under the leadership of Tamerlane (Timur the Lame), set out on a campaign of conquest. By 1392 Tamerlane's empire included: much of Russia, Turkistan, and India; all of Afghanistan, Baluchistan, Iran, Iraq, and Georgia (in the Soviet Union); and parts of Syria. Tamerlane's conquests put an end to the Ilkhans and to the minor Iranian kingdoms.

Shah Ismail, the first ruler of Persia under the Safavid Dynasty, reigned from 1499 to 1523. He is seen here leading his soldiers in the Battle of Chaldiran.

Shah Abbas the Great was one of the ablest military and government leaders in the modern period of Persian history. He reigned from 1586 to 1628.

Nadir Shah, who ruled Persia from 1736 to 1747, was the first shah under the Afsharid Dynasty.

Tamerlane surrounded himself with talented and intellectual men, and to his capital at Samarkand he brought craftsmen, artisans, and men of learning who had survived the years of war and anarchy.

Tamerlane's vast domains were the scene of bitter rivalries immediately after his death in 1405. For the remainder of the fifteenth century, internecine struggles weakened Turkic control over Tamerlane's empire and set the stage for the rise to power in 1499 of the first native Iranian dynasty to rule the whole of Iran since the coming of the Arabs over eight centuries before.

REVIVAL UNDER THE SAFAVID EMPIRE (1499–1736)

The first shah (king) of the Safavid Dynasty, Shah Ismail, was born and rose to power in the Ardabil area in modern East Azerbaijan province. His family was directly descended from the famous Shia religious leader, Shaykh Safi al-Din, and the Safavids had a reputation for piety even in the time of Tamerlane. A legend of that period tells how Tamerlane offered a boon to a member of this family, and this pious man asked for the release of some Turkic prisoners. Thereafter, the tribes from which these prisoners came attached themselves to the House of the Safavids and embraced the Shia religion. Around 1498 they helped Ismail to conquer Baghdad and to defeat several minor dynasties in the south of Iran, but their expansion was checked in the east by another Turkic group, the Uzbeks, who had replaced the Timurid heirs.

Upon his coronation in Tabriz in 1499, Shah Ismail proclaimed Shiism to be the official religion in Iran, and he coerced and persuaded the Sunnis among the Iranian people to give up their traditional faith. This attempt was relatively unsuccessful until the Ottoman Turks marched into the westernmost provinces of Iran. They had, by then, established their rule securely in Asia Minor and were looking eastward for new territory into which to expand their growing kingdom. This foreign challenge from the Ottoman Turkish ruler, who laid claim to the old Sunni title of caliph and assumed leadership of the entire Sunni Muslim world, was sufficient to cause the Iranians to rally around their new dynasty and embrace Shiism, which the Safavids made the state religion.

The greatest of the Safavids, Shah Abbas I, the Great, began his career inauspiciously in Khorasan, where, as one of the minor claimants to the Safavid throne, he was left as nominal governor under the guardianship of rival noble families of the region. When a weak shah was placed on the throne, a group of nobles in Khorasan proclaimed Abbas the shah, and by 1586 he had established his authority as far west as Qazvin, ninety miles northwest of modern Tehran. His first action was to sign a peace treaty with the Ottomans in order to turn his forces against the Uzbeks, who had progressed as far south as Herat in Afghanistan. After driving them back, Shah Abbas moved some Kurdish tribes to northern Khorasan to guard the eastern borders against

*Shah Safi I reigned from 1628
to 1642.*

*Shah Sulaiman I ruled
from 1667 to 1694.*

*Shah Abbas II ruled from 1642
to 1667.*

*Shah Husain I ruled from 1694
to 1722.*

future incursions and turned his own army against the
Ottomans. By the time of his death in 1628, he had rid
Azerbaijan, Georgia, Kurdistan, and Armenia of Turkish
rule and reestablished Iranian authority in these regions.

Shah Abbas was an excellent administrator. He moved
the capital to Isfahan in 1598, and he and his successors
supported art and architecture with such effect that the city
became, and has remained, one of the showplaces of Iran.

The generally receptive attitude that Shah Abbas maintained toward Europeans and their ideas caused considerable resentment and criticism on the part of the tradition-
oriented Shia clergy. In answer to this criticism, to prove
his piety and sincerity as a Muslim and to further consolidate the various tribes and peoples who lived in Iran into
one nation based on the Shia religion, Shah Abbas made
numerous pilgrimages to the tomb of Imam Riza at Mashhad, the most important Shia shrine located inside Iran.

Shah Abbas was followed after 1628 by weak rulers who
retained their empire primarily because of his reputation,
which sustained them to the end of the dynasty about a
century afterward. Attacks on the western boundaries were
resumed by the Ottomans, and in 1638 Baghdad fell under
the suzerainty of the Turks.

By the early eighteenth century the Safavid rulers had
become so weak that in 1722 an Afghan king named
Mahmud, whose family had asserted its independence from
Isfahan during its period of decline, was able to march into
Iran proper and lay siege to the capital. On October 23,
1722, the shah surrendered his starving city to Mahmud,
who was crowned shah of Iran. The new rulers, however,
could not enforce their rule throughout the Safavid Empire,

much less defend it against incursions by its neighbors, and in 1724 Russia and Turkey signed a treaty partitioning the westernmost provinces of Iran between them.

NADIR SHAH AND HIS SUCCESSORS (1736-96)

With the country once more without effective central authority, political factions and individual leaders contended for power. One of these, Nadir Quli, a Turkic tribesman from Khorasan, was able to build up his own military force, expel the Afghans from Iran, administer a decisive defeat to the Ottoman Turks, and put down rebellions initiated by other Iranians against his rule. In 1736 he deposed the last Safavid heir, who had continued to claim the title of shah, and crowned himself Nadir Shah.

Throughout his eleven-year reign Nadir Shah continued his military campaigns, fighting to consolidate his authority over the tribes of Iran and to extend the national boundaries. He was successful in driving the Ottomans from Georgia and Iranian Armenia, but the area of modern Iraq remained under Turkish control, thus cutting off the Shia Iranians from their most holy shrines. Peter the Great of Russia had died in 1725, and after the Iranian successes against the Turks the Russians evacuated the provinces bordering on the Caspian Sea. Nadir Shah obtained his greatest victory over the Moghul rulers of India; he seized Delhi in March 1739 and brought back to Iran enormous treasures, including the famous Peacock Throne. Thereafter, he defeated of Uzbeks, who had for many years raided the province the Khorasan, and established the Iranian boundary on the river called the Amu Darya, also known as the Oxus River.

Nadir Shah established his capital at Mashhad, in his home province of Khorasan, where he hoarded the fortunes amassed on his various foreign campaigns. During his rule the Persian countryside was impoverished by exorbitant taxes and the depredations of the army, which was allowed to live off the land. By the time of his assassination in 1747, there was widespread rebellion against his harsh rule. Numerous claimants to the throne gathered armed forces and quickly plunged Iran into civil war.

Around 1750 Karim Khan, a tribal leader of Fars, defeated all other major contenders for power in central Iran and established his capital at Shiraz. He ruled the major portion of Iran from 1758 to 1779, giving the war-torn countryside a much-needed rest.

MODERN IRAN

RISE OF THE KAJAR DYNASTY

Karim Khan died in 1779, and Iran was once again torn by civil war. The major contenders were the tribe of Karim Khan and the Kajars, a Turkic tribe from south of the

Agha Mohammed Khan was the shah of Iran from 1795 to 1797.

The Kiani crown of the Kajar Dynasty. When Shah Fath Ali commissioned it for his coronation in 1798, he revived a tradition that went back some twelve centuries. Crowns had been worn by Iranian monarchs since Sassanid days. The Safavid kings, for example, wore a jeweled aigrette in their turbans.

The genealogy table of the Quraysh shows the descent of the various dynasties from the Prophet Allah-Mohammed.

Nadir's victory at Karnal. The shah (1736–47) can be seen in this mural, lower center, on a white charger, swinging his sword in the middle of the battlefield.

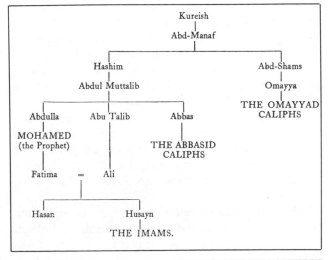

Caspian Sea. The Kajars had helped establish the Safavid Dynasty in 1499 and had fought with Nadir Khan to oust the Afghans in the early eighteenth century, but they had subsequently been repressed by Nadir and his successors. Under the leadership of a eunuch Kajar prince, Agha Mohammed Khan, the Kajars finally defeated their rivals in 1795. The capital was established at Tehran, in north-central Iran, where the Kajar power was strongest. Agha Mohammed was crowned shah in 1795 and established a dynasty that ruled Iran until 1925.

His campaigns to get and keep the throne were marked by extreme cruelty and pillage and, a year after becoming shah, he was killed by some of his own servants. His nephew and chosen successor, Fath Ali (1797–1834), was forced to suppress several rebellions before establishing his own authority in Tehran. Throughout the nineteenth and early twentieth centuries, the Kajar Dynasty continued to rule.

Hostilities broke out between Iran and Russia over control of the semi-independent kingdom of Georgia in 1804, and the war continued intermittently until 1813, when Iran was defeated. By the Treaty of Gulistan the shah gave up all rights to former Iranian provinces west of the Caspian Sea and also agreed not to maintain a navy on the Caspian. In 1825 another minor boundary dispute with Russia erupted into war; again Iran was defeated, and the 1828 Treaty of Turkmanchai gave the Russians further territorial and other types of concessions. The modern northwestern boundary was drawn.

After the death of Fath Ali in 1834, various claimants to the throne appeared. Supported by both the British and Russian governments, Mohammed, the grandson of Fath Ali, succeeded to the throne in 1834 and ruled until 1848 as Mohammed Shah. Early in his reign he resumed the campaign against the Afghans in the east. For their own reasons, the Russians encouraged Mohammed in this campaign, whereas the British were opposed to it. At first the shah rejected British advice that he withdraw from the siege of the Afghan city of Herat, but he finally did so in 1838 after being repulsed several times.

Nasir ul-Deen (1848–96) proved to be even more pro-Russian than his father, Mohammed. He occupied Herat in 1856 with the collaboration of a pro-Iranian Afghan prince. Meanwhile, the British had supported a pro-British Afghan ruler in the city of Kabul. British forces attacked Bushair and other southern Iranian cities, and the shah's forces were defeated. In the 1857 Treaty of Paris, Iran recognized the independence of Afghanistan and agreed to evacuate Herat. A British commission delimited the boundary between Afghanistan and Iran in 1881, dividing the province of Sistan between them and redefining it in 1893 to include the boundary between Iran and western Pakistan, then known as British Baluchistan.

During the reign of Peter the Great in the eighteenth century, and again in the nineteenth century, Russian troops had moved southward into the territories of the

Shah Muzaffar-ul-Deen (Din) at the time of his coronation in 1896

Shah Nasir-ul-Deen died in 1896, like many shahs before him, assassinated. He ruled Persia for forty-eight years amid constant strife from outside the country and within his own family and staff. This photograph shows him in early life.

Shah Nasir ul-Deen in his official royal photograph

Shah Mohammed Ali Kajar in his coronation pose in 1907

independent Turkic tribes around Khiva south of the Aral Sea and Bokhara. By 1884 Russia had overthrown the Uzbek power, taken Mary (formerly Merv) about one hundred fifty miles northeast of Mashhad, and established the modern boundary line with Iran in the northeast. This action illustrated the way in which the limits of the modern state of Iran were determined by territorial advances of European powers in the nineteenth century. In the further case of the Turko-Iranian boundary, a mixed commission including Russians and British had helped to delimit that frontier in 1847. By 1900 Iranian government finances were controlled by czarist Russian officials.

NATIONALISM AND REVOLUTION

Shah Nasir ul-Deen was assassinated in May 1896 by a young religious fanatic and was succeeded by his son, Muzaffar ul-Deen, who ruled from 1896 to 1907.

After the accession of Muzaffar ul-Deen, popular demands for reform and for constitutionalism grew in intensity. The new shah, however, adopted the personal extravagances of his father and brought the country to the verge of bankruptcy. One of the leaders of the popular movement was the pan-Islamic intellectual Jamal al-Din al-Afghani, who was to become well-known also in Egypt. Another leader was Malkom Khan, a senior officer of the Iranian foreign service. Both these men strongly opposed Amin al-Sultan, the shah's conservative grand vizier.

In 1905 two external events helped significantly to encourage Iran's nationalist movement. Russia was defeated by Japan in the Russo-Japanese war, and many Eastern nations took heart from this event, which showed them that European powers were not invincible. Secondly, an abortive revolt occurred in Russia against the czar's regime. Many of the escaping rebels fled to Iran, where they found intellectuals, merchants, bankers, and some Islamic clergy eager to listen to their revolutionary ideas.

In December 1905 and in 1906 Iranian nationalists, supported by many religious and business leaders, created a passive resistance movement. A number of these leaders took *bast* (mass refuge) in mosques in Tehran and Qom to protest actions by the shah's government and to demand that Grand Vizier Ayn al-Dawla, a son-in-law of the shah, be dismissed from his post.

The shah eventually yielded on August 5, 1906, and dismissed Ayn al-Dawla and appointed the more liberal Mirza Nasr Khan as grand vizier. Elections for a *majlis* (a permanent representative National Consultative Assembly) were held, and the first Majlis, convened on October 7, 1906, consisted of elected representatives from nobility, businessmen, landholders, and the Islamic clergy and teachers. On December 30, 1906, both the dying shah and his son and heir signed the constitution drawn up by this assembly; however, the new king. Mohammed Ali (1907–9), soon began attempts to disband the first Majlis and reimpose strong control over Iran. He reinstated as grand vizier the able but reactionary Amin al-Sultan, who had been exiled; the latter, however, was assassinated on August 31, 1907. On October 8, 1907, the shah signed the Supplementary Law that became an integral part of the Constitution of 1906. The Constitution of 1906 together with the Supplementary Law of 1907 (with further amendments) are often referred to simply as the constitution.

On August 31, 1907, Great Britain and Russia entered into an agreement under which Iran was divided by them into three zones for commercial development. Russia was to have primary rights in the northern part of the country, and Great Britain, in a much smaller area in the southeast. Between the two lay an irregularly shaped neutral zone.

This commercial partitioning aroused serious nationalist opposition in Iran. In May 1908 oil was discovered in southwestern Iran at Masjid Sulaiman, in the neutral zone, about 125 miles northeast of Abadan.

In June 1908 royal forces, in which Russian officers of the cossack troops played an important part, shelled the Majlis building in Tehran and killed a number of nationalist leaders. In other cities, notably Tabriz, Rasht, and Isfahan, the constitutionalists rallied volunteer fighters to their side, and a civil war began. These landmark events of the 1906-8 period, including constitutionalism and the establishment of the Majlis, the Anglo-Russian commercial partition and the reaction it engendered, and the discovery of oil in major quantities, are regarded by historians as ushering in the period of modern Iran.

The revolutionaries were greatly encouraged by the successful revolution in Turkey in July 1908, when the outcome of their own revolt was in doubt. Czarist Russian representatives, however, supported the shah in his efforts

The young crown prince Ahmed Mirza

The shah of Persia, Ahmed Mirza, started his reign in 1909 as the head of a country that was rich but financially incompetent. He died in 1925 without making very many inroads toward raising the level of learning and experience of the elite Persians.

The Shah Muzaffar ul-Deen   *Shah Ahmed on a 1911 stamp*

to reassert his controls. In April 1909, on the pretext of safeguarding European lives, Russian troops entered Tabriz, where the constitutionalists had until then managed to hold out against an Iranian army siege.

The revolutionaries, however, in July 1909 marched on Tehran and took the city from the shah's forces. The Iranian revolutionaries were able to depose Shah Mohammed Ali, who took refuge in the Russian legation and then fled to Russia. Ahmed Mirza, then only eleven years of age, was chosen by the nationalists, *mullahs,* and survivors of the Majlis and instated as Shah Ahmed Mirza in July 1909, with a regency under Nasr al-Mulk.

After their victory over the shah's forces in 1909, the constitutionalists continued attempts to modernize their government and rid their country of foreign influences. During the remaining years before the outbreak of World War I, Russia attempted to consolidate its influence in Iranian politics, going so far as to encourage the deposed shah, Mohammed Ali, in an unsuccessful attempt in 1911 to regain the throne.

Meanwhile, Iranian leaders attempted to find some other world power to serve as a balancing force against the Russians and British. Iran turned to the United States and requested it to send advisers to Iran; an American, William Morgan Shuster, served as treasurer-general in Iran until pressure from Russia, Great Britain, and the shah's ministers succeeded in having him discharged in 1911.

FOREIGN INFLUENCE
AND THE WORLD WAR I PERIOD

British and Russian troops entered Tehran soon after war broke out in 1914. The Majlis was dissolved, and the Iranian government declared its official neutrality in the war. While Iran's countryside was torn by war and the central government was weak, many tribal leaders seized the opportunity to assert their independence and take advantage of the peasant population.

By the end of the war the Russian revolution had caused the withdrawal of most of the czar's troops, and the British found themselves to be the dominant de facto influence in Iran. In 1919 Great Britain negotiated with the shah and his ministers an agreement that would have officially given Great Britain a paramount, monopolistic influence, but the Majlis refused to ratify it. The new Communist Russian government renounced the extraterritorial privileges that czarist Russia had held in Iran. In June 1920, however, Russian troops crossed the border into Iran and proclaimed their occupied area.

SHAH RIZA AND ESTABLISHMENT
OF THE PAHLEVI DYNASTY

When the Russian troops moved into the north of Iran, British troops were evacuating southern Iran, leaving a power vacuum in Tehran. In February 1921 Sayyid Zia al-Din Tabatabai, a prominent Iranian journalist and politician, engineered a bloodless coup d'etat with the military

backing of a little-known Iranian officer commanding the Persian Cossack Brigade, Brigadier General Riza Khan. This group seized control in Tehran on February 21, 1921. Tabatabai became prime minister with Riza Khan as his minister of war and commander in chief of the armed forces. Five days later a treaty with the Soviet government was signed, and the proposed Anglo-Persian Agreement of 1919 was denounced. Tabatabai resigned and left Iran some three months later; thereafter, Riza Khan was in control of the government.

In 1923 Riza Khan assumed the post of prime minister and assembled the Majlis. During 1924 the government regained minimal financial stability, assisted by a team of American economists under Arthur C. Millspaugh and royalties from the Anglo-Persian Oil Company (APOC).

In February 1925 the Majlis declared Riza Khan commander in chief of Iran's armed forces for life. On October 31, 1925, the Majlis declared the rule of the Kajar Dynasty ended and called for a new Majlis. The new body was elected and assembled, and on December 12, 1925, it formally vested the crown in Riza Khan, with right of succession to his heirs. On December 15 he took the oath to defend the constitution; on December 16 he was publicly proclaimed Riza Shah Pahlevi; and on April 25, 1925, the formal ceremony of coronation took place. Riza Pahlevi was born in Mazandaran province in 1878, of the Bavand clan. Upon becoming shah, he took as his dynastic name the word *Pahlevi,* the ancient word for the Persian language as used officially in the pre-Islamic Iranian Sassanid Empire (A.D. 226-641).

Both the British and the Soviet governments, for their own reasons, had either supported or not opposed the coup of 1921, and they later endorsed Riza Pahlevi's government. The Soviet Union had withdrawn from the north of Iran in 1921, and the area was quickly reoccupied by Iranian forces loyal to Riza Khan.

Riza Pahlevi, who ruled from 1925 to 1941, wished to adopt Western methods without succumbing to outside control. The new shah had observed the ineffectual attempts at administration made by the Tehran government during World War I, and he was determined to rid Iran of foreign control, to centralize his government, and to unite his people into a single, modernized nation. Major steps toward these goals were taken during the twenty years in which he governed Iran with a strong hand.

Although a Shia Muslim himself, Riza Pahlevi disregarded as backward and inappropriate many of the old particularistic religious edicts. He outlawed the veil for women on January 8, 1936, and introduced civil marriage and divorce, while expropriating Islamic clergy property holdings. In such ways he sought to loosen the tight hold that the Shia clergy had held on much of the Iranian population for almost thirteen centuries.

After the evacuation of British and Soviet troops in the early 1920s, Iran was free from foreign occupation for the first time in twenty years, and the shah worked to maintain

Shah Mohammed Riza at age five

The shah of Iran, Riza Pahlevi, was a former military leader who assumed control of the country in 1925 and served as the emperor until he was forced to abdicate in 1941. He was succeeded by his son, Mohammed Riza Pahlevi.

Shah Riza with three of his children. The successor shah is on his knee.

his country's new independence in international affairs. By 1928 he was successful in eliminating the extraterritorial custom of capitulations, by which Europeans in Iran had been immune from Iranian laws for one hundred years.

After withdrawing in 1921 from the Gilan area around Rasht on the Caspian Sea coast, the Soviet Union refrained from further attempts at territorial expansion at Iran's expense during Riza Pahlevi's rule. In 1931, at the shah's urging, the Majlis passed a law outlawing communism in Iran.

Like his predecessors, Shah Riza Pahlevi continued to look for a third world power to neutralize the influences of the Soviet Union and Great Britain. As in the pre-World War I period, Germany assumed this role. In the 1930s Germany supplied Iran with heavy machinery, technicians, and advisers for some of its industrial ventures, and by 1939 Germany rivaled the Soviet Union for a dominant role in Iran's foreign trade.

WORLD WAR II
AND THE AZERBAIJAN CRISIS

In February 1941 Iran declared itself neutral in World War II. Riza Pahlevi and certain Iranian political and military leaders had expressed some pro-German views, however, and the shah refused a British-Soviet request in June 1941 to allow transit of war supplies across Iran. On August 25, 1941, British and Soviet forces simultaneously invaded Iran and seized effective control. The British assumed responsibility in the southwest, while the Soviets occupied the northern provinces of Azerbaijan, Gilan, and Mazandaran. As a result of this invasion, the shah abdicated the throne on September 16, 1941, in favor of his eldest son, Mohammed Riza Pahlevi, then twenty-two years of age.

Riza Pahlevi left the country, resided briefly in Mauritius, and then moved to South Africa, where he died at Johannesburg on July 26, 1944. He had reestablished security and the authority of the central government throughout the country, initiated many social and legal reforms, fostered education, and promoted industry and communications, particularly the Trans-Iranian Railway. In his late years, however, his popularity had declined because of his increasing tendency to autocratic and arbitrary rule.

Riza Pahlevi's son, Mohammed, had been educated in Europe and, soon after his accession to the throne, he announced his intention to rule on a constitutional basis. Transition from the more arbitrary rule of his father, however, occasioned some political stress internally during the balance of World War II and the years immediately after. The abolition of Riza Pahlevi's tight political restraints permitted many previously repressed groups again to assert themselves. Tribal leaders secretly returned to their areas, regained lost authority, and resumed the old ways of tribal raiding and harassment of sedentary villages. The Shia clergy, silenced by Riza Pahlevi, regained importance. Many people went back to the traditional way of dressing; some women resumed wearing veils; and the clergy regained some lost ground in education. Numerous political parties sprang up.

Shah Mohammed Riza at the age of ten

The shrine of the sister of the Imam Riza, Fatimeh Ma'sumeh (Fatimah the Chaste) at Qum, south of Teheran

One party in Iran during World War II with a definite program was the Tudeh (Masses) party. It was composed initially of a group of rightists, liberals, and left-wing politicians, many of whom had been imprisoned during Riza's reign in the 1930s and had used their years in jail to organize a "party" in the Western sense of the word. Some of its members has studied for a time in the Soviet Union and belonged to the Communist Internationale; others were men who felt that the Tudeh offered the best opportunity for seeing their political concepts brought to fruition.

During the war the party came under the control of Communists, who were careful at first to minimize Communist elements in the party platform in an effort to attract supporters from among the intellectuals as well as from the working class.

On January 29, 1942, the Tripartite Treaty of Alliance was signed between Great Britain, the Soviet Union, and Iran, giving a formal status to the troops of the occupation powers and guaranteeing that they would "respect the territorial integrity, sovereignty and political independence of Persia." It also provided for the withdrawal of troops by Great Britain and the Soviet Union within six months after the end of hostilities.

On September 1, 1943, Iran declared war on Germany. In November 1943 the Allied leaders, Franklin D. Roosevelt, Winston Churchill, and Joseph Stalin, conferred at Tehran, without first requesting Iranian permission for the use of the capital. On December 1, 1943, the three leaders, at the suggestion of President Roosevelt, issued a Declaration on Iran, in which they formally thanked Iran for its assistance in the war effort, reaffirmed their commitment to Iran's independence, and promised economic aid after the war.

MOHAMMED MOSSADEQ AND OIL NATIONALIZATION

After the war, Iranian leaders in the Majlis and government turned their attention to more pressing internal problems. During both World War I and II, Iran had been occupied and used by foreign powers. To develop the power and wealth necessary to assure international prestige, Iranian leaders announced their intention to intensify the modernization and industrialization begun by Riza Pahlevi. In 1948 the Majlis approved the First Seven-Year Plan (September 21, 1948, to September 20, 1955) for industrial and agricultural development in Iran, which had been worked out by United States financial advisers, and a Plan Organization was set up to administer it. This ambitious plan was to be financed in large part by revenues derived from the agreement with the Anglo-Iranian Oil Company (AIOC), which was still operating under the terms of the 1933 agreement negotiated by Riza Pahlevi. Most politically conscious Iranians were aware that the British government derived more revenue from taxing the profits of the AIOC than the Iranian government did through royalties.

Mohammed Riza Pahlevi's cabinets changed many times in 1948 and 1949, and each prime minister tried to reach a more favorable settlement with the AIOC.

General Ali Razmara, who became prime minister in June 1950, urged the oil company to listen to the demands of the nationalists in the Majlis, but he was at first unable to get any concessions. Late in February 1951 the oil committee of the Majlis asked General Razmara to report on the practicability of nationalizing the oil industry. After consulting oil technicians and economists, he reported that nationalization was not practicable or in the best interests of Iran. Four days later, on March 7, 1951, he was assassinated by a follower of Mullah Kashani, a fanatically nationalistic and anti-British religious leader.

On March 15, 1951, the Majlis voted to nationalize the oil industry; when Prime Minister Hosein Ala made no move to take over the properties of the AIOC, the Majlis demanded that the shah appoint Mossadeq, then seventy-one years of age, as prime minister. His administration lasted from April 1951 to August 1953; during that time the nationalization law was put into effect, oil production in Iran almost came to a stop, and the Iranian government

The shah Mohammed Riza with Prime Minister Winston Churchill of Great Britain at the Teheran Conference

suffered greatly from the loss of oil revenues. Iran at that time had few trained technicians and engineers capable of continuing the production of oil once the British left.

The poorer people of Iran, however, were not at first directly affected by the loss of oil revenues and continued to hold Mossadeq in high esteem. Throughout his time in office, this emotional nationalist maintained a high pitch of excitement in the capital and, to a lesser extent, throughout the country. His major political weapons were the crowds that appeared in the streets to cheer his often near hysterical tirades against British colonial imperialists. The Tudeh party had been outlawed and had gone underground in 1949 after an attempt of February 4 of that year against the shah's life. It now emerged and resumed its activities. Mossadeq was not himself a Communist, but he did not suppress the Tudeh mobs, for, like Mullah Kashani, they supported him in his anti-British policies.

In the summer of 1952, when Mossadeq asked for absolute control over the government for a limited time, Mohammed Riza Pahlevi refused and made his first attempt to challenge Mossadeq's authority by appointing a new prime minister. Four days of rioting by Mullah Kashani's Devotees of Islam (Fadiyan al-Islam) forced the shah to change his mind; Mossadeq was reinstated, and for the remainder of 1952 he assumed almost absolute control over the government. Diplomatic relations with Great Britain were broken off by Iran in October. During this period the government became extremely repressive; censorship laws were enacted, prohibitions were issued against strikes by government workers and, in short, Mossadeq tried to prevent political opposition by means similar to those Riza Pahlevi had used. By January 1953 the increasing economic difficulties and repressive government measures caused Mossadeq's popular political support to decline. Even Mullah Kashani withdrew his support.

By early August Mossadeq's authoritarianism had alienated so many of his supporters in the Majlis that he lost his majority. He therefore called for a public referendum on August 3, 1953, to abolish the Majlis, and he claimed to have won the referendum. Taking advantage of the constitutional provision that, on the abolition of the Majlis, the shah could dismiss the prime minister, Mohammed Riza Pahlevi replaced Mossadeq with General Fazlollah Zahedi, a staunch supporter of the shah. Mossadeq refused to relinquish the government and arrested the shah's emissary. He then announced the deposition of Mohammed Riza and the formation of a regency council to act for the shah.

For four days, during which time the shah left Iran, near anarchy reigned in Tehran. By August 19, however, General Zahedi had rallied the army behind the shah, arrested Mossadeq and his supporters, and assumed the premiership. On August 22 the shah returned to Tehran amid great public enthusiasm. On December 2, 1953, Mossadeq was sentenced to three years of solitary confinement for high treason. After his release in 1956 he lived quietly and died in Tehran on March 5, 1967, at the age of eighty-seven.

MOHAMMED RIZA PAHLEVI AND THE WHITE REVOLUTION

After the overthrow of Mossadeq, the political climate in Iran changed markedly. The subsequent period was distinguished by the rise to preeminent national leadership of Mohammed Riza Pahlevi himself and by the program of national reforms and development, introduced by him, that became known as the White Revolution.

During and immediately after World War II, the Majlis, released from its period of subservience under Riza Pahlevi, had exerted substantial influence over the government. After the army assisted Mohammed Riza back into power in 1953, however, the political importance of the Majlis began to decline. Elections in 1954 and 1956, for the eighteenth and nineteenth Majlis, respectively, were closely managed by the government, which played an important part in nominating the candidates and in supervising the balloting. The Tudeh party continued to be outlawed, and Mossadeq's National Front, with its leader in jail, was prevented from obtaining substantial power in either of these assemblies.

Simultaneously, the influence of Shah Mohammed Riza, his immediate family, and his close associates at court and in the national security forces increased. The prime ministers of this period, as well as other members of the cabinets, were the personal choice of the shah, who also took an active part in determining the country's foreign policy. It was sometimes necessary, however, for the shah to accede to the advice or wishes of certain elite Iranian families of independent means. Through their influence in the Majlis, they could effect the passage of legislation desired by the shah. These influential families tended to be conservative in action, rather than socially progressive.

The fall of Mossadeq had removed the main obstacle to solution of oil dispute with Great Britain. In late 1953 a group of United States, British, and Dutch oil companies formed a consortium, in which the AIOC had a 40 percent share. In April 1954 the consortium opened negotiations with the Iranian government and the National Iranian Oil Company (NIOC), which was formed to take over the installations and assets in Iran of the AIOC. Agreement was reached in phases on August 5 and September 19, 1954, and was ratified by the Majlis in October 1954.

Shah Mohammed Riza at work at his desk in 1958

The Shah visits with President Harry S Truman in the White House in Washington, D. C., in 1951.

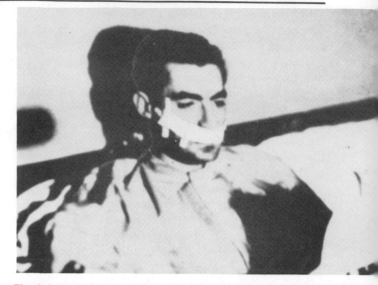

The shah in a hospital bed after an assassination attempt

The shah and his second wife, Empress Soraya, visit with President Dwight D. Eisenhower and the first lady Mamie Eisenhower at the White House in Washington, D.C.

The shah and the empress Farah Diba visited with President John F. Kennedy and First Lady Jacqueline Kennedy at Washington, D.C. in 1961. These photographs were taken upon their arrival at Andrews Air Force Base, located in nearby Maryland.

Relations between Iran and the Soviet Union after the fall of Mossadeq were correct but not cordial. In December 1954 agreements with the Soviet Union were reached by which the latter undertook payment to Iran in settlement of World War II claims and further agreed to a joint frontier survey, work on which commenced in August 1955. The shah visited the Soviet Union in 1956; the frontier demarcation commission completed its work in April 1957, when protocols were signed specifically defining the frontiers. Despite these accomplishments, relations were less than cordial.

With some countries of the Arab world frictions developed and continued after 1960. Some causes of disagreement were of older origin, such as the Iranian claim to the island of Bahrain, a claim not resolved until the spring of 1970. Other sources of differences of more recent origin lay in Iran's de facto recognition of Israel, which caused the severance of Iranian-Egyptian diplomatic relations in 1960, and in border incidents with Iraq connected with the Iraqi operations in 1963, 1965, and 1966 against dissident Kurds.

Relations with Jordan were consistently cordial, however, and in the late 1960s relations improved substantially with Saudi Arabia. Mohammed Riza Pahlevi and King Faisal of Saudi Arabia were instrumental in organizing and supporting the Islamic summit conference held in Rabat, Morocco, in September 1969. With its Islamic but non-Arab neighbors, Turkey and Pakistan, Iran's relations were good, being confirmed in a mutual cooperation agreement executed by the three in 1964.

Internally in Iran, much publicity was given during the middle and late 1950s to the need for firm action on chronic social problems, most of which had existed long before the Pahlevi Dynasty came to power. These included: over-centralization of government in the capital city and the resulting lack of control over their own affairs by provincial populations; concentration of land in the hands of a relatively few wealthy landlords; the enormous, often inefficient or venal, bureaucracy; and the inequality of tax laws and the manner in which they were administered. As early as 1949 the shah had indicated a firm intention to institute significant changes and to commence them with agrarian land reform. Before these were initiated, however, a preparatory period of economic recovery and of political stabilization, both internal and external, was needed. This recovery and stabilization period continued through the 1950s and early 1960s.

During the recovery period in the late 1950s, however, internal political stresses developed. Prime Minister Zahedi resigned in April 1955, and thereafter the shah took an increasingly active part in the national administration. Zahedi's successors included Hosein Ala, who remained in office until April 1957; Manuchehr Eqbal, who resigned in August 1960; Jafar Sharif Imami, who resigned in May 1961; Ali Amini, who resigned in July 1962; Asadollah Alam, who resigned in March 1964; Hasan Ali Mansur,

assassinated by a right-wing Islamic fanatic on January 21, 1965; Amir Abbas Hoveyda, who was designated at the latter time and held office until 1978 at which time he was executed; and Jamshid Amouzegar, who took office in 1978 and left Iran during the revolution of 1979.

Under Prime Minister Eqbal, martial law, which had been in force, was ended in 1957, and the foundation of a legal political party system was laid, in accordance with the desires of the shah. These parties included the Meliyuun (National) party, which later was succeeded in the majority role by the Iran Novin (New Iran) party and opposed by the Mardom (People's) party. The Tudeh party, the loose opposition alignment called the National Front, which was descended from Mossadeq's old organization, and the exiled "Free Iran" movement continued their underground subversive existence.

National elections were held in 1960 but were annulled by the shah because of supervisory irregularities. Elections were held again in January 1961. After this election, the shah, addressing the new Majlis, called upon it to enact a new electoral law. Subsequent to the resignation of Prime Minister Imami in May 1961, his successor, Ali Amini, took firm measures to correct irregularities in the civil service, to begin decentralization of administration, to limit luxury imports, and to initiate land redistribution reforms. In July 1962, because of budget controversies and dissatisfaction over postponement of elections, Amini found it necessary to resign and was succeeded by Asadollah Alam, of the Mardom party.

Prime Minister Alam was a firm advocate of close ties with the West and land reform. His government assisted the shah in preparing the historic reform program that the shah announced in January 1963 at the First All-Iran Farm Cooperatives Conference. This program, of major significance in the national life of the country, became known as the Revolution of the Shah and the People or, more commonly, as the White Revolution.

Six principles were initially embodied in this program: abolition of the feudal landlord-peasant system and redistribution of land; nationalization of public forests and pastures; compensation of former landlords by capital shares in government industry; profit sharing in all productive enterprises; ratification of a proposed new electoral law, including votes for women; and creation of a national literacy corps using educated youth in national service to raise the literacy rate. This program was overwhelmingly endorsed in a national referendum in January 1963. Six further points were added later. By the end of 1963 the shah had distributed the crown estates to the land distribution scheme or the Pahlevi Foundation. Prime Minister Asadollah Alam, who was a major landholder, also voluntarily distributed his land.

Early in June 1963 urban rioting occurred, animated by the opposition of landlords and reactionary Islamic clergy to land reform and the emancipation of women and by political opportunists in the old National Front or Tudeh party seeking to take advantage of political turmoil of any kind. At about the same time, tribal disturbances created sporadic disorder in southern Iran. The shah and his government held fast, however; the armed forces and gendarmerie remained loyal, order was restored, and elections were conducted in September 1963. In these elections, in which women voted in a parliamentary election for the first time in the history of Iran, Alam and his National Union coalition of political groups were overwhelmingly successful. The new Parliament, elected for four years by law, was formally opened in October 1963 by the shah, who was accompanied by Empress Farah. The shah called on Parliament to continue current efforts and to project a twenty-year program of reform and revivification of the nation.

Prime Minister Alam resigned his office in March 1964 and was succeeded at once by Hassan Ali Mansur, a former minister and progressive leader, who energetically supported and continued the reform program until his assassination on January 21, 1965, by a right-wing Islamic fanatic, an act that did much to discredit the reactionary clergy. The shah asked Amir Abbas Hoveyda, the minister of finance, to assume the prime ministership, and he did so with almost unanimous support of Parliament. He held the office continously from January 27, 1965 to 1978, actively administering the national objectives plan and receiving strong political endorsement in Parliament. In 1978 Jamshid Amouzegar took over the post of prime minister but was forced to flee during the 1979 revolution.

The shah himself was the target of a Tudeh-Communist assassination attempt on April 10, 1965, as he had been in 1949, but survived. About seventy-five persons were arrested; two were sentenced to death, but these sentences were later commuted by the shah to life imprisonment.

Serious internal opposition steadily decreased after 1963; the shah's program survived, and he showed progressively increasing strength in its implementation. On September 15, 1965, a grateful Parliament sitting in joint session of both houses conferred on the shah the personal title of *Aryamehr,* a word deriving from the ancient, pre-Islamic Achaemeni era and meaning "light of the Aryans." In the elections of August 1967 Prime Minister Hoveyda and the Iran Novin party supporting him received a large majority. This Parliament, being the twenty-second session of the Majlis and the fifth session of the Senate, was declared open by the shah on October 6, 1967, in a speech from the throne called "The Revolution—New Dimensions."

The formal coronation of His Imperial Majesty Mohammed Riza Pahlevi, Aryamehr, Shahanshah of Iran, was held on his forty-sixth birthday, October 26, 1967, twenty-six years after his accession to the throne on September 17, 1941. The impressive coronation ceremony was described as the crowning glory of the White Revolution, which the shah himself initiated in 1963. In public narrations of the event, the monarchy was said to be two thousand five hundred years old and, therefore, the oldest continuous

monarchy on earth. Immediately after placing the crown on his own head, the shah crowned Empress Farah, the first woman in the country's history to receive this honor, an act symbolizing the emancipation of Iranian women.

The Senate and Majlis, meeting in joint session on September 7, 1967, had resolved in a constitutional amendment that the empress should be recognized as regent in the event of the shah's death or incapacity before the twentieth birthday of the crown prince. The oldest son of the shah and Empress Farah, Riza Cyrus, born on October 31, 1960, was formally designated crown prince at the coronation ceremony.

From 1967 on, Mohammed Riza Pahlevi made special efforts to turn Iran into a viable modern state, and until late 1978 Iran was closely aligned with the United States foreign policies. (He permitted the United States to operate two key intelligence stations to monitor Soviet strategic weapons tests and he sold oil to Israel when other Arab nations would not.) The shah was a strong leader, both in backing United States military and economic interests in the Middle East and in pushing his people into the twentieth century. In addition to bringing about land reforms, he industrialized the towns, and offered education to the illiterate masses, and championed women's rights. But the shah knew the pitfalls of his aggressive policies, and for a country of 32 million subjects, he had to maintain a large military force.

The imperial crown that his father wore in 1924 was refurbished for the 1967 coronation.

The royal family in 1971

The "formal" coronation in 1967, twenty-six years after the shah's accession to the throne in 1941, represented to him the success of his "white revolution" over Communism. He had "whipped" the backward nation into a modern industrial country. But he had failed to move the minds of the people at the same rate. They were still living in the "Middle Ages."

The shah and empress visit the president and first lady (Richard M. Nixon and Pat Nixon) in the White House in Washington, D.C. on July 24, 1973. The shah was a much admired and close friend of President Nixon.

The empress Farah, left, *and to her left,* Queen Mother Frederika and Queen Anne- Marie of Greece.

Eventually, political unrest increased, for the students the shah had educated began to feel that feudal monarchy—no matter how enlightened—was still feudal monarchy. The middle class the shah had created by his policies began to resent the advantages the upper class and the royal family had over them.

The *mullahs,* Shiite Muslim leaders, feared their religion's authority and traditional Islamic social values were being destroyed by the shah's rule. (In 1963, Pahlevi had exiled his chief opponent, Ayatollah Ruhollah Khomeini, the spiritual leader of the Iranian Shiites.) From his home near Paris Khomeini continued to rally his followers in Iran to depose the shah.

From exile, Khomeini became the symbol of all the pent-up rage against Pahlevi's rule, with its authoritarianism, and emphasis on modernization instead of on the conservative Islamic tradition that the Ayatollah represented. Massive street demonstrations and the killing of many of Khomeini's followers by Pahlevi's troops created a powder-keg crisis. To avert a bloody civil war, Pahlevi left Iran on January 16, 1979. His departure set the stage for Khomeini's triumphant return on February 1.

From January 16, 1979, when he was forced to flee the gathering storms of revolution, the shah and his family moved from country to country looking for an asylum. First, they went to Egypt, at the beckoning of his good friend, President Anwar el-Sadat. Then to Morocco, then to the Bahamas, then to Mexico, and on October 22, 1979, the shah came to the United States for a gall bladder operation and for treatment of cancer. Thirteen days later, militant Muslim students invaded the United States embassy in Tehran and took some sixty Americans hostage in demand for the extradition of the shah, the return of his wealth, and a U.S. confession of "crimes they committed" in Iran. Mexico refused the shah reentry after his medical treatment in New York City, so the shah's next stop was San Antonio, Texas, at a military hospital facility. The shah then flew to Panama, and then back to Egypt, again at the request of President el-Sadat who was "tired" of seeing his friend a "king without a country."

Mohammed Riza Pahlevi was born on October 26, 1919, with a twin sister, later to become Princess Ashraf. Another sister, Princess Shams, was born in 1917. A brother Ali Riza, born in 1927, died in an accident in 1959. The shah married Princess Fawzia, eldest sister of Egyptian King Farouk, on March 15, 1939. She was only able to give birth to a daughter, Princess Shahnaz. The shah divorced her on November 19, 1948. The shah was married again, on February 12, 1951, to Soraya Esfandiary, the daughter of a tribal chieftain. She bore no children, so after several years transpired they were divorced (March 14, 1958). The shah then married Farah Diba on December 21, 1959. On October 31, 1960, she bore him a son, the crown prince Riza Cyrus, assuring a male succession to the throne. In 1963, the couple had a daughter, Princess Farahnaz, and in 1966, a second son was born, Ali, and in 1970, they had a second daughter, Princess Leila.

On July 27, 1980, the shah of Iran died in a military hospital in Cairo. His death was "a result of shock to the circulatory system caused by a general deterioration in his health."

President Anwar el-Sadat, who'd extended refuge for the deposed shah, arranged for the shah's body to be entombed in the mausoleum of Rifaie Mosque, where the shah's father had been interred briefly. The remains of Riza Shah, who died in South Africa after being forced to abdicate in 1941, were returned to Iran after World War II.

The mosque also holds the tombs of the last two kings of Egypt, Ahmed Fuad and Farouk. King Farouk, who was overthrown in the 1952 Egyptian revolution and died in exile in Italy in 1965, is buried under a white marble block near the west door of the mosque, overlooking the garden which was a favorite of his. King Ahmed Fuad, who died in 1936, and his mother, are buried in the southwest room. Just east of the Ahmed Fuad burial chamber is the room where Pahlevi is interred. Its thirty-foot-high walls of red marble are trimmed with ivory, ebony, cedar, and gold.

Princess Azzadeh Shafik, daughter of the shah's twin sister, Princess Ashraf, upon hearing of the shah's death said, "The King is dead. Long live the King!" in a paraphrase of an old English expression which means the old king is dead and long live the new king. There is total agreement among the surviving members of the shah's family that the automatic succession to the title of shah should go to the crown prince, Riza Cyrus.

The crown prince became the head of the royal Pahlevi family upon reaching his twentieth birthday on October 31, 1980. Until that time, his mother, Farah Diba served as the regent under the law enacted in 1967. On October 31, 1980, the crown prince, Riza Cyrus Pahlevi, in a quiet ceremony in the Kubbeh Palace in Cairo, Egypt, declared his "readiness to accept full responsibility as the lawful king of Iran." He called for "all patriotic groups inside and outside" of Iran to immediately rally behind him in "the common cause" of restoring him to the Peacock Throne and ending the "nightmare," he said his country was now passing through under the Islamic revolution of Ayatollah Ruhollah Khomeini.

The former empress of Iran, Farah Diba, after a period of recuperation in Egypt following the death of the shah, moved to the United States. She lives in two homes, one in New York and one in Massachusetts.

The late shah appeared on many postage stamps.

THE ROYAL SOVEREIGNS OF THE DYNASTIES OF IRAN (PERSIA)

Reign	Title	Ruler
ACHAEMENID DYNASTY (650–328 B.C.)		
600–559 B.C.	King	Cambyses I
559–529	King	Cyrus the Great (Cyrus I)
529–522	King	Cambyses II
522–486*	King	Darius I (Darius the Great)
486–465	King	Xerxes I
465–425	King	Artaxerxes I
425–424	King	Xerxes II
423–404	King	Darius II Ochus
404–359	King	Artaxerxes II
359–338	King	Ochus Artaxerxes III
338–336	King	Arses
336–330	King	Darius III
331–328	King	Artaxerxes IV
331–323	Emperor	Alexander the Great
SELEUCID DYNASTY (312–250 B.C.)		
312–281 B.C.	King	Seleucus I
ARSACID DYNASTY (250 B.C.–A.D. 226)		
250–248 B.C.	King	Arsaces I
248–214	King	Arsaces II Tiridates
214–196	King	Arsaces III Artabanus
196–181	King	Arsaces IV Priapatius
181–174	King	Arsaces V Phraates
174–136	King	Arsaces VI Mithridates
136–127	King	Arsaces VII Phraates II
127–124	King	Arsaces VIII Aratabanns II
124–87	King	Arsaces IX Mithridates II
87–77	King	Arsaces X Mnasciras
76–69	King	Arsaces XI Sanatroices
69–60	King	Arsaces XII Phraates III
60–56	King	Arsaces XIII Mithridates III
56–37	King	Arsaces XIV Orodes I
A.D. 37–2	King	Arsaces XV Phraates IV
2–40	King	Artabanus II
51–91	King	Vologesus I
107–130	King	Arsaces XXVI Osroes I
130–148	King	Arsaces XXVII Bolagases II
148–190	King	Arsaces XXVIII Bolagases III
190–208	King	Arsaces XXIX Bolagases IV
208–222	King	Arsaces XXX Bolagases V
209–226	King	Arsaces XXXI Artabanus IV (or V)
SASSANID DYNASTY (A.D. 226–641)		
226–241	King	Ardashir I
241–272	King	Sapor I
272–273	King	Hormisdas I
273–276	King	Baranes I
276–292	King	Baranes II
292–293	King	Baranes III
293–303	King	Narses I
303–309	King	Hormisdas II
309–379	King	Sapor II
379–383	King	Ardashir II
383–388	King	Sapor III
388–399	King	Baranes IV
399–420	King	Yazdegerd I
420–440	King	Baranes V (Bahram Gor)
440–457	King	Yazdegerd II
457–458	King	Hormisdas III
458–484	King	Peroz I
484–488	King	Balash I
488–531	King	Kobad I
531–578	King	Chosroes I (Khosrow) (Anushiruan)
578–590	King	Hormisdas IV
591–628	King	Chosroes II
628–628	King	Kobad II
628–630	King	Ardashir III

Reign	Title	Ruler
632–641	King	Yazdegerd III
641–1499—Persia under caliphates of Baghdad, the Seljaks, and the Mongols		
SAFAVID DYNASTY (1499–1736)		
1499–1523	Shah	Ismail I (Ishamael)
1523–1576	Shah	Tahmasp I (Tamasp) (Thamas)
1576–1577	Shah	Ismail II Murza
1577–1586	Shah	Mohammed Khodabanda Murza
1586–1628	Shah	Abbas (I) the Great
1628–1642	Shah	Safi I (Sophi)
1642–1667	Shah	Abbas II
1667–1694	Shah	Sulaiman I (Safi)
1694–1722	Shah	Husain I (Hussein)
1722–1725	Shah	Mahmoud
1725–1727	Shah	Ashraff
1727–1731	Shah	Tahmasp II
1732–1736	Shah	Abbas III
1749–1749	Shah	Sulaiman II (Safi)
1750–1751	Shah	Ismail III
1752–1752	Shah	Husain II
AFSHARID DYNASTY (1736–1750)		
1736–1747	Shah	Nadir
1747–1748	Shah	Adil (ah-Quli Khan)
1748–1749	Shah	Rukh (Rokh)
1748–1749	Shah	Ibrahim
1750–1750	Shah	Rukh
1750—Bakhtiari		
1750–1750	Shah	Ali Mardan Khan (central Persia)
ZAWD DYNASTY (1760–1795)		
1750–1779	Shah	Karim Khan (southern Persia)
1779–1779	Shah	Mohammed Ali
	Shah	Abul-Fath
1779–1779	Shah	Sadig
1781–1785	Shah	Ali Murad
1785–1789	Shah	Jafar
1789–1796	Shah	Lutf Ali
KAJAR (QAJAR) DYNASTY (1750–1925)		
1750–1758	Shah	Mohammed Hasan Khan
1795–1797	Shah	Agha Mohammed Khan
1797–1834	Shah	Fath Ali (Futteh)
1834–1848	Shah	Mohammed
1848–1896	Shah	Nasir-ul-Deen
1896–1907	Shah	Muzaffar-ul-Deen
1907–1909	Shah	Mohammed Ali
1909–1925	Shah	Ahmed Mirza
PAHLEVI DYNASTY (1925–1980)		
(Name changed from Persia to Iran)		
1925–1941	Shah	Riza Pahlevi
1941–1980	Shah	Mohammed Riza Pahlevi

*In 522 B.C. Pseudosmerdis the Usurper, attempting to attain the throne failed, but forever achieved fame with the word *pseudo*—"false," "sham," "counterfeiter."

10

The Ancient and Modern Kingdoms of Afghanistan

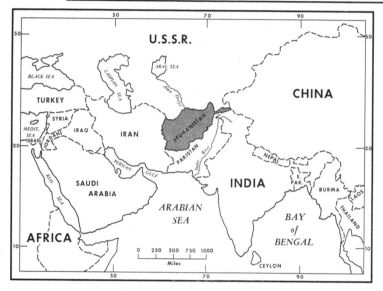

The geographical position of Afghanistan in southwest Asia

For centuries the course of historical events in Afghanistan has been linked with, and strongly influenced by, the activities of peoples and rulers beyond the country's present borders. Afghanistan continues to share cultural, linguistic, and ethnic ties with the people of central Asia immediately across the Amu Darya (classically, the Oxus River) on the north, with Pakistan on the east and south and with its western neighbor, Iran (Persia). As a result of a history complicated by invasions, foreign rule, and tribal movements across its borders, no single ethnic group in the country stands out as its authentic, original population.

Because of the country's position as a strategic meeting area of expanding cultures and clashing empires, early Afghan kings were deeply involved in the dynastic struggles of neighboring powers and principalities. In the modern era (the nineteenth century) of turbulent colonial expansion, Afghan rulers were embroiled, as pawns of conflict, in a shifting game of power politics as the British and Russians contended for control over the area comprising Afghanistan.

The Afghans strove to protect their independence either through noninvolvement or by expediently playing one foreign power against the other.

The year 1747 marks a significant point in the nation's history. Before that date Afghanistan did not exist as an integrated political entity; each tribe ruled its own territory; foreign conquerors—and occasionally a domestic despot—fought over the few population centers, usually hoping to control the Hindu Kush. It was an era of invasion and retreat with little continuity to mark the progress of the Afghans. In 1747, Ahmad Khan Sadozai, an Abdali (later known as Durani) tribal chief within the largest ethnic group, the Pashtuns, established a distinct political entity to be known as *Afghanistan* (the land of the Afghans). Nevertheless, it was not until 1919, when Great Britain recognized Afghanistan's independence in the Treaty of Rawalpindi, that the Afghans for the first time could regard their country as fully independent of foreign control.

Until the beginning of the twentieth century the country was mainly a confederation of tribes, held together by the intrigue and force of the ruler and subject to the machinations of rival chieftains and foreign governments, each trying to control the three centers of power—Kandahar, Herat, and Kabul. It was a period in which the Afghans demonstrated a fiercely independent spirit, acknowledging the power of rulership only when the ruler had a legitimate right, defined by their own tribal codes, to apply the controls of authority. Throughout this period Afghan rulers tried, with increasing success, to remove the nation's destiny from the hands of foreigners.

Afghanistan became what its present-day people call a modern nation during the reign of Abdur Rahman Khan (1881–1901), a powerful ruler who drew authority away from tribal chiefs and centralized it in Kabul. After his rule, Great Britain and Russia recognized the existence of Afghanistan as an independent state, delimited many of the country's borders (some without Afghan consent), and agreed that the country would be a buffer state between the two empires.

The evolution of national unity and development was a slow and painful process. An area inhabited by various linguistic and ethnic groups with conflicting loyalties and with no clearly definable areas of settlement, Afghanistan had for centuries been a battleground for Tajiks, Pashtuns, Turkomans, Uzbeks, Baluchis, and Mongols. Within the ethnic groups various tribes fought for ascendance either over the group itself or over the entire nation.

The word *Afghanistan* has been applied to the area by foreigners only since the beginning of the nineteenth century; to outsiders particularly the British, Afghan was synonymous with Pashtun. Many Pashtuns regard themselves as Afghan in an ethnolinguistic sense; others refer to themselves as Afghans only when talking to foreigners, generally identifying themselves by their tribal or ethnic names.

The historical themes of developing national unity and preserving independence have continued. The leaders have attempted to regain or acquire hegemony over all Pashtuns including many in what became Pakistan, and to steer a neutral course in the power conflict between the Soviet Union and the United States.

HISTORIC ORIGINS

The oldest elements of the Afghan population appear to be people of ancient Aryan stock, among them the Tajiks, Pashtuns, and the people of Nuristan. Yet in relation to the long history of human life around the Hindu Kush, these groups are new, because they began their habitation there after the eastward migrations of Aryan peoples in the second and first millennia B.C. Little is known of the peoples who lived in the area before that, but undoubtedly many of those in eastern Afghanistan were of Dravidian extraction as were most of the early inhabitants of the Indian subcontinent.

The movements of Aryan peoples some three thousand to four thousand years ago from central and western Asia onto the Iranian plateau and into the Indian subcontinent laid the foundations of the present population and gave it an Indo-European language base and racial characteristics of the people of the West. It was from these ancient peoples that the Vedas, part of the sacred literature of the Hindus, developed. By 600 B.C. they had either settled in or acquired rule over those Asian lands from the Aegean Sea in

Details of the location of regions and cities of Afghanistan

the west to the Indus River in the east, and from the Black and Caspian seas and the Pamirs in the north to the Arabian desert and the Arabian Sea in the south. The area around the ancient city and present town of Balkh in the north-central province of Balkh (formerly, Mazar-i-Sharif) was one of their major centers of settlement.

Afghan historians like to feel that this was the Aryan capital of the world—they term it the Mother of Cities—and that Afghanistan was known as Aryana. Present-day Iranians, on the other hand, like to believe that Iran, which means "land of the Aryans," was the center of Aryan civilization.

THE PRE-ISLAMIC PERIOD

THE ACHAEMENID EMPIRE
(ca. 550–331 B.C.)

Northern Afghanistan known in ancient times as Bactria (later as Afghan Turkistan) first entered recorded history around 550 B.C., when it was incorporated into the Achaemenid Empire by Cyrus the Great (559–529 B.C.), after whose tribe the empire was named. One of several satrapies, Bactria remained an integral part of its strategic borderland until 331 B.C., when the empire fell to Alexander the Great. The northern part of Bactria figured prominently as the home of the great religious teacher Zoroaster (Zarathustra), the Sage of Bactria, and the founder of Zoroastrianism, one of the first monotheistic religions. Vestiges of this faith still survive in parts of Iran, Pakistan, India, and among some hill tribes on the Hindu Kush.

GREEK INFLUENCE (325–50 B.C.)

Alexander, after conquering the Achaemenid Empire in 331 B.C. and occupying the area of Afghanistan for several years reached the Indus (in modern West Pakistan) in 325 B.C. and died two years later in Babylon. Although his expedition to the Aryana region was short lived, he and his brand of Greeks left behind a Hellenic cultural influence that lasted for centuries. The land east and south of the Hindu Kush fell to the Indian Mauryan rulers, who introduced Indic culture, including Buddhism, into the area. Faithful descendants spread the religion throughout Aryana, carved Buddhas into the cliffs at Bamiyan, northwest of Kabul, and built many stupas and sanctuaries in valleys, such as the Kabul. The land to the north and west was dominated by feuding Greek-descended *satraps* (provincial governors), most of whom had lost touch with their homeland and intermarried with Iranians. From these feuds the Graeco-Bactrian Kingdom (ca. 225–55 B.C.) arose north of the Hindu Kush. Demetrius, one of the greatest Graeco-Bactrian kings, who ruled about 187 B.C., expanded its boundaries eastward through Kabul across the Indus into India.

Under Menander (ca. 150 B.C.), who fused Hellenic and indigenous Indic forms to make a new "Indo-Greek" cul-

ture and empire, Buddhism and Graeco-Buddhist art flourished as did the commercial life of northern India and Afghanistan. After Menander's death Indo-Greek rule declined and was overrun by a fresh influx of Aryan-descended barbaric tribes, among them the Sakas (Scythians) and Pahlavas (Parthians). By 50 B.C. the Greek influence had lost much of its initial vigor and virtually all control.

KUSHANS (50 B.C.–A.D. 425)

Toward the middle of the first century B.C. five nomadic tribes from central Asia, called Yueh-chi by the Chinese, invaded Bactria and drove the last of the Indo-Greeks into India. It was the last invasion of Aryan-descended tribes into Afghanistan. One of them, the Kushans, gained supremacy and established a dynasty that was to dominate the Hindu Kush for nearly four centuries. They supplanted the Pahlavas to the south (Kabul) and the Sakas in India (Gandhara). Kanishka I (ca. A.D. 110 or 120–62), the Kushans' most famous king, ruled an empire containing present-day Afghanistan, Kashmir, and much of northern India, with capitals at Kapisa (near Kabul) and Purushupura (Peshawar). It was a period of great artistic and intellectual development; the Kushan kings, after Kanishka I, adopted the Mahayana form of Buddhism, promoted its propagation to China over the land routes of central Asia, and took over what remained of Graeco-Indian culture.

The brief expansion of the Iranian-Sassanid Empire (ca. A.D. 226–641) into Afghanistan and India greatly reduced the Kushan power. The empire was finally destroyed around 425 to 428 by the Ephthalites or White Huns, a Mongol people who dominated central Asia from 400 to 553. Sassanian power reasserted itself in the sixth century and regained control of most of Afghanistan; by the beginning of the seventh century, most of the country was under Sassanid control, divided into provinces governed by White Hun satraps.

THE COMING OF ISLAM (672–870)

In the seventh century Arab invaders and the tide of Islamic propagation reached Afghanistan, then considered by the Arabs as part of Iranian Khorasan. By the ninth century the Arabs had gained more or less full control of the region, and Islam triumphed over Zoroastrianism, Buddhism, Hinduism, and various forms of pagan worship which for centuries had been practiced in the region.

The first Arabic attempts to conquer Afghanistan directly were unsuccessful in spite of a temporary occupation around 672 of Kabul, Herat, and Balkh. Two centuries later, an Arab general, Yakub ibn Layth, again occupied Kabul, then ruled by a Hindu king, and established Islam permanently in Afghanistan. The inhabitants were gradually converted to the Sunnite branch of Islam.

During the eighth and ninth centuries, partly to obtain better grazing land, ancestors of many of the Turkic-speaking groups now identifiable in Afghanistan settled in the Hindu Kush area. Some of these Turki tribes settled in Ghor Ghazni and Kabul, and after a long period of cultural contact with existing Pashtun-Iranian tribes, apparently assimilated their language and characteristics. Some scholars hold that the Ghilzai Pashtuns may have descended from these tribes.

GHAZNEVID DYNASTY (962–1140)

In the mid-tenth century Alptagin, a former Turkish slave and commander in chief of the army of the Samanid Dynasty (874-999) in eastern Persia, gained control of the principality of Ghazni and founded the Ghaznevid Dynasty (962–1140), the first great Islamic empire in Afghanistan. The most renowned among his successors was Mahmud of Ghazni (998–1030), recognized by the caliph of Baghdad as the temporal heir of the Samanids. Known as a conqueror and destroyer of idols, he led seventeen expeditions into India and set a pattern of Sunnite ascendancy, and successfully prevented the Shiites of Iran from acquiring a dominant position in Afghanistan and India. Mahmud expelled the last of the Hindu rulers from the Kabul River valley and also tried to subdue some of the eastern mountain Pashtun tribes, who were then referred to as Afghans by Iranian historians. At his death his rule extended from western Persia to Kashmir and from the Amu Darya to the Ganges. A patron of the arts and of learning, he founded a university with the distinguished historian al-Biruni at its head. Among Mahmud's some four hundred resident poets were the famous Khwafa Abdullah Ansari and Firdawsi.

The empire survived for some one hundred twenty-five years after Mahmud's death, but its power had declined by the twelfth century. In 1152 the city of Ghazni itself, symbol of an empire noted for its plundering fury as well as for its intellectual attainments, fell to a neighboring Afghan principality, the Ghorid (southeast of Herat), climaxing a long feud between the Ghaznevids and the Ghorids.

The Ghorids, believed to be descendants of earlier Turkic-speaking people, lived in the mountains of Ghor. They ascended to dominance over Afghanistan under Muizuddin, known as Mohammed of Ghor—the most famous of the rulers of what became known as the Ghorid Dynasty. Unlike his Afghan predecessors, who invaded India chiefly for plunder, Muizuddin attempted to establish a permanent empire in India. In 1192 he led a strong force against the Hindu Rajputs (warrior caste group of northwestern and central India) and won a decisive victory that laid the foundations for the first Islamic Empire east of the Indus. One of his generals, Kutbuddin Aibak, a former Turkish slave, established himself as sultan at Delhi—the first of a long line of the so-called Turko-Afghan sultans.

MONGOL RULE (1220–1504)

In the early thirteenth century Mongols from the eastern plains of central Asia invaded Afghanistan and brought abrupt change to the social and dynastic history of the country. Under Genghis Khan (locally, Changez) they captured Herat and swept destructively eastward to the Indus by 1222. Genghis Khan's grandson, Hulagu, took the title of Il-Khan and ruled over Armenia, Iraq, Iran, and Afghanistan. Under the Il-Khans a local Tajik Dynasty, called Karts, was established and for nearly two centuries ruled the greater part of western Afghanistan. In the latter part of the fourteenth century, Timur (1336-1404)—known to the West as Tamerlane—son of a Turki tribal chieftain and a putative descendant, through his mother, of Genghis Khan, ended the Tajik rule. This represented the last effort of the Persian speaking people of Ghor and Herat to establish an independent domain in the area; no native dynasty, in fact, arose to rule the country until the ascendancy of the Pashtuns in the eighteenth century.

In the centuries preceding the first Mongol invasion of Afghanistan, the Pashtun tribes of the Sulaiman Range (between modern-day Afghanistan and Pakistan) had begun to emerge from their isolated valleys, making the best use they could of their rugged country to harass passersby. Tamerlane found them in such strongholds as Bannu and Kohat, now towns in Pakistan, as well as in their mountain fastnesses. Their fierce resistance not only to the Mongols and Turks but also to the inept attempts of the Turki sultans of Delhi to establish control over the passes of the Sulaiman Range, established a reputation of Pashtun independence that remains today. The hatred of the Pashtun for central Asian invaders persisted throughout the heyday of the Moghul Empire of India (1526-1707):

Tamerlane went on into India to build an empire, but dissension among the Timurid princes and the rise of Uzbek power under Shaybani Khan in central Asia caused the decline of this dynasty. A young descendant of Tamerlane, called Babar (1483–1530), who fled from his homeland in central Asian Ferghana under attack by the Uzbeks, moved south to Balkh, took Kabul in 1504 and laid claim to Tamerlane's empire.

His failure to reconquer Turkistan from the Uzbeks probably caused Babar to focus his attention on India, which was then ruled tenuously by Ibrahim Lodi, the Afghan sultan of Delhi. In winning the historic battle of Panipat near Delhi in 1526, Babar shattered the forces of the Lodi sultan and laid the cornerstone of the Moghul Empire in India. Babar died in India in 1530 but, as he had requested, was buried several years later in Kabul, which he claimed to have loved more than the Indian plains.

MOGHUL-IRANIAN RIVALRY (1526-1747)

Afghanistan entered a period covering two centuries during which it was fought over by the two great powers, Moghul India and Iran. The conflict set a pattern of foreign rivalry over Afghanistan that continues to affect the nation's position in the world. From Babar's capture of Delhi in 1526 to the collapse of Moghul power at the death of Aurangzeb (1658–1707), the rulers of Delhi sought to extend their control over Afghanistan either for territorial aggrandizement or to block the historic invasion routes into India across the Hindu Kush and Sulaiman Range. They were seriously concerned over the control of Kabul and Kandahar and over the fiercely independent tribes between these towns and the Indus Valley, essential to the safety of their domain. This was a strategic consideration later subscribed to by the British in India.

In Iran, the growing empire of the Safavids, beginning in 1499 and reaching its climax under Shah Abbas the Great at the turn of the seventeenth century, rivaled that of the Moghuls. The northwest and southeast of Afghanistan, with Herat and Kandahar as centers, lay in Iran's sphere of influence; the east, with Kabul, Ghazni, and Jalalabad its centers, and sometimes also Kandahar, lay within the claims of the Moghuls. The Uzbek tribes in central Asia contested for northern Afghanistan, particularly Badakhshan and Herat, where neither Persian nor Moghul power was ever strong.

Throughout this period of Moghul-Iranian rivalry the Pashtun tribes were steadily increasing in numbers and influence, and it was probably during this time that the Abdali and Ghilzai tribes spread from their mountain habitations over the more fertile lands of Kandahar, Zamindawar, and the Tarnak-Arghandab valleys. Their rise in power was facilitated by the decline in the position and influence of the Iranian Tajiks who had borne the brunt of the Mongol invasions.

Under Aurangzeb the governor of Kabul had to attempt to subsidize the tribes and create jealousy and distrust among them to keep open the road between Kabul and Peshawar. By deliberately stimulating the natural suspicions and dissensions among tribal peoples emerging from an isolated existence into the mainstream of events, Aurangzeb's policy destroyed whatever chance there might have been for a spirit of national unity among the eastern Pashtuns. By fostering the isolation of the frontier from the relatively advanced areas around it, he ensured the continuance of the no-man's-land that manifests itself even in modern times—a land whose people are united chiefly by their common hostility toward outsiders.

In Kandahar, an important trade center which was regarded by the Moghul emperors as their "indispensable first line of defense," the frequent shifts from Iranian to Moghul control and back again promoted dissensions and intrigue and enabled the powerful tribes in this area to play off one power against the other. Thus the Abdali tribes near Kandahar succeeded in obtaining concessions from the Iranian Safavid ruler, Shah Abbas the Great, and having one Sado Khan, an Abdali, recognized as chief. Sado's descendants, the Sadozai, became the ruling group and rebelled against the Iranians after Shah Abbas II reconquered Kandahar in 1648. To break Abdali power in Kandahar the Safavid shah

forced many of the Sadozai to migrate to Herat, where they eventually became powerful. This removal led to the ascendance of Ghilzai tribes near Kandahar, and their power increased as that of the Safavids' weakened. Under the Hotaki chief Mir Mahmud ibn Mir Wais the Ghilzai conquered Isfahan (in Iran) and came to rule most of southern Afghanistan and Iran, while the Sadozai Abdalis spread their control from Herat to much of the rest of Afghanistan, west of the Hindu Kish.

The Ghilzai overextended themselves and soon lost not only Iran but also Kandahar itself to Nadir Shah (1732-47), one of Iran's greatest monarchs, who, after defeating the Abdali, secured their support and broke Ghilzai power as well. Many Ghilzai fled to Kabul province, which gave Nadir Shah an excuse to capture Kabul and sever it from the Moghul empire in 1738. Nadir Shah, founder of the Afshar Dynasty, used Abdali as well as Iranian troops and moved on to plunder the great riches of India.

Shah Nadir, the king of Iran, conquered the city areas of Kandahar and Kabul and therefore was considered by some historians as the "first" king of Afghanistan. He reigned over them from 1736 to 1738.

EVOLUTION OF AFGHANISTAN AS A NATION

Ahmad Khan Sadozai, a chief in the Sadozai *kheyl* (lineage group) of the Abdali tribe, rose to a high position in Nadir Shah's army, and, when the shah was assassinated by plotting officers in Iran, Ahmad Khan with a strong contingent of Abdali troops seized a treasure convoy and marched to Kandahar. In 1747 he was elected by the chieftains of the Abdali tribes as ruler of all Afghans and assumed the power of the late shah in Afghanistan. He obtained possession of the whole eastern portion of Nadir Shah's empire, to which he added Kashmir and most of the Punjab by conquest. He made Kandahar his capital and in 1748 took the title of *dur-i-duran* (pearl of pearls); since then the Abdali have been called Durani, and Ahmad Khan used the throne name of Ahmad Shah.

By the time of Ahmad Shah's enthronment, the Pashtuns included many groups whose greatest single common characteristic was their Pashto language. Their origins were obscure; most were believed to have descended from ancient Aryan tribes, but some, such as the Ghilzais, may once have been Turki. To the east, in the impregnable hills of the central Sulaiman Range, the Waziris and their close relatives, the Mahsuds had been known to have been located since the fourteenth century. By the end of the sixteenth century and the final Turki-Mongol invasions, such Pashtun tribes as the Shinwaris, Yusufzais, and Mohmands had moved down from the upper Kabul River valley into the valleys and plains around Peshawar, near where Afridi Pashtuns had long been established around the Khyber Pass. Each Pashtun tribe was to play a role in the development of Afghanistan as a united national state. By producing men who excelled in battle or politics, or both, and who therefore were capable of wresting recognition from rivals or rebellious chieftains, the Pashtuns were able to achieve a measure of national unity and maintain independence. Since the middle of the eighteenth century, Durani leaders have held the title of *amir* (Arabic, chief or king) or its equivalent over all tribal leaders.

Ahmad Shah brought to the nation not only the skill of a conqueror but also the genius of an administrator. Although he followed the time-honored customs of raiding India, his main interest was consolidating the tribes under his rule. By levying light taxes and ruling through a council of noblemen *(sirdars)* who represented the Pashtun tribes, he forged the beginning of a unified state based on the ascendancy of the Pashto-speaking peoples. Ahmad Shah's son, Timur, was less of an able administrator, and internecine wars among the various Durani *kheyls* brought a return of near anarchy; Timur moved his capital to Kabul, where the population was mainly Parsiwan (of Persian descent and Persian-speaking). An assassination attempt on Timur in Peshawar brought reprisals, and many border chiefs, particularly among the Mohmands, were deeply alienated. At Timur's death in 1793 the Sadozai Durani Dynasty was

Timur Shah, the ruler of Afghanistan from 1773 to 1793

severely weakened by the quarrels of his twenty-three sons over succession to the throne.

The Sadozai family quarrel was ended in 1818 by a revolt of the Mohammedzai *kheyl* of the Durani. Led by Dost Mohammed Khan (1793–1863), the Mohammedzai extended their control over Kashmir and Peshawar. Dost Mohammed ascended the throne in Kabul in 1826 and declared himself amir of Afghanistan in 1835. The outer provinces of the former Sadozai Empire, however, were all lost; the Uzbeks of Balkh had claimed independence as had the people of Baluchistan and Sind; the Sikhs, an ethnoreligious group in the Punjab, in northern India, had retaken Peshawar; and Herat was ruled by Kamran, the last of the major Sadozai chiefs. To regain this territory— particularly Peshawar, which the Pashtun rulers of Kabul had long claimed—became Dost Mohammed's chief aim.

THE BEGINNING OF EUROPEAN INTERVENTION (1809)

While Durani Pashtun ascendancy was a prime factor in the evolution of a national state, European interests also played a contributing role. When British dominion over India began to expand while Napoleon looked covetously eastward, the East India Company, as Great Britain's represen-

Amir Dost Mohammed Khan served as king (khan) from 1826 to 1839 and from 1842 to 1863.

tative, approached the amir of Afghanistan for an alliance, and concluded the Anglo-Afghan Treaty of 1809. Dynastic strife in the ensuing decades once more isolated Afghanistan until 1837 when Dost Mohammed took firm control and appealed to the British for aid against Iran, which with Russian approval, had besieged Herat.

British distrust of Russia had been growing since the czar signed the Treaty of Tilsit in 1807 with Napoleon, subsequently attacked Iran, signed the Treaty of Turkmanchai in 1828 with the shah of Iran, supported the siege of Herat, and began diplomatic maneuvers in the court of Dost Mohammed. Yet the British declined Dost Mohammed's plea for assistance on the grounds that he had sought Russian support to help regain Peshawar from the Sikhs.

Instead, the British invaded Afghanistan in 1838 in what became known as the First Anglo-Afghan War (1838-42)—the first of three wars between them. British troops took Kandahar and Kabul and drove Dost Mohammed north; then they installed Shah Shuja, a Sadozai rival who had held the throne from 1803 to 1810, as amir. Dost Mohammed surrendered in 1840 and was exiled to India. Shah Shuja, who had in his earlier reign permitted the British to assist in organizing Afghanistan's first professional armed service, again depended upon British troops to protect his throne. British occupation of the country aroused tribal rebellions which ended in 1842 in complete disaster as the Afghans massacred all but a few of the expeditionary force. Although the British returned the same year to burn Kabul in retribution and restored Dost Mohammed as amir, enmity had been born; British occupation and destruction left a heritage of enduring hatred and suspicion of the British and other foreigners.

On his return from exile, Dost Mohammed set out to unite his people and consolidate his lands. He based his power on the willing political support of tribal chiefs and devoted his reign to pacifying the country, which included putting down two serious Ghilzai uprisings. In 1848, in expectation of recovering Peshawar, he joined the Sikhs in battle against the British, only to lose in the battle of Gujerat the following year all that he had gained. Between 1850 and 1855 he recovered Afghan Turkistan, Balkh, Kunduz, and Badakhshan, and in 1855 he regained Kandahar, which had

been lost to Kabul as a result of his exile.

Anglo-Afghan relations were cool during the initial years of Dost Mohammed's return to power, but events in other parts of the world forced both the British and the Afghan amir to come to an understanding. Russian ambitions in the Crimea and the threatening attitudes of Iran toward areas of British interest forced Dost Mohammed to conclude in 1855 the Treaty of Peshawar with the British. In 1856, however, Iran, with Russian support, captured Herat; in the Treaty of Paris between Iran and Great Britain in 1857, Iran gave up its claim to, but not its occupation of, the city.

In signing the treaty at the end of the Crimean war (1854-55) the great powers (Great Britain and Russia) recognized both Iran and Afghanistan as independent and named Great Britain as the arbiter in all future disputes between the two. The effect of the treaty and Dost Mohammed's faithfulness to his pledged word were soon apparent; despite considerable pressure from Muslims throughout Afghanistan, the amir refused to join the Indians in the rebellion of 1857 (called the Sepoy Mutiny). With British approval he captured Herat from the Iranians in 1863, shortly before his death.

THE RUSSIAN ADVANCE

During the next decade Russia advanced steadily southward and reached Samarkand (in Soviet Uzbekistan, north

This picture taken in 1869 shows the supremacy of the British over the Afghanistan royalty. His Excellency the earl of Mayo is "receiving" the king of Afghanistan at Ambala. The earl is seated, center, *with Sher Ali Khan,* left, *and his heir apparent,* right.

of Afghanistan) in 1868. Bukhara, immediately north of the Amu Darya, became a vassal state, and Russian influence was thus brought to the border of Afghanistan.

British policy at the time was one of noninterference. Amir Sher Ali's (1863–79) request for British guarantees against Russian encroachment was refused on the ground that by the Anglo-Russian Agreement of 1873 the Russians had formally accepted the Amu Darya as the limit of their southward extension. Sher Ali was able, with British subsidy, to start modernizing his army, but Anglo-Afghan relations deteriorated when a political shift in England inaugurated once again a "forward policy" on intervention. So, Sher Ali sought help from Russia.

THE SECOND ANGLO-AFGHAN WAR (1878–79)

Sher Ali's acceptance of a Russian envoy while refusing to allow entry to a British mission led to the Second Anglo-Afghan War. British troops drove Sher Ali out of Kabul and once more brought Afghanistan under foreign occupation. The bitterly hostile population and the relaxation of Anglo-Russian tension in Europe made it advisable for the British to withdraw and leave the country to Sher Ali's son, Yaqub Khan (1879). To ensure their future control of Afghanistan's foreign relations, the British dictated the Treaty of Gandamak in May 1879. This agreement left the new amir free to rule internally but bound him to follow British advice in all his relations with other powers; in effect this treaty restriction made the country a virtual British protectorate serving as a buffer between Russia and British India. The Afghan ruler also consented to the British occupation of the Khyber Pass. Abdur Rahman, who was placed on the throne by the British after Yaqub was deposed, reaffirmed the treaty.

In delayed reaction, the Russians invaded Afghan-held territory for the first time in 1885 by occupying Panjdeh, a Turkman village less than one hundred miles north of Herat. The British rushed in with aid for the defense of Herat and mobilized two army corps in India. For a while the two great powers were on the brink of war, but in September 1885, a compromise acceptable to Abdur Rahman was reached. By the Anglo-Russian Agreement of St. Petersburg in July 1887 the Russians agreed to make no further advance southward. The Anglo-Russian Pact of 1895 made the Wakhan (the eastern panhandle of Badakhshan) a permanent part of Afghanistan by establishing the border with Russia. The northern frontier was now clearly drawn and demarcated except for an exact definition of the boundary along the Amu Darya.

After gaining control of the amir's foreign relations, the British strove also to lay down the eastern and southern limits of the Afghan domain. In November 1893 Sir Mortimer Durand persuaded Abdur Rahman to sign an agreement fixing the border of Afghanistan along an irregular twelve-hundred-mile line running from Sinkiang (western China) to Iran through territories which Afghanistan had

Abdur Rahman Khan was king of Afghanistan from 1881 to 1901. He was appointed king by the British and as a strong ruler served them well—in the time of the Penjdeh incident his actions are credited with preventing a war between Britain and Russia.

regarded as its own. The agreement pledged each signatory not to interfere in the affairs of the other across the line.

MODERNIZATION AND NATIONAL INDEPENDENCE

ABDUR RAHMAN KHAN (1881–1901)

The surrender of control of foreign policy was the price Abdur Rahman paid for British recognition of his right to a free hand in the internal affairs of his country. A skilled general and statesman, Abdur Rahman set forth with British assistance to pacify the tribes and unite the country. He wrote in his autobiography:

> The country exhibiting a rebellious spirit, I appointed private detectives and spies to report to me all that went on among the people, thus finding out with abundant proofs those who were loyal and friendly . . . the ringleaders and worst offenders were the fanatical *mullahs* (Moslem religious leaders) and

headstrong chiefs who had been partisans of the late Shir Ali's family.

In 1881 Abdur Rahman captured Kandahar from Ghilzai rebels, secured Herat, and put down numerous tribal rebellions. In 1895 he invaded Kafiristan, later called Nuristan, the Land of Light, and converted the inhabitants to Islam.

Abdur Rahman stressed "the value of unity; unity and unity alone." Violating the Pashtun code that the king is essentially the "first among equals" he ignored the existence of tribal councils, set about to destroy the independent power of the tribal chiefs and religious leaders; and weakened tribal autonomy by transferring most of their military and administrative functions to the central government—moves which had the support of the British government of India. He established the royal prerogative of appointing and dismissing tribal chiefs. He built an effective administrative machine and secured the power and prestige of his position by developing a standing army and a police force. Above all, he departed from tradition by placing his sons in responsible positions in Kabul instead of appointing them governors of distant provinces. He redrew the boundaries of provinces to destroy the domains of tribal chiefs and issued new laws that would apply universally. Although harsh and autocratic, Abdur Rahman placed the nation on the road to progress, though many Afghans accused him of having pursued his policies at the behest of the British. His son, Habibullah, who succeeded him peaceably on his death in 1901, though less forceful, continued his policies.

In the early years of Habibullah Khan's reign (1901–19), Russia and Great Britain intensified their rivalry. Frontal clash was averted, however, because of their mutual interest in counteracting the growing German influence in Europe. In addition Russia, deeply shaken by its shattering defeat at the hands of Japan in 1904-5 and beset by internal unrest, was amenable to a conciliatory, comprehensive

This was the photograph of King Abdur Rahman Khan which was most often used by the Western newspapers and illustrated magazines.

settlement with Great Britain concerning major areas of friction, such as Afghanistan, Persia, and Tibet. The result was the Anglo-Russian Convention of St. Petersburg, signed in 1907, under which Afghanistan was formally recognized by both powers as a buffer state whose integrity would be respected by each; Russia also agreed that Afghanistan would be excluded from its sphere of influence. The agreement was to be ratified by Afghanistan before being implemented, but Habibullah was so incensed at not being consulted before the Anglo-Russian negotiations that he refused to endorse the convention. Nevertheless, Russia indicated in 1908 that, with or without the amir's approval, it would honor the agreement.

Habibullah's later years showed a diminishing hostility to Western influences. He introduced European medicine, surgery, automobiles, telephones, and telegraph and even opened a school organized on European lines.

After the Japanese victory over Russia, an increasing number of educated Afghans were moved by nationalist sentiments. Headed by Mahmud Beg Tarzi, nationalists, some of them leading religious figures, pressed for release of Afghanistan's obligations to Great Britain and closer ties with the Ottoman sultan in Turkey. World War I further accelerated the nationalist agitation because the war presented the Afghans with the prospect of winning complete independence by fighting against the British. Nonetheless, Habibullah chose neutrality throughout the conflict, apparently in the hope of obtaining full sovereignty through British goodwill. In February 1919, at the height of popular resentment over his stand, Habibullah was assassinated under mysterious circumstances. He was succeeded briefly by his brother, Nasrullah Khan, who was soon displaced by one of Habibullah's younger sons, Amanullah Khan.

AMANULLAH (1919–29)

Nationalistic, and regarded as anti-British, the new amir was deeply interested in social and economic reform at home and thereby antagonized the conservative, religious leaders of the country. Partly to divert internal discontent toward an enemy and partly because of his belief that an Indian nationalist revolution against the British was imminent, Amanullah, in May 1919, attacked the British forces in what came to be called the Third Anglo-Afghan War (May–August 1919). Afghanistan was not victorious despite some successes in Pashtun territory by an enterprising army commander and Mohammedzai chieftain named Nadir Khan. When Amanullah asked for an armistice in June the war-weary British, already exhausted from World War I and troubled by growing political unrest in India, elected to give the Afghans freedom of action in foreign relations and recognized their complete independence for the first time through the Treaty of Rawalpindi, signed on August 8, 1919. This treaty was supplemented and reaffirmed in November 1921. To the Afghans Amanullah emerged as the triumphant hero who had wrested independence from the world's mightiest empire.

King Amanullah Khan ruled from 1919 to 1929.

Amanullah rose on an anti-British wave to heights of popularity. The sentiment was helped considerably by repeated overtures from the Soviet Union which had backed Indian revolutionaries, and by Turkey, which had sent General Jamal Pasha to reorganize the Afghan army. In February 1921 Afghanistan and the Soviet Union signed a treaty of friendship, and the Soviet Union granted a subsidy of 1 million gold rubles and a supply of ammunition to Amanullah.

The Afghan amir's pro-Soviet ardor cooled, however, because of Soviet mistreatment of central Asian tribes, and in November 1921 he concluded a treaty with Great Britain reaffirming Afghan independence, accepting the Durand Line and agreeing to exchange diplomatic representatives. Amanullah's relations with the Soviet Union cooled further when in 1922 the Turkic-speaking Basmachi tribes in Bukhara, led by Enver Pasha, rebelled against the Soviet government. The revolt failed; Enver was killed; and many central Asian Muslims fled to Afghanistan. By 1926 the Soviets had regained their influence and signed a treaty of nonaggression with Afghanistan.

Amanullah was an imaginative ruler who dreamed of bringing Afghan society out of its traditional tribal ways, in which religious proscriptions dominated, to what he believed to be modern social behavior. In 1924 he organized the Royal Afghan Air Force and brought in Soviet technicians and Turkish officers to train his military forces. A trip through Europe, Turkey, and Iran in 1928, the first ever taken by an Afghan amir, imbued him with ideas of Western social and military reform. On his return to Kabul he ordered the emancipation of women by outlawing polyga-

my and decreeing compulsory education for both sexes. He set forth rules for the separation of religious and secular authority, established the first Afghan parliament, and ordered Afghans, even visiting tribesmen, to wear European dress in Kabul.

Afghanistan was not ready for such drastic changes. The mullahs, who were among the most powerful persons in the country, backed by tribal chiefs, especially among the Shinwari Pashtuns, reacted violently to the innovations. Amanullah attempted to backtrack and cancel many of his reforms, but he was too late. On January 14, 1929, faced with open revolt, he abdicated in favor of his elder brother Inayatullah, who in turn fled the capital after a Tajik bandit leader, Habibullah Ghazi (Bacha-i-Sawwo, "son of the water carrier"), attacked Kabul. Both Amanullah and his brother, after attempting a comeback from Kandahar but failing largely because of Ghilzai enmity in Kandahar and Ghazni, fled to India and eventual exile in Europe.

NADIR SHAH (1929–33)

Under the brief and turbulent rule of Habibullah Ghazi, Durani fortunes and the status of Afghanistan as a nation sank to the lowest depths since the advent of Ahmad Shah. The ignorant, illiterate Tajik ruler faced the enmity of most Pashtun tribes, but they were so divided among themselves that united action against him was virtually impossible until a dynamic new leader appeared. His name was Sardar Mohammed Nadir Khan, great grandson of one of Dost Mohammed's brothers.

Nadir Khan had exiled himself to France under circumstances still obscure after a distinguished military and diplomatic career under Habibullah and Amanullah. Although he was sick when news of Kabul's capture by Habibullah Ghazi reached him, he boarded a steamer for India to try to overthrow the usurper. Without funds, and at first without foreign or tribal support, he and his able brothers Mohammed Hashim Khan, Shah Mahmud Khan, and Shah Wali Khan, eventually won over enough support of the eastern Pashtun tribes, especially the Wazirs and Mahsuds, to defeat the forces of the Tajik ruler. Nadir Khan entered Kabul as a hero, and in October 1929, a gathering of tribal chieftains proclaimed him king, henceforth to be called Nadir Shah. The Tajik ruler was executed along with his leading lieutenants.

Nadir Shah faced a bankrupt country in which the animosities of the people against established government had

King Habibullah Ghazi served but nine months as king in 1929.

King Mohammed Nadir Shah ruled Afghanistan from October 16, 1929, until an assassin, Abdul Khaliq, shot him dead on November 8, 1933, while he was awarding ribbons to schoolchildren. Abdul Khaliq and twenty-eight of his relatives were punished for the crime by being tied to the mouth of a cannon and blown to bits before a public audience.

grown considerably. A zealous patriot and a pious Muslim, he disassociated himself from the modernism of Amanullah, proclaimed the supremacy of the Hanafi school of Islamic law, and repealed many of the laws and constitutional reforms instituted by his Durani predecessor. His tribal forces put down brief rebellions among the Tajiks of Kohistan, northeast of Kabul. After the Soviet-Afghan Treaty of Neutrality and Mutual Non-Aggression signed in 1931, he proscribed the activities of troublemaking followers of Russian counterrevolutionaries along the Amu Darya and returned Afghanistan to a semblance of peace.

Following tribal traditions, which Abdur Rahman and his sons had generally ignored, Nadir Shah restored tribal rule whereby the king becomes "chief among chiefs" who consults with the best available advisers before making major decisions. He had come to power with tribal help alone and hoped to preserve that power by means of consultations. To this end he promulgated a constitution which recognized by implication the national gathering of chiefs and notables, the *Loe Jirgah,* as the highest power in the land. His accession adhered to the tribal, religious, and dynastic traditions of Afghanistan.

Nadir Shah had received some of his education in British schools in India and, though he lacked the progressive zeal of Amanullah, hoped to modernize many of his country's institutions partly along European lines. With the aid of his brothers, who also had come in contact with European ideas, he set forth a program to "reeducate" the society's more conservative elements, particularly the mullahs and tribal chiefs. He planned new hospitals and clinics and brought in foreign advisers.

THE LAST MONARCHY

Nadir Shah's reign came to an end on November 8, 1933, when he was assassinated by a youth who was apparently motivated by personal revenge. He was succeeded by his son, Mohammed Zahir Shah, then nineteen years of age. The new shah generally continued his father's policies in matters of pacifying the tribes, pursuing economic and social development, and maintaining normal foreign relations, particularly with the Soviet Union, Iran, and India.

The tribal problems also had a major impact on the nation's foreign relations; nowhere was this more pronounced than on the Afghan-British Indian border. The military and political history of the Pashtuns in Afghanistan is mainly a story of revolt—against the Mongol and Turki invaders, against the Sikhs, and against the local dynasties of their own ethnic group, often including the rulers in Kabul. Most of all they rose against British India, an event not overlooked or impeded by most Afghan amirs who constantly used Pashtun hostility toward the British to help achieve or maintain Afghan security.

From 1933 to 1935 the Mohmands in the north were in constant ferment. In 1936, Haji Mira Ali Khan, commonly called the faqir of Ipi, led a group of *mullahs* and some Waziri tribesmen into battle against the British. The talented and ubiquitous faqir established a reputation for resistance and harassment, and continued his agitational activities, even after the departure of the British from India until his death in 1959.

Tribal unrest was sometimes directed against Kabul itself. In 1938, for example, Said al-Kailani, known as the *Shami Pir,* led an attack on Kabul allegedly to reinstate the exiled Amanullah to whom he was related. Gaining support from sympathetic Waziri and Mahsud tribesmen in the Sulaiman Range east of the Durand Line, he started for the frontier, attracting anti-Kabul Ghilzai tribesmen along the way. The attack was averted when the British, after frantic appeals by the Afghan government, bought off the *Shami Pir*. The near disaster prompted Prime Minister Mohammed Hashim Khan, Zahir Shah's uncle, to increase Kabul subsidies to Pashtun tribes along and across the Durand Line.

General resistance to the British in India led to a degree of Pashtun solidarity that had not previously existed. Probably the most dominant figure was Abdul Ghaffar Khan from the village of Utmanzai near Peshawar, east of the Khyber Pass. His professed goal, after 1927, was Pashtun independence initially by means of cooperating with the Indian nationalist movement of Mohandas K. Gandhi (popularly called Mahatma Gandhi). Known as the Frontier Gandhi himself, Abdul Ghaffar Khan continued to champion the Pashtun cause. This factor offered new opportunity for the Kabul government to assert its claims to Pashtun allegiance. The hope of incorporating British-controlled Pashtun territory east of the Durand Line into Afghanis-

The nineteen-year-old Zahir Shah became king of Afghanistan in 1933 upon the death of his father.

An official portrait of His Majesty al-Mutawakkil Ala Allah Mohammed Zahir Shah at the time of his departure from the throne in a bloodless coup d'etat in 1973.

tan—a dream nurtured among Kabul amirs since the Sikhs captured Peshawar and painfully strengthened by Afghanistan's failure to regain it in the Third Anglo-Afghan War—was particularly heightened as departure of the British from India became imminent after World War II. Afghan irredentism gradually became manifest in support for Pashtun independence after the partition of India and the creation of Pakistan in 1947. The *Pashtunistan* (land of the Pashtuns) issue calling for independence for the Pashtuns—but only those residing east of the Durand Line in Pakistan—came to the fore and continues to plague Afghan-Pakistan relations, although repeated efforts have been made, and continue to be made, to moderate the dispute and achieve a modus vivendi.

From the beginning of his reign, Zahir Shah, prompted primarily by the need to control restive tribes, began strengthening his army. For economic development he needed foreign assistance from many sources; in the years before and especially after World War II, the question of aid and foreign ties became increasingly important in Afghan affairs. In July 1937 Zahir Shah formally bound his nation with other Islamic states by participating in the Saadabad Pact signed in Iran under which Afghanistan, Iran, Iraq, and Turkey agreed to observe noninterference in each other's internal affairs, to respect border integrity, and to abstain from aggression on any member state. After World War II Afghanistan continued the traditional policy of nonalignment and generally maintained a neutralist posture in foreign relations.

In 1953 the elderly shah Mahmud Khan, who had assumed the prime ministership in 1946, resigned, and Mohammed Daud (1953–1963) a cousin of the shah succeeded him. The government's support of the Pashtunistan issue, strongly advocated by Prime Minister Daud, was accelerated. Under his direction the country's armed forces and economy were given greater attention—a policy continued by successor prime ministers.

With the 1964 constitution as the vehicle, Zahir introduced a program of social and political reform under a more liberal parliamentary rule. In practice, the so-called Experiment in Democracy produced few lasting reforms, and frequent executive-legislative deadlocks delayed or blocked vital legislation. Under this more relaxed rule, which allowed political expression but which did not provide for a legalized political party system, the country's moderate reformers were increasingly overshadowed by extremists of both the left and right. A two-year drought in 1971–72 worsened economic conditions. Amid charges of corruption and malfeasance, the monarchy was removed from power by a virtually bloodless military coup d'état led by former Prime Minister Mohammed Daud, on July 17, 1973. The 1964 constitution was abrogated, and Afghanistan was declared a republic with Daud as its first president and prime minister.

Since then, there has been political upheaval and it hasn't ended, including the Soviet Union's military intervention and occupation late in 1979 in support of a Communist faction.

THE ROYAL SOVEREIGNS OF THE ANCIENT AND MODERN KINGDOMS OF AFGHANISTAN

Reign	Title	Ruler
HOUSE OF DURRANI		
1747–1773	Khan	Ahmad Shah
1773–1793	Khan	Timur Shah
1793–1799	Khan	Zeman Shah
1799–1802	Khan	Mahmud Shah
1803–1810	Khan	Shah Shuja
1810–1818	Khan	Mahmud Shah
1818–1826—In family dispute		
HOUSE OF BARAKZAI		
1826–1839	Khan	Dost Mohammed Khan
1839–1841	Khan	Shah Shuja
1842–1863	Khan	Dost Mohammed Khan
1863–1866	Khan	Sher Ali Khan
1866–1867	Khan	Afzal Khan
1867–1869	Khan	Azam Khan
1869–1879	Khan	Sher Ali Khan
1879–1879	Khan	Yaqub Khan
1879–1879	Khan	Musa Khan
1880–1880	Khan	Ayub Khan
1881–1901	Khan	Abdur Rahman Khan
1901–1919	Khan	Habibullah Khan
1919–1929	Khan	Amanullah Khan
1929–1929	Khan	Inayatullah Khan
1929–1929	Khan	Habibullah Ghazi (Bacha-i-Sawwo)
1929–1933	Khan	Nadir Shah
1933–1973	Khan	Zahir Shah

II
The Dynasties and Princely States of India

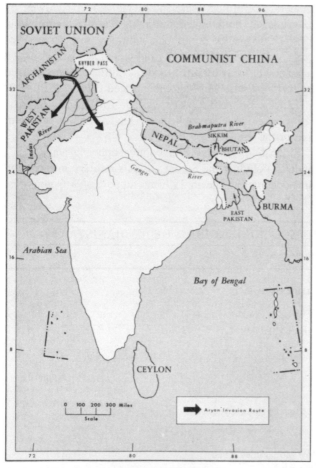

Ancient India, showing the Aryan invasion route

India is known to the Hindus as Bharata-Varsha, or the land of Bharata, who was a legendary ancient monarch. The name India was first applied to the country by the Greeks. It was derived from the Persianized form of the Sanskrit word *Sind,* which designated the Indus River valley, recognized as the cradle of India's earliest known civilization.

In 1947 India gained independence upon the partition of the subcontinent into the two sovereign states of India and Pakistan. Jawaharlal Nehru, leader of the Indian National Congress which led the independence struggle against British rule, became the first prime minister of India. Until his death in 1964 he dominated the political life of the country and assured its initial development as a nation-state in the face of formidable social and economic obstacles.

Indian history before independence may be divided into three major periods: ancient or Hindu, medieval or Muslim, and modern or British. Although the currents of Hindu culture continued to flow throughout history, this division reflects the most prominent feature of Indian history—the recurrent intrusion of new peoples and cultures and the continuous process of their acculturation, often accompanied by sharp conflict between old and new.

The people of India have had a continuous civilization for some five thousand years. The earliest known civilization of the subcontinent flourished during the third millennium B.C. in the Indus valley, now in West Pakistan. Its material remains, discovered forty years ago, contain elements echoed in later historic Indian civilization down to the present day. Modern, educated Indians are conscious and proud of the antiquity, richness, uniqueness, and continuity of their culture. Their early predecessors, however, had displayed little historical sense, and it was not until the coming of the Muslims that a tradition of recording and studying history began.

The history of India before the tenth century A.D. must be pieced together from archaeological findings and a large body of ancient literature and accounts of occasional Greek ambassadors and Chinese Buddhist scholars who traveled in India. The general outline of history that emerges from these sources deals mainly with northern India, largely because the principal dynastic struggles that had the greatest impact on the mainstream of Indian history were waged in northern India. Several kingdoms that flourished in southern India at various periods, however, made significant contributions to Indian cultures, as attested to by the richness of the surviving sculpture, architecture, and literature not only of that region, but also of those areas of Southeast Asia where the imprint of ancient Indian (Hindu and Buddhist) colonies and kingdoms is still discernible.

INDUS VALLEY CIVILIZATION (2500–1500 B.C.)

Evidently a highly developed urban culture based on commerce and trade and to a lesser degree on agriculture flourished from around 2500 to 1500 B.C. Two of its cities, Mohenjo-Daro, or Sind, and Harappa (in north Punjab), had well-planned streets, public baths, and an elaborate municipal drainage system far in advance of anything that was to appear again in India for many centuries. Some of the excavated articles indicate that the Indus cities carried on active trade relations not only with other parts of India but also with the Mediterranean world.

The religion of the Indus valley people, emphasizing the worship of nature gods, shows a fusion of elements from Mesopotamian cultures with concepts and practices that anticipate historic Hinduism. The cult of the Mother-Goddess, for instance, foreshadows the dominant position of female deities in Dravidian India; similarly, its cult of a male god evidently was the prototype of the later Hindu deity, Siva.

Although the origin and antecedents of the Indus valley people have not been conclusively established, the most widely held view is that they were speakers of a Dravidian language, perhaps the cultural ancestors of the people now living in southern India.

THE ARYAN INVASION AND VEDIC PERIOD (1500–500 B.C.)

The Indus valley civilization declined about the middle of the second millennium B.C., perhaps under repeated attacks from foreign warrior tribes. About the beginning of the second millennium B.C., tribes speaking an archaic form of Sanskrit, an Indo-European language, entered India through the northwestern passes. Originating in central Asia and known as the Aryans, they exerted such an enduring influence on Indian culture, particularly in literary and intellectual expression, that until the epoch-making discovery of the Indus valley civilization in the 1920s, it was generally held that civilization came to India with the Aryans.

The present-day knowledge of the Aryan society, known as the Vedic period, is derived solely from the literature of the times, the Vedas (Veda means "knowledge"), the four canonical collections of hymns, prayers, and liturgical formulas that were preserved in oral form for centuries. Set down in writing in their present form later on, they have become the fountainhead of subsequent literary and intellectual expression, and to the Hindus they are the most sacred scriptures. The Vedic literature, which covers the period from 1500 to 500 B.C., depicts the Aryans as pastoral tribesmen and warriors. Initially organized under patriarchal chieftains—giving way to kingdoms in the later Vedic period—the Aryans worshiped nature deities and at first were divided into two social classes: the nobility and the commoners; however, with the gradual eastward expansion of the Aryans, accompanied by increasing contact with the native peoples, the society came to be divided into the Aryans and non-Aryans, probably to preserve the purity of race by separating dark-skinned natives from fair-skinned Aryans. This social division began to crystallize into a rigid caste system in the later Vedic period when the Aryan power was firmly established in the Ganges River valley.

THE EVOLUTION OF HINDUISM

Hinduism, the most enduring and most important aspect of Indian civilization, has evolved slowly from the synthesis of the religion of the Vedic Aryans with those of the indigenous people they conquered. Although little is known about the nature and extent of this fusion, by the middle of the first millennium B.C. Hinduism was fully developed in its earliest form, embodying the concept of soul rebirth, and with such major non-Vedic features as the Siva cult and the sakti (literally, female principle) concept.

BUDDHISM AND JAINISM

As the Brahmans carried Hindu culture and Sanskrit literature out of the Ganges River valley around the sixth century B.C., social and spiritual reform movements were afoot against the entrenched power of the Brahmans and against the ritualism and the rigidity of the caste system that characterized Hinduism. The reaction to Brahmanism resulted in the rise of Jainism and its rival Buddhism, two dissident sects of Hinduism founded in the sixth century B.C. Sharing the belief in the transmigration of the soul and condemning animal sacrifices, both Buddhism and Jainism rejected the authority of the Vedas and the gods of the Hindu pantheon, opposed the Brahman-ridden caste system, and were joined by other reformists who challenged the claims of Brahmans to spiritual superiority. Although neither sect succeeded in altering the essential structure of Hinduism, they had a certain modifying influence. For instance, the Buddhist and Jain insistence on ahimsa (noninjury to animals, especially the cow), which was based perhaps on pre-Aryan popular sentiment, led ultimately to the suppression of those animal sacrifices that are described in the Vedas.

After flourishing nearly one thousand years on the strength of royal patronage, Buddhism was ultimately reabsorbed by Hinduism and has not survived within India, except as the religion of minorities on the northern and northeastern borders. Jainism survives today as the faith of a considerable minority in Gujarat and Rajasthan. Despite their common origin in Brahmanical Hinduism, Buddhists and Jains follow two distinct scriptures and diverge widely in both doctrine and practice.

THE EARLY EMPIRES

NORTHERN INDIA

The history of northern India, little known between the

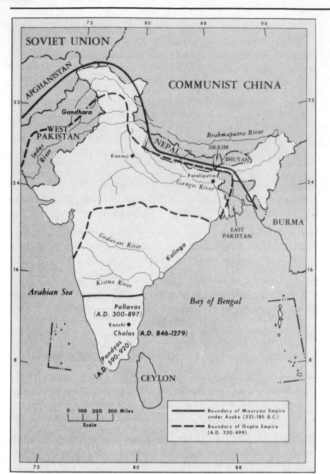

India from 300 B.C. to A.D. 1300 with the boundaries shown for the Mauryan and Gupta empires

the Himalayas except the southernmost region of the peninsula.

Buddhism, until then a mere sect in the Bihar region, acquired much prestige from the patronage of Asoka, who is called the first great royal patron of Buddhism. The edicts written on rocks and pillars record the spread of Buddhism not only to most of India but also Thailand, Ceylon, Burma and even to the Hellenistic world.

During the century after Asoka's death, his empire swiftly disintegrated, weakened probably by Buddhist pacifism. This was followed by political disunity for six centuries until the rise of the Gupta Empire in the early fourth century A.D.

THE GUPTA EMPIRE (A.D. 320–499)

In the fourth century A.D. the Gupta Empire arose in roughly the same area that gave rise to the Mauryan Dynasty. The two hundred years of Gupta rule were a period of political stabilization and of reactivated trade with east and west. This period is also noted for its revival of Hinduism and the decline of Buddhism, accompanied by the flowering of literature and the arts. The decline of Buddhism was largely caused by the imperial patronage which the Brahman caste enjoyed under the Gupta rulers. From their capital in Bihar, the Guptas ruled over an empire stretching from the Indus River to the Brahmaputra River in Bengal in northern India. Chandragupta II (not related to the founder of the Mauryan Empire), the most famous monarch of the Gupta Dynasty, was a great patron of the arts.

Around the middle of the fifth century A.D., the Gupta Empire began to decline because of repeated attacks from the White Huns invading from the central Asian steppes. These attacks were followed by general anarchy in northern India which lasted until the Harsha Dynasty, in modern Uttar Pradesh, in the early seventh century A.D.. Harsha was known as a great general, a just administrator, and especially as a patron of learning and the arts.

SOUTHERN INDIA

Archaeological findings and Greco-Roman writings suggest that a self-contained non-Aryan civilization flourished south of the Vindhya hills centuries before the Hinduization of the south, which began around 1000 B.C. Inhabited probably by the early Dravidians, who were pushed out of the Indus valley by the invading Aryans, the southern culture appears to have been supported by active sea trade with the Mediterranean world and eastern Asia. In general, the southern part of the peninsula has maintained a strong maritime tradition and had little direct impact on the history of India as a whole. In sharp contrast, northern India's history has been linked closely with that of central Asia.

Some of the more important kingdoms in the south were the Pallavas at Kanchi, now Conjeeveram in Madras; the Chola Dynasty on the Coromandel or eastern coast; and the Pandyas in the modern Mandura and Rinivelly areas. The Pallavas, who were eventually overthrown by the rising

seventh and fifth centuries B.C., generally becomes much clearer in the fourth century B.C., when Alexander the Great appeared briefly on the Indian scene. He entered the subcontinent in 326 B.C. through the historic invasion route leading through Afghanistan and what is now northwestern Pakistan. Although the political impact of the invasion was brief and negligible, it served to establish a cultural link between Indic civilization and Hellenism, as seen in Mauryan and later Buddhist art and architecture.

THE MAURYAN EMPIRE (321–185 B.C.)

Shortly after Alexander left Sind (the lower Indus valley in present-day West Pakistan), Chandragupta Maurya, whose origin is obscure, began to expand his power and ousted Alexander's successor in Gandhara, the northwestern region of West Pakistan. According to Greek records, Chandragupta's kingdom, with its capital at Pataliputra (modern Patna) in Bihar, was a highly centralized police state in which strict control was maintained over labor, trade, and the movement of foreigners.

The Mauryan Empire, the first great Indian empire, reached its zenith under Chandragupta's grandson, Asoka (ca. 273–232 B.C.), under whom the empire stretched from Afghanistan to Bengal and included all the lands south of

Chola Dynasty, are sometimes called the southern counterpart of the northern imperial Guptas for their cultural achievements and for their contributing role in the diffusion of Hindu culture into Southeast Asia. The Pallavas left an enduring imprint on the art, architecture, literature, and social institutions of Burma, Thailand, Indonesia, and Cambodia. An important sea power during and after the tenth century, the Chola Kingdom conquered Ceylon and southern Burma.

THE MUSLIM PERIOD

After the death of Harsha, northern and western India broke up into countless kingdoms that were seldom at peace with one another. Out of the ensuing political and social disintegration of the old Hindu order, the warlike clan-castes called Rajputs (sons of kings) arose in southern Rajasthan and Gujarat. Descending from the invading Hun chieftains and a mixed Hun-Indian nobility, and thoroughly Hinduized, they achieved great power and prestige, especially in what became known as Rajputana; however, these Hindu princes, weakened by continual internecine wars and hampered by tribal, sectarian, and caste divisions, were unable to bring about political stability.

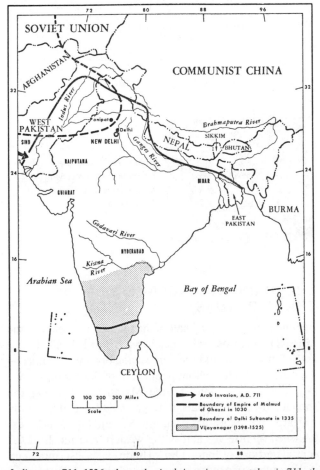

India, A.D. 711–1526, shows the Arab invasion route taken in 711, the boundaries of the empires of Malmud of Ghazni and the Delhi sultanate, and the Vijayanagar area

About this time, during the seventh and early eighth centuries, the eastward wave of Muslim Arab expansion hit India. In A.D. 711 the Arabs, led by Mohammed bin Qasim, gained a foothold in Sind, marking the beginning of Indo-Islamic cultural contact. By the end of the eighth century the Muslim scholars at Baghdad came to absorb Indian medicine, mathematics, and astronomy. They were also instrumental in transmitting the Hindu system of numerals, later to be known as Arabic numerals. Politically, however, the Arabs were unable to extend their power beyond the lower Indus valley, because of the resistance of the Rajput kings entrenched in northwestern India. It was only in the early eleventh century that Muslim Turks, led by Mahmud of Ghazni, the ruler of a small kingdom in what is now Afghanistan, effectively penetrated northern India. A zealous upholder of Islam and an ardent warrior against unbelievers and idolaters, Mahmud reduced northern India to debris through a series of wars of plunder and destruction. As a result, the economic foundation of northern India was laid waste, paving the way for subsequent Muslim invasions. By the close of the twelfth century, Mohammed of Ghor, known as Muizuddin, who had supplanted Mahmud of Ghazni, conquered the whole of the Ganges River valley up to Bengal, taking full advantage of the dissension among the Rajput kings and their inability to mobilize sufficient manpower and economic resources to counter the Muslims.

The Muslim invasion was one of the turning points in Indian history. The invaders brought with them a system of religious beliefs that was the very antithesis of Hinduism. Although in the past Hinduism succeeded in absorbing all invaders and their faiths into the Hindu hierarchical order of society, the monotheistic Muslims, with their belief in the brotherhood of mankind, refused to be overcome by the Hindu system and retained their distinct identity.

TURKISH SULTANATE (1206–1526)

Upon the death of Mohammed of Ghor, one of his generals, Kutbuddin Aibak, a former Turkish slave, set himself up as sultan at Delhi, thus becoming the first of a long line of so-called Turko-Afghan sultans. These sultanates expanded and contracted in response to pressures from Mongol and Afghan raiders from the northwest as well as from independent Hindu rulers to the south. During the years of its greatest power (1206–1388), the Delhi sultanate gave northern India a measure of political stability, and much of the peninsula was brought under Muslim influence. The ruling nobles consisted primarily of Turks, Afghans, Pathans, and Persians. They were not themselves directly involved with local administrative affairs, but ruled mainly through local princes, who were allowed a certain measure of autonomy in return for payment of prescribed amounts of tribute. The Delhi sultanate began to decline at the end of the fourteenth century, partly because of the destruction of Delhi by an invading Mongol named Tamerlane (Timur) and partly because of growing rebellions of Muslim and Hindu nobles. By the early sixteenth century northern and central India broke up into a number of warring Muslim and Hindu kingdoms. Some of the Hindu Rajput kings founded new kingdoms in less accessible parts of the country, such as Rajputana, central India, the foothills and valleys of the Himalayas, and even as far as Gihar. Although the expansion of the sultans was at first greatly facilitated by dissension among the Rajput rulers, their subsequent revolts against the Muslim rulers, although not coordinated, became the main obstacle to complete Muslim domination of India during the years of Muslim supremacy. The Delhi sultanate was ultimately deposed by the Mongols in 1526.

THE MOGHULS (1526–1707)

The Delhi sultanate was followed by the Islamic Moghul Dynasty. The history of the Moghuls is one of progressive political consolidation and cultural blending, and then of gradual disintegration under internal stresses. The first of the Moghul line, Babar, claimed direct descent from the Mongol emperor, Tamerlane. After defeating the Delhi sultan, Ibrahim Lodi, at Panipat in 1526, Babar established himself in Delhi and, in the following year, crushed the forces of the Rajput confederacy.

The most renowned king of the Moghuls was Akbar (1556–1605), who was the grandson of Babar and the greatest sovereign since Asoka. His rule was characterized by exceptional military and administrative skill combined with an unusual degree of religious tolerance. Recognizing that his vast empire could not last unless he was supported by all peoples, he promulgated policies that were designed to secure the loyalty of Hindus and even won over many of the Rajput kings. To show his tolerance, Akbar had Hindu and Christian, as well as Muslim, wives. Akbar's successors—his son, Jahangir, and grandson, Shah Jahan—were better known for their patronage of the arts than for their administrative skill. Shah Jahan in particular was a master builder and was responsible for the construction of the Taj Mahal at Agra in 1648.

During the reign of Aurangzeb (1658–1707), the last of the Moghul Dynasty, the empire, comprising nearly all of India, began to decline. Though the reasons for this decline are complex, the onus falls on Aurangzeb himself. A devout Muslim, he intensified the persecution of non-Muslims, a policy which he inherited from Shah Jahan. The policy, reversing Akbar's religious tolerance, aroused the hostility of the Rajputs and other Hindu powers. The Moghul Empire, too large to be governed by one man or from one center, rent with internecine strife, regicide, and revolt, and further undermined by the resultant breakdown of economic order, was ill prepared to cope with both internal and external stresses. Following the death of Aurangzeb the empire was torn in pieces, and various provincial governors and adventurers swiftly carved out independent principalities for themselves.

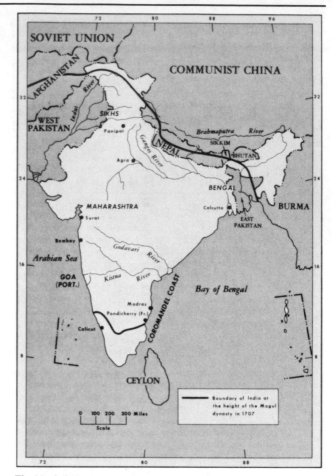

The Moghul Empire area in India, 1526–1707

Babar, the first of the Moghul rulers in India, receiving gold tribute from a lesser ruler, in his domain

THE HINDU RESURGENCE: THE MARATHAS

Beginning in the second half of the seventeenth century, the Moghul power was challenged by such hostile Hindu forces as the Rajputs, the Sikhs and, most notably, the Marathas—the warlike Hindu peasant population of the region known as Marahashtra, "land of the Marathas." Sapping the strength of the Moghuls through banditry and guerrilla warfare, the Marathas, led by Shivaji (1625–80), established themselves across the western and much of the central portions of India. Other Hindu states also sprang up in the southern tip of the peninsula and along the Himalayan foothills. The Sikhs, a militant theocratic order, acquired a powerful foothold in the northwest.

The Great Moghul Babar on his favorite elephant, leading his soldiers into battle

Humayun, the second of the Great Moghuls, reigned from 1530 to 1540. He was called Humayun the Timid.

Akbar, who reigned from 1556 to 1605, was the third of the Moghul emperors of India. He is seen in this manuscript hunting deer and rabbit with tamed cheetahs (Victoria and Albert Museum, London).

A sketch of Akbar in the year he died—1605.

Akbar the Great was considered at the time of his reign to be one of the most powerful rulers in the world. This sketch shows him in his later years when he traded lion hunting for falconry.

Akbar was succeeded by his son Jahangir, who considered himself to be a deity. Here a page in an album of his reveals a painting that shows him to be aligned with Jesus Christ but one level higher.

Nur (Empress) Jahan

Akbar on his throne holding court

An allegory painting of the accession to the throne of Jahangir in 1605

Another allegorical painting of the Great Moghul Jahangir. In this one he is, right, embracing Shah Abbas of Persia. This was a condition that in reality was only on the surface.

Shah Jahan, the fifth of the Great Moghuls, reigned from 1628 to 1657. He appears in a painting at the time of his marriage to Mehrunissa in 1615. After the wedding he changed her name to Mumtaz Mahal.

Shivaji's political ideals were reversed by one of his shortsighted descendants, who thus alienated the sympathies and support of many of the Rajputs and Hindu chiefs as well as of the peasantry. This estrangement contributed to the eventual downfall of the Maratha power. Regarded as the hero of all Hindus during his lifetime, Shivaji later became the symbol of incipient Hindu nationalism directed against both Western and Muslim influences.

For a time it appeared as though the Hindu hopes of political supremacy were to be realized. The ascendancy of the Marathas, however, also coincided with the expansion of the Afghans invading from the northwest and of British power on the subcontinent. In the battle of Panipat in 1761, the Maratha confederacy was dealt a crushing defeat by the Afghans. But neither the Afghans nor the Marathas, who recovered some of their former strength shortly after 1761, could establish supremacy, since they were both weakened as the result of dynastic wars.

THE COMING OF THE EUROPEANS

India had indirect trade relations with Europe by way of the overland caravan route, as well as the maritime route, dating back to the fifth century B.C., but the lucrative spice trade with India was mainly in the hands of the Romans and later the Arab merchants. By the fifteenth century European traders came to believe that the commissions they had to pay the Arabs were prohibitively high and therefore sent out fleets in search of new trade routes direct to India.

The arrival of the Europeans in the last quarter of the fifteenth century marked another great turning point in Indian history. The dynamics of Indian history, hitherto mainly intertwined with those of central Asia, came to be affected chiefly by the Europeans' political and trade relations with India as India was swept into the mainstream of European power politics. Since the arrival of the Europeans generally coincided with the gradual decline of Moghul

power, India became the scene of power conflict not only between Europeans and the native powers, but also among the Europeans themselves. As a result, for four and a half centuries the Portuguese, Dutch, French, and British left varying degrees of political and cultural imprints in India.

The Portuguese were the first to arrive. In 1498 Vasco da Gama anchored off Calicut on the western coast of India, inaugurating the first direct maritime contact with the Indians. Under Admiral Alfonso de Albuquerque, the Portuguese successfully challenged and eliminated the maritime power of the Arabs in the Indian Ocean. To strengthen their maritime power, the Portuguese also seized strategically located Goa on the Indian west coast in 1510. For the next one hundred years the trade and control of the Indian Ocean were a Portuguese monopoly.

The United Dutch East India Company, founded in 1602 under government patronage with power to maintain fleets and armed forces, replaced Portuguese hegemony on the Coromandel coast, in Ceylon, and in the East Indies. It established "factories" (trading posts) along the Coromandel coast and in the interior, along the lower reaches of the Ganges.

The British East India Company, a private company formed in 1600 during the reign of the great Moghul, Akbar, and operating under a charter granted by Queen Elizabeth, was slower to expand its trade in the area but, as Portuguese influence was reduced to a few coastal enclaves and with the arrival of the more powerful Dutch and English fleets, the rivalry between the Dutch and the British mercantile establishments intensified.

This contest continued well into the last decade of the eighteenth century, when the Dutch were forced from the Indian scene by the British and thereafter focused their primary attention on the East Indies.

The French, whose East India Company was founded under government support in 1664, were the last of the European powers to arrive. After their initial settlement near Madras in 1670, they set up trading posts on the southwestern and eastern coasts and moved their main base

The Taj Mahal was built as the tomb for Mumtaz Mahal, the wife of the
Great Moghul Shah Jahan. She died at the age of thirty-nine after giving
birth to their fourteenth child. It took the employ of 22,000 men, 22 million
dollars, and 22 years to complete the beautiful mausoleum that, although
not the greatest of Shah Jahan's architectural endeavors, became one of
the seven modern wonders of the world.

Shah Jahan as he appeared
in later years

Mumtaz Mahal

Murad Bakhsh, younger son of
Shah Jahan, served as the
Moghul emperor for a few
months in 1657 upon the death
of his father. A great warrior,
he is seen here in battle in 1658
with his brother Dara Shukoh,
for the throne, but neither won.

This sketch was made of Aurangzeb at about the time of his death in 1707. The throne and crown passed on to his son, Azam Shah and, successively to his brother Kam Bakhsh in 1707. His brother Shah Alam I took over before the close of 1707, but there were no truly great Moghuls to ever serve India again.

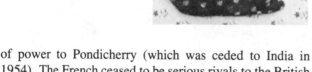

Aurangzeb, the last of the Great Moghuls, reigned from 1658 to 1707.

Azam Shah, third son of Aurangzeb, reigned for a short period of time in 1707. He was more fond of sports than of the rigors of the throne. He is seen here engaged with his servants in falcon hunting.

of power to Pondicherry (which was ceded to India in 1954). The French ceased to be serious rivals to the British by the last quarter of the eighteenth century.

Although the initial aim of the British East India Company was to seek trade under concessions obtained from local Moghul governors, the collapse of the Moghul Dynasty forced the company into a gradual involvement in internal politics and in military activity for the protection of its trade interests. Capitalizing on the political division of India among the native powers—the Rajputs, the Marathas, the Sikhs, and independent Muslim governors—the British ultimately rose to supremacy through the use of military expeditions, annexation, bribery, the system of "subsidiary alliance," and by playing one party against another.

The first British settlement on the western coast of India, at Surat in 1612, was followed by the establishment of factories at Madras, Bombay, and along the lower Ganges River valley. In 1690 another strategic settlement was established at Hooghly, the present site of Calcutta, in Bengal. The slow pace of British encroachment was hastened after the acquisition of the wealthy and strategically situated province of Bengal from its Muslim governor, Siraj-ud-Daulah, who had unwisely provoked a military confrontation with the British at Plassey in 1757. Although allied with the French, he was defeated by Robert Clive, a young official of the British East India Company. By 1760 the French were driven out of southern India by the British, who then methodically proceeded to subjugate the native

The sultan of Delhi's power began to decline at the end of the fourteenth century, partly due to the near destruction of Delhi by the invading Mongol, Tamerlane (Timur), who is seen here on the outskirts of Delhi.

powers. By 1815 the supremacy of the East India Company, which was reinforced by British victories over the French in Europe and North America, was unchallengeable. By the 1850s the British control and influence had extended to the territories essentially the same as those which became the independent state of India in 1947, with the exception of Baluchistan and Upper Assam.

In England in the early nineteenth century, when the industrial revolution was in full swing, the Indian market had to be thrown open to competing private interests. Accordingly, in 1813 the company's trade monopoly was terminated by Parliament. Along with these measures, an imperialist policy of annexing those territories remaining under Indian princes was efficiently carried out. The British annexed the Maratha states of Nagpur, Satara, and Jhansi and the Muslim state of Oudh by means of the so-called doctrine of lapse, under which the sovereignty over a state reverted to a superior power whenever the direct line of succession died out.

The puppet Moghul emperor, Shah Alam, handing Lord Robert Clive the formal grant of sovereign rights to Bengal

The emperor Shah Alam I, who ruled from 1707 to 1712

The visit of the first of England's ambassadors to a ruler in India. Queen Elizabeth I sent Sir John Mildenhall in 1599 to Akbar, the Great Moghul, to apply for a trade commission with India. The result eventually became the East India Company of England.

A caricature of the sepoy soldier

THE MUTINY OF 1857 AND AFTER

By the middle of the nineteenth century dissatisfaction with British hegemony and with efforts to reform India on Western lines aroused strong hostility among Muslim and Hindu feudal princes who had vested interests in the old Indo-Persian culture and the old political order.

The mutiny of 1857, or Sepoy Mutiny, as it is called by the British historians, but regarded today in both India and Pakistan as the first war of independence, was sparked by the alleged use of cartridges greased with pig or cow fat, which is offensive to the religious beliefs of Muslim and Hindu *sepoys* (Indian soldiers employed by the British). Although confined more or less to northern and central India (southern India was untouched) and limited mostly to the sepoys, the mutiny lasted more than a year.

The mutiny marks a great divide in modern Indian history, contributing to the end of British rule by the East India Company. In 1858, as a consequence of the mutiny, the British crown assumed a direct responsibility for the government of India, which was to be headed by the governor-general, called viceroy when acting as the direct representative of the British crown. The governor-general was the supreme legislative and executive authority. British administrators also developed a highly efficient administrative machinery known as the Indian Civil Service, which was based on competitive examination held in London. Initially, the Indian Civil Service consisted almost exclusively of Europeans, but limited numbers of Indian nationals were gradually admitted. In 1871 the system of local self-government, modeled along British lines, was introduced in limited scope.

The mutiny also brought a swift reversal of British policy from that of reforming zeal and expansion to noninterference in the social and political affairs of the native states. Formal annexations under the doctrine of lapse virtually ceased, and the political boundaries of British territories vis-à-vis the native states were frozen thereafter. By this time the British territories constituted about three-fifths of the India-Pakistan subcontinent, and some 562 native states of varying sizes occupied the remainder. The British relationship with the native states was governed by the so-called principle of paramountcy, whereby the princely states exercised sovereignty in their internal affairs, but their external relations were handled by Great Britain, the

paramount power. On its part, the paramount power assumed responsibility for the defense of the native states, but reserved to itself the right to intervene in cases of maladministration and gross injustice. The native princes remained loyal to the British and did not support the Indian nationalist movement. The social complexity and the disparities in technological, social, and economic development in different parts of India today are derived in large measure from this division of the subcontinent into two spheres of political patterns. Although the impact of Western education and modern economic techniques greatly facilitated the growth of political consciousness and the development of economy in British-controlled territories, the princely states generally remained unaffected by the modernizing impact.

NATIONALISM AND THE STRUGGLE FOR INDEPENDENCE

British Indian policies had beneficent effects on many fields of human endeavor and unwittingly paved the way for the rise of nationalism. In its formative stage, especially in the third quarter of the nineteenth century, the nationalist movement in India found most of its supporters among the middle-class intellectuals and drew its leadership mainly from Bengal and Maharashtra. Also during this stage religious and racial overtones were features of the movement, and it was not until after World War I that political and economic goals became overriding.

It is not surprising, then, that nationalism was fomented first in Bengal and Maharashtra. Bengal, the center of British rule in India, had had the longest contact with the British and had the most highly developed political consciousness on the subcontinent. Bengal was also the home of Raja Rammohan Roy, a towering personality who was deeply versed in Hindu-Muslim culture and in the English and Greek civilizations. A scholar, social reformer, and political thinker, he has been called the "originator of all the more important secular movements in India" and "the first modern man in India." In Maharashtra, with its warlike Hindu traditions, its tough peasantry, and its vigorous Brahman elite, militant nationalists in the 1890s spearheaded a movement for a Hindu national renaissance directed against all non-Hindu peoples.

The Indian National Congress was founded in 1885—the first significant event in the evolution of Indian nationalism. The congress was founded mainly on the initiative of Allan Octavian Hume, a retired British civil servant who had envisioned it as "the germ of a native Parliament" serving as "an overt and constitutional channel for discharge of the increasing ferment which had resulted from Western ideas and education."

Subsequently, however, the British administration be-

Modern-day India, showing its fifteen states

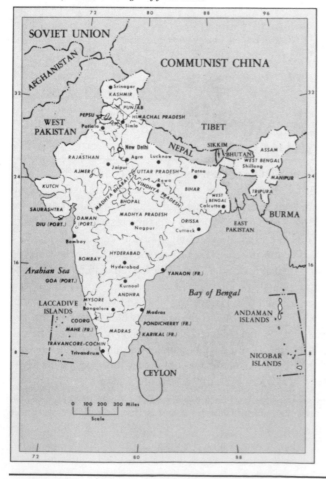

Lord Curzon, viceroy of India, riding in state celebration of the accession of Edward VII, 1901

The formal royal ceremony after the arrival of the king and queen with the principal princes of India in attendance

King George V and Queen Mary, 1917, arrive in Delhi, India, on their royal railroad coach.

The legendary raja of Gwalior

The king of Oojein on his royal throne

The Prince of Wales with the maharaja of Patiala

The modern-day raja of Gwalior, Maharaja Sindia, aboard the royal elephant with the Prince of Wales (Edward VIII) during his 1921 visit to India

Ranjit Singh of Lahore

The maharana of Udaipur

A portrait of the maharaja of Patiala

Both the Indian princes and the British officers loved the pomp and ceremony of official parties. Seen here are four princes of distinguished lineage. Left to right: nawab of Bahawalpur, the maharaja of Jodhpur, the nawab of Malerkotla, and the maharaja Rana of Dholpur.

Maharaja Ranjit Singh, ruler of Punjab from 1780 to 1839, is honored on a 1966 Indian stamp.

Bubbles and Joey, the sons of the maharaja of Jaipur, bedecked with gold court dress and emerald necklaces. The former maharaja of Jaipur is one of the wealthiest of the princes.

The maharaja of Bikaner served in the British armed forces along with his camel corps. Many of the princes served as officers in the British army.

The maharaja of Jammu and Kashmir

The maharaja of Jammu

The heir apparent of Boroda is about to ride into the state capital on his favorite elephant. Note that his elephant chair has a lantern for night riding.

The maharaja of Patiala, who was known as the statesman and the Casanova of the princes of India

The maharaja Dulip Singh of Punjab, who was exiled to Great Britain's mother islands and "lost" the famous Koh-i-noor diamond to Queen Victoria

The nizam of Hyderabad

The Chamber of Princes—pre-Constitution. The Chamber of Princes was a ruling body composed of native rulers who usually did the bidding of the British envoys in India. Left to right: the maharaja of Bikaner, the maharaja of Gwalior, the nawab of Bhopal, and the maharaja of Patiala.

came wary of what it called "the constitutional agitation" of the congress. In addition to its annual meetings, the congress sought to arouse and organize public opinion in both India and England by sending petitions and holding lectures urging steps toward self-government for India.

After the turn of the century the congress movement took on a new militant spirit, aroused in part by the Japanese victory over the Russians in 1904–5, but most of all by the partition of Bengal in 1905. The partition into pre-

dominantly Muslim and Hindu zones also led to the founding of the All-India Muslim League in 1906 and to the Muslim demand for constitutional safeguards and separate electorates.

During World War I, British India made substantial contributions in troops, money, and resources to Great Britain's war efforts. The great majority of the Indian people, led by the moderate-dominated congress, supported the British with the expectation that the chances for

Mahatma Gandhi

Jawaharlal Nehru

obtaining self-rule would be greatly enhanced. Despite India's role in the war, the British not only continued to repress militant nationalist activities, especially in the Punjab and Bengal, but also became involved in war with the Islamic sultan of Turkey, who was then regarded by Indian Muslims as their spiritual leader.

As World War I drew to a close, British policy toward India became somewhat liberal as much because of the exigencies of the war as because of the growth of the nationalist movement in certain anti-British terrorist activities.

Indians were granted greater self-government in their local affairs under the Government of India Act of 1919, but the congress, then controlled by the militant elements, rejected the act as "inadequate, disappointing, and unsatisfactory." Meanwhile, many moderate members left the congress, protesting that the 1919 reforms should be given a fair trial. The liberal intention of the British government was undone, however, by the enactment in early 1919 of the Rowlatt Act, which sought to perpetuate the extraordinarily repressive powers exercised by the government during the war—e.g., trial without counsel, jury, or the right to appeal against a death sentence. A leading nationalist leader described this act as "the parent of the Non-Cooperation Movement" in India.

It was against this background that Mohandas Karamchand Gandhi, popularly called Mahatma (great soul) Gandhi, entered Indian history. Gandhi promptly organized a passive protest movement against the act, but the repressive measures undertaken in the Punjab to put down mass demonstrations and strikes were so gruesome that they evoked mass support for the congress movement for the first time since its inception.

In 1920 Gandhi's famous nonviolent, noncooperation movement was launched. Through his charismatic appeal to all segments of the population, he succeeded in converting the middle-class nationalist agitation into a mass revolutionary movement, thus inaugurating a new chapter in the evolution of the nationalist movement.

Beginning in 1922, the nationalist movement became increasingly radical under the influence of young militant nationalists, including Nehru and Subhas Chandra Bose. In 1929 the congress adopted a resolution changing the goal of the movement from self-rule within the empire, as declared in 1906, to one of complete independence. Also in that year Nehru was elected president of the Indian National Congress for the first time and took further steps to launch a campaign of civil disobedience. In 1930 Gandhi signaled a major civil disobedience campaign by leading his famous "salt march" to the sea, in order to dramatize his protest against the government's salt monopoly.

The civil disobedience movement prompted the holding of three roundtable conferences in London between November 1930 and November 1932. Failing to elicit any enthusiasm from the Indian congress, which boycotted the first and third conferences, the British government made new proposals in March 1933 for India's constitutional reform in the light of all three conferences, and referred them to the joint Committee on Indian Constitutional Reform. Although opposed by the congress, the 1933 proposals as deliberated by the committee ultimately became the basis of the Government of India Act of 1935.

The act of 1935 gave a new constitution to India, certain portions of which were later incorporated into the Constitution of 1950. The act provided for an all-India federation of all provinces and the native states; it also granted provincial autonomy to the eleven British provinces, Bengal, Bombay, Bihar, Assam, Central Provinces, Madras, North-West Frontier Province, Orissa, Sind, Punjab, and the United Provinces, by means of an executive government responsible to an elected legislature in each province. The provision for the all-India federation was never put into effect because most Indian princes were reluctant to risk the loss of their political powers and privileges. The act of 1935 also provided for a complex system of separate communal electorates. It fell far short of the congress demand for complete independence, and at that time Nehru termed it as the "new charter of slavery."

In December 1936 the congress, somewhat reluctantly, decided to try out the provincial portions of the 1935 act and to contest the elections, vis-à-vis the Muslim League, to the provincial legislatures without committing itself to any definite policy. In the elections held in 1937 the congress won a clear-cut majority in six of the eleven provinces and a plurality in two others. Only in Bengal, the Punjab, and Sind was it in a minority. Shortly thereafter, it became the ruling authority in eight of the provinces and continued to administer these provincial governments until October 1939.

As the result of the elections, the Muslim League became convinced that the Muslims could expect neither justice nor fair play under the congress movement and began to seek an alternative to the congress rule in India. On the other hand, many of the congress leaders gained valuable experience in politics and government as elected provincial officials from 1937 to 1939. These experiences formed the basis of administrative stability after India gained independence and were helpful in the formulation of the constitution in 1950.

The two years preceding the drawing up of the constitution of 1950 were occupied with the enormous problem of integrating the many Indian states. There were 363 states, all varying in size tremendously. Some were the size of states in the United States, but many others were merely "estates." The most populated state was Hyderabad with 17 million people, and the smaller ones were but a few square miles with only several thousand people.

The British had renounced all of the special treaty rights they had given to the old states and recommended that all of them join into one of the new states. There was a period when the old states attempted to form around a political figure. One group turned to the nawab of Bhopal, but the other princes' jealousies were too great to overcome.

Aga Khan III on his fiftieth birthday received his weight in diamonds from the Muslim sect at Bombay, India, in 1946.

The Aga Khan III (center) *is seen here with Mahatma Gandhi and Mrs. Sarojani Naidu. The Aga was closely associated with the Mahatma.*

By Independence Day, all but Travancore, Kashmir, Hyderabad, and Junagadh had joined into new states. Travancore joined in at the last moment; but, the latter three were eventually formed into new states along linguistic or political lines. Several old states like Baroda, the Kathiawar and the Rajput states were combined to form the new federal unit of Saurashtra and Rajasthan. Mysore became its own new state. Travancore was lined up with Cochin and became Kerala. Only a few princes survived, such as the rajas of Mysore and Travancore, who were allowed to remain as the titular heads of the new states, and their new princely title was "Rajpramukh." With the constitution, by and large the Indian government had done away with the royal properties and domains. However, the princes survived with their personal wealth, which in most cases was valued in the millions of dollars.

THE AGA KHANS

A book on India's royalty, which includes the princes of the states, would not be complete if it didn't contain a section on the Aga Khans. The origins of the Aga Khan family can be traced directly back to the Prophet Mohammed and the Middle East. Aga Khan III, the best known of the Aga Khans, who have been the heads of the Muslim sect, has operated out of India. He has been closely associated with the Indian government. Aga Khan III, who was an Indian citizen, was the most popular of the leaders of the Muslims. At the time of his death in 1957 it was believed by most of his religious followers that he would name his son Aly as his successor upon his death. But, at the reading of his will, it soon became apparent that he would name his grandson, Aly's son Karim, as the new Aga Khan. When the reading was over it was Karim who became the Aga Khan IV.

Aga Khan III at his installation as imam in Bombay in 1885

Aga Khan III (left) at the time of his son Aly's second marriage. This one was to the beautiful movie star, Rita Hayworth, in 1949. Begum Yvette, Aga Khan III's beautiful fourth wife, is present to the right in the photograph. Aly Khan died in an automobile accident in 1960.

On October 28, 1969, Karim, Aga Khan IV, was married to Lady James Crichton-Stuart, who had been married to the marquess of Bute's brother, Lord James, a marriage which, because there was no issue, was dissolved in 1966 and annulled by the Vatican in 1970.

Some views of the palaces of the princes. Several palaces are now serving as tourist hotels.

Jaipur—Rambagh Palace Hotel

Jodhpur—Ummaid Bhavan Palace Hotel

Musore Palace illuminations

Jodhpur—Ummaid Bhavan Palace Hotel

Udaipur—Lake Palace Hotel

Udaipur—Lake Palace Hotel, Kush Mahal suite.

THE ROYAL SOVEREIGNS OF THE DYNASTY OF INDIA

Reign	Title	Ruler	Reign	Ruler
1526–1530	Emperor	Babar	*First Dynasty—Sangama*	
1530–1540	Emperor	Humayun	1377–1404	Harihara II (son of Bukha I)
1540–1555—Suri Dynasty of Afghanistan			1404–1406	Bukha II (disputed succession)
1555–1556	Emperor	Humayun	1406–1422	Devaraya I
1556–1605	Emperor	Akbar	1422–1425	Vira Vijaya (disputed succession)
1605–1627	Emperor	Jahangir	1425–1447	Devaraya II (once co-ruler with
1627–1628	Emperor	Davar Bakhsh		Vira Vijaya: sole
1628–1657	Emperor	Shah Jahan		ruler from ?1425)
1657–1657	Emperor	Murad Bakhsh		
1657–1658	Emperor	Shah Shuja		
1658–1707	Emperor	Aurangzeb (Alamgir I)	**THE MARATHA PESHWAS 1713–1818**	
1707–1707	Emperor	Azam Shah	1713–1720	Balaji Visvanath
1707–1707	Emperor	Kam Bakhsh	1720–1740	Baji Rao I
1707–1712	Emperor	Shah Alam I (Bahadur Shah I)	1740–1761	Balaji Baji Rao
1712–1712	Emperor	Azim ash-Shan	1761–1772	Madhava Rao I
1712–1713	Emperor	Jahandar Shah	1772–1773	Narayan Rao
1713–1719	Emperor	Muhammad Farrukh Siyar	1773–1774	Raghunath Rao (Raghoba)
1719–1719	Emperor	Rafi ad-Darajat	1774–1796	Madhava Rao II
1719–1719	Emperor	Shah Jahan II (Rafi ad-Daula)	1796	Chimnaji Appa
1719–1719	Emperor	Nekusiyar	1796–1818	Baji Rao II
1719–1748	Emperor	Muhammad Shah		
1720–1748	Emperor	Muhammad Ibrahim		
1748–1754	Emperor	Ahmad Shah	**THE SIKH KINGDOM OF THE PUNJAB 1798–1849**	
1754–1759	Emperor	Alamgir II	1798–1839	Ranjit Singh
1759–1759	Emperor	Shah Jahan III	1839–1840	Kharak Singh
1759–1788	Emperor	Shah Alam II	1840	Nao Nehal Singh
1788–1806	Emperor	Bidar Bakht	1840–1843	Sher Singh
1806–1837	Emperor	Akbar Shah II	1843–1849	Dulip Singh
1837–1858	Emperor	Bahadur Shah II		

Reign	Ruler		Reign	Ruler
			THE NIZAMS OF HYDERABAD 1713–1948	
SULTANS OF THE BAHMANI DYNASTY OF THE DECCAN 1347–1518			1713–1748	Nizam-ul-mulk, Asaf Jah (created subadar [governor] of the Deccan by Mughal emperor)
1347–1358	Ala-ud-din		1748–1750	Mir Muhammad Nasir Jang
1358–1373	Muhammad I		1750–1751	Muzaffar Jang
1373–1378	Mujahid		1751–1761	Mir Asaf-ud-daula Salabat Jang
1378	Daud		1762–1803	Nizam Ali
1378–1397	Muhammad II		1803–1829	Mir Akbar Ali Khan, Sikandar Jah
1397	Ghiyas-ud-din		1829–1857	Nasir-ud-daula Farkhundah Ali Khan
1397	Shams-ud-din		1857–1869	Afzul-ud-daula
1397	Firuz		1869–1911	Mir Mahbub Ali Khan
1422–1435	Ahmad		1911—State absorbed into	H. E. H. Nawab Mir Usman Ali
1435–1457	Ala-ud-din II		the Indian Union 1948, Nizam	Khan Bahadur Fateh Jang
1457–1461	Humayun		remaining as constitutional	
1461–1463	Nizam		Governor.	
1463–1482	Muhammad III			
1482–1518	Mahmud			
THE SULTANS OF BIJAPUR 1490–1686			**THE NAWABS AND KINGS OF OUDH 1722–1856**	
1490–1510	Yusuf (governor, under the Bahmani sultan)		1722–1739	Sa'adat Ali I
			1739–1754	Safdar Jang
1510–1534	Ismail		1754–1775	Shuja-ud-daula
1534–1535	Mallu		1775–1797	Asaf-ud-daula
1535–1557	Ibrahim I		1797–1798	Wazir Ali
1557–1580	Ali		1798–1814	Sa'adat Ali II
1580–1626	Ibrahim II		1814–1827	Ghazi-ud-din assumed title of 'king' 1819
1626–1656	Muhammad (tributary of Shah Jahan, 1636)		1827–1837	Nasir-ud-din
1656–1673	Ali II		1837–1842	Muhammad Ali
1673–1686 (captured by Aurangzeb, and dynasty ended)	Sikandar		1842–1847	Amjad Ali
			1847–1856	Wajid Ali
THE RULERS OF VIJAYANAGAR 1336–1585			**THE NAWABS OF BENGAL 1740–1770**	
1336–1354	Harihara I (chief, not of royal rank; traditional date of the founding of Vijayanagar, 1336)		1740–1756	Alivardi Khan
			1756–1757	Siraj-ud-daula
			1757–1760	Mir Jafar
			1763–1765	
1354–1377	Bukha I (disputed succession; chief, not of royal rank)		1760–1763	Mir Kasim
			1765–1766	Najim-ud-daula
			1766–1770	Saif-ud-daula

12

The Kingdoms of Nepal, Bhutan, and Sikkim

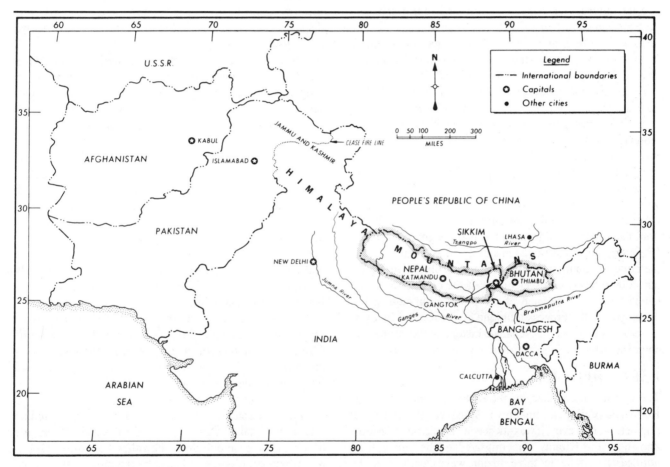

Nepal, Bhutan, and Sikkim

THE KINGDOM OF NEPAL

For all but the last several centuries there is an absence of reliable information on the history of the area now known as Nepal. Although there are ancient monuments, coins, and other cultural artifacts and archaeological remains that have survived as objects of study, they are isolated pieces of evidence which are of little assistance in penetrating the obscurity of the country's past and constructing a continuous narrative of the experience of its people from earli-

est times. Written materials date only from the fifth century A.D., and even though historical sources gradually increase in volume after that time, they fail to provide a basis for anything more than a vague and fragmentary description of the country's history.

An accurate and detailed account of Nepalese history does not become possible until the latter part of the eighteenth century, when the nation became unified under the king of the Gurkhas. The great body of the country's history before that time consists of folklore and legend—handed down through the centuries—in which gods and demons mingle with authentic persons, and myths and miracles merge with real events. About the sixteenth century these legendary accounts, sometimes extending back to many centuries earlier, began to be committed to writing in documents known as *vamsavalis*. These are essentially genealogical chronicles of the kings and dynasties of Nepal, recounting the achievements, real or imaginary, of its monarchs and glorifying their reigns. Despite the fact that what little verifiable data they contain have become heavily encrusted with the accumulated fantasies of centuries of storytellers, the *vamsavalis* are the single most important category of source material on most of the country's history and the only source for the period before the fifth century A.D.

Such information as is available on Nepalese history pertains almost exclusively to the Katmandu Valley; it deals very little, if at all, with all of that part of the Himalayan area now forming the state of Nepal. The legendary dawn of Nepalese life opens with the story of the supernatural creation of the valley, and from that time to the present it has been the focal point of the country's history. It has long been the largest population center, the site of a vigorous culture, a major trading entrepôt and one of the strongest military and political areas in the central Himalayas.

Lying athwart the main Himalayan routes, Nepal's development has been profoundly influenced by its relations with India, Tibet, and, to a lesser extent, China. Indian culture manifested through centuries of war, trade, migration, and religious pilgrimage has had the greatest impact. However, Nepal has not been simply a passive receiver of the cultural radiations of others, but has played an important role in transmitting elements of the cultures of India, China, and Tibet to each of the others. Although it has developed in the process a unique civilization of its own, the dominant theme of Nepalese history is the strong and enduring effects of its relations with other nations.

EARLY HISTORY

The origin and character of the earliest inhabitants of the Katmandu Valley are unknown. Whatever the aboriginal population, however, it was succeeded by a group of people known as the Kiratas who migrated to the valley from northeastern India in three major waves ending in the seventh century B.C. Racially Indo-Mongoloid and speaking a Tibeto-Burman language, the Kiratas lived under a system of tribal government and appear to have remained undisturbed in the valley for a period of seven hundred years. Gautama Buddha was born about 563 B.C. in Lumbini, which is now the Nepalese village of Rummin-dei in the Tarai, and by the end of the Kirata period Buddhism had become the common faith of the people of the valley, who in the course of time became the Newar.

About the first century A.D., immigrants from India, the Lichavis, established themselves as the rulers of the Kiratas, and from then until the present time all the ruling

dynasties of Nepal have been drawn from the plains of northern India. The Lichavis ruled the valley with brief interruptions from the first to the ninth centuries, and during that period the Indian impact on Nepal was in one of its most extensive and significant phases. Powerful monarchs of India—initially the Kushans and after the fourth century, the Guptas—exercised considerable influence over Nepal without extinguishing its independence. The Guptas, for example, were responsible for the establishment of a monarchical system of government in the valley, replacing the "republican tribal democracy" which had existed up to that time. Another result of this relationship was the introduction of Hinduism into Nepal. It gained its initial foothold through the conversion of the ruling class about the fourth century and later received acceptance from most of the people. The growth of Hinduism did not result in the displacement of Buddhism, but led to the fusion of the two religions.

Throughout the latter part of the Lichavi period, Tibet was becoming increasingly powerful and, under the great king Srong-btsan-sgam-po, it eventually came to dominate large areas of China, central Asia, and the Himalayas. For more than a hundred years, between the seventh and the ninth centuries, Tibet held Nepal in vassalage, and for several centuries the influence of Tibet rather than that of India was paramount in Nepal. At this time Buddhists were migrating northward out of India and Nepal mediated much of the transfer of Buddhist culture from India to Tibet; Mahayana Buddhism, the Guptan script, and Sanskrit literature, as well as Nepalese artistic and architectural forms, entered Tibet from Nepal with lasting effect. The seventh and eighth centuries also marked the beginning of fairly frequent contacts not only between Nepal and Tibet but also between Nepal and China.

Near the end of the ninth century the Lichavis were replaced by the Thakuri Dynasty, which held control of the valley intermittently for the next several centuries. During the latter part of their reign the valley was under repeated invasion not only from Indian states to the south but also from the mountain kingdoms to the west.

In the thirteenth century yet another dynasty of Indian origin, the Malla, was established in Nepal. Under the Mallas, the Newar culture of the valley flourished, Orthodox Hinduism was strengthened by the introduction of the caste system, and the power of Nepalese kings was ex-

Nepalese stamps issued to honor (left to right) Amsu Varma, seventh-century ruler and reformer; Ram Shah, seventeenth-century ruler and reformer; and Bhim Sen Thapa, eighteenth–nineteenth–century administrator and reformer

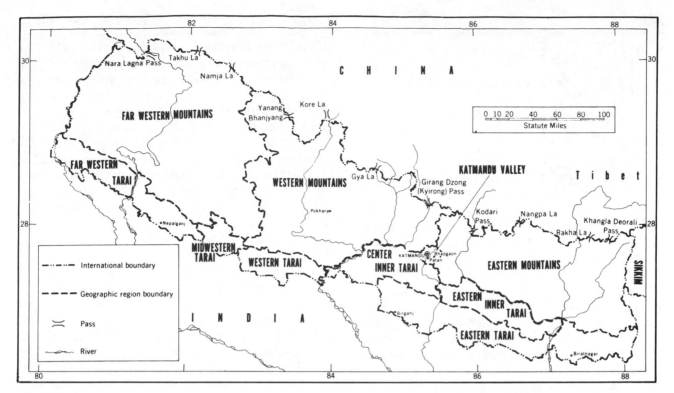

The regions of Nepal

tended far beyond its previous limits. The domain of the Mallas reached its greatest extent under Jayayakshamalla in the middle of the fifteenth century. Upon his death, however, the kingdom was divided among his descendants and quickly fell into a state of anarchy.

FORGING THE MODERN STATE OF NEPAL

During the sixteenth century the territory now contained within the boundaries of Nepal was fragmented into scores of minor principalities which were gathered into four major groupings. In the east were the various tribal states of the Kiratas; in the Katmandu Valley were the three Newar kingdoms ruled by the Mallas; to the west of the valley lay a group of petty lordships known as the Chaubisi rajas; and on the far west was a similar set of states, the Baisi rajas. Although many of the states of these four groupings nominally recognized the supremacy of several of the more powerful among them or, in the case of the Baisi and Chaubisi rajas, of the Moghul emperor in Delhi, they were virtually independent and engaged in continual warfare. The absence of any political system embracing these states and the turbulence of their relations made possible the rise of the Gurkhas and, ultimately, the formation of the state of Nepal.

In 1559, Drabya Shah, the younger son of the raja of the Chaubisi kingdom of Lamjung, brought Gurkha—a small, adjacent principality west of the Katmandu Valley—under his dominion and established the line of kings which later became the monarchs of Nepal. During the next two centuries the position of the dynasty was consolidated by Drabya Shah's successors, and the territory of the kingdom was extended to include most of the area between the Marsyandi and the Trisuli rivers.

The main thrust of Gurkha expansion, however, did not occur until the middle of the eighteenth century with the accession to the throne of the tenth in the Shah line, Prithvi Narayan (reigned 1742–75). Extolled as a fierce and resourceful warrior king even among a people renowned for their martial qualities, Prithvi's overriding aim was the conquest of vast areas of the Himalayas and their incorporation into the territories of the House of Gurkha. In the second year of his reign he embarked upon a relentless campaign for the systematic subjugation of the surrounding kingdoms that lasted until his death and, continued by his successors, did not come to a complete halt until almost three-quarters of a century later.

The first and most critical phase of this undertaking was the conquest of the Katmandu Valley, a task which required twenty-five years to accomplish. Katmandu was not taken until 1768, Patan and Bhadgaon fell the following year, and by the end of 1769 the whole of the valley was under the control of the kingdom of Gurkha. Moving his capital to Katmandu, Prithvi Narayan established a policy which strictly excluded Europeans from the country, reformed the systems of land tenure and taxation, and executed large numbers of people whom he felt might constitute a potential threat to his position as the first king of Nepal. Domestic affairs occupied his attention only briefly, however, and the Gurkha advance was soon resumed. Meeting only slight opposition, Prithvi's armies subjugated the entire Kirata area to the east and by the time of his death were in possession of territory as far east as Darjeeling (now a part of India).

Nepalese stamp issued in memory of Raja Prithvi Narayan (1769–1775), founder of modern Nepal

The conquests of the Gurkhas continued under the leadership of Prithvi Narayan's descendants, most notably his younger son, Bahadur Shah, who ruled from 1837 to 1857. The Gurkhas turned west and overran Chaubisi, Baisi rajas, Kumaon, and Garhwal. Most areas were brought by conquest under the direct control of Katmandu. However, to avoid conflict with a few particularly strong adversaries, treaties of subsidiary alliance were concluded which often granted them a large measure of autonomy. Thus, by the end of the eighteenth century the territory of the kingdom of Nepal extended from the southern frontier of present-day Kashmir all along the arc of the Himalayas to the heart of Sikkim.

While these conquests were being made in the west, Nepal became engaged in a quarrel with Tibet over a number of questions—primarily the circulation of Nepalese coinage in Tibet and the taxation of goods traveling between India and Tibet—which eventually involved Nepal in war with China. Nepalese invasions of Tibet in 1788 and 1791 challenged the suzerainty which the Chinese Empire, then at the zenith of its power under the Manchu Dynasty, had established over the domains of the Dalai Lama during the preceding century and a half. In 1791 a Chinese ultimatum demanded the withdrawal of Nepalese troops. When it was rejected a Chinese army said to number seventy thousand entered Tibet, put the Nepalese to flight, and then—culminating a campaign regarded as even more extraordinary than Hannibal's crossing of the Alps— passed through the Himalayas and approached within a day's march of the Nepalese capital. Forced to terms in 1792, Nepal agreed to return territory earlier taken from Tibet and to send a tribute mission to Peking every five years, thereby assuming the nebulous tributary relationship to the Manchu emperor that China had already established over Tibet and such other countries as Siam, Korea, and Burma.

After this encounter with China, Nepal's expansionist energies, blocked in all other directions, turned toward the south. At the same time, however, the British in India were moving northward. They had arrived in India in the late sixteenth century and by the latter part of the eighteenth century the territory under their control extended up through the area of what is now East Pakistan and the Indian provinces of Bihar and Bengal to the lower reaches of Nepal. During this period their primary interest in the

Himalayas lay in exploiting the commercial potential of the mountain states and in acquiring trade routes through them into Tibet and thence, it was hoped, to China. Although the British had been hostile toward Prithvi Narayan, fearing that the extension of his power throughout the Himalayas would jeopardize their plans, by the time of the Sino-Nepalese war they were seeking to put their dealings with Nepal on a more amicable footing. However, treaties of 1792 and 1801 between Great Britain and Nepal providing for the establishment of diplomatic and commercial relations were subsequently nullified by the opposition of ruling circles in Nepal.

After continued acquisitions by the British East India Company made its territories contiguous with the southern frontier of Nepal in 1801, Nepalese depredations on British possessions across the frontier caused relations between the two countries to deteriorate still further. Turmoil along the frontier continued for more than a decade and by 1814 it, along with the persistent refusal of Nepal to enter into trade and diplomatic relations, had become intolerable to the British. When Nepal rejected a British proposal that a joint boundary commission be established to recommend a settlement for the disputed territories and ignored an ultimatum which followed, Great Britain sent troops to occupy the contested areas and declared war against Nepal in November 1814.

The confrontation with British power decisively brought the course of the Nepalese expansion to an end. Resisting until British troops menaced the Katmandu Valley, Nepal capitulated in 1816 and met Great Britain's demands in a settlement known as the Treaty of Sagauli. The territorial provisions of the agreement greatly reduced the area of Nepal and established the general outline of its present boundaries. Nepal was stripped of all its conquests west of the Kali and east of the Mechi rivers, as well as large portions of the Tarai.

STRUGGLE FOR DOMESTIC SUPREMACY

After 1816 the militancy of the Nepalese expressed itself primarily in a factional struggle for internal supremacy. The major contestants in this internal competition were two major families of the nobility, the Thapas and the Pandes. Their bitter animosities had resulted in conflict and bloodshed for generations, and their rivalry was directed toward possession of the prime-ministership, a position which had grown increasingly powerful since the days of Prithvi Narayan because of the incompetence or extreme youth of a succession of monarchs.

The internal struggle also came to involve the question of who was actually to wield the authority of the throne, enervated though it had become. A single monarch, Rajendra Bikram Shah, reigned from 1816 to 1847 but because of his impotence, initially the result of his youth and later of his passivity, he seldom actually ruled. Consequently, there were continual machinations within the royal family to fill the vacuum around the throne. The conflicts which arose within the royal family became interlocked with the feud between the Thapas and the Pandes, and in the fluid tactical alliances which resulted the Pandes were usually found supporting the king or his legitimate heirs while the Thapas aligned themselves with other members of the royal family. Earlier it was the judicious disposition of the power of the throne which had preserved a semblance of equilibrium between the Thapas and the Pandes and prevented either from dominating the king completely. When the influence of the royal family was dissipated by the widening of the rifts within it, however, these divisions were exploited by a collateral member of the Thapa family to eradicate all remaining vestiges of monarchical power and establish himself as ruler of Nepal.

The primacy of the Thapas came to an end in 1837 when Bhim Sen Thapa was toppled from power, and there followed a chaotic decade, punctuated frequently by assassinations, unrest, and foreign difficulties, in which the internal struggle for supremacy moved toward a final resolution. It culminated in a bloody slaughter in 1846 when the younger wife of King Rajendra, Queen Lakshmi Devi, gathered the nobles and ministers of the court at the Kot (Royal Court of Assembly) to determine who was responsible for the murder of her lover, a contender for the prime-ministership. Jang Bahadur, nephew of Bhim Sen Thapa and commander of a quarter of the armed forces, seized the opportunity to establish his own predominance. Troops under his command exterminated all those unable to escape the Kot, destroying virtually all of the Nepalese government, and during the massacre he managed to have the queen appoint him prime minister and commander in chief of the army. Thereafter, with the full backing of the army, he expelled from the country all those from whom he could not expect complete loyalty, confiscated their lands, filled the government with members of his family, and conferred on them and on himself the honorific name Rana. Forcing the king and queen into exile in India, he kept the heir apparent, Prince Surendra, a prisoner in Katmandu to confer the legitimacy of the throne on his thorough and comprehensive control of the government.

THE RANA PERIOD (1846–1951)

With Jang Bahadur's assumption of the prime-ministership, a pattern of rule and a system of politics were established which prevailed virtually without alteration until the end of the Rana era in 1951. Jang Bahadur's de facto control of all governmental affairs was given royal sanction in edicts of 1846 and 1856 which transferred to the prime minister, or maharaja, all the absolute powers previously vested in the king and provided the legal basis for the authority of the Rana maharajas. Moreover, the practice whereby the appointment of the prime minister lapsed each year and had to be renewed by the king was abolished and the position of prime minister was made a hereditary possession of the Rana family.

According to the rule laid down by Jang Bahadur to govern succession within the Rana family to the prime-ministership after his death, the position was to pass, not from eldest son to eldest son in lineal descent, but laterally to his brothers, from eldest to youngest. After the last of his brothers had died, the eldest member of the next generation was to become prime minister, and the succession was then to run through the entire generation of brothers and cousins—to the eldest in turn—and in that manner through each following generation. Jang's purpose in instituting this procedure was to ensure that the prime-ministership would always be in the hands of a Rana of mature years. Having come to power partly as the result of the fact that the system of primogeniture governing succession within the royal family had often produced infant kings who were easily dominated by their prime ministers, he sought to prevent Rana control from ever becoming enfeebled in a similar fashion. In this he was entirely successful, although the system possessed inherent defects which were as grave as those he had tried to avoid.

In addition to the sovereign authority conferred on the Ranas by the throne, the strength of their position was buttressed by numerous other means. Ranas were placed in high positions throughout the government, the importance and rank of their office depending on their place on the roll of succession. They were also strongly entrenched in the army, a major source of their support. Traditionally, the position of commander in chief of the army was held by the person who stood first in the line of succession to the prime-ministership, and all male members of the family were automatically accorded high military rank at the time of their birth. It also became customary for the Ranas to intermarry with the royal family. Moreover, the Ranas cultivated good relations with the British in India, and the continuing influence of Great Britain in Katmandu was a major factor in the continuance and stability of Rana rule.

The system of rule brought into being by Jang Bahadur was oligarchical rather than dictatorial, however, for the extensive authority held by the prime minister was limited by the power which rested with other members of the Rana family. Few decisions of the maharaja could be sustained, nor could he hope to remain in office against the opposition of the most highly placed Ranas. Several prime ministers, felt to be either incapable or too progressive, were forced from office by combinations within the family. The most serious challenges to the control of the maharaja always came from other members of the family.

The establishment of Rana control, therefore, did not fundamentally alter the nature of politics. Possession of the prime-ministership was still the crucial objective, power and initiative were possible for only a small number of individuals, and conspiracy and assassination remained commonplace. Moreover, the royal family, despite the diminution of its influence and prestige, continued to be drawn into the familial intrigues of the Ranas by those who sought to exploit its latent authority. Thus, though the structural effect of Rana ascendancy was the preeminence of the prime minister over the king, its major political effect was the exclusion of all other groups from competition for and exercise of power and the monopolization by a single family.

RELATIONS WITH TIBET AND CHINA

Nepal's relations with Tibet, which had been marked by continual friction since 1792, became inflamed shortly after the Ranas assumed control. The major sources of discord were the ill treatment of the Nepalese tribute missions passing through Tibet en route to Peking and the abuse of Nepalese traders residing in Lhasa. These issues, combined with a desire in Nepal to repossess the territories north of the Kodari (Kuti) and Kyirong passes which it had been forced to return to Tibet in 1792, caused Nepal to declare war against Tibet in 1854. The war was fought to a stalemate and a settlement was reached in the Treaty of Thapathali of 1856. In the major political provisions of the agreement both parties reconfirmed their special relationship to the Chinese emperor, and Nepal agreed to come to the assistance of Tibet if it should ever be invaded by a foreign power. In addition, Tibet agreed to pay Nepal an annual tribute.

Despite the agreement, relations between Nepal and Tibet failed to improve appreciably during the rest of the century and were severely strained when Tibet was invaded by a British expeditionary force in the early twentieth century. Great Britain had been trying to establish political and commercial relations with Tibet since 1774, but all of its efforts were frustrated by Tibetan opposition. The aggravations of this situation to Great Britain were increased when it began to fear that czarist Russia—one of its major diplomatic antagonists not only in Europe but in the Near East, central Asia, and the Far East as well—was attempting to bring the government at Lhasa under its influence as a means of threatening the British position in India. Although the danger of Russian interference in Tibet was later seen to be largely imaginary, a contingent of British troops under the command of Colonel Francis Younghusband was sent into Tibet in 1904 to secure Great Britain's predominance at Lhasa, settle a number of longstanding issues between Tibet and British India, and open trade and political relations between the two countries. Although Nepal had agreed to assist Tibet in the event of invasion, the Nepalese government recognized that compliance with the treaty would only earn the enmity of Great Britain and result in defeat. Therefore, Nepal withheld all aid from the Tibetans and continued its policy of giving full support to Great Britain, supplying the Younghusband expedition with several thousand pack animals and urging the Tibetan authorities to accede to British demands.

The circumstances surrounding the dispatch of the expedition provided a vivid demonstration of the pivotal importance of Tibet to the security of India, Nepal, and the other Himalayan states. Although Tibet had become a dependency of the Chinese Empire in the eighteenth century,

by the time British expansion reached the foothills of the Himalayas the effective influence of China in Tibet was beginning to ebb, and it soon disappeared altogether.

This was demonstrated several years later when China attempted to reassert its authority over Tibet and concurrently tried to revive its influence in Nepalese affairs. China's suzerainty over Nepal, which was at most only nominal, had largely evaporated by the time the Ranas came to power. The tribute missions which Nepal sent to China rested more on commercial motives than on any sense of obligation or compulsion, and they appear to have been the only form of regular diplomatic intercourse between the two countries throughout the nineteenth century. From 1905 to 1911, however, the Chinese were pressing forward with a vigorous military campaign in Tibet to enforce their suzerainty there and made repeated assertions that Nepal was still a vassal of China. The Chinese military and diplomatic campaigns against Tibet were only temporarily abated in 1911 when a revolution overthrew the Manchu Dynasty. Although a republican form of government was established, its policy on Tibet was the same as that of its predecessor. In 1912 the new government announced that Tibet was to be considered an integral part of the Republic of China and the military offensive was renewed. Tibet had declared its independence in 1911, however, and with the aid of Great Britain was able to hold off the Chinese armies on its eastern frontier.

Similarly, with the fall of the Chinese emperor, Nepal considered any justification for the tribute missions as having ceased; the last was in 1908—the one scheduled for 1912 was never sent. Thereafter, a succession of events—World War I, growing internal conflicts during the 1920s and 1930s, invasion by the Japanese, World War II, and civil war—intervened to preoccupy China for the next half-century, and consequently the threat to the independence of Tibet and Nepal, and to the security of India, was removed.

THE FALL OF THE RANAS

Conflict within the Rana clan rather than forces external to it was the decisive factor in the dissolution of Rana despotism. In establishing the procedure for the transfer of power, Jang Bahadur had foreseen neither the longevity nor the fecundity of his descendants.

The monarchy played a significant role in the activities of the groups which were coalescing in opposition to the Ranas. King Tribhuvan, whose reign began in 1911, was an early supporter of anti-Rana activities, lending them his covert encouragement and financial support. The palace was implicated in a number of plots against the Ranas in the 1930s and 1940s and Tribhuvan ran serious personal risks to serve as a symbolic rallying point for the various opposition elements.

The first organized efforts against the Ranas from outside the clan itself took place in the 1930s. Several groups were formed secretly in Nepal—among them the People's party (Praja Parishad) in 1935—by young men who sought the overthrow of the Ranas and the establishment of democratic government, but these groups were discovered and suppressed before they became a threat to the regime. No organized activity against the Ranas took place during the war, but after 1945 political agitation resumed. A number of political parties came into being during the next several years, the most prominent of which was the Nepali National Congress, founded in India in 1946. The congress opened its campaign against the Ranas with a *satyagraha* (passive, nonviolent resistance movement) in support of a strike in Biratnagar in 1947 which had been forcibly suppressed by the government. Obtaining a withdrawal of the *satyagraha* by agreeing to institute liberal reforms, the prime minister, Padma Shamsher (1945–48), promptly established a reforms committee and early the next year promulgated the country's first constitution, the Government of Nepal Act, 1948. Padma's conciliatory spirit, however, and the liberal tendencies exhibited by the 1948 constitution alarmed a powerful group of the more conservative Ranas headed by Mohan Shamsher. After forcing Padma to resign, Mohan took over as prime minister, postponed promulgation of the new constitution, and declared the Nepali National Congress illegal.

India was deeply concerned with these developments in Nepal. Having become independent in 1947, India had adopted the principles of political democracy and a mixed Socialist economy and sought to persuade the Ranas of the desirability of moving rapidly in a similar direction. In the Indian view such reform measures became all the more urgent and necessary in 1949 when the Communists came to power in China and their invasion of Tibet appeared imminent, with ominous implications for Nepal at such a critical juncture. The Ranas acquiesced in the establishment of a bicameral legislative body, which was convened in the Nepalese capital in September 1950.

A crisis was reached in the fall of 1950. Neither the scope nor the pace of the reforms reluctantly granted by the Ranas were sufficient for the major political parties. They instigated sporadic uprisings in various parts of the country during the summer of 1950, and in late September the government announced the discovery of a plot by the Nepali Congress to assassinate the prime minister and other high officials. The invasion of Tibet by Communist Chinese troops in October added to the tension. Shortly thereafter, on November 6, King Tribhuvan, allegedly implicated in the Nepali Congress conspiracy and fearful for his safety, took refuge in the Indian embassy in Katmandu and two days later was flown to India where he was granted asylum. Simultaneously, a general rebellion erupted throughout the country under the loose coordination of the Nepali Congress. By the end of November, however, regular government troops succeeded in breaking the insurrection. In the meantime, Tribhuvan's three-year-old grandson had been proclaimed king by Mohan Shamsher.

The Rana victory was transitory, however, for the Indian government continued to recognize Tribhuvan rather than his grandson as head of state and demanded not only that he be returned to the throne but also that constitutional reforms be made immediately to render the Nepalese government more representative of the public will. Amenable to the latter proposal, Prime Minister Mohan refused to allow Tribhuvan to return. He was soon forced to capitulate, however. In the middle of December a second offensive was launched by rebel forces; government troops, previously loyal, began to desert to the other side; and forty Ranas resigned from high civil and military positions and another one hundred demanded that India's conditions be met. The adamancy of India, the danger from China, the deterioration of the domestic situation, and the staggering loss of support from large sections of the Rana family compelled Mohan to meet India's terms. In January 1951 he agreed to an amnesty for insurgents, the restoration of King Tribhuvan, the formation of a constituent assembly, the inclusion of popular representatives in the cabinet on the basis of parity with the Ranas, and the holding of elections by 1952. The following month the Rana political monopoly came to an end when King Tribhuvan returned to the throne and an interim cabinet was formed which included five representatives of the people drawn from the Nepali Congress and five Ranas, with Mohan Shamsher as prime minister.

REVIVAL OF ROYAL POWER

Although King Tribhuvan had declared at the time of the formation of the new government that a parliamentary democratic system under a constitutional monarchy would be established, the creation of such a system was delayed for eight years by the turmoil which followed the overthrow of the Ranas. In the period from 1951 to 1959 the chaos and fragmentation of the country made political stability—let alone the inauguration of democratic government—impossible and fostered the gradual reacquisition of supreme power by the king. For eight years the power relinquished by the Ranas was held by a succession of interim governments appointed by the king, interspersed with brief intervals of direct rule by the monarch himself, and political parties became progressively enfeebled by internal dissensions. Chronic political instability was accompanied by frequent disturbances throughout the country, which the government was often powerless to deal with. As the formation of a constituent assembly and the holding of elections were repeatedly postponed, politics became increasingly divorced from the objectives of the popular movement against the Ranas and disregarded the insistent necessity of relieving the country's economic stagnation. The great mass of the people, disillusioned when the hopes and expectations aroused by the overthrow of the Ranas were not fulfilled by the actual course of events, turned to the king as the only source of continuity and the major pivot of unity and strength.

Between 1951 and 1955 there were three different cabinet governments and one period of direct rule by the king. The coalition cabinet formed in early 1951 under Mohan Shamsher quickly proved unworkable and was dissolved in November. It was succeeded by a cabinet dominated by the Nepali Congress party in which M. P. Koirala held the prime-ministership but, due to conflicts within the Congress, it fell from power in August 1952. King Tribhuvan then ruled directly until May 1953, when he called a second time upon M. P. Koirala—who by then had split entirely with the congress—to form a government from his newly formed National Democratic party. Koirala's second regime was so weak, however, that in February 1954 he transformed it into a coalition government to strengthen its position. This precarious alliance, which included representatives of three other parties in the cabinet, was immobilized by disagreements between the constituent parties and survived only until January 1955.

With the disintegration of the coalition, Crown Prince Mahendra flew to Switzerland to consult with his ailing father—abroad for medical treatment—and returned in the middle of February vested with full royal powers to deal with the cabinet crisis. He attempted to organize a new government but the effort failed, and he announced at the end of the month that he would rule directly for the time being. Two weeks later, on March 13, 1955, King Tribhuvan died while still in Europe and Mahendra ascended the throne.

By the end of Tribhuvan's reign the general situation in the country had deteriorated dangerously. Four years of freedom from Rana rule had brought none of the benefits expected, and in many respects the outlook was even more discouraging than it had been before 1951. Chaos prevailed in the country's politics. After 1951 the popular movement against the Ranas lost its cohesion and momentum and dissolved into numerous factions and groups. Concerned only with the attainment of power for its own sake and preoccupied by internal conflicts which nullified their effectiveness, the rivalries between and within the various parties produced chronic instability and paralysis in the government.

Because of the defaults of other potential centers of leadership, therefore, the crown became the strongest political force in the country during Tribhuvan's reign. Under King Mahendra, the monarchy was to become still more powerful. He conceived of the king's role as a much more active and forceful one than had his father, and immediately after the latter's death he began systematically to augment further the power of the throne. This earned him the hostility of most of the political parties, particularly the larger ones, who felt that the expansion of royal influence and the return to royal councils of Ranas and members of their regime jeopardized their chances of arriving at power through elections. The king was subsequently unable to remain aloof from political conflict and criticism, as had been possible for Tribhuvan. With Mahendra on the throne, royal actions began to be publicly challenged, and many of the major issues of succeeding years were merely facets of the larger debate over definition of the limits of monarchical power.

King Mahendra remained in direct control of the government until January 1956, when he invited Tanka Prasad Acharya to become prime minister and form a government. Initially composed of an equal number of royal nominees and members of Acharya's own party, the People's party, the cabinet was later expanded to include more supporters of the king. Acharya demanded their removal and, when the king refused to do so, submitted his resignation in July 1957. Mahendra soon called upon K. I. Singh, a colorful *enfant terrible* of Nepalese politics, to form a new cabinet. The daring and ambitious Singh immediately set out to challenge Mahendra's position by attempting to acquire independent control of important sources of power. The threat was easily countered, however, and in November Mahendra announced suddenly that he had accepted Singh's resignation. The king then ruled directly until elections were held in February 1959, although he was advised by a coalition Council of Ministers which was formed at the beginning of 1958.

During the period from 1955 to 1959 one of the major political issues concerned the purpose and timing of elections. The compromise agreement of January 1951 between the king, the Ranas, and the political leaders had stipulated that the formation of a constituent assembly was to be the purpose of the elections. This was reaffirmed in 1954 by an amendment to the constitution, the Interim Government of Nepal Act of 1951. Although Mahendra had declared in July 1955 that general elections would be held in October 1957, he strongly opposed the formation of a constituent assembly. There could be no more fundamental challenge to the monarch's claim to ultimate sovereign authority than the preparation of a new constitution by elected representatives of the people. Skeptical of the sincerity of the king's promise and eager to validate their claims of strength by success at the polls, the political parties—particularly the Nepali Congress and the Communist party of Nepal—continued to demand elections for a constituent assembly at the earliest possible date.

The issue of elections developed greater intensity during Singh's brief regime, and it was finally resolved in the period of direct rule which followed. On October 6, 1957, two days before the scheduled date for elections, Mahendra announced that it would be impossible to hold them due to the failure of the Acharya government to make adequate preparations. Since the king had not rescheduled the elections, a coalition of the major parties responded by threatening to begin a civil disobedience movement on December 8, 1957, unless a new date for elections had been fixed by then. On December 17, after ten days of demonstrations, Mahendra designated February 18, 1959, as the date on which elections would be held. Although the coalition had wanted them to be held within six months, it acquiesced in the king's action and suspended the movement. Mahendra later announced that he was appointing a commission to draft a new constitution which would provide that a legislative body rather than a constituent assembly was to be the purpose of the impending elections. Although it had always opposed such a move, the Nepali Congress accepted the king's decision without protest, as did the other parties, and the final obstacle to the holding of general elections was thereby removed. A year later, on February 12, 1959, King Mahendra promulgated the new constitution, and a week later Nepal's first general elections began. The Nepali Congress party, a moderate Socialist group, gained a substantial victory, and its leader, M. P. Koirala, was called upon to form a government and serve as prime minister.

In December 1960 King Mahendra dismissed the Koirala government, suspended the constitution, and resumed direct rule. The king charged the Nepali Congress party's government with corruption, misuse of power, and an inability to maintain law and order throughout the country. King Mahendra declared that Nepal was not yet ready for Western parliamentary institutions and needed a democratic political system closer to Nepalese traditions. To meet this need the king initiated, under a constitution promulgated on December 16, 1962, a partyless system of *panchayat* (council). This system draws its theoretical inspiration from the traditional local government institution found in parts of Nepal—the village panchayat.

The constitution specifies that the king (chief of state) is the sole source of authority for all government institutions in Nepal. He exercises broad powers over the country's panchayat system of government.

The Council of Ministers (cabinet) is the executive arm of the government and gives policy advice to the king. The prime minister (head of government) and cabinet ministers are appointed by the king from the membership of the National Panchayat (Parliament).

With the panchayat system firmly established by 1967, King Mahendra began working out an accommodation with the former political party members, and participation in the government by former political leaders has been encouraged.

The reactions to this accommodation attempt were mixed. Some former Nepali Congress party leaders favored participation in the panchayat system while others urged continued opposition to the system.

In January 1972 King Mahendra died of a heart attack and was succeeded by his twenty-seven-year-old son, the crown prince Birendra, who has continued the partyless *panchayat* system.

THE KING

The monarchy is the center of political life. The king is the most powerful political force and the most significant political institution in the country. He is the symbol of national unity, the source of all important government policy, and the major defender of tradition as well as the principal agent for change. The strength of the monarchy has been and

Their Majesties King Mahendra Bir Bikram Shah Deva, left, the ruler of Nepal, and Queen Ratna Rajya Lakshmi Shah visited the United Nations headquarters in New York City in 1960. They are seen here with the UN secretary-general Dag Hammarskjöld, right.

The king and queen of Nepal visited the United Nations headquarters again in 1967. They are seen here with Secretary-General U Thant, right.

The commemorative postage stamps for the 1975 coronation of Nepal king Birendra Bir Bikram Shah Deva

A 1978 stamp commemorates the queen mother's birthday.

The king and queen of Nepal visited with the president of the United States, Lyndon B. Johnson, in October 1967. This photograph was taken in the Rose Garden of the White House in Washington, D.C.

A close-up of a lighter moment between President Johnson and King Mahendra

remains under constant challenge from those who seek to diminish his authority by the establishment of governmental institutions less subject to his will. Disagreement over the legitimate bounds of royal power and its position in the evolving political system has been the most basic, enduring and pervasive political issue.

The king's power ultimately rests on his ability to attract and retain the support of the key elements in a scattered, locally isolated, multiethnic population. He enjoys the advantage of the prestige of a role traditionally held to have supernatural attributes and of being the most widely known national political figure. Much of the king's support comes from elements who are endowed with high hereditary status, land holdings, or commercial wealth and who suspect or oppose reforms of which they see themselves as the underwriters rather than the beneficiaries.

The incompatibility of these interests confronts the king

with a particularly difficult political problem in determining the rate at which reform and development are to progress. He is the focus of popular expectations for action which will compensate for over a decade of delay in carrying out economic reforms, and there is a degree of urgency required in meeting these demands which he cannot ignore without risking serious discontent. He must act with sufficient speed to prevent the eruption of a potentially explosive problem which would deprive him of any control in its solution, yet he must not move so swiftly as to provoke serious reactions from conservative groups close to the throne.

As of early 1964, King Mahendra had been able to deal with these opposing pressures without markedly diminishing his support from either group. A limited but increasing number of the peasantry recognized that he was virtually the only figure able to bring about the desired improvement in economic conditions. Similarly, the privileged elements, realizing that some change is unavoidable and that they would be even more directly threatened under any other regime, also continued to look to the king to protect their basic interests.

The king's power is also dependent to a very large extent on his control of the armed forces. He appears to be in firm possession of the allegiance of the army and has been highly successful in inoculating it against the infection of political rivalries by cultivating and rewarding reliability as the primary military virtue. Consequently the army, while a potential force of major importance, is a passive one. It has not exhibited any political initiative of its own, and it has exerted no political influence independently of the king's direction.

The stature of the king is heightened by the fact that he is regarded by many of the people as an incarnation of the Hindu god Vishnu. A majority of the population is Hindu, and by the Constitution of 1962 Nepal was officially proclaimed a Hindu state. As a result of centuries of intermingling of Buddhism and Hinduism, many of the Buddhist minority also worship gods of the Hindu pantheon; at least some would also probably acknowledge the divinity of the king to some extent. It would appear that in some areas of the country there is even a greater awareness of the religious significance of the king than of his political role.

The monarchy is the one political concept most widely shared by the people, and King Mahendra made vigorous efforts to broaden and strengthen its popular support. One of the primary means by which this is being done is through the panchayat system, which, as the first uniform system of local government to operate on a national scale, may be expected to have an important influence on attitudes toward the government if it remains in operation for a sufficient length of time.

In January 1972, when King Mahendra died of a heart attack, he was succeeded by his twenty-seven-year-old son, Crown Prince Birendra.

King Mahendra appeared on many stamps of Nepal. Here are six different poses.

Queen Ratna with a playing child

Nepalese stamp issued to commemorate the wedding of Crown Prince Birendra Bir Bikram Shah Deva and Crown Princess Aishwarya Rajya Lakshmi Devi Rana on February 27–28, 1970

King Birendra also appeared on a number of Nepal's stamps.

In the spring of 1979, a round of student demonstrations and antiregime activities resulted in a call by King Birendra for a national referendum to decide on the nature of Nepal's government—either the continuation of the panchayat sys-

tem or the establishment of a multiparty system. In a December 1979 speech, the king promised to amend the constitution, in the event the panchayat system was retained, to further democratize it.

The referendum was held in May 1980, and the partyless panchayat system won a narrow victory. As he had promised, the king reformed the panchayat system, providing for election to the National Panchayat on the basis of universal suffrage. The amendments also granted to the National Panchayat greater power than it previously had.

A second round of voting was held in the spring of 1981 to elect a new National Panchayat. The election was boycotted by most of the major political groups which had expressed unhappiness with the king's political reforms. Nevertheless, the election attracted a broad array of candidates and a respectable turnout at the polls. Surya Bahadur Thapa, prime minister from the time of the student uprisings in 1979 until the election, was renominated to that post by an overwhelming majority of the Panchayat members when that body convened in June.

THE KINGDOM OF BHUTAN

Little is known of the history of Bhutan before the late eighteenth century. It is generally assumed that the forebears of the dominant ethnic group, the Bhote, came from Tibet, but the period of their arrival is uncertain. Of the several versions suggested by modern scholars, the most probable is that expansion across the mountains began in the ninth century when Tibet, at the height of its power, sent troops to seize control of the area. According to this account the Tibetan invaders met with little resistance in Bhutan, which at that time was a Hindu state ruled by a maharaja, and they easily brought it under their control.

Development of the government began early in the seventeenth century when a Tibetan lama, believed by his followers to be a reincarnation of Buddha, established his authority over the others and was given the title of *Dharma Raja* (spiritual leader). His successor is said to have organized the country into several territories, or provinces, each of which included one or more forts within its jurisdictional area. The governors *(penlops)* who administered these territories were appointed officials, who in turn appointed subordinate governors (called *jungpens)* from among the leaders in their respective forts. The Dharma Rajas concerned themselves primarily with religious matters, leaving authority over secular affairs to an appointed minister, who soon became known as the *Deb Raja* (temporal leader).

Subsequently, as the Dharma Raja became increasingly preoccupied with spiritual matters, the Deb Raja came to be regarded as the actual head of state, and his post was given to persons "elected" by a council of *penlops* and *jungpens.* In practice the most powerful *penlop,* usually the most influential landlord in the country, either appointed the Deb Raja or usurped the post for himself. Thus, a change in the

The king of Nepal, Birendra Bir Bikram Shah Deva and Queen Aishwarya Rajya Lakshmi Devi Shah with President Ronald Reagan and First Lady Nancy Reagan at the White House on the way to a formal dinner in December 1983, during a state visit by the monarchs of Nepal. (Official White House photograph by Pete Souza)

post of Deb Raja frequently resulted in a change of *penlops* and their subordinate *jungpens,* a system which bred intense rivalries for rulership, as the ousted officials customarily would occupy their time in making preparations to regain power by any possible means.

Beset by internal difficulties, Bhutan nevertheless followed an aggressive policy toward its neighbors during the eighteenth century, sending frequent raiding parties across the western and northern borders. Its warriors plundered wide areas in Sikkim, kidnaped the king, and carried off many captives, emerging from a series of engagements in possession of the Ha Valley and the Kalimpong region (then a part of Sikkim and now in West Bengal).

Bhutan's aggressions on the southern border, however, were far less successful. In 1771 when the Deb Raja sent troops into Cooch Behar—possibly to prevent any British attempt to set up a trade route through his country to Tibet—the British intervened, drove the Bhutanese out, and pursued them into their own territory. Peace was arranged in 1773, largely through the intercession of Tibet.

Disputes along this border nevertheless continued into the early nineteenth century, with the result that in 1841 the government of British India annexed the Duars Plain to Assam, placing its northern frontier along the general line

of the present boundary. The British in return agreed to pay a small annual subsidy to the Bhutanese as long as they remained peaceful. Bhutanese raiders continued to operate across the border, carrying off Indian subjects of the British as slaves.

In 1863 a British representative, sent to Bhutan to protest against these infractions, was kidnaped and forced to sign an agreement returning the Duars Plain to Bhutan. After escaping, he repudiated the agreement, stopped the subsidy, and demanded restoration of the captives. When the demands were rejected in 1865, British troops invaded Bhutan and forced the Bhutanese authorities to sue for peace. Under the terms of the Sinchu La treaty, which terminated hostilities, the Duars Plain and Kalimpong were ceded back to British India, the Bhutanese agreed to refer any dispute with Sikkim or Cooch Behar to the British government for negotiation, and Bhutan's annual subsidy was greatly increased. Thereafter, relations with the British government in India remained satisfactory.

The dual system of government, which has been in existence for some three hundred years, was discontinued in the early twentieth century when the incumbent Dharma Raja died and no successor who could qualify as the reincarnation of Buddha could be found. The Deb Raja then took on the added responsibility of administering to the spiritual needs of the people. The post of Dharma Raja finally was abolished in 1907, when with British support Ugyen Wangchuk, the *penlop* of Tongsa province in the eastern region, was elected hereditary maharaja of the country. Hereditary secular and religious rule vested in the Wangchuk family facilitated the establishment of a unified, centrally administered government for the first time in Bhutan's history.

After World War II, India achieved independence and took over Great Britain's responsibilities in the realm of Bhutan's foreign affairs. With Indian support the country, under a forward-looking maharaja who has completely reversed the former policy of isolation, has made a slow but steady beginning toward entering the modern world.

THE MAHARAJA (KING)

During the twelve years of his incumbency as a theoretical absolute monarch, the maharaja has introduced certain features of modern representative government. The latter include an Advisory Council, comparable to a cabinet, and a Tsongdu or National Advisory Assembly, created in the mid-1950s. Although the maharaja appoints the Advisory Council and about 25 percent of the assembly members, the remaining assemblymen are elected indirectly every five years from among village headmen.

As many of the assemblymen are illiterate, most of the legislative bills are initiated by the maharaja. Free expression of opinion is encouraged, however, and debates on some issues reportedly become quite stormy. Members may criticize the monarchy, even the maharaja himself.

The assembly meets once or twice each year, sometimes in Thimbu, the winter capital, and sometimes in Punakha, the summer capital. Each session, lasting one or two weeks, is presided over by the speaker, who is also chief secretary to the government. Voting is by show of hands, and the maharaja has final veto power. Presumably a proposed bill can be defeated by a majority vote, but there is no record of such an action.

THE WANGCHUK ROYAL FAMILY

Political leadership has been virtually a monopoly of the Wangchuk family since 1907, when it was vested with power to rule over secular and religious affairs. It appears to be confronted with no serious sources of opposition. The maharaja himself is deeply involved in the broad task of modernization, but leaves the handling of ordinary administrative matters to the governors of Bhutan's four regions.

Several factors contribute to the apparent apathy of the population toward political issues. Living standards are relatively good compared to most other Asian states. Over-

Bhutan

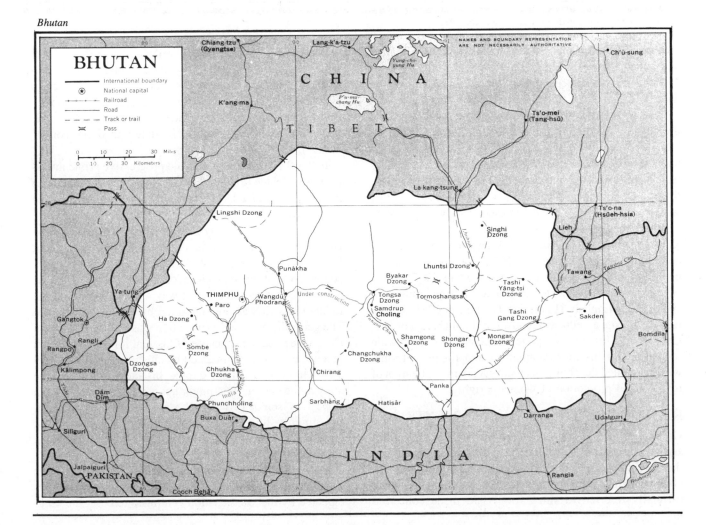

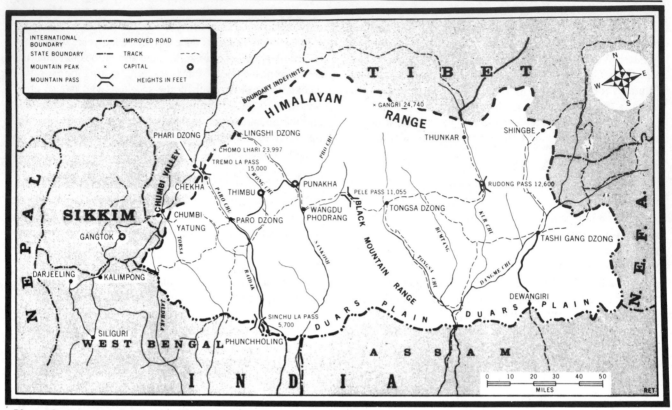

Bhutan showing terrain features described in this chapter

crowded and impoverished urban settlements don't exist, and almost all families own their own land.

Moreover, until the Chinese Communist aggressions in Tibet and against the neighboring Indian frontier, the people had been virtually isolated from the political turmoil of the outside world. Because of the high illiteracy rate and lack of communications facilities, political organization and the dissemination of information on political issues have been seriously handicapped. It is probable, however, that the creation of a National Advisory Assembly with a large proportion of elected representation will gradually diminish this apathy.

The late maharaja Jigme Dorji Wangchuk, born in 1929 and enthroned on October 27, 1952, was the third in the hereditary line of maharajas established in 1907 by the British. Although educated in Bhutan by royal tutors, he spoke fluent English, Hindi, and Tibetan. In 1951 he married the European-educated cousin of the maharaja of Sikkim. During his brief reign he established a countrywide reputation for his humanitarianism and for his reforms, which included the abolition of slavery, democratization of royalty, and promotion of women's rights.

RECENT POLITICAL DEVELOPMENTS

On July 24, 1972, the seventeen-year-old crown prince Jigme Singhye Wangchuk ascended the throne, succeeding the enlightened and liberal monarch Jigme Dorji Wangchuk. The late *druk gyalpo* (as the monarch has been officially referred to since 1963) had made concerted

efforts during his twenty-year reign to bring this remote mountain kingdom into the twentieth century. In this undertaking he had achieved considerable progress. He not only initiated a series of political, social, and economic reforms but also broadened contacts with the outside world. The new *druk gyalpo* expressed his determination to continue his father's unfinished work.

In April 1964 the dynamic and progressive prime minister Jigme Polden (Palden) Dorji was assassinated while the *druk gyalpo,* Jigme Dorji Wangchuk, was away in Europe for medical treatment. More than fifty persons were arrested, including nearly forty military personnel led by Brigadier Bahadur Namgyal, deputy commander in chief of Bhutan's army. One of the arrested suspects reportedly confessed that he had close connections with Chinese agents. Although this account was widely reported in the Indian press, it was not supported by any firm evidence. The generally accepted explanation was that Jigme Polden Dorji made enemies because of his zeal for modernization in a society where feudal and clannish influences still remain deeply rooted. For example, his attempt to reform the army at the end of 1962 might not have been popular with some fifty senior officers who were retired on pension. Presumably he also antagonized some conservative religious elements by his efforts to reduce the power of the church.

The *druk gyalpo* named Lhendup Dorji, brother of Jigme Polden Dorji, to succeed him. But the instability precipitated by the assassination continued to beset the kingdom for more than a year. In November and December 1964, a power struggle apparently broke out between royalists and those supporting Lhendup Dorji. Circumstances surrounding this political infighting are still unclear, but it would appear that the army commander, Brigadier Ugyen Tyangbi, backed Prime Minister Lhendup Dorji in a losing cause. Having incurred the serious displeasure of the *druk gyalpo* and fearful for their safety, the oppositionists escaped to Nepal, where they asked for and received political asylum and established their exile headquarters at Katmandu (Kathmandu). Whatever their personal differences with the *druk gyalpo,* they did not advocate the overthrow of the monarchy; instead, their avowed political objective was to win for Bhutan "full freedom from Indian interference." Their main complaint was that India was behaving as a neoimperialist power in Bhutan and that India was to be blamed for the circumstances leading to the oppositionists' estrangement from the *druk gyalpo* and to their self-exile in Nepal. After this aborted coup, the *druk gyalpo* took over the duties of the premiership.

The political situation settled into a relative calm in 1965 and 1966, despite a brief crisis in July 1965 when an attempt was made on the life of the *druk gyalpo,* Jigme Dorji Wangchuk. Evidently the Lhendup Dorji group was not implicated in this attempted assassination. Who was behind this plot remained obscure. Two of the would-be assassins were caught on the same day but were later freed on royal pardon and were exiled to a remote border village.

Potentially a far more revolutionary change was the surprise announcement of the *druk gyalpo* in May 1968 that the Tsongdu should be made the kingdom's sovereign institution and that it should have the inherent power to remove not only ministers but also the ruling monarch himself. In November 1968 he also astonished the Tsongdu by declaring that he renounced his royal prerogative to veto bills passed by the Tsongdu and that he would step down if two-thirds of the Tsongdu members demanded his abdication on a vote of no confidence. He made it explicit, however, that, in the event of his abdication, the successor must be a member of the current Wangchuk royal family. In May 1969 he asked the Tsongdu, in the face of its own reluctance, to adopt a rule by which he was to seek a vote of

King Wangchuk in a tribal meeting with his four jongpons, *the commanders of the border forts. (They are the ones with the embroidered caps.)*

The second king of Bhutan, Jigme Dorji Wangchuk (photo: John Claude White)

nonaligned and neutral between India and China. As early as August 1964, during a visit to India, then Prime Minister Lhendup Dorji expressed Bhutan's desire to establish direct contacts with foreign countries without being bound to the Indo-Bhutan Treaty of 1949, under which Bhutan had "agreed to be guided by the advice" of India in regard to its external affairs. In exchange India pledged not to interfere in the kingdom's internal administration. In 1966 Bhutan formally notified India of its wish to join the United Nations.

India was not eager to loosen its grip on Bhutan because of its strategic factor in New Delhi's northern frontier defense. Foreigners wishing to enter the kingdom or Bhutanese wanting to travel outside both the kingdom and the Indian subcontinent were required to obtain permits from Indian authorities. It was in recognition of the kingdom's defense value that the government of India provided the equivalent of US$50 million to Bhutan between 1961 and 1971. Moreover, India agreed to underwrite almost the entire cost of Bhutan's Third Five-Year Plan (1971–76), which was estimated to cost an equivalent of approximately US$45 million.

The People's Republic of China (PRC) was an important factor in Bhutan's external affairs. The PRC persisted in its efforts to detach Bhutan from India or to weaken Indian influence in the kingdom. It reiterated that Bhutan was an independent and sovereign state and had the right to conduct its own foreign relations. At the same time the PRC reminded the kingdom that any Chinese-Bhutanese boundary disputes could be peacefully solved through direct negotiations without India's interference.

From January 1968 Bhutan's relations with India came under the charge of a newly created "special officer of India in Bhutan." This officer reported directly to New Delhi rather than to the political officer in Gangtok, Sikkim (until 1968, the Indian political officer at Gangtok had handled Bhutanese affairs in addition to his responsibility for Sikkim). Administratively, however, the special officer in Thimbu still remained under the jurisdiction of the Indian political officer who was stationed in the neighboring king-

This 1975 Bhutan stamp commemorates King Jigme Singhye Wangchuk's twentieth birthday, in a lithograph embossed on gold foil.

confidence from the Tsongdu every three years. The renewal of his mandate was to be decided by a simple majority vote but, at the insistence of the Tsongdu, the *druk gyalpo* accepted a two-thirds majority requirement.

On the diplomatic front, Bhutan made steady progress in getting its sovereignty accepted by the world outside India. It also sought actively to reduce its traditional dependence on India and to emulate Nepal's successful efforts to remain

dom. Observers interpreted this new development as an indication of growing Indian sensitivity to Bhutan's search for a self-reliant posture in world affairs. In any case, in October 1968, Bhutan sent its first observers to the United Nations. In 1969 the Tsongdu adopted a resolution urging India and the United Nations (UN) to admit Bhutan as a member of the world organization.

In December 1970 Bhutan applied for admission to the UN, and its application, supported by India, was endorsed by the UN Security Council in February 1971. Bhutan was welcomed as a new member in September 1971—in time to vote favorably for a resolution that would remove the Republic of China (Nationalist China) from the United Nations and set the PRC in its place. It opened a permanent mission in New York; nonetheless, Bhutan's diplomatic representation at the end of 1972 was limited to India only. India in turn was the only foreign state with a diplomatic mission in Thimbu, the capital. The new king, Jigme Singhye Wangchuk, stated that he had no immediate plan to expand diplomatic contacts.

The late king Jigme Dorji began to guide his country toward constitutional monarchy. His son, Jigme Singhye Wangchuk, who ascended the throne on July 24, 1972, has pledged to continue the work begun by his father.

The king was earlier subject to a vote of confidence every three years, but this practice was dropped after King Jigme Singhye assumed the throne.

THE INDIAN PROTECTORATE OF SIKKIM

Sikkim, to the east of Nepal, is a compact square-shaped country situated between two massive mountain spurs jutting southward from the main Himalayan range. Slightly smaller than Yellowstone National Park, it has an estimated population of about 165,000, composed mainly of Lepcha and Bhote ethnic groups and of relatively recent emigrants from Nepal. Most of its people live in rural areas in detached homesteads, generally a mile or more apart. Gangtok, the capital and largest town, with only about 7,000 inhabitants, is an overgrown village rather than an urban center. The country has common frontiers with Tibet on the north and east, Bhutan on the southeast, and India on the south, as well as with Nepal on the west.

Of these four neighbors, Tibet has had the major role in influencing Sikkim's development and in shaping its cultural identity. Bhote (Bhotia) people began entering the country from eastern Tibet in the early fourteenth century, spread along the valleys of the Tista River and its tributaries, and gradually extended their control over the local Lepcha inhabitants. When Sikkim emerged as a distinct national entity in 1642, a family of Tibetan ancestral origin sat on the throne, and the foundations of a theocratic state, based on Tibetan Lamaism, had been established.

Although it was theoretically a kingdom ruled by its own maharaja (until 1975), the country is now actually a state of India, particularly in respect to its foreign relations and the defense of its territorial integrity. It had no constitution, but several political parties had been formed. The maharaja by proclamation of March 23, 1953, introduced certain features of a democratic system of government. The proclamation recognized the authority of an Indian-appointed *dewan*, whose responsibilities were similar to those of a prime minister. It also established a State Council, which had limited legislative functions, and an Executive Council, which served as a cabinet. The *dewan* presided over both bodies.

The basic character of this governmental structure remains essentially unchanged. In the aftermath of the aggressions of Communist Chinese forces in the Himalayan area in late 1962, however, certain modifications, possibly of a temporary nature, have been introduced. Chief of these were the replacement in early 1964 of the *dewan* by an Indian "principal administrative officer" and the substitution of a Consultative Committee for the State Council.

Political issues stem mainly from the demands of the Nepalese community for increased representation in governmental affairs. The Lepcha-Bhote politicians, led by the ruling family, contend that since many of the Nepalese are recent arrivals in the country, they should be regarded as temporary residents unqualified to have a dominant voice in state councils until their permanent assimilation into Sikkimese society is assured. Overshadowing all political activities is the Chinese Communist threat from Tibet. As in

Sikkim

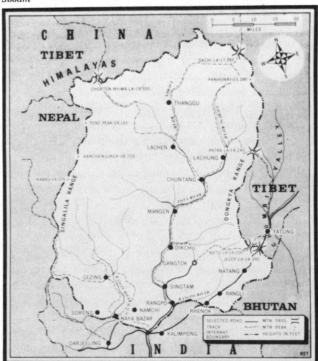

Nepal, this threat is particularly intensified by the Chinese aggressions of 1962 in the Himalayan region.

HISTORY

Of the three main ethnic groups, the Lepcha were the first established in the area. Nothing certain is known about their time of arrival, but it is commonly believed they were Sikkim's original inhabitants. Lepcha settlements were encountered in the early fourteenth century by the Bhota when they began coming into the country from eastern Tibet, the largest influx moving southwestward through the Chumbi Valley (now in Tibet) across the 14,200-foot Natu La (Natu) pass, and on to various points along the Tista River and its tributaries. A smaller number pushed across the still higher passes on the northern frontier.

During the fifteenth and sixteenth centuries the newly arrived Bhote readily gained ascendancy over the less sophisticated local people. Some Bhote established themselves on the land and built up large estates. Others devoted themselves to the propagation of Tibetan Lamaism among the animist Lepcha, succeeding in converting many of them to the Buddhist faith. Of the lamas engaged in missionary endeavors in this period, those who were to play a major role in the nation's history congregated at Yoksam on the Rangti River, a tributary of the Tista River in the southwestern region.

In the mid-seventeenth century several of the chief monks at Yoksam, realizing the need for a formal government structure in Sikkim, established a wealthy Bhote from Gangtok as ruler of a Lamaistic theocratic state. He was Phuntso (Phunshog, Penshoo) Namgyal, a seventh-generation descendant of a Tibetan nobleman, who according to legend was helped to this position in fulfillment of a sacred prophecy. The coronation took place in 1642 at Yoksam. Shortly thereafter the newly crowned maharaja appointed twelve Bhote and twelve Lepcha as civil officials and gave them large tracts of land; they were the forebears of Sikkim's nobility, later called *kazi.* Lamaist monasteries and shrines multiplied throughout the countryside and Buddhist emigrants not only from Tibet but from eastern Nepal entered the country in increasing numbers.

Cordial relations with the Dalai Lama V in Lhasa were quickly established, developing in later years to the point that Sikkim, whose royal family customarily intermarried with Tibetan nobility, became a virtual dependency of its neighbor to the north. This relationship continued until well into the nineteenth century, during most of which time Tibet itself was under suzerainty of the Chinese Empire.

The boundaries of the country, fixed at the time of Phuntso Namgyal's coronation, extended beyond their present outlines on the east across the Chumbi Valley to the Ha Valley of Bhutan; on the south to the plains of India just below Darjeeling and Kalimpong; and on the west across the Ilam province of Nepal. During the eighteenth century, however, Sikkim was attacked first from the east, later from the west, and lost much of its territory. The Bhutanese invaders struck during the reign of the third maharaja, Chakdor (Chagdor) Namgyal, who ascended the throne in 1700. Having occupied the country and forced the maharaja to flee to Lhasa, they were eventually expelled with Tibetan help but by terms of the settlement allowed to retain the Kalimpong area.

At the close of the Anglo-Nepalese war (1814–16), the government of British India returned this territory (exclusive of Ilam) to Sikkim, an act which marked the start of effective British influence in the area. In 1839, however, Sikkim was forced to cede the Darjeeling district to the East India Company, in return for which Great Britain provided an annual subsidy to the maharaja of three thousand Indian rupees. Trade and commercial relations between the two countries shortly thereafter produced friction, aggravated in 1849 by the arbitrary imprisonment of two British citizens who had been traveling in Sikkim.

To safeguard its interests the government of British India in 1861 imposed the Treaty of Tumlong under which Sikkim was forced to recognize British authority and responsibility in its internal and foreign affairs. The annual subsidy, withheld since 1850, was restored. However, the situation was not to the liking of the maharaja, who in 1886 sent a plea for support to the Chinese resident in Lhasa. In response a small Tibetan force was dispatched to Sikkim, where it established fortifications in the southeastern region near the Jelep La (Jelep pass). These troops continued to harass the British until finally driven out in 1888.

Soon afterward China capitulated on the matter of British supremacy in Sikkim and signed a convention at Calcutta in 1890 confirming the British protectorate there; further, it agreed in 1893 to a supplementary treaty on trade and internal matters. This accomplished, the British appointed an Indian political officer and a council composed of civil officials and lamas to assist the maharaja in dealing with affairs of state. The maharaja fled, later dying in exile. He was succeeded in 1914 by his son, who succumbed in 1918, and was followed on the throne by his half-brother, Tashi Namgyal, father of the present maharaja. The annual subsidy, which had been forfeited in 1889, was resumed.

In 1947, India assumed the British protectorate, a status confirmed by a treaty of December 1950, when an Indian civil official was appointed to assist the maharaja.

THE MAHARAJA (KING)

Since emerging as a state in 1642 the country has been ruled autocratically by a king, commonly called the maharaja. His absolute powers were curtailed in 1861, when the government of British India under the Treaty of Tumlong formally established a protectorate and assumed control of foreign relations.

To check a growing spirit of resistance against their controls, the British in 1890 appointed a political officer to reside in Gangtok and assist the maharaja in administering governmental affairs through a *durbar,* or council, composed of the chief civil officials and lamas. This general restriction on the maharaja's powers continued until 1918, when Sir Tashi Namgyal, after prolonged negotiations, was vested by the British with autonomy over internal affairs.

Further changes developed soon after the government of India took over the British protectorate in 1947. In view of the threat imposed by the entry of Chinese Communist forces in Tibet in 1950, Indian authorities felt the need for even greater assurance of close cooperation from the Sikkimese government than was accorded the British. The new relationships were formalized in 1950 by the Indo-Sikkim treaty in which India undertook the responsibility for Sikkim's foreign affairs, territorial defense and strategic communications. The British political officer, responsible also for Bhutan since 1904, was replaced by an Indian incumbent. Furthermore, the Indian administration added a *dewan* who, with functions similar to those of a prime minister, acted as the maharaja's chief adviser.

Early in the 1950s the maharaja began experimenting with several types of advisory bodies. By proclamation of March 23, 1953, he established the State Council and the Executive Council, which with minor modifications continue to be the central elements of the new governmental structure. Despite the presence of various Indian officials and advisers on political, technical, and other special matters, the maharaja retained supreme authority over internal affairs.

The changes in governmental organization and procedures since 1950 have been in the nature of adjustments in response to internal political pressures and to external tensions, particularly those induced by the disputes between neighboring India and Communist China. By 1958 communal representation on the State Council had been somewhat broadened by the addition of three members, one elected by all the voters at large, one selected by the lamas from those monasteries recognized by the ruling family, and the third appointed by the maharaja.

The first general elections in Sikkimese history were held during 1952 and 1953, but the electorate was politically immature and only about 40 percent voted. In the second elections, held late in 1958, demands for a constitutional monarchy and relaxation of Indian controls became major issues. The third general elections, scheduled for 1962, were postponed a year because of the continued state of emergency which, following India's example, had been declared on November 13, 1962, after Communist China's aggressions into Assam on the eastern, and Ladakh on the western, Himalayan border of India.

The State Council had been dissolved since the expiration of its term in 1963. During the emergency it was replaced by a "People's Consultative Committee" and the Executive Council was reduced to four members. Moreover, the Indian *dewan* had, by mutual agreement, been replaced by an Indian "principal administrative officer" who headed the Consultative Committee and the Executive Council.

The maharani of Sikkim

The country's most popular leader was Maharaja Palden Thondup Namgyal, ruler after the death of his father, Sir Tashi Namgyal, on December 2, 1963. The maharaja, eleventh in the Namgyal family dynasty, was married twice. His first wife, a Tibetan, bore him three children before she died in 1957. On March 20, 1963, he married Miss Hope Cooke, an American woman. They had a son, born in February 1964. The maharaja was a devout Buddhist and played an active role in Sikkimese affairs after 1950, when he represented his country in the Indo-Sikkim treaty negotiations. He later became a leading figure in the National party. Besides having an expert knowledge of Sikkim and its neighboring countries, he was well read on world affairs and received special training in government administration and civil service procedures. A world traveler, he made repeated visits to Tibet, India, the United States, Japan, Moscow, England, the Continent, and the Soviet Union.

In September 1974, the Indian Parliament voted to make Sikkim an associate Indian state, which action absorbed it into India. The monarchy shortly thereafter (April 1975) was abolished in a referendum.

In 1975 the Sikkim lawmakers voted to abolish the monarchy and declared King Palden and his family ordinary citizens and commoners.

The former king was divorced in 1978 from Hope Cooke. He died in New York on January 29, 1982. After his funeral in Sikkim, the monks and priests (lamas) named his son from his first wife, Wangchuk, as Sikkim's chogyal, the political and spiritual head of the Sikkimese Buddhists. The appointment did nothing more than slightly annoy the Indian government, which had earlier annexed Sikkim as the twenty-second state of India.

The king of Sikkim, Palden Thondup Namgyal, right, and his queen, the former Hope Cooke, are seen in this artist's sketch. The queen was the first American-born citizen to become a foreign queen when, in 1963, she married Namgyal. She divorced the king and returned, in 1973, to live in New York City with their two children. (Sketch by Jay O'Leary)

THE ROYAL SOVEREIGNS OF THE KINGDOMS OF NEPAL, BHUTAN, AND SIKKIM

Reign	Title	Ruler	Reign	Title	Ruler
NEPAL			ca. 1061–1067	King	Pradyumnakamadeva
			ca. 1062–1065	King	Nagarjunadeva
THAKURI DYNASTY			ca. 1065–1082	King	Sankaradeva II
881–943	King	Raghavadeva	1082–1085	King	Vamadeva
923–933	King	Jayadeva	1085–1098	King	Harshadeva
933–943	King	Vikramadeva I	1098–1126	King	Sivadeva III
942–1008	King	Gunakamadeva I	1110–1125	King	Si(m)hadeva
943–962	King	Sankaradeva I	1124–1136	King	Indradeva
962–996	King	Sahadeva	1136–1140	King	Manadeva
996–997	King	Viramadeva II	1140–1147	King	Narendradeva II
997–999	King	Narendrdeva I	1147–1166	King	Anandadeva
998–1004	King	Udayadeva	1167–1175	King	Rudradeva II
1004–1009	King	Nirbhayadeva	1175–1177	King	Amritadeva
ca. 1005–1018	King	Rudradeva I	1178–1182	King	Somesvaradeva
1008–1041	King	Lakshmikamadeva I	1183–1184	King	Ratnadeva
1009–1020	King	Bhojadeva	1184–1192	King	Gunakamadeva II
ca. 1041–1061	King	Jaya(kama)deva	1192–1198	King	Lakshmikamadeva II
1043–1050	King	Bhaskaradeva	1192–1200	King	Vijayakamadeva
ca. 1050–1062	King	Bala(nta)deva			

Reign	Title	Ruler	Reign	Title	Ruler
MALLA DYNASTY					
1200–1216	King	Arimalla	1396–1428	King	Jayajyotirmalla
1216–1255	King	Abhayamalla	1428–1480	King	Jayayakshamalla
1255–1258	King	Jayadeva	ca. 1440–	King	Jayajivamalla
1258–1291	King	Jayabhimadeva	ca. 1457–1467	King	Rayamalla
1271–1274	King	Jayasimhamalla	1480–1775—In political dispute		
1274–1310	King	Anantamalla	1775–1778	King	Pratap Singh
1310–1330	King	Jayanandadeva	1778–1799	King	Rana Bahadur
1310–1326	King	Jayarudramalla	1799–1816	King	Firban Juddha Bikram Shah
1320–1334	King	Jayarimalla	1816–1847	King	Rajendra Bikram Shah
1344–1347—Interregnum			1847–1881	King	Surendra Bikram Shah
1347–1347	King	Jagatsimha	1881–1911	King	Prithvi Bir Bikram Shah
1347–1385	Queen	Rajalladevi	1911–1950	King	Tribhuvan (Tribhubana) Bir Bikram Shah
1347–1347	King	Pasumipatimalla			
1347–1361	King	Jayarajadeva	1950–1952	King	Bir Bikram
1360–1361	King	Jayarjunadeva	1952–1955	King	Tribhuvan (Tribhubana) Bir Bikram Shah
1382–1382	King	Jayasimha Rama			
1382–1395/6	King	Jayasthitimalla	1955–1972	King	Mahendra Bir Bikram Shah Deva
ca. 1392	King	Ratnajyotirdeva			
1396–ca. 1408	King	Jayadharmamalla	1975–	King	Birendra Bir Bikram Shah Deva
1396–ca. 1405	King	Jayakirttimalla			

Reign	Title	Ruler
SOVEREIGNS OF BHUTAN		
1926–1952	King	Jigme Wangchuk
1952–1972	King	Jigme Dorji Wangchuk
1972–	King	Jigme Singhye Wangchuk
SOVEREIGNS OF SIKKIM		
1642–1670	Maharaja	Phuntso Namgyal
1670–1700	Maharaja	Tensung Namgyal
1700–1717	Maharaja	Chakdor Namgyal
1717–1734	Maharaja	Gyur-me Namgyal
1734–1780	Maharaja	Penchoo Namgyal
1780–1790	Maharaja	Tenzing Namgyal
1790–1861	Maharaja	Cho-phoe Namgyal
1861–1874	Maharaja	Sikhyong Namgyal
1874–1914	Maharaja	Tho-tub Namgyal
1914–1963	Maharaja	Tashi Namgyal
1963–1975	King	Palden Thondup Namgyal

13
The Kingdom of Burma

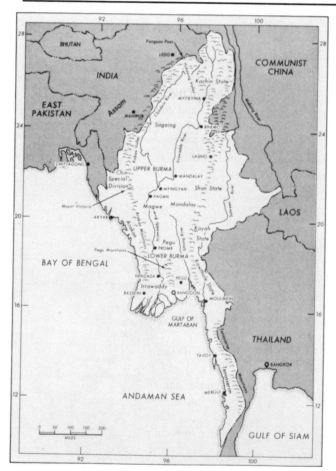

Burma in its Southeast Asia setting

The history of Burma is conditioned above all by its geography—physical, human, and economic. All around the inland frontier it is shut off from the rest of Asia by mountains clothed with thick tropical forests. Within its boundaries, fixed by mountains and the sea, Burma has been, and still is, working out the two main themes in its historical development—welding into one nation the peoples within its boundaries and adapting to the environment and pressures of the wider world outside.

There is general agreement that the modern peoples of Burma are descendants of immigrants from the north. Their racial affinities point to a northern center of dispersion. Linguistically, the contemporary inhabitants of Burma are related to peoples in China to the north, and the occurrence of migrations from the north in historic times is well-established.

The southward drive of migrants from the Asian mainland spread far beyond the limits of Burma to Indonesia and the Philippines. These migrants all have in common a Mongoloid physique and a cultural heritage distinct from that of China and India, notable especially in the comparatively high status of the women. In speech, however, they differ from one another. The earliest to find a permanent resting place in Burma, the Mons, speak an Austro-asiatic language which has some affinity with Indonesian. Almost all other indigenous languages of Burma are classified as Tibeto-Burman.

The best guide to the order of arrival of the peoples surviving to the present day is the ecological law that newcomers push their predecessors to either side, so that dispersal is an index to antiquity. On this assumption the Karens seem to have been the first of the Tibeto-Burman peoples to have arrived—perhaps about the same time as the Mons. They were in such close touch with them and with other tribes that the affinities of their speech have long been disputed. Apparently the Karens were followed by the Chins, and these in turn were split up by the pressure of the Burmans, who began to cross the border from Yunnan into Burma not much later than A.D. 500. Still later, the Thai, in their turn driven south, settled in Thailand (Siam) and spread through the eastern hills of Burma, where they are known as Shano. Last of all came the Kachins, who never penetrated beyond the extreme north of Burma.

Among all these various peoples the Burmans have long been the most prominent, and it is from them that Burma takes its name. Yet, thanks to continuing improvement of

232

communications and to regional exchanges—rice from the southern deltas, cotton and oilseeds from the drier central tract, and timber and bamboos from the hills—that are now customary, the greater part of the people speak the Burman language and most of them are at least beginning to share a common culture. They are all people of Burma and may be classed indiscriminately as Burmese, distinguishing as Burmans those who speak that language by right of birth.

EARLY HISTORY

As a result of Indian influence in Burma two considerable kingdoms—the Pyus and Mons—emerged during the first millennium of the Christian Era. The Pyu Kingdom was centered in the Irrawaddy Valley, with capitals at Prome and Pagan. East and south of this lay the Mon Kingdom, with capitals at Thaton and Pegu in the lower Sittang Valley. Farther north across the frontier of modern Burma, was the kingdom of Nanchao. Presumably, it was in order to reopen and control the trade route to India through Burma that Kolofeng, the second king of Nanchao, attacked the Mons and Pyus. In A.D. 832, when Thai tribes from Nanchao sacked the capital, the Pyu Kingdom disappeared from history.

The place of the Pyus was taken by new arrivals, the Burmans. On their way south from the Tibeto-China borders they seem to have halted for some time in Nanchao. In the ninth century they filled the political vacuum created by the Thai attacks on the Mons and Pyus, and began to emerge as a new force in the history of Burma. By the middle of the tenth century they had established their seat of power at Pagan near the confluence of the Irrawaddy and Chindwin rivers, and some of them had crossed the hills west of the river into Arakan where now, as Arakanese, they still preserve an archaic form of Burman language.

Thereafter, the history of Burma, at first glance, presents a confused struggle between rival elements aiming to hold and extend their territories. Yet, close analysis reveals a pattern. Before the days of modern communications there were two natural centers of power. A kingdom in central Burma could control both of the two main river valleys, the Irrawaddy and the Sittang; it could dispatch armies to either valley and launch a sudden attack downstream. Also, it was a meeting point for trade with India and China. All the chief capitals of Burma lay in this region—Pagan, Sagaing, Ava, Amarapura, Mandalay. The only exception was Shwebo, a little farther north.

The spread of Buddhism, however, rather than force of arms, was the main factor in Burman supremacy, although religion alone could not overcome ethnic animosities. Until some progress had been achieved in political unification the peoples of the country were not united, even in religion. One of the earliest attempts at political unification was made by a Burman hero, known today as Anawrahta (or Anorata), who made himself master of Pagan in 1044. By the end of his reign, in 1067, he had brought practically the whole of Burma under one rule and had established a dynasty that was to reign for over two centuries. He also had done much to establish Hinayana Buddhism as the dominant religion.

At this point in history, Burma seems to have been in contact with centers of both the Hinayana, the earlier, and Mahayana, the later, varieties of Buddhism. Mahayanism lent itself more readily to ritual, magic, priestcraft, and priestly domination than did Hinayanism. The Hinayana form of Buddhism, which by its disciples was called Theravada, had no elaborate ceremony or priestly hierarchy.

At the time of Anawrahta animism prevailed among the Burmans, but there existed also the Mahayanist Buddhism that had spread from Bengal to China and Tibet. During the latter part of the eighth century the rise of Lamaism in Tibet led to the attainment of supreme power by Mahayanist priests. Tibet was then in close contact with Nanchao, to which the Burmans had long been subject. Anawrahta must have known what had happened in Tibet and been a far-sighted statesman, wise enough to take warning from this example and to prefer Hinayanism or Theravadism, which did not sanction claims by monks to supernatural powers.

During the latter half of the thirteenth century, the Mongol invasion of China and the conquest of Yunnan by Kublai Khan stirred up forces that shook all the thrones in Southeast Asia. The kingdom of Pagan fell to Kublai Khan's warriors in 1287 after its ruler refused to submit to Chinese sovereignty. The Mongol emperors endeavored to govern the territories acquired in Burma through a number of puppet rulers, but these soon fell to blows among themselves. After several decades of confused warfare, the rulers of China abandoned attempts to maintain control in Burma, and two centers of power gradually emerged, one in central Burma under the Shans and the other in southern Burma under the Burmans. The period was marked by the advent of Muslim traders from Bengal toward the end of the fourteenth century and the spread of Muslim influence and power. This was the general situation in Burma when the Portuguese led by Vasco da Gama entered the seas around India in 1498.

After the Portuguese gained control of the Malay archipelago from their headquarters at the port of Malacca, Portuguese free lances sought fortune elsewhere in Southeast Asia in the service of local princes. In Toungoo, the lands in the Sittang River valley of Lower Burma, a new Burman Dynasty, dating from the beginning of the sixteenth century, enlisted the aid of the Portuguese against the Mons. The third of this Toungoo line, Bayinnaung (1551–81), extended his sway over almost the whole of Burma, driving the Shans back into the eastern hills where he compelled them to accept his suzerainty. Like Anawrahta, he reinforced his rule by religion. He was diligent in spreading Buddhism in the newly conquered states, building pagodas and monasteries, supporting monks and distributing copies of the Buddhist scriptures, while sternly suppressing the more barbarous practices of animism. His activities against the Shan princes inevitably embroiled him with their cousins in Siam, and from this time onward war between Burma and Siam was a recurrent theme in the history of both countries.

In 1635 the Toungoo capital was shifted from Pegu to Ava, a move that has often been misinterpreted by modern historians as signifying an abandonment of the dream of national kingship and a relapse into the tribal homeland. The rulers, however, realized that only from this strategic center could they enforce their rule over the whole of Burma. In Ava successive kings reigned in seclusion for more than one hundred years while the Dutch were building up their strength in Indonesia and the English and French were contesting supremacy in India. The Dutch displayed only a passing interest in the Irrawaddy route to China until they felt secure at sea against the Portuguese, as later did the English until they could traverse eastern waters without serious fear of molestation by the Dutch. The kings of Ava, however, no longer were in close touch with Pegu, where the Mons had rebelled and set up a separate kingdom in 1740. The Mons prospered, and in 1752 they sacked Ava and carried the last king of the Toungoo Dynasty into captivity.

After this catastrophe the Burmans rallied under a new leader, Alaungpaya (or Alompra), who rapidly subjugated the Mons and infused a new vigor into his own people. Under Alaungpaya and his immediate successors the Burmans devastated Siam, destroying its capital, Ayuthia. They repelled a Chinese invasion, ravaged Manipur and gained control over Assam. Here at last the country was brought into immediate contact with the outer world, for, as the triumphant Burmans were expanding toward India from the east, British rule in India was extending its frontier to meet them from the west. At the same time, the war with Napoleon and the closing of the European markets was compelling England's merchants to seek new markets in Asia for their cotton goods, the first fruits of the industrial revolution. Thus, Burma came into contact with the West on two fronts—political and economic.

The British East India Company in India made various attempts after 1795 to establish diplomatic relations with Burma. But the king, Bodawpaya (1782–1819), a son of Alaungpaya, despised the East India Company as a mere trading concern. He failed to appreciate its strength and, after a succession of victories, confident in the invincibility of his arms, he repelled the company's overtures. At the same time he excited the company's apprehension of hostile action by efforts to form alliances with independent Indian princes.

THE BRITISH CONQUEST OF BURMA

It was impossible that the social order which had evolved in Burma during its long seclusion should withstand the impact of the modern West. Confronted with a more dynamic system which was buttressed by superior technology, the Burmese had to adjust their customs and institutions to the requirements of the new environment. The rulers, knowing only their own little world and flushed with the triumph of conquest, did not realize their danger.

Petty frontier collisions led eventually to the first war with Britain in 1824, which ended in 1826 with the surrender of the two maritime provinces, Arakan and Tenasserim.

Despite this stern lesson the rulers in Burma continued to refuse the trading facilities which the West demanded and still hoped for better fortune in a new trial of strength. In 1852 a trivial incident arose out of complaints by two British ship captains of unfair treatment in the Burmese courts. Lord Dalhousie, the govenor-general of British India, dispatched an expedition to enforce redress, and before the end of the year a successful campaign was crowned by the annexation of the delta provinces, Pegu and Martaban, which corresponded approximately to the former Mon Kingdom of Pegu. The new conquest gave the British control of all of Lower Burma and cut off from the sea the kingdom of Ava.

By now the outer world was pressing on Burma from all sides, not because of its intrinsic value, but as a key to the interior of China. British manufacturers had been urging the potential importance of new markets in that region. The opening of the Suez Canal in 1869 gave a new stimulus to trade between Europe and the East. The completion in the same year of a railway across the United States pointed to increased United States commercial involvement on the seaboard of China. The French had an eye on Yunnan and were exploring access to it. The Burmese court welcomed the chance to escape the dominance of Britain and sent missions to Europe in a vain attempt to secure aid from France and other Western powers. Thus, Burma, left almost to itself for centuries, suddenly became a center of intrigue in world politics.

In domestic affairs the king, Mindon Min, did what he could toward equipping his people to meet on equal terms the outer world now at Burma's borders. He modernized the administration, improved communications, experimented in industrial enterprise, and sent young men abroad for foreign studies. His throne was insecure, however, and in 1866 the heir apparent, the prince whom he had selected to continue his reforms, was assassinated. To secure his throne and crush rebellion, he urgently needed a better and stronger army. In 1867 he granted trading concessions to the British on condition that he be allowed to import arms, but the British-controlled government in Lower Burma refused to sanction the import of even a few rifles. The immediate effect of this action was to throw Mindon more closely toward France, and his concessions to French interests exposed him more dangerously to the British. On his death in 1878 his successor, Thibaw, was left to reap the harvest.

Thibaw, an incompetent youngster raised to the throne

by a palace intrigue, had no military force to overawe rival claimants. He was at the mercy of events and of the British government. When Britain discovered the impending expansion of French interests, it took advantage of a dispute between the government of Burma and a British timber firm to send an ultimatum demanding the immediate acceptance of terms amounting to a surrender of Burmese sovereignty. Thibaw, who had neither contemplated nor prepared for war, was unable to resist. After a brief and almost bloodless campaign late in 1885, Thibaw was taken captive and exiled to India, and his territory was annexed. On January 1, 1886, Burma ceased to be an independent kingdom and became instead a province of the Indian Empire.

During the period of the monarchy, Burmese urban society was built around the royal court. Urban society was highly stratified, with persons in the upper ranks almost totally dependent upon the king's patronage for their positions. Unlike the king, the high-ranking officials did not inherit their positions. These royal favorites were engaged in rivalry among themselves, a competition that often evolved into conspiracy and revolt. The villages were essentially egalitarian and were at pains to perpetuate the great social distance between the countryside and the court. A traditional Burmese prayer includes the phrase "spare me the five evils," by which is meant flood, fire, kings, thieves, and enemies.

Under their own rulers the people of Burma had never found a solution for the twin problems of internal unification and external adjustment. Anawrahta's vision of a united national state had never been realized. The spread of Buddhism had done much to unite the various ethnic elements in a common faith but had not consolidated them into one people. Even in the homeland of Upper Burma as late as 1886, and despite Mindon's administrative reforms, the social order still embodied elements of tribal rather than territorial organization.

The final extension of British power in 1886 brought the whole country under one rule, stronger than it had ever known under its own kings. This rule implied contact between Burma and the outer world. It might seem that the two conflicting themes of Burmese history had been woven together in a harmonious resolution. This, however, required an effort of creative imagination not to be found in those days. At that time there was a general belief in economic progress as the key to welfare. British colonial policy had always claimed to be enlightened and benevolent, and in accordance with the spirit of the times, the new rulers of Burma aimed to foster economic progress. In order to effect their benevolent intentions, however, it was necessary to ensure the security of British rule.

Annexation of Upper Burma in 1886 and the consequent extension of British rule to the whole of Burma encouraged ethnic particularism. In Lower Burma direct rule along Western lines was necessary for the growth of trade, but there was little prospect of much trade in the frontier hills, and direct rule would have been too costly. The British

The last king and queen of Burma—King Thibaw Min and Queen Soupayalat. Their unsuitable conduct helped the British to decide on annexation of Burma. The king reigned from 1878 to 1885.

The royal headdress, ornamented in gold and set with precious stones, including the native star rubies, in use for centuries, is now preserved in a national museum.

British arrest King Thibaw   The royal palace in Mandalay

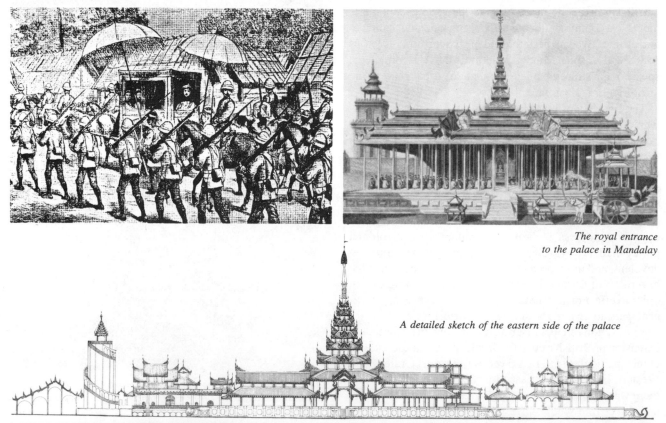

The royal entrance
to the palace in Mandalay

A detailed sketch of the eastern side of the palace

The royal white elephant served several kings of Burma.

colonial government accordingly adopted the policy of ruling the frontier tribes indirectly through their own chieftains, thereby dividing them from one another and from the people, mainly Burmans, in the lowlands. This increased the security of British rule by hindering anti-British combinations. The resulting sense of ethnic differences was strengthened by the colonial government's practice of recruiting Karens for the armed forces, together with some Chins and Kachins, and excluding Burmese and Shans.

At the same time, in the interest of economic progress, the British government threw Burma open to the world.

Anyone, European or Asian, without regard to nationality or color, could carry on business in Burma on practically equal terms with British subjects and with no tariff discrimination in favor of Britain. Burma was flooded with immigrants, especially from India and China. This multiplied the racial diversity in Burma and transformed its social structure. Under the pressure of economic forces the society took on the character of a business concern, but with a division of labor along racial lines.

Industry and commerce were developed by foreigners, to the exclusion of Burmese. The latter were employed as judges, magistrates, and police, but their economic activities were practically confined to agriculture, especially the production of rice for export. This exposed the people of the countryside to the direct impact of the world market, with the result that large areas of riceland passed into foreign hands, and the Burmese farmers became a sort of rural proletariat. Economic progress required the introduction of Western law, which frequently conflicted with traditional ties and custom. It required also the introduction of Western methods of education, which struck at the basis of the Buddhist monastic schools. As a business concern, Burma flourished with great economic progress, yet this brought the people less into contact with world civilization than with the world market.

The twentieth century saw the growth of political and cultural nationalism and its spread among the Burmese people of all classes, and independence.

THE ROYAL SOVEREIGNS OF THE KINGDOM OF BURMA

Reign	Title	Ruler	Reign	Title	Ruler
KINGS AND DYNASTIES OF BURMA			902	King	Geinda
Before 1044—Rulers of Pagan			917	King	Migadeippagyi
1044–1287—Pagan Dynasty			932	King	Geissadiya
1298–1364—Kingdom of Myinsaing and Pinya			942	King	Karawika
1315–1364		Sagaing	954	King	Pyinzala
1364–1555		Ava	967	King	Attatha
1486–1752—Toungoo Dynasty			982	King	Anuyama
1752–1885		Alaungpaya or Konbaung Dynasty	994	King	Migadeippange
1752–1760	King	Alaungpaya of Shwebo (Alompra)	1004	King	Ekkathamanta
1760–1763	King	Naungdawgyi	1016	King	Uppala
1763–1776	King	Shinbyushin	1028	King	Pontarika
1776–1781	King	Singu Min	1043–1044	King	Tissa
1782–1782	King	Maung Maung	1044–1287—Under the rule of Pagan		
1782–1819	King	Bodawpaya	1287	King	Wareru
1819–1837	King	Bagyidaw	1306(?)	King	Hkun Law, brother
1827–1846	King	Swebo Min	1310	King	Saw O, nephew
1847–1853	King	Pagan Min	1324	King	Saw Zein, brother
1853–1878	King	Mindon Min	1331	King	Zein Pun, usurper
1878–1885	King	Thibaw Min (Theebaw)	1331	King	Saw E Gan Gaung, nephew of Saw Zein
1886—Burma became a province of British India			1331	King	Binnya E Law, son of Hkun Law
			1353	King	Binnya U, son
			1385	King	Razadarit, son
MON KINGDOM OF PEGU (HANTHAWADDY)			1423	King	Binnya Dammayaza, son
Territory comprised part of present-day southeastern Burma and west-central Thailand, with the capital at Pegu.			1426	King	Binnya Ran I, brother
			1446	King	Binnya Waru, nephew
			1450	King	Binnya Kyan, cousin
825	King	Thamala, legendary founder of Pegu	1453	King	Mawdaw, cousin
837	King	Wimala, brother	1453	King	Shin Sawbu, daughter of Razadarit
854	King	Atha, nephew	1472	King	Dammazedi, son-in-law
861	King	Areindama	1492	King	Binnya Ran II, son
885		A monk	1526–1539	King	Takayutpi, son, driven out by Burmese

Reign	Title	Ruler
1539–1550—First Burmese occupation		
1550	King	Smim Sawhtut, minor prince of the old dynasty, leader of revolt against Burmese, eliminated by Smim Htaw
1551	King	Smim Htaw, son of Binnya Ran II, defeated and killed by the Burmese king Bayinnaung
1551–1740—Second Burmese occupation		
1740	King	Smim Htaw Buddhaketi, son of a Burmese governor of Pagan, leader of revolt against Burmese, exiled
1747–1757	King	Binnya Dala, father-in-law and chief minister (murdered) Rangoon 1773) d.
1757		Pegu captured by Bumese and Mon independence finally ended

KINGDOM OF ARAKAN

Territory comprised part of present-day southwestern Burma.

LAUNGGYET DYNASTY

Reign	Title	Ruler
1237	King	Alawmahpyu, son
1243	King	Yazathugyi, son
1246	King	Sawlu, son
1251	King	Ossanagyi, son
1260	King	Sawmungyi, son
1268	King	Nankyagyi, son
1272	King	Minbilu, son
1276	King	Sithabin, usurper
1279	King	Minhti, son of Minbilu*
1374–1385—Burmese nominees of the blood		
1385	King	Ossanange
1387	King	Thiwarit, brother
1390	King	Thinhse, brother
1394	King	Razathu, son (for first time)
1395	King	Sithabin, usurper
1397	King	Myinhsainggyi, usurper
1397	King	Razathu (for second time)
1401–1404	King	Theinhkathu, brother

MROHAUNG DYNASTY

Reign	Title	Ruler
1404	King	Narameikhla (or Minsawmun), son of Razathu
1434	King	Ali Khan, brother
1459	King	Basawpyu (or Kalima Shah), son, murdered
1482	King	Dawlya, son
1492	King	Basawnyo, uncle
1494	King	Yanaung, son of Dawlya
1494	King	Salingathu, uncle on mother's side
1501	King	Minyaza, son
1523	King	Kasabadi, son

*Traditionally assigned a reign of one-hundred six years.

Reign	Title	Ruler
1525	King	Minsaw O, brother of Salingathu
1525	King	Thatasa, son of Dawlya
1531	King	Minbin, son of Minyaza (d. 1553)
1551	King	Dikha, son
1555	King	Sawhla, son
1564	King	Minsetya, brother
1571	King	Minpalaung, son of Minbin
1593	King	Minyazagyi, son
1612	King	Minhkamaung, son
1622	King	Thirthudamma, son, murdered
1638	King	Minsani, son
1638	King	Narapatigyi, great-grandson of Thatasa, lover of Thirithudamma's chief queen
1645	King	Thado, nephew
1652	King	Sandathudamma, son
1684	King	Thirithuriya, son, murdered

Reign	Title	Ruler
1685	King	Waradhammaraza, brother, placed on throne by the Moghuls, deposed
1692	King	Munithudhammaraza, brother, murdered
1694	King	Sandathuriyadhamma, brother
1696	King	Nawrahtazaw, son
1696	King	Mayokpiya I, usurper
1697	King	Kalamandat, usurper
1698	King	Naradipati, son of Sandathuriyadhamma
1700	King	Sandawimala, grandson of Thado
1706	King	Sandathuriya, grandson of Sandathudamma
1710	King	Sandawizaya I (formerly Maha Danda Bo), usurper, murdered
1731	King	Naradipati II, son
1735	King	Narapawara, usurper
1737	King	Sandawizaya II, cousin
1737	King	Katya, usurper
1737	King	Madarit, brother of Sandawizaya II
1742	King	Nara-apaya, uncle
1761	King	Thirithu, son
1761	King	Sandapavama, brother
1764	King	Apaya, brother-in-law
1773	King	Sandathumana, brother-in-law
1777	King	Sandawinala, usurper
1777	King	Sandathaditha
1782–1785	King	Thamada, deposed
1785—Burmese conquest		

KINGDOM OF PAGAN

Territory comprised part of present-day southern Burma, with the capital at Pagan.

Reign	Title	Ruler
1044	King	Anawrahta
1077	King	Sawlu, son, murdered
1084	King	Kyanzittha, brother
1113	King	Alaungsithu, grandson
1167	King	Narathu, son, killed
1170	King	Naratheinhka, son
1173	King	Narapatisithu, brother
1210	King	Nantonmya (or Htilominlo), son
1234	King	Kyaswa, son
1250	King	Uzana, son
1254	King	Narathihapate (called *Tarokpyemin*, i.e. "the king who ran away from the Chinese"), son, defeated by the Mongols at the battle of Ngasaunggyan 1277, fled from Pagan during the Mongol invasion of 1283, murdered
1287	King	Kyawswa, son, Mongol vassal, murdered by the Shan chiefs
1298	King	Sawhnit, illegitimate son, placed on throne by the Shan chiefs
1325	King	Uzana, son, ruled at Pinya (see Shan kingdom of Myinsaing and Pinya)

SHAN KINGDOM OF MYINSAING AND PINYA

Territory comprised part of present-day northern Burma, with the capital initially at Myinsaing and later at Pinya.

Reign	Title	Ruler
1298	King	Athinhkaya, Yazathinkyan, and Thihathu, the three Shan brothers; the last surviving brother, Thihathu, transferred his capital from Myinsaing to Pinya 1312
1324	King	Uzana (see Kingdom of Pagan)
1343	King	Ngashishin, half-brother
1350	King	Kyawswange, son

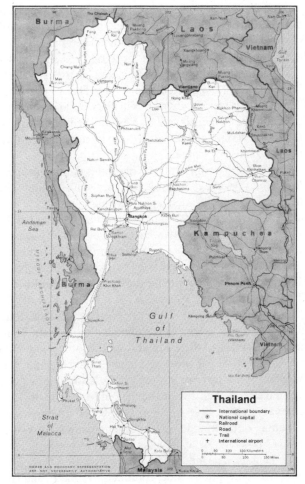

14
The Dynasties and Kingdom of Thailand (Siam)

A map of Thailand showing the geographic details of the country within the setting of southeast Asia

The Thai were preceded by other ethnic groups in migrating to Thailand. Some of the earlier groups established sophisticated courts that were centers of Southeast Asian art and culture three or more centuries before the Thai's coming. The Thai set up their first kingdoms in Thailand during the thirteenth century and soon became the overwhelmingly dominant group.

The first Thai state within the borders of modern Thailand was founded in the thirteenth century and had its capital at Sukhothai in the north. During the next five hundred years Sukhothai, and the kingdom of Ayuthia that succeeded it, struggled against neighboring states in Southeast Asia to maintain and expand sovereignty. Wars were fought against other Thai states, against the Khmer of Cambodia, against the Malays in the south and, most importantly, against Burma.

The destruction of Ayuthia by the Burmese in 1767 was soon countered by military victories of the Thai, which resulted in the unification of all of Thailand and parts of what are now neighboring countries under the sovereignty of a new dynasty in Bangkok in 1782. The new Chakri Dynasty retained absolute rule of the country (then known as Siam) until 1932.

Certain traits have been characteristic of the country's society and history through the centuries. From the time of Nanchao, the earliest known Thai state (in Yunnan, China), the Thai have been primarily rice cultivators, have believed in a type of Buddhism that does not exclude certain animistic practices, have been predominantly rural in residence, and have been willing to leave government in the hands of an elite educated to rule. Although the kings had virtually absolute power over their subjects from the fourteenth to the early twentieth centuries, the people have suffered little from oppression. There have been no instances of class warfare or mass revolt.

Wars with neighboring states have been frequent. The result has been that Thailand frequently has expanded and contracted in size as the result of changes in the strength of the kingdom and that of its neighbors. The territory included within the 1980 borders seldom has been subject to foreign rule, and then only for brief periods. The country has, however, at all times been heavily influenced by foreign cultures. The people have borrowed consciously and liberally those foreign ideas and techniques that they found suitable.

Takeover by one of the Western powers during the nineteenth-century period of colonial expansion was avoided by the policies of two extraordinarily able Thai kings who reigned between 1851 and 1910. The modernization of Thailand's governmental, legal, and social institutions was begun by these kings. These royal initiatives enabled the kingdom to command the respect of the Western powers without the conservative Thai society being unduly disrupted. The skillful diplomacy of the kings preserved independence at a time when colonial powers dominated the surrounding area.

In 1932 members of a small Western-educated group that had recently developed staged a successful coup d'etat. The result of this coup was that the king was transformed from an absolute to a constitutional monarch. Power shifted from the throne to a cabinet composed of Western-educated leaders of various factions in the armed and civil services. Although there have been numerous changes of government since 1932, through coups d'etat and new constitutions, power has remained with the cabinet, and elections and political parties have played a relatively minor role.

Under the various post–World War II regimes, Thailand has been allied unequivocally with the non-Communist world. Thailand has also been actively involved in promoting regional cooperation with non-Communist neighbors and was an active supporter of United States policies in Southeast Asia during the Vietnam War period.

EARLY SETTLEMENT

Thailand lies along the path of migration out of southern China that most scholars now believe resulted, over the course of thousands of years, in the peopling of Southeast Asia and the southwest Pacific. Ethnic groups descended from some of the earliest migrants can be found in Thailand. For example, the Semang Negritos continue an aboriginal way of life in the jungles near the Malaysian border. Tools have been found in abundance that indicate the existence of a Paleolithic culture in Thailand. A corpse from the Mesolithic period and many corpses from the Neolithic period also have been found.

Traces of the existence of a later group of migrants who probably appeared between 1500 B.C. and A.D. 300 include ten magnificent bronze objects, shaped like large kettle-drums, that have been unearthed in various parts of the country. Each drum has the same distinctive ornamentation that connects it stylistically to the archaeological site of Dong-son in North Vietnam, where sizable remains of this metalworking culture were first discovered.

The Dong-son culture was carried south by migrants, possibly of Malay stock, who left a trail of these drums from Indochina, down the Chao Phraya valley, the length of the Malay Peninsula, and out to the eastern islands of Indonesia. The drums found in Thailand are thought to date from the first or second century B.C. A similar drum, found in neighboring Malaysia, however, was radiocarbon-tested in 1965, with results indicating a date several centuries earlier.

THAI MIGRATION INTO SOUTHEAST ASIA

The Thai, one of the ethnic groups dwelling south of the Yangtze River, established the kingdom of Nanchao (Mandarin Chinese for "south of the clouds") in northwest Yunnan, possibly as early as the middle of the seventh century A.D. Successfully resisting Chinese efforts at conquest in the eighth century, Nanchao slowly spread its domain southward and eastward. By the ninth century it had invaded Tonkin in what is now North Vietnam.

Nanchao fell to Mongol armies in 1253 when Kublai Khan was conquering China. Considerably before Nanchao's fall, however, bands of Thais had already moved into the Shan states of Burma and into parts of North Vietnam, Laos, and northern Thailand. The Thai of Burma later came to be called Shans; those of Laos were called Lao; and those of Vietnam were called Thai *Dam* (Black Thai) and Thai *Deng* (Red Thai). The Thai of the Chao Phraya valley were known to outsiders as Siamese until 1939. Thai settlements were also established eventually as far west as Assam and as far east as Hainan Island off the southeast coast of China.

By the early twelfth century Thai states dotted the upper Chao Phraya valley, and by the thirteenth century the stream of Thai migration into the valley had become a flood, released by the Mongol conquest of Nanchao in the north and the simultaneous weakening of Khmer power in the south. The Khmer lost control over the old Mon kingdom of Dvaravati in Lavo to the Thai, and the independent Mon state of Haripunjaya in the north fell to another band of Thai conquerors.

In 1238 a powerful Thai warrior-chief named Phra Ruang defeated the Khmer at Sukhothai in northern Thailand and established there a mighty and vigorous, although short-lived, Thai kingdom. Another Thai kingdom was founded shortly thereafter by a Thai warrior-chief named Mangrai after he had conquered the old Mon state of Haripunjaya. In about 1296 Mangrai established Chiengmai as the capital of his kingdom. The Chiengmai Kingdom was never as powerful or as large as the Sukhothai Kingdom, but it maintained its independence as a separate Thai polity, with brief interruptions under Ayuthian, Burmese, and Lao control, until the eighteenth century. Conquered by forces sent by King Taksin in 1775, Chiengmai was absorbed by the Bangkok Kingdom in 1782.

SUKHOTHAI, 1253–1378

The defeat of the Khmer that led to the founding of Sukhothai was followed by the gradual removal of Khmer control from all of modern Thailand, including the peninsular area. Sukhothai is regarded by the Thai as having paved the way for the creation of the kingdoms at Ayuthia and Bangkok that resulted, by the eighteenth century, in the formation of the modern state of Thailand.

Although the first king of Sukhothai, Phra Ruang (whose name means glorious prince), is a great hero celebrated in Thai legend and credited with superhuman powers, the Sukhothai king of whom the fullest historical record survives is the third of the dynasty, King Ramkemhaeng (Rama the Great), who reigned from 1275 to 1317.

Chinese records indicate that during Ramkemhaeng's reign diplomatic relations were established between Sukhothai and China. From then until the mid-nineteenth century the Thai kings sent frequent missions to the Chinese emperors, acknowledging China's overlordship over the kingdom of the Thai. During Ramakemhaeng's reign Chinese artisans were imported to establish the famous pottery works at Sawankhalok, some twenty-five miles north of Sukhothai. The king also maintained friendly relations with other Thai kings in the area, including Mangrai, king of Chiengmai.

Ramkemhaeng was a noted warrior before he came to the throne, and his success in war continued after he became king, with the result that Sukhothai's sovereignty was extended over parts of Laos, Burma, and the Malay Peninsula. His cultural contributions to the kingdom were also great. After conquering the Theravada Buddhist kingdom of Nakhon Si Thammarat, a peninsular state on the site of ancient Tambrálinga, he established its chief abbot as the chief prelate of the Sukhothai Kingdom and declared Theravada Buddhism the official religion. He is credited by a contemporary inscription (dated 1292) with having created the first Thai alphabet, adapting Mon and Khmer scripts, derived in turn from a south Indian script, to his purpose.

During Ramkemhaeng's reign the kingship was the font of paternal justice and magnanimity. Accessible to hear the complaints of any subject who would ring the bell at the palace gate, King Ramkemhaeng saw his role as that of moral leader, supreme magistrate, and protector of his subjects. Although his power was absolute, he chose not to exert it over the economy of his country. The 1292 inscription boasts of the latitude given the Thai by their king: "The lord of the country levies no tolls on his subjects. . . . Whoever desires to trade elephants, does so; whoever desires to trade horses, does so; whoever desires to trade silver and gold, does so."

The kingdom of Sukhothai weakened after Ramkemhaeng's death, and in 1378 it was absorbed into the new southern kingdom established in 1350 by a prince from Uthong at Ayuthia, forty miles north of Bangkok. Sukhothai continued to struggle against its new Thai overlords during the first century of the new regime.

AYUTHIA, 1350–1767

The new capital was established on an island in the middle of the Chao Phraya River. Its location in the midst of a fertile agricultural area accessible to Angkor, the Gulf of Thailand, and the southern peninsula was to prove advantageous. It helped Ayuthia maintain its existence through numerous wars during the four-hundred-year period that it was the capital of the Thai Kingdom.

The founder of Ayuthia took the kingly name of Rama Thibodi I and ruled for two decades until 1369. During his reign the borders of the Thai Kingdom, which had shrunk under Sukhothai's last two kings, stretched again, southward to include peninsular Malaya and Burma and eastward into Khmer territory. Attempts were also made to take and keep Angkor, the Khmer capital (near modern Siem Reap) famous for the colossal Hindu-Buddhist monuments of Angkor Wat. These efforts were not immediately successful because of frequent rebellions of Sukhothai, abetted by independent Chiengmai, that diverted Rama Thibodi's attention from the eastern campaign.

Although the Khmer continually lost ground to Rama Thibodi I, they exercised a great cultural influence upon his kingdom. From the Khmer the Thai court adopted the elaborate court etiquette, language, and politicoreligious regalia and rituals that had made the Khmer ruler not merely the chief magistrate and father of his people but a *devaraja* (Sanskrit for divine king), whose powers were more than mortal, who in his person provided the essential link between the kingdom and the sacred order of the universe. As a result of the acquisition of these semidivine attributes from the Khmer tradition, the Thai monarch in the Ayuthia period became sacred and remote behind a wall of taboos and sumptuary rituals and was no longer accessible to his subjects as the Sukhothai kings had been.

In Rama Thibodi's reign the government services became more functionally organized than they had been during the Sukhothai era. Four great offices of state were created: the ministry of Wieng (town or city, also country or land), which was, in effect, in charge of the internal affairs of the kingdom; the ministry of Klang (the treasury); the ministry of Wang (the king's household); and the ministry of Na (agriculture). The king also examined the laws and customs of the Thai from the time of Nanchao to his own day, discarded some, and compiled the remainder into a legal code for his kingdom.

In 1370, the year after Rama Thibodi I died, an official emissary arrived in Ayuthia from the Ming emperor. This visit led to the prompt recognition of Ayuthia as the legitimate successor to China's former vassal, Sukhothai. This recognition by the major power in Asia was worth the cost in tribute and nominal vassalage of the Thai kingdom to the Chinese throne.

In the early fifteenth century, shortly after the great Malay trading port of Malacca was founded on the western coast of the Malay Peninsula, attempts were made by Malacca's ruler to bypass the Thai throne, which claimed sovereignty over the entire Malay Peninsula, and to establish direct relations as a vassal of China. The Thai, however, insisted on tribute from Malacca and, when it was refused, sent armed forces against the new port by land and sea between 1440 and 1460.

The court of Malacca had been converted to Islam by 1409. Malacca resisted the Thai invasions, and Islam served thereafter as a symbol of Malay solidarity against the Thai. This sentiment spread with Islam to the northernmost Malay states in the isthmian region of southern Thailand.

Throughout the fifteenth century Ayuthia's wars with neighboring Thai states continued, first with Sukhothai, which lost its last rebellion against Ayuthia in 1438, and then with Sukhothai's former ally, the northern Thai kingdom of Chiengmai. A decisive victory for Ayuthia against the Khmer Empire, which had waned as Ayuthia waxed, came in 1431 when the Ayuthian king, Baromaraja II, so devastated Angkor that the Khmer abandoned it as a capital.

By the mid-fifteenth century, in their rivalry with the Malay states, which were at the time the bases for trade between the West and the Far East, the Thai had lost the battle to make a vassal of Malacca. Malacca controlled the trade through the Strait of Malacca, but Ayuthia continued to control the substantial trade on the isthmus. The isthmian ports were attracting Chinese traders who were seeking at the source the various Southeast Asian specialty goods that had been introduced to the Chinese court by tribute missions and were in growing demand in the luxury markets of China.

The greatest ruler of the Ayuthia Dynasty during the fifteenth century was King Trailok (1448–88). His contributions to Thai governmental institutions were numerous and enduring. One of his innovations was the creation of the position of *uparaja* (deputy king or heir apparent) as part of an attempt to prevent the violent scrambles for the kingship that have marred earlier reigns of the dynasty. Another enduring institution that was reorganized during King Trailok's reign was the *sakdi na* system of granting irrigated ricefields to persons holding positions in the government. The granting of ricefields to persons of rank predated his reign, but King Trailok established for the first time definite allotments for each title. For example, the governor of a first-class town, who held the title of Chao Phraya, could have four thousand acres, and the acreage of other officials tapered off according to rank; the ordinary free farmer was entitled to ten acres.

During the reign of Rama Tibodi II (1491–1529), Ayuthia received its first European envoys. Alfonso de Albuquerque, viceroy of Portuguese India, conquered Malacca in 1511 and in the same year sent an envoy to Ayuthia. This envoy was probably the first European to visit the country. A treaty between Ayuthia and Portugal was concluded in 1516 granting the Portuguese permission to live and trade in the kingdom. Two Dominican missionaries from Malacca arrived in 1555. In the seventeenth century Portuguese influence declined as that of the Dutch, English, and French grew.

The royal silver (twenty-fifth) wedding anniversary of King Bhumibol Adulyadej and Queen Sirikit commemorated on a 1975 stamp

This 1965 stamp commemorates the fifteenth wedding anniversary of King Bhumibol Adulyadej and Queen Sirikit.

Foreigners were cordially received, and missions were sent from Ayuthia to some European capitals. The Thai court skillfully played off one power against another—the French against the British and the Dutch against the French—thus avoiding excessive influence by any single foreign power. Pretexts for European takeovers were avoided by promptly granting the European demands for extraterritorial rights. The first such grant was given to the Dutch East India Company, making its employees subject only to Dutch courts.

Toward the end of the reign of King Narai (1657–88), the attitude toward Westerners became less tolerant. In their competition for special advantage, the trading companies had not hesitated to intervene in domestic politics, and fear of European military power (that of the French in particular) was growing.

In his conduct of foreign relations, King Narai was greatly influenced by a Greek adventurer, Constantine Phaulkon, who was one of his more powerful advisers. Phaulkon was a senior officer in the ministry of Klang (treasury), which was also responsible for the conduct of foreign relations. Through Phaulkon, French traders and Jesuit priests were able to enlarge their influence in the kingdom, but they aroused the suspicions and resentment of the Thai aristocracy and Buddhist clergy. The situation came to a crisis in 1688 when King Narai fell ill. Phaulkon, isolated from his royal patron, was arrested by his enemies and put to death. Ruthless persecution of Westerners followed. Only a few Dutch and Portuguese remained after this incident. For nearly a century and a half thereafter the Thai cut themselves off from the West.

Throughout the Ayuthia era relations with China continued, in the form of tribute missions to the Chinese throne once every five to ten years, and the number of Chinese living and working in Thailand grew. In the early sixteenth century a Chinese source recounts that Ayuthia already had "a street where the Chinese live," and sixteenth-century Portuguese accounts state that Chinese merchants were found everywhere the Portuguese went. The takeover of Malacca by the Portuguese had led to a shift of indigenous Asian trade away from that port to the isthmian town of

Pattani, a Malay city-state that had been under Thai domination for centuries. In the early seventeenth century a Chinese wrote of Ayuthia that "the inhabitants accept the Chinese very cordially, much better than do the natives of other countries; therefore Siam is a country that is really friendly to the Chinese."

Shortly after this was written, however, King Prasat-Tong in 1630 introduced royal trade monopolies. All traders thereafter had to receive permits from the king. Tin and lead mined in the kingdom had to be delivered to the king's warehouse in Ayuthia before it could be exported. This setback to the Chinese business community in Thailand was soon overcome as Chinese traders found employment as hired factors of the royal monopolies in trade and industry.

After the revulsion against the Europeans in 1688 by the Thai court, the Chinese fell heir to the European trade with Ayuthia. A similar revulsion against the Japanese traders in the 1630s had resulted in the Chinese inheritance of the substantial trade with Japan. Chinese came to the country in increasing numbers throughout the sixteenth and seventeenth centuries, and their favorable position as compared to other foreigners continued to the end of the Ayuthia era in the mid-eighteenth century.

Frequent wars with neighboring states plagued Ayuthia from its earliest reigns to its end. The most dangerous enemy was Burma, which subjugated the Thai Kingdom for a fifteen-year period in the sixteenth century. In 1584 the Thai regained their independence, led by Thailand's greatest military hero, Prince (later King) Naresuan, who had been absent from Ayuthia at the time of the Burmese conquest. During King Naresuan's reign (1590–1605) the Thai Kingdom came to include Chiengmai, much of modern Cambodia, and southern and peninsular Burma. Most of these territorial gains, however, were lost during subsequent reigns.

The Laotian kingdom of Lan Xang broke up after 1694 into three segments. Two of these, Luang Prabang in the north and Champassak in the south, became nominal vassals to Ayuthia.

In the eighteenth century the Burmese returned to the Thai Kingdom in strength. In 1767 they sacked and destroyed Ayuthia, bringing to a close the era that bears its name.

EARLY BANGKOK PERIOD, 1767–1851

As had been the case after the earlier conquest by Burma in the sixteenth century, the Thai made a rapid recovery under a new military leader called Phya Taksin, a man of mixed Thai-Chinese extraction. In 1767, after the fall of Ayuthia, Taksin established a new capital in Thon Buri across the river from modern Bangkok and was proclaimed king that year. By 1776 King Taksin had reunited the Thai Kingdom, which had fragmented into small states after Ayuthia was destroyed, and had also conquered Chiengmai.

King Bhumibol Adulyadej's fiftieth birthday anniversary is commemorated on this stamp.

King Taksin eventually developed delusions of personal divinity and, as a result, his ministers had him executed in what they believed were the interests of the state. His accomplishments, however, won him a secure place among Thailand's national heroes.

CHAKRI DYNASTY FOUNDED

King Taksin was succeeded by General Chakri, also of mixed Thai-Chinese extraction, who had taken a leading part in the struggle against Burma. As Rama I (1782–1809), he founded the present dynasty of Thailand and established its capital, Bangkok, at its modern-day site.

FOREIGN RELATIONS

During the reign of Rama I the Thai successfully resisted repeated invasions by Burma. They were unsuccessful in recovering the Burmese states of Tenasserim but were able to expand their control over parts of Indochina. In 1795 the Thai extracted five Cambodian provinces, including Battambang, Siem Reap (Angkor), and parts of Khorat, from the Cambodian king in payment for earlier support. After 1802 the Cambodian ruler acknowledged both the Thai and the Vietnamese as overlords; the Laotian kingdom of Vientiane had done the same since 1778.

The expansionist tendencies of the new Chakri Dynasty caused anxiety among some of the Thai throne's nominal vassals on the Malay Peninsula. In 1786 the sultan of Kedah, a Malay vassal whose holdings included modern Perlis, Kedah, Penang Island, and Province Wellesley in Malaysia, ceded Penang Island to the British. Penang Island became the first British acquisition along the Malay Peninsula. The sultan's reason for ceding the territory was his hope, later proved to have been unfounded, that the British would help Kedah protect itself from anticipated Thai attempts to bind the state closer to Bangkok.

Under Rama II (1809–24) an invasion of Kedah by Thai forces under the command of the raja of Ligor (as the Malays called Bangkok's viceroy at Nakhon Si Thammarat) took place in 1821. The sultan of Kedah fled to Penang Island, where the British had built a commercial center and fort. Later that year the British sent a mission headed by John Crawford to see if the sultan of Kedah could be restored to his throne and also to attempt to negotiate a trade agreement with the Thai king. In neither effort was Crawford successful, although a few Western traders, including one Englishman named Hunter, had been permitted to live in Bangkok after 1818.

Under Rama III (1824–51) more substantive relations

with Western powers were established. In 1824 the first Anglo-Burmese war broke out. The war ended two years later with the cession by the Burmese of Arakan (along the northeast coast of the Bay of Bengal) and Tenasserim to Great Britain. A stronger power thus gained provinces that the Thai and Burmese had disputed for centuries.

Much of Rama III's reign was devoted to maintaining Bangkok's authority in Indochina against rebellions in Laos and Vietnamese incursions into Cambodia. In this he was successful, but the outermost limits of Thai authority had been reached. The expansionism of the Chakri Dynasty had been halted in all directions by the end of Rama III's reign.

After 1840 the king sought more revenue from his foreign trade monopoly. More Chinese tax collectors were employed, and the government increased the charges and restrictions upon foreign traders. The king also ordered the construction of a number of trading ships, for royal use, that would be duty-free. The number of British and other Western ships visiting Bangkok was greatly reduced. Efforts by British and other Westerners in the last years of Rama III's reign to get these restrictions removed met with determined resistance at the Thai court.

POLITICAL AND SOCIAL CONDITIONS

The first three Chakri kings, by succeeding each other without bloodshed, brought the kingdom a degree of political stability that had been lacking in the Ayuthia period. There was, however, no automatic rule governing succession to the throne. If no *uparaja* was alive at the time of the king's death—and this was frequently the case—the choice of the succeeding monarch from among the royal family was left to the Senabodi, the council of senior ministers, princes, and prelates that assembled at the death of a reigning monarch.

The power of the kings, although in theory absolute, was in practice limited by the looseness of civil administration. Provincial officials were independent of the central trea-

Rama III, King Nang Klao, was the eldest son of King Rama II but not the son of a royal mother. However, he had the political backing necessary to take the throne. The favorite of the king, Prince Maha Mongkut, the eldest son of a royal mother, had to wait his turn. The reign of Rama III, on the whole, was not an impressive one.

sury. The most senior ministerial positions in the central government, those of minister of defense, minister of interior, and minister of finance and foreign affairs, had become more or less inherited positions dominated by an influential family, the Bunnags, who had been connected by marriage with Rama I, founder of the Chakri Dynasty. (Connections through marriage were often used by the Thai kings as the means of maintaining alliances with powerful families. The king's wives, as a result of this policy, usually numbered in the dozens.)

By the early nineteenth century approximately one-third of the people of the kingdom were slaves. There were also prisoners of war who served as slave troops of the king. They usually lived separate from the Thai in their own ethnic enclaves, with a few less privileges than Thai freemen, except for their military obligation to the throne.

Aside from the enclaves of alien prisoner-slaves, the Chinese were the only large alien group resident in the kingdom. Their control of foreign trade and of the commercial operations of the king was such that Bangkok, the center of commerce, gave the appearance of a Chinese city. China was the major trading partner with the Thai crown during the early Chakri period. Between 1782 and 1854, the last year of royal monopoly of trade, there were thirty-five tribute missions sent to China. The tribute missions, often three hundred men strong, were permitted to sell goods in China duty-free and were permitted to buy whatever they wanted, except for a few strategic goods. Such generous trading privileges in China were not granted to the Europeans until the 1840s.

King Rama I (Buddha Yot Fa) was best known as the Siamese ruler who moved the capital from Ayuthia to Bangkok. Also, during his reign, Siam had control over Cambodia due to his expertise in the battlefield.

SIAM MODERNIZED, 1851–1925

KING MONGKUT AND THE MISSIONARIES

Rama IV, or Chom Kloa, known as King Mongkut (1851–68), is the Thai monarch best known in the West as a result of reportedly colored and distorted accounts of life at his court written by Anna Leonowens, a widowed lady employed by King Mongkut between the years 1862 and 1867 to teach English to the royal family. Incidents from Mrs. Leonowens's books were subsequently fictionalized and romanticized by Margaret Landon in a 1944 novel, *Anna and the King of Siam*, from which the popular musical play and film *The King and I* were derived. The Thai have continued to find it unfortunate that King Mongkut should be popularly portrayed in front of Western audiences as a sensual and childish man leaning on the supposed wisdom of Anna Leonowens when the facts are at considerable variance.

An ascetic who spent most of his adult life as chief abbot of a Buddhist monastery, King Mongkut knew more of Western civilization and languages than any Oriental monarch of his day. His knowledge of the West dated in fact from long before he took the throne.

King Mongkut had many Western mentors and friends, especially among the missionaries that his elder half-brother, King Rama III, permitted into the country after 1828. During his twenty-seven years as a monk, Mongkut's chief interest was in establishing a reform movement to purify Thai Buddhist practice. During these years the future king also studied with several Christian missionaries, ex-

King Mongkut (Rama IV) depicted in his older age on a postage stamp

tracting what he thought would be useful from Western thought and technology without absorbing the accompanying religious doctrines. He is alleged to have said, "What you [Christians] teach us to do is admirable, but what you teach us to believe is foolish." From a French Catholic bishop the future king learned Latin and science; from a Protestant missionary from the United States, he learned English and science. Another Protestant missionary from the United States, Dan B. Bradley, became Mongkut's personal physician, lifelong friend, and intellectual adversary.

The contributions of the missionaries to the intellectual development and public welfare of the Thai court and kingdom were many, although their converts were few. Bradley, the most famous of the missionaries, was personally responsible for numerous contributions. He introduced smallpox vaccinations and vaccinated many thousands of Thai, including the king and royal family. He performed the first surgical operation in the kingdom and many others to follow, all without charge. He had brought a Thai-lettered printing press with him when he came in 1835 and in 1844 produced the first Thai newspaper, the *Bangkok Recorder*. He introduced modern obstetrical practices into the royal harem and was on call day and night to advise the king on various matters.

The beginnings of modern education are found in the efforts of King Mongkut and King Chula Chom Klao, called Chulalongkorn (1869–1910), to train people to deal with Western nations and to better perform government tasks. Western teachers were engaged to teach officials, and English tutors were appointed for the royal children. Traditionally the bulk of formal education was provided by the Buddhist monks in the *wat* (Buddhist temple complex) schools.

King Mongkut's experience with Westerners greatly affected his policies after he assumed the throne in 1851. The year before Mongkut was chosen king, Rama III had spurned requests by British and United States diplomats for more generous trade privileges, such as the Western powers were then enjoying in China. When Mongkut came to the throne his superior knowledge concerning the power and motives of the Westerners led him to take a more conciliatory policy and thus avoid the humiliations to his kingdom that China had recently undergone.

The Chinese turned from foreign trade and the operation of various royal monopolies and foreign trade tax collection to the sale and distribution of opium and domestic tax collection. Wars were fought between rival Chinese secret societies for the tax concessions.

Rama IV, King Mongkut (Chom Klao), in royal dress and wearing the crown of Siam. He was the subject of the best-seller book, movie, and stage play, Anna and the King of Siam. *King Mongkut was the forty-third child of Rama II. He learned a number of foreign languages and became the first ruler of Siam to bring the country out of its medieval ways.*

King Mongkut early in his reign

The summer palace was a frequent hideaway for King Mongkut and Queen Debserin.

The King (Mongkut) designed a magnificent royal throne for himself and kings to follow.

The royal barge of King Mongkut

Queen Debserin and King Mongkut

A family portrait of Rama V. Left to right: *Prince Asdang, King Chulalongkorn, Crown Prince Vajiravudh, Queen Saowabha, Prince Prajadhipok, Prince Chakrabongse, and Prince Chutadhuj.*

Toward the end of his reign, King Mongkut was obliged to apply his conciliatory policy toward Western powers to the demands for territorial concessions. In 1867 he relinquished to France Siam's claim to the remainder of Cambodia in exchange for French recognition of Thai sovereignty over two western Cambodian provinces, Battambang and Siem Reap.

KING CHULALONGKORN'S REFORMS

At the time of King Mongkut's death in 1868 there was no *uparaja*. The second king, Mongkut's younger brother, had died in 1866, and Mongkut's eldest son, Chula Chom Klao, or Chulalongkorn, was only fifteen. The Senabodi, nevertheless, chose the young prince to succeed his father and, until his majority, appointed as regent a close friend and adviser of King Mongkut and member of the powerful Bunnag family, Chao Phraya Sri Suriyawongse. Sri Suriyawongse had been a friend and patron of the missionaries

and was able to continue the trend toward Westernization of the kingdom. During the regency period the young king traveled to Singapore, Java, and India, the first Chakri king ever to leave his kingdom.

At the coronation ceremony that marked the end of the regency in 1873, King Chulalongkorn (1869–1910) began the transformation of the Thai political and social systems that was his explicit goal. The new king's first act was to read a decree abolishing the ancient practice of prostration before the king on the grounds that it was an act unsuitable in a modern state. Other social reforms soon followed, of which the most important were the abolition of slavery and an end to the forced labor system.

King Chulalongkorn also reorganized the government. The local rulers of distant regions were replaced by royally appointed governors, and the central government was reorganized into twelve functional ministries along European lines. Communications between Bangkok and the

King Chulalongkorn, Rama V, loved to travel abroad in his earlier years, and is seen here with Emperor Nicholas II of Russia. He was the ninth of King Mongkut's eighty-two children (by thirty-five wives). King Chulalongkorn followed in his father's ways. He carried forward a modernization program for the country and gradually abolished slavery. The king had seventy-seven children by thirty-seven wives.

The young Rama V in Western clothes at a garden party in England, leading Queen Alexandra and followed by King Edward VII.

The young king's supporters in his struggle against the older generation of nobles and princes of the Senabodi included members of the court who, as the result of King Mongkut's policies, had received the benefits of Western education. The younger Westernized courtiers, known as the Young Siam party, gained some official status when King Chulalongkorn drew upon them to man two new governmental bodies, the Council of State and the original Privy Council. These bodies were created in 1874 to advise the king on legislation.

In recognition of the need for more educated personnel to administer his reforms, the king set up schools for children

rest of the kingdom were improved by the building of postal and telegraph systems and railroads. An efficient army under a unified command, manned by conscription, and a central treasury, which took charge of all state sources of revenue (including a head tax, introduced at this time), replaced the inefficient, decentralized, and oppressive forced labor and tax collection systems that had enriched various government officials in the past at the expense of both the crown and the general public.

King Chulalongkorn was convinced that modernization was essential if the kingdom was to survive as an independent state in the era of Western colonization of Southeast Asia. He also believed that such modernization could only be achieved if it were planned and led by the king. Since he felt that only a strong king could modernize Siam, King Chulalongkorn's social and governmental reforms were carefully formulated in ways that increased the power of the king at the expense of the nobility. The result was that, as the kingdom became more modern, the king grew more powerful.

A postage stamp issued in 1908 of the statue of King Chulalongkorn, which has the inscription at the bottom of the stamp, "Coronation Commemoration—Forty-first year of the reign—1908."

of officials. He later established the *Suan Khularb* (Rose Garden School), the forerunner of Thai government secondary schools and the first to be open to nonofficials. At the opening ceremony, the king voiced his wish that "all children from my own to the poorest should have an equal chance of education." He sent most of his own sons to Europe for their advanced education and encouraged officials and others to do so also. This practice resulted in the birth of a Western-educated group of royal and commoner stock that has led the kingdom socially and politically in modern times.

King Chulalongkorn's relations with reigning monarchs in Europe were extremely cordial, partly as a result of his lifelong friendship with Prince Waldemar of Denmark, youngest son of King Christian IX and brother of the consorts of the king of England and the czar of Russia. Prince Waldemar came to Bangkok acting as the agent of the Danish East Asiatic Company, which had teak concessions as well as considerable other business in the kingdom.

In the last years of his reign, King Chulalongkorn traded border territories to the Western powers in return for increased legal jurisdiction over their resident protégés, and in 1909 a similar exchange was made with Great Britain, relinquishing all claims to the four Malay provinces of Kedah, Perlis, Kelantan, and Trengganu in exchange for sovereignty over Great Britain's Asian protégés in Siam.

Rama VI, King Vajiravudh, was the son of King Rama V by his half-sister, Sauvabha. He was very talented in the arts—an essayist and playwright and was educated at Sandhurst and Oxford. He had little political sense but did survive two military plots against him. This king had but three wives and one child.

King Mongkut Klao (Vajiravudh) honored on Siamese postage stamps

King Chulalongkorn on 1883 and 1887 postage stamps

King Prajadhipok and Chao Phya Chakri. This stamp commemorates the 150th anniversary of the Chakri Dynasty, the founding of Bangkok in 1782, and the opening of the bridge across the Chao Phya River.

BEGINNING OF THAI NATIONALISM

King Mongkut Klao, or Vajiravudh (Rama VI, 1910–25), son of King Chulalongkorn and *uparaja* from 1895, was the first Thai king to be educated abroad. His entire education was received in England and included study at Oxford University and Sandhurst military academy. He was also the first Thai nationalist and wrote under various pen names in the local press on the subject of love of country.

In addition to introducing Thai nationalism, King Vajiravudh's reign is noted for the return of virtually complete sovereignty over all persons and businesses in the kingdom. This was accomplished as an indirect result of the anglophile king's decision to send a small expeditionary force to serve on the Allied side in World War I. This entitled Siam to participate in the Versailles peace conference and led by 1925 to the signing of new treaties with the Western powers. Siam also became a founding member of the League of Nations. The kingdom's international prestige was higher than ever before.

Another contribution of King Vajiravudh's reign was the introduction in 1924 of the first law in Thai history to regularize the succession to the throne, by male primogeniture. Another enduring innovation of his reign was the introduction of a legal requirement that Thai persons have surnames (although these have seldom been used in ordinary social intercourse). The king also founded Chulalongkorn University as a memorial to his father. When King Vajiravudh died without a son in 1925, the kingdom passed to his younger brother Prajadhipok (1925–35), who became the last absolute monarch of the Thai.

BEGINNING OF THE CONSTITUTIONAL ERA

The new king, the youngest of his line, had never expected to assume the throne. He was a diffident and retiring person and, like King Vajiravudh, was Western-educated. He was

King Prajadhipok, Rama VII, was the younger brother of King Vajiravudh by the same mother. He abdicated in 1935 after two coups d'etat and one revolt. He had but one wife and no children.

King Prajadhipok on a 1928 postage stamp

King Naresuan on a war elephant honored on a 1955 stamp issued to commemorate his four-hundredth birthday anniversary (1555–1955)

Two 1931 stamps issued to honor King Ananda Mahidol.

the first Thai king to have only one wife. Early in his reign he showed his preference for sharing governmental responsibility with others rather than holding all the reins of power himself. He investigated the possibility of granting the kingdom a constitution and, in the meantime, set up an advisory Supreme Council of five princes and the Committee of Privy Councilors, composed of forty distinguished persons chosen by himself, to represent the intellectual, commercial, and professional interests in the country.

The king did not demonstrate the same political astuteness that had characterized his father, King Chulalongkorn. Neither he nor his advisers appeared to realize a need for haste in granting a constitution and, accordingly, they decided in April 1932 to postpone its promulgation. The king was faced with great discontent among the public caused by the world depression that began in 1929 and with the extreme unhappiness among members of the political elite caused by drastic retrenchments in government spending. These entrenchments involved the forced removal from government service of large numbers of civil and military personnel and the demotion of others.

THE 1932 COUP

The long era of absolute monarchy came to a sudden end on June 24, 1932, with a coup d'etat led by a group of civilian officials and army officers with the support of military units in the Bangkok area. Three days later the military junta

headed by three colonels announced that a provisional constitution was in effect and that the kingdom had become a constitutional one. The coup, like most of the others that have followed it in rapid succession, was bloodless and had little public participation.

The king, who with his queen had spent several months in the United States during 1931 for an eye operation, had only recently returned to Thailand at the time of the coup. He was away from the capital when it occurred and, when he returned two days later, he readily accepted the provisional constitution, although he was held prisoner by the coup leaders for a brief period. The provisional constitution had been drafted by the group's leading intellectual, Pridi Banomyong, a holder of a French doctor of law degree and professor of law at Chulalongkorn University.

The key figures in this coup, who are often called the promoters, included several men who had been educated in Europe in the 1920s. The promoters continued to be major figures in Thai politics for the ensuing three decades. Pridi, a man in his early thirties, son of a wealthy Chinese merchant and his Thai wife but who had been brought up as a Thai, was the most influential civilian promoter. There were also several military promoters, of whom Colonel Phya Phahol Pholphayuhasena was the senior representative of the disaffected old-line military officers and Phibul Songgram was the most important of the young, ambitious army officers.

These three men were the most influential members of the cabinet or Commissariat of the People elected by the new seventy-member National Assembly. The National Assembly had been appointed by the coup leaders immediately upon their assumption of control. It met for the first time on June 28, four days after the coup. The prime minister, called the president of the Commissariat of the People, was a former high court judge, Phya Manopakorn, who had not participated in the coup but was chosen by the promoters to assuage conservative opinion.

A permanent constitution was promulgated on December

10, 1932, to replace the provisional one of June 27, 1932. The new constitution maintained the status of the government as it had been since the June coup—no longer under the control of the king but not yet in the hands of the people. The promoters and their supporters, who called themselves the People's party, held the power.

Under the terms of the new Constitution of December 1932, the legislature was to have half its members chosen by adult suffrage and half appointed. The constitution stated that the entire legislature would be elected after half the electorate had received four years of schooling or ten years had elapsed, whichever came sooner.

The assumption underlying this provision was that constitutionalism should be a gradual development and time would be needed before the people would be ready to benefit from unalloyed democracy. The promise of eventual rule by a popularly elected government, made for the first time in this 1932 constitution, remained substantially unfulfilled in 1970. Although there have been various constitutions in force in the intervening period, almost all reserved a sizable proportion of legislative seats for appointed members.

Conflict between civilians and members of the military in the cabinet developed. Pridi proposed an economic plan in 1933 that involved nationalization of all natural and industrial resources, including land. This proved intolerable to the more conservative military group and to the conservative civilian prime minister, Manopakorn. The prime minister closed the National Assembly and ruled by decree. A law against communism was proclaimed, and Pridi, accused of being a Communist, fled into exile. The military leaders of the coup group, disapproving of the policies of Pridi and the methods of Manopakorn, seized power by staging a coup d'etat on June 20, 1933, less than a year after the first coup. The government was now headed by the conservative military promoter of the previous year, Phya Phahol, who maintained the government's anti-Communist stance but recalled the National Assembly.

In addition to factionalism within the cabinet, the government also faced in October 1933 a serious revolt of military troops led by the king's cousin, Prince Bovaradej, who had been minister of defense. Although the king gave no support to the prince, who demanded the resignation of Phya Phahol and his cabinet, relations between the king and the political leaders deteriorated thereafter, according to historians of the period.

Public sentiment in favor of Pridi, the promoter least tolerant of royal or aristocratic interference in government, became widespread. Pridi had been permitted to return to Bangkok a month before Prince Bovaradej's revolt, and in March 1934 a government commission cleared him of charges of Communist activities.

During the mid-1930s, in addition to the decline in popularity and influence of the conservative civilian elements, particularly those with royalist leanings, and the rise in popularity of Pridi, the left-wing intellectual, there also developed a faction within the military led by Phibul Songgram. Phibul was an army officer of obscure origin who had won national acclaim for his role in the first coup of June 24, 1932, and the coup of June 20, 1933, and in the successful suppression of Prince Bovaradej's revolt.

In 1934 Phibul became minister of defense and proceeded to build the Thai army into a powerful political instrument. He launched a campaign to show the need for a strong military organization to keep the country from being controlled by outsiders. He also took every opportunity to assert the superior efficiency of his military administration to the rival civil administration, in which Pridi was the most influential cabinet member, although the prime minister from 1933 to 1938 remained Phya Phahol.

Thailand's first election, held in November 1933, confirmed Pridi's popularity with the voters, although fewer than one-tenth of eligible voters cast their ballots. Prime Minister Phya Phahol maintained a balance between Pridi and Phibul factions.

The king's prestige continued to fall after the October 1933 rebellion by his cousin. He left the country in 1934, saying that he needed medical help for his worsening eye condition. In March 1935 he abdicated without naming a successor and went into retirement in England. The ten-year-old son of the king's deceased younger brother was chosen. Rama VIII, or King Ananta Mahidol (1935–1946), was at the time still attending primary school in Switzerland. Pending attainment of his majority, a regency council of three members was appointed to carry out these limited functions of the monarchy that were retained under the constitutional system. The new king did not return to his country until 1945.

NATIONALISM AND WAR UNDER PHIBUL

The three years before the outbreak of the Pacific phase of World War II were marked by a wave of Thai nationalism, led by Phibul with support from Pridi.

Phibul declared war on the Allies in 1942, but his ambassador to the United States, Seni Pramoj, a civilian aristocrat

Rama VIII, King Ananda Mahidol, the grandson of King Chulalongkorn, spent most of his life in Switzerland. He was found dead of a gunshot wound on a visit to Bangkok in 1946. To this day the circumstances involved are very mysterious.

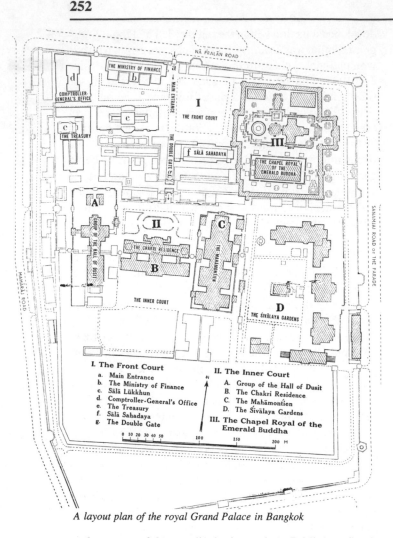

A layout plan of the royal Grand Palace in Bangkok

I. The Front Court
  a. Main Entrance
  b. The Ministry of Finance
  c. Sālā Lūkkhun
  d. Comptroller-General's Office
  e. The Treasury
  f. Sālā Sahadaya
  g. The Double Gate

II. The Inner Court
  A. Group of the Hall of Dusit
  B. The Chakri Residence
  C. The Mahāmontien
  D. The Śivālaya Gardens

III. The Chapel Royal of the Emerald Buddha

and a man of less radical views than Pridi but firmly anti-Japanese, refused to deliver the declaration of war to the government of the United States. (The Thai ambassador's behavior, coupled with the work of Pridi's underground organization, which maintained contact after 1944 with the Southeast Asia Command at Kandy, Ceylon, led the United States not to deal with Thailand as an enemy country in the postwar peace negotiations.)

As the war dragged on and Japan began to lose, the Japanese presence in Thailand grew more irksome. Trade came to a stop, and the Japanese military personnel stationed in the country confiscated whatever they needed, as if Thailand were a conquered territory rather than an ally. The infamous "death railway" being built between Burma and Thailand by Allied prisoners of war imported from Malaya and elsewhere helped to make the Thai public sympathetic to Pridi's underground movement. In July 1944 Phibul's government fell and was replaced by the first predominantly civilian government since the 1932 coup.

PRIDI AND THE CIVILIAN REGIME, 1944–47

The new government was headed by a civilian, Khuang Aphaiwong, who had no known commitment to either side

in the world war and was associated with Seni Pramoj and the conservative civilian elements domestically. The most influential political figure of the regime, however, was Pridi, whose anti-Japanese views were increasingly attractive to the Thai. Under the new government, United States military intelligence agents were given tacitly the freedom of Bangkok. At the end of the war Khuang and Pridi disagreed; since Pridi was more powerful, the prime minister was replaced by the Pridi nominee, Seni Pramoj.

In the early postwar period the United States had the most cordial relations with Thailand of all the Allies as a result of the United States' refusal to recognize the 1942 Thai declaration of war. Great Britain demanded war reparations from the Thai in the form of rice for British Malaya and insisted on the return of the four northern Malay states. France refused to permit Thailand to participate in the newly formed United Nations organization until the Indochinese territories, annexed during the war, were returned. The Soviet Union insisted that Thailand repeal its anticommunism law or face a veto of its admission to the United Nations. These various demands by the Allies were acceded to.

The Seni regime lasted only until an agreement was signed with Great Britain in January 1946. Then Pridi restored Khuang as prime minister, but he was obliged to take over the post himself in March 1946. The discontent of the Thai public was growing at this time, the result of inflation, the reparation payments of rice to British Malaya, the relinquishment of all the wartime territorial gains, and the high level of mismanagement at all levels of government.

Pridi, who felt that his political strength and that of any civilian regime depended upon there being a more important role for parliamentary and civilian politics, worked with his cabinet and the parliamentarians to draft a new constitution to achieve that purpose. The new basic law was promulgated on May 9, 1946.

As a result of the 1946 elections Pridi became the first prime minister to have a popularly elected Parliament supporting him. Pridi's prestige and popularity suffered severe and permanent damage two weeks after the election of the upper house, however, when King Ananta Mahidol, who had just returned in December 1945 from Switzerland, was found dead in his bed at the palace, a bullet wound through his head.

The successor to the throne, the nineteen-year-old King Bhumibol Adulyadej, was the younger brother of the dead king. King Bhumibol Adulyadej was born in the United States and spent his childhood years with King Ananta Mahidol and their mother in Switzerland. He had come back to Bangkok with his brother in December 1945. The new king returned to Switzerland to complete his education after his brother's death and did not come back to Bangkok to take up his royal duties until 1951.

The country was shocked by the death of King Ananta Mahidol. Although the official account attributed it to an

An aerial view of the Chapel Royal on the palace grounds.
Recent kings of Siam and Thailand have had strong affiliations with Buddhism and its way of life.

The Chakri royal residence is as imposing a palace today as it was decades ago when it was built from the plans of a British architect in the style of the Italian Renaissance but covered with roofs in pure Siamese style.

accident, there were widespread expressions of doubt since few facts were made public. Many of the rumors circulating in Bangkok at that time mentioned Pridi in connection with the tragedy. In August, two months after the king's death, Pridi resigned on grounds of ill health and left the country to take a world tour.

RETURN OF PHIBUL
AND THE MILITARY

For a few months after Pridi's resignation the government continued with a new prime minister, Thamrong Nawasawat. This period was notable for economic difficulties and widespread discontent with the way in which the regime had handled the investigation of the king's death.

King Bhumibol Adulyadej appears on many of his country's postage stamps

The royal summer palace in Chiengmai—Phu Phing Rajanives

His Majesty King Bhumibol Adulyadej in his official portrait

Her Majesty Queen Sirikit in her official portrait

COUP D'ETAT OF NOVEMBER 8, 1947

By November the military faction had regained some of the morale and popularity that had been lost as the result of its association with the Japanese defeat. Phibul had been arrested as a war criminal in the early postwar period but had been released by the courts soon afterward. A strong and efficient leader, renowned for his anti-Communist stance, Phibul became increasingly attractive to the Thai politically elite group as a candidate for political power. Governmental mismanagement, concern over possible regicide, and economic disorder were threatening domestic stability, and communism threatened the kingdom's neighbors—Burma, Malaya, Vietnam, and China.

On November 8, 1947, a group called the Khana Rathap-

rahan (Coup d'Etat Group), led by two retired army generals with support from Phibul, seized power in a bloodless coup. Pridi, who had returned from his world tour, fled the country. Thamrong and other Pridi supporters went into hiding.

An interim government was appointed by the coup leaders under Khuang Aphaiwong, making this his third time as prime minister. A provisional constitution was promulgated by the coup leaders on November 9, and the promise of a new permanent constitution was made. General elections held the following January confirmed the coup leaders' control of the government, although they retained Khuang as prime minister in an effort to placate Khuang's conservative civilian supporters.

In April 1948 Phibul, then a field marshal, took over as prime minister, removing Khuang by force.

For the next three years Phibul worked successfully to maintain his government against numerous attempted coups and revolts. Disaffected political factions included Khuang's conservative civilians of the Democrat party, some of whom participated in drafting the new permanent constitution that had been promised by the coup group in November 1947 and that was promulgated in March 1949.

The military group, too, had serious fissures. An anti-Phibul army group was arrested in October 1948. Supporters of former prime ministers Pridi, Thamrong, and Khuang could be found in the navy and the marines. In February 1949 a revolt that is commonly alleged to have been sponsored by Pridi supporters in the marines was attempted and failed. This revolt was followed by a violent purge by the government of senior politicians and officials. In June 1951 troops of marines and navy men took part in a rebellion and abducted Phibul. The rebellion was suppressed in a three-day war between the rebels and loyal troops of the army and air force.

Phibul's policies during this period were similar to those he had initiated in the late 1930s. The use of the name Thailand was restored in 1949. (There had been a reversion to the name Siam in 1946 with the defeat of Japan.) The regulation of Thai social behavior by legislation to make it conform to modern standards, begun by Phibul before the war, was continued. Secondary education was improved, and the military organizations were given large sums to improve themselves in quantity and quality. The harassment of Chinese and the tendency to regard resident Chinese as likely to be disloyal and, after 1949, Communists were notable features of the Phibul regime. Communist revolts in Laos, Malaya, Burma, and Vietnam and the fall of China to the Communists helped to make Phibul's policies popular with the Thai.

Phibul's anti-Communist position had great influence on his foreign policy. Thailand refused to recognize Communist China, supported the United Nations against North Korea in 1950, and became the most loyal supporter of United States foreign policy in mainland Southeast Asia.

SILENT COUP OF NOVEMBER 29, 1951

By the time of the rebellion of the navy and marines in June 1951, Phibul had begun to share political power with two associates who had participated with him in the 1947 coup that overthrew the civilian regime of Pridi. One of these was General Phao Siyanon, director general of police and a close associate of Phibul since the original coup of 1932. The other man, more junior, was General Sarit Thanarat, commander of the Bangkok army.

As time passed, the two associates grew more powerful than Phibul, who was able to retain the prime ministership because of the rivalry of Phao and Sarit for the succession. All three, however, were in opposition to the 1949 constitution, a basic law that had been formulated by a committee with a civilian bias.

On November 29, 1951, military and police officers announced over the radio that the 1949 constitution was suspended and the December 10, 1932 constitution was in force. The reason given for restoring a unicameral parliament with half its membership appointed by the government was the danger of Communist aggression.

Shortly after this radio announcement, King Bhumibol Adulyadej returned to Thailand, having completed his Swiss education, and for the first time since 1935 an adult monarchy was on duty in the palace in Bangkok. His first

Four stamps depicting royal houses: Top to bottom: *Sivalaya-Mahaprasad Hall, Cakri-Mahaprasad, Mahisra-Prasad, and Dusit-Mahaprasad*

This postage stamp honors the crown prince Vajiralongkorn.

Queen Sirikit—various portraits of Queen Sirikit in different dress designs on 1968 postage stamps

governmental action was to insist that certain revisions be made before the December 1932 constitution was adopted. The cabinet agreed to this. The revised constitution was promulgated on February 26, 1952.

THE MONARCHY

Although all power is exercised in the name of the king, he has very little real power in his own right. Since the 1932 coup the monarch has generally been restricted to exerting limited influence behind the scenes, usually not decisive. Since the coronation in 1950 of King Bhumibol Adulyadej, who reigned as the ninth in the Chakri line of Thai monarchs, the prestige of the throne has been greatly enhanced. The relationship between the king and the government has also been most cordial. The real significance of the monarchy in national politics, nevertheless, has been in the king's symbolic representation of national unity and the need of the ruling group in any given period for the king to legitimize its rule through royal appointment to the major ministerial offices of the state.

The king is aided by three agencies: the Privy Council,

which advises the monarch and, under certain conditions, appoints a regency to exercise royal powers; the Office of the Royal Household, which organizes ceremonial functions and administers the finances and housekeeping of the royal court; and the Office of His Majesty's Private Secretariat, which performs clerical and secretarial tasks for the king.

For centuries one of the important functions of the government was to conduct elaborate ceremonies, rituals, and acts of religious merit that were regarded as efficacious in bringing to the people not only spiritual benefits but also a host of material benefits. These ceremonies, as well as other displays of power and wealth by the state, made it possible for the people to see in their king the living symbol of the hierarchy of respect that was operative throughout Thai society. The court and the capital represented to the people the highest realization of their cultural values.

Before 1932 the monarch had held power and prestige by virtue of his representing both political powers and religious sanctions. When the 1932 coup separated the power from the absolute monarch, it failed to diminish the traditional royal prestige. Although the king was reduced to

Queen Sirikit's favorite snapshot of her daughters. The queen in Thailand has very important duties in government. When the king went into priesthood during 1956, Queen Sirikit became the regent during that period. She performed her duties so well and so satisfactorily that on the recommendation from the government she was given a title of higher distinction. She is now Somdech Phraborom Rajininath. Such a title is given to a queen who has ably performed the function of head of state on behalf of the king when he is absent from the realm or when for some reason he is unable to exercise his function for a certain period of time.

The king in 1960 when visiting the United States, his birthplace, toured the Library of Congress. He is seen here, left, before the exhibit containing the first and second drafts of Lincoln's Gettysburg Address, with the librarian of Congress, L. Quincy Mumford.

King Bhumibol Adulyadej and Queen Sirikit visiting with children in an outlying province. The king and queen are very much revered by the people of Thailand, especially the children.

King Bhumibol Adulyadej during a state visit to England with Queen Elizabeth II of Great Britain

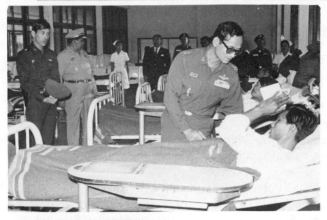

The king maintains close rapport with the armed forces personnel. Here he is seen visiting Thai soldiers in a hospital.

King Vajiravudh honored on a recent Thailand centennial anniversary stamp

The royal family is a talented group of musicians. Here the royal princess Ubol Ratana is singing a song and playing guitar for a charity dance. Her father, the king, and her brother, the crown prince, may be seen in background with their saxophones, an instrument they both excel in playing.

A 1982 issue of stamps for the bicentennial of the city of Bangkok honoring the Chakri Dynasty of kings from Rama I to Rama IX. Left to right and top to bottom: Buddha Yod-Fa, 1736–1809; Buddha Lert La Naphalai, 1767–1824; Nang Klao, 1787–1851; Mongkut, 1804–1868; Chulalongkorn, 1853–1910; Vajiravudh, 1880–1925; Prachathipok, 1893–1941; Ananda Mahidol, 1925–1946; and Bhumibol Aduldej 1927–.

The king and queen on an official visit to the United States, June 28, 1960, being greeted on arrival at Washington, D.C., by the president, Dwight D. Eisenhower. Secretary of State Christian Herter can be seen in the background, left, center.

The king and queen of Thailand, His Majesty King Bhumibol Adulyadej and Her Majesty Queen Sirikit on an official state visit to the United Nations headquarters in New York City in 1967.

the position of being merely one of a number of national symbols, the people continued to respect their monarch much more than any other leader or emblem of the state.

Popular respect for the king is enhanced in part through the playing of the royal anthem ("*Sanrasorn Phra Bara-*

mi"—literally, "Anthem Eulogizing His Majesty"), at all public functions attended by the king or the queen; it is also played at the end of public entertainments.

Thailand's government is a constitutional monarchy which functions through a cabinet, a national legislature, and a highly centralized administrative system. The king has little direct power but is a popular symbol of national identity and unity. A fourteen-member Privy Council is appointed by the king to advise him and, under certain conditions, to appoint a regency for the exercise of royal powers.

Thailand's eleventh constitution was signed by the king and promulgated October 7, 1974. It provides for a 100-member Senate appointed by the king; a 269-member House of Representatives, or Assembly, elected to four-year terms by direct suffrage and secret ballot; and a cabinet of not more than 30 members.

The country's judicial system is patterned after European code models. Supreme Court justices are appointed by the king.

The monarch, His Majesty King Bhumibol Adulyadej, and Queen Sirikit have four children, including one son, Prince Vajiralongkorn (born July 28, 1952), who was invested as crown prince in December 1972. Their other three children are Princess Ubol Ratana (born April 5, 1951), Princess Sirindhorn (born April 2, 1955), and Princess Chulabhorn (born July 4, 1957).

THE ROYAL SOVEREIGNS OF THE DYNASTIES AND KINGDOM OF THAILAND (SIAM)

KINGDOM OF SUKHOTHAI (SIAM)

Reign	Title	Ruler	Reign	Title	Ruler
1238–1269	King	Sri Intaratitva	1610–1628	King	Songtam (Intharaja)
1269–1275	King	Ban Muang	1628–1630	King	Jettha
1275–1317	King	Ramkemhaeng (Rama the Great)	1630–1630	King	Athityawong
1317–1347	King	Loetai	1630–1656	King	Prasat-Tong
1347–1350	King	Mahr Tammaraja Latai	1656–1656	King	Chao-Fa-Jai
			1656–1657	King	Sri Suthammaraja
			1657–1688	King	Narai
AYDHYA (AYUTHIA) DYNASTY			1688–1703	King	Phra-Phetraja
1350–1369	King	Rama Tibodi I	1703–1709	King	PhraChao Sua
1369–1370	King	Ramesuen	1709–1733	King	Puhmintharaxa (Tai Sra)
1370–1388	King	Baromaraja (Boromaraja) I	1733–1758	King	Baromakot (Maha Thammaraja II)
1388–1395	King	Ramesuen	1758–1758	King	Utumpon
1395–1408	King	Ram Raja	1758–1767	King	Baromoraja V (Ekathat) (Suriyamarin)
1408–1424	King	Intaraja	1767–1782	King	Phya Taksin
1424–1448	King	Baromaraja II			
1448–1488	King	Trailok (Baroma Trailokana)	**BANGKOK DYNASTY (CHAKRI)**		
1488–1491	King	Baromaraja III	1782–1809	King	Rama I, Buddha Yot Fa (Tong Duang)
1491–1529	King	Rama Tibodi II	1809–1824	King	Rama II, Buddha Loes-La Nabhalai
1529–1534	King	Baromoraja IV	1824–1851	King	Rama III, Nang Klao (Chesda)
1534–1534	King	Ratsada	1851–1868	King	Rama IV, Chom Klao (Mongkut)
1534–1546	King	Phra Chai	1869–1910	King	Rama V, Chula Chom Klao (Chulalongkorn)
1546–1548	King	Keo (Yodfa)			
1548–1548	King	Khun Worawongsa	1910–1925	King	Rama VI, Mongkut Klao (Vajiravudh)
1548–1569	King	Maha-Chakrapat	1925–1935	King	Rama VII, Prajadhipok (Phra Pok Klao)
1569–1569	King	Mahin (Thara-Thirat)	1935–1946*	King	Rama VIII, Ananta Mahidol
1569–1590	King	Maha Tammaraja	1946–	King	Bhumibol Adulyadej
1590–1605	King	Naresuan			
1605–1610	King	Ekathotsarot	*Changed name from Siam to Thailand, 1939.		

15

The Kingdoms of Malaysia

Malaysia's position in Southeast Asia

The early Buddhist Malay kingdom of Sri Vijaya, based in east Sumatra, dominated much of the Malay Peninsula from the ninth to the thirteenth centuries. The powerful Hindu kingdom of Majapahit, based on Java, gained control of the Malay Peninsula in the fourteenth century. The conversion of the Malays to Islam, beginning in the early part of the fourteenth century, was accelerated with the rise of the state of Malacca under the rule of a Muslim prince.

The arrival of the Portuguese in Malacca in 1511 marked the beginning of European expansion in this area as the power of the sultanates declined. The Dutch ousted the Portuguese from Malacca in 1641 and in 1795 were replaced in turn by the British, who had occupied Penang in 1786.

Sir Thomas Stamford Raffles founded a British settlement at Singapore in 1819. In 1826 the settlements of Malacca and Penang were combined with Singapore to form the Colony of the Straits Settlements. In the nineteenth and early twentieth centuries the British concluded treaties establishing protectorates over the nine Malay states on the peninsula. Four of these states were consolidated in 1895 as the Federated Malay States.

West Malaysia, then known as Malaya, enjoyed a century of prosperity with the gradual establishment of a well-ordered system of public administration, extension of public services, and development of large-scale rubber and tin production. This period was interrupted by the Japanese invasion and occupation from 1942 to 1945.

The Federation of Malaya was established from the British territories of peninsular Malaysia in 1948. The British colonies of Singapore, Sarawak, and Sabah (North Borneo) joined the Federation of Malaya to form Malaysia on September 16, 1963. The Sukarno government of Indonesia objected to the formation of Malaysia and conducted a program of "confrontation" against the new state, which included economic, political, diplomatic, and military offensives. This "confrontation" continued through Singapore's withdrawal from Malaysia on August 9, 1965, and ended only after the fall of the Sukarno regime in 1966. Relations between Malaysia and Indonesia have subsequently become very cordial.

After World War II the local Communists, almost all Chinese, expanded their influence and made plans for an armed struggle. A state of emergency was declared in June 1948, and a long and bitter guerrilla war ensued.

The emergency ended in 1960 as Malaya, in partnership with the United Kingdom, gained the distinction of being one of the few countries in the world to control a large-scale Communist uprising. However, what remained of the Communist force regrouped in southern Thailand and over the years was able to rebuild its strength. In the past few years, small bands of Communist guerrillas have once again been encountered in the northern portion of West Malaysia, and in light of Communist successes in Indochina appear to have renewed their efforts. However, government forces are apparently well in control of the situation. A small-scale Communist insurgency in the East Malaysian state of Sarawak has also been contained, and in 1973–74 skillful government counterguerrilla activities resulted in the surrender of most of the insurgents there.

EARLY PERIOD

Evidence of human residence in parts of Malaysia goes back more than thirty-five thousand years. There is widespread evidence of a Mesolithic culture beginning about ten thousand years ago. The people of this culture are thought to have been small, dark-skinned Veddoids similar to the Melanesians and to some of the aboriginal peoples still living a Stone-Age existence in the inland jungles of the Malay Peninsula. These Veddoids were cave dwellers who hunted, fished, and collected jungle produce. They buried their dead and engaged in ritual cannibalism and possibly headhunting.

About 2500 to 1500 B.C., a Neolithic people, believed to have migrated from southwest China, moved down the peninsula and also beyond it to the Indonesian archipelago. These proto-Malays were good woodworkers and carvers. They grew food crops, including yams and possibly rice; they had pottery and stone jewelry and may have worn bark-cloth clothing. Of the same racial stock as the proto-Malays are the deutero-Malays, who are credited with having introduced the Bronze–Iron Age to Southeast Asia. Beautiful and intricately decorated bronze drums and bells have been unearthed in various parts of West Malaysia testifying to the ubiquity and skill of these early migrants.

In the first century A.D., the more advanced portion of the populace, who for the most part dwelled near the coast, had an irrigated rice agriculture, mixed gardening, and domesticated cattle. They had the ability to work metals and had considerable navigational skill. They lived in bamboo houses raised on stilts. Their social system included matriarchal descent and an important place for women. Their religious practices involved ancestor and phallic worship, horizontal and vertical megaliths, burials in jars or horizontal cists, and a tendency to categorize things dualistically—for example, high versus low, mountain versus sea.

Malaysian culture was never uniform, however. Depending upon accessibility to foreign influence and other factors, there were, and have continued to be, great variations in culture among different ethnic groups and tribes.

THE HINDU-BUDDHIST PERIOD, SECOND TO FIFTEENTH CENTURIES A.D.

The Indian traders who visited Malaya in the first centuries A.D. inaugurated a process of cultural influence that was to continue for more than a thousand years. From India came many of the Malays' basic political ideas and practices, art forms, and popular legends. Indian traders introduced, successively, Hinduism, Buddhism, and Islam. Indian influence came in waves, and the Indian contributions to Malaysian culture represent several periods of history and geographic regions.

Indianized city-states began to develop in Southeast Asia at the start of the Christian Era as the result of trade contacts. Although there is no evidence of large-scale settlement, control, or invasion by Indians, Indian concepts adopted by the indigenous Southeast Asian elite soon became the basis of political organization in the trading communities. This organization transformed independent subsistence villagers into citizens of city-states and kingdoms, subject to a ruling class, indigenous or foreign, who lived off the trade profits and justified the new hierarchical social structure by reference to Hindu and Buddhist religious doctrines.

The first Southeast Asian city-state of lasting importance

was Funan, a trading settlement on the Mekong Delta. Smaller city-states also sprang up. One of these was Kedah, on the west coast of the Peninsula. A vassal to Funan, Kedah was, by the seventh century, the last port of call in Southeast Asia for Chinese pilgrims on their way to the Buddhist holy places in India. By the third century A.D., Chinese were trading at an entrepôt in the Malacca Strait, perhaps on the island of Singapore.

In the seventh century Funan fell to the Khmers of Cambodia. Kedah soon became a vassal of a new empire, Sri Vijaya, which was growing on the profits of the trade through the Malacca Strait. Sri Vijaya's capital was in southern Sumatra, but gradually the empire incorporated the coasts of peninsular Malaya and parts of western Borneo, the isthmian city-states that had formerly been Funan's vassals, and, for a time, parts of Java.

Through its control of the Malacca Strait and its suzerainty over the region's seaports, Sri Vijaya became the richest and most powerful kingdom in Southeast Asia. It also became a major center for the propagation of Mahayana Buddhism. A seventh-century Chinese pilgrim reported finding one thousand Buddhist monks studying in Sri Vijaya's Sumatran capital near modern Palembang.

All traffic through the Malacca Strait paid duty at the Sri Vijayan ports. A Chinese account of the time states that "if some foreign ship passing Sri Vijaya should not enter the port, an armed party would certainly board it and kill the sailors to the last man."

Perhaps in reaction to the high-handedness of the Sumatra-based empire, King Rajendra Chola I of the Chola Dynasty of southern India led a raid on Sri Vijaya's capital and on the vassal states on the Malay Peninsula. Kedah, which had become a leading city of Sri Vijaya, never fully recovered from this attack.

The trade of Sri Vijayan days was essentially luxury trade. Arabs came to the northwest of the peninsula to buy tin and jungle produce in exchange for Western goods such as glassware and cloth. The Chinese trade with maritime Southeast Asia, an area the Chinese called Nanyang (southern seas), was more exotic. Ivory, rhinoceros horn (used in Chinese traditional medicine), hardwood, and camphor from Southeast Asia were exchanged for Chinese wine, rice, silk, and porcelain.

In the eleventh century there developed a lucrative and well-organized East-West trade to provide Europe with Moluccan spices. Arab traders carried the trade between Venice and Cambay in western India through the Red Sea and the Persian Gulf. Gujerati Indians from Cambay and other southern Indian ports operated the trade across the Indian Ocean to the northern coast ports of East Java, the chief collection point for spices from Indonesia's eastern islands.

By the thirteenth century the demand in the West for goods from China increased and exceeded China's demand for Western goods. In order to maintain the balance of trade with China, the Indian and Arab traders expanded their trade with indigenous Malaysians. The Indian traders exchanged Western goods for Southeast Asian jungle produce, which found a ready market in China. By 1225 a new port on the east coast of the Malay Peninsula, possibly in the present-day state of Trengganu, had become the chief emporium of this Indian, Arab, and Chinese trade. Malaysian jungle produce, including tree resins, hornbill ivory, and edible birds' nests from the caves of Borneo, formed an important part of the trade between China and the West.

By the end of the thirteenth century Sri Vijaya had gone into eclipse, and the land empire of the Khmers in the north of the peninsula had fallen to the Thai. A new city-state, established by a Sumatran prince on the island that is now Singapore at the end of the thirteenth century, was raided alternately by the Thai and by the new southern power, the Javanese empire of Majapahit, throughout the fourteenth century.

The trade through the Strait of Malacca was constantly harassed by pirates inhabiting the old Sri Vijayan Sumatran ports including Palembang. When the Mongol Dynasty fell in the mid-fourteenth century and the Ming emperor banned private Chinese trade in the Nanyang, Chinese outlaws joined the other pirates of the strait.

By the end of the fourteenth century, the Thai had extended their control to most of the Malay Peninsula. A Javanese attempt to capture Singapore was repulsed, and Java could no longer exact allegiance from the Sumatran ports. New Muslim city-states were growing on Sumatra's northeast coast that were engaged in an effort to establish safe ports along the pirate-infested strait between Sumatra and the Malay Peninsula.

MALACCA'S GOLDEN AGE, 1400–1511

Malaysian history before the beginning of the fifteenth century must be mainly deduced by arranging in meaningful order the scant archaeological fragments that have survived the centuries in a damp, tropical climate. Much of what is known of early Malaysia has been gleaned from the occasional comments of passing foreign travelers, most of them Chinese.

With the start of the fifteenth century, however, Malaysia entered into the fully historical period with the rise of the entrepôt of Malacca, celebrated in Malaya's first known indigenous chronicle, the *Sejarah Melayu* (Malay Annals). The *Sejarah Melayu* was written before 1536 and is still a useful source for Malaysian social history despite some evident distortions.

Covering much of the same period are historical summaries written by the Portuguese who conquered Malacca in the sixteenth century. There are also two detailed first-hand accounts by Chinese officials who accompanied the emperor's envoy, Admiral Cheng Ho, to Malacca during the early days of the Malacca sultanate. Although there are conflicting details in these various accounts, the century during which Malacca was under Malay rule is fully described. With the addition of historical romances, such as the famous *Hikayat Hang Tuah* (Tale of Hang Tuah), the first original romance in the Malay language that dates back to the sixteenth century or earlier, the flavor and character of this time have been preserved. Although the sultanate lasted in Malacca only a century, its customs and organizations survive, especially in the traditions of the Malay royal courts.

For all Malaysians who regard themselves as culturally Malay, fifteenth-century Malacca still provides cultural heroes, dynastic ancestors, patterns of statecraft, and traditional examples of ideal public and private behavior. For the Malays of Malaysia (some 44 percent of the population) modern civilization began here.

THE FOUNDING OF MALACCA

Shortly before the end of the fourteenth century, a Sumatran-born refugee from Majapahit Java fled to Singapore. His name, *Sri Parameswara,* meaning "prince consort," suggests that he had married above himself, possibly a Javanese or Sumatran princess.

Singapore at that time was being ruled by a relative of the Thai king. Parameswara promptly murdered the ruler and, with his band of followers, took over the town. The Thai king sent, one source recounts, "three thousand troops and war elephants" to avenge the murder and retake the town. Parameswara and his group, which now included adventurers collected along the way and bands of indigenous aborigines who lived a sea-nomad existence along the peninsula's coasts, retreated from Singapore, which was thoroughly devastated by this siege.

In approximately 1400 the refugees took over a small fishing village at the mouth of the Melaka River and started to operate a trading port of the Sri Vijayan type. It was a good time to start a new trading port: China's overland routes to the West had been blocked by Tamerlane (Timur Lenk), and the new Ming emperor who came to the throne of China in 1402 was anxious to open a sea route to the West. In 1403 the emperor sent the first of seven expeditions to Southeast Asia to arrange for a new system of controlling the traffic through the strait. Thailand, China's vassal, was instructed not to molest Malacca. More important for Malacca's success, in 1407 Admiral Cheng Ho and a fleet of sixty-two vessels and thirty-seven thousand men destroyed the pirate's den in Palembang, removing a serious threat to Malaccan power. Grateful Malaccan kings went to China four times between 1411 and 1433 to demonstrate their loyalty as vassals of the emperor, although to avoid trouble they continued paying tribute to the Thai until 1446.

The Muslim city-states of north Sumatra benefited from the strait being made clear for trade again. Parameswara (or possibly his son), by converting to Islam and marrying a princess of the north Sumatran port of Pasai, became the ally of the Sumatran Muslim traders who soon moved their headquarters to Malacca.

Malacca's chief asset was its location; it was convenient for controlling the trade through the strait and provided safe anchorage where the monsoons met. Malacca's rulers wisely kept the toll and customs charges reasonable, and it was relatively easy to police the forty miles between Malacca and the Sumatran coast to prevent ships bypassing the entrepôt.

THE GOLDEN AGE

Although as time went on Malacca received tribute from vassals, the bulk of her wealth came from a 6 percent duty on foreign trade and lesser taxes on domestic trade, including sales in the local food markets and even licenses for peddlers. Of the foreign trade, the most important was the trade between the Gujerati Indian traders, now converted to Islam, and Javanese traders who met in Malacca to exchange Western manufactures, chiefly cloth, for Moluccan spices.

One effect of the prominence of the zealously missionizing Gujeratis in the Malacca trade was the spread of Islam throughout the archipelago, especially among the coastal populations who were most directly involved in the spice trade. Islam became the religion of the commercial fraternity. Another shared feature of the Malacca population was a facility in the Malay language, which became the lingua franca of trade and from which developed the national language of Malaysia, Bahasa Malaysia.

Malacca, however, was by no means a social melting pot. Rather, it was a large foreign settlement subdivided into smaller foreign enclaves on the sparsely settled Malay coast. Gujeratis, Malays, Javanese, Sumatrans, Bugis (from the Celebes), Borneans, Filipinos, Persians, Arabs, and Chinese each lived apart. A *capitan* (headman) chosen by each enclave from among its members represented the community in its dealings with outsiders. Above the *capitans* came the four *shahbandars* (harbormasters and controllers of customs). Each *shahbandar* dealt with the traders from prescribed areas; one *shahbandar* dealt with the Gujeratis, and another dealt with the Sumatrans, the Javanese, and the people of the islands to the east. Frequently, the harbormaster was of the nationality of one of the groups with whom he dealt. Above the *shahbandars* was the Malay court, headed by Parameswara's successors.

Although after 1446 the ruler of Malacca bore the Muslim title of sultan, the court officials continued to use Sanskrit titles, and court ritual showed the persisting influence of Hindu ideas. As the personification of the state, the sultan drew upon many Hindu symbols of divine kingship, such as the royal umbrella, the sacred *kris* (dagger), and the reservation to royalty of the colors yellow and white, symbols that had become part of court ritual in the city-states of Southeast Asia since the time of Funan.

As this elaborate ritual developed around the throne of

the sultan, the actual wielding of power tended to come under the control of the chief minister *(bendahara)*. The *bendahara* more or less inherited his claim to the office, as did the sultan's other chief officers, the treasurer, the admiral, and the military commander. Below this inner council of four there were eight other major chiefs, and below them thirty-two territorial chiefs.

These courtiers lived well on the proceeds of the various taxes and presents from traders. In return, they held together the mosaic of small and mutually suspicious transient communities so that trade could take place for everyone's profit.

The *bendahara* during the period of Malacca's greatest wealth and power was Tun Perak. He was the power behind the throne during the reigns of four sultans from behind the throne during the reigns of four sultans from 1456 to 1498. He led Malacca's forces against land and sea invasions by the Thai and made vassals of the ports of central and southern Sumatra. Pahang, Kedah, Perak, Johore, and Trengganu became part of the empire before Tun Perak's death in 1498. As Malacca successfully wrested territory from the Thai, Islam spread on the Peninsula, taking root among the people as an expression of opposition to Buddhist Thailand.

Sultan Mansur Shah (1459–77) reigned at the height of Malacca's power. He was a devout Muslim, and during his reign Malacca became a center for the study of the Sufi mystic sect of Islam.

One problem that was to plague Malacca and subsequent Malay sultanates was that of the royal succession. A king generally nominated one of his sons, by no means always the eldest, to the post of *raja muda* (crown prince) during his lifetime. This choice, however, was not binding on his subjects. At the funeral of a sultan, the senior chiefs of the kingdom gathered and made the final choice among candidates whose royal blood entitled them to consideration. The chiefs often passed over the dead sultan's favorite and conferred the title on a pretender who, they anticipated, would be grateful to and dependent upon his electors. It was a system upon which intrigue thrived and usually resulted in weak elderly sultans and strong petty chieftains.

Potential troublemakers among the pretenders were sent away from the capital to govern outlying posts of the empire. In this way, for example, a dynasty of rulers in Pahang was founded by sons of Sultan Mansur Shah who had been passed over by the chiefs.

The establishment of new dynasties and intermarriage with old ones ensured the spread of Islam among the ruling families of Malaysia. The court of Brunei in northwest Borneo became Muslim at this time. Majapahit, with whom Brunei had had close connections, had been gradually declining. In converting to Islam, Brunei severed its ties forever with the Javanese Empire.

On Mansur Shah's tombstone, dated A.D. 1477, appears the verse, "The world is but transitory/the world has no permanence/the world is like a house made by a spider."

The transitoriness of Mansur Shah's Malacca became clear shortly after the death of his *bendahara*, Tun Perak, in 1498.

TRADERS, PIRATES, AND MIGRANTS AFTER THE FALL OF MALACCA

THE PORTUGUESE

During the time of Malacca's sultanate, the trade between Southeast Asia and Europe was in the hands of Muslim traders as far as Venice, which was the sole distributor of Asian goods in Europe. The Portuguese in the early sixteenth century sought to damage the Muslim trade and break the control of Venice over the European market.

By 1509 they had partly destroyed the Muslim monopoly on the India-Arabia leg of the trade route, and a peaceful attempt to establish a trading post at Malacca was unsuccessful. In 1511 Alfonso de Albuquerque led a large fleet from the Portuguese fort at Goa eastward to Malacca and, after a long battle, captured the town. The sultan fled, first to Pahang and then to Johore, and the Portuguese began immediately to fortify their new emporium.

Within the thick stone walls of the fort, called *A Famosa* (the famous one), a Eurasian, Christian, Portuguese-speaking community emerged that continued into the twentieth century. Portuguese Malacca, like the sultanate that preceded it, was dependent on imports from abroad for food. The Javanese provided the bulk of the rice during the Portuguese period, although at the beginning they were hostile and sent a fleet of one hundred ships to attack Malacca in 1513.

A Famosa was attacked almost continually during the one hundred and thirty years of Portuguese control. From Johore, the new center of the displaced Malacca sultanate, there were serious attacks leading to vigorous Portuguese counterattacks for a century after the Portuguese takeover. In the period from 1540 to 1640 an aggressive and zealously Muslim dynasty in Acheh (Atjeh), north Sumatra, sought to gain a monopoly over the Strait of Malacca and alternately attacked Johore and Malacca. Alliances between the two Muslim kingdoms, Johore and Acheh, were occasionally attempted to destroy the Europeans, but mutual suspicion kept the two sultanates apart.

BRUNEI

Another Malay sultanate, Brunei on Borneo, fared better in the Portuguese era. Brunei was much like Malacca, a Muslim state with Hindu rituals and an elegant court given to display of wealth. Never as powerful as Malacca, it had only one *shahbandar*. At the height of its power in the sixteenth century, Brunei claimed all North Borneo and the Sulu Archipelago in the southern Philippines, and it even received tribute from Manila for a few years.

The Portuguese kept on friendly terms with Brunei, and

their ships stopped there en route to the Moluccan spice gardens. Brunei had habitually sent gold and jungle produce to Malacca to be exchanged there for cloth and beads from India and the West. The Portuguese city inherited that trade, but the bulk of Brunei's trade was with Chinese merchants, many of whom had moved from Malacca to Patani in the Thai part of the Malay Peninsula, which became in the seventeenth century the chief entrepôt for the Chinese goods in Southeast Asia.

THE DUTCH

As the sixteenth century came to a close, another European power entered the contest for control of the Malacca Strait. The Dutch had for a century handled the European distribution of the Portuguese Eastern trade, collecting their goods in Lisbon. In 1594 the Spaniards closed Lisbon to the Dutch, who now had to obtain Eastern produce directly from the source.

By 1619 the Dutch East India Company had established its headquarters on Java and attempted to form alliances with Acheh and Johore to destroy Malacca. Dutch fleets tried to cut off rice supplies from Java and Sumatra on their way to Malacca. In 1640, after more than twenty years of harassment and attacks, the Dutch, allied with Johore, laid siege to the walled community. A breach on the land side of the famous fort admitted the invaders to the starving town after a siege of six months.

Malacca's period as a major trade emporium was over. During the Portuguese era it had been declining, with some of the trade following the Muslim traders to northern Sumatra and to the Riau Islands of the Johore sultanate. The Dutch, with their new entrepôt Batavia (modern-day Djakarta) in Java, regarded Malacca more as a fortress on the strait to maintain Dutch trade monopoly of spices, pepper, gold, and tin than as a trading port.

THE SULU SULTANATE

Brunei's power also waned in the seventeenth century. Attacks by Bruneis and Sulus on the Spanish settlements in the Philippines resulted with the sacking and burning of Brunei Town in 1645 by Spaniards. With Brunei weakened, Sulu gained its independence.

At the end of the seventeenth century, the rivalry of two heirs to the Brunei sultanate brought on a civil war. One of the pretenders asked the sultan of Sulu for military aid in return for that portion of what is now Sabah running from the island of Sebatik on the east coast to Kimanis on the west coast. Although Sulu's ally won the war, it later became unclear whether the promised cession actually took place or whether the Sulus unilaterally claimed the promised territory as their reward. This question of overlapping claims was to become important in the late nineteenth century when some adventurous Western businessmen sought to obtain a grant of the disputed territory. Some of the ramifications of this dispute also carried over into the twentieth-century controversy between Malaysia and the Philippines over title to the area.

THE BUGIS AND THE MINANGKABAU

Dutch trade policies had a more deleterious effect on indigenous trade than had the Portuguese. Whereas the Portuguese were interested primarily in monopolizing the Eastern trade reaching Europe by controlling the shipping from the East to the West, the Dutch were determined to take over the trade between the Asian ports as well. Garrisons and blockades in Kedah and Perak were built by the Dutch to prevent tin shipments from slipping past them, and in 1667 the seagoing *prahus* (small sailing craft) of the Bugis people of the Celebes were cut off from their traditional control of the Celebes-to-Java spice trade by a Dutch garrison in Makassar.

The frustrated Bugis turned to piracy and migrated to other parts of the archipelago. Many settled in Selangor, West Malaysia. Ambitious and aggressive, the Bugis were ready to fill the power vacuum that occurred in the Johore Empire at the beginning of the eighteenth century.

Johore, the direct descendant of the Malacca sultanate, had squandered its wealth gained from its entrepôt at Riau in a twenty-year war with the Sumatran state of Jambi, but the Bugis found Johore's empire (which included the tip of the peninsula and the Riau and Lingga islands) an excellent base from which to attack Malacca and the Dutch shipping monopoly. Another foreign Malay group, the Minangkabau of Sumatra, many of whom had migrated to farm the hinterland of Malacca since the time of the Portuguese, were also determined to gain political power on the peninsula.

The two foreign Malay groups allied to take the throne of Johore in 1717, after the last heir to the Malacca Dynasty had died in 1699 and the *bendahara* had come to the throne. There was bad faith on both sides of the alliance, and by 1721 the Bugis had effective control of the Johore empire. A puppet sultan, the son of the former *bendahara*, was installed under the authority of a Bugis regent with a new royal title, *yam tuan muda* (deputy king).

Conflict between the Minangkabau and Bugis broke out again in Kedah in 1724 when they intervened on opposite sides in a dynastic war. Again the Bugis were the victors, and for more than forty years they extracted war-debt payments from Kedah. The Bugis fought the Minangkabau again in Perak, and in 1740 they established a Bugis dynasty in Selangor.

The Dutch grew concerned over the increasing Bugis power and especially over their attempts in Perak and elsewhere to break the Dutch monopoly on tin. In mid-century the sultan of Johore offered the Dutch trade and tin monopolies if the Dutch would rid him of his Bugis overlord. The Dutch and the Bugis fought each other intermittently for nearly thirty years until finally the Bugis power was broken, and the Dutch established a garrison at the Bugis stronghold at Riau. The sultan of Johore now had a Dutch, instead of a Bugis, overlord.

NINETEENTH-CENTURY MALAYSIA

THE STRAITS SETTLEMENTS

Singapore, Penang, and Malacca, called the Straits Settlements, were important to the British for the command of the strait and as links in the long chain of bastions protecting the shipping lanes from Gibraltar to Hong Kong. They were also important as trading centers where the exchange of Eastern and Western goods could take place.

In both respects, Singapore was more successful than the other Straits Settlements because its location was best for controlling the strait, and by 1825 Singapore had double the trade of Penang and Malacca together. It was the British East India Company's first unqualified success at establishing a trade center in the area, the original purpose for which the company had been founded two centuries earlier.

A free-trade area, Singapore was soon the greatest trading port in Southeast Asia. In 1832 Singapore became the administrative capital of all the Straits Settlements.

Unwilling to abandon its free-trade policy and tax the entrepôt trade, the company depended for its revenue upon so-called tax farms. The tax farmers were businessmen, almost always Chinese, who were granted the right to collect taxes on gambling, luxury goods, and imports for local use. The tax farmer retained any sums received above the amounts promised to the government. It was the least expensive way to collect revenue and, since the taxes were collected on items used predominantly by the Chinese, such as opium, whiskey, and pork, and on gambling, a large Chinese community was welcomed in the Straits Settlements.

Like the Dutch and the Portuguese before them, the British were interested primarily in trade and not in acquiring territory on the peninsula. A small, costly, and ill-advised war against the Minangkabau settlers in Malacca's hinterland, Naning, provided proof that the British East India Company had nothing to gain and much to lose by interfering in the Malay Peninsula.

THE THAI, 1816–63

The first permanent British settlement in Malaysia, Penang, had been granted to the British East India Company by the sultan of Kedah in the hope of protection against his enemies, chiefly the Bugis and the Thai. In 1823 the Thai, unsatisfied with Kedah's cooperation in its efforts to gain Perak, sent an expedition into Kedah that destroyed much life and property. The sultan begged Penang in vain for the aid that Frances Light had promised but which the company had never endorsed.

To the British East India Company, with its major investments in India, Thai friendship was more important

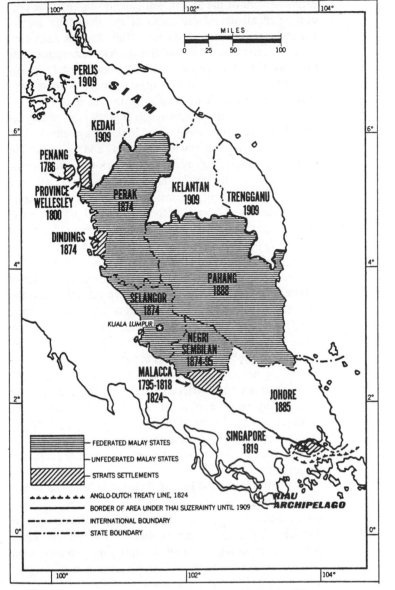

The extension of British rule in Malaysia clearly established the thirteen independent kingdoms (sultanates). The king is elected by and from the nine states who have hereditary rulers. Through 1979, there have been seven rulers (kings) since Abdul Rahman, who was the first to assume the throne in 1957.

than that of Kedah, whereas to interfere for Kedah's protection would be very expensive. In a treaty with Thailand in 1826, the company sacrificed Kedah to the Thai in exchange for a promise that the Thai would no longer molest Perak. The Thai then attempted to assert control over the eastern coast, and soon Kelantan and Trengganu were vassals. An attempt to gain control over Pahang, however, was unsuccessful, and by 1863 the Thai wave of expansion southward in the Malay Peninsula was over. The Thai retained their suzerainty over Kedah (including what later became Perlis), Kelantan, and Trengganu until 1909.

THE MALAY STATES BEFORE 1874

Life in the Malay states was little changed at first by the

establishment of the Straits Settlements. In 1850 the population of all the Malay states of the Peninsula did not exceed three hundred thousand. The Borneo territories, later to become Sarawak and Sabah, had very sparse populations. Only the Straits Settlements had substantial populations, with the majority Chinese. In 1857 there were seventy thousand Chinese in Singapore alone.

Malay society in the nineteenth century consciously retained as much as possible of the Malacca system. Malays were divided into two classes, the rulers and the ruled. The ruling class, including royal heirs and non-royal aristocrats, was headed by the state's sultan, whose capital was at a strategic place along the main river mouth of the area. Surrounded by elaborate protocol and ritual going back to Malacca times and earlier, the sultan was charged with the defense of the state against outsiders. Within the portion of the state over which his strategic riverine position gave him control, the sultan acted as the district chief, collecting tribute in crops, minerals, and jungle produce. Other district chiefs, appointed by the sultan in return for their allegiance and a portion of their income, collected from the trade of major tributaries and nearby rivers.

A sultan ruled for life but, as at the time of Malacca, his son did not necessarily inherit the title. At the funeral of the reigning sultan, the district chiefs met to select the new one from among a number of royal candidates; the chiefs usually preferred a weak or aged ruler who could be expected not to interfere seriously with the chiefs' administration of their districts, and civil wars over the succession were a frequent occurrence.

The chiefs depended less on their noble birth and letters of appointment from the sultan than on their armed followers to enforce their authority over the villages in their districts. A successful chief collected a substantial labor force—an entourage of relatives, hired mercenaries, debt bondsmen, and pagan slaves—to enforce his rule and provide the amenities of civilization.

A small but prestigious immigrant group to be found at the trading ports and elsewhere along the coast was the Arab community, composed primarily of persons of mixed Arab-Malay parentage. Often wealthy traders, they had additional prestige because of their association with the land of Islam's origin. Many of these Arabs prefaced their names with the honorific sharif or sayyid, titles reserved for direct descendants of the Prophet Mohammed.

The Muslims of part Arab or Indian descent were less easily assimilated into the Malay community than were, for example, the Bugis and Minangkabau. Their wealth and intellectual attainments were admired, but their bias toward urban residence and shopkeeping in the British-governed Straits Settlements made them foreign culturally.

In the early nineteenth century, most Chinese lived in the Straits Settlements. Although there were small Chinese enclaves at district capitals and other larger settlements inland on the peninsula, there was little to induce Chinese to settle in large numbers away from the big entrepôt towns.

This situation changed in midcentury when large tin deposits were discovered in the west of the peninsula, in Perak, Selangor, and Sungei Ujong (part of what later became the state of Negri Sembilan).

Disputes over land concessions and taxes involving rival Malay chiefs and rival *kongsis* (village organizations) and involvement of Chinese militias on both sides of dynastic wars resulted in widespread disorders throughout the tin-mining areas. The Malay political hierarchy also suffered sudden changes as petty chieftains downstream from newly developed mines found themselves more rich and powerful than their sultans.

BRITISH INTERVENTION IN THE MALAY STATES

In the 1870s British policy in the Malay states changed. Until then the officially proclaimed policy was noninterference in the affairs of the Malay states, except where "necessary for the suppression of piracy or the punishment of aggression on our people or territories." By 1874, however, the British government policy became one of employing its influence "to rescue, if possible, these fertile and productive countries from the ruin which must befall them if the present disorders continue unchecked."

The wars over the mines in West Malaysia were largely responsible for this change in policy. Chinese born in the Straits Settlements, and therefore British subjects, were demanding protection of their interests in the Malay states. Improved communications with Europe, especially after the Suez Canal opened in 1869, meant an increase in European business interests, including British investments that needed protection. There was also the fear that foreign interests might gain control of the Malay states if Great Britain hesitated.

Another factor in creating a more activist policy was the establishment of a crown colony composed of the Straits Settlements and Labuan Island in 1867. The interest of the British crown in the Malay territories was greater now that the Straits Settlements were under its direct authority and not, as formerly, a mere appendage to the Indian Empire. Singapore's role in Western trade with China and Indonesia was being reduced by the new port at Hong Kong and by the Dutch shipping network directly connecting the Netherlands with her colonies. The handling of the west coast tin exports from Malaya offered a new source of income to the Straits Settlements.

Great Britain extended its influence over the Malay states by a combination of persuasion, pressure, and an occasional show of force rather than by actual conquest. The Pangkor Treaty of 1874, which became the model for similar agreements signed later with the states of Selangor, Negri Sembilan, and Pahang, bound the sultan of Perak to accept British protection and to have no dealings with foreign powers except through Great Britain. In internal affairs the advice of a British resident had to be asked and followed except in matters concerning Malay religion and custom.

The Chinese *kongsi* war in Perak was also brought to an end at Pangkor through the arbitration of Great Britain's first Chinese-language officer in the Malay states, W. A. Pickering. After the extension of protection to Malay states of Selangor and Negri Sembilan, the *kongsi* wars subsided.

In exchange for accepting British advice, the sultans received very substantial stipends, as did other royal claimants and aristocratic chieftains. Efforts were made to maintain intact the forms of the Muslim monarchies, although basic changes were made, for example, in the way taxes were collected and justice administered.

State councils were established by the residents in the protected states. Headed by the sultan, the typical council membership included the resident, the major Malay chiefs, and the leading Chinese and, later, Western businessmen. The councils, to some extent a formalization of the Malay tradition of consultation between a sultan and his territorial chiefs, discussed all problems as they arose and approved estimates of revenue and expenditure and the appointment of lesser chiefs and village headmen (*penghulu*).

The resident, in theory responsible to the governor of the Straits Settlements but in practice virtually autonomous within his state, took the initiative in all matters except those concerning Malay religion and custom. A successful resident always tried to win genuine support and help from the Malay counselors by tact and patience, especially when venturing into areas regarded by the Malays as reserved to their control, such as slavery and customary criminal law.

By centralizing the power of each state in the hands of the resident, nominally the sultan, and at the same time remunerating the territorial chiefs and maintaining their formal prestige, the British brought an end to most of the causes for war that had previously troubled the states. For the villagers the abolition of feudal taxes, slavery, and the arbitrary rule of the territorial chiefs led to a more settled and peaceful life. In the protected states the villagers no longer felt the need to flee an oppressive chieftain. A penal code, based on British practice in India, was established, and European and Malay magistrates were appointed to administer it.

By the 1890s it became apparent that greater coordination of policy in the several states was necessary if they were to develop similar institutions. Sir Frank Swettenham, the resident in Perak, was largely responsible for developing a plan to federate the states and gaining its acceptance by the several sultans.

The federation came into effect in 1896. Included were the protected states of Perak, Selangor, Pahang, and the confederation of Negri Sembilan—which had been re-formed with British advice the previous year—but not the Straits Settlements, over which the British ruled directly. In the Federated Malay States each ruler retained a theoretical sovereignty, even if he surrendered many of his functions to the British residents. Thus, the Malays in each state were subjects of the sultan, whereas residents of the Straits Settlements could become British subjects. Although the vaguely worded federation treaty had promised no lessening of the sultan's authority, it led, in effect, to considerable centralization. Under the first resident general of the federation, Sir Frank Swettenham, a central administration was developed at Kuala Lumpur; the decisions of its departments were implemented in each of the states. Laws were often drafted by a British legal adviser, approved by the resident general, and automatically passed by the state councils. During this era in Malaya the civil servants, recruited by examination in Great Britain, exercised much of the authority usually belonging to legislative or executive bodies.

Under the British resident, British district officers administered the districts within each state and, within each district, administration was executed by salaried Malay *penghulu* appointed by the British after consultation with the Malay community. The *penghulu* were responsible for maintaining law and order in their territories.

Material prosperity increased greatly in the next decade. Revenues nearly tripled; exports nearly doubled; population increased; and roads, railroads, hospitals, schools, postal services, and savings banks appeared where none had been before. In 1900 the Institute for Medical Research was founded at Kuala Lumpur, and within a few years a concerted campaign against malaria was under way. British capital holders began to invest in the tin mines and in estate agriculture. A major innovation, one to play an important part in Malaya's future, was the introduction of rubber cultivation. The first seedlings had been smuggled from Brazil to Great Britain and brought to Malaya in the 1870s. By 1905 considerable acreage was planted in rubber, and from then on, with the continued increase in world demand, new land was put into rubber cultivation even faster. The estate owners faced a serious labor shortage, as had the owners of tin mines before them. Indian laborers were brought in to tap the rubber trees, as well as to work in railroad construction and on coffee plantations. By 1911, when the first census was taken, Malaya's plural society had been created. The population was composed of nearly 1.5 million Malays, over 900,000 Chinese, and 267,000 Indians. No restrictions were placed on immigration until 1930, when the world depression led to serious unemployment among Malay's alien workers.

THE BRITISH COME TO SARAWAK AND SABAH

By the nineteenth century the sultanate of Brunei had declined from its former greatness. Although theoretically the ruler of a territory covering all of northern and western Borneo, from the Sibuku River in the east to Cape Datu in the west, the sultan was unable to enforce his rule much beyond his capital city at Brunei Town. The sultan of Sulu also claimed ownership of part of north Borneo eastward from the Kimanis River and, although he could not enforce his rule over much of the territory, Brunei's power was strongest in the west and was negligible in the areas claimed by Sulu.

In 1842 the sultan of Brunei ceded a large tract of land embracing the Sarawak River area to a young British adventurer, James Brooke, as reward for the help Brooke had given in putting down a rebellion against the sultan's district chief in the area. Brooke was appointed the new district chief, or raja, of Sarawak, by the sultan. Within a few years he eliminated piracy and headhunting in his dominions with the occasional help of gunboats of the British Navy. In 1845 the "white raja's" regime survived a Malay rebellion led by the ousted district chief, and by 1853 Sarawak was independent of Brunei.

In the decade after 1850 a number of Chinese gold miners migrated to Sarawak from Dutch Borneo, joining the smaller community of Chinese gold miners in Bau, twenty miles from Kuching. In a bid for political power, the Chinese *kongsi* struck Kuching in 1857 and forced the raja to flee his residence. A combined force of Malays and Land Dayaks led by the raja's nephew put down the rebellion, but Brooke suspicion of Chinese political and secret society activity continued to the end of Brooke rule a century later.

Headhunting was an essential feature of Iban and other Borneo religions and cultures, and piracy, including, by Brooke definition, all seaborne opposition, was prevalent. In fighting these and in responding to requests for relief from the oppression of Brunei's appointed district chiefs, James Brooke and his heir, Charles Brooke, greatly expanded the borders of Sarawak. By the 1880s Brunei was surrounded by Sarawak territory except on the seaside. The sultan generally favored cessions to the Brookes, since he thus received annual payments that were greater than those he had previously received from his district chiefs.

Under the Brooke regime, the country was not open to commercial exploitation or large-scale migration in the manner of Malaya. This was largely because the raja felt a paternal concern that his subjects not be overwhelmed. Commerce and cash crops, however, were soon in the hands of Chinese merchants and farmers, and revenues for the raja came mainly from tax farms on Chinese opium, gambling, and other luxuries, as in the Straits Settlements. A handful of British residents and district officers governed according to the raja's personal instructions. Malay traditional leaders provided some measure of political backing as advisers, and Malays and other indigenous leaders filled minor administrative positions.

Enforcement of Brooke rule was achieved by letting loose upon disobedient tribal communities punitive expeditions of fearsome bands of Iban volunteers led by the Brookes. This unusual method of policing their territory earned the raja notoriety in Great Britain, which never gave its unqualified support to the Brookes's highly personal autocracy.

The Sarawak people, however, enjoyed a measure of physical security, which had previously been totally absent, and a modest amount of economic development without severe disruption of the way of life of the tribal interior peoples.

British control did not come to Sabah until 1881, when the British government granted a royal charter to the British North Borneo Company. The company, formed by a group of British and Austrian entrepreneurs, had already received grants from the sultans of Brunei and Sulu for their overlapping claims in northern Borneo and had bought out the rights to other earlier business ventures in the area.

The acquisition of the territory brought immediate objections from the Spanish, Dutch, and German governments, all of which claimed certain rights in the area, which were eventually quieted. The Spanish claim was revived by the Philippines in the twentieth century.

The royal charter was essentially one of restraint rather than privilege. The British North Borneo Company was to remain British in character and domicile; all directors and officials were to be British subjects; territory was not to be alienated without the consent of the British government; foreign affairs were to be controlled by the British government; slavery was abolished; religious freedom was guaranteed; general commercial monopoly was prohibited; and the appointment of the governor was made subject to British approval. Great Britain assumed, in fact, the role of protector.

Two major tasks faced the company: the economic development of the country and its territorial consolidation. Land and loans were offered to various groups to encourage development, and the immigration of Chinese was encouraged in order to provide a labor supply. Serious attempts were made to exploit what were considered the three major assets—timber resources, mineral deposits, and an abundance of arable land. Although timber proved to be an asset, mineral deposits were disappointing, and development of the land resources for tobacco plantations became, after 1890, the salvation of the company for a period of twenty years. A serious economic crisis was averted by the development of a boom in the production of rubber in the early twentieth century, and rubber became the mainstay of the country's economy. A west coast railroad linking Kota Kinabalu (formerly Jesselton), Weston, and Melalap, completed in 1905, opened up land ideal for rubber production. A degree of economic security resulted from these developments, which were also accompanied by a rise in population.

Territorial consolidation occurred mainly between 1884 and 1902 and involved the absorption of coastal enclaves through pressure either directly on local chieftains or on the sultan of Brunei. The extensive hinterland, a kind of terra incognita, fell to company control by default. In 1905, through the sale of the Lawas district to Sarawak, the boundary with that state was defined. Between 1890 and 1906 the company also administered the crown colony of Labuan.

Determined to keep on good terms with the Colonial Office in London, the chartered company modeled its administration on Malayan practices. With little money and few men, it kept the peace and abolished piracy and headhunting. As in Sarawak, the government was benevolent and paternalistic, although the gains in self-government and social services were modest.

CONSOLIDATION OF BRITISH RULE

At the turn of the century the British were consolidating their control over the Malaysian territories. In 1888 Sarawak, Sabah, and Brunei had accepted the protection of the crown, and in the next two decades Sarawak's and Sabah's boundaries acquired the shapes that they had in late 1969. In 1906 the sultan of Brunei accepted a British resident, thereby interposing the British government between what was left of Brunei and the continuing territorial ambitions of Sarawak. This had an unexpected result when, a few years later, northern Borneo's major oilfields were developed in territory that Brunei had been on the verge of ceding to Sarawak. The Brunei resident, with the help of civil servants borrowed from the Malayan Civil Service, ran the government on behalf of the sultan.

In 1909 the Federated Malay States government was further centralized by the creation of a federal council in Kuala Lumpur, which came gradually to take over much of the legislative initiative previously exercised by the state councils. The great rubber boom had begun, and the large-scale British investment required a more efficient government than separate state councils could provide. Improved transportation and communications within the peninsula made centralized administration possible for the first time.

The new priority placed on modern technical knowledge and skills left little place in the administration for Malays, whose skills were primarily political. The Malay establishment objected to the increase in centralized administration, since it lessened further the influence on British policy of the indigenous Malay state leadership. Pro-Malay sentiment among the British civil servants also opposed the increased centralization of the government of the Federated States. They felt that since the Malays were not partaking in the phenomenal economic development of their country, they should at least be allowed consideration in political matters.

The decentralizing faction grew in strength when the Thai government signed a treaty with Great Britain in 1909 transferring the states of Perlis, Kedah, Kelantan, and Trengganu from Thai to British protection. These four states and the southernmost state, Johore, refused to enter into the federation and became known as the Unfederated Malay States. Gradually, these states agreed to accept British "advisers," whose authority was somewhat less than that of the residents of the Federated States.

Other developments in Malaya during this period were largely continuations of trends begun in the previous century. Railroads, roads, and communications were extended into the Unfederated States. Social services increased throughout the peninsula. Malays, Indians (who had been

Iskandar, the sultan of Perak, the grandfather of Sultan Idris Almutawakkil Alalahi Shah, is honored on a 1938 postage stamp.

imported in quantity after 1870 to work in the rubber estates), and Chinese were given slightly more opportunity to advise the government of their opinions, but neither the fact of nor the demand for representative government existed.

THE JAPANESE OCCUPATION

MALAYA AND SINGAPORE

On December 8, 1941, when Japan declared war on Great Britain, Singapore's sea defense included only two capital vessels, which were soon sunk. The Japanese moved easily from Thailand to Kedah and on down the peninsula; on February 15, 1942, the British surrendered.

In occupying Malaya, the Japanese diverged from the tactics used in other parts of Southeast Asia in that they made no pretense of permitting Malayan self-government. Malaya and Sumatra were briefly combined in an attempted union. The Japanese made few changes in government on the peninsula and, for the most part, the Malays neither opposed nor actively aided the invaders. In 1943 Kedah, Perlis, Trengganu, and Kelantan were returned by the Japanese, for the duration of the war to the Thai, who placed Thai governors at the head of the existing state administrations. The civil servants in Malaya continued to function much as they had done under the British; they had, however, slightly more authority during the war than before it, with the result that the eventual return of the British was felt to be a loss.

Although the whole population suffered during the war years, particularly because the cessation of rice imports led to widespread malnutrition, the most marked hardships were borne by the Chinese community. Thousands of Chinese were killed in the first days of occupation, and many thousands more fled to the interior, where they became squatters on the fringes of the jungle. The British, in preparing to leave Malaya, had given rapid training in the arts of sabotage to the members of the only group sufficiently organized and anti-Japanese to carry on armed resistance—the Chinese of the Malayan Communist party.

SABAH AND SARAWAK

Resistance against the Japanese was carried on also by the people of Sabah and Sarawak. In Sabah the biggest single action took place on October 9, 1943, when a few hundred Chinese, Sulus, and Bajaus killed all fifty Japanese in the

Kota Kinabalu area. Japanese retribution was fierce, and during the remainder of the occupation executions, death marches, and disease overtook much of the Asian population and annihilated the Allied prisoners of war.

At the start of the occupation Sarawak's monarch was out of the country, and the civil servants left in charge were without instructions. With the arrival of the Japanese in Kuching on Christmas Day, 1941, the entire government collapsed. The civil servants were put in prison camps, and the Japanese took charge. As the occupation continued, food and other basic imports grew more scarce, and the town populations suffered hardship; attempts to resist the Japanese, generally led by Chinese, were easily crushed. In the beginning of 1945 Allied guerrilla leaders parachuted into the Sarawak interior to organize the indigenous resistance that preceded the Allied liberation of Borneo beginning in June.

THE REESTABLISHMENT OF BRITISH RULE

When the British returned to their Malaysian territories, they found them devastated by war. Sabah's major cities, Kota Kinabalu and Sandakan, had been leveled by Allied bombs during the fight for liberation. Hunger was widespread, and throughout the territories racial animosities had intensified.

Great Britain's status had been irrevocably altered by the war. The success of the Japanese in East and West Malaysia was a defeat for British prestige and a boost to Asian and communal nationalism. With the growth of nationalism also came demands for better economic and social conditions.

THE FEDERATION OF MALAYA

During the war the British Colonial Office had drawn up plans for the Malayan Union to be imposed on British Malaya (the Malay states of the peninsula and the Straits Settlements) when the Japanese were driven out. The union, involving great concessions by the Malay rulers and the state governments to a British-led central government, was conceived with little discussion and considerable haste and was implemented by the MacMichael treaties between Great Britain and the Malay rulers in 1946.

The imposition of centralization upon the Malay states with allegiance to the British crown replacing that sworn to the individual sultans was a threat not only to the long-recognized prerogatives of the ruling class but also to the special position of all ethnic Malays, since the plan called for the incorporation of Penang and Malacca, with their large Chinese and Indian populations, into the union and the granting of Malayan citizenship to all on an equal basis. Singapore, with its one million Chinese, was omitted from the union as a concession to Malay sentiment.

The Malayan Union came into legal effect in April 1946,

This is a photograph taken of "King" Hisamuddin Alam Shah, the elected ruler of Malaya, shortly before he became ill and died on September 1, 1959. He was to have replaced Sir Abdul Rahman. Ironically, Hisamuddin's death came on the day that he was to have been enthroned.

The sultan Yussuf Izuddin Shah, father of the present sultan, is honored on a 1950 stamp.

The Malaysian state of Negri Sembilan commemorates the coronation of Queen Elizabeth II, June 2, 1953, on this postage stamp.

Yussuf Izuddin Shah, the sultan of Perak, appears on a 1953 Perak postage stamp.

Sultan of Johore, Ibrahim, honored on a 1949 postage stamp. He was the father of Sultan Ismail.

The fourth Yang di-Puertuan (king), the sultan of Trengganu, Sultan Ismail Nasiruddin Shah, was elected to the throne and sworn in on September 21, 1965.

The Sultan of Trengganu on a postage stamp.

The first king of Malaysia after its independence from Great Britain, Sir Abdul Rahman, Yang di-Pertuan Agong and his queen, Raja Permaisuri Agong, in the garden of the Royal Palace (Istana Negara), near the capital, Kuala Lumpur. He became king in 1957 and died of a heart attack before serving out his five-year term of office.

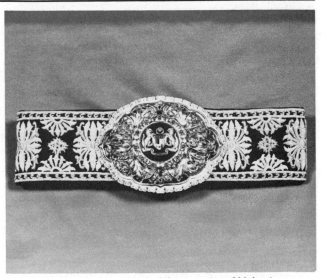

The official cummerbund of the sovereign of Malaysia

A closeup of the royal "crown" of the king

The official "sword" of office, which is worn in the cummerbund on ceremonial occasions.

King Rahman in his official costume.

Lee Kuan Yew, prime minister of Singapore, left, on his arrival at Kuala Lumpur airport in a 1963 visit to Malaysia, being greeted by Prince Abdul Rahman, right. Prince Rahman, the former prime minister of the Federation of Malaya, became Malaysia's first prime minister when the nation was born on September 16, 1962. Singapore, a member of the Malaysian Kingdom, separated from it in 1965 to become a nation by itself.

The sultan of Kedah, His Royal Highness Sultan Abdul Halim Mu'adzam Shah.

The sultan of Kedah became king on February 20, 1959. His coronation is commemorated on this postage stamp.

The sultan of Perlis on a
Perak postage stamp

The sultan (raja) of Perlis, His Royal Highness Tuanku Syed Putra ibni
al-Marhum Syed Hassan Jamalullah

The king and queen of Malaysia visit with the emperor and empress of
Japan.

The raja of Perlis ascended the throne as king (Yang di-Pertuan Agong) on
January 4, 1961.

Also, the queen was enthroned the same day.

King Ismail Nasiruddin Shah on the throne on coronation day

Also, his queen was enthroned the same day.

King Ismail Nasiruddin delivers the official royal message of enthrone-ment from the royal state proclamation and responds to congratulations from other rulers, the government, and the people of Malaysia.

With the official enthronement over, the new king arrives with a full smile at the banquet place.

King Ismail Nasiruddin and his queen (Raja Permaisuri Agong) in 1968, about to depart by airplane for a royal visit to the territory of Sabah.

The sultan of Selangor, His Royal Highness Sultan Salahuddin Abdul Aziz Shah

The sultan of Selangor on two of his country's stamps

but unexpectedly strong Malay resistance induced the British to delay its implementation. The resistance was led by the new United Malays National Organization (UMNO), founded and led by Dato Onn bin Ja'afar, a Johore Malay. Months of discussions between British and local leaders resulted in the abandonment of the centralized government scheme. On February 1, 1948, the Federation of Malaya came into being. The Federation of Malaya was a revival of the method used by the British to govern the Federated Malay States. A British high commissioner appointed by the crown ruled as the representative of the crown and the Malay rulers. An appointed executive council advised the high commissioner, and the Federal Legislative Council included representatives from the state and Straits Settlements councils. The federation included the nine Malay states and the two Straits Settlements of Penang and Malacca. It returned to the states many of their traditional rights; to the rulers, their prerogatives, and to the Malays, the assurance by its citizenship provisions that the Chinese would not in the near future become politically dominant.

THE EMERGENCY

In the year the federation came into being, the Malayan Communist party began an insurrection. Partly because the Communists' former tactics in Malaya, mainly the infiltration of labor unions, were being successfully opposed by British policy and partly because of the change in tactics of Asian Communist groups, the Malayan Communist party began to follow a policy of terrorism. Their targets were local, mainly police stations and communications lines, and many Chinese Kuomintang leaders and European planters were murdered. On June 16, 1948, the British authorities declared a state of emergency.

Gradually, the guerrillas were driven into isolated jungle areas, but the operations against them were a tremendous drain on the country's economy. To cut the guerrillas' supplies of food and equipment, the government was obliged to resettle in fenced and protected new villages nearly half a million persons, among them thousands of Chinese families who since World War II had been squatters on the jungle's fringes.

The Emergency, as the guerrilla war was called, lasted twelve years, claimed eleven thousand lives, and cost the Malayan government the equivalent of US$567 million. The nadir came in 1951 when a convoy protecting the British high commissioner, Sir Henry Gurney, was ambushed in daylight on one of the main roads of Malaya and Sir Henry was killed.

THE PATH TO INDEPENDENCE

The British had promised in the Federation Agreement of 1948 to grant eventual self-rule to Malaya. Nevertheless, the colonial government insisted upon evidence of national unity before granting independence.

Independence came for the Federation of Malaya in 1957

The sultan of Pahang, His Royal Highness Sultan Abu Bakar Ri'ayatuddin al-Mu'adzam Shah

The sultan of Pahang on two Malaysian postage stamps

The sultan of Kelantan, His Highness Sultan Yahya Petra ibni al-Marhum Shah, became the sixth king of Malaysia on September 21, 1975.

Sultan of Kelantan, Ibrahim, on a 1951 state postage stamp

after a relatively brief period of preparation for self-government. The independent government inherited from the colonial period two major problems that have confronted the successor government of Malaysia—a need to create national harmony out of diverse ethnic groups and a need to diversify an economy overly dependent upon the world prices of a few primary products.

GOVERNMENT

The country has a constitutional monarchy, nominally headed by the *yang di-pertuan agong,* or "paramount ruler." The ruler is elected for a five-year term by the sultans of nine states of West Malaysia from among their own members. He performs the duties of a constitutional monarch and is the leader of the Islamic religion for Malaysia.

Executive power is vested in the cabinet, led by the prime minister, the leader of the political party that wins the most seats in a parliamentary election. The cabinet is chosen from among the members of Parliament and is responsible to that body.

The bicameral Parliament consists of a Senate and a House of Representatives. Of the fifty-eight members of the Senate, twenty-six are elected by universal adult suffrage (two from each state) and thirty-two are appointed by the *yang di-pertuan agong.* All sit for six-year terms. Representatives of the house are elected in single constituencies by universal adult suffrage. The one hundred and fifty-four members in the House of Representatives—one hundred and fourteen from the states of West Malaysia and forty from the states of East Malaysia—are elected to maximum terms of five years. Legislative power is divided between federal and state legislatures.

The Malaysian legal system is based on English common law. The Federal Court, the highest court in Malaysia, reviews decisions referred from the High Courts and has original jurisdiction in constitutional matters and in dis-

His Highness Tengku Ismail Petra ibn al-Sultan Yahya Petra became the regent of Kelantan upon his father's enthronement as the sixth king of Malaysia. Then, upon his father's death in 1979, he became the sultan of Kelantan.

The sultan of Johore on a postage stamp

The sultan of Johore, His Highness Sultan Ismail ibni al-Marhum Shah

The Yang di-Pertuan Besar of Negri Sembilan, His Highness Tuanku Munawir ibni al-Marhum Tuanku Abdul Rahman

The sultan of Perak, His Highness Paduka Sri Sultan Idris al-Mutawakkil Allallahi Shah

The seventh Yang di-Pertuan Agong (king) of Malaysia, Tuanku Haji Ahmad Shah at the time of installation (coronation)—July 10, 1980. The queen (Raja Permaisuri Agong), Tuanku Hajjah Afzan (right).

putes between states or between the federal government and a state. West Malaysia and East Malaysia each have a High Court.

The federal government has authority over external affairs, defense, internal security, justice (except Islamic and native law), federal citizenship, finance, commerce, industry, communications, transportation, and other matters. The states of East Malaysia enjoy guarantee of states' rights with regard to immigration, civil service, and customs matters.

The heads of the thirteen states in Malaysia are titular rulers. Effective executive power in the states rests in the hands of the chief ministers. The chief ministers and the members of their state cabinets are selected from the state legislatures and operate under a parliamentary system.

On February 9, 1984, the nine Malaysian hereditary sultanate rulers chose Sultan Mahmood Iskander of Johore to be king for the next five years. Mahmood Iskander was convicted on a homicide charge resulting from a shooting incident in 1977. He was later pardoned by his father and reinstated as crown prince. His father died in 1981, and he succeeded him to the throne of Johore. His name and title as the Monarch of the Malaysian States is Yang di-Pertuan

Agong. During his term of office, the Paramount Ruler relinquishes all authority in his state. The Paramount Ruler is the nominal source of all government authority in Malaysia and the official leader of its Islamic community.

THE ROYAL SOVEREIGNS OF THE KINGDOMS OF MALAYSIA

September 16, 1963—Federation of Malaysia formed from Singapore, Sarawak, and British North Borneo

Reign	Title	Ruler
1957–1959	Paramount Ruler	Sir Abdul Rahman
1959–1961	Paramount Ruler	Abdul Halim Mu'adzam Shah
1961–1965	Paramount Ruler	Tuanku Syed Putra
1965–1970	Paramount Ruler	Ismail Nasiruddin Shah
1970–1975	Paramount Ruler	Tuanku Abdul Halim Mu'adzam Shah
1975–1979	Paramount Ruler	Tuanku Yahya Putra
1980–1984	Paramount Ruler	Tuanku Haji Ahmad Shah
1984–	Paramount Ruler	Yang di-Pertuan Agong

The king and queen of Malaysia visiting the United Nations headquarters in New York City on April 14, 1978. Left to right: the queen, Seri Paduka Baginda Raja Permaiguri Agong Tuanku Zainab binti Tengku Muhamed Petra; the king, Seri Paduka Baginda Yang di-Pertuan Agong Tuanku Yahya Putra ibni al-Marhum Sultan Ibrahim, with Ambassador Tan Sri Zaiton Ibrahim, the permanent representative of Malaysia to the UN, showing them the interior of the building. The king died in 1979 and was replaced by Tuanku Haji Ahmad Shah of Pahang.

The seventh king of Malaysia, the former sultan of Pahang, Tuanku Haji Ahmad Shah

The Malaysian sultanate rulers elected Yang di-Pertuan Agong as Paramount Ruler in 1984.

16
The Kingdom of Laos

The Kingdom of Laos, the name by which the country was known until 1975, came into being in 1946 under French guidance. It became a constitutional monarchy the following year and achieved full independence from France in 1953.

The first ruler of the new kingdom traced his descent from the royal line of the ancient Lao kingdom of Lan Xang, founded in 1353. Lan Xang at the end of the seventeenth century had split up into several smaller states, each subject at various times to Burmese, Siamese, and Vietnamese suzerainty, sometimes to two at once. Throughout the eighteenth and nineteenth centuries—until the imposition of French domination in the late 1800s—the fortunes of these Lao states were to a major extent determined by the shifts in power relationships among the more powerful states surrounding them.

The Laotian government, newly independent in 1953, was immediately threatened by rightist and leftist factional dissidence; the leftist elements received external support first from the Communist Viet Minh forces and later from the government of the Democratic Republic of Vietnam (North Vietnam). By the early 1960s the country was on the brink of civil war, the international implications of which brought about the convening of a conference of Geneva in 1962. At the conference agreements were reached that have permitted Laos to survive as an independent and neutralist state.

On December 2, 1975, the monarchy was abolished and the Lao People's Democratic Republic was established. The new regime proclaimed its alignment with the Communist bloc but stated its intention to participate actively with "nonaligned countries."

ORIGIN OF THE LAO

The kingdom of Laos derived its name from the Lao, a branch of the Tai ethnic group. In their earlier history the Tai occupied most of the present-day Szechwan and Yunnan provinces in southwest China, where they established the kingdom of Nanchao in the eighth century A.D.; its capital was in Yunnan. A relatively well-organized state with strong military forces, Nanchao existed until 1253, when it was destroyed by the Mongols under Kublai Khan.

Chinese expansion, even before the destruction of Nanchao, had brought pressure on these Tai peoples, who gradually migrated farther south. Some Tai, including the present-day Lao, followed the Mekong River into the rugged, sparsely populated northern hinterland of the Khmer Empire, which was centered in the modern Khmer Republic (Cambodia). The few inhabitants of this region consisted of two distinct groups. One group was dark skinned, believed by some to have been in the area since the time land bridges linked the continent with the major archipelagoes near southeastern Asia. The second group was Malayo-Polynesian, who had migrated there sometime between 500 B.C. and A.D. 500. There were also some Cham, Mon, and Khmer peoples, who may have been of Malayo-Polynesian origin.

The early Lao migration was peaceful—not an invasion—and did not involve large movements of population. The Lao accepted Khmer domination of their tribal organization and later appeared to have been under the suzerainty of a Tai state to the west in what is now Thailand. Gradually, as their numbers increased, they occupied the valleys of the Mekong and its tributaries for their wet-rice cultivation, displacing earlier inhabitants who then moved to higher altitudes. The breakup of Nanchao accelerated the southward migration of the Tai, who reached the areas of modern Assam in India, Burma, Thailand, North Vietnam, and Hainan Island.

In their long association with the Chinese, the Tai peoples assimilated from the Chinese the arts of war, use of the bow, terracing of hill slopes for cultivation, and wet-rice cultivation on the plains. They did not, however, adopt writing from the Chinese but from the culturally Indianized Mon and Khmer. This indirect Indian influence on the Tai, including the Lao, was also evident in the mythology and rites that provided supernatural sanction for rulers. One of these myths concerns the origin of the Lao. It relates how the King of Heaven sent down to earth a semidivine an-

The Kingdom of Laos

cestor, Khoun Borom, to rule the Celestial Kingdom (probably an allusion to China). Mounted in royal splendor on a white elephant and accompanied by two wives, he arrived in the vicinity of present-day Dien Bien Phu. There he found two enormous gourds, which when pierced with a poker produced men, women, seeds, animals, and all the materials useful in populating the world. The darker peoples were said to have emerged sooty from a hole burned with the poker. Khoun Borom divided the land among his seven sons, the divisions corresponding to the region into which the Tai migrated. Khoun Lo, the eldest son, was given the lands of Muong Swa (present-day Luang Prabang province), from which the Lao empire of Lan Xang developed.

THE KINGDOM OF LAN XANG

The recorded history of the Lao started in the fourteenth century with Fa Ngoun, by legend the twenty-third successor of Khoun Lo. Fa Ngoun was brought up at the Khmer court of Angkor and was married to a Khmer princess. With Khmer assistance he returned to Muong Swa and conquered the small states that constitute present-day Laos as well as much of the Khorat Plateau in northeastern Thailand. In 1353 he united these territories into the Lao kingdom of Lan Xang (literally, million elephants), one of the largest, though sparsely populated, states in the region.

Fa Ngoun was converted to Theravada Buddhism and received from his father-in-law a mission of Cambodian Buddhist monks who brought, in addition to the Buddhist scriptures, a famous gold statue of the Buddha, known as the Prabang, which was believed to have come from Ceylon originally. The statue became the principal religious symbol of Lan Xang and remains so in modern Laos. Fa Ngoun established Buddhism as the state religion; however, it had only a superficial effect on the majority of the people.

Fa Ngoun, called the Conqueror, continued to expand Lan Xang's territory. Its eastern borders eventually reached Champa and extended along the Annamite Chain; on the west it was bordered by three Tai kingdoms along the Menam River. Fa Ngoun may have received tribute from one of these kingdoms as well as a princess for marriage to his son. Constant warfare exhausted his people, however, and Fa Ngoun's excesses and the ruthlessness of his military commanders finally caused his ministers to drive him into exile in 1373.

His successor was known as *Phya Sam Sene Thai* (literally, lord of three hundred thousand Tai), a title derived from a census of adult males taken in 1376. The census showed about three hundred thousand men in the kingdom to be of Tai origin; another four hundred thousand were of non-Tai origin. Sam Sene Thai's reign was one of consolidation and administrative development under strong Siamese influence. He was a devout Buddhist, building *wat* and schools; under his rule the Buddhist priest began to assume in the Lao communities the place of honor that was traditional in other Buddhist countries. The *wat* developed into the center of community life and social gathering as well as a place of worship.

The king established a standing army said to have had 150,000 men consisting of infantry, cavalry, and an elephant corps, supported by a supply corps of 20,000. His capital was well placed economically, and under his rule Lan Xang became an important center of trade, its gumlac and benzoin being much in demand by the Siamese. Lan Xang grew larger than any of its neighbors and became embroiled in struggles with Siamese and Burmese states, a continuing feature of Laotian history.

Sam Sene Thai's administrative structure was based on the principle of absolute monarchy. It employed princes of royal blood as the king's main advisers. There was a hierarchy of officials, tax collectors, and minor functionaries holding their positions at the pleasure of the king; however, positions of the royal family were hereditary. Next to the king in power was the *maha oupahat* (second king or viceroy) who, although not necessarily of royal blood, was the king's most intimate adviser, often acting in his stead. Governors of *muong* (districts) might either be royal appointees or selected by a local council of notables from the family of the previous incumbent. In theory, any qualified person could rise to high office.

In 1520 King Phothisarath I succeeded to the throne of Lan Xang and moved the capital to Vientiane (Vien Chang). He was notable for his devotion to Buddhism, the construction of Buddhist *wat,* and his attempt at suppression of the cult of *phi* (spirit worshipers). He strengthened the official position of the established religion, but the people were as much in reverence with the spirits as they were with Buddha.

Phothisarath warred with his neighbors and in 1545 obtained the throne of Lan Na for his son Setthathirath. The son inherited the throne of Lan Xang in 1547. He returned to Muong Swa (to which the capital had again been moved), taking with him an important religious object and symbol of sovereignty known as the Emerald Buddha, to safeguard it from Burmese attack. Under pressure from the Burmese, however, he again moved Lan Xang's capital to Vientiane (at that time the old capital of Muong Swa was given its present-day name of Luang Prabang). At his new capital, King Setthathirath built the temple compound, Wat Keo, and a stupa, That Luang, in which the Emerald Buddha and other Buddhist relics were then enshrined.

Setthathirath mysteriously disappeared in 1571 on his way home from a punitive expedition against Cambodia, perhaps in battle with the unconquered tribes in the highlands. Lan Xang then entered a period of twenty years of anarchy and Burmese domination. A decline of Burmese power, however, permitted the restoration of Laotian independence in 1591. In 1637 Souligna Vongsa seized power after another dynastic struggle. His long rule, from 1637 to 1694, has been called the golden age of Laos. The country's boundaries were redefined, and Laos was probably at its zenith in territory and in power among its neighbors. Souligna Vongsa did, however, alienate the small but strategically important kingdom of Xieng Khouang.

PERIOD OF LAO FRAGMENTATION

Souligna Vongsa contributed to the fall of Lan Xang by refusing to stay the execution of his only son. Upon the king's death in 1694 there was a struggle for succession that destroyed the unity of the kingdom.

Three Lao states emerged from competition for the throne. Souligna Vongsa's nephew controlled from Vientiane a considerable area on both sides of the middle Mekong, under the suzerainty of Annam, which had helped him to get the throne. A separate kingdom was established at Luang Prabang in 1707 by Souligna Vongsa's grandsons; this area remained independent of the Vietnamese. A third kingdom, Champassak, which controlled the southernmost provinces on both sides of the Mekong, was established in 1713 by another prince. This kingdom was increasingly influenced by Siam.

The kingdom of Vientiane declined steadily and in 1778 was occupied by Siam, which also exacted tribute from Luang Prabang. Double vassalage existed during this period. For example, the kingdom of Vientiane paid tribute—subsequently restored by Siam—not only to Siam but also to Vietnam after the revival of Vietnamese power by Emperor Nguyen Anh in 1802. This was possible because tribute was little more than a symbolic act implying virtually no obligation from either party.

In the 1820s Prince Anou, a former *maha oupahat,* who then ruled Vientiane, involved his kingdom in a disastrous war with Siam. His capital was destroyed in 1829; its inhabitants were forcibly resettled in Siam, and much of the central Mekong area in Laos was depopulated. In 1873 a European traveler found Vientiane still in ruins. The Siamese during this time also carried off the sacred Prabang Buddha and other booty. Later Siamese campaigns resulted in a virtual depopulation of the area between the Mekong and the Annamite Chain; Xieng Khouang was the only surviving Lao state in this buffer zone.

In the latter 1800s the kingdom of Luang Prabang was reduced in size by the Siamese to no more than a small portion of the buffer zone between Siam and Vietnam. Xieng Khouang continued to exist during part of this period through a policy of neutrality under which it paid tribute to both sides, but in 1885 it was occupied by Siamese troops. In the same year another Siamese conquest of Vientiane occurred, and both Luang Prabang and the kingdom of Champassak were reduced to being Siamese satellites. Vietnam annexed Sam Neua, then an autonomous hill state in northeast Laos, in the same year.

THE FRENCH COLONIAL PERIOD

In the course of the intense European colonial activity that occurred in Southeast Asia generally in the nineteenth century, the French were the first to make contact with Laos. After the establishment of French protectorates over Annam and Tonkin in 1882, the French started active intervention in the Lao territories. The Siamese troops that occupied Xieng Khouang and Sam Neua in 1885 had done so ostensibly to suppress Chinese bandits but in reality to counter French moves. The French recognized Siamese suzerainty there but secured the right to maintain a vice-consul at Luang Prabang. The appointee, August Pavie, was credited with subsequently winning the area for France by persuading the royal court at Luang Prabang to request French protection.

Because of French pressure, the Siamese by successive treaties between 1893 and 1907 renounced all claims to territory east of the Mekong and to islands in the river as well as to territory along the lower west bank. The upper portions west of the Mekong—part of the former Lan Xang Kingdom—remained a part of present-day Thailand.

In 1899 the French stationed a chief resident in Vientiane to unify the administration of the territories of Luang Prabang, Xieng Khouang, Champassak, and Vientiane into a single administrative entity, called Laos for the first time. Only the royal house of Luang Prabang retained its royal title and prerogatives under French protection. The son of the king of Champassak was appointed governor of Bassac province but without royal status. The other principalities were reduced to provinces; no effort was made to restore their royal families, and the entire area was ruled directly or indirectly by French officials.

On the whole, the hand of France rested lightly on Laos. The French generally accepted the advice and employed the services of the local elite, especially the tribal chiefs. Patterns of local rule and custom compatible with French sovereignty were unmolested. The French were adamant only in abolishing slavery and in tightly controlling all fiscal administration. Gradually, however, they also began influencing the judicial and educational systems and later made an innovation by establishing government health and sanitation services.

The Lao caused the French little trouble. The crown prince, Sisavang Vong, who returned from studying in Paris in 1904 to assume the throne of Luang Prabang, accepted French overlordship. The use of French military force did not involve the Lao. French action was directed, between 1901 and 1907, at a group of southern Mountain Mon-Khmer who rebelled to protest suppression of their customary slave trading. Chinese bandits from Yunnan province in China kept the colonial army occupied between 1914 and 1916. The final major action occurred from 1919 to 1921 and was against Meo raids on the Lao and other groups.

WORLD WAR II AND TRANSITION

During World War II the Japanese, with concessions made by the Vichy regime in France, occupied French Indochina in 1941: A few Lao engaged in underground resistance against the Japanese, but most showed little resentment, and life went on much as usual. Thailand seized and, after Japanese "mediation," kept portions of the Lao provinces of Bassac and Sayaboury lying west of the Mekong. In compensation for Lao acquiescence in this loss of territory the Vichy French made the kingdom of Luang Prabang a protectorate and extended it to include the provinces of Vientiane, Xieng Khouang, and Houa Khong. King Sisavang Vong was authorized to form a cabinet, adapted from

King Sisavang Vong was the official king of Laos from 1904 until his death in 1959. He appeared on many of the kingdom's postage stamps.

This set of stamps was issued to honor the memory of King Sisavang Vong. Left to right, top to bottom: Funeral urn under canopy with monks, April 23–29, 1961; urn under royal canopy; catafalque on a seven-headed dragon carriage; and King Sisavang Vong.

the traditional king's council, in which his eldest son, Prince Phetsarath, was prime minister.

In March 1945 the Japanese declared the French colonial regime ended; the princely rulers were to become an independent part of Japan's "new order." King Sisavang Vong at first proclaimed through the crown prince his loyalty to France but was later forced by the Japanese to declare his independence. The viceroy and prime minister, Prince Phetsarath, who had a relatively free hand in running the country, in August 1945 confirmed that Japanese-instigated declaration of independence and decreed that Laos was to be an independent monarchy under King Sisavang Vong. The prince formed a committee called the Lao Issara (Free Lao) to resist any attempt to return to colonial status; however, Free French paratroopers landed in Vientiane and Luang Prabang and announced the resumption of the French protectorate.

The king, apparently under French pressure, stripped Prince Phetsarath of his titles and positions in October 1945. This action strengthened the Lao Issara, which in October 1945 formed the Committee of the People and proclaimed a provisional constitution of an independent Laos. The king refused to approve the constitution and the government, whereupon the new National Assembly deposed him on the grounds that he was not a free agent. Later the king realized the strength of the movement, accepted the constitution, and was reinstated as a constitutional monarch after agreeing to install a Lao Issara government. Prince Phetsarath continued to be the main force in the Lao Issara, though he did not become prime minister. Sisavang Vong was enthroned as king of all Laos in traditional ceremonies in April 1946.

The Free French meanwhile had moved to restore French authority in Laos. A force of Franco-Lao guerrillas and French detachments was mustered in the south and advanced up the Mekong. It smashed the resistance of Vietnamese troops sent by Ho Chi Minh and of the small Lao Issara forces, and two days after Sisavang Vong's enthronement French ground forces entered Vientiane. The Lao Issara forces broke up into guerrilla bands; many escaped into Thailand, where they were joined by the whole Lao Issara government. In Thailand Prince Phetsarath, calling himself the regent of Laos, set up a government-in-exile.

The French became more conciliatory after occupying Vientiane and Luang Prabang. A Franco-Laotian commission was formed that produced a modus vivendi, signed on August 27, 1946, which confirmed the autonomy of Laos and provided for the election of a constitutional assembly. Despite some guerrilla action in the countryside, the election was held in January 1947, and in September of that year a constitution was officially promulgated.

Meanwhile, dissension arose in the Lao Issara government-in-exile. Prince Phetsarath refused to have any contact with the French and continued to press for a completely independent Laos. Opposing him was a half-brother,

Stamp issued on tenth anniversary of King Sisavang Vong's death also shows the "resting place."

Prince Souvanna Phouma, who also wanted independence but was inclined to work with the French to get it. Another half-brother, Prince Souphanouvong, who had commanded the Lao Issara forces, demanded active cooperation with Ho Chi Minh's Viet Minh forces.

In 1947 the Lao Issara's operations in Thailand were adversely affected by a change in the Thai government, and many of its adherents returned to Laos. In 1949 a new Franco-Laotian convention fulfilled many of the Lao Issara's demands, and the organization dissolved; most of the exiles returned to reenter the service of the Lao government. Prince Phetsarath, however, remained in Thailand until 1957.

Under the 1949 Franco-Laotian convention, France recognized Laos as an independent associate state, and Laos affirmed adherence to the French Union. The convention gave Laos greater authority in foreign affairs, including the right to apply for membership in the United Nations. Several Western countries, including the United States, extended recognition, as did Thailand. The French, after the Viet Minh launched their offensive in Vietnam in 1950, hastened progress toward full Laotian independence in order to

devote more attention to Vietnam. Full sovereignty was given Laos by the Franco-Laotian Treaty of 1953.

INDEPENDENCE AND CIVIL WAR

Independent Laos immediately encountered economic, military, and political difficulties. The French withdrew their troops to meet the threat in Vietnam, and Laos was compelled to form its own army. This was accomplished under French tutelage and with French financial and logistic support furnished from funds and stocks supplied to France by the United States.

An overriding complication was the constant threat of intervention by North Vietnam. Prince Souphanouvong, who had gone to Hanoi in 1948, later headed a Communist movement that was formed in 1950. It was originally known as the Free Lao Front but later was renamed the Lao Patriotic Front (Neo Lao Hak Sat—NLHS). This organization, whose military arm was popularly known as the Pathet Lao, presented itself as the free government of all Laos and the refuge of all true opponents of French colonialism and United States "imperialism."

In 1953 Viet Minh troops, with support from Pathet Lao units, crossed into northern Laos, forced French and Royal Lao government units from the area, and established what Prince Souphanouvong called a resistance government in the province of Houa Phan (the government designation for the province of which Sam Neua is the capital). From this base the Viet Minh were within striking distance of Luang Prabang.

The Geneva Conference of 1954, convened primarily to end the fighting in Vietnam between the French Union forces and the Viet Minh, also reached a settlement for Laos. It decided that the dissident forces in Laos, both Viet Minh and Pathet Lao, be regrouped in the two northern Laotian provinces of Phong Saly and Houa Phan "pending a political settlement" that would integrate the NLHS into the national community. The conference also established the International Commission for Supervision and Control (commonly known as ICC) in Laos, composed of representatives of India, Canada, and Poland. Because of its makeup, the ICC was incapable of reaching the unanimous agreement required for effective action.

From 1955 to 1957 a series of negotiations to find an acceptable domestic political settlement took place among the various Laotian factions. Prolonged efforts primarily directed at political and military integration failed, the chief issue being the government's right to assume the administration of Phong Saly and Houa Phan provinces. Eventually, at the end of 1956, agreement in principle was reached as a basis for national reconciliation, for which the first step was to be a coalition government under Prince Souvanna Phouma. The initial attempt failed. Another effort resulted in November 1957 in the detailed settlements called the Vientiane Agreements for civil and military reintegration of the Pathet Lao into a united government.

The Government of National Union under Prince Souvanna Phouma was formed after Prince Souphanouvong surrendered the two northern provinces and swore allegiance to the kingdom of Laos for himself and the NLHS. Supplementary elections to fill seats in the National Assembly for the two provinces, under terms of the Geneva Conference of 1954, were held in May 1958 and resulted in a victory for the NLHS and its ally, the Peace party; together they won thirteen of the twenty-one seats contested. The reaction of the United States government to this electoral result was unfavorable and was a factor in the suspension, in June 1958, of the United States aid program in Laos, which had begun in 1953 and by 1958 amounted to all but a fraction of the Laotian budget.

The Government of the National Union fell, and its successor, under Phoui Sananikone as prime minister, excluded the Pathet Lao. Prince Souvanna Phouma was made ambassador to France. Also in 1958 the ICC adjourned. There were difficulties in integrating the Pathet Lao military forces, a move that was not completely accomplished, and Prince Souphanouvong was put under house arrest and later jailed. The Committee for the Defense of National Interests (CDNI), a group of educated persons and military officials considered strongly rightist, was dominant in the government. Within the CDNI, Colonel (later General) Phoumi Nosavan was dominant.

After almost a year in jail, Prince Souphanouvong and his NLHS colleagues escaped and rejoined the Pathet Lao in the north. The NLHS resumed its rebellion in 1959. It subsided somewhat after a special United Nations Security Council Investigation Subcommittee reported it could find no evidence that the Pathet Lao were using regular North Vietnamese troops. United Nations Secretary-General Dag Hammarskjöld then advised the government to adopt a more neutral policy, and an uneasy peace followed that lasted until mid-1960.

The next important development occurred in August 1960 when a young paratroop commander named Kong Le, dismayed by the constant war, seized Vientiane in a coup and proposed establishment of a neutral government. Prince Souvanna Phouma was recalled from Paris to form the new government proposed by King Savang Vatthana. General Phoumi Nosavan at first agreed to serve in this government but soon changed his mind and established a military headquarters in southern Laos from which he hoped to retake the capital. This he did in December, at which time Prince Souvanna Phouma's government and the forces under Kong Le retreated to the northeast, where Kong Le's troops seized the Plain of Jars in January 1961.

The neutralist forces were joined by the Pathet Lao and were aided additionally by North Vietnamese units and by supplies furnished by the Soviet Union. A combined attack was launched, and by the spring of 1961 the combined forces appeared to be in a position to take over the entire country.

Sri Savang Vatthana, king of Laos from 1959 to 1975

The United States warned that it would intervene to prevent a Communist takeover. The situation became an international issue and, to abate the crisis, a fourteen-nation conference was convened at Geneva in May 1961 that intended through both international and internal Lao negotiations, to give a neutral status to Laos. After long and difficult negotiations, new Geneva agreements were signed in July 1962 providing certain international guarantees for the independence and neutrality of Laos. These guarantees were to be supervised by the revived ICC.

Internally, the three Lao factions—the rightist, represented by Prince Boun Oum; the neutralist, represented by Prince Souvanna Phouma and backed by Kong Le's forces; and the Communist NLHS under Prince Souphanouvong—reached agreement and formed the Government of National Union under the premiership of Prince Souvanna Phouma in June 1962. General Phoumi Nosavan and Prince Souphanouvong were appointed deputy premiers, and it was agreed that government decisions generally would be unanimous and that the unanimity of the three leaders would be required in matters concerned with foreign relations and national defense and security.

After this settlement disagreements arose between the Pathet Lao forces and those of Kong Le. Minor skirmishing broke out, which turned into serious hostilities in early 1963 when the Pathet Lao opened an attack on Kong Le's troops. The troops had to withdraw from many of their positions on the Plain of Jars. The neutralist forces thereafter realigned themselves with the right-wing forces against the Pathet Lao.

Fighting between the neutralists and the Pathet Lao continued sporadically throughout 1963 and into 1964 despite efforts by Great Britain and the Soviet Union—who were cochairmen of the Geneva Conference of 1962—to arrange a cease-fire. A meeting of Prince Souvanna Phouma, Prince Souphanouvong, and General Phoumi Nosavan to work out an agreement finally took place in April 1964 but without success. A right-wing coup then overthrew the government, but the government was almost immediately reinstated, after consultation with King Savang Vatthana, by coup and government leaders; however, Prince Souvanna Phouma continued as prime minister.

The reinstated prime minister announced soon afterward, in May 1964, that agreement had been reached between the neutralist and the right-wing groups; the rightists accepted his leadership. When he appealed for cooperation from the Pathet Lao, however, Prince Souphanouvong refused to accept the government, maintaining that in effect it had been established by the right-wing coup leaders. The Pathet Lao then started heavy attacks on the neutralists on the Plain of Jars. Kong Le's forces were driven from the area.

The loss of the Plain of Jars resulted in international consultations, though without full-scale conferences because of disagreements among the powers. At the request of the prime minister and in view of Pathet Lao refusal to allow

King Savang Vatthana on a 1962 stamp

Prince Souvanna Phouma has served, off and on, as the prime minister of Laos since 1962.

ICC inspection of its territory, the United States began reconnaissance flights over Pathet Lao-held areas; this action was reported to Great Britain. In June 1964 the reconnaissance flights were accompanied by armed escorts authorized to fire back if fired upon.

Leaders of the three Laotian factions met in Paris in September 1964 in a further effort to resolve their differences. These meetings were once again unsuccessful. Lower level talks at Vientiane were continued, however; they went on sporadically until 1966 but without results.

Another coup by right-wing forces was attempted in Vientiane in January 1965 but was defeated by the government. General Phoumi Nosavan, one of the alleged leaders, fled to Thailand. One result was the reorganization of the Lao police force, previously a paramilitary force under right-wing control, into a civilian force.

National Assembly elections were held in July 1965. The NLHS refused to participate or to allow the election to be held in their territory. Souvanna Phouma, continuing as prime minister, made efforts to maintain the tripartite structure, which he considered his obligation because of the Geneva agreements, by retaining Prince Souphanouvong as one deputy premier and a representative of the right-wing group as the other. Cabinet posts were allocated among the three factions also: eleven to the neutralists, four to the NLHS, and four to the rightists.

In September 1966 the National Assembly rejected the government's budget. King Savang Vatthana dissolved the assembly, and in January 1967 new elections were held in which about 80 percent of the electorate voted. The NLHS again refused to participate, and polling for provinces occupied by the Lao People's Liberation Army (until 1965 known as the Pathet Lao) was confined to refugees from those areas. The new assembly met on January 30, 1967; the majority of its fifty-nine members, though without sharply defined party alignment, supported Prince Souvanna Phouma.

THE KING

From 1967 until the country abolished the monarchy form of government, the control of Laos seesawed back and forth among the leaders and parties. However, the king during this period was titular head of state and commander in chief of the armed forces, and he played a significant role in the country. He promulgated, in the form of royal ordinances, laws passed by the National Assembly as well as ministerial regulations countersigned by responsible cabinet ministers. The king signed and ratified all treaties when they had been "favorably received" by the National Assembly and could have declared war with the consent of two-thirds of the National Assembly membership.

Under exceptional circumstances when the National Assembly was unable to meet, the king could have assumed legislative power after having consulted with the officers of the assembly; however, royal decree issued under those conditions would have been subject to "ultimate ratification by the National Assembly." The king's emergency power extended also to the executive domain. During national crises the monarch could directly exercise executive prerogatives or appoint a cabinet of his own choice after consulting the King's Council and National Assembly. When the cabinet, or "the exceptional government" as the constitution described it, was appointed by the king, the life of the government was fixed by the National Assembly; in this instance the parliamentary confirmation of the cabinet was to be dispensed with.

In addition, the king was authorized to establish government positions, civil and military, and make appointments to them according to law. He also presided over sessions of the Council of Ministers, but this function was rarely performed. The king also exercised the power of pardon and commutation of sentences and conferred military and civilian honors.

The constitution provided for hereditary succession "in accordance with the dynastic rules . . . and the ordinary laws" governing this matter. It reserved the throne for the prince designated as heir by the king or a male descendant of the late king Sisavang Vong. When the king died without an appointed heir, the choice of the successor was determined by the National Congress from a list of nominees submitted by the King's Council.

If the king became incapable of carrying out his duties for any reason, a regent was to be appointed by the King's Council. The regent, who must have attained his majority, also would have been designated (by the King's Council with the concurrence of the National Assembly) as heir to the throne, provided he was a member of the royal family. Appointment of a regent was mandatory if the king was a minor. During the king's temporary absence from the country or pending designation of a regent, the King's Council meeting in continuous session was charged with carrying out the functions of head of state.

Executive power was exercised by the prime minister and the Council of Ministers. The prime minister, who was appointed by the king in consultation with political leaders, was president of the Council of Ministers, which included ministers and secretaries of state (who headed major ministerial subdivisions called secretariats of state). The basic responsibility of the prime minister and his council was to implement the laws enacted by the National Assembly.

The prince, in his role as prime minister, conferring with Secretary-General Kurt Waldheim, during a visit to the United Nations headquarters in 1972

FROM 1967 TO ABOLISHMENT OF THE MONARCHY

In 1968 the Lao Communists began making overtures toward negotiations for a peace settlement. Their proposal of March 1970 called for an internal Lao settlement, withdrawal of all American and Thai assistance to Laos, and a stop to all American bombing, which had offset North Vietnam's preponderance on the ground. Prime Minister Souvanna Phouma countered with demands that controls be put on North Vietnamese troops in Laos. In July 1972 the Communist Lao Patriotic Front (LPF) and Royal Lao Government (RLG) representatives met in Vientiane to resume negotiations. After lengthy discussions, they reached agreement on a ceasefire, to take effect February 27, 1973.

The agreements of February 27, 1973, together with an implementing protocol concluded in September, laid the basis for the third coalition. After protracted negotiations among the factions, a Provisional Government of National Union (PGNU) was finally established on April 5, 1974, with Prince Souvanna Phouma again as prime minister. The cabinet of the PGNU was composed of equal numbers of LPF members and "Vientiane side" members.

After the collapse of the non-Communist governments in Cambodia and South Vietnam, the Lao Communists' initiation of small-scale military clashes west of the Plain of Jars, and Communist-instigated demonstrations in Vientiane against the leading figures of the "Vientiane side," the key non-Communist leaders fled the country in May 1975, leaving the LPF in charge. By the end of June, while the fiction of a coalition government was preserved, its non-Communist side was wholly ineffective.

On December 2, 1975, the monarchy was abolished and the Communist Lao People's Democratic Republic (LPDR) was established. The new regime proclaimed its alignment with the Communist camp and also stated its intention to participate actively in "nonaligned" councils.

In the governmental structure of the LPDR, the only political party is the Marxist-Leninist Lao People's Revolutionary party (LPRP). The titular head of state, the president, is Prince Souphanouvong. But real power rests with the prime minister, Kaysone Phomvihan, who is also the secretary-general of the party.

THE ROYAL SOVEREIGNS OF THE KINGDOM OF LAOS

Reign	Title	Ruler	Reign	Title	Ruler
1486–1496	King	La Sene Thai	1778–1782—Interregnum		
1496–1501	King	Som Phou	1782–1792	King	Chao Nan
1501–1520	King	Visoun	1792–1805	King	Chao In
1520–1547	King	Phothis Arath I	1805–1828	King	Chao Anou
1548–1571	King	Setthathirath	1828—Under control of Siam		
1571–1575	King	Sene Soulintha			
1575–1580	King	Maha Oupahat	**UPPER LAOS**		
1580–1582	King	Sene Soulintha	1707–1726	King	Kitsarath
1582–1583	King	Nakhone Noi	1726–1727	King	Khamane
1583–1591—Interregnum			1727–1776	King	Intha Som
1591–1596	King	Nokeo Koumane	1776–1781	King	Sotika Koumane
1596–1622	King	Thammikarath	1781–1787	King	Tiao-Vong
1622–1623	King	Oupagnouvarat	1787–1791—Interregnum		
1623–1627	King	Phothis Arath II	1791–1817	King	Anourout
1627–1631	King	Oupagnaovarath	1817–1836	King	Mantha Thourath
1631–1637	King	Tone Kham	1836–1850	King	Souka Seum
1637–1637	King	Visai	1851–1869	King	Tiantha-Koumane
1637–1694	King	Souligna Vongsa	1869–1872	King	Oun Kham
1694–1700	King	Tan Thala	1887–1894—Interregnum		
1700–1700	King	Nan Tharat	1893—Became French protectorate		
1700–1707	King	Sai Ong Hue	1894–1904	King	Zakarine
			1904–1959	King	Sisavang Vong
LOWER LAOS			1959–1975	King	Baromo Setha Khatyk Sourya Vongsa Phra Maha Sri Savang Vatthana
1707–1735	King	Sai Ong Hue	1975—Rule divided politically among royal male offspring.		
1735–1760	King	Ong Long			
1760–1778	King	Ong Boun			

17
The Kingdom of Cambodia

Throughout the early centuries of the Christian Era there were many contenders for the rich, fertile lands that form the Mekong River valley and the central plain of present-day Cambodia. From legends, inscriptions on ancient monuments, and fragmentary references in Chinese records, it appears that the Khmer, who have emerged as the dominant group in the area, fought fiercely to gain control of their lands. Then they defended them against the encroachments of invaders from the neighboring Thai kingdom of Siam to the north and the Cham kingdom of Champa that once dominated large parts of what are now Cambodia, Laos, and South Vietnam. The Cambodian royal chronicles, dating from the middle of the fourteenth century, continue the tale of strife in which periods of triumph and conquest alternated with eras of defeat and vassalage.

Although the connection between the Khmer kings of the chronicles and the ancient Khmer dynasties celebrated in legend has never been established, the people regard Prince Norodom Sihanouk as the direct descendant of an ancient lineage in whose accomplishments they take great pride. The vicissitudes of their past have welded them into a cohesive political force that continues to stress independence and the integrity of the country's borders as paramount goals. They acknowledge the contributions of foreign cultures to their own, but they remain deeply devoted to their Buddhist religion, their arts, and their distinctive traditions and customs.

History, for most Cambodians, is legend symbolizing the subjective experiences of their ancestors rather than the more or less factual record of events usual in the West. Such legends contain facts, of course, but facts handled with great freedom. The reigning dynasty, for example, claims direct descent from the sovereigns of the Angkor Wat period, and most Cambodians not only admit the claim but take pride in it. At the same time, however, they reject any attempt to identify themselves with the people who built Angkor Wat, explaining them away in a legend about a people who built stone monuments, then disappeared.

Cambodian legends have reinforced the cohesiveness of the people, forming a bond of common heritage and significance. One example is provided by the symbols river and mountain—important in Cambodian thinking since the second Bronze Age. In the ancient tales mountain men were pitted against river men. This dualism was also a feature of the social organization; tribes were divided into factions which derived their principal livelihood either from high country or from the river. The mountain chiefs and sorcerers were considered descendants of Garuda, the divine bird, and they commanded fire and lightning. The river chiefs and sorcerers were considered descendants of Naga, the divine fish or serpent, and they ruled over the waters and rain.

The legendary origin of Indian civilization in Cambodia is linked to this theme. Chroniclers record the legend of the Hindu prince, Kaundinya (king of the mountain), who married a female serpent, a Nagi, and founded the "lunar" dynasty which long ruled the country. A variation of the story recounts that Fu-nan (the Chinese name given the country) was governed by a woman. A prince of a "southern province" (India) dreamed that a spirit gave him a bow and arrows and told him to conquer the sea. He took to the sea and arrived in Fu-nan, where the queen's troops were massed in defense. When an arrow from the magic bow struck one of the defenders the queen surrendered. Prince and queen married, and the prince taught the people to wear clothes and make cloth. It is essentially this version of early history that is taught in Cambodian schools today, presenting in legendary form the historical fact that Indian culture was brought into Cambodia at a very early date.

Social mobility and the immediate reward of merit are illustrated in the legend of the Old Man of the Sweet Cucumbers. Once an old peasant named Ta-chey planted sweet cucumbers in his kitchen garden. One season the cucumbers were so good that he offered some to the king. The king liked them so much that he gave Ta-chey a lance with which to protect the garden. To test the old man's watchfulness, the king one night stole into the garden and in the dark was killed by Ta-chey. Whereupon the dignitaries of the realm, seeing that Ta-chey was a meritorious man, called him to the throne and crowned him king.

MONGOLIA

Sinkiang

C H I N A

Tibet

SHANGHAI•

Cambodia's position in Southeast Asia

•CHUNGKING

INDIA

EAST
PAKISTAN

CALCUTTA
•

•KUNMING

TAIWAN

B U R M A

NORTH
VIETNAM

HANOI•

HONG KONG
•

RANGOON
•

L
A
O
S

VIENTIANE
•

Hainan

PHILIPPINES

THAILAND

Paris
Isl

MANILA•

BANGKOK
•

CAMBODIA

SOUTH CHINA SEA

ANDAMAN

PHNOM
PENH•

SOUTH
VIETNAM

SEA

SAIGON•

GULF OF SIAM

MALAYSIA

STRAIT OF MALACCA

S
u
m
a
t
r
a

KUALA
LUMPUR
•

INDIAN OCEAN

SINGAPORE•

B o r n e o
(Kalimantan)

Celebes

0 50 100   200   300
Statute Miles

I   N   D   O   N   E   S   I   A

DJAKARTA
•

J a v a

THE ASCENT TO GREATNESS

Cambodia's documented history begins with remains that place man in Cambodia in the Neolithic period. The people who lived there in prehistoric times probably included the proto-Malayan or Indonesian forebears of today's Chams and of the mountain peoples known as *Khmer Loeu* (literally, upper Cambodians). None of the other prehistoric peoples of Cambodia have survived. The first habitations are said to have been in the delta of the Mekong, an area now part of South Vietnam.

EARLY PERIODS

FU-NAN AND CHEN-LA (A.D. 200–802)

The first inhabitants of the area were said to have lived in the delta of the Mekong, an area now part of South Vietnam. Three distinct, politically independent people—the Funanese, the Chams, and the Khmer—were present during the first century A.D. The area of Funanese control

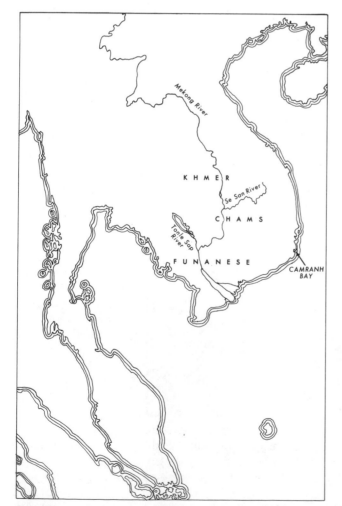

Indochinese civilizations in the first century A.D.

extended as far north as the Tonle Sap River and eastward to the coast, possibly as far as Camranh Bay. The Chams were farther north, perhaps as far as the Se San River, and the Khmer were north of the Chams in the Mekong valley.

By the third century the Funanese had overcome the neighboring tribes, and the area became known as Fu-nan (Chinese terminology). According to Chinese documents an Indian Brahman ruled the country and in the fourth century Indianized the customs of Fu-nan. During that time the Laws of Manu, the Indian legal code, were put into effect, and the use of the Indian alphabet was introduced. Modified forms of the alphabet and parts of the legal code are still used.

The chief vassal state of Fu-nan was Chen-la to the north. The Khmer, in their expansion southward, had defeated the Chams and established the kingdom of Chen-la and its first capital on the Mekong River near the present-day Laotian town of Pakse. In the middle of the sixth century Chen-la gained control over Fu-nan, first making it a vassal state and then annexing it. Fu-nan may have been weakened by Malay incursions along its coastal regions. Chen-la's conquest of Fu-nan has been cited as an example of the recurrent drive to the south in the history of the Indochinese peninsula.

During the next two hundred and fifty years, in which Chen-la was dominant over Fu-nan, the empire was extended northward to the border of present-day China. Then, divided by civil strife, it fell under Malayan rule for a while and once more became independent.

The name Cambodia derives from this time. The founder of the Khmer Dynasty, according to legends, was Kambu Svayambhuva. *Kambuja,* hence the French *Cambodge* and the English *Cambodia,* is traceable to his name. *Kambujadesa* (sons of Kambuja) was the name sometimes given the country in later years, but the Chinese documents of the time used the name Chen-la. The legendary importance of the river and the mountain was given historical substance by a series of eighth-century civil wars, which split Chen-la into two parts: Land Chen-la, the upland area to the north, and Water Chen-la, the maritime area which formed the nucleus of the Khmer empire.

KAMBUJA, OR ANGKOR (802–1432)

At its peak the empire extended from the Annamite chain (in present-day South Vietnam) to the Gulf of Siam. The buildings at Angkor that were erected at that time have become a national symbol; a representation of the Towers of Angkor is the central design on the national flag. The kings of that period are still hailed; outstanding among them are Jayavarman II and Jayavarman VII.

Jayavarman II, who was placed upon the Khmer throne in 802 as vassal to the Malays, asserted his independence. He reunited the old Chen-la Empire, including the northernmost part, which bordered on China's Yunnan province. All of present-day Laos and much of present-day Thailand were added to his kingdom. The sacred royal sword, treasured as a symbol of authority today, is said to be that of Jayavarman II.

Jayavarman VII (1181–1215) was reported to have founded over a hundred hospitals, built resthouses for travelers on the pilgrim routes and distributed tons of rice to the needy. The arts flourished. Angkor Wat and the Bayon of Angkor Thom, two of the most famous temples, were built in the twelfth and thirteenth centuries, respectively. Many of the kings excelled as scholars, and Sanskrit literature was raised to new heights by royal patronage. Jayavarman VII was an accomplished warrior and was considered the greatest of the Khmer emperors, as the empire reached its greatest extent during his reign. He conquered the kingdom of Champa, which occupied the eastern portion of present-day South Vietnam, in 1190 and had some form of hegemony over a part of the Malay Peninsula.

The empire began to disintegrate after the death of Jayavarman VII. One reason for this was the complete exhaustion of the people because of the continuous wars of conquest and the frenzied building program. Every important Khmer king built his own capital, which had a temple that usually was larger and more ornate than his predecessor's and served as the center of religion during his reign and later as his mausoleum.

Champa regained its independence in 1220. Mongol pressure on the Thai Kingdom in Yunnan in the thirteenth century gave greater impetus to Thai penetration. By the end of the thirteenth century independent Thai kingdoms had been created in former Khmer territory. In 1353 a Thai army captured Angkor; the Kambujans recaptured it later, but wars with the Thai continued. Angkor was looted a number of times, and thousands of artists and scholars were carried away to slavery in Siam (now Thailand), including the entire Cambodian ballet. At this time, too, Khmer territory north of the present Laotian border was lost to the Lao kingdom of Lan Xang.

In 1430–31 the Thai again captured Angkor, this time aided by treachery within the Khmer capital. The Khmer recaptured their city but abandoned it as a capital, probably because it was too close to the Thai capital. Moreover, the steady infiltration of Theravada Buddhism made the vast temples no longer vital to their life. In the course of centuries the jungle was allowed to encroach upon and almost conceal Angkor Wat, Angkor Thom and many other beautiful temples, which for centuries remained as hidden chronicles of the once-great Khmer Empire.

WARS FOR SURVIVAL (1432–1864)

During the next four centuries Cambodia expanded its energies in resisting aggression on the part of Siam (Thailand) and Annam (parts of present-day North and South Vietnam). Siam claimed suzerainty over Cambodia and for years tried to validate its claim by forceful means as well as through a puppet king.

King Ang Duong reigned from 1841 to 1859.

King Norodom I reigned from 1859 to 1904.

In 1593 the Thai again captured the Cambodian capital—then Lovek (now Longvek) on the Tonle Sap River. The Khmer recovered their capital, and ten years of internal strife resulted during which time the Thai attempted to place a submissive monarch on the throne. At some time during the sixteenth century the monarch moved his capital to the Angkor area, and an attempt was made to restore Angkor Wat.

The Khmer king, fearing another attack by the Thai, sent two emissaries to the Spanish governor-general in Manila to request assistance. They were two adventurers, one Spanish and one Portuguese. They convinced the governor-general of the desirability of dispatching a military expedition to explore the possibility of establishing Spanish domination over the kingdom. Two small military expeditions were sent from Manila, one in 1596 and the other in 1598. During the summer of 1599, while the leaders of the Spanish expedition were attempting to negotiate with King Barom Reachea III, an armed altercation occurred between Spanish soldiers and some Malays camped nearby. Khmer went to the assistance of the Malays, and the Spaniards, including the leaders who had rushed from the palace to help their men, were all killed.

Siam and Annam struggled for control of Cambodia for the next two hundred and sixty years, each encroaching upon its territory. Land won in the north by Siam and in the south by Annam is the basis of present-day disputes between Cambodia and its neighbors. Cambodian kings sometimes tried to set Siam and Annam against each other, but in 1846 they joined in crowning Ang Duong as the Cambodian king. Subject to dual vassalage, Ang Duong looked to a stronger power for protection. He believed that British policy was more aggressive in Burma and Malaya, so he turned to France, and Cambodia became an ally of France, which was then fighting Annam.

Ang Duong died during the course of the war, and the coronation of his eldest son, Norodom, who had become a Thai protégé, was a point of conflict with the French. After Norodom had ceded two western provinces to Siam as a price for its acquiescence to his acceptance of French protection, a treaty was made with the French in 1863, and a French protectorate was proclaimed in April 1864. Two

King Sisovath, center, *in an annual appearance (1925) before the ancient gold throne in Pnom-Penh, the capital of Cambodia. He ruled from 1904 to 1927.*

months later Norodom was crowned in his own capital by representatives of France and Siam.

FRENCH PROTECTORATE (1864–1949)

Despite implied joint suzerainty, France increasingly ignored Thai claims. France exploited Cambodia commercially and profited thereby, but the protectorate was never a vital element of the French Empire.

The Franco-Cambodian Treaty of 1863 gave France exclusive control of foreign affairs and the right to defend Cambodia against external and internal enemies. A French resident general was installed in the capital as executive officer. Widespread political, economic, and social powers were granted the French, but even more were demanded.

King Norodom was forced to sign a new treaty in 1884. An unsuccessful rebellion expressed the popular reaction.

Cambodia was placed under direct French control through a parallel administration. The resident general was the actual ruler; the king was merely the symbol of the country and the religion. Cambodian social and political structures were left largely intact, but sweeping reforms were instituted. After 1887 Cambodia became part of the Indochinese Union, which also included Tonkin, Annam, and Cochin China (parts of present-day North and South Vietnam), Laos, and Kwangchow Wan, a French coastal leasehold in South China.

When King Norodom died in 1904, after a forty-year reign, his kingdom was peaceful, prosperous, and powerless. His brother Sisowath was king until 1927, and his son Moivong reigned until 1941. After his death his sons were excluded from the royal succession, and Prince Norodom Sihanouk, the son of his eldest daughter and a great-grandson of Norodom through the paternal line, became king.

The French administration considered Moivong's son Monireth too independence-minded at a time when the French had suffered defeat in Europe and the Japanese had received permission from the Vichy government to send troops to Hanoi and Saigon and were demonstrating a growing importance to Southeast Asia. King Sihanouk was descended from both the Norodom and Sisowath families, and the French saw in him a young, malleable person who would be subservient to their directives, but they were wrong.

After the defeat of the French armed forces and the establishment of the Vichy government, Japanese military units entered Hanoi and Saigon, where they moved into the French barracks, forcing the French units to set up tent camps in public parks. The Thai government, enjoying the friendship of the Japanese, sent a message to the Vichy government, stating in part: "The Thai Government would appreciate it if the French Government would give its assurance that in the event of an interruption of French sovereignty, France would return to Thailand the Cambodian and Laotian territories."

The request was rejected by the Vichy government. After a series of Mekong River border incidents a Thai force invaded Cambodia in January 1941. The land fighting was indecisive, but the Vichy French defeated Thai forces in a naval engagement off the Thai island of Ko Chang in the Gulf of Siam.

King Sisovath on a French Indochina stamp

The Japanese intervened and compelled the Vichy French authorities to agree to a treaty which surrendered the provinces of Battambang and Siem Reap to Thailand. Until the spring of 1945 the Japanese allowed the Vichy French to maintain nominal control of Indochina, but they forced the French to give the governor general in Saigon the power to sign agreements in the name of Vichy France.

In the spring of 1945 the Japanese removed the whole Vichy French colonial administration and authorized Cambodia, Laos, and Vietnam to declare their independence within the Japanese-sponsored Greater East Asian Co-Prosperity Sphere. The Japanese also appointed Son Ngoc Thanh, a nationalist leader, as foreign minister of Cambodia; on his advice, King Sihanouk declared the independence of Cambodia on March 12, 1945.

After the surrender of Japan, British troops and some French units arrived in Saigon and later in September an Allied unit occupied the capital city, Phnom Penh, and arrested Son Ngoc Thanh for collaboration with the Japanese. King Sihanouk agreed to send delegates to Saigon to negotiate a new set of rules to govern France's relations with Cambodia, provided they would be considered delegates from an independent country. The French made some concessions, and in January 1946 Cambodia was recognized as an autonomous kingdom within the French Union.

EMERGENCE OF THE MODERN STATE

THE ROYAL MANDATE

A Constituent Assembly was elected in September 1946, and a constitution was promulgated on May 6, 1947. The lower and upper houses of the legislature were convened in January and February 1948, and parliamentary government began. Political factionalism emerged almost immediately and threatened the government, which up to that time had

On the fifth day of his coronation, King Monivong took a ceremonial tour of Pnom-Penh, symbolizing taking possession of the kingdom of Cambodia.

King Monivong is seen here in his coronation robes and gold headdress. His coronation took place between July 20 and 25, 1927, and his reign lasted until 1941.

been dominated by King Sihanouk and the members of his family.

In the first full representative elections, opposition to French rule was the basic issue. Many Cambodians were opposed to collaboration with France. They either organized themselves as dissident groups, which collectively were called Khmer Issarak (Free Cambodia), or joined the Communist Viet Minh who had crossed the borders from Laos to Vietnam. A new party, known as the Democrat party, emerged; it was opposed to the government of King Sihanouk and was also the legal front for the Khmer Issarak. This party won an overwhelming majority in the National Assembly and began systematically to block all legislation sponsored by the king or his followers.

King Sihanouk dissolved the National Assembly in September 1949 and ruled for two years without it, aided by ministers of his own choice. New elections were held in September 1951, and a new National Assembly was seated in October. The Democrat party, again the winner, failed to produce a firm program and replaced many able civil servants with persons whose primary qualification was loyalty to the party.

In June 1952 the king announced that he was assuming control again until he could restore order in the national administration and security throughout the country. This

measure was not based on any constitutional provision but was an autocratic action outside the constitution. The king, on his own initiative, dissolved the two houses of the National Assembly in January 1953.

The period during which the king ruled directly (June 1952 to February 1955) was known as the Royal Mandate. The king created a temporary advisory council to serve in place of the national legislature. The number of governmental crises was greatly reduced but not entirely eliminated, since members of the advisory council were still free to resign even though they were selected by the king. The king devoted his energies to obtaining major concessions from the French.

A treaty had been signed in 1949 which gave Cambodia the first prerogatives of internal sovereignty. There were limitations on the country's sovereignty in defense and economic policy, and non-Cambodians residing in the country were outside of Cambodian jurisdiction, as in the time of the protectorate. Negotiations continued, and by 1953 the greatest problem faced by the French was their military involvement with the Viet Minh.

In March 1953 King Sihanouk departed for what he called a pleasure trip to Europe, Canada, and the United States, but he made statements highly critical of the French refusal to grant full independence to his country. After his return in June, he left Phnom Penh and went to Bangkok; he stated he would not return to Cambodia until the French gave assurances that all the prerogatives of full independence would be granted. He did, however, return to Siem Reap, which was then controlled by the Khmer armed forces, and prepared plans, with other leaders, for resistance to be carried out if the French were not ready to negotiate on Cambodian terms.

Faced with a difficult military situation in Vietnam and Laos, on July 4, 1953, the French government declared itself ready to grant complete independence to the three associated states. The Cambodians, however, insisted on their own terms, which included sovereignty over their defense establishment, their tribunals, and their currency. The French yielded. Both the police and the judiciary had been transferred to Cambodian control at the end of August, and on September 1, 1953, all of Cambodia was placed under its own military command. By virtue of an additional agreement in October, the French army retained only operational control east of the Mekong River and tactical command of the Khmer battalions operating in the area.

King Norodom Suramarit and Queen Kossamak were joint rulers of Cambodia from 1955 to 1960.

King Sihanouk, a hero in the eyes of his people, returned to Phnom Penh, and on November 9, 1953, Independence Day was celebrated.

INDEPENDENCE

The French still retained extensive powers in the economic field, but by a quiet exchange of letters Cambodia obtained in February 1954 the transfer of all residual economic and technical services still in French hands. Cambodia became a truly independent nation before Vietnam and Laos. It was represented at the conference in Geneva in July 1954, which reached an agreement, signed by both the French and Viet Minh delegations, calling for a cessation of hostilities in Indochina and stipulating that all Viet Minh military forces be withdrawn above the seventeenth parallel. In a separate agreement, signed by the Cambodian representative, the French and Viet Minh agreed to withdraw all forces from Cambodia by October 20, 1954.

The four-power (France, Cambodia, Laos, and South Vietnam) ties were severed in December 1954; the quadripartite system was dissolved, and each of the three associated states was given full sovereignty over services which previously had been subject to joint administration. In September 1955 Cambodia had withdrawn from the French Union.

THE SANGKUM

On February 7, 1955, a nationwide referendum was held to decide whether or not the king had fulfilled his mandate of attaining independence and security for his country. As a special privilege, members of the armed forces and monks were given permission to vote. King Sihanouk obtained 925,000, or 99.8 percent, of the approximately 927,000 votes cast. Soon afterward he abdicated in favor of his father Norodom Suramarit, in order to enter politics.

Prince Sihanouk immediately began building an organization known as the People's Socialist Community (Sangkum Reastr Niyum—usually called Sangkum). Although he was no longer king, he was still a prince of the royal family, and he had gained considerable prestige during the years leading up to independence. He had applied himself to the dual task of suppressing armed rebels and achieving freedom from the French. Doubt as to his patriotism, a key point in some Cambodians' justification of their seeming disloyalty to him, had been removed. Many rebel chiefs, convinced that he was working sincerely for Cambodian independence, came over to his side and were commissioned in the Royal Cambodian Army.

New national elections were held in September 1955, and the Sangkum won all the seats of the ninety-one-member assembly. Aware that its opposition stems mainly from the discontented younger generation, the Sangkum has made special efforts to secure its active support through a youth auxiliary called the Royal Khmer Socialist Youth (Jeunesse Socialiste Royale Khmère—JSRK).

The government began an ambitious program of economic, financial, and educational reforms—improvements in transportation and industry; civic action; preparedness for national defense; and consolidation of political power. It also entered the arena of international politics as a member of the United Nations.

CAMBODIAN NEUTRALITY

The central element of Cambodian foreign policy during the fifties and sixties was neutrality, and both the defeated

French Indochina stamp shows young Sihanouk as the king of Cambodia.

Prince Norodom Sihanouk appears on this 1964 Cambodian postage stamp.

King Norodom Sihanouk in royal military garb at the time of his enthronement in 1941.

A familiar pose of the flamboyant Prince Sihanouk

Khmer Republic and their opponents publicly claimed neutrality as an attribute of the state during the 1970–75 war. The 1976 Constitution of Democratic Kampuchea specifies that neutrality is a goal of the new government, named Kampuchea.

Prince Norodom Sihanouk took the first steps to reaffirm neutrality in early 1956 by rejecting the Southeast Asia Collective Defense Treaty's protocol which permitted the former French Indochinese nations to apply for help in the event of an attack. In September 1957, Cambodia enacted a law to define neutrality as noncommitment to a military alliance or ideological bloc. By the mid-1960s, however, sections of Cambodia's northeast provinces served as bases for North Vietnamese and Viet Cong (NVA/VC) troops operating against South Vietnam. In 1969 the prince finally publicly noted the fact.

THE WAR

After the National Assembly deposed Sihanouk as chief of state on March 18, 1970, he took refuge in Peking. The anti-Vietnamese and anti-Communist orientation of those who overthrew him prompted the Vietnamese to reject the Cambodian government's proposals for withdrawal of NVA/VC troops and to reinfiltrate the two thousand five hundred to eight thousand Khmer who had gone to North Vietnam for military training after the Geneva Accords. These men acted as a cadre for an indigenous insurgency. Sihanouk had cast his lot with the growing insurgency, drawing new recruits into it, and the small Communist party of Cambodia assumed leadership under the NVA/VC shield.

In Phnom Penh, the leadership, under Prime Minister Lon Nol, abolished the monarchy October 9, 1970, and established the Khmer Republic.

Initially, the Communists attacked small government units and interdicted lines of communications, while the NVA/VC hit major objectives. By 1973, however, the insurgents had grown strong enough to fight full battles, and by 1974 they had organized themselves into divisions. At no point did fighting in Cambodia follow classical guerrilla warfare.

The Cambodian government surrendered to the Communist Khmer Rouge, April 6, 1975, ending five years of warfare. Sihanouk was renamed head of state but resigned in 1976. The Domino Theory proponents could be seen pointing the finger of their prediction at the rest of the world.

The new government, under Premier Pol Pot in 1977, evacuated all cities and towns and shuffled the rural population into slave labor camps to clear the jungle which covered half the country, converting the recovered land into rice fields. At least one million people were killed in executions and enforced hardships by Pol Pot's government. U.S. President Jimmy Carter accused Cambodia of being the world's worst violator of human rights.

Heavy fighting broke out along the Vietnam border in 1978, which developed into a full-scale invasion by the Vietnamese. Pol Pot took to the jungle in January 1979 with about 18,000 of his troops, where he continues to be active as military commander of these Khmer Rouge guerrilla forces. The fighting continues today between the Communist troops and the anti-Communist forces including about 5,000 guerrillas who are backing Sihanouk. Prince Sihanouk is still standing in the wings ready to return on stage.

THE ROYAL SOVEREIGNS OF THE KINGDOM OF CAMBODIA

Reign	Title	Ruler	Reign	Title	Ruler
1486–1512	King	Srey Sukonthor	1702–1702	King	Thommo Reachea II
1512–1515	King	Kan	1703–1706	King	Chettha IV
1516–1565	King	Ang Chan I	1706–1710	King	Thommo Reachea II
1566–1576	King	Barom Reachea I	1710–1722	King	Ang Em
1576–1594	King	Chetta I	1722–1738	King	Satha II
1594–1596	King	Reamea Chung Prei	1738–1747	King	Thommo Reachea II
1596–1598	King	Barom Reachea II	1747–1747	King	Thommo Reachea III
1599–1599	King	Barom Reachea III	1747–1749	King	Ang Tong
1600–1600	King	Chau Ponhea Nhom (nephew, deposte)	1749–1755	King	Chettha V
			1755–1758	King	Ang Tong
1603–1618	King	Barom Reachea IV	1758–1775	King	Outey II
1618–1632	King	Chettha II	1775–1779	King	Ang Non II
1622–1628	King	Family dispute	1779–1796	King	Ang Eng
1628–1628	King	Ponhea To	1796–1806—Interregnum		
1628–1629	King	Outey	1806–1836	King	Ang Chan II
1630–1639	King	Ponhea Nu	1837–1841	King	Ang Mey
1640–1641	King	Ang Non I	1841–1859	King	Ang Duong
1642–1659	King	Chan	1859–1904	King	Norodom
1659–1672	King	Batom Reachea	1904–1927	King	Sisovath
1672–1672	King	Chettha III	1927–1941	King	Monivong
1673–1674	King	Ang Chei	1941–1955	King	Prince Norodom Sihanouk
1674–1675	King	Ang Non	1955–1960	King (joint rule)	Norodom Suramarit
1675–1694	King	Chettha IV			
1695–1695	King	Outey I	1955–1960	Queen	Queen Kossamal
1695–1699	King	Chettha IV	1960–1970	King	Prince Norodom Sihanouk
1699–1701	King	Ang Em	1970–		Cambodia became a republic (Khmer).
1701–1701	King	Chetta IV			

18
The Empire of Vietnam

Throughout two thousand years of recorded history—to which legend adds two thousand more—the Vietnamese have been sustained by a feeling of unity based on common origin, language, and cultural heritage. They are intensely proud of having been an independent and unified nation for centuries, although they also experienced periods of disunity and foreign domination. They take equal pride in their cultural heritage, regarded by them as an eloquent testimony to their eclectic and creative talents for absorbing foreign cultures without themselves losing distinct political identity.

In the evolution of Vietnamese society and culture much of the formative influence came from China, whose colonial officials and traders were largely responsible for the transmission of the Chinese way of life. The Chinese influences intermingled freely with the indigenous culture, known as Dong-Son (Indonesian), which dates from around the fourth century B.C. and was then centered in the Red River Delta.

A striking feature of Vietnam's history is the story of its relations with China, its vastly larger and more powerful neighbor to the north. Over the centuries the Vietnamese have admired China for its superior culture and feared it for its power. During the one thousand years (second century B.C. to the tenth century A.D.) that the country was ruled directly by China, the people accepted discriminately much of the dominant culture, but politically they were inclined to be militantly anti-Chinese.

Freeing themselves from direct Chinese control in A.D. 938, they thereafter jealously guarded their independence by various means, at times holding off invading Chinese and Mongolian armies and at others, resorting to hard bargaining, the payment of tribute, or the acceptance of nominal Chinese overlordship. Negotiating from weakness, they became adroit bargainers, expert in obtaining through suppleness and patience the best terms under a given circumstance.

In their long resistance to Chinese domination, they came to regard China as the traditional enemy. This old antagonism profoundly affects their thinking and attitude,

and many Vietnamese continue to see danger in any relationship with China.

The Chinese rule was followed by varying degrees of independence under a succession of Vietnamese emperors presiding over a powerful bureaucracy of the Chinese type. Revolts were numerous, and with brief periods of reasserted Chinese control one dynasty fell to be replaced by another, but the outcome was always a transfer of authority without basic change in the sociopolitical structure.

The Vietnamese are prone to regard themselves as peaceful people, but they assign high importance to valor and fighting ability in their survival as a nation. The heroes and heroines of their history are those who rebelled against invading armies from the north. To the prowess of their ancestors they attribute not only successful resistance to Chinese encroachment but also the extension of their territory to the present boundaries of North and South Vietnam by victories over neighboring kingdoms to the south and west.

Because of powerful China to the north and apart from defending themselves against occasional northern invaders, the main thrust of Vietnamese history usually has been directed southward, as epitomized in *nam-tien* (march southward). Aided by superior organizational skill and military techniques acquired from the Chinese, the people of the overcrowded Red River Delta moved down the coastline in search of more rice paddies. In the process they pushed the original settlers of the lowland coastal areas farther back into the highlands to gain the fertile foothills for themselves. This process of southern expansion continued at the expense of the peoples of the kingdom of Champa to the south of Hue and of Cambodia to the west until the Vietnamese acquired the fertile lands of the Mekong River Delta in the eighteenth century. Through the absorption of these peoples, who had been under the cultural influence of India, the Vietnamese came into contact with the Hindu civilization of India.

This pattern of expansion left an indelible imprint on the differing cultural orientation between the north-central section of the country on the one hand and the southern part of

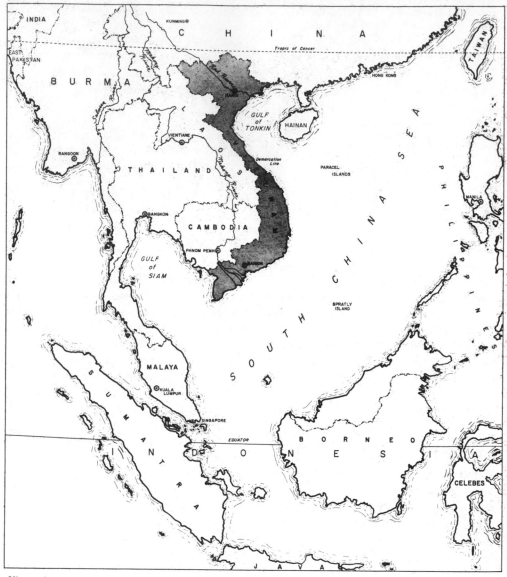

Vietnam's geographic position in southeast Asia

the country on the other. The people of the northern (Tonkin) and central (Annam) regions came to be regarded as keenly conscious of a traditional way of life. Those in the southern part (Cochin China)—perhaps because of their exposure to Indian influence—were thought to be more eclectic and less tradition-bound.

Moreover, during nearly a century of French rule, which had begun in the latter part of the nineteenth century, the varying pattern of French control gave further solidity to the country's cultural variation. Because the French rule was more direct and all-pervasive in the south than in the northern and central regions, the impact of French influence was correspondingly more pronounced in the south, resulting in a more culturally heterogenous society there.

The French, much more than the Chinese before them, remained alien to the people. The Vietnamese, as they always had, reacted to foreign control with reluctant acquiescence and, when they could, with open resistance. During World War II, French rule was exercised by repre-

sentatives of the Vichy regime at the sufferance of Japan until March 1945, when it was ended by a Japanese coup d'etat. After Japan's surrender the French returned to a position which the events of the war years had made irretrievable.

In the Indochina war, which broke out at the end of 1946 and ended nearly eight years later in the French defeat at Dien Bien Phu, the French found themselves confronted by skillful and determined Communist leadership under Ho Chi Minh. The Communists, exploiting popular opposition to the continuation of any form of foreign control, soon came to the forefront in the increasingly bitter struggle. Under a nationalist disguise within the Viet Minh—a Communist-led coalition group—they attracted the active or passive support of most of the population.

With the achievement of independence and the partitioning of the country in 1954, Vietnam entered a new phase of conflict. The struggle was between the non-Communist government in the South, supported by the United States and its allies, and the Communist regime in the North, backed by Communist China and the Soviet Union. Beginning in 1958, the Northern regime stepped up its efforts to subjugate the South through a well-organized campaign of subversion and terror. Eventually the United States, at South Vietnam's request, intervened to help the Saigon government repel armed aggression from the North.

HISTORIC ORIGINS

Legend establishes the first Vietnamese Kingdom in what is now North Vietnam. According to one story, Lac Long Quan, the first Vietnamese king, was the descendant of a line of Chinese divine rulers. He married Au Co, an immortal, and, according to the legend, fathered one hundred sons. The king and queen then parted, dividing sons between them. The king went south; the queen, north into the mountains near Hanoi. The eldest of the boys accompanying the king was then installed on the throne and founded the Hong Bang Dynasty, the dates of which are given as 2879 to 258 B.C. This legendary account, which probably was not developed in literary form until A.D. 1200, differs in substance from Chinese mythical history but shares some themes and figures with it. The resemblance suggests not only Chinese influence but an effort by the Vietnamese chroniclers to show that in origins and antiquity Vietnam (literally, the Viet of the South or Southern Viet) was in no way inferior to dominant China.

The first historical records pertaining to the people in the Red River Delta were written by the Chinese after they had conquered the area in the third century B.C. Still earlier Chinese accounts mention a Viet (*Yüeh*, in Chinese) Kingdom which existed about 500 B.C. south of the Yangtze River. This kingdom fell in 333 B.C., and its inhabitants, one of the many tribal peoples in southern China at the time, moved farther south.

Basically Mongoloid, like the Chinese, they seem to have shown, both physically and culturally, the results of mixture with Mon–Khmer- and Malayo–Polynesian-speaking peoples. Some of the Viets remained in China and over the centuries were integrated into the developing Chinese

A 1974 issue of stamps—Hung Vuong, founder of the Vietnamese nation and the Hong Ban Dynasty (2879–258 B.C.), with bamboo tallies and a flag inscribed "Hung Vuong"

civilization, the dynamic center of which was then in northern China. Others, under pressure from the north, pushed south, reaching the Red River Delta in the mid-fourth century B.C., and encountered a mixed Indonesian population with which they both fought and mingled.

After the fall of the Ch'in Dynasty of China (255–207 B.C.), there emerged a number of small, competing states, which, after 207 B.C., had been united as the kingdom of Nam Viet under a Chinese general. This kingdom is referred to as Nan Yüeh (Southern Viet) in ancient Chinese chronicles. It controlled the areas west of the present site of Canton and extended through the Red River Delta down to Hai Van pass, forty miles south of Hue.

CHINESE DOMINATION

The overthrow of the kingdom of Nam Viet in 111 B.C. by the armies of the Chinese Han Dynasty (206 B.C.–A.D. 220) marked the end of the legendary period of Vietnamese history. The Red River valley and a coastal strip to the south as far as Hue became Giao Chi, the southernmost Chinese province, and for the next one thousand years the events in the area were an integral part of imperial China.

The Chinese found the Viets organized along feudal lines. Villages and groups of villages led by hereditary local chiefs were in vassalage to provincial lords, who, in turn, owed allegiance to the king, to whom many of them were related. The primitive agriculture of the people included some knowledge of irrigation but not the plow and the water buffalo, which were introduced by the Chinese. Fish and game supplemented the cereals raised in the fire-cleared fields. Bronze had made its appearance in the form of ceremonial objects and arrowheads, but the principal agricultural tool was the stone hoe, and the people hunted and fought with spears and bows and arrows.

Chinese rule was not initially oppressive, and the Vietnamese feudal chiefs, although required to recognize the authority of a few Chinese high officials and pay taxes to the Chinese throne, were left largely undisturbed. Chinese agricultural technology, intellectual culture, and method of making weapons were readily accepted. Life in the delta was enriched but not overwhelmed. Later, when a growing Chinese officialdom began to expand its direct controls, the local aristocracy rallied against the alien encroachment on their hereditary prerogatives. Armed revolt in A.D. 39 briefly threw off the Chinese yoke. The struggle was led by two sisters, Trung Trac and Trung Nhi, who ruled jointly until A.D. 43, when, with the defeat of their forces by the Chinese, they drowned themselves. The memory of the warrior queens has been preserved in Vietnam as a symbol of resistance to foreign oppression.

The revolt was harshly suppressed, and those of its leaders who were not killed were exiled or degraded. With the old feudal order weakened, direct Chinese rule was imposed, and only subordinate places in the bureaucracy were left to the Vietnamese. The process of introducing

Chinese culture, which now began in earnest, remade many aspects of Vietnamese life.

In attempts to strengthen central authority by destroying feudal vestiges at local levels, China introduced, around A.D. 50, a system of communal administration under which groups of five to fifty families formed communes. As the basic administrative and social unit, the commune had considerable freedom to manage local affairs through its council, which was chosen by influential villages and family heads from among their own number. The council was responsible for public order, implementation of official decrees, the collection of taxes, and the recruitment of conscripts for the army. In discharging these functions the village council was financially independent of the central government because its operating expenses were derived mostly from village communal land, which also served to support the landless and needy people of a village. By installing their own administrative institutions, the Chinese gave the Vietnamese a new political structure, the cohesion and strength of which later made it possible for Vietnam to resist and expel invaders from the north.

There were important areas of thought and action over which the process of acculturation simply spread a Chinese gloss without essentially altering the resistant material beneath. This was especially true of the peasantry from whom the Chinese rule meant mainly the payment of taxes and the giving of labor service. Conscious of their distinctive ethnic identity, the peasants continued to use their traditional language and clung to animist beliefs and other customs preserved from long before the arrival of the Chinese. When confronted with oppressive Chinese officials, the peasants resisted them, rallying around their communes, which served as the focus of social and political activities. It was in acknowledgment of the debt the country owed to these village communes that all the Vietnamese dynasties, after those of China, took great care to preserve village autonomy. The autonomous village tradition is perhaps best epitomized by a popular saying, "The king's laws bow before village customs."

The Vietnamese language, the origin of which remains controversial, was retained though it was enriched by Chinese words and expressions. Nevertheless, the Chinese language and learning were essential to any who aspired to office under the Chinese. Educated Vietnamese were largely oriented toward Chinese culture, but their native roots were also preserved through their continuing contacts with the ordinary people whom they helped the Chinese to govern.

In a parallel process, Chinese officials, acquiring land and wealth and marrying Vietnamese, developed local loyalties and personal ambitions which rendered increasingly remote the claim of Peiping. Out of this mingling of cultures and convergence of interests there was to emerge a new breed of Chinese elite, owing allegiance to their homeland but displaying increasing Vietnamese orientation.

Chinese domination survived the collapse of the Han Dynasty in A.D. 220 and the ensuing period of confusion, during which several anti-Chinese revolts were attempted. In 248, Trien An, a woman, incited an uprising which was put down the following year. Ly Bon led a revolt in 542 and proclaimed himself emperor in 544 but the Chinese ousted him by the following year. Ly Xuan in 589 and Ly Phat Tu in 602 also tried unsuccessfully to overthrow the Chinese authorities. The leaders of the revolts are honored as national heroes in Vietnam today.

In 679 the T'ang Dynasty (618–907) made the province of Giao Chi a protectorate-general and renamed it *Annam* (pacified South), a term resented by the Vietnamese. Under more liberal policies, Annam thrived, the population increased, and reclamation and resettlement of the Red River Delta proceeded more vigorously. Culture was further enriched under Buddhist influence, first introduced by a Chinese monk around A.D. 188.

Prosperity and the continued penetration of Chinese influence did not, however, check the growth of incipient national feeling. The Vietnamese were frequently in revolt, and although these uprisings usually involved only upper-class elements and were invariably short lived, they produced an array of national heroes and heroines celebrated in Vietnamese history and still venerated at many village and city shrines.

INDEPENDENCE

The disorders following the fall of the T'ang Dynasty provided the opportunity the Vietnamese had long sought. In 938 one of their generals, Ngo Quyen, in a struggle culminating in the Battle of Bach Dang, drove out the occupying Chinese forces from the Red River Delta and founded the short-lived Ngo Dynasty. Chinese attempts to retake the Red River valley were repelled, and by 946, though by no means entirely secure and out of danger from the Chinese, the first independent Vietnam became a historical reality. With the exception of a twenty-year interlude of Chinese reoccupation early in the fifteenth century, it remained independent for the next nine hundred years.

THE DINH DYNASTY

The formation of stable institutions of government which could function without the sustaining influence of a foreign occupying power proved difficult, and during the latter part of the tenth century there were no less than a dozen autonomous local leaders in the Red River valley. One of them, Dinh Bo Linh, defeated his rivals in 968 and called his new state Dai Co Viet (Great Viet State). The Chinese continued to refer to it as Annam.

Aware of the superior power that the newly established Chinese Sung Dynasty (960–1279) could bring against him, Dinh Bo Linh embarked on a course which was to establish the basis for future relations with China for many centuries. He sent an embassy to the Sung court, requesting confirmation of his authority over Dai Co Viet. This embassy agreed to accept, on his behalf, the title of vassal king and to send a triennial tribute to China.

Acceptance of Chinese suzerainty was softened by the understanding that the Chinese would not attempt to restore their authority over the country. Moreover, Dinh Bo Linh was permitted to call himself emperor at home and in dealing with countries other than China. Peace with China was maintained during most of the Dinh Dynasty. Relations with the kingdom of Champa to the south, however, were unfriendly, and the two kingdoms were in frequent conflict. Champa was then within the Indian rather than the Chinese cultural sphere.

THE LY DYNASTY

The Dinh Dynasty did not outlast the first emperor, whose throne was usurped. The Ly Dynasty, established in 1009, was the first of the great Vietnamese dynasties and, after an interval of confusion, ushered in a period of population growth, territorial expansion, prosperity, cultural development, and stability. An efficient central government with a strong administrative and military organization was formed. The Ly rulers, adapting the Confucian Chinese model, gave the government the form it retained until the French conquest.

The emperor had three roles. He was at once the father of the nation-family, the absolute temporal monarch in whom all powers of the state resided, and, finally, the religious head of the realm and intermediary between it and heaven, the highest realm of the supernatural. The work of administering the country was carried on by a civil bureaucracy—the so-called mandarinate. Six administrative departments were created: personal, finance, rites, justice, armed forces, and public works. A board of censors kept watch over the civil servants and advised the emperor of any infractions.

The first literary examinations were held in the mid-eleventh century; a college for prospective civil servants and an imperial academy were founded—all geared to the mandarinate system. Ranked in nine grades, the mandarins were recruited through public examinations in which knowledge of the Chinese Confucian classics and skill in literary composition were the central requirements. This method of recruitment survived until the second decade of the twentieth century.

Public revenues were used to complete the drainage and resettlement of the Red River Delta and to build new dikes, canals, and roads. More land was opened up for rice cultivation to feed the expanding population. An army was created which not only repelled a Chinese invasion in 1076 but also checked aggression from the kingdom of Cambodia and seized territory from the kingdom of Champa (192–1471), which then controlled territories corresponding roughly to the northern half of what is now South Vietnam. It was after one of the victories over Champa in 1069 that Thanh-Tong, the third Ly emperor and one of the greatest Vietnamese sovereigns, renamed the country Dai-Viet (Greater Viet). The country kept this name until 1802, when Emperor Gia Long (Nguyen Anh) changed it to Vietnam.

It was during the Ly Dynasty that the expansionist policy of *nam-tien* began in earnest. This policy was continued down through Vietnamese history until 1780, when the southern tip of the Indochinese peninsula was acquired from Cambodia.

During this dynasty, Buddhism reached its height on the strength of royal patronage. It was made the state religion. Many of the better-educated Buddhist monks filled high official posts. The Ly rulers also encouraged Confucianism and Taoism. Taoism, in particular, penetrated the countryside, adulterating popular Buddhism. Art depicting Buddhist themes also flourished. Another notable achievement was the perfection of ceramic art.

THE TRAN DYNASTY

In 1225 the throne was seized by the Tran Dynasty, which held it for one hundred seventy-five years of repeated military crises, including prolonged conflict with the kingdom of Champa. Three invasions by the Mongol armies of Kublai Khan—1257, 1278, and 1284—were repelled. The Vietnamese victory under General Tran Hung Dao in the last of these encounters is one of the most celebrated in the annals of the country's history. After the Mongol withdrawal, the Tran monarch sent a mission to Kublai Khan and reestablished peace as a tributary of Mongol-ruled China.

During this dynasty, Confucianism, with its emphasis on learning, replaced Buddhism in importance. This scholarly atmosphere produced a number of literary accomplishments. The first extant historical records—a thirty-volume official history of Dai-Viet *(Dai-Viet Su-kyh)*—date from the Tran. Other historical writings and biographies also appeared—all written in Chinese.

THE CHINESE INTERREGNUM

Economic and social crises, following the devastation of war, were intensified by the aggrandizement of big landlords at the expense of the peasantry and by incompetence and corruption in the bureaucracy. An ambitious regent, Ho Qui Ly, took advantage of the situation to usurp the throne, thereby giving the Ming Dynasty (1368–1644) of China the occasion to intervene on the pretext of restoring the Tran Dynasty. Within a year of the Chinese invasion in 1406, Dai-Viet was again a province of China. Under the Ming the country was heavily exploited, and radical measures were instituted to sinicize the Vietnamese. Within little more than a decade, oppression had brought into being a powerful movement of national resistance.

THE LE DYNASTY

The leader of the movement to restore independence was Le Loi, an aristocratic landowner. Employing guerrilla tactics, he waged a ten-year fight against the Chinese, defeating them in 1427. Shortly after the Chinese left the country, he ascended the throne under the name of Le Thai To. His dynasty lasted for three hundred sixty years.

During the early years of the dynasty, the kingdom grew more powerful than it had ever been, particularly under Le Thanh-Tong, one of the most celebrated rulers in Vietnamese history. The triennial tribute to China was paid regularly, and relations with the Chinese were peaceful. At the same time, war was vigorously pushed against the kingdom of Champa; when it was finally conquered in 1471, all Champa territory north of Mui Dieu (formerly called Cap Varella or Varella Cape) was annexed. The remaining territory became a vassal state in tribute to Dai-Viet. The Vietnamese, however, continued to absorb Champa until it disappeared as a political entity. All that remains of this once-advanced culture in present-day Vietnam is a small rural ethnic minority called Cham and impressive ruins in the central lowlands.

The power and prestige of the Le Dynasty declined after the death of Le Thanh-Tong in 1497. In 1527, General Mac Dang Dung usurped the throne and established a new dynasty for which he was able to purchase the unenthusiastic approval of the Chinese. Shortly thereafter, another powerful family, the Nguyen, set up a descendant of the deposed Le Dynasty as head of the government-in-exile south of Hanoi—an event which marked the beginning of a century and a half of regional strife and of division between the north and the south which lasted until the latter part of the eighteenth century. In this struggle, the place of the Mac was taken by another family, the Trinh, which in 1592 defeated the Mac ruler and reinstalled a puppet Le emperor on the throne in the north. Meanwhile, the Nguyen were able to consolidate power in the region south of the seventeenth parallel.

It was in the name of the Le emperor, the symbol of national unity, that the Nguyen and the Trinh carried on their war against each other. Both the Trinh, who controlled the Le emperors at this time, and the Nguyen, who ruled as independent autocrats, claimed support of the Le as justification for the legitimacy of the respective regimes. In 1673, after half a century of bloody and inconclusive fighting, a truce was concluded which lasted for one hundred years.

This one hundred years of peace brought a great cultural resurgence, especially to the north, where the Vietnamese civilization was well established. Along with the Buddhist renaissance that occurred, there was much literary and artistic effort. The north produced great works of history and historical criticism.

Under the Nguyen, Vietnamese expansion, at the expense of Cambodia, was vigorously pursued. The remaining coastal territories of the Champa were gradually absorbed, and in the seventeenth and eighteenth centuries a series of short but decisive wars were waged with the Cambodians, who then occupied the Mekong Delta and

A 1972 issue of stamps—King Quang Trung (1752–92)

most of the south-central portion of the Indochinese peninsula. The acquisition of the vastly fertile Mekong Delta represented a gain of major proportion for the land-hungry Vietnamese. By the end of the eighteenth century, Vietnamese control extended to the limits of contemporary South Vietnam.

THE TAY SON UPRISING

Late in the eighteenth century three brothers of a Nguyen family in the village of Tay Son in central Vietnam led an uprising against the ruling Nguyen (to whom they were not related). The rebellion had popular support, both of the peasants and of the merchants. The oldest of the brothers, Nhac, drove the Nguyen lords out of the south by 1778 and proclaimed himself emperor over southern Dai-Viet. The youngest brother, Hue, led the attack on the Trinh in the north, defeating them in 1786. In 1788, after abolishing the decrepit Le Dynasty and extending his power to the south at the expense of his brother, he made himself emperor of a reunited Vietnam. A new Chinese invasion attempt was repelled by him in 1788. He is known as the Quang-Trung emperor. Hoping to cultivate a Vietnamese national consciousness free of Chinese influence, he substituted *chu nom* (the vulgate script using Chinese characters to express Vietnamese sounds) for Chinese in all public acts and military proclamations.

A bloody struggle ended with the defeat of the last Tay Son king in 1802 and the installation of Nguyen Anh as the emperor Gia Long—Gia Long being the contraction of Gia Dinh (then Saigon) and Thanh Long (Hanoi). With the founding of the Nguyen Dynasty at Hue, the reunified country was renamed Vietnam. In 1803 the emperor's authority was formally recognized by the Chinese Ching Dynasty, to which he agreed to pay tribute biannually. The Nguyen Dynasty lasted until the abdication of Bao Dai at the end of World War II.

THE FRENCH CONQUEST

Toward the middle of the nineteenth century pressure was

mounting in influential French quarters for positive action to establish a position for France in Vietnam of the kind other European powers enjoyed, or were acquiring, elsewhere in Asia. The missionaries had been roused to an angry militance by the imprisonment or execution of some of their number and by the periodic persecution of Vietnamese Christians. The imperial ban had not halted missionary activity in the country, but it was clear that the authorities would never cease to obstruct Christianity unless forced to do so. Considerations of French national prestige and military advantage were also present, as was the desire for a share of the economic benefits to be had from an aggressive policy in Asia.

In September 1857 all these factors led to France's decision to take Tourane (Da Nang). The city was captured in 1858, and the French thereafter turned their attention to the south. Inflicting heavy losses on the Vietnamese, they took Saigon by July 1861. In June 1862 the Vietnamese court at Hue ceded Saigon and the adjacent area to France and agreed to pay a war indemnity. They also promised not to cede territory to any other power without French permission. The western part of the southern delta, which was virtually cut off from the rest of Vietnam, was annexed by France in 1867, thus completing the territorial formation of what later became the French colony of Cochin China.

Until the nineteenth century Vietnam had been a relatively static and conservative society. Essentially agrarian and peasant based, it was ruled by an emperor and his royal family, governed by an intellectual elite organized in a civil bureaucracy, and stratified on the basis of education and occupation into four classes: scholars, farmers, artisans, and merchants.

French rule challenged this entrenched order, signaling an era of rapid social change. The upper stratum of society became oriented toward modernization, reflecting the impact of French education, technological development, and an expansion of private enterprise in all fields. Along with this, the traditional elite was gradually superseded by a new group based on wealth and French education. This new group was schooled in the traditions of liberalism and individualism.

With the collapse of the colonial regime and the rise of Communist influence in the mid-twentieth century, the stage was set for still further change. Lao Dong party leaders and the government undertook to impose their Communist social model on the weakened base of what they defined as a capitalist society. They were explicit as to the structure of the new society to be expected under communism. In theory the Communist system allegedly rests on a broad social base consisting of an alliance between the workers and peasants and other groups of working people—under the leadership of the workers. Communist doctrine was adapted, however, to fit the special circumstances of North Vietnam, which is an essentially agrarian society lacking a sizable urban proletariat. The collective peasantry, along with the working class, would therefore constitute

the main force of the revolution.

By late 1966 certain changes in the class structure had almost certainly resulted from agrarian reform, economic reconstruction, and restrictions on the functioning of the former intellectual elite. Statements by party leaders to the effect that social transformation could not be accomplished either swiftly or by harsh methods suggested, however, that the measure of changes was not sweeping. Moreover, detailed information regarding such changes as may have occurred was not available, and the precise character of social structure at that time was a matter of speculation.

One assumption could, nevertheless, be made with relative certainty. Whatever pattern of stratification emerged, party members would control both the social structure itself and the channels for upward mobility within that structure, for, backed by a strong army, the party membership enjoyed a virtual monopoly on prestige and privilege. Members were dispersed in key positions throughout the society, and the influence of the party was pervasive. Within the party itself a still smaller element could be distinguished from the rank and file by its greater degree of prestige and privilege and by its exclusive control of the machinery both for making and carrying out policy decisions.

Other social groupings based on ethnic origin and religious adherence could be distinguished within the society. Cultural and linguistic differences, for example, set apart some two million members of the ethnic minorities from the rest of the population. Among the ethnic Vietnamese themselves, a social distinction was made between the estimated five hundred thousand to eight hundred thousand adherents (in 1966) of Roman Catholicism and the majority of the population, which had traditionally identified itself with Buddhism. In the past, differentiation between urban dweller and villager also had had important social implications, but with the massive population shifts of the early 1960s that distinction had become less meaningful.

HISTORICAL BACKGROUND

PRE-FRENCH

When the French arrived in Vietnam, there was no permanent nobility status, except for the emperor and his royal family. An older feudal nobility, originally deriving its position from large land grants from the emperors and enjoying hereditary titles, powers, and privileges, had already been abolished and replaced by an elite which received, for special services rendered to the court, only small token grants of land. Their titles bore no power or privilege and, moreover, in each generation were successively downgraded through five ranks until, in the sixth generation, they were lost entirely. Anyone, whether of royal or common extraction, could receive a title. Collectively this elite had no special mutual interests and did not form in any sense a class; their titles might give them prestige in their own communities, but their status in the country at large depended on their wealth as landowners.

The annexation of Cochin China by 1867 and the subsequent political subordination of Annam and Tonkin by France changed the political and economic structures of those areas and led, consequently, to changes in the social structure. Political subordination, the introduction of French education, the beginnings of modern industrialization, the stimulation of urbanization, and the growth of commercial agriculture affected the whole country.

The most important social change was the introduction of a foreign governing class. There had been a few French missionaries in the area since the sixteenth century, and the French had had a hand in establishing the Nguyen Dynasty in the eighteenth century, but the 1860s brought the French in as governors. First reducing Cochin China to the status of a colony, the French soon extended their power to Annam and Tonkin, which were made protectorates. In 1887 these political units, together with Cambodia and, later, Laos, were formed into the Indochinese Union. Vietnamese tribunals were replaced by French courts. In the protectorates of Tonkin and Annam the indigenous administration was largely retained, but over all was the French resident superior in each protectorate plus a French resident in each province. At the royal court in Hue, French administrators were assigned to each minister.

With the establishment of this new foreign ruling class, the power of the royal family and the civil bureaucracy began to decline. The emperor remained on the throne, but his dominion over Cochin China and, in practice, over Tonkin was lost; he became, in effect, an appointed and usually obedient servant of the French. If the emperor rebelled, he was replaced by another member of the royal family.

The royal family was a restricted group, being limited to the emperor's household and lineage. Families related by blood or marriage to the royal family had no formal prerogatives because of this fact, and the further they were removed genealogically from the emperor's line of descent, the more tenuous became their claim even to royal blood. Thus, although thousands of persons claiming royal blood surrounded the court and although they might consider themselves for reasons of descent socially superior to commoners, in fact their real weight in the society depended more on other attributes—mainly wealth in land or status in the governmental bureaucracy.

CONSOLIDATION OF COLONIAL RULE (1883–1900)

The French next turned their attention to the Red River, having found the Mekong unsuitable as a trade route to China because of its rapids. A treaty was signed in 1874 which opened the Red River to French traders, but Chinese pirates largely nullified the value of the concession. In 1883 an expeditionary force brought northern Vietnam under French control, and the signing of a Treaty of Protectorate

on August 25, 1883, formally ended Vietnam's independence.

The treaty of 1883 and one of June 1884 established French protectorates over northern Vietnam (Tonkin) and central Vietnam (Annam). All of southern Vietnam (Cochin China) had been in French hands since the conquest in 1867 and now, with the abrogation of what was left of the country's independence, the name Vietnam itself was officially eliminated. In Annam the emperor and his officials were left in charge of internal affairs, except for customs and public works, but they functioned under the eye of the French, who had the right to station troops in the area. The protectorate over Tonkin made a few concessions to the appearance of autonomy, and French resident officers in the larger towns directly controlled the administration.

These developments did not go unchallenged. The Chinese denied the validity of treaties made with the Vietnamese without their approval. The French defeated a Chinese force sent in to win control of a part of Tonkin. China in 1885 formally recognized the French protectorate over Tonkin and Annam. The Vietnamese were more difficult to cope with. Beginning in 1885, under the twelve-year-old emperor Ham-Nghi, a general uprising broke out against the French. It failed, and Ham-Nghi was exiled in 1888. Active armed resistance, led by such men as De Tham and Phan Dinh Phung, continued into the early twentieth century but failed largely because the movements were localized and made no systematic attempts to arouse popular nationalist sentiments.

The final phase of French consolidation was marked by the formation of an Indochinese Union in 1887. Consisting of Tonkin, Annam, Cochin China, and Cambodia (a French protectorate since 1863), the union was administered under a French governor-general who was responsible directly to the Ministry of Colonies in Paris. In 1893, Laos, following annexation by France, was also added to the union.

The basic political structure of French Indochina was completed by 1900. Each of Vietnam's three regions was treated differently, although basic policy decisions for all usually originated in Paris. Cochin China was administered directly by a French-staffed civil service under a governor and a colonial council. It also sent a representative to the Chamber of Deputies in Paris. The colonial council, a legislative body, consisted of both French and Vietnamese members. In the administrative apparatus, only subordinate positions were open for Vietnamese. In the protectorate of Tonkin, the mandarinate was retained for administration purposes, but important executive powers were vested in a French senior resident at Hanoi. In Annam, where the emperor was still nominally in power and the mandarinate continued to function, French rule was only a little less direct.

On the whole, French rule was much more liberal in Cochin China than in Annam or Tonkin. Cochin China was administered under the French judicial system, whereas in

Tonkin and Annam the traditional judicial system, marked by extreme severity, was retained and applied by using the bureaucracy as a front.

THE IMPACT OF FRENCH RULE

French influence permeated nearly all walks of Vietnamese society. With the aid of modern science and technology, the French undertook to develop a society which would be patterned after their own but, at the same time, uncritically submissive to colonial rule. In the process, stabilizing forces of the traditional order were disrupted, and workable alternatives were lacking. The resulting social tensions and stresses paved the way for the political awakening of the people.

Meanwhile, French nationals took over all important governmental administrative and managerial positions. The traditional community of scholar-officials declined sharply in social prestige and political influence. As a direct consequence, aspiring Vietnamese turned to Western-type rather than to Chinese-type schooling, traditionally the most important means for the attainment of power and wealth. This shift exposed educated Vietnamese to liberal and radical political ideals of the West, stimulating them to question the capability of their Confucian-oriented social order to withstand new challenges from the West. Direct contact with French culture, especially during World War I when about one hundred thousand Vietnamese served on the European front, further accelerated the introduction of new ideas. At the same time many educated people began to demand the right to self-determination.

French influence, especially pronounced in urban areas, also left a discernible imprint on the rural society. The traditional village institution was gradually affected by stimulating forces emanating from the highly centralized administrative system, the improved network of communications and transportation, and the penetration of cash economy. The village notables could no longer command the authority they once had, and, as a result, social cohesion weakened. The French policy of establishing large landed estates, especially in Cochin China, tended to strip villages of communal land, which had been the major source of social insurance to the needy peasants. Much of the communal land fell into the hands of speculators and absentee landowners. As a result, the rural society became in-

Emperor Khai Dinh (left) *during a state visit to Paris in 1923*

creasingly subjected to disruptive forces beyond its control. A growing tax burden, combined with rapid increases in the number of landless peasants and in total population, brought about progressive impoverishment in rural areas. Surplus rural manpower was absorbed partially by industries in the north and by rubber plantations in the south, but in the absence of protective labor legislation the plight of urban workers proved to be equally distressing.

In the economic sphere the colonial policy was geared mainly to benefit metropolitan France. Indochina was transformed not only into a source of raw materials but also into an exclusive market for tariff-produced French goods. To facilitate French domination, canals, drainage systems, railroads, harbors, and highways were extensively constructed. Large tracts of virgin land in the Mekong Delta were opened for rice cultivation, thereby making Indochina an important rice exporter. Most of the new land fell into French hands or into the hands of Vietnamese landlords who collaborated with the French. These landlords derived substantial portions of their wealth from high rents and from practices of usury.

Although much French profit went out of the country, some remained for investment in light industries and rubber plantations, from which the Vietnamese were virtually excluded. By 1938 nearly 95 percent of all foreign investments were in French hands. As a result, Vietnamese capital continued to be invested in land. On the whole, industry became the exclusive domain of the French investors, whereas the control of agriculture was shared by French and Vietnamese elements. The two sectors were linked by Chinese middlemen, dominating rice trade and retail business in both urban and rural areas.

The impact of French rule was most pronounced in Cochin China, which was directly ruled by French officials and dominated by French business. Western influences, however, also penetrated some industrial cities of Tonkin. Annam was least affected, as the area afforded little opportunity to French entrepreneurs, compared with the rubber plantations in the south and the industrial potential of the north. Furthermore, the presence of the Vietnamese court at Hue with its ceremonial rites kept alive the traditional structure.

THE RISE OF NATIONALISM

Early in the twentieth century nationalist movements began to develop, initially among urban intellectuals. Japan's victory over Russia in 1905 gave impetus to nationalist sentiment by demonstrating that an Asian nation with sufficient technical knowledge and equipment could prevail over a Western power. Despite the watchfulness of the French authorities, numerous anti-French secret societies sprang up, but most of them were loosely organized and had no well-defined political objectives. Nascent nationalism drew its inspiration from outside sources—Europe, China, and Japan.

A distinguished scholar, Phan Boi Chau, is popularly regarded as the founder of nationalist movements. Vietnamese independence, he thought, could best be achieved by enlisting the support of, or emulating Japan, and in 1906 he went to Japan to promote his cause. Through his writings and the leadership of a group of Vietnamese intellectuals who shared his exile, he gained a wide following. His activities were a source of embarrassment to the Japanese government, and he was expelled in 1910, but he continued his work from exile in China, where he succeeded in uniting most of the nationalist groups outside of Vietnam in the Association for the Restoration of Vietnam (Viet Nam Quang Phuc Hoi). He organized a government-in-exile under Prince Cuong De, a direct descendant of Gia Long and claimant to the throne of Annam. Despite intensive clandestine propaganda efforts, his movement—whose objective was to oust the French and restore monarchical rule in traditional form and to promulgate a constitution on the Japanese model—failed to enlist mass support.

While Phan Boi Chau led a nationalist movement from outside the country, others worked in Vietnam for similar goals. Phan Chau Trinh, another scholar, led a group of nationalists who sought French rather than Japanese assistance. Believing that the French could be persuaded to prepare the Vietnamese for eventual independence, he presented a memorandum along these lines to the French governor-general in 1906. His proposals were ignored, however, and when he continued to agitate for reforms and formed various study groups he was imprisoned by the French authorities.

From the group of scholar-officials also came the leaders of an uprising in 1916 to which young Emperor Duy-Than lent his support. Several hundred of the participants were executed or deported, and Duy-Than himself was sent into exile. After this disaster, resistance by the scholars subsided, but it did not disappear.

By the early 1920s a new socioeconomic group had emerged that had been made wealthy by the acquisition of newly developed lands through cooperation with the French. Many of these persons, especially in Cochin China, sought the privileges of French citizenship for themselves and frequently sent their children to France to be educated. Some of them, however, still cherished nationalist sentiments and advocated Franco-Vietnamese collaboration and gradual reform. In 1923 two such leaders, Bui Quang Chieu and Nguyen Phan Long, founded the Constitutionalist party in Saigon. This was the first Vietnamese political organization to be sanctioned by the French authorities, but lukewarm French response and lack of mass support only brought disillusionment to its leaders.

A number of nationalist groups found inspiration in the Chinese nationalist movement. Of these, the best known and most important was the Vietnamese Nationalist party (Viet Nam Quoc Dan Dang—VNQDD). It was established first in 1925 in Canton, then the center of the revolutionary ferment in China, in opposition to the Association of Vietnamese Revolutionary Youth (Vietnam Thanh-Nieu Cach-Mang Dong-chi Hoi), precursor of the Indochinese Communist party.

Two years later the VNQDD was also established secretly in Hanoi by Nguyen Thai Hoc, a schoolteacher. Impressed by the Chinese efforts to modernize their country and simultaneously to repel foreign encroachments, Nguyen Thai Hoc's supporters adopted the organization, methods, and programs of the Chinese Nationalist party (Kuomintang), but failed to create an effective organization within the country. Their greater shortcoming was the lack of an imaginative social program. An uprising staged in 1930 at Yen Bay, northwest of Hanoi, was severely repressed by the French. The VNQDD was nearly destroyed, and many of its surviving members fled to Yunnan in southwest China. They returned to Vietnam after World War II to confront both the French and the Communists.

After the Yen Bay insurrection, the leadership of the clandestine Nationalist movement in Vietnam was taken over by the opportunist Indochinese Communist party (Dong Duong Cong San Dang), which chose not to participate in that uprising. Formed in Hong Kong in 1930, it united several existing independent Communist groups under the leadership of Nguyen Ai Quoc (Nguyen the Patriot), later known as Ho Chi Minh.

UNFULFILLED REFORMS

The thoroughness with which the Yen Bay uprising was repressed for a time rendered the more militant nationalists inactive. Some Vietnamese did, however, attempt to advance the cause of national liberation through reforms from above. They looked to the young emperor Bao Dai as their best hope. Bao Dai had ascended the throne in 1926 at the age of twelve on the death of his father, Emperor Khai-Dinh, but did not return to Vietnam until 1932 after he had completed his education in France.

Bao Dai was greeted with enthusiasm by the Vietnamese, who expected that he would be able to persuade the French to install a more liberal regime. He attempted to reign as a constitutional monarch, according to the terms of the treaty of 1884 establishing the protectorate, and he strove to modernize the ancient imperial administration at Hue.

Among his young collaborators was Ngo Dinh Diem, governor of the Phan Thiet area in Binh Thuan province (approximately one hundred miles east of Saigon), who was given the portfolio of minister of the interior and appointed head of the secretariat of a Vietnamese-French commission which was charged with the responsibility of implementing Bao Dai's reform proposals. When it became obvious that the French had no intention of granting real power to the Vietnamese administration and would make no concessions toward unification of the country, the

Emperor Bao Dai in royal ceremonial garb on the palace steps

Emperor Bao Dai, who ruled Vietnam from 1925 to 1945, was considered by historians to be a most able administrator.

Emperor Bao Dai (right) *and the French commander in Indochina, General Joost Van Vollenhoven, visit with a mountain tribe and sample their wine.*

A 1943 issue of stamps—Bao Dai, emperor of Annam, and Nam Phuong, empress of Annam.

youthful emperor appeared to lose interest, and Ngo Dinh Diem resigned his official position.

For a brief time in 1936, during the period of the Popular Front government in France, the Vietnamese had hopes that autonomy might be granted. The French Socialists, however, made no important concessions, and the colonial administration continued as before.

THE JAPANESE OCCUPATION (1940–45)

After the fall of France in June 1940, the Vichy government acceded to Japanese demands, which ultimately led to the establishment of Japanese controls over all of the French Indochinese peninsula. In August 1940 the Vichy authorities agreed to accept Japan's "preeminent" position in the Far East and to grant the Japanese certain transit facilities in Tonkin in return for Japanese recognition of its sovereignty over Indochina. Under this accord the French colonial administrative structure was kept intact, and the French community maintained its privileged position with little change to indicate to the population the eclipse of French power in Indochina. This arrangement gave the Japanese the benefit of the services of the French officials and freed Japanese personnel for duties elsewhere. There were clashes between Japanese and French forces along the northern border of Tonkin, and Japan's aircraft bombed the port of Haiphong. After the Vichy government had agreed, however, in September, to the stationing of Japanese troops in areas on the northern side of the Red River, the French troops did not offer further military opposition and continued their traditional garrison duties.

An economic agreement was signed in May 1941 which reserved all of the important exports of Indochina for Japan; these included rice, manganese, tungsten, antimony, tin, and chrome. A shortage of Japanese shipping, however, contributed to a sharp decline in exports, which in turn drastically curtailed imports, and shortages developed in many items which the Vietnamese had been accustomed to import from Europe.

The Japanese position was further consolidated in July 1941 when the two governments signed a military agreement providing for the "common defense of French Indochina," under which Japan was permitted to station troops in southern Indochina. The agreement also enabled Japan to control virtually all airfields in the south and important port facilities and railroads elsewere. Immediately after Japan's attack on Pearl Harbor, the French made another agreement reaffirming the existing Franco-Japanese cooperation, and this uneasy relationship continued until the Japanese coup d'etat in March 1945.

The Japanese occupation and French reaction to it had the effect of further stimulating nationalist sentiments. Fearing that Japan would capitalize on the strong anti-French feelings of the people, the French administration undertook to liberalize certain of its repressive policies. It improved technical and vocational education programs, opened new schools, and launched a youth movement presumably in hopes of winning the support of youth groups. It also opened additional civil service posts for the Vietnamese. The French apparently intended, however, to reinforce the colonial order through these token concessions, while they continued to impose restrictions on nationalist activities.

COMMUNIST MOVEMENT

Nguyen Ai Quoc (Ho Chi Minh), a Communist since 1920 and founder of the united Indochinese Communist party in 1930, was still in the forefront of the Vietnamese Communist movement ten years later. Allied with and deftly exploiting the non-Communist nationalist groups, Nguyen Ai Quoc eventually emerged as the dominant political figure of the country.

To broaden the social and political bases of its activities, the Communist party, in May 1941, adopted a policy of collaboration with all non-Communist nationalists. This decision led to the formation of a united front organization, the Vietnam Independence League (Viet Nam Doc Lap Dong Minh), better known as the Viet Minh.

One of the first actions of the Viet Minh was to form guerrilla bands, under the direction of Vo Nguyen Giap, to operate in Vietnamese territory against the Japanese and the French. He also began implanting agents and setting up intelligence networks in Tonkin. Meanwhile, comparable efforts by the non-Communist groups, beset by factional wranglings, were virtually nonexistent. Although Nguyen Ai Quoc was jailed for his Communist activity by the Chinese authorities in 1942, the Viet Minh continued its vigorous efforts to win popular support.

During the same period, the Chinese, who urgently needed intelligence on Japanese activities in Tonkin, attempted to make use of the non-Communist Vietnamese exiles for this purpose. At Chinese urging, a new organization, called the Revolutionary League of Vietnam (Vietnam Cach Minh Dong Minh Hoi), usually abbreviated to Dong Minh Hoi, was formed in October 1942 and given financial support by the Chinese Kuomintang. Although all the major nationalist groups—including the Vietnamese Nationalist party and the Viet Minh—were represented in it, the new organization, without active Viet Minh cooperation, remained ineffective. It was against this background that in 1943 the Chinese released Nguyen Ai Quoc in exchange for his offer to help them. Thereupon he took the name of Ho Chi Minh (he who enlightens), presumably to conceal his Communist affiliation from the Vietnamese people.

Ho Chi Minh was expected to work through the Dong Minh Hoi, but, in fact, he worked only through the Viet Minh and used the funds which the Dong Minh Hoi received from the Chinese Nationalist government to strengthen his Communist organization. His organization produced some intelligence of use to the Allies, and Vo Nguyen Giap's guerrilla bands engaged in minor forays against the Japanese. In return, Ho Chi Minh received an undetermined amount of small arms, munitions, and communication equipment from the United States for counteraction against the Japanese. This aid later formed the basis for his claim that the Viet Minh enjoyed Allied support.

Working in nationalist disguise, Ho Chi Minh effectively strengthened the organization of Communist cells throughout Vietnam. In the subsequent struggle for leadership in the Nationalist movement as the war ended, the superior organization of the Communists enabled him to gain control of the Viet Minh and to claim all the credit for Nationalist activities during the war. Capitalizing on the anti-colonialist propaganda organized by Moscow, Vietnamese Communists claimed to be fighting only against economic misery and for national liberation. They were not recognized by Vietnamese as representing an alien force except by those with superior education and keen political insight.

The Imperial Palace in Hue

Crown Prince Bao Long in Annamite costume and in Western uniform (1952)

Empress Nam Phuong on a 1952 stamp supporting the Red Cross

President Ngo Dinh Diem

NATIONAL INDEPENDENCE REGAINED

In September 1944 the Tokyo government, alarmed over growing indications of anti-Japanese activities, decided to displace the French and grant independence to the Vietnamese. Initially, this plan was to be executed on April 25, 1945, but the reoccupation of the Philippine Islands by the United States forces in October and the growing awareness that Japan was losing the war advanced the date of the Japanese coup d'etat to March 9, 1945.

At the instigation of the Japanese, Emperor Bao Dai proclaimed independence of Vietnam under Japanese "protection." He formed a new government at Hue, proclaimed a political amnesty and attempted to create a Vietnamese administration to replace the French administration which had been ousted. An effective government could not be established, however, because of administrative difficulties arising from the sudden French ouster, the breakdown of communications owing to Allied bombing, crop failures

Ho Chi Minh, the Communist leader who formally took control of Vietnam when Emperor Bao Dai abdicated in 1945

effective because of factional differences. The Viet Minh exploited this situation by launching a skillful propaganda campaign which portrayed the Viet Minh as a strong Nationalist movement enjoying the support of the Allies. In ignorance of the organization's actual character, the United National Front agreed to accept Viet Minh leadership.

While these events were taking place, Bao Dai, apparently convinced that a united and independent nation offered the only possibility of preventing the return of French control, decided to abdicate. Recognizing only the nationalist character of the Viet Minh movement and assuming that it had Allied support, he abdicated in its favor on August 25, 1945, and handed over his imperial seal and other symbols of office to Ho Chi Minh. To the overwhelming majority of the people this clearly meant that Ho Chi Minh was endowed with legitimacy and that they would be expected to follow the Viet Minh leadership.

On September 2, Ho Chi Minh formally proclaimed the independence of Vietnam and the establishment of the so-called Democratic Republic of Vietnam. To facilitate the negotiations directed toward gaining international recognition of its legitimacy, Communist domination of the new government was carefully concealed and emphasis placed on the "democratic" Vietnamese character of the regime. Bao Dai was made high counselor to the new government.

and famine in Tonkin and Annam, and the imposition of direct Japanese military rule over Cochin China.

Meanwhile, at Hanoi, the Viet Minh went into action, refusing to support the Bao Dai regime. Ho Chi Minh began to refer to the Viet Minh guerrilla units as the National Liberation Army and announced the formation of a Committee for the Liberation of the Vietnamese People, with himself as president. By late August 1945 the Viet Minh partisans and agents gained administrative control over the Tonkin area by a show of force.

In Cochin China, where Communist activity had been negligible because of strict French control measures, nationalist groups of various political leanings formed a United National Front and took over administrative functions from the Japanese. It was, however, politically in-

THE ROYAL SOVEREIGNS OF THE EMPIRE OF VIETNAM

Reign	Title	Ruler
1802–1820	King/Emperor	Nguyen Anh (Gia Long)
1820–1841	King	Minh Mang
1841–1848	King	Thieu Tri
1848–1883	King	Tu-Duc
1883–1883	King	Nguyen Duc Duc
1883–1883	King	Nguyen Hiep-Hoa
1883–1884	King	Kien-Phuc
1884–1885	King	Ham-Nghi
1885–1889	King	Dong-Khanh
1889—French Indo-China formed		
1889–1907	Emperor	Thanh-Thai
1907–1916	Emperor	Duy-Than
1916–1925	Emperor	Khai-Dinh
1926–1945	Emperor	Bao Dai

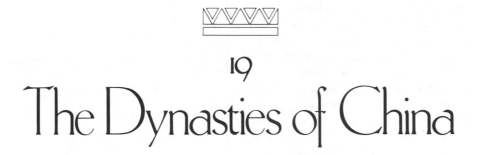

19
The Dynasties of China

The Chinese kept voluminous historical records since very early times. It is largely as a result of these records that information concerning the ancient past, not only of China but also of the rest of Asia, has survived.

Chinese history, until the twentieth century, was written by members of the ruling class and was meant primarily to provide the ruler with established precedents to guide or justify his policies. The official historians confined their accounts almost exclusively to events pertaining to the king or emperor and to the relatively small circle of people with whom the ruler dealt. Their histories told of a succession of dynasties, each one following a cyclical pattern of rising, flourishing, decaying, and falling.

The official historians had a duty to make their history serve the dynasty that patronized them. Nonetheless, they were expected to be accurate and impartial, not mere propagandists. Since the Communist takeover after World War II historians in China have been expressly instructed to write history that serves the purposes of the regime.

In the attempt by Communist historians to make Chinese history fit into the authorized Marxist pattern of progression—from primitive communism to slavery to feudalism to capitalism to socialism—most of the imperial period has been termed feudal and given scant attention. The little that has been written by Chinese Marxists about the imperial period (which lasted, with brief interruptions, from 212 B.C. to A.D. 1911) has emphasized the activities of, and conditions among, the common people. The imperial historians had concentrated almost exclusively upon the political elite. The chief concern of the Marxist historians has been the role of the class struggle in China's evolution and, therefore, attention has been focused on peasant uprisings during the imperial period.

Of various recurrent patterns identified by independent historians, an important one has been the tendency of the Chinese to absorb into their civilization the people of contiguous areas by the superiority of their technology, by the refinement of their artistic and intellectual achievement, and by the weight of their numbers. This process continued until virtually all of what is now known as China Proper had

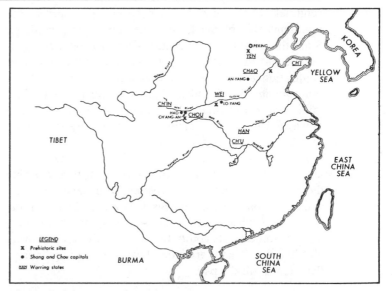

China's early beginnings

become Chinese and the people of the periphery, especially the Koreans, Japanese, and Vietnamese, had become deeply influenced by Chinese civilization.

A theme related to this tendency of the Chinese to absorb neighboring peoples has been the great and ever-increasing size of China's population. From an estimated 65 million in the late fourteenth century, 150 million in 1600, and 430 million in 1850, the population by 1971 had grown to approximately 800 million, or one-quarter of the world's population. The great size of the country's population and, in particular, the dense settlement over many centuries of the north China plain and the Yangtze Delta have greatly influenced China's history and society.

Another recurrent theme has been the struggle of the Chinese people, who have always been primarily sedentary and agrarian, to deal with the threat posed to their safety and their way of life by predatory foreigners. At first the chief threat came from nomadic tribesmen from the steppes of northern and northwestern Asia, but later it came from traders and missionaries from the Near East and Europe and eventually from modern business, missionary, and military personnel from Europe, America, and Japan.

For thousands of years virtually all of the foreigners that the Chinese ruling class saw came from the less developed societies along China's land borders, and this conditioned the rulers' view of the outside world. For millennia China saw itself as the self-sufficient Middle Kingdom (*Chung-kuo*—the traditional Chinese name for China), surrounded on all sides by so-called barbarian peoples whose cultures were demonstrably inferior by Chinese standards.

By the time of the first serious confrontation with men from the Western world, China had long taken for granted that it alone was civilized, that its empire included "all under heaven," and that all relations between China and foreigners should be conducted according to the prescribed pattern of patronage and tribute that had evolved over the centuries to govern relations between the emperor and representatives of the lesser states on China's borders. Since the mid-nineteenth century China has been engaged in an effort to reassess its position in respect to Western civilization and to determine what aspects of that civilization could be usefully adapted to serve China's needs. The millennia-old dynastic system of government was brought down in 1912 by its inability to successfully make this reassessment and readjustment.

It is possible to find many contemporary elements that are without precedent. The denigration of the family and of the past and the admiration of youth, of dynamic change, and of the common man and his work are total reversals of traditional Chinese values. The technological capability of the government—its ability to exert effective control over all of the people at the grassroots level—is also a significant departure from the past.

THE ANCIENT DYNASTIES

Chinese tradition traces civilization back to P'an Ku, the creator, the first in a succession of divine and semidivine beings who taught men the essential skills. Then came a train of legendary rulers, beginning with Huang Ti (the Yellow Emperor), who is alleged to be the progenitor of the Chinese people. Among Huang Ti's successors, the best known are Yao and Shun, who are considered model rulers and whose reigns constituted a golden age. They are reputed to have governed wisely and well, and they also chose the ablest and most virtuous men, rather than their own sons or brothers, to succeed them. As Yao chose Shun, so Shun chose Yu, the hero who is said to have drained off the waters of the great flood of Chinese legend. The legend asserts that Yu left his throne to a son, thus originating the dynastic system of inherited succession to the throne by males of the male line.

The dynasty that Yu founded is known as the Hsia Dynasty. No archaeological evidence of the Hsia Dynasty has yet been identified, but many scholars believe that the traditional account of it has a basis in fact. The last Hsia

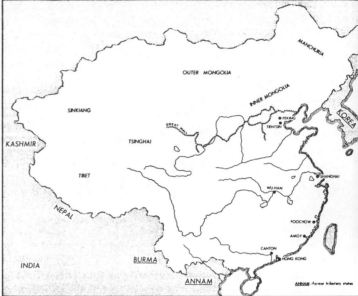

Imperial China's territory in 1911

ruler is said to have been a tyrant who was overthrown in a popular uprising led by a nobleman named T'ang. This semilegendary event provided a precedent for the ancient Chinese doctrine that the people have a right to depose unjust rulers.

THE DAWN OF HISTORY

The rebel leader T'ang is believed to have founded the Shang Dynasty, in which China's known written history had its origin. A wealth of archaeological evidence has been unearthed in the Yellow River valley—also the area of numerous prehistoric sites—that confirms the Shang Dynasty's existence during the second millennium B.C. The traditional dating for the dynasty is 1766–1122 B.C.

In addition to the specimens of archaic Chinese writing found on the oracle bones (animal bones and shells used by priests in divination), there are also inscriptions on a number of ceremonial bronze vessels that date from this period. The workmanship on the bronzes attests to a high level of civilization.

Shang civilization was based on agriculture, augmented by animal husbandry. The Shang kings ruled over much of north China, and Shang forces, often numbering as many as five thousand troops, fought frequent wars with neighboring settlements and nomadic herdsmen. The capitals—one of which was at Anyang—were centers of glittering court life. Court ritual to propitiate natural spirits and to honor sacred ancestors was highly developed. In addition to his secular powers, the king was the head of the ancestor and spirit worship cult. By the last years of the dynasty the king had become an absolute despot. Evidence from the royal tombs at Anyang indicates that royal personages were buried with much ceremony and with articles of value, presumably provided for use in the afterlife. Perhaps for the same reason, hundreds of commoners, who may have been slaves, were buried alive with the royal corpse.

THE CHOU PERIOD

The last Shang ruler was denounced as oppressive and was overthrown by Wu, chief of a vigorous people from the Wei River valley in Shensi province, west of the Shang area in Honan province. Wu founded the Chou Dynasty which, through conquest and colonization, gradually sinicized much of China Proper north of the Yangtze River. The early Chou rulers established their capital at Hao (near modern Sian) in the Wei River valley, west of the right-angle bend of the Yellow River. The Chou Dynasty lasted longer than any other—from the twelfth or eleventh century until 255 B.C. Official historians of the Chou Dynasty first enunciated the doctrine of the "mandate of Heaven," the notion

that the ruler (the "son of Heaven") governed by right of the power divinely invested in him and that, if he were overthrown, his fall from power was proof that he had lost the divine sponsorship. The doctrine permitted them to explain and justify the demise of the two earlier dynasties and, at the same time, provided the chief justification for the authority of China's rulers that would be used by royal apologists from then on.

Chou kings parceled out their kingdom into hereditary fiefdoms granted to royal vassals in a pattern of landholding and personal loyalty relationships similar to that which prevailed during Europe's Middle Ages. In the first half of the Chou period the Middle Kingdom (which in early Chou

Chronological chart of China's main dynastic regimes

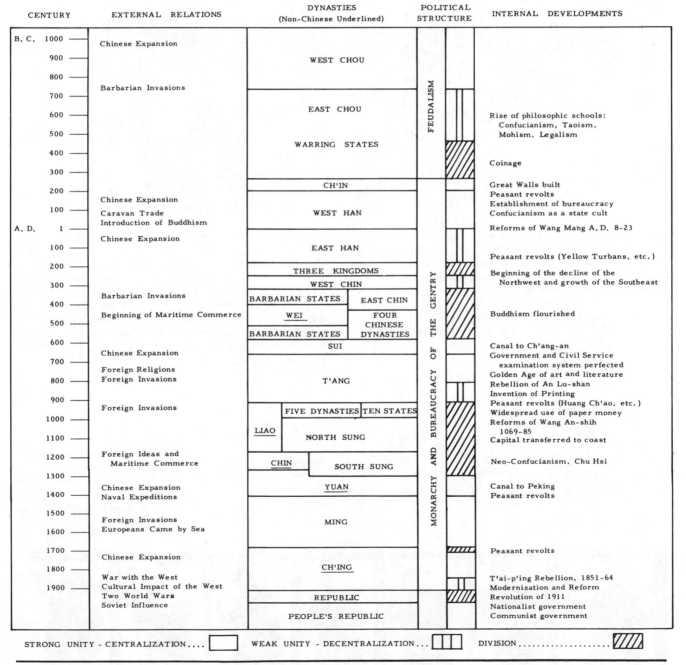

CENTURY	EXTERNAL RELATIONS	DYNASTIES (Non-Chinese Underlined)		POLITICAL STRUCTURE		INTERNAL DEVELOPMENTS
B.C. 1000	Chinese Expansion			FEUDALISM		
900		WEST CHOU				
800	Barbarian Invasions					
700		EAST CHOU				
600						Rise of philosophic schools: Confucianism, Taoism, Mohism, Legalism
500		WARRING STATES				
400						Coinage
300						
200		CH'IN				Great Walls built / Peasant revolts
Chinese Expansion						Establishment of bureaucracy
100	Caravan Trade	WEST HAN				Confucianism as a state cult
	Introduction of Buddhism					
A.D. 1	Chinese Expansion					Reforms of Wang Mang A.D. 8-23
100		EAST HAN				
200						Peasant revolts (Yellow Turbans, etc.)
		THREE KINGDOMS		GENTRY		Beginning of the decline of the Northwest and growth of the Southeast
300		WEST CHIN				
Barbarian Invasions	BARBARIAN STATES	EAST CHIN				
400		WEI	FOUR CHINESE DYNASTIES			Buddhism flourished
Beginning of Maritime Commerce						
500		BARBARIAN STATES				
600		SUI				Canal to Ch'ang-an
Chinese Expansion						Government and Civil Service examination system perfected
700	Foreign Religions					Golden Age of art and literature
800	Foreign Invasions	T'ANG				Rebellion of An Lu-shan / Invention of Printing
900	Foreign Invasions					Peasant revolts (Huang Ch'ao, etc.)
		FIVE DYNASTIES	TEN STATES			Widespread use of paper money
1000						Reforms of Wang An-shih 1069-85
1100		LIAO	NORTH SUNG			Capital transferred to coast
1200	Foreign Ideas and Maritime Commerce	CHIN	SOUTH SUNG			Neo-Confucianism, Chu Hsi
1300						
1400	Chinese Expansion / Naval Expeditions	YUAN				Canal to Peking / Peasant revolts
1500						
1600	Foreign Invasions / Europeans Came by Sea	MING				
1700						Peasant revolts
1800	Chinese Expansion	CH'ING				
1900	War with the West / Cultural Impact of the West					T'ai-p'ing Rebellion, 1851-64 / Modernization and Reform
	Two World Wars / Soviet Influence	REPUBLIC				Revolution of 1911 / Nationalist government
		PEOPLE'S REPUBLIC				Communist government

(Political Structure center label: MONARCHY AND BUREAUCRACY OF THE GENTRY)

STRONG UNITY - CENTRALIZATION.... [ ]   WEAK UNITY - DECENTRALIZATION... [|||]   DIVISION................... [////]

In this portrait of the legendary Emperor Yao standing, his official regalia are painted in red. At the top is the title "Yao," and there follows an eulogy. Emperor Yao was a ruler of remote antiquity who it is said was the son of the emperor K'u. Yao's patronymic was I-ch'i, for the characters of which there are two variants. At first he was enfeoffed at T'ao, and later at T'ang, and hence he is also known as T'ao-t'ang.

Fu Hsi, the "first" emperor of China. Legend has it that he reigned about 2990 B.C. Here Fu Hsi is seen seated, his hair loose and a deerskin cast over his shoulders. At the top is a preface and an eulogy in standard script by the emperor Li-tsung of the Sung Dynasty, which refer in particular to Fu Hsi's association with mystic diagrams. It is said that he invented writing from the eight mystic diagrams. His capital was at Ch'en.

This is a standing portrait of Yu of the Hsia Dynasty wearing a crown and holding a jade scepter. At the top is the title "Yu," and this is followed by an eulogy. King Yu, the traditional dates of whose reign are 2205–2197 B.C., was the founder of the Hsia Dynasty. His patronymic was Szu, and his given name Wen-ming. His father, Kun, was unsuccessful in controlling the waters, and was executed. Yu continued his father's work, being made superintendent of works, in which post he brought the waters and land under control. He traveled for thirteen years through the nine prefectures of what is now the north of China, establishing the tribute that it was suitable for each area to give to the court. At first he was enfeoffed as earl of Hsia, and so is sometimes known as Yu the Earl. He succeeded Shun as "Son of Heaven."

Portrait of legendary ancient emperor Shao Hao (2974–41 B.C.)

Emperor Ch'i (reigned 2176–67 B.C.), son of the great emperor Yu

Seven Chinese emperors from a relief in the Wu Liang Temple in Shantung Province. Left to right: Yu, Shun, Yao, Ti K'u, Chuan Hsii, Huang Ti, and Shen Nung. All seven are from the early legendary period.

times corresponded approximately to the region now included in Shensi, Shansi, and Honan provinces) gradually absorbed the peoples and lands to the south and east until all China Proper as far south as the Yangtze and as far east as the ocean was part of the Middle Kingdom. The barbarians of other areas, particularly those of the inhospitable steppes and deserts of the north and west, were hardier and more warlike and successfully resisted the Chinese, even invading the Middle Kingdom whenever Chinese power waned.

In 771 B.C., under threat of barbarian invasion, the Chou court was obliged to abandon Hao, its western capital in the Wei River valley, and move its seat of government eastward to Loyang in the present-day province of Honan. Because of the shift, historians divide the Chou Dynasty into Western Chou and Eastern Chou periods. The phenomenon of the capital being withdrawn away from danger in times of dynastic decay and being restored to an advanced position at a time when the central government was strong has occurred repeatedly in the course of Chinese history.

From 722 to 481 B.C. (an era called the Spring and Autumn Period after a famous historical chronicle of the time), the influence of the central government greatly diminished, and warfare between the feudal states increased in violence and frequency. The power of the Chou ruler continued to fade until the dynasty was finally extinguished in 255 B.C.

Although the so-called Era of the Warring States (402–221 B.C.) was one of unceasing warfare, it also coincided with the greatest flowering of Chinese thought and culture. The centuries of civil strife were accompanied by fundamental economic and social changes. Aristocrats became commoners, and commoners rose to high rank. Upward mobility was aided by the spread of education and the development of domestic interregional commerce. Commerce was stimulated by the introduction of coinage and technological improvements. Iron came into general use, making possible not only the forging of deadly weapons of war but also the manufacture of plows and tools. Public works on a grand scale were executed by the various states. Enormous walls were built to fortify long stretches of the northern frontier against horsemen from the steppes. Large-scale irrigation and water control projects were undertaken, and transport canals were dug. These public works were constructed by a huge labor force, drawn from what by the third century B.C. was probably the world's largest population. By that time many of China's domestic arts had also taken their enduring forms. Chopsticks, lacquerwork, and silk were being used.

THE FLOWERING OF PHILOSOPHY

The increase in government activity, for such purposes as the directing of public projects and the collecting of taxes, had obliged the rulers of the various states to supplement their aristocratic administrative staffs with skilled, literate professionals chosen for their talent, not just their class

順天應人 本乎仁義
以賢繼患 眄曰宗典
盤銘一德 桑林六事
人紀肇修 垂千萬世

湯

King T'ang of the Shang Dynasty stands in this portrait wearing a royal crown and robes. Beside him there is a wild animal. At the top is the title "T'ang," and there follows an eulogy. It is said that while T'ang was in Po cultivating his moral virtues a spirit leading a white wolf by a ring came to the Shang court. Hence the animal beside T'ang in this portrait is a white wolf.
T'ang, the traditional dates of whose reign are 1783–52 B.C., was the founder of the Shang Dynasty. His personal name was Lu, and he was a descendant of Ch'i. T'ang attacked King Chieh of Hsia and having driven him to the Nanchao barbarians, took possession of the empire, naming his dynasty the Shang.

Emperor Wu ting, 1336–1281 B.C.

In this portrait King Wu of Chou is standing dressed in red patterned robes, with his hair in a topknot, that is covered by a piece of cloth and held in place by means of a hairpin. At the top is the title "King Wu," which is followed by an eulogy. King Wu of the Chou Dynasty (1134–15 B.C.), whose personal name was Fa, was the son of King Wen of the Chou Dynasty. King Wu gathered the feudal lords for an expedition to the east in which he defeated King Chou of Shang at Mu-yeh, and Chou burned himself to death in his palace. King Wu thereupon succeeded to the empire, making his capital at Hao. His posthumous name was Wu.

origins. The new recruitment procedures led indirectly to a revolution in patterns of thought.

So many different ideas arose that the Chinese accounts refer, figuratively, to a "hundred schools" of philosophy. Many of the philosophers were itinerant professional government workers who, besides teaching their disciples,

大成至聖文宣王

Confucius (551–479 B.C.), whose personal name was Ch'iu, and style name Chung-ni, was the founder of the school which bears his name. At first he served in the state of Lu as minister of crime, with general charge over affairs. Later, when out of office, he wandered throughout the various states. On his return to Lu he set about editing and establishing the texts of what were later to become the Confucian classics. He did this in order to transmit the true way of the former kings. He had three thousand disciples.

In the twenty-seventh year of the K'ai-yuan period of the T'ang Dynasty (A.D. 739) Confucius was given the posthumous title of "Prince of Culture." In the second year of the Shun-chih period of the Ch'ing Dynasty (1645) his titles were increased to "Confucius, All-Encompassing Supreme Sage and Cultivated First Teacher." In 1657 this was changed to "Confucius, Marvelous Supreme Sage and First Teacher."

Confucius preaching his doctrine to his disciples

Mencius, the principal disciple of Confucius. He developed the humanism of Confucianism, declaring that man is by nature good and becomes bad only when corrupted by adverse environment.

Authentic history of China may be said to begin with the Yellow Emperor (2698–2598 B.C.), who is looked upon as the ancestor of the Chinese race. He unified China, extending Chinese territory from the Yellow River valley eastward to the sea and southward to the Yangtze River. He gave China the magnet and the wheel, corrected the calendar, built the first brick structures, and invented the writing systems. His wife developed sericulture.

Afterward, eight heroes of culture, all of whom were descendants of the Yellow Emperor, formed China's early history and molded the pattern of her culture. Emperor Yao (reigned 2357–2255 B.C.), the sixth emperor in the line of the Yellow Emperor, introduced a new political concept by choosing the unrelated but virtuous Shun to be his successor. Emperor Shun (reigned 2233–2184 B.C.), the seventh emperor in the line of the Yellow Emperor, was the model of filially devoted sons and a patient hero who fought flood.

Yu the Great (reigned 2205–2197 B.C.), a minister of Emperor Shun, drained the land of the flood waters and opened up waterways. Because of his accomplishment, Emperor Shun chose him to be his successor. Yu the Great founded a dynasty named Hsia (2183–1802 B.C.). During the Hsia Dynasty China entered the bronze age, for Yu the Great cast the renowned Nine Tripods which later became the symbol of orthodox sovereignty.

The last of the Hsia rulers was so corrupt that his people revolted against him under the leadership of King T'ang (reigned 1783–1752 B.C.), who founded the Shang Dynasty (1766–1122 B.C.). This was China's first recorded revolution and has often been used in the course of Chinese history as a precedent to justify any revolution against tyranny.

Findings of excavations in the 1920s in the vicinity of Anyang on the north China plain have confirmed traditional Chinese records of that dynasty. Hence, modern historians have regarded the Shang as the beginning of recorded Chinese history.

King Wen (reigned 1171–22 B.C.) was a contemporary of the last ruler of the Shang Dynasty, a corrupt and tyrannical despot. King Wen was succeeded by his son King Wu (reigned 1134–15 B.C.). With less than 50,000 troops but aided by other states, King Wu defeated the powerful forces of the Shang ruler, numbering 700,000, and set up the Chou Dynasty (1111–255 B.C.). He declared, "Heaven sees and hears through the eyes and ears of the people."

The duke of Chou (Chou Kung) aided King Wu, his brother, in his war with the Shang. When King Wu was followed by his young son, the duke of Chou became a wise and saintly consolidator of the new dynasty. He formulated the Law of Chou (Chouli), which became the basis of the Chinese conception of government.

It was Confucius (551–479 B.C.), the last of China's eight culture heroes, who collected and edited the records and teachings of earlier dynasties before his time, and assembled them into classics on divination, history, songs, rituals, and music. These classics, later known as the "Five Classics," constitute the authentic source of Chinese learning and established the pattern of Chinese culture. Subsequent history of China has been largely a record of the enlarging and expansion of this pattern of Chinese culture.

Dr. Sun Yat-sen said that his Three Principles of the People, upon which the Republic of China has been founded, is a continuation of the orthodox teachings of the eight culture heroes.

The eight culture heroes have been featured on definitives of 1972 and 1973. The designs of these stamps are based on the paintings which were originally kept in the Forbidden City of Peiping (Peking).

The last five-hundred years of the Chou Dynasty are known in Chinese history as the Age of the Spring and Autumn and the Age of Warring. The contending states fought for hegemony both on the battlefield and at the conference table. Despite prolonged chaos, this was the greatest age of Chinese thought: Confucius, Mencius, Lao-tse, and the Naturalists, the Dialecticians, the Legalists, Mo-tzu, Hsun Tzu and Chuan-tze were all of this age.

During these turbulent years, the state of Chin finally emerged victorious, and the Ch'in Dynasty (255–207 B.C.) was founded by the First Emperor, one of China's worst tyrants. Although he standardized Chinese characters, initiated common systems of communications and currency *and standards of weights and measures, built the Great Wall to shut out invaders in the north, he is usually denounced for burning books to keep the people ignorant and burying scholars to silence opposition.*

Continuing the short-lived Ch'in Dynasty, a peasant revolutionary named Liu Pang (Han Kao Tsu), (reigned 206–194 B.C.) founded the Han Dynasty in 206 B.C., which remained in power for four centuries interrupted only by an interval of seventeen years when a reform-minded usurper held sway. The Han era saw China steadily grow in power and prosperity. Confucianism was elevated to the status of almost a state religion. The famous silk route led from Changan, the imperial capital, through a corridor west of the Yellow River and central Asia to Europe.

The Han Empire disintegrated during the early third century into Three Kingdoms—Wei in the northwest, Shu Han in the southwest, and Wu in the southeast.

China was united again in 265 A.D. under new rulers, the Tsin Dynasty. But peace and stability continued only for a brief time. Barbarian tribes on the borders to the north started a massive invasion. This invasion resulted in a mass population migration southward, making the Yangtze River valley a new economic and cultural center of China. Barbarians in the Yellow River valley were gradually assimilated into Chinese culture.

After these disorders China prospered again with the founding of the Sui Dynasty in 589 and the T'ang Dynasty in 626 A.D.

The civil service examination system, begun in the Han Dynasty and designed to pick civil servants through a series of graded competitive examinations, was perfected. The system was copied by succeeding dynasties with only minor variation.

Printing and gunpowder were invented; the arts and sciences flourished.

The Changan metropolitan area, both the center and the symbol of the highly centralized, carefully regulated T'ang Empire, had a population reaching 1,960,186. Students from Japan, Korea, and central Asia flocked to Changan in pursuit of knowledge.

The T'ang Dynasty crumbled because of civil strife. After a brief period of disorder from 907 to 960, which is known as the Epoch of Five Dynasties and Ten Kingdoms, the Sung Dynasty (960–1279) was founded in 960 by the famous Chinese general, Chao Kuang-yin (reigned 960–76). The Sung Dynasty rivaled the T'ang epoch in cultural and scientific developments.

Mongol invasions interrupted this golden age, but the Kublai Khan (1216–1294), the grandson of Genghis Khan (1162–1227), and the most enlightened and progressive of the Mongol emperors, encouraged Chinese culture and contact with the outside world.

Under the rulers of the Ming Dynasty (1368–1644), the richness and variety of Chinese life became the envy of foreign traders, travelers and missionaries. But the Manchus, who succeeded the Ming Dynasty to form the Ching Dynasty (1644–1912), made a deliberate attempt to isolate China from the rest of the world. This policy led to internal stagnation and, with a final futile explosion of the "Boxer Incident" in 1900, ended in the collapse of Imperial China.

The heroes of Chinese culture. Top to bottom, left to right: *Emperor Yao, Emperor Shun, Yu the Great, King T'ang, King Wen, King Wu, the duke of Chou, and Confucius.*

were employed as advisers to one or another of the various state rulers.

The school of philosophy that had the greatest effect on subsequent Chinese thought was the one founded by K'ung Fu-tzu, or Master Kung (551–479 B.C.), known to the West as Confucius. The ablest scholar-teacher of the age, Confucius sought to restore China to the peaceful feudalism of early Chou times but felt that the only way the hierarchical system could be made to work properly was for each person to perform correctly his assigned role. "Let the ruler be a ruler and the subject be a subject," he said, but he added that to rule properly a king must be virtuous and set an example of proper ethical conduct. To Confucius, social stratification was a fact of life to be sustained by morals, not force. He laid much stress on the possibility of remolding men's minds through education and taught that proper inner attitudes could be inculcated through the practice of rituals and the observance of rules of etiquette and decorum.

Mencius, or Meng-tzu (372–289 B.C.), developed the humanism of Confucian thought further, declaring that man is by nature good and is corrupted by adverse environment. Mencius also introduced the idea that a ruler cannot govern without the people's tacit consent. If the people successfully depose or assassinate the ruler, this is proof of the fact that he has lost the mandate of Heaven. Thus Mencius took the Chou justification for dynastic conquest and turned it into a justification for popular rebellion.

Taoism, the second most important and enduring stream in Chinese thought, also developed at this time. Its formulation is attributed to a legendary figure, Laotzu (Old Master), who is alleged to predate Confucius. Taoism deals with man in nature, not man in society, which was Confucius's sole concern. For the Taoist the goal of life for each individual is to find his own private adjustment to the rhythm and patterns of the natural (and supernatural) world, to follow the Way *(tao)* of the universe. This is achieved by means of nonintellectual disciplines: through mysticism, trance, and periods of solitude in natural surroundings; through spontaneous response to nature; and through the

Han Kao Tsu (Liu Pang), the first Han Dynasty emperor (206–196 B.C.). This is a contemporary sketch.

Huang Ti, "the Yellow Emperor," the first emperor to be officially crowned

Probably the best known of the Chinese emperors was Shih-huang Ti (reigned 246–209 B.C.), who stopped the Tatars and extended China's borders while spending the entire treasury of China in building the Great China Wall—at the cost of 400,000 lives. However, he was very popular with the people and is seen in this old sketch performing the emperor's chore at the annual spring ceremony of ploughing and sowing the seed.

Shih-huang Ti was called "the first emperor" by the Chinese historians. By destroying the fortifications of the separate Chinese states and assassinating their feudal lords, Shih-huang created a centralized nation that could withstand foreign intervention.

The first great emperor, Shih-huang Ti in his royal carriage on the way to meeting with the Taoists

avoidance of action, change, or making distinctions between things. In many ways the opposite of Confucian activism, Taoism proved to many of its adherents to be complementary. A scholar on duty as an official would usually subscribe to Confucian principles but on holiday or in retirement might well seek the harmony with nature of a Taoist recluse.

Another idea that can be traced back to philosophies current in the Eastern Chou period is the belief that all nature is composed of interlocking, mutually complementary opposites: *yang,* which is male, light, hot, and positive; and *yin,* which is female, dark, cold, and negative. Other beliefs that have survived from this period are the concern with numerology, especially the number five—as in the five elements, the five directions (including the center), the five senses, and the five colors. Chinese astrology and geomancy also developed at this time.

One school of thought that originated during this period and has had an enduring influence on China, although it did not attain widespread popularity, is the philosophy of legalism. According to this belief, man's nature is incorrigibly selfish, and therefore the only way to preserve social order is to impose discipline from above. The ruler should promulgate laws for his own purposes, and these laws must be inflexibly enforced. The punishment for infraction of the law must be so harsh that man's selfish interest will keep him law abiding.

The legalists exalted the state and sought its prosperity and martial prowess above the welfare of the citizens. They believed that the state should consist of a strong central government overseeing a mass of producers of primary goods, or peasant farmers. Big landholdings were thought to be a threat to the central power, whereas merchants and intellectuals were regarded as nonproductive and therefore not to be tolerated.

Noted legalists advised the kings of the state of Ch'in and, when a Ch'in ruler became the first emperor of a unified China, legalism became the philosophic basis for the imperial form of government. In post-Ch'in times the use of Confucian-trained scholar-officials to administer the empire eventually led to a humanizing element being introduced into the administration, which helped to mediate between the people at large and the legalist imperial framework.

THE IMPERIAL ERA

THE FIRST IMPERIAL PERIOD

In the Wei River valley, where the Chou state had begun, there arose, after the Chou capital moved eastward, the state of Ch'in. By the fourth century B.C. the state had established a centralized, nonfeudal administration. The state was divided into prefectures *(hsien),* each under a prefect sent out from the capital, not a local lord or hereditary vassal. All persons were obliged to work in what the regime held to be productive occupations. Conformity to government policy was demanded at the local level. Clusters of families were made collectively responsible for individual actions, and citizens were encouraged to spy on one another.

By 221 B.C. Ch'in armies had gained control of all of the warring states. The king of Ch'in took for himself the grandiloquent title of First Emperor *(Shih-huang Ti)* and proceeded to apply Ch'in administrative practices to the empire. Provinces, administered by officials appointed by the central government, replaced the feudal system of the warring states. The forms of writing, the codes of laws, the coinage, and even the axle length of vehicles were standardized. Interregional commerce and agriculture were encouraged, and private ownership of land was extended throughout the empire.

To further the standardization of thought and to silence criticism of imperial rule, virtually all books (except technical works) were burned, and many scholars were banished or put to death. To prevent regional concentration of wealth, the population was redistributed; to forestall rebellion, the arms of the people were confiscated; and to fend off barbarian intrusion, the various northern fortification walls were incorporated to make a fourteen hundred-mile-long Great Wall. Ch'in armies pushed forward the frontiers of the empire, and settlers and political offenders were sent to open up virgin lands, especially in south China.

These activities required tremendous levies of manpower and resources from the people. Revolts broke out as soon as the First Emperor died in 209 B.C., and the dynasty was overthrown less than fifty years after its triumph. The imperial system it initiated, however, persisted, with brief interruptions for more than two thousand years, and the name of the first imperial dynasty survives in the name "China."

Civil war raged until 202 B.C., when a military man of peasant origin named Liu Pang (d. 195 B.C.), who had in 206 B.C. gained the title king of Han, was able to defeat his warlord rivals and gain control of the empire. Under the dynasty of Han (206 B.C. to A.D. 220), which Liu founded, most of the political machinery of Ch'in was retained, although some of the harsher aspects were modified or abolished. The capital was located at Ch'ang-an (now Sian) in the Wei River valley, and Confucian scholars, who had been out of favor during the Ch'in period, were employed in high offices.

Intellectual and artistic creativity revived and flourished and, with Confucianism given official patronage, Confucian ideals began to be adopted by the government. Men of talent were recruited for government service by examinations that stressed the Confucian literature. Technological advances also marked this period. Two of the great Chinese inventions, paper and porcelain, date from Han times. The Han period was such a time of military and cultural prowess that to the present day members of the majority ethnic group of China proudly call themselves men of Han.

The Han emperors extended their domains westward to include the Indo-European population clusters in small farming oases scattered along the rim of the Tarim Basin, making possible relatively secure caravan traffic across central Asia to Antioch, Baghdad, and Alexandria. The paths of the caravan traffic are often called the silk route because they comprised the route of importation of Chinese silk by the Romans.

The expansion of the empire into central Asia came in response to the persistent threat to the plains-dwelling Han Chinese of Mongoloid Turkish-speaking nomads from the northern steppes. About 52 B.C. the danger was eliminated. The southern half of Horde submitted to being a tributary people of the Han emperor; others of the group moved westward. Chinese armies also invaded and annexed parts of Korea and Indochina toward the end of the second century B.C.

Han society consisted chiefly of the ruling class and the peasantry. The ruling class was headed by a small hereditary aristocracy. There were also merchants, but the Han rulers regarded commerce as parasitic, and merchants were forbidden to buy land or become officials and were popularly ranked as the lowest in a status hierarchy of the four main occupations, below scholars, farmers, and artisans. Nonetheless, those merchants with great wealth gained considerable power. At the bottom of the scale were some serfs and a small number of domestic slaves.

Han dynastic rule was interrupted early in the Christian Era but was subsequently restored and enjoyed another two centuries of power. In A.D. 220, however, a combination of palace intrigues, internal unrest, and external pressures brought the dynasty to an end.

Imperial rule had already been undermined by the grad-

ual concentration of wealth, especially land, into the hands of a few families whose political influence helped them avoid the imperial taxes. As these landholding families increased in wealth and power, the central government, relying on an ever-diminishing tax base to support ever-rising expenses, grew progressively more odious to the ordinary tax-paying public. This succession of events—concentration of wealth, a diminished tax base, and excessive taxation upon that base—has marked the onset of decay for every major dynasty since the Han period.

The collapse of the Han Dynasty may also have been accelerated by the weakening of the intellectual and religious consensus in the empire resulting from the introduction into China of Buddhism, propagated by missionaries from India in the late Han era.

ERA OF DIVISION

With the collapse of the Han Dynasty, the unity of empire dissolved. For three and one-half centuries, which Chinese historians call the Six Dynasties Period, the empire remained divided. At first there emerged three kingdoms—one in the north, another in Szechwan, and a third in the Yangtze River valley. The Era of the Three Kingdoms (as this period is traditionally called) is remembered by the Chinese as an age of chivalry, valor, and adventure. The Shu-Han Dynasty reunited most of China for a relatively brief period (A.D. 221–420), but it was too weak to hold back the tide of barbarian advance from the north.

Foreign influences were important in this period. North China came under the domination of several successive dynasties of non-Chinese-speaking barbarians, although gradually the various barbarian ruling groups became increasingly sinicized in culture and through intermarriage. The northerners were at first more receptive to Buddhism than was the conservative population of south China, but gradually Buddhism became a popular religion in both north and south.

Pilgrimages by Chinese converts to the sacred Buddhist sites in India greatly expanded China's knowledge concerning the peoples and countries to be found between India and China. As Chinese knowledge in various fields expanded, major technological advances were made. The invention of gunpowder (at that time for use in fireworks only) and the wheelbarrow and advances in medicine, astronomy, and cartography date from the Six Dynasties Period.

RESTORATION OF EMPIRE

In 589 a general of Han Chinese family with ties to the barbarian aristocracy brought about the reunification of the Chinese Empire. The Sui Dynasty that he founded lasted for only twenty-eight years. Its early demise was the result of the government's excessive demands on the people to carry out ambitious public projects and military adventures aimed at expanding imperial control over much of central and Southeast Asia as well as Manchuria and northern Korea.

In this bust portrait Emperor Wu is shown dressed in a wide gown and a hat affixed with a hairpin, while in his left hand he holds a jade scepter. Emperor Wu (reigned A.D. 502–48) came from southern Lan-ling. His surname was Hsia, his personal name Yen. He beseiged Chien-k'ang and killed the Ch'i ruler, eventually taking the imperial title himself.

In this standing portrait Emperor Kao Tsu is depicted as having a black beard, and is dressed in a cloth turban, a belted silk robe, and leather boots. Emperor Kao Tsu (reigned 618–25) was the founder of the T'ang Dynasty. Surnamed Li, and with the personal name Yuan and style name Shu-te, he came from Ch'eng-chi in Lung-hsi (Kansu). Though at first he served under the Sui Dynasty he later revolted and established himself as emperor.

In this standing portrait the emperor T'ai Tsung is depicted with curly beard and black hat of silk, dressed in a yellow belted gown with narrow sleeves. Emperor T'ai Tsung (reigned 626–49), whose personal name was Shih-min, was the second son of Emperor Kao Tsu.

In this standing portrait Emperor T'ai Tsung is depicted wearing a "p'u-t'ou" style hat and a jade-belted brown gown.

The Empress Wu (Son of Heaven) Hou, who ruled from 690 to 704, was the only woman to rule China as a sole sovereign on the throne. In ancient Chinese times the emperor was called the "Son of Heaven" to emphasize the rights of equality and universal brotherhood, which in Wu Hou's situation meant equality of gender.

After a chaotic period following the popular revolt that overthrew the dynasty, there emerged the T'ang Dynasty (618–907), which is regarded by historians as a high point in Chinese civilization equal, or even superior, to the Han period. A governmental system was built on Sui foundations that was to survive for three centuries under T'ang emperors. Civil service examinations based on a Confucian curriculum, first instituted in Han times, became standard T'ang recruitment procedure. The bureaucratic machinery of the empire was refined, and the T'ang government and its code of laws became models for neighboring states.

The flowering of Chinese culture that occurred during the T'ang period was partly the result of stimuli received from abroad that contributed to a renewal of Chinese creativity in all fields. It was the golden age of Chinese literature and art. Block printing was invented, making the written word available to a vastly greater audience. Government schools at the regional and national level were introduced.

Foreigners came from afar to receive the polish of a Chinese education, and their presence enhanced the cosmopolitan atmosphere of the T'ang capital, Ch'ang-an. In the tolerant climate of early T'ang, foreign missionaries came to propagate their faiths—Zoroastrianism, Manichaeism, and Nestorian Christianity—and Muslim merchants and soldiers of fortune introduced Islam. Colonies of foreign merchants sprang up in Chinese ports. The Chinese did not hesitate to employ foreigners in their government, to use foreign imported goods in daily life (such as tea, introduced from Southeast Asia), and to gain ideas and technological information from the foreigners.

The most significant development in the social system during the T'ang Dynasty was the gradual development of a new social group. This group, which English-speaking Chinese scholars have termed the gentry, included those persons who passed the Confucianist government examinations, becoming degree holders in literature, the classics, or other fields and thus eligible to be appointed to office in the imperial bureaucracy. The term *gentry* has also been used, more loosely, to describe local landowners who lived in the provincial towns, receiving rents from their rural tenants, and who were members of the families from which the degree holders came. The landowning class supplied the bulk of the scholars because it had the money to pay for the lengthy classical education necessary to pass the examinations.

The presence of the gentry made possible the governing of the great and populous empire by a relatively small group of officials. The gentry, with its enduring status in the local community and its family ties and shared values connecting it to the officialdom, mediated between the rural population and the imperial government from T'ang times until the end of the empire in 1912. It was also the case, however, that candidates who failed the examinations and degree holders

The Great Wall of China

who sought but did not obtain official employment constituted an articulate, discontented group within the gentry, ready to support or lead rebellions.

By their military prowess the early T'ang rulers built up a larger empire than that of the Han. In the west they defeated the Turks and established a protectorate over Turkestan. Tibet, unified for the first time in the seventh century, soon came under T'ang suzerainty. In the east the imperial troops vanquished the land and sea force of the Japanese and Koreans. A Chinese-led army even penetrated India.

By the middle of the eighth century T'ang power had ebbed. Military defeats were suffered by the imperial forces at the hands of the Tai people of the kingdom of Nanchao (in modern Yunnan province) and at the hands of Arabs who were beginning to gain control over parts of central Asia. Uighurs and Tibetans sacked the T'ang capital.

A barbarian general in the T'ang army, An Lu-shan, led a revolt in 755 that, although quickly crushed, permanently impaired the effectiveness of the imperial government. Regional military commanders came to exert more power at the expense of the central government. The T'ang capital became a center of factionalism and conspiracy. Popular uprisings in the late ninth century further weakened the

empire, facilitating the efforts of northern invaders, who brought the T'ang Dynasty to an end in 907.

The Sung Dynasty was founded in north China in 960. Although in 979 it was able to reunite much of the empire, it was not a total reunification. The advent of barbarian regimes in the north forced the Sung regime to move its capital to Hangchow in the southern coastal area, abandoning the interior provinces.

The Sung period marks the commencement of modern life in China. For the first time private trade overshadowed government enterprise, and urban communities that had begun not as administrative centers but as centers for commerce sprang up. Urban sophistication became characteristic of the Chinese opinion-makers. The landed gentry, although largely dependent upon rural rents for their incomes, lived in the towns alongside the officials and the merchants.

The spread of printing, the increase in the number of schools, and the growth of private trade and of a money economy gave rise to a new group of wealthy and influential commoners. Land and the holding of public office stopped being the chief means of gaining wealth and the sole means of gaining prestige and entry into the gentry

In this full length portrait Emperor T'ai Tsou is seated wearing a yellow robe. The emperor T'ai Tsou (reigned 960–75) was the founder of the Sung Dynasty. His surname was Chao, his personal name K'uang-yin, and he came from Chuo-chun. He named his dynasty Sung. The year periods during his reign were Chien-lung (960–63), Ch'ien-te (963–68), and K'ai-pao (968–75).

Lu Chih is portrayed with a black hat and purple gown, and the title is inscribed in "clerical" script: "Portrait of Lu Chih of Wu." Lu Chih (754–805), whose familiar name was Ching-yu, came from Chia-hsing during the T'ang Dynasty. He was both loyal and righteous, and was a keen student of Confucianism. He took his chin-shih degree for entrance into official life at eighteen, and during emperor To-Tsung's reign became a member of the Han-lin Academy. During the Chien-chung period the emperor was forced to flee to Feng-t'ien because of the Chu Tz'u revolt, and it was Lu Chih who wrote the many imperial proclamations during this period. He rose to high office, but was later demoted because of slander and banished to Chung-chou where he died. His posthumous name was Hsuan.

In this standing portrait Emperor Chuang Tsung of the later T'ang Dynasty is depicted with a black beard, dark silk cap with side flaps, and a jade-belted blue robe. Emperor Chuang Tsung (reigned 923–26) was the son of Li K'o-yung. His personal name was Ts'un-hsu.

In this standing portrait Emperor T'ai Tsung is wearing a yellow robe with long wide sleeves, and the "p'u-t'ou" style headdress. He has a black beard. Emperor T'ai Tsung (reigned 976–97) was the younger brother of Emperor T'ai Tsou. His original personal name was K'uang-i, but he was later granted the name Kuang-i. After his succession to the throne he changed his personal name to Chung. He was both political and decisive, and proved an able ruler. In his youth he had helped Emperor Tai Tsu in the founding of the dynasty, and on his brother's death he became emperor. His reign periods are T'ai-p'ing hsing-kuo (976–84), Yung-hsi (984–88), Tuan-kung (988–90), Ch'un-hua (990–95), and Chih-tao (995–97).

class. Industry and commerce were also important sources of income, and the stigma that had been attached to trade since the empire began faded to some extent. Maritime commerce was encouraged and, with the aid of the mariner's compass, the Chinese were able to wrest from the Arabs the Far Eastern leg of the East-West maritime trade.

Culturally, the Sung was a period in which developments that had occurred in late T'ang times were refined. Among these was the T'ang ideal of the universal man who was scholar, poet, painter, and statesman. Another development of the late T'ang period was the decline of interest in, and tolerance for, foreigners and foreign things and concepts.

Among the Sung neo-Confucianists who wrote commentaries on the classics, the most famous and influential was Chu Hsi, whose synthesis of Confucian thought and Buddhist, Taoist, and other ideas became the official imperial philosophy. Chu Hsi's neo-Confucianism became by the fourteenth century an unyielding orthodox official creed, which stressed the one-sided obligations of obedience and compliance by subject to ruler, child to father, and wife to husband.

The development of an urban way of life and the emergence of urban amusements and tastes—for example, the appearance of wine shops, tea shops, restaurants, theaters, and brothels—were contemporaneous with the development of urban pauperism, as those without land gravitated to the towns. There also began a decline in the status of women. Among the town elite there was a growth in the popularity of concubinage, the taking of secondary wives. A preexisting ban on remarriage of widows also grew more inflexible at this time and, among upper-class women, there began the practice of footbinding—the mutilation from childhood of female feet to make them conform to a shape held to be pleasing to Chinese men of the time. The practice of binding women's feet was later to spread to all classes of society.

The growth and development of a refined civil life was accompanied by a decline in enthusiasm for military life. This decline in military capacity left the empire prey to barbarians from the north. After a protracted struggle with the Khitan and the Jurched, the Chinese were in a weakened position when confronted by a stronger enemy, the invading Mongol army.

MONGOLIAN INTERREGNUM

The new invaders already had subjugated north China, Korea, and the Muslim kingdoms of central Asia and had twice penetrated Europe. Thus Kublai Khan (1214–94), grandson of Genghis Khan, the founder of the Mongol Empire, had the resources of Asia behind him when he began his drive against the Sung. Finally, after having successfully defeated the Chinese army and fleet in the south, the Mongol leader established the first non-Chinese dynasty to control all of China.

This is a sitting portrait of a consort of the emperor Chen Tsung. Her face is covered by a silk veil, and she wears a hat decorated with a dragon pattern. According to the official history of the Sung Dynasty, Emperor Chen Tsung had four empresses: the first was the Chang-huai empress P'an from Ta-ming, the second the Chang-mu empress Kuo from T'ai-yuan, the third the Chang-hsien-ming-su empress Liu of Hua-yang, and the fourth the Chang-yi empress Li of Hang-chou.

In this portrait the emperor Jen Tsung is depicted sitting. He is lightly bearded, and is dressed in a brown robe and the 'p'u-t'ou' style of headdress. Emperor Jen Tsung (reigned 1022–62) was the sixth son of Emperor Chen Tsung. His personal name was Chen. He succeeded to the throne as a child, and during his minority the empress acted as regent. On her death he assumed the reins of government himself. His reign periods were T'ien-sheng (1023–32), Ming-tao (1032–34), Ching-yu (1034–38), Pao-yüan (1038–40), K'ang-ting (1040–41), Ch'ing-li (1041–49), Huang-yu (1049–54), Chih-ho (1054–56), and Chia-yu (1056–63).

In this sitting portrait Emperor Shen Tsung is depicted in the "p'u-t'ou" style headdress. Emperor Shen Tsung was the eldest son of Emperor Yin Tsung. His personal name was Hsu. His reign periods were Hsi-ning (1068–78) and Yuan-feng (1078–85).

In this sitting portrait of a consort of the emperor Jen Tsung the subject has her face covered by a gauze veil under which pearl ornaments have been set on her skin. She wears a hat with dragon decoration. The hair on her temples is allowed to show, and she wears a plumed dress with a silken girdle from which hang jade pendants. At either side is a lady-in-waiting, one holding a spittoon, the other a cloth. According to the official history of the Sung Dynasty the emperor Jen Tsung had two consorts: Empress Kuo and the Tz'u-sheng-kuang-hsien empress Ts'ao. Since Empress Kuo was discarded, this is doubtless a portrait of the other, who was made empress in 1034. She came from Cheng-ting.

Ssu-ma Kuang is seen here wearing a silk hat and purple gown, with an official tablet at his waist. (This is the frontispiece by an anonymous Sung artist to a chuan on Ssu-ma Kuang's appointment as chancellor of the left). Ssu-ma Kuang (1019–86) came from Su-shui prefecture in Chou-hua hsien in Shansi. His style name was Chün-shih, but contemporaries knew him as Sou-shui Hsien-sheng.

In this bust portrait, a consort of the emperor Che Tsung is shown with unadorned hair, wearing a blue dress. According to the official history of the Sung Dynasty the emperor Che Tsung (reigned 1085–1100) had two empresses: the Chao-tz'u-sheng-hsien empress Meng, and the Chao-huai empress Liu. Since Empress Liu hanged herself, the subject of this portrait is doubtless Empress Meng. She came from Lo-chou, and was made empress in 1092.

This is a bust portrait of Kublai Khan (reigned 1259–94). He is known in Chinese history as Emperor Shih-tsu. He established his capital at Yen-ching, the modern Peking, and formally founded the Yang (Yuan) Dynasty. After destroying the Southern Sung Dynasty and thereby unifying China, he launched expeditions against Japan in the east and Burma, Annam, Champa, Java, and other countries to the south. His reign period was Chih-guan.

The Yuan Dynasty (created by Kublai Khan in 1260) gained all of China by 1279, after roughly fifty years of Mongol campaigning. By 1267 Kublai Khan had begun construction of a new capital at Peking, which had been his headquarters in China since 1263. Later, the Grand Canal (which had been built in Sui times to connect north China with the fertile Yangtze River valley) was extended to the new capital. His summer capital remained in Mongolia, however, at Shang-tu (Xanadu), north of the Great Wall.

The Mongol regime was never accepted by the men of Han, as the north Chinese continued to be called, or by the southerners, as the Mongols called the Chinese of the Southern Sung Kingdom. Kublai Khan, who, as the Great Khan, was head of the entire Mongol realm as well as of the Chinese Empire, preferred employing non-Chinese from other parts of the Mongol domain—Russia, the Near East, and central Asia—in those positions for which no competent Mongol could be found.

The influence of other foreigners upon the Yuan Dynasty was also considerable. Related to this time are the first records of travel by Westerners, including both merchants and missionaries, into China after the fall of the Roman Empire. In the last years of the thirteenth century Franciscan monks reached China, and one of them built a church in Peking with the consent of Kublai Khan. The most famous European traveler of the period was the Venetian Marco Polo, whose account of his trip to China and life there astounded the people of Europe. The effect of Europeans upon China, however, was neither as great nor as lasting as

that of the peoples and cultures of the eastern half of the Mongol Empire. From this period dates the conversion to Islam, by Muslims of central Asia, of large numbers of Chinese in the northwest and southwest. At this time also the Mongols acquired Tibetan Buddhism, also known as Lamaism. The Mongols attempted to promote Tibetan Buddhism in China and gave it a favored position at court.

THE CHINESE REGAIN POWER

Rivalry among the Mongol imperial heirs, natural disasters—especially frequent floods of the Yellow River (which had drastically changed its course in 1194 from north to south of the Shantung Peninsula, reaching the sea through the mouth of the Huai River)—and numerous peasant rebellions against the unpopular Mongol regime led to the collapse of the Yuan Dynasty. In 1368 Chu Yuan-chang, a Han Chinese peasant and former Buddhist monk who had become a rebel army leader, emerged as successor to the Great Khan as ruler of China Proper. He founded the Ming Dynasty, with its capital at Nanking. After his death the capital was moved, in 1421, to Peking, the city Kublai Khan had built.

The zenith of Ming power was reached during the reign of the third Ming emperor, Yung Lo, who reigned from 1402 to 1424. The Chinese armies reconquered Annam and kept back the Mongols, while the Chinese fleet ranged the China seas and the Indian Ocean, cruising as far as the east coast of Africa. The maritime Asian nations sent envoys to perform the *kowtow* (formal prostration) in homage to the Chinese emperor. The tribute they sent, together with the gifts China gave in return, were of a volume substantial enough to constitute international trade.

Between 1405 and 1433 the eunuch admiral Cheng Ho led seven separate voyages of the imperial fleet to the Nan Yang (southern ocean). After 1433, however, Ming policy was to concentrate its energies on preventing another barbarian land invasion, either by the Mongols or, later, by a northern ethnic group related to the Mongols, the Manchus. Trade expeditions to the Nan Yang were banned.

The cessation of imperial interest in maritime Southeast Asia may have been in part caused by the development of a conservative climate at court, brought about by pressure from the powerful neo-Confucianist bureaucracy, which

This is a bust portrait of Emperor Shun-chih's consort. The official history of the Yuan Dynasty states that Emperor Shun-chih's consort was the empress Chao-hsien yuan-sheng, whose personal name was Ta'-chi. At first she had been Shun-chih's concubine, but gave birth to the later emperor Wu Tsung. On coming to the throne he gave his mother the title of empress.

Emperor Hung Wu is seen sitting wearing a hat of black silk and a yellow gown. Emperor Hung Wu (reigned 1368–98) was the founder of the Ming Dynasty. Originally his name was Chu Yuan-chang, his style name Kuo-tuan. At the end of the Yuan Dynasty military leaders arose in many different areas. One of these, Kuo Tzu-hsing, seized Hao, and Chu Yuan-chang joined him. He proved militarily invincible, and these forces eventually became his own. On Kuo Tzu-hsing's death Chu Yuan-chang was proclaimed duke of Wu, and later king of Wu. He then

captured Peking, thus extinguishing the Yuan Dynasty and making himself ruler of China.

In this bust portrait the Hsiao-tz'u-kao empress Ma wears a hat decorated with dragons and phoenixes and a pale yellow imperial robe with a cape. According to the official history of the Ming Dynasty Emperor Hung Wu's consort, the Hsiao-tz'u-kao empress, came from Su-chou and was surnamed Ma. Her mother was named Chang Wen.

This is a bust portrait of the Jen-hsiao-wen empress wearing imperial robes and crown. The Hsiao-jen-wen empress, whose surname was Hsu, was the consort of Emperor Yung Lo and the eldest daughter of Ta, prince of Chungshan. In 1377 she became the concubine of the prince of Yen, and when he came to the throne as Emperor Yung Lo she was made empress. She was the mother of Emperor Jen-tsung.

led to the revival of the traditional denigration of trade and commerce. The low esteem in which these occupations were held was enforced by the fact that the path to power and prestige in Ming times was through internal politics and Confucian erudition, not through trade. The stability of the two and one half centuries of the Ming Dynasty, which were without major disruptions of the economy, arts, society, or politics, promoted a belief among Chinese that they had achieved the most satisfactory civilization on earth and that nothing foreign was needed or welcome.

This belief in China's self-sufficiency impeded relations with the Portuguese and other European traders and missionaries who began to appear along the coast of China and elsewhere in the Far East during the sixteenth century. The Portuguese were the first to be permitted to establish a trading settlement, in Macao, but all the Western traders were severely restricted in their activities by the emperor. The efforts of the Portuguese missionary Saint Francis Xavier to Christianize China were frustrated by the imperial ban on his entry into the mainland. He died off the coast of China.

The focus of Chinese pride was not as much their ethnic group or territory as it was their way of life, their arts, their governments, and their social arrangements. Aware of the Chinese cultural pride, the Jesuit Matteo Ricci (1552–1610) gained a foothold in Peking by familiarizing himself with Chinese customs, institutions, and classical learning so that he could present Christianity in terms comprehensible to the Chinese. The fact that the criteria for being Chinese were chiefly cultural rather than racial was to prove of great importance to the Manchus when they became China's new rulers in the seventeenth century.

Long wars with the Mongols, incursions by the Japanese

In this portrait Emperor Hsuan Te gallops forward with a falcon on his arm. In front of him a flock of wild geese rises up startled from the rushes. The inscription on this painting reads: "Emperor Hsuan Te's Amusements."

In this sitting portrait Emperor Chia-ching is shown with a light beard. Emperor Chia-ching (reigned 1522–66) of the Ming Dynasty was the grandson of Emperor Hsuan Te. His personal name was Hou-ts'ung. In his later years the emperor became addicted to Taoist practices for gaining immortality, dispatching his servants in search of new formula. Eventually he died from taking a cinnabar potion.

Emperor Shun-chih of the Ming Dynasty is depicted returning to the palace on board a boat after a visit to the tombs of his ancestors. He wears the "p'u-t'ou" style of hat decorated with a pair of dragons, and a purple gown embroidered with dragons. He is sitting in the center of the boat.

into Korea, and harassment of Chinese coastal cities by the Japanese in the sixteenth century weakened the Ming Dynasty. Its overthrow in 1644 by the leader of the last of numerous rebellions against it, in turn, weakened China so that it was once again ripe for an alien takeover.

THE LATE IMPERIAL PERIOD

Rivalry among the rebels after the fall of the Ming regime left a power vacuum that the Manchu armies easily filled. In 1644 the Manchus took Peking and became masters of North China, establishing the Ching Dynasty (1644-1912). Ming adherents resisted the Manchus for many years, however. By 1683 the last Ming pretender had been taken prisoner, the Ming stronghold on Taiwan had been captured, and the last vestiges of rebellion in south China had been quelled. The empire was to remain in Manchu hands until the twentieth century.

Although the Manchus were not Han Chinese, they had, in contrast to the Mongols, been sinicized to a great degree before coming to power and, realizing the importance of doing things the Chinese way if they were to dominate the empire, they took over many institutions of Ming and earlier Chinese derivation. They buried the last Ming emperor (who had committed suicide) with full honors and claimed that they had come to suppress the anti-Ming rebels and restore order. They also continued the Confucian cult rituals, over which the emperors had traditionally presided.

The Manchus also retained, until 1905, the Confucian civil service examination system for recruiting Chinese officials. Many Chinese found employment with the new regime. Although Chinese were barred from the highest offices, outside the capital Chinese officials predominated over Manchu officeholders, except in military positions. The Manchus retained the Chinese administrative system that had been perfected in Ming times. Under this system the administration was divided among civil, military, and censorial branches, the last branch being a systematized inspector corps assigned to check on the other two and report back to the throne. The neo-Confucianist philosophy, with its emphasis on obedience by the subject to the ruler, was also retained and was enforced as the state ideology.

Jesuit Father Matteo Ricci (1552–1610), left, *head of the Society of Jesus (Jesuits), the first religious leader to bring Christianity to China, is seen in this early English illustration with his first "primary" convert, Paul-hsu,* right, *who was the Chinese government chief "law interpreter."*

Emperor K'ang-hsi, who ruled from 1662 to 1723, is seen in this early drawing in a royal procession celebrating his sixtieth birthday traveling down the main street of Peking.

Emperor Shun-chih, the first Manchu emperor of China, founded the Ching Dynasty. He reigned from 1644 to 1661.

Ch'ien-lung, the Chinese emperor from 1736 to 1796, is seen in this old contemporary painting receiving Mongol horses in tribute.

The Manchu emperors also patronized Chinese literary projects of enormous scope. Great dictionaries and encyclopedias were compiled; a complete collection of Chinese literature was assembled; and an edition of the twenty-four dynastic histories was published. Since it is known that the dominant concern of the Ching Dynasty was to retain its control of China, it has been suggested by historians that the purpose of the emperors in sponsoring these massive literary projects was to keep Chinese scholars harmlessly occupied so that they would not trouble the foreign regime. The imperial literary projects also made possible an official review of Chinese literature. Connected with the review was the imperial suppression of many works on the grounds that they either criticized foreign rule in China or praised the Ming Dynasty. Nonetheless, the survival of much of China's ancient literature is the result of the Ching imperial projects.

As part of their policy to ensure Manchu dominance over

Emperor Chien-lung reigned for sixty years, from 1736 to 1796. He abdicated in favor of his son, Chia-ch'ing.

Emperor Tao-kuang in the "enthronement" ceremony in 1821 above the palace gate in Peking

successfully all danger to China Proper from across its land borders, and during its regime the Chinese Empire grew to include a larger area than ever before or since. In addition, the Ching emperors received tribute from the various states situated just beyond the empire's borders—Burma, Annam, and Korea.

Unanticipated by the Ching emperors, the chief threat to China's integrity and to the continuance of the dynasty did not come overland, as it had so often in the past, but instead it arrived by sea, reaching the southern coastal area first. Western traders and missionaries began to arrive in large numbers. The dynasty's inability to evaluate correctly the nature of the challenge these foreigners posed or to respond adequately to it resulted in the collapse of the Ching Dynasty and of the entire millennia-old framework of dynastic rule.

FOREIGN MISSIONARY AND TERRITORIAL ENCROACHMENT

In the last quarter of the nineteenth century foreign imperialism and the disruption caused by the introduction of foreign culture into all parts of China by Christian missionaries contributed to the decline of Ching dynastic rule. By 1894 there were more than five hundred thousand Roman Catholics and tens of thousands of Protestants in China. More than two thousand foreign missionaries were active in various parts of China, most of them Protestants from Great Britain and the United States. Their doctrines shook the foundations of Chinese traditional society and were opposed by hundreds of anti-Christian riots, but the missionaries had the protection of foreign gunboats.

The most serious anti-Christian uprising came as the century ended when a fanatical group of anti-Christian and anti-imperialist members of a secret society called the I-ho ch'uan (Righteous and Harmonious Fists), known to the West as the Boxers, killed over two hundred missionaries and other foreigners in north China and Manchuria. In the summer of 1900 the Boxers, with the complicity of Manchu princes, laid siege for two months to the foreign legation quarters of Peking. The foreigners were eventually rescued by an allied expeditionary force.

The end of the nineteenth century also brought additional

China, efforts were made by the Ching emperors to prevent the absorption of the Manchus into the Han Chinese population. Han Chinese were prohibited from migrating into Manchuria. No agriculture was permitted in northern Manchuria, and Manchus were forbidden to engage in trade or manual labor and to bind their women's feet. Intermarriage between Manchus and Han Chinese was forbidden. Manchu emperors never lost their suspicion of the Han Chinese. In many positions a system of dual appointments was used, the Chinese appointee to do the substantive work and the Manchu to supervise and prevent treachery.

The Ching regime was determined to protect itself not only from internal rebellion but also against invasion from without. From earliest times the chief threat to an established dynasty in China had always come from the barbarians on China's land frontier. The Ching dynasty carried out a policy designed to prevent its being toppled in this way. The Manchus had absorbed the Mongols of Inner Mongolia (present-day Inner Mongolian Autonomous Region) into the Manchu state before they conquered China. After all of China Proper had been subdued, the Manchus conquered Outer Mongolia (now the Mongolian People's Republic) in the late seventeenth century, and in the eighteenth century the Manchus conquered central Asia as far as the Pamirs and established a protectorate over Tibet.

The Ching thus became the first dynasty to eliminate

The lake entrance to the Summer Palace

The main entrance to the Imperial Palace in Peking as it appeared in the early twentieth century

A view of the Imperial Summer Palace grounds as seen from the lake

The Palace of Heavenly Purity in the center of the Great Within as it existed in the early nineteenth century

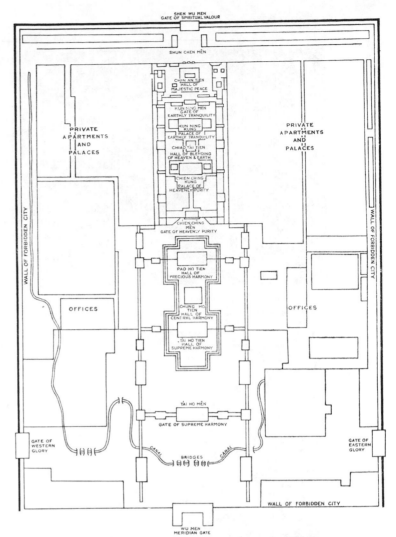

A schematic sketch of the Imperial City (Forbidden City) in Peking

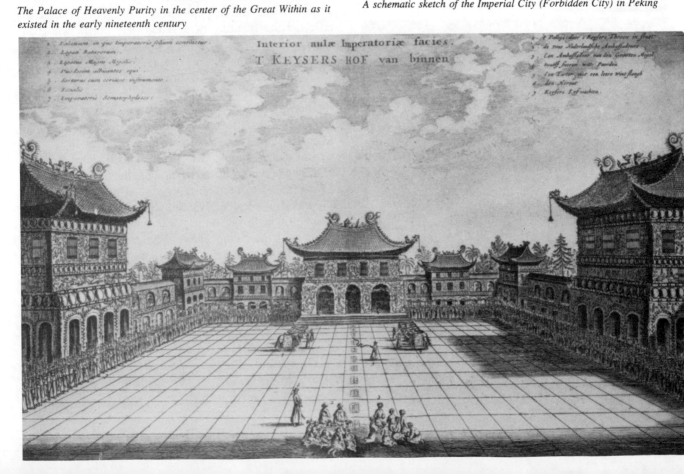

Emperor Tung-chih gives a public audience to a group of foreign ambassadors in 1873, in the first such official recognition of foreigners.

Emperor Kuang-hsu in the year of his enthronement

The new emperor on his first charger

economic concessions to the foreigners. By then, Europeans administered China's maritime customs and postal system and set the schedule of tariffs for the import of their goods into China. They also had the right to establish factories, open mines, operate coastal and inland shipping, construct railroads to funnel commerce through ports under their control, and patrol the rivers and coasts with their warships and gunboats to ensure the execution of the provisions of the "unequal treaties."

The foreign powers also at this time took over the peripheral states that had once acknowledged Chinese suzerainty and given tribute to the emperor. France, victorious in a war with China in 1883, took Annam (Vietnam). The British took Burma. Russia penetrated into Chinese Turkestan (Sinkiang). Japan, newly emerged from its century-long seclusion, annexed the Liu-ch'iu (Ryukyu) Islands and, by defeating the Chinese in Korea (1894–95), began to exert control over that peninsula as well as the island of Taiwan.

The defeat by Japan stripped China of its remaining prestige. Too weak to resist, the Chinese yielded to the foreign powers' plans to carve up the empire. In 1898 the British acquired on a ninety-nine-year lease the so-called New Territories of Kowloon, which greatly increased the size of their Hong Kong colony. Great Britain, Japan, Russia, Germany, France, and Belgium each gained spheres of influence elsewhere in China. The various powers were moving to take control of the communications and industries of whole provinces. The breakup of the empire into colonies seemed imminent for a time.

The United States, which had not acquired any territorial cessions, in 1899 proposed that there be an "Open Door" policy in China, whereby all foreign trade would have equal duties and privileges in all treaty ports within and outside the various spheres of influence. Great Britain, Germany, France, Italy, and Japan agreed to this.

THE HUNDRED DAYS OF 1898

In 1898, in the hundred days between June 11 and September 21, the Manchu court launched a series of edicts aimed at basic social and institutional reforms. These measures reflected the thinking of a group of scholars who had impressed the court with the necessity of making drastic changes if the dynasty were to survive the next few years.

The edicts covered a broad range of subjects and were aimed especially at remaking and revising basic institutions: the school and examination systems, the legal system, the defense system, and the postal system. The edicts also attempted to promote modernization in agriculture, medicine, mining, and other practical studies. To help achieve modernization in these fields, the Chinese government planned to send students abroad to learn from the more technologically advanced countries.

Opposition to the reform was widespread among the gentry and the ruling class. With the support of these groups, the empress dowager Tz'u-hsi, who had previously exercised power as a result of a palace coup in 1861 but had been in retirement since 1889, engineered a second coup on September 21, 1898. On that date she forced the young reform-minded emperor Kuang-hsu into seclusion and took over as regent. The Hundred Days of reform ended with the execution of six of the reformers and the flight of the two chief reformers, K'ang Yu-wei and Liang Ch'i-ch'ao, to Japan.

The conservatives then gave clandestine backing to the

A photograph of Emperor Kuang-hsu when he was a youth. The emperor avoided having his photograph taken later in life.

Kuang-hsu, the emperor of China from 1875 to 1908. In the last decade of the nineteenth century, the emperor was in strong conflict with the dowager queen. He wanted to let the Western world have a wedge into China because he believed that it would bring business and prosperity into a poor and backward nation. The dowager queen wanted to keep the traditional Chinese way of life.

The "defeated" empress dowager in 1903 meets with the Western legation wives who won her over and vice versa.

The empress dowager queen Tzu-hsi as she appeared in her youth

The dowager queen in her younger days

In October 1907, the empress dowager queen, contemplating abdication, surprised the world by issuing an edict declaring China henceforth a constitutional monarchy. In November of the following year, both she and the emperor, Kuang-hsu, died within four days of each other. Hsung-tung (P'u-yi), the two-year-old son of Prince Chun, brother of the late emperor, was placed upon the throne, with his father as regent.

xenophobic Boxer Rebellion. The rebellion was crushed by expeditionary forces of the foreign powers, and the court was made to consent to the Boxer Protocol of 1901. This agreement provided for the payment of a large indemnity, for the stationing of foreign troops in China, and for the razing of some Chinese fortifications. As a result of the Boxer debacle, the conservative cause lost much of its appeal to the empress dowager, and many of the reforms of the Hundred Days were put into effect in the decade that followed.

In 1905, the year that Japan emerged victorious from the Russo-Japanese war, the civil service examination, with its classical Confucian bias, was abolished. In 1901 efforts had already begun to modernize the education of Chinese and to introduce Western logic, science, political theory, and technology. Thousands of students were sent abroad to study, chiefly to Japan.

CONSTITUTIONAL REFORM

One characteristic feature of the Chinese system of government from ancient times had been that all power resided in

The empress dowager queen in later life

the emperor or his nominees. The emperor's power, in theory at least, was limited only by his moral principles. Rebellion and conquest were the only means of opposing the ruler. The concept of loyal opposition did not exist, although the scholar-adviser had possessed (in the days before neo-Confucian thought had rigidified) an obligation to warn the emperor of any danger to the regime, even of the emperor's own making. Since early Ching times, however, the educated people (the degree holders) had been expressly

forbidden to make statements concerning policy or to "associate with large numbers of others, or to form alliances or join societies." The only way of opposing the court was to do so secretly.

In the years after the Boxer Rebellion and Japan's victory over Russia, the movement among the leading intellectuals to reform China's basic institutions included an effort to introduce constitutional elements into the dynastic system, as had been done in Japan. In 1906 the ministries were reorganized into a cabinet system. In 1908 the empress dowager proclaimed a nine-year program to achieve constitutional self-government, and in the following year consultative assemblies in Peking and the provinces met for the first time. The suddenness and ambitiousness of the reform movement hindered its achievement.

There also came in 1908 a change in the imperial leadership. The empress dowager, who had been at the center of power for half a century, died on November 15, 1908. On that day it was also announced that the reform-minded emperor Kuang-hsu, whom the empress dowager had forced into retirement, had predeceased her by one day. The empress dowager had named as her successor a three-year-old grandnephew, Hsuan-tung (P'u-yi), whose father, Prince Ch'un, was made regent. The experienced, if autocratic, rule of the empress dowager was followed by the rule of inexperienced Manchu princes.

THE REPUBLICAN REVOLUTION

By the time the court began to institute constitutional reform, many Chinese had already become convinced that the only solution lay in outright revolution, in sweeping away the old regime and erecting a new order. The leadership and the revolutionary organizational structure came from the Westernized southern coast of China and from the secret society tradition that had grown up there in the period of the Ching conquest. The secret societies, the only organizations through which the common people could seek to bring about a change in conditions, were highly organized in south China, with lodges in several provinces and elaborate systems of passwords and signs used to identify fellow members.

By 1894 a new secret society, the Hsing Chung Hui (Revive China Society), had come into being with branches in the Macao-Hong Kong-Canton area and in Hawaii. The

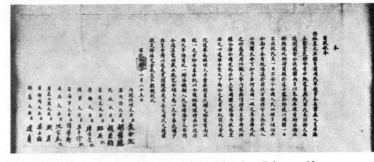

Emperor Hsuan-tung's abdication document rendered on February 12, 1912, ended two thousand years of royal rule.

new organization was founded by Sun Yatsen, the leader of the Chinese republican revolution.

Sun was born into a Cantonese-speaking peasant family living in a village near Macao that had long been in the habit of sending its surplus males to the Nan Yang to seek their fortune. Sun was sent to an Episcopalian boarding school in Hawaii and later attended Queen's College in the British colony of Hong Kong. He became a Christian (Congregationalist) in 1884. His patriotism was aroused by the aggression of the foreign powers in China in the 1880s. From 1886 to 1892 he studied medicine at schools in Canton and Hong Kong and began to practice in Macao, but his medical career was ended when he was forbidden to continue practicing because he lacked a Portuguese diploma. Already a reformer, he became a revolutionist.

In 1895 Sun plotted to seize the Canton provincial government offices. The plot was discovered; several of his associates were executed; and Sun escaped to Japan in disguise. In 1896 he was in London, where he was recognized at the Chinese legation and kidnapped. While he was being held inside the legation building before being sent home to be executed, Sun got a message to Sir James Cantlie, his former medical missionary teacher from Hong Kong who lived near the legation in London. Cantlie brought pressure to bear upon the British government to intervene. As a result of the publicity attendant upon his rescue, Sun at the age of thirty was an internationally famous anti-Manchu revolutionary.

By 1905, when the reform movement was gaining impetus in the wake of the Japanese victory over Russia, Sun had already begun organizing revolutionary activity among the overseas Chinese throughout Asia and the Pacific. For this purpose Sun developed his connections with the powerful Triad Society and with the officer corps of the newly modernized imperial army.

In 1905 Sun issued the first statement of his political philosophy, the Three People's Principles *(San Min Chu I).* These principles were: nationalism—to achieve political unity so as to resist imperialism; democracy—the establishment of a centralized government on a popular base; and people's livelihood—by which was meant improved living standards and popular welfare.

Sun's secret society had grown to over forty branches by

The dowager queen was carried into the garden in a daily ritual at the Imperial City.

Ex-Emperor Hsuan-tung (P'u-yi) in 1931, photographed with his consort

P'u-yi abdicated in 1912 and ten years later married the daughter of Jung Yuan, a Manchu noble.

1905, and in that year he reorganized the society and renamed it the T'ung Meng Hui (Together Sworn Society). Japan, where most of the overseas students were, as well as a few reformers who had fled China after the termination of the Hundred Days of reform in 1898, became the headquarters for Sun's revolutionary group. This group took an oath to overthrow the Manchus and establish a republic.

The revolutionaries began publishing and smuggling into China a monthly newspaper aimed at the modern Chinese student group. They also made numerous unsuccessful revolutionary plots. The tenth such effort was discovered in April 1911 in Canton, and the imperial government had seventy-two conspirators executed. Another plot was scheduled for the fall but was accidentally uncovered when a bomb being saved for the event exploded prematurely in a warehouse.

Organized protests had already occurred in the provinces of Szechwan, Hunan, and Kwangtung. These demonstrations were led by shareholders in Chinese companies against an imperial plan to nationalize the rights to build private railroad trunklines, preparatory to mortgaging the lines to foreign powers. By the time of the bomb explosion, fighting over the railroad issue had already broken out in Szechwan. On the night of October 10, 1911, the imperial garrisons at Wu-ch'ang, influenced by Sun's revolutionary propaganda, rose in revolt against the dynasty. This date, often referred to as the double ten—the tenth day of the tenth month—is celebrated by Chinese as the birthday of the republic.

The revolution spread quickly, attracting as adherents various groups who had reason to be dissatisfied with the imperial rule. Sun, who was in the United States on October 10, learned from the newspapers that his revolution had come to fruition. Upon returning to China, Sun was inaugurated on January 1, 1912, in Nanking as provisional president of the Republic of China, but power in Peking had already passed to Yuan Shih-k'ai, commander in chief of the modern imperial army, upon the regent's resignation in December.

In order to prevent division in the country from destroying the new republic, Sun agreed to Yuan's insistence that China be united under a Peking government headed by himself. On February 12, 1912, the Manchu emperor Hsuan-tung abdicated, and on March 10 Yuan took the oath as provisional president of the Republic of China.

REPUBLICAN CHINA

Although the Ching regime had been overthrown, the republic that Sun and his associates envisioned did not immediately come into existence. The revolutionists lacked an army, and the power of Yuan, as the new chief executive, began rapidly to outstrip that of Parliament. Yuan revised the constitution at will and became engaged in reasserting the central government's control over the civil

In 1912, when Emperor Hsuan-tung abdicated, Yuan Shih-Kai took control of the government. By the end of 1915 Yuan had proclaimed himself president for life, but while he got his wish, it was for only one year, for he died in 1916. He is seen here in 1912 offering sacrifices to God in thanks for his victory over the throne, a scene which the rest of the world thought a mockery of Christianity.

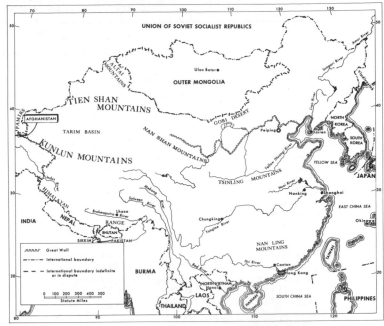

Communist China today

Commander-in-chief of the armies Yuan Shih-K'ai, personally, through his cleverness and desire to replace the emperor, brought about the abdication.

Sun Yat-sen, the first president of the Chinese Republic in 1911

administration, the provincial military governors, and the peripheral parts of the empire, namely Mongolia and Tibet.

In August 1912 a political party was brought into being by one of Sun's revolutionary associates, Sung Chiao-jen. The new party, called the Kuomintang (Nationalist party, often abbreviated as KMT), was an amalgamation of small political groups with Sun's revolutionary secret society, the T'ung Meng Hui. During the national elections held in February 1913 for members of the new bicameral Parliament, Sung campaigned widely for his party and against the administration in power. The new party gained a majority of seats in Parliament. President Yuan had Sung assassinated in March 1913. Yuan already had arranged the assassination of several prorevolutionist generals.

Revulsion against Yuan grew because of his tactics and also because his government signed in April 1913, without Parliament's approval, a loan agreement with a consortium of banks from Great Britain, France, Germany, Russia, and Japan for 25 million pounds sterling to maintain his armies and his administration. The agreement with the banking consortium had, in addition to a high interest rate, the pledge of China's salt taxes as security, to be collected by a joint Sino-foreign collection agency. In the summer of 1913 seven provincial governments staged an attempted second revolution against Yuan's government and, when it was suppressed, Sun and other revolutionary leaders fled to Japan.

In October 1913 an intimidated Parliament elected Yuan president of the Republic of China, and the major powers extended recognition to his government. To achieve international recognition for the republic, Yuan had to agree to autonomy for Outer Mongolia and Tibet. China was still to be suzerain but would have to allow Russia continuance of its domination of Outer Mongolia and Great Britain continuance of its influence in Tibet.

In November Yuan, legally president, ordered the KMT dissolved and its members removed from Parliament. Within a few months Yuan suspended Parliament and the provincial assemblies and became the dictator. By the end of 1915 Yuan had proclaimed himself president for life and would have had himself proclaimed emperor had it not been for the opposition of the provincial military governors. Yuan died of illness in 1916, having failed to found a new dynasty.

THE ROYAL SOVEREIGNS OF THE DYNASTIES OF CHINA

Reign	Title	Ruler	Reign	Title	Ruler
2183–1802 B.C.	Hsia Dynasty		88–105	Emperor	Ho Ti
1766–1121	Shang (Yin) Dynasty		105–105	Emperor	Shang Ti
			106–125	Emperor	An Ti
			125–125	Emperor	Shao Ti
CHOU (CHOW) DYNASTY			125–146	Emperor	Shun Ti
1121–1105	Emperor	Wu want	145–145	Emperor	Ch'ung Ti
1104–1066	Emperor	Cheng want	145–145	Emperor	Chih Ti
1067–1041	Emperor	K'ang want	146–169	Emperor	Huan Ti
1041–1023	Emperor	Chao wang	168–189	Emperor	Ling Ti
1023–982	Emperor	Mu wang	189–189	Emperor	Shao Ti
982–967	Emperor	Kung wang	189–220	Emperor	Hsien Ti
966–954	Emperor	I wang I			
954–925	Emperor	Hsiao wang	**SHU-HAN DYNASTY**		
924–878	Emperor	I wang II	220–222	Emperor	Chao Lieh Ti
878–841	Emperor	Li wang	223–263	Emperor	Hou Ti
841–827	Emperor	Kung-ho	264–289	Emperor	Wu Ti
827–782	Emperor	Hsuan wang	290–306	Emperor	Hui Ti
781–770	Emperor	Yu wang	306–312	Emperor	Huai Ti
770–719	Emperor	P'ing wang	313–316	Emperor	Min Ti
719–697	Emperor	Huan wang	317–321	Emperor	Yuan Ti
696–681	Emperor	Chuang wang	322–324	Emperor	Ming Ti
681–675	Emperor	Hsi wang	325–341	Emperor	Cheng Ti
676–651	Emperor	Hui wang	342–343	Emperor	K'ang Ti
651–618	Emperor	Hsiang wang	344–360	Emperor	Mu Ti
618–613	Emperor	Ch'ing wang	361–364	Emperor	Ai Ti
612–607	Emperor	K'uang wang	365–371	Emperor	Hai Hsi Kung
606–585	Emperor	Ting wang	371–371	Emperor	Chien Wen Ti
585–571	Emperor	Chien wang	372–395	Emperor	Hsiao Wu Ti
571–544	Emperor	Ling wang	396–417	Emperor	An Ti
544–519	Emperor	Ching wang	418–420	Emperor	Kung Ti
519–475	Emperor	Ching wang			
475–468	Emperor	Yuan wang	**SOUTHERN SUNG DYNASTY**		
468–440	Emperor	Cheng-ting wang	420–421	Emperor	Wu Ti
440–425	Emperor	K'ao wang	422–423	Emperor	Shao Ti
425–401	Emperor	Wei-lieh wang	424–452	Emperor	Wen Ti
401–375	Emperor	An wang	453–464	Emperor	Hsiao Wu Ti
375–368	Emperor	Lieh wang	464–465	Emperor	(Ch'ien) Fei Ti
368–320	Emperor	Hsien wang	465–472	Emperor	Ming Ti
320–313	Emperor	Shen-ching wang	472–476	Emperor	Fei Ti
314–255	Emperor	Nan wang	477–479	Emperor	Shun Ti
CH'IN (TS'IN) DYNASTY			**SOUTHERN CH'I DYNASTY**		
255–250	Emperor	Chao-hsiang wang	479–482	Emperor	Kao Ti
250–250	Emperor	Hsiao-wen wang	482–493	Emperor	Wu Ti
249–247	Emperor	Chuang-hsiang wang	493–493	Emperor	Yu-lin wang
246–209	Emperor	Shih-huang Ti	494–494	Emperor	Hai-ling wang
209–207	Emperor	Erh-shih	494–498	Emperor	Ming Ti
			498–500	Emperor	Tung-hun
WESTERN HAN DYNASTY			501–502	Emperor	He Ti
206–196	Emperor	Han Kao Tsu (Liu Pang)			
195–188	Emperor	Hui Ti	**SOUTHERN LIANG DYNASTY**		
188–180	Emperor	Kao Hou	502–548	Emperor	Wu Ti
180–157	Emperor	Wen Ti	549–551	Emperor	Chien Wen Ti
157–141	Emperor	Ching Ti	551–551	Emperor	Yu-chang
141–87	Emperor	Wu Ti	552–554	Emperor	Yuan Ti
87–74	Emperor	Chao Ti	555–555	Emperor	Chen-yang hou
74–49	Emperor	Hsuan Ti	555–557	Emperor	Ching Ti
49–33	Emperor	Yuan Ti			
33–7	Emperor	Cheng Ti	**SOUTHERN CHEN DYNASTY**		
7–1	Emperor	Ai Ti	557–558	Emperor	Wu Ti
1 B.C.–A.D. 9	Emperor	P'ing Ti	559–566	Emperor	Wen Ti
A.D. 6–8	Emperor	Ju-tzu Ying	566–567	Emperor	Fei Ti
ca.9	Emperor	Wang Mang	568–581	Emperor	Hsuan Ti
23–25	Emperor	Huai-yang wang	582–589	Emperor	Hou Chu
EASTERN HAN DYNASTY			**SUI DYNASTY**		
A.D. 25–58	Emperor	Kuang-wu Ti	589–603	Emperor	Wen Ti
57–75	Emperor	Ming Ti	604–616	Emperor	Yang Ti
75–88	Emperor	Chang Ti			

Reign	Title	Ruler	Reign	Title	Ruler
617–618	Emperor	Kung Ti	1274–1275	Emperor	Kung Tsung
618–625	Emperor	Kao Tsu	1276–1277	Emperor	Tuan Tsung
			1278–1279	Emperor	Ti Ping

T'ANG DYNASTY

YUANG DYNASTY

Reign	Title	Ruler	Reign	Title	Ruler
626–649	Emperor	T'ai Tsung			
650–683	Emperor	Kao Tsung	1206–1227	Emperor	T'ai Tsou
684–684	Emperor	Chung Tsung	1227–1228	Emperor	Tolui
684–689	Emperor	Jui Tsung	1229–1241	Emperor	T'ai Tsung
690–704	Empress	Wu Hou	1241–1246	Empress	Toregene Khatun
705–710	Emperor	Chung Tsung	1246–1249	Emperor	Ting Tsung (Guyuk)
710–711	Emperor	Jui Tsung	1249–1250	Empress	Oghul Ghaimash
712–755	Emperor	Hsuan Tsung	1251–1260	Emperor	Hsien Tsung (Mongke)
756–762	Emperor	Su Tsung	1260–1294	Emperor	Shih Tsung
763–779	Emperor	Tai Tsung	1294–1307	Emperor	Ch'eng Tsung
779–804	Emperor	To Tsung	1307–1311	Emperor	Wu Tsung
805–805	Emperor	Shun Tsung	1311–1320	Emperor	Jen Tsung
805–820	Emperor	Hsien Tsung	1320–1323	Emperor	Yin Tsung
820–824	Emperor	Mu Tsung	1323–1328	Emperor	T'ai Tin Ti
824–825	Emperor	Ching Tsung	1328–1328	Emperor	Wen Tsung
826–840	Emperor	Wen Tsung	1329–1329	Emperor	Ming Tsung
840–846	Emperor	Wu Tsung	1329–1332	Emperor	Wen Tsung
846–859	Emperor	Hsuan Tsung	1332–1332	Emperor	Ning Tsung
859–873	Emperor	I Tsung	1333–1368	Emperor	Shun Ti
873–888	Emperor	Hsi Tsung			
888–903	Emperor	Chao Tsung			
904–907	Emperor	Chao Hsuan Ti			

LATER LIANG DYNASTY

MING DYNASTY*

Reign	Title	Ruler	Reign	Title	Ruler
			1368–1398	Emperor	Hung Wu (Chu Yuan-chang)
907–911	Emperor	T'ai Tsu	1398–1402	Emperor	Chien Wen
912–912	Emperor	Ying wang	1402–1424	Emperor	Yung Lo
913–923	Emperor	Mo Ti	1424–1425	Emperor	Hung Hsi
			1426–1435	Emperor	Hsuan Te

LATER T'ANG DYNASTY

Reign	Title	Ruler	Reign	Title	Ruler
			1435–1449	Emperor	Chen T'ung
923–926	Emperor	Chuang Tsung	1449–1457	Emperor	Ching T'ai
926–933	Emperor	Ming Tsung	1457–1464	Emperor	T'ien Shun
933–936	Emperor	Min Ti	1464–1487	Emperor	Ch'eng Hua
			1488–1505	Emperor	Hung hsi

LATER CHIN DYNASTY

Reign	Title	Ruler	Reign	Title	Ruler
			1505–1521	Emperor	Cheng-Te
936–941	Emperor	Kao Tsou	1522–1566	Emperor	Chia-ching
942–946	Emperor	Ch'u Ti	1566–1572	Emperor	Lung-ch'ing
			1573–1619	Emperor	Wan-li

LATER HAN DYNASTY

Reign	Title	Ruler	Reign	Title	Ruler
			1620–1620	Emperor	Tai-ch'ang
947–947	Emperor	Kao Tsou	1620–1627	Emperor	Tien-ch'i
948–950	Emperor	Yin Ti	1627–1644	Emperor	Ch'ung-ch'en

LATER CHOU DYNASTY

CHING (MANCHU) DYNASTY†

Reign	Title	Ruler	Reign	Title	Ruler
			1644–1661	Emperor	Shun-chih (Fu-lin) (Shih-tsu)
951–954	Emperor	T'ai Tsou			
954–959	Emperor	Shih Tsung	1662–1723	Emperor	K'ang-hsi (Hsuan-yeh)
959–960	Emperor	Kung Ti	1723–1736	Emperor	Yung-cheng (Yin-chen)
			1736–1796	Emperor	Ch'ien-lung (Hung-li)

SUNG (SONG) DYNASTY

Reign	Title	Ruler	Reign	Title	Ruler
			1796–1821	Emperor	Chia-ch'ing (Yung-yen) (Jen-tsung)
960–976	Emperor	T'ai Tsou			
976–997	Emperor	T'ai Tsung	1821–1851	Emperor	Tao-kuang (Min-ning) (Hsuan-tsung)
997–1022	Emperor	Chen Tsung			
1022–1062	Emperor	Jen Tsung	1851–1862	Emperor	Hsien-feng (Yi-chu) (Wen-tsung)
1063–1066	Emperor	Yin Tsung			
1067–1085	Emperor	Shen Tsung	1862–1875	Emperor	Tung-chih (Tsai-ch'un) (Ki-tsiang)
1085–1100	Emperor	Che Tsung			
1100–1124	Emperor	Hui Tsung	1875–1889	Empress Dowager	Tzu-hsi
1125–1127	Emperor	Ch'in Tsung	1875–1908	Emperor	Kuang-hsu (Tsai-t'ien)
1127–1162	Emperor	Kao Tsung	1898–1908	Empress Dowager	Tzu-hsi
1162–1180	Emperor	Hsiao Tsung	1908–1912	Emperor	Hsuan-tung (Pu-yi)
1180–1193	Emperor	Kuang Tsung			
1194–1223	Emperor	Ning Tsung			
1224–1264	Emperor	Li Tsung			
1264–1274	Emperor	Tu Tsung			

*Mongol names used starting with Ming Dynasty.
† Both Chinese and Mongol names used in Ching Dynasty.

20

The Empire of Mongolia

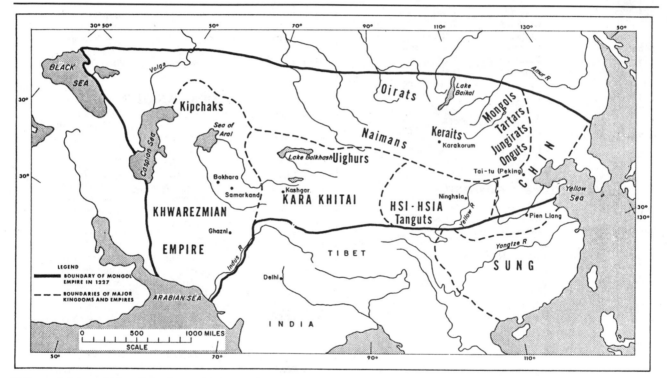

Tribes and nations of Mongolia and central Asia, A.D. 1150

The Mongolian People's Republic comprises approximately half of a vast central Asian region known generally throughout history as Mongolia. That region originally extended roughly from the Sungari River valley of modern Manchuria in the east to Lake Valkash and the Irtysh River valley in the west, and from the Tien Shan Mountains and the southern limits of the Gobi Desert in the south to Lake Baikal and (approximately) the fifty-fifth parallel of latitude in the north. The territory which is the present Mongolian People's Republic was the heartland of that older and larger region, and is today the only portion of the region in which a majority of the population are descended from the Mongols of history. Thus the modern state is truly the successor of historical Mongolia.

Until relatively recent times the peoples who inhabited Mongolia were nomads, and even today a substantial proportion of the rural population is essentially nomadic. At the dawn of history there were many warlike tribes living a nomadic life in Mongolia, and apparently most of these belonged to one or the other of two possible racially distinct, and linguistically very different, groupings. One of these groupings, the Yueh Chih, was related linguistically to the ancient nomadic Scythian peoples who inhabited the steppe and desert lands extending generally from the Danube valley in the west to the Altai Mountains in the east and therefore they are Indo-European. The other grouping, racially Mongoloid, was known to the early Chinese as the Hsiung Nu, and might be the same people known to the ancient and medieval Europeans as the Huns.

Although, over the course of history, other peoples dis-

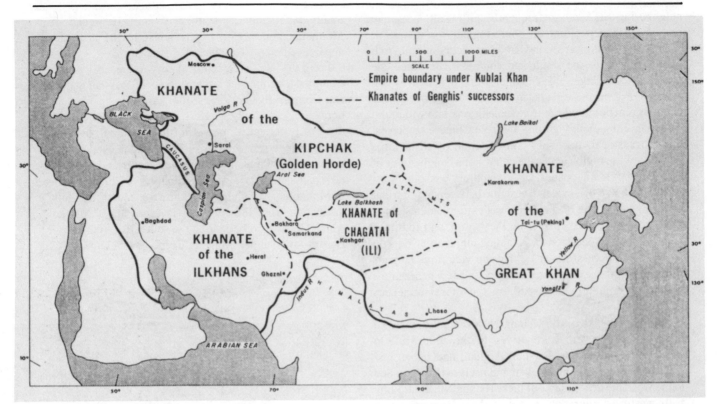

The Mongol Empire, A.D. 1280

Kublai Khan's mobile throne was mounted on four elephants for use in the field.

In 1274, the great Tatar emperor Kublai Khan, angered because the Japanese were killing his ambassadors and emissaries to that country, led a powerful force to conquer Japan. In this scene he is bottled up by the Japanese archers. After two attempts, the emperor decided that his revenge wasn't worth the loss of life and gave up his goal of conquering Japan.

placed the confederations of the Yueh Chih and the Hsiung Nu, their activities, conflicts, and internal and external relationships established a pattern which continued almost unchanged—with one momentous deviation—until the eighteenth century A.D. There were three principal themes in this pattern: first, constant and fierce struggles among neighboring tribes, whose frequently shifting alliances may have been independent of ethno-logical, or racial, or linguistic distinctions; second, frequent incursions into rich Chinese lands to the south and southeast, in which the pleasures of pillage and slaughter were matched by the rewards of loot; these raids, in turn, prompted occasional Chinese reaction, and punitive expeditions into Mongolia by some of the more vigorous and able Chinese emperors; third, occasional, transitory consolidation of all or large portions of the region under the control of a conqueror or of a coalition of similar tribes; such temporary consolidations could result in a life-or-death struggle between major tribal groupings until one or the other was exterminated, joined the other, or was expelled from the region; and fourth, a result on several occasions was raiding into North China on so vast and successful a scale that the victorious nomads settled down in the conquered land and in a few generations became completely absorbed by the more numerous Chinese.

Within this pattern the Hsiung Nu eventually expelled the Yueh Chih, who were driven to the southwest, to become the Kushans of Persian, Afghan, and Indian history. In turn, the Hsiung Nu were themselves later expelled to the west; the descendants of these Hsiung Nu, continuing their westward migration, established the Hun Empire in central and eastern Europe, which reached its zenith under Attila.

The continuation of this pattern was abruptly and dramatically interrupted in the latter years of the twelfth century and throughout the thirteenth, by Genghis Khan and his descendants. While completing the consolidation of Mongolia and during some of the invasions of north China, Genghis created sophisticated military and political organizations, exceeding in skill, efficiency, and vigor the institutions of the most civilized nations of the time. Under him and his immediate successors, the Mongols conquered most of Eurasia.

After a century of world preeminence by the Mongols, the traditional patterns reasserted themselves. In China and elsewhere the Mongols were absorbed by the conquered populations, and Mongolia again became a land of incessantly warring nomadic tribes. True to the fourth pattern, a similar tribe, the Manchus of easternmost Mongolia, conquered China in the seventeenth century, and ultimately became sinicized.

Here the pattern ended. The Manchu conquest of China came at a time when the technologically inspired expansion of Europe was beginning to have a significant impact upon east Asia. Russian colonial expansionism was sweeping rapidly across Asia, at first passing north of Mongolia, but bringing incessant pressure against the Mongolian nomad tribes from the west and the north, and by conquests and protectorates beginning to establish firm footholds in Mongolian territory. At the same time the dynamic Manchu-Ching Dynasty began to bring similar pressures against Mongolia from the east and south. This was partly the

traditional attempt at control over nomadic inroads from Mongolia, but was also in response to the now clearly apparent threat of Russian expansionism.

From the late seventeenth century to the early twentieth century Mongolia was a major focus of Russian and Manchu-Chinese rivalry for predominant influence in all of northeast Asia. In the process Russia absorbed those portions of historical Mongolia to the west and north of the present Mongolian People's Republic, and Manchu-China absorbed those regions to southwest, south and east that are now included in the People's Republic of China. The heart of Mongolia—which became known as Outer Mongolia in distinction from the four provinces of Inner Mongolia, which China absorbed along the southern rim of the Gobi Desert—was under Manchu-Chinese sovereignty. Con-

This is a portrait of Kublai Khan's empress. The official history of the Yuan Dynasty records that Kublai Khan's consort was known as Empress Chao-jui shun-sheng. Her personal name was Ch'a-pi.

tinuing Russian interest in Mongolia was discouraged by the Manchus.

But as the power of the Manchu (Ching) Dynasty gradually waned in the nineteenth and early twentieth centuries, Russian influence in Mongolia grew. Thus Russia supported the Outer Mongolian assertions of independence in the period immediately after the Chinese Revolution of 1911. The change from empire to Soviet Republic did not diminish this Russian interest, and the Russian civil war spilled over into Mongolia in 1919–21. Chinese efforts to take advantage of internal Russian disorders by reestablishing control over Outer Mongolia were thwarted in part by China's own internal instability, and also by the vigor of Soviet reaction once the Bolshevik Revolution had secured its triumph in Russia. Soviet predominance in Outer Mongolia was unquestioned after 1921, and when the Mongolian People's Republic was established in 1924, it was as a Communist-controlled satellite of the Soviet Union.

GENGHIS KHAN AND HIS PROGENY

RISE OF GENGHIS KHAN

In the year 1162 a first son was born to the Mongol chieftain Yesukai, a son of Kabul. The boy was named Temuchin. Yesukai, who was chief of the Kiut subclan of the Borjigin Mongols, was treacherously killed by neighboring Tatars in 1175, when Temuchin was only twelve years old. The Kiuts, acutely aware of the hazards of community and individual existence in the fierce and never-ending struggles of the steppes, rejected the boy as their leader, and chose one of his kinsmen instead. Temuchin and his immediate family were abandoned and apparently left to die in a semi-desert mountainous region.

Temuchin did not die, however. In an intensely dramatic struggle, first for life, and later for power, he had by the age of twenty become the leader of the Kiut subclan, and by 1190 had become the unquestioned chief of the Borjigin Mongols. There followed sixteen years of nearly constant warfare as Temuchin greatly increased his power in the region north of the Gobi Desert. At first he was allied with the neighboring Kerait clan. Much of his early success was due to this alliance, and to subsidies which he and the Keraits received from the Chin emperor in payment for punitive operations against Tatars and other tribes which might threaten the northern frontiers of Chin China. Later Temuchin broke with the Keraits, and in a series of major campaigns defeated all of the Mongol and Tatar tribes in the region from the Altai to Manchuria. His principal opponents in this struggle had been the Naiman Mongols, and he selected Karakorum (Kharakhorum), their capital, as the seat of his new empire.

In 1206 Temuchin's leadership of all the Mongol tribes was formally acknowledged by a *khuraltai* (or council) of Mongol chieftains as their *khagan* (great khan). They also

Artist's concept of Genghis Khan

An old temple painting of Genghis Khan and his family

gave to Temuchin the honorific title of Genghis (correctly spelled and pronounced Chingis, a variant also written Jenghiz) in an effort to signify the unprecedented scope of his power. The word may have come from the Turkic word for ocean, meaning that his dominion spread out over all of the earth, or it may have been a completely new Mongol word, coined especially for him, with a meaning incorporating the concepts of great, supreme, unflinching, and invincible.

During the quarter of a century in which Genghis had risen to supremacy in Mongolia, he had developed a new and unprecedented military system and organization. As a result, he now had a highly organized, superbly trained, and exceptionally flexible cavalry army which comprised one of the most formidable instruments of warfare that the world had ever seen. Building on a permanent base of perhaps thirty thousand warriors under arms at all times, Genghis could, by levies upon the Mongol tribes, raise armies of more than two hundred thousand men on short notice.

At the time of his first *khuraltai* at Karakorum, Genghis Khan was already engaged in the first of his wars of conquest. A dispute had broken out with the Tangut Kingdom or empire of Hsi-Hsia, and in 1205 the Mongol *tumen* (a *tumen* was roughly equivalent to a modern division, comprising ten thousand men) had easily defeated the much larger Tangut forces in Kansu and Ninghsia. The Mongols had been baffled, however, by the strong fortifications of the Hsi-Hsia cities. The results were the same in the campaigns of 1207 and 1209. When peace was concluded, in 1209, the Hsi-Hsia emperor, with reduced dominion acknowledged the suzerainty of Genghis Khan.

EARLY WARS IN CHINA

War with the Chin Empire broke out in 1211. At first the pattern of operations against the Chin was the same as it had been against the Hsi-Hsia. Genghis and his warriors were victorious in the field, but were frustrated in their efforts to take major north Chinese cities. In his typical logical and determined fashion, Genghis and his highly developed staff studied the problems of the assault of fortifications. They gradually built up a siege train and, with the help of impressed Chinese engineers slowly developed the techniques that would eventually make them the most accomplished and most successful besiegers in the history of warfare.

By 1213, as a result of a number of overwhelming victories in the field, and a few successes in the capture of fortifications in raids deep into China, Genghis had conquered and consolidated Chin territory as far as the Great Wall. He then advanced with three armies into the heart of Chin territory, between the Wall and the Yellow River. He completely defeated the Chin forces, spread devastation through north China, captured numerous cities, and finally in 1215 besieged, captured, and sacked Peking (then known as Yenching or Chungtu). The Chin emperor was forced to recognize the suzerainty of the Mongol conqueror.

Meanwhile the deposed khan of the Naiman Mongols, Kushluk, had taken refuge at the court of Kara Khitai. Kushluk treacherously overthrew the khan of Kara Khitai, and seized the throne. He prepared for war with Genghis, whose spies kept him informed of these events.

By this time the Mongol army was exhausted by ten years of continuous campaigning against the Hsi-Hsia and the Chin. So Genghis sent only two *tumen* (twenty thousand men) under brilliant young General Chepe against Kushluk. An internal revolt was incited by Mongol agents; then Chepe overran the country. Kushluk's forces were defeated west of Kashgar; he was captured and executed; Kara Khitai was annexed by Genghis.

CONQUEST OF KHWAREZM

In 1218 several of Genghis's ambassadors were mistreated by Alaud-Din Mohammed (Mohammed Shah), Khwarezmian-Turkish ruler of Persia.

Genghis began to gather a force of more than two hundred thousand men, divided into four main armies under himself and his sons Juji, Jagatai, and Ogadai. He planned to advance into Persia from the northeast while Chepe also moved in from Kara-Khitai with a small force. In 1219 Juji and Chepe, with not more than thirty thousand men between them, fought a draw battle in the Ferghana Valley against Mohammed's vastly superior forces (perhaps two hundred thousand), but Chepe was able to continue his mission.

Early the next year the main Mongol armies struck from the north and northwest, to the amazement of the Khwarezmians, who were expecting an invasion across the Pamirs. The speed of the Mongol advance seems to have terrified Mohammed Shah, who had earlier gained a reputation as a warrior and conqueror. He fled to Persia, abandoning his homeland to the conquerors. The strongly fortified cities of Samarkand, Otrar, and Khojend were sacked and destroyed, and many of their inhabitants were slaughtered. Genghis spared Bokhara, which had surrendered without resistance, although he made the population raze its walls.

Sending a small force of three *tumen* under his best generals, Chepe and Subotai, in pursuit of the fleeing shah, Genghis and the remainder of the army overran the eastern portion of the Khwarezmian empire. He now encountered the only serious resistance of the war, from Jellaluddin, the son of Mohammed Shah. But Genghis defeated Jellaluddin in a hard-fought battle on the west bank of the Indus River, ending effective Khwarezmian resistance.

RECONNAISSANCE INTO EUROPE

Meanwhile, after a pursuit of five months by Chepe and Subotai, Mohammed Shah fled to an island in the Caspian Sea, where he died on February 1221. The Mongol generals now received permission from Genghis Khan to continue around the Caspian Sea, through the Caucasus, to make a

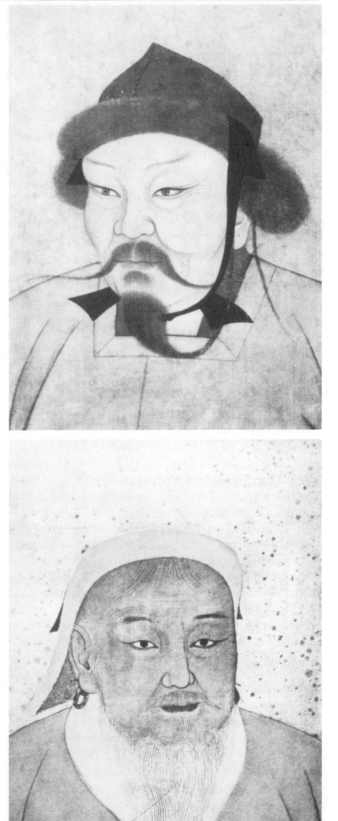

reconnaissance in force into eastern Europe.

In 1222, after smashing the Georgians and the Cumans of the Caucasus, the small Mongol expedition advanced into the steppes of the Kuban. Combining rapid movement with guile, the Mongols again defeated the Cumans, captured Astrakhan, then pursued across the Don. Penetrating into the Crimea, they stormed the Genoese fortress of Sudak on the southeast coast, then turned north into the Ukraine.

The Mongol leaders now felt they had accomplished their mission. Before returning to Mongolia, however, they decided to rest their *tumen* and to gain more information about the lands to their north and west. They camped near the mouth of the Dnieper River, and their spies were soon scattered all over eastern and central Europe.

Meanwhile, under the leadership of Mstislav, prince of Kiev, a mixed Russian-Cuman army of eighty thousand marched against the Mongol encampment. Chepe and Subotai sought peace, but when their envoys were brutally killed, they attacked and practically annihilated the Russians on the banks of the Kalka River. The expedition then marched eastward, in compliance with a courier message from Genghis. As they were marching north of the Caspian Sea, Chepe sickened and died. In 1224 Subotai brought the expedition back after a trek of four thousand miles to a rendezvous with the main Mongol armies, now returning from their victories over the Khwarezmians.

THE LAST CAMPAIGN OF GENGHIS KHAN

The vassal emperor of Hsi-Hsia had refused to take part in the war against Mohammed Shah, and Genghis had vowed punishment. While he was in Persia, the Hsia and Chin

Three portraits of famous Mongol rulers preserved in the Imperial Portrait Gallery Museum in Peking. Kublai Khan, Ogadai Khan, and Genghis Khan.

Genghis Khan (Temujin) proclaims himself emperor of the Mongols and supreme authority over Mongolian territory.

empires had formed an alliance against the Mongols. After rest and reorganization of his armies, Genghis prepared for war against the allies.

By this time advancing years caused Genghis to feel that he should prepare for the future and ensure an orderly succession among his descendants. He selected his son Ogadai as the successor to his throne and established the method of selection of subsequent *khagans* (now khan) specifying that they should come from his direct descendants. Meanwhile he studied intelligence reports from Hsia and Chin and readied a force of 180,000 men for a new campaign.

Late in 1226, when the rivers were frozen, the Mongols struck southward with their customary speed and vigor. The Tanguts, well acquainted with Mongol methods, were ready, and the two armies met by the banks of the frozen Yellow River. The Hsia army numbered something more than three hundred thousand men. In a great battle, fought on and beside the frozen river, the Mongols virtually annihilated the Tangut host.

Pursuing energetically, the Mongols killed the Hsia emperor in a mountain fortress. His son took refuge in the great walled city of Ninghsia, which the Mongols had vainly besieged in earlier wars. Leaving one-third of his army to invest the Hsia capital, Genghis sent Ogadai eastward, across the great bend of the Yellow River, to drive the Chin from their last footholds north of the river. With the

remainder, he marched southeast (evidently to eastern Szechwan) taking a position in the mountains where the Hsia, Chin, and Sung empires met, to prevent Sung reinforcements from reaching Ninghsia. Here he accepted the surrender of the new Hsia emperor, but rejected peace overtures from the Chin.

A premonition of death caused the *khagan* to start back to Mongolia but he died en route. On his deathbed he outlined to his son Tului the plans which would later be used by his successors to complete the destruction of the Chin Empire.

OGADAI AND CONTINUING CONQUESTS

In compliance with the will of the dead emperor, a *khuraltai* at Karakorum selected Ogadai as *khagan*. The new ruler completed the conquest of the outlying territories of the Western Hsia. In 1231 he sent an expedition to conquer Korea.

That same year Ogadai decided to destroy the Chin Empire. He formed an alliance with the Sung, then sent his brother Tului southward with a large army into Chin territory. In 1232, in the middle of the campaign Tului died, and Subotai took command. He continued on to besiege the great city of Pien Liang (Kaifeng), the Chin capital. Despite skillful use of explosives by the defenders, the city finally fell to Mongol assault after a year's siege. Subotai then

This is a portrait of Ogadai Khan. Ogadai reigned 1229–41. He was the son of Emperor T'ai-tsu (Genghis Khan). He was both loyal and compassionate, and of wide sympathies. He aided his father in the Mongolian conquests, and on Genghis Khan's death succeeded to his throne. He also continued his father's policy of allying with the Sung to conquer the Chin Dynasty, and followed this with an invasion of Korea. In the west he sent generals to attack Russia, where he obtained the submission of the king and other rulers. His armies reached Poland and the western border of Hungary.

completed the conquest of the Chin Empire. Ogadai refused to divide the conquered region with the Sung, who then (1234) attempted to seize the former Chin province now called Honan. This was the signal for another war, destined to last for forty-five years.

Incredible though it may seem, Ogadai deliberately committed his nation, with a total population that could not have exceeded 1 million, to an offensive war against the most populous nation on earth, while other Mongol armies were ranging in offensive warfare through Persia, Anatolia, and Syria, as well as across the steppes of western Siberia and Russia. By this time Mongols probably made up less than half of the so-called Mongol armies, the remainder being Turks, Tatars, Tanguts, Cumans, Bulgars, and other of the mixed peoples of central Asia. Nonetheless the audacity and confidence with which the Mongols embarked on these far-flung wars were almost as remarkable as the invariable success of their operations.

In compliance with the wishes of Genghis, as expressed in his *yassa* (will, or law), his vast empire had been apportioned among his sons and their descendants, subject to the overall authority of the *khagan* at Karakorum. Batu, son of Juji (who had predeceased Genghis), was ruler of the region to the north and west of Lake Balkash. Jagatai was given the southwestern region which includes modern Afghanistan, Turkestan, and central Siberia. He and his successors were known as the khans of the Jagatai Mongols. By implication, this realm extended indefinitely to the southwest, as Batu's did to the northwest. Ogadai and his progeny were awarded China and the other lands of east Asia. Tului, the youngest of the four principal heirs, was to have had central Mongolia, the homeland, in accordance with Mongol custom. However, he and his descendants were to have shared Mongolia's precious fighting manpower with the other three khanates.

In 1235 or 1236 Ogadai authorized at least two more major offensive operations, one against Tibet, the other in Europe. The Tibetan expedition was led by Godan, son of Ogadai, and the conquest was completed in 1239.

SUBOTAI
AND THE EUROPEAN EXPEDITION

The European expedition was to be a major Mongol effort, comparable in scope to the war against China. Nominal command was to be exercised by Batu, since this was the part of the world which he had inherited in the will of Genghis Khan. But the actual commander was aging, but still brilliant, Subotai. He was probably the most gifted of all Mongol generals, after Genghis Khan himself, and had been one of the commanders of the momentous reconnaissance that had swept through south Russia fifteen years earlier.

The expedition was ready by late 1237. Subotai and Batu led an army of 150,000 warriors across the frozen Volga River in December 1237. The Mongols spread destruction and death through Russia in 1237 and 1238. Moscow,

Vladimir, and other north Russian principalities were completely destroyed before summer. Subotai then turned south to the steppe region around the Don, to allow his army to rest, regain strength, and prepare for new advances. Apparently his timetable was delayed for a year by a dispute among Batu and the other royal princes who were commanding various hordes (a horde was a force of several *tumens*, roughly equivalent to a modern army corps) of the army. Nonetheless, this additional time gave Subotai opportunity to accumulate still further information about central and western Europe from his spies.

In late November of 1240, after the rivers and marshes of the Ukraine had frozen hard enough to take the weight of Mongol horsemen, Subotai and his army crossed the Dnieper River. On December 6 Kiev was stormed and conquered. Subotai continued westward, his army advancing on a typically broad front in three major columns.

To the north was the horde of Prince Kaidu, three *tumen* strong, protecting the right flank of the main body. Kaidu swept through Lithuania and Poland and on March 3 he destroyed the army of Boleslaus V of Poland at Cracow. He detached a *tumen* to raid along the Baltic coast and with the remainder headed westward into Silesia. On April 9 at Liegnitz he met a mixed army of Germans, Poles, and

Hulagu, the Mongol emperor from 1260 to 1265, the last of the Mongol Empire rulers, is seen here directing the artillery during the siege of Baghdad in 1258.

Teutonic Knights under Prince Henry of Silesia. In a bitterly contested battle the more numerous Europeans were decisively defeated; Henry and most of his knights were killed.

Meanwhile, to the south another horde of three *tumen* under Prince Kadan was to protect the southern flank and advance through Transylvania, into the Danube Valley, and thence into Hungary. In mid-April Kadan and Kaidu joined the main body—under Batu and Subotai—in central Hungary.

Subotai had led the central force across the Carpathians in early April. He had lured the army of King Bela IV of Hungary into battle at the Sajo River on April 11, and had totally destroyed it. The Mongols then seized Pest and spent the rest of the year consolidating their control of Hungary east of the Danube.

Late in 1241 the Mongols were ready to move again. In December the army crossed the frozen Danube. Scouting parties raided into north Italy past Venice and Treviso, and up the Danube toward Vienna. But suddenly the advance halted. Word had come, by the way of the incredibly swift Mongol messenger service, that Ogadai had died on December 11.

The law of Genghis Khan explicitly provided that "after the death of the ruler all offspring of the house of Genghis Khan, wherever they might be, must return to Mongolia to take part in the election of the new *khagan*." Reluctantly Subotai reminded his three princes of their dynastic duty. From the outskirts of trembling Vienna and Venice, the *tumen* countermarched, never to return. Their ebb went through Dalmatia and Serbia, then eastward across northern Bulgaria. They virtually destroyed the kingdoms of Serbia and Bulgaria before they vanished across the lower Danube.

REIGN OF KUYUK

It was not until the summer of 1246 that a *khuraltai* to select a successor to Ogadai assembled at Karakorum. This was mainly because of political maneuvering by Batu and other royal princes who had hopes of being elected. While deliberately stalling in south Russia in 1243 Batu selected Sarai, on the Volga, as the capital of his khanate of the Kipchak, best known to history as the Golden Horde.

At Karakorum, in July, 1246, Kuyuk, son of Ogadai, was chosen as the new *khaghan*. Present during the colorful *khuraltai* was Friar John di Piano Carpini, who had been sent to the Mongol capital by Pope Innocent IV to try to ascertain the intentions of the Mongols in Europe. Carpini learned a great deal about the Mongols, but little of their intentions. He nevertheless recognized that the conquest of Europe was definitely planned.

Kuyuk was apparently torn between completing the conquest of China and continuing the conquest of Europe. The latter project was complicated, however, by Kuyuk's continuing rivalry with Batu. Just as this seemed to be verging upon civil war, in 1248, Kuyuk died.

MAUGU AND THE WAR IN CHINA

Except for the descendants of Ogadai and Jagatai, most of the royal princes thought that Batu should be elected *khagan*. By this time, however, Batu had decided that he preferred the steppes of the Volga to the steppes of Mongolia. He declined the offer, and nominated Maugu—eldest son of Tului—unquestionably one of the most gifted descendants of Genghis Khan. This nomination was confirmed by a *khuraltai* in 1251. Maugu Khan executed several of the sons of Ogadai who had opposed his election. He at once restored the force and vigor to Mongol rule which had been lacking since the death of Genghis, taking seriously the legacy of world conquest.

Maugu decided to place primary emphasis on completing the conquest of Asia, and particularly of China; Europe would be dealt with later. Because the Sung had had the benefit of a lull of nearly ten years to recuperate and reorganize, the task had become more difficult than it would have been earlier. Maugu himself took the field in command, but also placed great responsibility on his younger brother Kublai. Another brother, Hulagu, he sent to Persia to renew the expansion of Mongol control in Southeast Asia. He encouraged Batu to renew Mongol raids into

A close-up of the Kublai Khan and his empress Cl'e-po-erh taken from the center of the hunting scene.

central Europe, but did not send him additional resources. Thus, although Batu's armies raided deep into Poland, Lithuania, and Esthonia, and again overran Serbia and Bulgaria, these were not major offensives such as were being undertaken in Southeast and southwest Asia.

Maugu made some major administrative changes in the khanates which had been established by the will of Genghis. He completely disinherited the surviving sons of Ogadai. He and his brother Kublai were to inherit the lands of east Asia. He also placed a limit on the domains of the successors of Jagatai; these were to end along the Oxus River and the Hindu Kush Mountains, instead of extending indefinitely to the southwest. Southwest Asia was to be the inheritance of Maugu's brother Hulagu, the first of the Ilkhans.

Maugu prosecuted the war in Chin with intensity and skill. His principal assistant was his brother Kublai, who was appointed his viceroy in China. In 1252 and 1253 Kublai conquered Yunnan (then known as Nanchao), possibly accelerating the southward migration of the Tai or Shan people who then inhabited the region. Tonking was then invaded and pacified, the conquest ending with the fall of Hanoi in 1257.

Sung resistance in south China was based upon determined defense of their well-fortified, well-provisioned cities. The Chinese Empire began to crumble, however, under the impact of a series of brilliant campaigns, personally directed by Maugu between 1257 and 1259. However, his sudden death in August of 1259 from dysentery caused another lull in the war.

KUBLAI KHAN AND THE WORLD EMPIRE

The overwhelming choice of the *khuraltai* as Maugu's successor was his equally brilliant younger brother, Kublai. The selection of Kublai was violently opposed, however, by his younger brother, Arik-Buka. This precipitated a civil war, which Kublai won by vigorous action in 1261. For the next few years the new *khagan* devoted his attention to administrative reforms for his vast empire.

Finally, Kublai could turn his full attention again to the war in China (1268). A series of campaigns, distinguished by the skill of the general Bayan (grandson of Subotai) was culminated in 1276 by the capture of the capital city of Hangchow. It took three more years to subdue the outlying provinces. The last action of the war took place in 1279; a naval battle in the Bay of Canton, in which the Sung ships were all destroyed by a Mongol fleet.

Kublai Khan did not share his elder brother's fierce desire to conquer the world. He had prosecuted the war against China with equal determination, but apparently he realized that there was a limit to Mongol capability to consolidate and control conquered territory. It is likely that he recognized that this limit was being approached from an event that occurred during the interregnum after the death of Maugu and before his own accession.

Hulagu, who had been carrying out the conquest of Mesopotamia and Syria with typical Mongol thoroughness and ferocity, had returned to Mongolia upon receiving news of the death of Maugu. This was in compliance with the carefully observed terms of the will of Genghis Khan. While he was gone, in 1260, his deputy was defeated and killed by a larger Mamluk army at the Battle of Ain Jalut, near Nazareth, in Palestine. This was the first significant Mongol defeat in seventy years. The Mamluk had been led by a Turk named Baibars, a former Mongol warrior, who used Mongol tactics.

Neither Kublai nor Hulagu made a serious and intensive effort to avenge the defeat of Ain Jalut. Both devoted their attention mainly to the rounding out of their conquests, suppressing dissidence, and reestablishing law and order. Like their uncle Batu and his successors as khans of the Golden Horde, they limited their offensive activities to occasional raids or limited objective offensives in unconquered neighboring regions. After the failure of two relatively small invasion attempts against Japan (1274 and 1281), Kublai also gave up that project. There was a brief invasion effort on Java in 1292–93, which was partially successful. The Mongols withdrew, however, after the ruler of the island recognized Mongol suzerainty.

Kublai had moved his capital from Karakorum to Peking

The enthronement of Emperor Kublai Khan and his empress

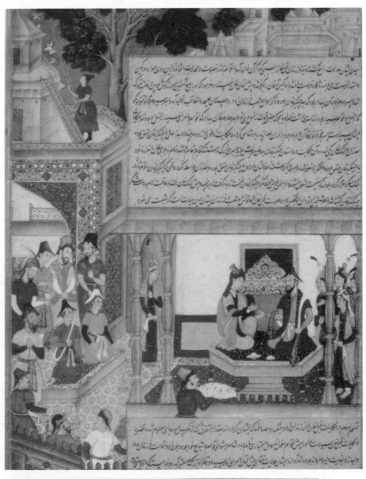

Tamerlane impressed Europe more than any other Asiatic conqueror. Genghis Khan, a century and a half earlier, did not make contact with the Near East or Europe but conquered lands remote from the West, and it was not until after his death that his descendants subdued Russia to the north and Mesopotamia (Iraq) to the south. Tamerlane, on the other hand, overran Persia and Mesopotamia, and subsequently entered Russia and attacked the Kipchaks of the lower Volga valley. He also sacked Moscow. He then turned toward India, which he invaded. Here he passed the limits both of Alexander the Great and of Genghis Khan, the former having halted on the shore of the Beas River, while the latter barely crossed the Indus. Westward, too, Tamerlane took Damascus and weakened the power of the Mamluks, and finally defeated and captured Sultan Bayezid I of Turkey on the field of Angora. No other Asiatic conqueror in history has performed such military feats.

Kublai Khan on a hunting party. Kublai Khan, wearing a white fur, rides a black horse while nine followers, both ladies and gentlemen, amuse themselves with bows and arrows, falcons and dogs.

Batu Khan, the first of the Golden Horde emperors, ruled from 1223 to 1256.

Marco Polo, left, *descending from his carriage, hand on his ceremonial sword, is welcomed at the court of Kublai Khan*, right, *with arm extended for a handshake, in the year 1271.*

Tamerlane on his throne, holding the spear, the symbol of his conquests

Marco Polo

Kublai Khan welcomes Marco Polo and his Venetian merchants.

in 1263. After the Sung Dynasty was destroyed, in 1279, he declared himself emperor of a united China, and established the Yuan Dynasty. Kublai proved himself to be one of the most able and beloved rulers of Chinese history. His death, in 1294, was mourned as sincerely by his Chinese subjects as by the Mongols. He was enough of a Mongol, however, to have left instructions that he was to be buried in a simple grave on the side of Mount Burkan-Kaldun, beside his grandfather, his father, and his elder brother.

Much that the Western world of the thirteenth and fourteenth centuries knew about the Mongols and Asia was the result of the famous missions of the Venetian Polo family in

1262 and later in 1271. Marco Polo was trusted by Kublai Khan, and undertook a number of diplomatic missions for the *khagan* throughout the empire. The story of his travels, the *Book of Marco Polo,* appeared about the year 1299.

DECLINE OF THE YUAN DYNASTY

Kublai's successors were more Chinese than Mongol, and soon lost all influence on the other Mongol lands across Asia. They gradually lost influence in China as well. The reigns of these later Yuan emperors were short and marked by intrigues and rivalries. They were separated from both their Mongolian army and their Chinese subjects, and cared very little about the administration of the country. China was torn by dissension and unrest; bands of thieves raged the country without interference from the weakening armies of the Yuan.

The last of the nine successors of Kublai was driven from China by a peasant Buddhist, Chu Yuen-chang, a leader of one of the robber bands. Chu—who proclaimed himself Emperor Hung Wu, founder of the Ming Dynasty—adopted Mongol military methods. With an army of 250,000 men he pursued the defeated Yuan armies into Mongolia and won a final decisive victory at the Battle of Puir Nor in 1388. Some seventy thousand Mongols were made prisoner, and Karakorum was destroyed.

THE ILKHANS

The defeat at Ain Jalut in 1260 led directly to the first important war between grandsons of Genghis Khan. The Mamluk leader, Baibars, made an alliance with Birkai Khan, brother of Batu and his successor as ruler of the Golden Horde. Birkai had been converted to Islam, and thus was sympathetic to the Mamluk for religious reasons, as well as because of jealousy of his nephew Hulagu. When Hulagu sent an army into Syria to punish Baibars, he was suddenly attacked by Birkai. Hulagu had to turn his army back to the Caucasus to meet this threat. However, Birkai withdrew when Kublai sent thirty thousand troops to aid Hulagu.

This chain of events marked the end of the Mongol expansion in southwest Asia. The successors of Hulagu did not exhibit the austere soldierly qualities of their forebears. They devoted themselves to pleasure and let their provinces be governed by Turkish viceroys. Finally these viceroys seized control, and the Ilkhan Empire fell apart seventy-five years after it had been founded by Hulagu.

THE GOLDEN HORDE

The Golden Horde of Batu had more room for expansion of its territories than any of the other Mongol khanates. Furthermore, the Golden Horde was not directly faced by a powerful enemy, or by an ancient civilization which could absorb it. So this portion of Genghis's empire had the longest and greatest influence on world history.

The court of Batu at Sarai became a prosperous center of commerce under Birkai. Here, as in China, Mongol rule meant free trade and the transport of goods between the west and east, and also the toleration of all religions. But the Mongols remained a nomad people completely at home in the steppes of Russia. They preserved their simplicity along with their power, in part because they mixed with the Turkish tribes of the steppes to become the Tatars of Russia.

But the power of the khans of the Golden Horde slowly declined, particularly as a powerful new state rose in central Russia. The princes of Moscow, vassals and tributaries to the Mongols, took advantage of this weakness to assert independence under Ivan III in 1480.

One cause of the Mongol decline had been a bitter war against Tamerlane (Timur Lenk) during the latter part of the fourteenth century. This Turkish conqueror claimed to be a descendant of Genghis Khan through the family of Jagatai, and he reunited all of Turkestan and the lands of Ilkhans under his rule. In 1391 he invaded Russia and defeated the Golden Horde; he again ravaged the Caucasus and south Russia in 1395.

The effects of this defeat, as well as internal struggles, led to the breakup of the Mongol or Tatar Kingdom in Russia. Three separate khanates—Astrakhan, Kazan, and the Crimea—lasted into the sixteenth century. That of Astrakhan—the Golden Horde itself—was destroyed in 1502 by an alliance of the Crimean Mongols or Tatars, with the Muscovites. The last reigning descendant of Genghis, Shanin Girai, khan of the Crimea, was deposed by the Russians in 1783.

The Mongols, or Tatars, through influence and through intermarriage with other Russian rulers, left a lasting effect on Russia. This Tatar heritage has much to do with Russia's distinctiveness from the nations of central and western Europe.

MONGOLIA IN TRANSITION

RETURN TO THE NOMADIC PATTERNS

By the early fifteenth century the main tribal groupings of the Mongols had begun to stabilize. The most important of these were the Khalkhas, who lived north of the Gobi Desert and the Oirats, who inhabited the Altai region of western Mongolia. These tribes were almost constantly at war with each other or with external neighbors. The strife between the Oirats and the Khalkhas was particularly bitter.

By the middle of the fifteenth century the Oirats were predominant, under the leadership of Esen Tayi Khan, who was able to unite much of Mongolia under his control, and who then continued the Mongol war against the Ming. He was so successful in this, in fact, that in 1449 he defeated and captured the Ming emperor. However, after he was killed in battle four years later, the brief resurgence of Mongolia came to an abrupt halt, and the tribes returned to their traditional disunity.

After nearly two more decades of Oirat-Khalkha con-

flict, another Oirat chieftain, Dayan Khan, a descendant of Genghis Khan, undertook to reunite the Mongols. By the end of the fifteenth century he was the leader of an Oirat confederation inhabiting a vast region of north-central Asia, between the Ural Mountains and Lake Baikal. Soon after this he extended his control eastward to include the remainder of Khalkha Mongolia. They were surrounded by the Turkic descendants of the Jagatai Mongols who occupied the lowlands to the east and west, in the three independent sultanates of Yarkand (modern Chinese Turkestan south of the Tien Shan), tiny Ferghana, and Khwarezm (or Khiva), with capital at Samarkand. Early in the sixteenth century these three khanates were overwhelmed, however, by the Uzbek Turks, who had earlier broken loose from the authority of the Golden Horde. The Uzbeks consolidated their control over Turkestan—the regions now known as Sinkiang province of China and Soviet Central Asia.

After the death of Dayan in 1543 the Uzbek khanate remained relatively stable in central Asia. The eastern Khalkhas and the Oirats disintegrated once more into insignificant and quarrelsome tribal groupings. The Torgut subclan of the Oirats was now perhaps the most vital of the Mongol peoples. They raided frequently across the Urals into the Volga valley, which by now had been completely conquered by the new Muscovite or Russian Empire. Further east the Khalkhas roamed the region north and south of the Gobi; the Ordos and Chahar became loosely grouped in a confederation holding most of the area now known as Inner Mongolia.

Throughout all of this internal bickering among the Mongols, they shared a continuing hostility to the Ming, with the struggle maintained principally by the Khalkhas. Although the title had become almost meaningless, the line of the *khagans* had continued among the Chahar tribe, whose leader was thus the rallying point for the conflict against China.

The war with China was renewed with considerable energy after Altan Khan of the Tümed clan united the Khalkhas. Although not so prominent in history as his predecessor, Dayan, or his successor, Galdan, it appears that Altan Khan was probably the greatest of the Mongol princes in the centuries following the collapse of the Yuan Empire. By 1552 he had also defeated the Oirats, and reunited most of Mongolia. It soon became obvious to Altan that there was nothing to be gained by continuing the war with Ming; the empire of Genghis could never be restored. Accordingly, in 1571 he concluded a treaty with the Ming emperor, ending a struggle that had lasted for almost three centuries, perhaps the longest war in history.

In the remaining eleven years of his life Altan aggressively pushed Mongol power to the south and southwest, and raided extensively into Tibet. The conqueror was in turn conquered by a Buddhist revival in Tibet, and became a fervent convert. In 1577 he proclaimed Buddhism as the state religion of Mongolia.

SQUEEZED BETWEEN RUSSIA AND THE MANCHUS

During the seventeenth century a process began which would, in the following century, completely extinguish the traditional independence of the Mongols as well as that of their Turkish neighbors and kinsmen. This was the steady expansion of czarist Russian from the west, and of Manchu from the east. That the Mongols and Turks, traditionally conquerors, should themselves now be conquered was not due to any decline in their warlike proclivities, but rather to the fact that the evolution of the art of war had progressed beyond the capacity of essentially nomadic peoples. Their economic resources would not permit the production or purchase of muskets and cannon, and their cavalry could not stand up to musketry and artillery.

This process began when most of the area now known as Manchuria was overrun and consolidated by the Manchus. This people was essentially nomadic in origin, being descended from the Juchen who had earlier established the Chin Dynasty. Early in the seventeenth century, under their leader Nurhachi, the Manchus began to press southward into Inner Mongolia.

This westward movement of the Manchu soon involved them in a struggle with the last of the *khaghans*, Ligdan Khan of the Chahar Mongols. Ligdan had been attempting to reestablish Chahar predominance among the khalkhas, and particularly among those tribes inhabiting the region south of the Gobi. These efforts alarmed his neighbors, who called upon Nurhachi for assistance. For several years it appeared that the Manchu conqueror had met his match, because Ligdan possessed some of the military prowess of his ancestors. While he could not prevent the Manchus from gaining control of the territory of the neighboring Ordos Mongols, Ligdan repulsed every Manchu effort to move farther west. After his death in 1634, however, Mongol resistance to the Manchus collapsed in Inner Mongolia. This is the period of the Mongolian national hero, Tsogto Taji, who is said to be the only northern Mongol aristocrat to lead his subjects against the Manchus in defense of the southern Mongols.

Meanwhile, in about 1620 many of the Torguts, westernmost of the Oirat Mongols, began to migrate westward. Possibly the movement was a reaction to the growing truculence of the Dzungar Mongols, the Torguts' neighbors to the south. In any event, the Torguts fought their way through Kirghiz and Kazakh territory, to cross the Embe River. Becoming better known as the Kalmyk tribe, they subsequently settled in the Trans-Volga steppe, raiding Russian settlements on both sides of the river. Finally submitting to Russia in 1646, they maintained autonomy under their own khan. They became an excellent source of light cavalry for the Russians, who later used them in their campaigns against the Crimean Tatars and in central Asia.

The Mongolian interest in Tibet that had been aroused in Altan's campaigns seems to have been transmitted to the Dzungar tribe. This Oriat subclan inhabited a region east of Lake Balkash which extended eastward into northern Sinkiang. They carried out a number of campaigns into Tibet, and by 1636 had established a virtual protectorate over the region. Because of the generally high quality of their leadership at this time, the Dzungars dominated the history of Mongolia for much of the seventeenth century.

Farther east, the religious revival begun by Altan Khan had continued unabated, and was perhaps the greatest single influence on Mongol life and culture during this and succeeding centuries. In 1635 the khan of the Tüshetü tribe proclaimed that his son was the reincarnation of an ancient and respected scholar who had achieved such a state of virtue that he had become known as a buddha. Thus the young Tüshetü prince was a "Living Buddha," or *Jebtsun Damba Khutukhtu*. This was the beginning of a line of Living Buddhas which was to continue unbroken for nearly three centuries; all of the reincarnations of the Jebtsun Damba Khutukhtu were found among the Tüshetü.

By the middle of the seventeenth century the Russian process of exploration and annexation had become very worrisome to all of the Mongols and to the Turks, to the southwest. In 1672, in response to this pressure, Ayuka Khan of the Torgut Mongols raided through western Siberia across the Urals and the Volga, and into Russia. He then made peace with the Russians on terms that enabled him to maintain his lands in relative peace for the remainder of the century.

In the later years of the seventeenth century a new effort toward Mongolian unity was attempted by Galdan (Kaldan) Khan (also known as Bushtu Khan) of the Dzungars. He conquered most of Kashgar, Yarkand, and Khotan from the Kirghiz, and also expanded into Kazakh territory. He then turned eastward, about 1682, intending to conquer the Khalkhas. In 1688 the hard-pressed Khalkhas appealed to the Manchus for aid. The Manchus were more than pleased to respond, and a Chinese-Manchu army marched to help.

By this time the Manchus had conquered all of China and had established the Ching Dynasty. They had become much concerned by the steady Russian eastward expansion. Up until this time the Russians had kept themselves in the high latitudes, carefully avoiding the still-formidable Torguts, who inhabited the region which now comprises central Siberia. By this process the Russians had by midcentury reached the Pacific Ocean and the Amur Valley.

In the period between 1641 and 1652 the Russians slowly conquered the Buryat Mongols, to gain control of the region around Lake Baikal. The Manchus observed with considerable apprehension the growing pressure of Russia on the Turks and Mongols of central Asia. As early as 1653 there were clashes between Manchus and Russians in the Amur valley. In 1660 the Manchus ejected the Russians from the Amur region, only to see them reappear when the Manchus became occupied with internal troubles in south China.

In 1683 a Manchu military expedition began systematic

operations to eject the Russians again. These culminated in 1685 when a small Manchu army marched on the Russian stronghold at Albasin and forced the garrison to surrender. But, when the Manchus withdrew, later that year, another Russian contingent reconstructed the fortifications. The Manchus began to prepare for a more extensive war. It was at this time that the Khalkha Mongols appealed for aid. The Manchus promptly responded, seeing an opportunity to gain control over all of Mongolia as a base for possible war with Russia.

This Chinese move was probably clearly understood by Peter the Great of Russia, who was engaged in serious wars in Europe. He decided that the dispute with China must be settled peacefully. This led to the Treaty of Nerchinsk, in August 1689, in which the Russians agreed to abandon Albasin and the area north of the Amur River. The terms of the Treaty of Nerchinsk, supplemented by the later Treaty of Kyakhta, regulated Russian-Chinese relations for one hundred seventy-five years.

THE END OF INDEPENDENCE

Meanwhile the Manchus had sent a large army into Mongolia to settle the dispute between the Khalkhas and the Dzungars. This led to the calling of a *khuraltai* at Dolonor. There in 1689 most of the Mongol tribes formally accepted Manchu suzerainty in return for protection against the Dzungars.

By this time the Jebtsun Damba Khutukhtu had been forced to flee to escape the advance of Galdan, the Dzungar Khan. After five years of continued raiding by the Dzungars into central Mongolia, Manchu-Chinese emperor K'ang-hsi led eighty thousand troops across Mongolia and in 1696 crushed Galdan near Chao-Modo (Urga, now known as Ulan Bator). The employment of Manchu artillery had a decisive effect. The Dzungar leader fled, but committed suicide next year. This ended Dzungar influence in most of Mongolia, although they retained control of the western regions, and in parts of Sinkiang and Tibet.

Despite the punishment meted out to them at Chao-Modo by K'ang-hsi, twenty years later the Dzungars were again embroiled in war with that formidable emperor. In 1718, Galdan's nephew and heir, Tzewang Rabtan, led his warriors into Tibet to settle a prolonged dispute over the succession to the Dalai Lama. The Dzungars seized Lhasa, imprisoned the incumbent Dalai Lama, and ambushed a Manchu force coming to his aid. Emperor K'ang-hsi retaliated in 1720; two Chinese armies defeated the Dzungars and drove them from Tibet. This was the first war in which Mongol forces made extensive use of musketry; they were not very effective, however, against the larger, better-armed, better-equipped Chinese forces. After the death of the then Dalai Lama, a new Dalai Lama was installed by K'ang-hsi, and a Manchu garrison was left in Lhasa. Meanwhile another Chinese army invaded Dzungaria, to capture Urumchi and Rutfan.

Continuing Dzungar opposition to Chinese policy in Tibet, and frontier depredations in western China, resulted in a series of Chinese punitive expeditions. At first, largely due to poor management, the Chinese were not very successful. However, after reorganization, the Chinese soundly defeated the Dzungars in 1732. This virtually ended the history of independent Mongolia for nearly two centuries.

The Russian and Chinese empires continued their expansions into Inner Asia. They found it expedient in 1727 to delimit the borders between the areas of ancient Mongolia that they had conquered in the previous century. This was done by the commercial Treaty of Kyakhta, which established the border between Outer Mongolia and Siberian Mongolia that is largely unchanged to this day.

In 1755 a serious revolt against Chinese rule broke out among the Oirats in the Ili valley, in Dzungaria. This was promptly and ruthlessly suppressed by General Chao Hui, who seized this opportunity to strengthen Chinese control over western Mongolia, also Oirat territory. It has been estimated that half a million Mongols were slaughtered between 1755 and 1758. As a result, a few years later, in 1771, the Chinese government persuaded part of the Kalmyk tribe to return from Russia to repopulate the region devasted by Chao Hui.

During the next century the Chinese generally neglected most of Mongolia. The southern provinces—Suiyuan, Chahar, and Jehl, known as Inner Mongolia—were in time virtually absorbed into China. The remainder of the region, which became known as Outer Mongolia, was a largely ignored colony. During the late nineteenth century, however, China again became alarmed by Russia's continuing policy of expansion and colonial development in the regions north and west of Outer Mongolia. This increased Chinese colonial attention brought about some economic and social improvement in Outer Mongolia. It also revealed to the Mongolians some possibilities of playing off the two great empires against each other, in order to achieve further progress.

During this period of Chinese-Manchu dominance, Mongolia had become an increasingly theocratic society. Buddhism had relatively early absorbed shamanism, and the result was a unique local religion. The flight of manpower to the ever-expanding monasteries was such that by the late nineteenth century probably one quarter of the male inhabitants of Outer Mongolia were monks. Contributing to the theocratic nature of the society was the increasingly important position of the Jebtsun Damba Khutukhtu as a temporal as well as a religious leader. The Chinese colonial rulers did everything in their power to reduce the influence of the tribal khans, and to make Mongolia completely dependent upon China.

THE SECULAR STRUCTURE

Historical sources refer to a class system among the Mongols as early as the thirteenth century. Traditionally, this was a very simple structure, consisting of two main classes: the nobles, or "white bone" *(tsagan yasun),* and the commoners, or "black bone" *(kara yasun)*. These distinctions were hereditary and were ultimately based on Mongol theories of kinship.

As early as the days of empire, political and other power corresponded to hereditary social rank. Under the system as it was organized until 1402, the *khagan,* in direct descent from Ghenghis, was at the head of the empire, with members of his clan in other important governing positions. Nobles of other tribes and clans held lesser status. Commoners could be divided into such occupational categories as warrior, herdsman, merchant, artisan, cultivator, or slave. In Mongolia proper, the last four categories were overwhelmingly foreigners.

Many elaborations were imposed on the basic framework, however, particularly by the Manchus, who may be said to have come into full power in 1757 when, after defeating the Oirat, the Chinese emperor assumed the long-vacated title of *khagan,* ruler of all Mongolia.

Northern and eastern Mongolia, or Khalkha, at this time, was composed of the same two social classes, the nobility, representing the descendants of Genghis Khan and still holding the chief ruling positions, and the commoners. Politically, it was divided as it had been in 1691 when Manchu suzerainty was accepted, into three *aimaks,* or provinces, each headed by an hereditary khan (the modern form of *khagan*), and leagued together under one of the khans of the senior line. Below each khan and his officials were a variety of hereditary princes who with the assistance of still other nobles ruled the principalities *(khoshuns),* totaling thirty-seven, which composed the *aimaks.* When the Manchus reorganized this administrative structure, the result was that the traditional structure of hereditary power was considerably altered.

First, the Manchus reduced the power and prestige of the khans by making the headship of the *aimak* league an elective post filled by the vote of the assembled *khoshun* princes, the *jasaks.* A khan retained his title and his hereditary social preeminence, but without power it became an increasingly empty honor. The next move of the Manchu emperor was to standardize the *khoshuns* as the basic structural units of society by breaking them up into more and more *khoshuns* and parceling them out to petty princes.

The position of *jasak* remained hereditary, but was subject to confirmation by the emperor. By the end of the nineteenth century a considerable number of appointive, nonhereditary *jasaks* has been created. The social dilution of hereditary prestige and status was furthered by the establishment of six ranks within the princely class, also appointed at the will of Peking.

THE NOBLE CLASS

Despite Manchu tampering, for political motives, with the system of ranks and authority, the Mongolians of the noble classes clung to their traditional, kinship-based relationships. The Khalkha noble families preserved genealogies to prove their claim of direct male descent from the family of Genghis Khan, and registered within them births, deaths, and attainment or loss of political rank and social status. Appointive *jasaks* were looked down upon socially by the Khalkha nobility.

The nobility constituted a small group, estimated in various sources as comprising 7 to 8 percent of the total population of the early twentieth century: thirteen thousand males, or seven hundred families. It may be divided into two subclasses, the upper nobility, composed of princes (noyan), both ruling *(jasak)* and nonruling; and the lower nobility, the *taiji.* Membership in these subclasses was hereditary, and was apparently allocated according to directness of descent from Genghis Khan.

The upper nobility, comprising the members of the male lines of descent from Genghis, are estimated as having numbered two hundred males, of whom only approximately one hundred might be *jasaks.* As well as controlling the leading political positions, this group on the whole was very rich in livestock. Figures available give average holdings of fifteen hundred head, or twenty times that of most commoners.

MODERN MONGOLIA

REVOLUTION AND CHAOS

In 1911 the Republican Revolution of October 10, 1911, overthrew the decadent Ching Dynasty of China. There had been considerable revolutionary ferment in Mongolia in the years before the Revolution, to a large degree encouraged by czarist Russia. Now Russian officials in Siberia provided arms and equipment to Mongolian princes who hoped to gain independence from China in the wake of the Manchu collapse.

On November 18, 1911, Mongolia proclaimed its independence on the basis that its allegiance had been to the Ching Dynasty, and not to China. The Jebtsun Damba Khutukhtu was named Bogdo Khan, or ruler, of Outer Mongolia. An army of twenty thousand troops was created, and Russian officers appeared in Urga to help train and organize the army. The new government in China refused to recognize Mongolian independence, but was too busy with internal discord in China to do anything about enforcing its sovereignty. Meanwhile Russia was moving rapidly to take advantage of the situation. On November 3, 1912, a Russian-Mongolian treaty was signed in Urga, affirming Mongolia's separation from China, but not recognizing Mongolian independence. The treaty, in fact, created a Russian protectorate over Outer Mongolia.

Although additional Russian-Mongolian treaties were signed in 1913, and again in 1915, Russia's involvement in World War I reduced the attention that the czar's government could pay to Mongolia. This situation seemed to offer an opportunity in Mongolia to the new power in northeast Asia: Japan. When the Russian revolution broke out, Japanese interest was further encouraged. At the same time, the various warlord rulers of northern China saw in the Russian revolution an opportunity to reassert Chinese sovereignty over Mongolia, and also to prevent further Japanese penetration into the continent.

The Mongolian government of the Living Buddha was shocked by the outbreak of Russian revolution, and at first refused to recognize the new Bolshevik government. While the Mongols now completely isolated from the outside world, were wondering what they should do, the Chinese began to move in. In October 1919 a small Chinese army occupied Urga, and received an acknowledgement of Chinese sovereignty from the Mongolian government. The new Mongol army was disarmed and disbanded.

Soon, however, the tides of the Russian civil war began to lap into Mongolia from the north. In October 1920 the White Russian troops of Baron Roman von Ungern-Sternberg moved into Mongolian territory from Siberia. On February 3, 1921, Ungern-Sternberg drove the Chinese out of Urga and occupied the city. At first the White Russians were hailed as deliverers by the Mongolians, but soon the repressive policies of the Mad Baron, as Ungern-Sternberg was called, aroused popular opposition. During the next several months he instituted a reign of terror across much of Mongolia.

NATIONALISM AND COMMUNISM

The Chinese and White Russian invasions greatly stimulated the growing spirit of Mongolian nationalism. Two nationalist revolutionary parties had been established in 1919, one under Sukhe Bator and Danzan Khorlo, the other headed by Khorloghiyin Choibalsan. On the advice of representatives of the Moscow Comintern, the two parties merged in 1920, in order to be able to present a strong and united nationalistic front to the foreign invaders. The Jebtsun Damba Khutukhtu gave his encouragement and support to the revolutionary leaders, and in his name they appealed to Moscow for more assistance.

In Siberia the Japanese were pressing ahead with their efforts to take advantage of the chaos of the Russian revolution. Nominally as part of an Allied Expeditionary Force intervening in eastern Siberia to facilitate the evacuation of the Czech legion, a large Japanese force had taken over much of the Trans-Siberian Railway between Vladivostok and Lake Baikal. Japanese funds were provided to Ungern-Sternberg and the other White Russian dissidents, in order to prevent the Soviet government from reestablishing control in Eastern Siberia or from obtaining too much influence in Mongolia. The Japanese efforts were to a large degree thwarted, however, by the strictly neutral attitude taken by the American elements of the Allied Expeditionary Force, and slowly the Red Russians established control over Siberia.

The improved Communist position in Siberia enabled Moscow to give some response to the appeals of the Mongolian nationalists. On March 13, 1921, a Revolution-

ary Provisional Government of Mongolia was established at Kyakhta, just inside Siberia from Mongolia. Here a joint Russian-Mongolian military force was established. The Mongolian contingent, under Sukhe Bator, was a very small proportion of the assembling army.

In early June, Red troops, together with Sukhe Bator's small Mongolian force, defeated Ungern-Sternberg's forces at the border town of Altan Bulak. Moscow apologized to Peking for this violation of the Chinese border. Yet the continued existence of the Baron and his scattered troops in Mongolia, although no threat to Russia, gave the Bolsheviks an excuse for the reestablishment of Russian power in Outer Mongolia. On July 3, a joint Russian-Mongolian army invaded Mongolia and marched on Urga. On July 6, the capital city was occupied. Ungern-Sternberg was soon captured and executed. The Communist victors established a new national government at Urga, with the Jebtsun Damba Khutukhtu as the nominal head of state but actual direction under a monk named Bodo, who in turn was controlled by the three revolutionary leaders. The government was maintained in power by the Soviet troops, who virtually occupied the country.

On November 26, 1924, The Mongolian People's Republic was proclaimed as an independent state, with a new constitution on the Soviet model.

THE ROYAL SOVEREIGNS OF THE EMPIRE OF MONGOLIA

Reign	Title	Ruler
MONGOL EMPIRE		
1206–1227	Khan	Genghis Khan
Sons of Genghis Khan		
1227–1232	Khan	Tului (Tule)
1227–1229	Khan	Jagatai
1229–1241	Khan	Ogadai and Juji
1241–1255	Khan	Batu Khan
1246–1248	Khan	Kuyuk
1248–1248	Khan	Kaidu
1251–1259	Khan	Maugu Khan
1259–1294	Khan	Kublai Khan
1260–1265	Khan	Hulagu
GOLDEN HORDE		
1223–1256	Khan	Batu Khan
1257–1267	Khan	Birkai
1267–1280	Khan	Mangu
1280–1312	Khan	Toktai
1313–1340	Khan	Uzbek
1340–1357	Khan	Janibeg
1357–1369	Khan	Berdibek
1370–1381	Khan	Mamai
1381–1395	Khan	Taktamish
1395–1405	Khan	Tamerlane (Timur Lenk)
1921—Outer Mongolia—remained under Russian control		
1947—Inner Mongolia—remained under Chinese control		
1920–1924	Khan	Bogdo Gegen Khan (Eighth Jebtsun Damba Khutukhtu)
1924—Mongolia became a republic		

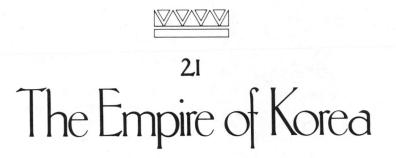

21

The Empire of Korea

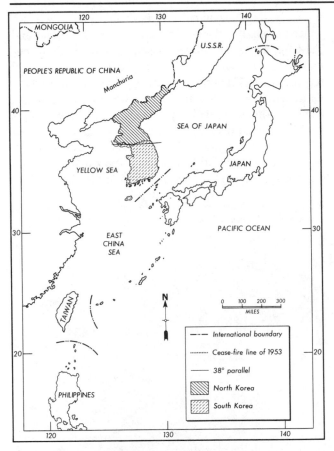

Korea in its geographical setting

According to a legend, Korea was founded in 2333 B.C. by a mythical figure named Tan'gun in what is now the lower Taedong River basin in the northwestern region of the peninsula. This myth was popularized after the twelfth century A.D., especially in times of foreign invasions, to foster the development of national solidarity. The legend is dismissed as a fairy tale in North Korea; the myth is regarded as an important national heritage in South Korea (Republic of Korea), where the government has adopted 2333 B.C. as the year of Korea's birth. Another legend

given some substance by several Chinese chronicles states that a Chinese prince named Chi-tzu, or Kija in Korean, established the country around 1123 B.C. after the decline of Tan'gun Korea. This account, however, is disputed by nearly all Korean historians.

The earliest Korean peoples are believed to have been migrants and invaders from present-day Manchuria, northern China, and Mongolia of either Tungusic or Mongoloid origin; their language was probably related to the Altaic family. Neolithic remains found in all parts of the peninsula indicate that the earliest settlers had, by the third millennium B.C., moved into the country along the northwestern coastal lowlands as well as into the Tumen River valley in the extreme northeast. Initially subsisting as fishermen, the early inhabitants of the peninsula later moved inland and took up hunting and pastoral pursuits. They are believed to have been divided into large extended kin groups, possibly prototypes of the clans that were to become an integral part of Korean social organization. They most likely practiced the shamanism common to the tribal groups of northeast Asia, a belief system that centers on worship of nature of ancestral spirits. This pattern too persisted through the centuries.

Ancient Korea, known as *Choson* (literally, the Land of the Morning Freshness), developed into a league of tribal groups centered in the northwestern part of the peninsula around the fourth century B.C. By this time agriculture and animal husbandry had become more important than hunting and gathering. In about the third century B.C. an indigenous Han tribal family ruled in the lower Taedong River region. In 194 B.C. Wiman, a tribal chieftain of either Korean or Chinese origin, overthrew the Han family and established the kingdom known as Wiman Choson. The deposed family migrated south to the Han River basin, then controlled by a tribe called Chin. The Han family regained power shortly thereafter, and the three major tribal powers—Ma Han, Chin Han, and Pyon Han, which ruled the southern half of the peninsula before the rise of the Three Kingdoms—were all named after the Han family.

King T'aejo (Yi Songgye), founder of the Choson (or Yi) Dynasty. He ruled from 1392 until his death in 1399.

In 108 B.C. Emperor Wu Ti of the Chinese Han Dynasty destroyed Wiman Choson and established four colonies in the northern half of Korea, of which the most important was Lolang (Nangyang in Korean), roughly coterminous with the present-day P'yongan provinces in North Korea. As the political, cultural, and trade center of Chinese colonists, Lolang left an enduring cultural imprint on Korean society. Its officials, scholars, and merchants introduced metal and bronze culture, their form of writing, and early Chinese classics. The brilliance of the Lolang culture is demonstrated by a large number of material remains excavated in the vicinity of modern P'yongyang.

Chinese rule was not welcomed by the indigenous tribes. By 75 B.C. all but one of the colonies had to be abandoned because of local resistance and revolts. Lolang remained the only Chinese outpost until it was destroyed in the early fourth century A.D.

THE THREE KINGDOMS

From the late fourth century A.D. to the mid-seventh century A.D., three Korean kingdoms competed for hegemony; Koguryo in the north, Paekche in the southwest, and Silla in the southeast. Koguryo, the first to emerge, originated in the Yalu River basin around 50 B.C. Founded by a group from the Tungusic Puyo tribes of northern Manchuria, it conquered Lolang in A.D. 313 and ruled much of the area

north of the Han River and a substantial portion of southern Manchuria.

The Koguryo people were culturally advanced; they were also warlike, frequently fighting off hostile, aggressive tribes north and northwest of the Yalu River. One of the most celebrated wars in Korean history, for example, took place in 612 when an invading Chinese army of more than one million was crushed by the Koguryo army of three hundred thousand in a series of battles at Liao-tung ch'eng (present-day Liao-yang, southwest of Mukden in Manchuria), at P'yongyang, and along the Ch'ongch'on River. According to Korean chronicles, only twenty-seven hundred Chinese survived the battles. Ulchimundok, commanding general of the Koguryo army, is honored throughout Korea.

Under a branch of the Puyo tribes from the north, the kingdom of Paekche developed south of the Han River in the early fourth century A.D. Paekche culture was advanced, strongly influenced by its contacts with Lolang and Tai-fang, a Chinese colony formed early in the third century south of Lolang in order to pacify the increasingly rebellious anti-Chinese local tribes. The new colony was destroyed shortly after the fall of Lolang in the fourth century. Although relatively affluent, Paekche was troubled by internal disunity and frequently had to ally itself with its eastern neighbor, Silla, and sometimes with Japan in order to counter warlike Koguryo. The kingdom of Silla had emerged in the late fourth century to the east of Paek-

A gold crown which was a headdress for the kings of the old Silla Dynasty, was discovered recently in a royal tomb in Kyongju, Korea.

che. It was the least developed of the Three Kingdoms, at least in part because of its early isolation from Chinese influences. It was continually harassed by Japanese pirates, by Koguryo, and by its sometime ally, Paekche.

As they progressed into statehood, each of the Three Kingdoms developed institutions of centralized power and authority. These included both the strengthened power of their kings and a hierarchical class of nobility, drawn from former tribal chiefs. In Silla political and military leaders came from an elite circle of five hundred to one thousand youths chosen exclusively from the nobility; their ability as ministers and generals proved to be crucial during Silla's rise to supremacy. Inspired by Confucian as well as Buddhist precepts, this leadership corps stressed five virtues: loyalty to the king, filial piety, sincere friendship, no retreat in battles, and no unnecessary killing.

Buddhism and Confucianism, both from China, were introduced to Koguryo in 372 and, subsequently, Paekche and Silla. As vehicles for the transmission of Chinese culture, they were to influence Korean society in the ensuing centuries. Buddhism spread more rapidly than Confucianism. Korean rulers actively aided its propagation, believing—as did Chinese rulers—that Buddhism exerts magical influences in bringing about prosperity and in repelling evils. Stressing tolerance, harmony, and secular rather than transcendental and speculative matters, Buddhism was able to win many people by offering colorful and awe-inspiring features that had been lacking in the traditional spiritworshiping cults.

Confucianism, a philosophy developed by Confucius (551–479 B.C.), was less popularly appreciated because of its exclusive identification with the ruling literati. The philosophy spread through a Chinese-style academy that was founded in Koguryo in 372 to teach Chinese classics and Confucian scriptures. During the fourth century A.D. scholars from Paekche were responsible for the transmission of important Confucianist texts to Japan, as they were later, during the sixth century, for passing Buddhism on to Japan.

The kingdom of Silla, allied with the T'ang Dynasty of China, ultimately conquered Paekche in 660 and Koguryo in 668. This alliance proved costly because T'ang was quick to annex Koguryo's territory in southern Manchuria and establish a garrison in P'yongyang. Aroused further by T'ang's other maneuvers to assert authority over the defeated Paekche, Silla waged war against T'ang expeditionary forces and in 676 forced them to retreat north of the Taedong River. Establishing itself south of the river and paying tribute to China, Silla was recognized by China as a self-governing state.

UNIFIED SILLA (676–935)

Korea emerged as a unified political entity in 676 under the domination of the Silla Kingdom. The century that followed is usually described as a golden age of artistic and

The Nojong Spring site in Kyongju is, according to legend, the place where King Hyokkose-Wang, the founder of the Silla Dynasty, was born, hatched from an egg found at this well.

cultural achievement, as the diminished threat of invasion from the north permitted Korean scholars to travel to China and to return bringing with them the elements of advanced Chinese culture.

The country was ruled by a king and hereditary nobles, whose status and function were determined solely by birth and legitimized by a highly rigid system of rank classification. Under the system only the Kim families of the first rank were entitled to the throne. The administrative structure was organized mainly on the Chinese model, and Silla was divided into nine provinces, the northern territorial limits being marked by the Taedong River. To ensure compliance with central authority, each provincial lord was required to send a hostage to the capital, Kyongju, fifty-five miles northwest of present-day Pusan.

After a decline of central authority that began in the mid-eighth century, the royal court attempted to regain its authority and to improve administrative efficiency by introducing a new system for recruiting talented people. The court adopted the Chinese examination system, knowing that by the eighth century in China the new system had blossomed into an effective means for providing able leaders. The Chinese system, however, was not well-received by many important families whose privileged position depended on hereditary and family connections.

Despite these changes, Silla continued to decline and at the beginning of the ninth century was plagued by mounting peasant insurrection and outlawry. Various landlords impoverished the peasantry, and many peasants were forced to sell themselves into slavery in order to avoid starvation, most particularly in the springtime, when provisions ran critically short.

The Silla society was basically a three-tiered structure. At the top were the kings, aristocrats, provincial lords, senior civil and military officials, and Buddhist monks, many of whom were also scholars. The middle tier included the peasants, merchants, and craftsmen; at the bottom were the outcastes (*ch'ŏnmin;* literally, despised people). The outcastes included slaves and their offspring, prisoners of war, criminals and their families, and individuals convicted

Tomb of King Munjon (1450–52) of the Yi Dynasty

of treason or charged with rebellion. In some instances a whole village or a group of villages was branded as disaffected and was discriminated against. The outcastes were required to maintain segregated residential areas. Silla's social stratification was inherited by succeeding dynasties and grew more rigid as centuries passed.

The study of Chinese classics was stimulated after the establishment of a national college in 682. This, in turn, led to the invention of a script by Solch'ong, one of the most honored Confucian-Buddhist scholars in the literary history of Korea. The script, called *idu*, was developed in the late seventh century, using Chinese characters for the approximate phonetic value to indicate participles and verbal endings in the spoken Korean language. Used mainly by monks, who were also the largest literate segment of Silla society, *idu* contributed to the development of a native folklore literature *(hyangga). Idu* also inspired the invention of Korea's first phonetic alphabet many centuries later.

The foreign relations of Silla were predominantly cultural and commercial. Each year several hundred monks and lay students studied in China, and some had traveled as far as India. Silla traders carried on a thriving maritime trade with China and Japan and maintained a number of settlements along the eastern coast of China. It was probably through such seafaring activity that Silla first became known to the Arab geographer ibn Khurdadhbih who, in the mid-ninth century, correctly recorded the location of "al-Shila."

Five tombs in one location—Kyongju: Silla monarchs, King Saji (479–500), his queen consort, King Namhae, King Yurye (A.D. 57–80), and King Pasa

KORYO DYNASTY (935–1392)

Koryo, a shortened version of Koguryo, from which the English name of the country is derived, was established by a general, Wang Kon, during the last days of Unified Silla. The new state was regarded by its founders as a successor to Silla. To extend governmental authority uniformly throughout the country, four regional capitals were created—the central capital at Kaesong, the eastern capital at Kyongju, the northern capital at P'yongyang, and the southern capital at Seoul. Of these, Kaesong (known variously as Kaeju, Song'ak, and Songdo) was the most important.

The governmental structure remained along Chinese lines, and officials were chosen through highly rigorous civil service examinations. The bureaucracy was divided into two broad categories, civil and military, forming what was then known as *yangban* (literally, two groups). The civilian officials were more highly regarded than their military counterparts because many of the military officials, coming from the commoner class *(sangmin),* lacked the scholarly qualifications held to be essential to the Confucian ideal of enlightened rule.

The state continued to own all lands, the historic foundations of political and financial stability. Private ownership was not recognized. Under an elaborate system of distribution, designed to check the concentration of lands in the hands of a few great families, the government assigned farmlands to its various departments, the royal household, temples, monasteries, and public officials, including certain meritorious subjects who had helped to found the dynasty.

Two centuries of relative calm were disrupted by the gradual ascendancy of aristocrats who, by means of intermarriage with the royal line, had gained important powers in the government. Through shifting matrimonial alliances they undermined the authority of kingship and precipitated incessant court intrigue. The resulting chaos at the court led to a military seizure of power in 1170.

The takeover was led by General Chong Chung-bu, who had been biding his time after a humiliating incident in which his whiskers were scorched by a civilian official. Because of social prejudices against the military, General Chong had been unable to demand an apology. During and after his assumption of power, however, he ordered a wholesale massacre of ranking civil officials.

The reason for the coup, however, went beyond the apparent personal vengeance of General Chong. As early as 1014 a group of officers had publicly voiced their dissatisfaction with the social and political discrimination against the military—treasonable conduct in those days of civilian supremacy.

The coup was followed by two decades of rebellions by peasants and slaves and by a breakdown of the old political and social order. Army officers reduced the monarch to the position of a puppet, and many aspiring commoners and lowborn persons managed to rise to high government positions. Political anarchy hastened a disintegration of the landholding system, resulting in the steady, illegal transfer of public lands to private estates. Individuals and groups aspiring to power, including many Buddhist monasteries, built private armies to protect their holdings. State revenues declined, and the government found itself defenseless against foreign invasions.

The seal of the Yi Chosun emperor

Tombstone of King Kwanggaet'o-Wang (reigned 391–412), nineteenth king of Koguryo Dynasty.

Tomb of King Munmu (reigned 661–81) of the Silla Dynasty

The tombs of King Sejo (1417–68) and his consort, Queen Chonghui of the Yi Dynasty

MONGOL INVASIONS

The collapse of the T'ang Dynasty in China forced Koryo to contend with powerful tribes from the north without any Chinese help. The last one hundred and sixty years of the kingdom were especially turbulent, punctuated by waves of Mongol invasions that laid waste large areas of the country. After nearly thirty years of resistance, Koryo capitulated to the Mongols in 1259 because its economic resources had been systematically destroyed by the invaders and its manpower was critically depleted. In 1254 alone about 206,000

Korean male captives were said to have been carried off by the Mongols.

In 1259 the northern part of the country was incorporated into the Mongol Empire, soon to be known as Yuan (1271–1368); the Koryo royal line became a branch of the Mongol ruling family through intermarriage between its kings and Mongol princesses. The crown princes of Koryo were obliged to reside in Peking, the capital of Yuan, as hostages, and in time the customs and language of the Mongols became part of the Koryo court. Koryo was required to pay tribute, including large numbers of virgins, and was subjected to additional hardships after 1274 as the result of heavy burdens imposed by the Mongols in their two unsuccessful attempts to invade Japan in 1274 and 1281. On both occasions Koryo expended a large part of its treasury on ships and manpower.

Koryo regained national freedom in 1368 when Yuan was succeeded by the Chinese Ming Dynasty (1368–1644).

King Sejong composed this poem for his deceased consort, Queen Sohon, in 1447 and distributed it throughout Korea. It is still widely reprinted.

The Pine Tree of Chong, a national monument, is by legend reported to have been given court rank by King Sejong (1418–50) because it lifted its branches every time he passed by on the road beneath it.

For a while the fate of Koryo was undecided as its ruling officials split into two rival factions, one favoring continued vassal ties with the Mongols and the other advocating a pro-Ming policy. The issue was resolved in 1388 when the pro-Ming group, led by General Yi Songgye, seized control of the government. In 1390 and 1391 he destroyed all land registers, confiscated all private estates, and instituted a new landholding system. The economic backbone of leading Koryo families was effectively broken.

CHOSON (YI) DYNASTY (1392–1910)

In 1392 General Yi Songgye ascended the throne and soon moved his capital from Kaesong to Seoul, then called Hanyang. The Yi Dynasty also adopted the ancient name of Choson, apparently to claim antiquity as well as continuity for the Korean people.

The new dynasty adopted Confucianism as the official state doctrine, promoted Confucian scholarship, and reformed the governmental system. Early in the fifteenth century King Sejong—the greatest monarch of the five-hundred-year dynasty—recovered the northwestern and northeastern fringes of the peninsula south of the Yalu and Tumen rivers, the territories previously lost to China in the latter half of the seventh century A.D. The king divided the country into eight provinces: Kyonggi, Ch'ungch'ong, Cholla, Kyongsang, Kangwon, Hwanghae, P'yongan, and Hamggyong.

The Yi society was even more rigidly stratified than that of Koryo. At the top were the royal family and members of the *yangban,* the civil and military bureaucracy; as a rule, the civil officials enjoyed greater social prestige than the military. The monks, the favored group under previous dynasties, were no longer held in high regard, partly because of their own moral degeneration and partly because of the pro-Confucian policy of the Choson Dynasty. From 1456 onward the monks were forbidden to enter Seoul because of their alleged subversive potentiality; this restriction was lifted only in 1895, partially as a result of mounting reformist sentiments.

The most notable intellectual achievement of the dynasty was the invention in 1443 of a Korean phonetic vernacular writing system. The public was slow to accept the new system because the ruling class of scholar-officials continued to favor the traditional Chinese written language and ridiculed the new as fit only for persons of little education, women, and commoners. Efforts to link the two writing systems culminated in the mixed use of both Chinese characters and native alphabet for the first time in 1886.

PATTERNS OF POLITICS

The politics of the Choson Dynasty, especially after the fifteenth century, were characterized by rampant factional strife. Political competition was organized around a faction brought together by kinship, by the commonality of regional and school affiliation, or by teacher-disciple relationships. Factionalism became deeply rooted in Korean society, and its residual effect persisted well into the mid-twentieth century.

Two factors contributed to the growth of factional strife. The first was the institution of a new landholding system in the mid-fifteenth century that prevented newer government officials from being granted lands they could have expected

The tombs of two Yi kings, Kojong and Sunjo (Sunjojk) (1800–34), with the traditional animals and other figures lining the entrance path

The tomb of King Honjong (1817–49) of the Yi Dynasty

to receive under the old system. This established a natural division between senior officials with vested interest and junior officials who were discontented with their inferior position. The second factor related to the limited number of government positions available. Since Confucian ethics deemed civil service the only appropriate occupation for *yangban*, those unable to secure official positions were left to plot and intrigue among themselves or to found private Confucian academies that often became centers of dissident political activity.

The triumph of one faction ultimately led to sweeping purges of rivals through execution, dismissal, or banishment to such undesirable areas as the northwestern, northeastern, and southwestern fringes of the peninsula.

Moreover, the localities of purged officials were usually branded as disaffected and were politically discriminated against for generations. The families of these officials were similarly subjected to political discrimination. Because of the Confucian exhortations to filial piety and to upholding the family name, feuding was invariably handed down along family or clan lines.

Factionalism thus became socially and politically institutionalized during the Choson Dynasty. Even at the height of the Japanese invasions in the late sixteenth century, political leaders at all levels of society were unable to unite effectively across factional lines. Eventually, the practice of recruiting officials through the examination system was eroded by favoritism and nepotism.

The ceiling decoration in the Kunjongjon building

A tombstone of King Muryol-Wang, the last king of the Silla Dynasty, who ruled from 654 to 661. It is located in Kyongju.

The main entrance to the Toksu Palace grounds in downtown Seoul

The main audience room (Injongjon) of the king at the Changdok Palace of the Yi Dynasty

The pond at Kyongbok Palace

The Toksu Palace grounds in Seoul

The throne building (Kunjongjon) on the Kyongbok Palace grounds in Seoul, Korea. Royal palaces and castles from the various dynasties are in evidence throughout Korea.

The throne room in the Injongjon

JAPANESE AND MANCHU INVASIONS

Korea's leadership was divided and its military forces demoralized and defenseless against the Japanese invasions of 1592 and 1598. The attacks, both directed by the Japanese general Toyotomi Hideyoshi, were the first steps in his efforts to conquer China, efforts that ended with his death in 1598. The military operations devastated nearly the whole peninsula and were followed by recurrences of famines, epidemics, and peasant revolts. Admiral Yi Sun-sin, who became one of the country's most celebrated heroes during the war against the Japanese, invented the world's first iron-plated, turtle-shaped warship. The admiral is credited with having destroyed much of the Japanese fleet in 1592 and cut off its supply lines with such warships. Posthumously awarded the honorary title of *Ch'ungmu* (Loyalty-Chivalry), the admiral is honored throughout Korea.

Korea had scarcely begun to recover from the disasters when the Manchus overran the country in 1627 and 1637, causing further depletion of manpower and economic resources. The Choson Dynasty became a vassal state of the new Ching Dynasty of China, which was founded by the Manchus in 1644.

THE OPENING OF KOREA

Alarmed by the increasing number of foreign ships appearing in its waters, Korea adopted a policy of isolation from the non-Chinese world. Debilitated earlier by foreign invasions, it had neither the strength to resist external pressure nor the courage to initiate internal reforms.

SOCIAL, CULTURAL, AND ECONOMIC CONDITIONS

Early in the eighteenth century, nearly one hundred and thirty years after the first Japanese invasion, the country had not yet fully recovered from the devastations wrought by the Japanese and Manchus. The amount of taxable land under effective state control was still less than half of the preinvasion level. Destruction of land registers during the invasions had enabled landowning officials to transfer public land illegally to their estates. The consequent decline in state revenue had to be supplemented by harsh taxation schedules. Many peasants left their lands, some moving to the interior mountains for slash-and-burn farming, others migrating to Manchuria across the Tumen River in the extreme northeastern corner of the peninsula, and still others joining gangs of bandits. The government's ineptness in mitigating the grievances of the people resulted in frequent local insurrections.

The social and economic depression of the seventeenth and eighteenth centuries fostered the rise of a new intellectual movement of advocating that human knowledge be put to practical use. Pioneered by a Confucian scholar-official named Yi Su-kwang (1563–1628), the new movement—soon to be called *Silhak* (practical learning)—was partly inspired by his firsthand knowledge of occidental

Yi Ha-ung, father of King
Konjong

Emperor Kojong entered the
throne in 1864, reigned for
forty-three years, but had to
abdicate in 1907, taking the
blame for the decision to send a
secret mission to the International
Peace Conference in the Hague in
1907. The mission met with the
displeasure of the Japanese. His
successor, Emperor Sunjong, the
last monarch of Korea, reigned
until 1910.

Syngman Rhee takes the oath of
office to become the first
president of the Republic of
Korea.

Public procession of Emperor Kojong

Emperor Kojong (seated) with
his son, Sunjong

Queen Min, wife of Emperor
Kojong

sciences that he had acquired while on official visits to Peking.

The Silhak movement, brought to maturity by Chong Yak-yong (1762–1838), was in effect an antiestablishmentarian protest against sterility and formalism of neo-Confucian orthodoxy, a protest undertaken first by early Ching scholars. It was supported by a group of discontented scholars, lower officials, ex-officials, and some commoners. Although the movement had little political impact, its followers contributed a number of pioneering studies in medicine, geography, mineralogy, agriculture, botany, and mapmaking. Several encyclopedias dealing with these subjects were also written by Silhak scholars.

The germination of Silhak thought was accompanied by and, in turn, aided the spread of Roman Catholicism, which had reached the country early in the seventeenth century through the Jesuit mission in China. Along with occidental knowledge, the new religion was associated with what was then known as Sŏhak (Western learning). Roman Catholicism was accepted by a limited number of reformist Silhak scholars and by many socially oppressed commoners and lowborn persons. It was refected by the yangban as heretical and subversive. The Christian disapproval of the Confucian customs of ancestor worship was especially singled out as endangering the very fabric of the family system and hence of society. A government ban on the Christian movement in 1786 was followed by ruthless and systematic persecutions.

FOREIGN RIVALRIES
AND INTERNAL DISUNITY

The first half of the nineteenth century witnessed an increasing number of foreign vessels seeking trade. As a dependent state of China, however, Korea was unprepared to conduct foreign relations independently. The government sought refuge in its policy of seclusion after the First Opium War (1839–42) because it was shocked by the spectacle of the imperialist exploitation of China, the traditional protector and the fountainhead of civilization. Internally, Christians were persecuted; in 1866 some thirteen thousand Roman Catholic converts were executed.

The Japanese were the first to succeed in penetrating Korea's isolation. After warlike provocation in 1875 and the failure of China to come to Korea's aid, the Japanese forced an unequal treaty on Korea in February 1876, giving

Japanese nationals extraterritorial rights and opening three Korean ports to Japanese trade.

Confronted with the impending danger of losing its traditional vassal state, China sought to counter Japan by widening Korea's external relations and by playing off one occidental power against another. In 1882, through China's good offices, Korea signed a treaty of friendship and commerce with the United States; in 1883 it sent the first diplomatic mission to Washington. The treaty culminated almost two decades of American efforts to establish trade relations with the country; in 1866 an armed American merchant vessel had cruised up the Taedong River as far as P'yongyang, defying the Korean ban on trade with foreign states other than China. When it had refused to withdraw, the vessel had been attacked and set on fire and, according to Korean chronicles, its crew members were killed. Korea also concluded treaties with Great Britain and Germany in 1883, Italy and Russia in 1884, and France in 1886. Each was accompanied by a letter from the Korean king enunciating his country's dependency on China.

Despite Chinese attempts at counteraction, by the mid-1890s Japan had emerged as the most influential foreign power in Korea. In 1893 Japan accounted for 91 percent of Korea's annual export trade and over 50 percent of its imports. Moreover, although alarmed by Japan's aggressiveness, a growing number of Korean reformists became inspired by their neighbor's successful modernizing experiences.

Internally, the Korean court was divided into three major factions: pro-Chinese, pro-Japanese, and pro-Russian, the last two being more reformist than the first. The shifting political fortunes of these factions were determined in part by the ebb and flow of foreign influences in the country. The intensity of internal struggles and of foreign rivalries was indicated by the turbulent cabinet changes that occurred between 1876 and 1910. Thus, the reformist cabinet in power from 1876 to 1882, inclined to follow Japan's lead in modernization, was succeeded by the prince regent's isolationist leadership, June–July 1882; a pro-Chinese cabinet, July 1882–October 1884; a three-day pro-Japanese cabinet in October 1884; a pro-Chinese cabinet, October 1884–June 1894; a pro-Japanese cabinet, June 1894-June 1895; pro-Chinese and pro-Russian coalitions, June–August 1895; a pro-Japanese cabinet, August 1895–February 1896; a pro-Russian cabinet, February 1896–February 1904; and a pro-Japanese cabinet, March 1904-August 1910.

In 1885, in an attempt to exclude all foreign influences from the country, the German consul general in Seoul proposed a plan for the permanent neutralization of Korea. Under foreign pressures, however, the plan was rejected by the Korean court.

TONGHAK REBELLION AND THE REFORM OF 1894

The internal and external tensions, especially after the

Palace favorites of Emperor Sunjong

A royal portrait. Left to right: *Crown Prince Sunjong, King Kojong, and Queen Min.*

Emperor Sunjong's funeral procession in 1926. His death marked the end of a very long reign of monarchs for Korea.

mid-nineteenth century, gave rise to an indigenous social and religious movement inspired by Buddhism, Confucianism, Taoism, and even Roman Catholicism. Founded in 1860, *Tonghak* (Eastern learning), as it was then called in distinction to Sohak, was critical of the neo-Confucian social and political order and was antigovernmental as well as antiforeign. Although it was suppressed by authorities because of its reformist thrust, Tonghak gained popular support, mainly from the socially oppressed, impoverished peasants and some discontented scholars.

The Tonghak Rebellion of 1894, which is alleged by North Korea to be the greatest struggle in the history of the Korean peasants' movement, began in January as a minor peasant insurrection and soon spread beyond the government's ability to suppress it. At the government's request, China dispatched troops to aid in the repression of the rebellion; this move precipitated the intervention of Japanese forces, culminating in mid-1894 in the Sino-Japanese war (1894–95), which was fought entirely on Korean soil, despite the fact that the rebels had voluntarily laid down their arms in an attempt to avert such an occurrence. The victorious Japanese formally established their hegemony over Korea in the Treaty of Shimonoseki in 1895 and dictated to the Korean government a wide-ranging series of reforms. Westernization was to be accelerated, and a Western-style cabinet was adopted along with several other governmental reforms. Civil service examinations were discontinued. Economic innovations were introduced, including new taxation and monetary measures. The class structure was legally abolished, as was slavery.

These sweeping reforms were legitimized by a fourteen-point governmental program promulgated by the king in January 1895, partly as a result of Japanese instigation. Sometimes referred to as Korea's first constitution, the fourteen-point royal edict enumerated the spirit of the 1894 reforms. Modernizing efforts continued in 1895 with the opening of postal services and adoption of a solar calendar. The school system was reorganized along Japanese lines.

For the most part, the people greeted the change with skepticism and apprehension. Distrustful of authorities and resentful of the Japanese, they were neither enthusiastic nor saddened over the new edict. To those senior officials whose immediate political fortunes depended on the outcome of factional infighting, however, the only recourse was either to support the Japanese and seek their assistance or to turn for support to one of Japan's adversaries. Many of the powerful, conservative officials adversely affected by the reform sought aid from the Russians.

RUSSO-JAPANESE RIVALRY

Russia's acquisition in 1860 of the Manchurian coastal region, known as the Maritime Provinces, from a weak and troubled China resulted in a common frontier with Korea. Covetous of Korea's ice-free ports, mineral resources, and strategic location, Russia had managed to emerge as the principal rival to Japan by the mid 1890s. Through a friendly cabinet formed after the palace coup that it had backed in February 1896, Russia secured timber concessions along the Korean side of the Yalu River and on the island of Ullung in the Sea of Japan. Other concessions included mining rights in the northeastern corner of the peninsula and rights to link the Seoul-Wonsan telegraph line with that of Siberia. In addition, Russia prevailed on the Korean court to reorganize its army along Russian lines, using weapons and advisers from St. Petersburg. It also acquired de facto control of fiscal affairs through a financial adviser. The Russian example set in motion a scramble for concessions among foreign powers, including Japan, France, Germany, Great Britain, and the United States.

The strategic rivalry between Russia and Japan exploded in the Russo-Japanese War of 1904–5, ending with Japan's victory. Under the peace treaty signed at Portsmouth, New Hampshire, in September 1905, Russia acknowledged Japan's "paramount political, military and economic interest" in Korea.

Two months later, Korea was obliged to accept a Japanese protectorate; it became a Japanese colony under the Treaty of Annexation, signed on August 22, 1910. The treaty recognized the dignity of the Korean royal family and awarded titles of nobility to important pro-Japanese collaborators. Prime Minister Yi Wan-yong, who had signed the treaty although he had figured prominently between 1896 and 1901 in the anti-Japanese pro-Russian cabinet, has since become the symbol of treason to the Korean people.

JAPANESE RULE (1910–45)

From 1910 until 1945 Korea, or Chosen as the Japanese called it, was ruled from Seoul by a governor general who was appointed by the Japanese emperor and who reported directly to Tokyo. Under Japanese rule all civil liberties were revoked. Japanese authorities closed many private schools and established their own public school system, which was designed to assimilate Korean youth into Japanese cultural patterns by omitting Korean history and language and stressing those of Japan.

The colonial experience is often recalled with bitterness by Koreans, and much of the resentment generated by Japanese colonial rule persisted into the 1970s. Almost all important positions of authority were occupied by Japanese nationals, and this authority was harshly enforced. Although major improvements were instituted in transportation, health facilities, and the financial sectors, exploitive economic relations were arranged to serve the interests of Japanese landowners and businessmen. Colonial authorities appropriated enormous tracts of land, in some cases for infractions of an ordinance requiring landowners to report the size of their holdings and in other cases because land was owned by clans or communally. Much of this land was sold to Japanese immigrants, and the land tenure system was run solely for the benefit of Japanese landlords, who exported to Japan such a large proportion of the increased rice production that per capita rice consumption in Korea actually declined. Large numbers of Koreans were forced into slash-and-burn farming, the most meager of agricultural existences. Many displaced farmers migrated to Manchuria, the Soviet Union, and Japan; a relatively small number found jobs in newly built factories.

Rapid industrialization promoted by Japanese capital, management, and technology led to a substantial decline in the importance of agriculture relative to industry and mining in national production. In a pattern that would be repeated when North Korea achieved political independence after World War II, industrialization relied on capital-intensive production techniques and was concentrated on producer-goods industries.

INDEPENDENCE MOVEMENT OF 1919

Nationalist sentiments were particularly stimulated in January 1918 after Woodrow Wilson, president of the United States, enunciated the principle of self-determination for all dependent, oppressed peoples. In February 1919, aroused by a rumor that King Kojong, who had been dethroned in 1907, had been poisoned in January 1919 by the Japanese, some six hundred Korean students in Tokyo drafted a resolution demanding independence and submitted it to Japanese authorities. Inspired by these students, a group of thirty-three leaders in Seoul proclaimed a Declaration of Independence on March 1, 1919, precipitating spontaneous, peaceful demonstrations throughout Korea protesting Japanese rule.

Although caught by surprise, the Japanese gendarmerie and police crushed the demonstrations in which about 370,000 people participated. According to Korean sources, the total casualties included 6,670 killed; 16,000 wounded; and 19,525 arrested. In commemoration of this event, symbolic of the Korean struggle for independence, March 1 is celebrated each year as March First Movement Day.

The demonstrations marked the beginning of a more intensified phase of the independence struggle, especially among Korean exiles abroad. In Shanghai a Korean provisional government was formed in April 1919 with Syngman Rhee, who was then in the United States, as president. Some Koreans promoted the nationalist cause in the United States and in Japan.

In Korea the resistance movement continued, especially among students, factory workers, and urban intellectuals. In the early 1920s a strongly nationalistic labor union movement was started. In April 1925 a group of intellectuals in Seoul organized the Korean Communist Party; the party soon joined the Communist International but, on the Soviet Union's order, was disbanded in 1928 because of factional fighting within the organization. A student uprising in Kwangju in 1929 continued to underscore the weighty role of youth in the country's political scene. Lasting nearly five months and participated in by as many as fifty-four thousand students, the uprising has since become, for Korean youth, a symbol of protest against repression and injustice.

The March 1919 demonstration also occasioned a new phase in Japan's colonial policy. The Japanese administrators softened their earlier police-state tactics and began limited efforts to placate the local population. They improved farming methods and encouraged local industry and commerce. An increasing number of Koreans were given administrative positions but mostly at local subdivision levels. As a result, some Koreans were able to improve their social and economic positions.

The Japanese, nevertheless, continued to deny the Koreans the advantage of association and experience in political and economic management. They intensified the policy of eradicating Korean cultural identity by forbidding the use of the Korean language in schools, banning the study of Korean history, and stopping Korean publications. They forced Japanese surnames upon the people, introduced Shintoism in schools, and encouraged Confucianism in order to take advantage of its authoritarian features.

The policy of Japanizing the peninsula was accelerated after 1937, when the Sino-Japanese War (1937–45) broke out. To satisfy growing military requirements, Japan began to fashion the economy into a so-called continental logistical base; it developed northern Korea's rich mineral resources, built dams for hydroelectrical generation, and constructed factories to process iron ores and to produce chemical fertilizers. In time the peninsula evolved economically into two distinct halves—the industrial north and the agricultural south—and emerged as an integral part of Japan's expanded wartime economic structure.

Japan also utilized the country's manpower for war efforts in 1937 by instituting a so-called voluntary enlistment system for male adults; in 1942 this system was changed to conscription. A great number of laborers were drafted into wartime service in Japanese mines and munition factories. Some of them chose to settle in Japan after World War II and, together with those who had migrated earlier as wage earners, formed the nucleus of the Korean minority in Japan.

CAIRO DECLARATION

Korea reentered the limelight of world history during World War II, when its struggle for independence was given formal recognition on December 1, 1943, by representatives of the United States, Great Britain, and China in a joint statement issued in Cairo. After deliberating on the future course of military operations against Japan, the three Allied powers declared their determination to strip Japan, once defeated, of all the territories Japan had taken after the Sino-Japanese War of 1894–95. "Mindful of the enslavement of the people of Korea," they also resolved that "in due course Korea shall become free and independent."

The Cairo Declaration, as it is commonly called, was reaffirmed at the Potsdam Conference of July 1945 by the three powers, who specifically stated that "Japanese sovereignty shall be limited to the islands of Honshu, Hokkaido, Kyushu, and Shikoku and such minor islands as we shall determine." On August 8, 1945, by which time Japan's defeat was certain, the Soviet Union declared war on Japan although the countries had been on nonbelligerent terms under the Russo-Japanese neutrality treaty of April 1941. On the same day, the Soviet Union announced its adherence to the Potsdam statement and, hence, to the Cairo Declaration and secured for itself a legitimate pretext for gaining a foothold in Korea. Soviet troops entered the peninsula on August 10 by land and sea, meeting minimal Japanese resistance.

KOREA DIVIDED

To accept the surrender of Japanese forces in the peninsula after August 15, 1945, the United States and the Soviet Union agreed to divide the country at the thirty-eighth parallel into two occupation zones, the Soviet forces in the northern half and the American forces in the south. The line of demarcation was intended to be temporary, but all ensuing diplomatic efforts to lift the line and unify the country ended in failure.

The first significant attempt to unite the country was made in December 1945 by representatives of the United States, the Soviet Union, and Great Britain. Meeting in Moscow, they agreed to establish a trusteeship under four powers, including China, for the country for a period of up to five years "with a view to the reestablishment of Korea as an independent state." Their agreement also provided for the formation of a joint American-Soviet commission to assist in organizing a single "provisional Korean democratic government." The trusteeship proposal was immediately opposed by all Koreans except the Communists, who also objected at first but, under Soviet pressure, quickly changed their position.

These huge stone figures represent the principal courtiers of the king's court and they line the walk to the Royal (Neung) Tomb of the kings and queens near the city of Seoul. There are fifty-one of these royal tombs scattered throughout Korea.

The Imperial Library building still stands intact and its charm and contents are a tribute to those in power who followed and chose to preserve the archives.

The throne palace, one of the few remaining buildings in Korea that attests to its royal heritage

Kim Il Sung, the premier of North Korea, was offered the position of Successor King of Korea in addition to his title as premier, but he declined. So the line of kings ended with King Sunjong's reign, which formally was over in 1910.

The joint commission met in Seoul intermittently from March 1946 until it adjourned indefinitely in October 1947. The Soviet insistence that only those "democratic parties and social organizations" upholding the trusteeship plan be allowed to participate in the formation of an all-Korean government was unacceptable to noncommunist nationalist leaders. The nationalist leaders, represented by the United States, argued that the Soviet formula, if accepted, would put the Communists in controlling positions through Korea.

In September 1947 the United States submitted the Korean question to the General Assembly of the United Nations (UN), which in November, over Soviet objection, adopted a resolution stipulating that elected representatives of the Korean people should establish the conditions of unification and determine their own form of government. The United Nations Temporary Commission on Korea was formed to observe nationwide free elections and to carry out the terms of the November resolution. After the Soviet refusal in January 1948 to admit the commission to the northern half, elections were held on May 10, 1948, only in the southern half. Four days later the communist authorities completed the severance of north-south ties by shutting off power transmission to the south.

Throughout Korean history, the peninsula as a whole has been influenced in varying degrees by the culture and activity of neighboring peoples. As a result, many Koreans accept the popular belief handed down for generations that their national destiny has been determined less by internal than by external factors.

Foreign influences penetrated the country long before the Christian Era in the form of tribal and Chinese intrusions from the north across the Yalu and Tumen rivers. The Chinese ruled part of the northern half of the Korean peninsula for more than four hundred years (108 B.C.–A.D. 313), leaving an indelible imprint on the culture of Korea. Among other events underlying what the Koreans describe as their historic fate (*yŏksajŏk sukmyŏng*) were the centuries of vassal ties to China (with an interregnum of vassalage to the Mongols from 1259 to 1368) lasting well into the last days of the nineteenth century; the devastation wrought by the Mongols in the thirteenth century, by the Japanese in the sixteenth century, and by the Manchus in the seventeenth century; the frontal clash during 1904 and 1905 between czarist Russia and Japan in the expansionist machinations for control of the strategically located peninsula; and the thirty-five years of colonial experience under the Japanese. The post-World War II involvement of the Soviet Union and the United States is seen by the people as still another confirmation of the historical trend.

THE ROYAL SOVEREIGNS OF THE EMPIRE OF KOREA

Reign	Title	Ruler	Reign	Title	Ruler
KOGURYO DYNASTY			545–559	King	Yang-won-Wang
37–19 B.C.	King	Tongmyongsong-Wang	559–590	King	P'yong-won-Wang
19 B.C.–A.D. 18	King	Yurimyong-Wang	590–618	King	Yong-yang-Wang
A.D. 18–44	King	Taemusin-Wang	618–642	King	Yongnyu-Wang
44–48	King	Minjung-Wang	642–668	King	Pojang-Wang
48–53	King	Mobon-Wang			
53–146	King	T'aego-Wang			
146–165	King	Ch'adae-Wang			
165–179	King	Sindae-Wang	**PAEKCHE DYNASTY**		
179–197	King	Kogukch'on-Wang	18 B.C.–A.D. 28	King	Onjo-Wang
197–227	King	Sangsang-Wang	A.D. 28–77	King	Taru-Wang
227–248	King	Tongch'on-Wang	77–128	King	Kiru-Wang
248–270	King	Chungch'on-Wang	128–166	King	Kaeru-Wang
270–292	King	Soch'on-Wang	166–214	King	Ch'ogo-Wang
292–300	King	Pongsang-Wang	214–234	King	Kusu-Wang
300–331	King	Mich'on-Wang	234–234	King	Saban-Wang
331–371	King	Kogugwon-Wang	234–286	King	Koi-Wang
371–384	King	Susurim-Wang	286–298	King	Chaekkye-Wang
384–391	King	Kogugyang-Wang	298–304	King	Punso-Wang
391–412	King	Kwanggaet'o-Wang	304–344	King	Piryu-Wang
413–491	King	Changsu-Wang	344–346	King	Ke-Wang
492–519	King	Munja-Wang	346–375	King	Kunch'ogo-Wang
519–531	King	Anjang-Wang	375–384	King	Kun-gusu-Wang
531–545	King	Anwon-Wang	384–385	King	Ch'imnyu-Wang

Reign	Title	Ruler	Reign	Title	Ruler
385–392	King	Chinsa-Wang	897–912	King	Hyogong-Wang
392–405	King	Asin-Wang	912–917	King	Sindok-Wang
405–420	King	Chonji-Wang	917–924	King	Kyongmyong-Wang
420–427	King	Kuisin-Wang	924–927	King	Kyong'ae-Wang
427–455	King	Piyu-Wang	927–935	King	Kyongsun-Wang
455–475	King	Kaero-Wang			
475–477	King	Munju-Wang	**KORYO DYNASTY**		
477–479	King	Samgun-Wang	918–943	King	T'aejo (Wang-kon)
479–501	King	Tongsong-Wang	943–945	King	Hyejong
501–523	King	Munyong-Wang	945–949	King	Chongjong
523–554	King	Song-Wang	949–975	King	Kwangjong
554–598	King	Widok-Wang	975–981	King	Kyongjong
598–599	King	Hye-Wang	981–997	King	Songjong
599–600	King	Pop-Wang	997–1009	King	Mokchong
600–645	King	Mu-Wang	1009–1031	King	Hyonjong
645–660	King	Uija-Wang	1031–1034	King	Tokjong
660–663	King	P'ungjang-Wang	1034–1046	King	Chongjong
			1046–1082	King	Munjong
SILLA DYNASTY			1082–1083	King	Sunjong
57 B.C.–A.D. 3	King	Hyokkose-Wang	1083–1094	King	Sonjong
A.D. 4–24	King	Namhae-Wang	1094–1095	King	Honjong
24–57	King	Yuri-Wang	1095–1105	King	Sukjong
57–80	King	T'alhae-Wang	1105–1122	King	Yejong
80–112	King	P'asa-Wang	1122–1146	King	Injong
112–134	King	Chima-Wang	1146–1170	King	Uijong
134–154	King	Ilsong-Wang	1170–1197	King	Myongjong
154–184	King	Adalla-Wang	1197–1204	King	Sinjong
184–196	King	Porhyu-Wang	1204–1211	King	Huijong
196–230	King	Naehae-Wang	1211–1213	King	Kangjong
230–247	King	Chobun-Wang	1213–1259	King	Kojong
247–261	King	Ch'omhae-Wang	1259–1274	King	Wonjong
262–284	King	Mich'u-Wang	1274–1308	King	Ch'ungnyol-Wang
284–298	King	Yurye-Wang	1308–1313	King	Ch'ungson-Wang
298–310	King	Kirim-Wang	1313–1330	King	Ch'ungsuk-Wang
310–356	King	Hulhae-Wang	1331–1332	King	Ch'unghye-Wang
356–402	King	Naemul-Wang	1339–1344	King	Ch'unghye-Wang
402–417	King	Silsong-Wang	1344–1348	King	Ch'ungmok-Wang
417–458	King	Nulchi-Wang	1348–1351	King	Ch'ungjong-Wang
458–479	King	Chabi-Wang	1351–1374	King	Kongmin-Wang
479–500	King	Soji-Wang	1374–1388	King	Sin-u
500–514	King	Chijung-Wang	1380–1389	King	Sinch'ang
514–540	King	Pophung-Wang	1389–1392	King	Kongyang-Wang
540–576	King	Chinhung-Wang			
576–579	King	Chinji-Wang	**CHOSON (YI) DYNASTY**		
579–632	King	Chinp'yong-Wang	1392–1399	King	T'aejo (Yi Songgye)
632–647	King	Sondok-Yowang	1399–1400	King	Chongjong
647–654	King	Chindok-Yowang	1400–1418	King	T'aejong
654–661	King	Muryol-Wang	1418–1450	King	Sejong
			1450–1452	King	Munjong
UNIFIED SILLA			1452–1455	King	Tanjong
661–681	King	Munmu-Wang	1455–1468	King	Sejo
681–692	King	Sinmun-Wang	1468–1469	King	Yejong
692–702	King	Hyoso-Wang	1469–1494	King	Songjong
702–737	King	Songdok-Wang	1494–1506	King	Yonsan-gun
737–742	King	Hyosong-Wang	1506–1544	King	Chungjong
742–765	King	Kyongdok-Wang	1544–1545	King	Injong
765–780	King	Hyesong-Wang	1545–1567	King	Myongjong
780–785	King	Sondok-Wang	1567–1608	King	Sonjo
785–798	King	Wonsong-Wang	1608–1623	King	Kwanghae-gun
799–800	King	Sosong-Wang	1623–1649	King	Injo
800–809	King	Aejang-Wang	1649–1659	King	Hyojong
809–826	King	Hondok-Wang	1659–1674	King	Hyonjong
826–836	King	Hungdok-Wang	1674–1720	King	Sukchong
836–838	King	Huigang-Wang	1720–1724	King	Kyongjong
838–839	King	Minae-Wang	1724–1776	King	Yongjo
839–839	King	Simmu-Wang	1776–1800	King	Chongjo
839–857	King	Musong-Wang	1800–1834	King	Sunjo
857–861	King	Honan-Wang	1834–1849	King	Honjong
861–875	King	Kyongmun-Wang	1849–1863	King	Ch'oljong
875–886	King	Hon-gang-Wang	1864–1907	King	Kojong (became Emperor Kwangmu)
886–887	King	Chonggang-Wang	1907–1910	Emperor	Sunjong (Yun-heui)
887–897	King	Chinsong-Yowang	1910–1945—Japanese rule		

22

The Japanese Empire

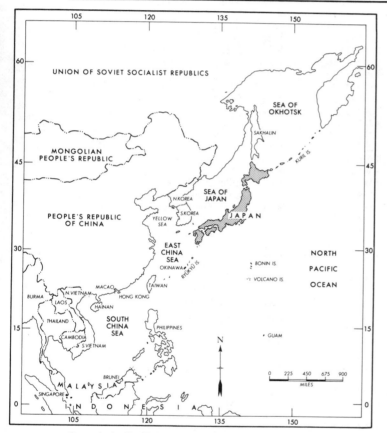

Japan in its Far East setting

Geographic isolation has played a major role in Japanese history. The country's island setting was remote from all centers of early civilization except China, which was not close enough to impose its influence on Japan; rather, the Japanese consciously borrowed from China and adapted what they borrowed to their own traditions and environment. The result was a distinctive Japanese culture within which some elements, such as the written language, remained identifiable as importations. Still other features originally adopted, for example, Chinese military organi-

zation, were discarded. The same pattern was repeated in later periods of Japanese history.

Japanese receptivity to foreign influence has varied to extreme degrees. For example, in the thirteenth century they repelled an attempted Mongol invasion but in the sixteenth century welcomed European Roman Catholic missionaries. Two centuries of self-imposed isolation followed until 1854, when the Western world forcibly reopened the country. During the period of isolation Japanese social and political institutions evolved into their premodern form of a centralized feudal state under dual authority. The functions of the emperor—of a single imperial house throughout Japanese history—were limited to religious ritual, as they had been for centuries, but an independent *shōgun* (military ruler) was dominant in all other respects. Both emperor and shogun, however, were usually figureheads.

After 1868 another major change occurred in Japanese attitudes toward the rest of the world. A small group undertook, in the name of the emperor, the purposeful political, economic, and social transformation of Japan to enable the country to compete with the Western powers that had forced Japan into a position of inferiority by the imposition of "unequal treaties." The dramatic success attained in the Meiji Restoration, measured by victorious wars with China and Russia, brought with it a degree of social evolution and a large measure of economic modernization. Parliamentary government was the chief political innovation; it was, however, alien to Japanese tradition and was not fully successful. Executive power in the new government was diffuse, and by the 1930s ultranationalists and militarists were therefore able to abrogate power to themselves, resulting first in an attempt to impose Japanese hegemony over China, then over the western Pacific and Southeast Asia. Both efforts were unsuccessful.

The military defeat in 1945 brought the Japanese a period of total foreign control. The reforms directly imposed by occupation forces resulted in major changes in Japanese society. In the political sphere a new constitution defined and fixed the executive responsibility in the government.

Japan's relations with the world were vastly different in the second half of the twentieth century from what they had been earlier. The Japanese appeared to have accepted the loss of autonomy in defense and the resultant reliance on the United States. In the same period, however, they regained and further enhanced their position as a major economic power engaged in worldwide competition. The material gains were highly visible and to most Japanese apparently satisfactory.

EARLY HISTORY TO A.D. 710

Archaeological evidence has not established beyond debate the sequence of migrations that produced the remarkably homogeneous Japanese race and culture. There are indications of the existence in the islands of an identifiable culture by 20,000 B.C. These early inhabitants were not necessarily related to the modern Japanese.

Theories popular among the Japanese trace their origin to peoples migrating from the south through Formosa (Taiwan) and the Ryukyu Islands. The evidence does not support such an origin for most ancestors of the Japanese, who migrated from the Asian mainland by way of Korea. Some also came from farther north to Hokkaido. Some may have come from the south as well, perhaps from south China.

Despite the uncertainties of detail, the Japanese are predominantly Mongoloid in physical type and inheritors of a language derived from Altaic roots, as are the Mongolian, Manchu, Turkic, and Korean languages. The known exception to Mongoloid origin is the modern Ainu, whom some believe to be descended from early Caucasoid peoples of northern Asia. The "hairy Ainu" left little imprint on Japanese history in their losing competition with the Mongoloid peoples, but they may well have contributed to Japanese physical characteristics in that the modern Japanese have a relatively greater amount of body hair as compared with the other Mongoloid races.

Three major periods are identified in that part of the prehistoric era of Japan dating from about 4500 B.C. to the sixth century A.D. The first period, ending around 250 B.C., is called Jomon because of the distinctive cord impressions found on most of the pottery; this period had a hunting, fishing, and gathering culture. It was followed by the Yayoi period, named after a section of modern Tokyo, which lasted until A.D. 250. During this period further migrations through Korea brought the bases for many of the characteristics of later Japanese culture. The Japanese language and the indigenous religion of Shintoism evolved during this time, irrigated rice agriculture was practiced, bronze and iron implements were in use, and hereditary ruling families had emerged.

The third period, called Yamato, from about A.D. 300 to 710, linked the semihistoric with the fully historic period of Japan. Among its legacies are great burial mounds attesting

Empress Jingo was the first empress to rule Japan. The great-granddaughter of Emperor Kaikwa, she reigned from 201 to 269. Her story is the greatest legend in Japanese history. The legend, believed to have a historical basis, recites that the empress Jingo had a revelation from the god Sumiyoshi, who told her that Korea (Shinra) should be "conquested" to pay for the revolt Korea had incited in Japan. At the time, the empress was the consort of Emperor Chuai. Emperor Chuai died shortly after the revelation. So Empress Jingo, upon assuming the throne, started a sea invasion of Korea. The god Sumiyoshi served as the empress's pilot on the open sea. Just before arriving at landfall for Korea, he caused a great storm to take place and big fishes came to the surface to support the war boats toward the journey's end. The king of Korea, upon seeing this fateful armada approaching, decided to capitulate. He promised never ever to interfere again in the in-

The fifteenth emperor of Japan, Ojin, who ruled Japan from his birth in 201 until his death in 310 at the age of 109, was the longest-ruling sovereign in the history of kings. Of course, Empress Jingo served as regent in Ojin's learning years, for sixty-nine of them, and it was only after her death in 269 that he was able to rule with the great judgment that he learned from her. He was considered to have brought culture to Japan. In 284 of his reign he brought two Korean scholars to Japan, Ajiki and Wani, who brought with them Chinese literature and Confucianism, which were introduced throughout the empire by Ojin.

ternal operations of Japan. He formally recognized the total "suzerainty" of Japan. Empress Jingo left her minister, Yada no Sukune, in Korea to control the government, and she returned to Japan, where she gave birth to a son, who became the emperor Ojin in the year 201.

its large-scale organization and the high degree of control exercised by its clan leaders. The long iron swords used by the mounted warriors who headed these groups were evidence of their recent migration from Asia, again through Korea. These swords, which were among their most valued objects; their bronze mirrors, which were of Chinese origin; and their comma-shaped jewels carved from semiprecious stones became in time the symbols of Japanese imperial authority.

Successive migrations from Korea expanded the area of control of this militarily superior group northeastward along the Inland Sea. One element settled in the Yamato plain near the eastern end of the sea, in the vicinity of modern Osaka. From this base it gradually extended its authority over central and western Japan—and into parts of southern Korea as well. Along with the development of Yamato political authority went the ascendancy of the Yamato clan cult headed by its priest-chiefs, thereby making its divine progenitor, the Sun Goddess (Amaterasu Omikami), paramount in the Shinto pantheon.

The ranks and relationships of clan structure provided the model for the Japanese state that emerged from the suzerainty of the Yamato clan. Within the clans, social stratification was based on occupation. Distinctions among clans, based originally on relative power, came in time to be rationalized in terms of claims to divine origin. The Yamato claimed the highest descent—from the Sun Goddess—through the first emperor, Jimmu (660–585 B.C.). The second category, the so-called inner clans, claimed descent from lesser divinities. A third class, lacking any divine origin, was known as the outer clans. The association of clans of the Yamato period was the beginning of the Japanese state; the concepts of hierarchy and kinship and the importance of heredity persisted in the state's subsequent evolution.

There was some contact with Chinese culture beginning in the early years of the Yamato period; part of this contact was indirect through the immigrants from Korea. Some knowledge of writing and of the arts and sciences reached Japan at a relatively early date. By the late sixth century A.D. Chinese influence had become direct and was consciously accepted by the Japanese. The initial vehicle of the transmission was Buddhism, then a vigorous missionary religion.

After the opposition that developed with the Yamato clan to the new religion and its associated innovations was defeated, about 587, the regent prince Shotoku Taishi instituted in 607 the dispatch of large official embassies to China, a practice that continued at average intervals of twenty years until 838. This period coincided with the political and intellectual vigor of the Sui and early T'ang dynasties in China. During this time the foundations of historical Japanese civilization were formed through the synthesis of indigenous elements and imported Chinese art, literature, religion, ethics, politics, and technology. The influence in this direction exerted by the young men of the aristocracy who were members of the embassies was supplemented by that of the Chinese and Korean immigrants, who were welcomed at that time to Japan.

NARA PERIOD, 710–84

Between 645 and 702 imperial edicts, codes, and reforms had established a Chinese system of government in Japan, a country then without towns or cities and therefore lacking a fixed center for administration. In 710 the Japanese undertook the building of a capital on the model of Ch'ang-an, the T'ang capital. The site chosen was near the modern city of Nara in the Yamato plain, where palaces, residences, and Buddhist temples were constructed. Several temples have survived. They are among the oldest wooden structures in the world and are the only known examples extant of Chinese architecture of the period, as those in China apparently have all been destroyed.

For administrative purposes the empire was divided into provinces, prefectures, and subprefectures similar to those in China. In practice, however, the authority of the central government was vague because the autonomy of the non-

Emperor Nintoku entered the throne in 313 when he was twenty-three years of age. The sixteenth emperor, he was a most popular ruler, having had the interest of the people at heart, foremost. He built dikes for protection from the flooding, dug canals for transportation, and built government storage houses for rice. After a reign of eighty-six years, he died at the age of 109. According to most records he was born when his father was 90 years of age.

The thirty-second emperor, Sujun, who ruled from 588 to 592, was the twelfth son of the twenty-ninth emperor, Kimmei. Sujun was a scholar as well as a ruler and is credited with bringing the Chinese scales of weights to Japan. Sujun was assassinated in 592.

Prince Shotuku-Taishi, one of the greatest figures in Japanese history, is seen here with his two sons. Crown Prince Shotuku was the second son of Emperor Jomei and the regent for his Aunt Tenno (Suiko) from 593 to 621. He brought Buddhism to Japan and is also credited with adopting the Chinese calendar for Japan in 604.

The empress Jito ruled Japan from 686 to 696, and history records that she was responsible for bringing "modern" agricultural methods to rural Japan and that she struck the first silver coins. She was the daughter of Emperor Tenji and the consort of Emperor Temmu, and upon his death, succeeded him.

The imperial seal of Emperor Junnin (757–64)

Yamato clans was strong enough to prevent direct rule by the new bureaucracy. Provincial governorships became sinecures, held by clan aristocrats who remained at the imperial court. Prefectural governorships emerged as the most import; nt positions in the new hierarchy. Appointments to this post were originally only for lifetime tenure but became in time hereditary. The incumbents were for the most part local notables.

Innovations in landownership, taxation, and military organization were put into effect, at least nominally, during the short period of imperial rule from Nara. None proved to have a lasting effect, and probably they were enforced only within the Yamato clan areas. The clans were in theory deprived of their landholdings, which were to be redistributed equally among peasant cultivators as the basis for equitable taxation. It appears that many members of the clan aristocracy managed to keep control of their land, although many did accept the compensation of livelihood and administrative positions offered by the central government. The bureaucracy centered on the court, which the aristocracy entered, soon became hereditary in contrast to the Chinese system of qualification by examination.

Taxes were payable by the peasants in produce, labor, or military service. Conscript armies of foot soldiers were created, but they did not prove effective in frontier wars against the Ainu. Eventually, these forces became demoralized and weak. The unsuccessful effort to reorganize Japanese military forces on the basis of conscription left the mounted warrior as the Japanese military ideal.

The short Nara period was marked by a number of disputes over the right of succession to the throne. Palace intrigue and factional disputes involving Buddhist priests were common. Three empresses reigned, one of whom ruled at two separate intervals; they were the last female occupants of the Japanese throne until the seventeenth century.

The writing of dynastic history as practiced by the Chinese was adopted by the Nara court. Imperial patronage resulted in the production of two important works in the early eighth century. The first, the *Kojiki* (Record of Ancient Matters), said to have been written in 712, was perhaps a draft of the great official history, the *Nihonshoki* (Chronicles of Japan), which appeared in 720. Both works were in Chinese. The history incorporated the mythology of the Yamato line's descent from the Sun Goddess, thus establishing Japan's claim to a standing similar to that of China. The historians sought to establish that Japan's culture was superior and more ancient than China's. This same rationale was used many centuries later by the ultranationalists of the nineteenth and twentieth centuries who succeeded at times in making it official Japanese policy to accept the two works as factual history. During the 1930s and early 1940s, especially, the works had a great impact.

Arts and crafts flourished in Nara, and the examples that survive are evidence of the early development of the high

The fiftieth emperor was Kwammu (782–805), the eldest son of Emperor Konin. He moved the capital from Yamashiro to Kyoto in 794, where it remained for ten centuries. Also, he commissioned the learned Omi no Mifune to fix the dates, times, and names of all previous emperors back to Jimmu.

Jimmu, the first emperor of Japan, looked something like this in his official garb.

The fifty-ninth emperor of Japan was Uda, who ruled from 888 until he resigned in favor of his son, Daigo. Upon his abdication in 897, he shaved his head and became a monk.

aesthetic standards characteristic of Japanese culture. The first anthology of Japanese poetry, *Man'yōshū* (Collection of a Myriad Leaves), appeared sometime after 759.

The Buddhist temples in and around Nara received great amounts of imperial wealth as the Yamato court continued to accord a special status to Buddhism and its institutions. In 752, for example, the emperor dedicated the statue of the Great Buddha, still to be seen in the temple known as Todaiji; Todaiji is now one-third smaller than the original structure but is claimed by the Japanese to be the largest wooden building in existence.

HEIAN PERIOD, 794 -1185

Motivated at least in part by a desire to escape the political intrigue and influence of the numerous and wealthy Buddhist temples in Nara, the Yamato court moved from Nara—first to Nagaoka in 784 and then to Heiankyo (later shortened to *Kyōto,* which means the capital) in 794. The new, larger city was constructed at enormous expense, again on the model of Ch'ang-an. It was to remain the seat of the imperial court until 1868.

The Heian period is celebrated for its cultural achievements. By the tenth and eleventh centuries, the principal characteristics of Japanese literature, art, and architecture had evolved under the patronage and participation of court circles. The second great anthology of poetry, the *Kokinshu* (Collection of the Old and New) was completed around 905; it was composed of poems of classical Japanese style. The most famous literary form of the period was the novel based on court life. The best known—and still widely read—is the *Genji Monogatari* (Tale of Genji), written around 1000 by Shikibu Murasaki; it reflected the court life of which the authoress was a part. By that time the development of the Japanese syllabary *(kana)* had made possible writing in Japanese, in contrast to the earlier exclusive use of Chinese characters to transliterate Japanese sounds.

The Chinese system of government developed in the Nara period was extensively modified during the Heian era. Measures were taken to control local officials, establish a dependable civil service, restore revenues to the government, and reorganize the army; their cumulative effect was a radical change in government structure. Government authority on the other hand was reduced at the same time by the expansion, often by illegal means, of the tax-free estates of the great monasteries and families. On these estates, known as *shōen,* the position of farmers was little better than that of serfs. As the manors, including those of the imperial family, became autonomous domains, the Heian court gradually lost its power as a central authority.

The most striking feature of the Heian system of government was the role played by regents of the Fujiwara family (the family had been prominent since the seventh century), which had immense landholdings. Manipulation of court politics and intermarriage with the Yamato, its main tactics, gradually gave the Fujiwara complete control of the imperial family. The Fujiwara did not replace the Yamato line, choosing to act instead as hereditary regents or, from the end of the ninth century, as hereditary *kampaku* (chancellors or civil dictators). At the zenith of Fujiwara power, from 995 to 1027, the head of the clan was the father-in-law of four emperors and grandfather of another four. The large number of emperors in this thirty-two-year period was owing to the practice of early abdication. An emperor was easily persuaded to resign from his onerous ritualistic position; he was then succeeded by a child emperor with a Fujiwara regent. In the eleventh century the power of the Fujiwara declined, and by 1100 they had lost most of the important posts to other clans, especially the Minamoto clan. Imperial abdication continued to be practiced but with a new objective—that of the indirect exercise of authority by the retired emperor through domination of the son succeeding him, thereby bypassing the authority of the Fujiwara.

There was widespread disorder in Japan in the tenth century as the power of the central government declined. Armed groups under local leaders tried to protect their properties and to restore local order. The armed forces of the new power centers were raised and led by the aristocracy, who once again were the mounted warriors of Japanese military tradition. Regional associations gradually formed; the greatest movement toward such essentially military groupings was in the Kanto plain, on which modern Tokyo is located. This transfer of effective power eventually brought about the feudal age in Japan.

Official relations with China continued during the early Heian period; the last Japanese embassy to China sailed from Japan in 838. Unofficial travelers introduced two major new schools of Buddhist thought, Tendai and Shingon, in the first decade of the ninth century. By the end of the Heian period both schools had acquired extensive estates and had become as powerful and influential as their predecessors. The final Japanese mission reported a decline of Buddhism in China, and later accounts of disorder there, including persecution of Buddhists, led the Japanese to end formal diplomatic relations with China.

Ainu defeats of Heian conscript armies forced the government to find an alternative. A generalissimo, the literal meaning of *shōgun,* appointed at the end of the eighth century to organize military units led by members of families owning land in the regions involved won decisive victories. His example showed that Japanese military strength lay in local volunteer forces rather than in conscripted ones.

Imperial power declined toward the end of the period, and disputes arose among factions, often concerning succession to the throne. The capital was, moreover, often at the mercy of groups of marauding warrior monks from the great temples, causing the authorities to call in the forces of provincial leaders to restore order at various times.

By then the military associations in the countryside had produced two great warrior leagues, the Minamoto and the Taira, both of which claimed imperial descent. In 1156 a succession dispute brought both provincial forces into Kyōto to stay. An epic struggle started between the two groups that ended in a Minamoto victory in 1185 and ushered in the feudal period.

FEUDAL PERIOD, 1185–1867

Japan's feudal period was not characterized by the same political disunity as that of its European counterpart. Institutions that developed after the transfer of power from the emperor eventually produced a degree of central authority. This political system has been termed by Japanese historians centralized feudalism.

KAMAKURA SHOGUNATE (1185–1333)

The almost seven-hundred-year feudal period in Japan began formally in 1192 when Yoritomo Minamoto, who had

The eightieth emperor of Japan (1169–80) was Takakura. At eight years of age he succeeded his nephew, Emperor Rokuju. When Takakura was twenty, Kiyomori talked him into abdicating in favor of Takakura's son Antoku, who was but two years of age. The following year, 1181, Takakura died of unknown causes. Kiyomori's actions with the throne created a rebellion between the nobles and Kiyomori which the nobles won. In the course of the rebellion, Antoku was removed from the throne.

Go-Toba was the eighty-second emperor (1184–99). He entered the throne at the age of four. At the age of twenty, Go-Toba abdicated in favor of his son, Tsuchimikado, who in turn was succeeded by his brother Juntoku, in 1211. During these two reigns, Go-Toba governed in the name of his sons.

The shogunate began in 1185 when Yoritomo (1147–99), head of the Minamoto family was appointed by the mikado (the crown) as the sei-i-tai, governor-generalissimo ("a barbarian-subduing generalissimo"), called the shogun. He was formally invested in 1185. Yoritomo instituted a system of military administration that prevailed for many centuries.

established his *bakufu* (military office) at Kamakura, near modern Tokyo, was given the title of *shōgun* by the emperor. In theory the delegation of authority to the shogun was limited to command of the military forces but, in fact, because generations of unrest had resulted in a social order dominated by the military, control of the military was tantamount to control of the country. The new shogunate attempted to restore some central control by the installation of *shugo* (constables or guards) in each province and *jitō* (stewards or district headmen) in the taxable areas. The *jitō* not only ensured the shogunate of a source of revenue but also provided positions with which to reward the loyal. The new posts were often held concurrently by the same local family and in time became hereditary. In 1232 the *bakufu* promulgated an organizational code that institutionalized its national military organization.

The developing customary law of the time showed the influence of the feudal environment but did not lose all vestiges of the kingship orientation of the past. The relationship between lord and vassal, for example, resembled the kinship tie of father and son. Locally, social relationships were regulated by the house laws of the principal noble families. Differing in detail, these codes rested on the basic assumption that the lord's interests and wishes were supreme.

The samurai class crystallized in this period in a social order in which all males were expected to contribute to local defense. The class comprised feudal lords, mounted armored noblemen, and foot soldiers. The samurai became responsible for administration, and as a result other social groups became subordinate to them.

The ideal virtues of the samurai were unquestioning obedience and unconditional loyalty to his lord, spartan self-control, and courage. Influenced by the new sect of Zen Buddhism, which stressed emotional discipline rather than intellectual attainment, the samurai code of Bushido, the way of the warrior, was exalted in the literature of the period.

The power of the Minamoto clan did not long survive the death of Yoritomo in 1199. In 1226 a member of the opposing Fujiwara line became shogun. During the thirteenth century, however, the shogun were in reality puppets of the Hojo clan, the family of Yoritomo's wife, which had established a hereditary regency over the shogunate after Yoritomo's death. The reigning emperor was usually the tool of an emperor who had abdicated and of the Fujiwara courtiers; together they constituted the nominal government. This government, however, did the bidding of the shogun, who in turn was the puppet of the Hojo regent. Hojo chiefs generally were able men who used personal relationships as the basis of their power.

A great religious revival took place in the early part of the Kamakura period. New sects (schools) of Buddhist teaching achieved rapid dominance at all levels of society; they maintained this dominance to the modern era. They included the Pure Land (*Jōdo*) and True Pure Land (*Shin*) sects, which had wide popular appeal. An evangelical sect, Nichiren Buddhism, was also an active military force during this era of almost constant political unrest. In contrast, Zen Buddhism, newly imported from China, had a nar-

In 1219, the last of the Minamoto shoguns, Sanetomo, was assassinated, and the shogun power was taken over by Hojo Yoshitoki. The ex-emperor Go-Toba made war with Hojo, lost, and was exiled to Sado. Miura Yoshimura, who had sided with Hojo in his fight with Go-Toba, is seen here delivering his brother's head to Hojo to show his loyalty. Yoshimura's brother, Miura Taneyoshi, was aligned with Go-Toba.

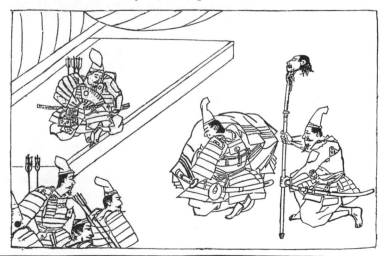

rower appeal; its mystic, antischolastic, and disciplined teachings soon became the philosophical basis of the warrior class, which gave it continuing prestige.

In time Kamakura power decreased as some provincial lords achieved great wealth and strength and as social changes, such as the emergence of a merchant class, affected the basis of the shogunate's authority. The expense of defense against Mongol invasions in 1274 and 1281 had further serious consequences for the shogunate. The first Mongol attack was repelled with difficulty, although it was less than full scale. In the second, Japan was saved by a typhoon—a *kamikaze* (literally, divine wind)—that wrecked the invader's fleet. Unlike the aftermath of internal warfare, there were no spoils from this defensive fighting, and the Hojo leaders' inability to reward their vassals lost them much support.

The Kamakura shogunate ended in 1333 when a retired emperor, known by his posthumous name of Go-Daigo, attempted to restore imperial rule and was joined by the Kamakura general Takauji Ashikaga. Takauji soon turned against Go-Daigo and assumed the title of shogun, at the same time placing a noble from another branch of the imperial line on the throne. Go-Daigo set up a separate court, which continued to function from 1335 until it was destroyed in 1392.

ASHIKAGA SHOGUNATE (1358–1573)

The Ashikaga shogunate established its seat in Kyōto in the district of Muromachi, from which the arts of the period take their name. Politically, the Ashikaga shogunate was a time of chaos; culturally and economically, it was a period of rapid change and advance. There was vigorous commercial expansion and technological improvement resulting from overseas trade with China and, from the 1500s, with Europe. These developments were accompanied by a great increase in social mobility and changes in the character of feudal institutions. By the late sixteenth century, the boundaries between the ruling warrior and commoner classes had blurred considerably.

Internal strife, general after 1467, led to a breakdown of the last vestiges of the old system of loyalties based on clan relationships. Kinship as a principle of social organization now operated within smaller groups. New political units were formed on the basis of local residence, economic needs, and common interests. A typical unit centered on a *daimyō* (local lord) who in most cases was the successor of the *shugo*, over whom the Ashikaga never attained more than a precarious control. The daimyo's domain comprised within its territory the families of his vassals and retainers and the peasants, artisans, and merchants of the common causes. His military forces were groups of peasant foot soldiers. The mounted samurai lost their military and administrative positions in the revised feudal order. Increased social mobility, both upward and downward, resulted.

The authority of the various Ashikaga shogun was exercised on the sufferance of the daimyo, whose numbers and independence caused fragmentation of power. The new daimyo sought to consolidate their local power by demanding personal loyalty from their vassals and retainers. Vassals were usually the heads of small family units that had replaced the extended clan-family as the basic social unit; they did not necessarily have kinship ties to the daimyo or to other families. Within such families individual interests were subordinated to those of the group, headed by the senior male. The position of women was inferior to that of men, who inherited by right of primogeniture.

In Kyōto the various Ashikaga shogun devoted themselves to the cultivation of art and literature. Scholarship flourished under the auspices of the monasteries, especially those of the Zen monks, who became active in Chinese learning. New cultural influences from China were assimilated, such as monochrome landscape painting, architectural styles, landscape gardening, flower arrangement, and the tea ceremony. Purely Japanese art forms were created, among them the *Nō* (Noh) drama. This cultural flowering is often compared with that of the Heian period.

The exercise of authority by the imperial court and bureaucracy came to an end early in the Ashikaga period because of the location of shogunate headquarters in Kyōto and because the shogunate lost its control over the daimyo. Some poverty-stricken aristocrats, descendants of the Heian court nobility, retreated into Shinto, which they revived in an eclectic form incorporating Buddhist elements.

Kinkakuji Temple, or Gold Pavilion, Kyoto, was originally built in 1394 by Yoshimitsu, the third Ashikaga shogun. It was restored in 1955.

Go-Daigo, the ninety-sixth emperor, reigned from 1318 to 1339. However, the Hojo family head, Takatoki, in 1331, sent a large army against Go-Daigo in Kyoto, took over the throne, and exiled the emperor to Oki. Prince Kazuhito was placed on the throne by Takatoki. But, in 1333, Go-Daigo escaped, gathered an army, defeated Takatoki, and returned to the throne.

Despite feudal strife and social confusion, trade, manufacturing, and commerce developed steadily. By the fifteenth century foreign trade was an important factor in Japan's economy. It was extended beyond the original trade with China in the sixteenth century when the first Westerners reached Japan. Japanese took to the seas not only as traders but also as pirates who in Ashikaga times were the scourge of the coasts of Korea, China, and Southeast Asia. Some Japanese also settled in sizable communities at such foreign ports as Manila in the Philippines. Japanese exports included fine handicraft items, such as screens, folding fans, and laminated steel swords.

Foreign commerce was sponsored by the daimyo and the abbots of monasteries but was conducted mainly by lesser daimyo and the merchants of western Japan. The formation of guilds and the emergence of a merchant class reflected the rapid increase in manufacturing and commerce. The site of modern Osaka, under the protection of a castle-monastery of True Pure Land Buddhists that remained impregnable until the late sixteenth century, developed as a trading center free of daimyo control.

Portuguese traders from Macao, an enclave in southeastern China, were the first Westerners to reach Japan, arriving in the 1540s. They were followed by Jesuit missionaries, among them Saint Francis Xavier, who were welcomed by the Ashikaga and the leading daimyo and who quickly made many converts. The traders also introduced potatoes, tobacco, muskets, and gunpowder.

A movement toward political unity occurred in the latter half of the sixteenth century as a result of the concentration of power in the hands of a few daimyo as the more powerful defeated the weaker. This political development was owing in part to the changes in warfare brought about by the use of firearms. The musket and the cannon revolutionized Japanese strategy. The daimyo now based their military operations on large fortified castles that commanded considerable expanses of territory and in major campaigns used mass armies of foot soldiers armed with the new weapons. Mounted samurai lost their relative military superiority to the peasantry who, as infantrymen, were equally effective. The possession of firearms by the True Pure Land Buddhists was the reason they were able to successfully challenge the power of the daimyo in the Osaka area.

National unification was finally achieved by a celebrated military triumvirate—Nobunaga Oda (1534–82), Hideyoshi Toyotomi (1536–98), and Ieyasu Tokugawa (1542–1616). Oda, a Taira daimyo in central Japan, achieved dominance in that region by 1578. His power over the imperial court was sufficient to cause the abolition of the shogunate in 1573. Oda, who was the first to make full use of the musket's firepower, also demolished the most powerful of the great Buddhist monasteries around Kyōto and captured the Osaka castle-monastery, breaking the secular power of the monks. It was he who welcomed the Jesuits to Japan.

After Oda was murdered in 1582, his vassal and ablest commander, Hideyoshi Toyotomi, a commoner, completed the unification of the country. Hideyoshi Toyotomi established an efficient countrywide administration from Azuchi (part of modern Osaka) and introduced monetary reform and a land survey. In 1592 he took the title of *kampaku* (chancellor or civil dictator) because his social status did not qualify him for the rank of shogun. Hideyoshi Toyotomi assigned friendly and unfriendly daimyo to domains adjacent to one another in order to reduce the possibility of plots against him—a tactic continued by the succeeding Tokugawa shogunate.

Hideyoshi Toyotomi was not as friendly toward Christian missionaries as Oda had been because he suspected them of being political agents for foreign powers. He issued an edict in 1587 banning missionaries. This was not strictly enforced, however, until ten years later, when, annoyed by feuding between religious orders, he ordered the execution of several missionaries and Japanese converts. Hideyoshi Toyotomi organized two invasions of the Asian mainland, in 1592 and 1598, with the objective of conquering China and moving his capital there. His campaigns began in Korea and were at first successful, but he was eventually defeated by the combined Chinese and Koreans.

Hideyoshi Toyotomi died in 1598 and was succeeded by Ieyasu Tokugawa, a man of Minamoto lineage, who had been a close collaborator and ally of Oda. His accession to power was challenged by a coalition of daimyo, which he defeated decisively at Sekigahara in central Honshū in 1600. Tokugawa power was consolidated by 1616 and remained unchallenged for the next two hundred and fifty years.

TOKUGAWA SHOGUNATE (1603–1867)

The Tokugawa shogunate (the title was granted in 1603) was a military dictatorship that operated through the bureaucracy of the *bakufu*. Its policies were designed to create political stability not by coping with change but by preventing it. To this end the country was isolated from all but the most rigorously supervised contact with the outside world. The *bakufu* organized the population into a rigidly stratified and supervised social system. The *bakufu* vigorously promoted a national orthodoxy compounded of samurai and neo-Confucian ideals. The Tokugawa shogunate adopted neo-Confucianism in 1790 as the state ideology. Confucian teachings became the official rationale for the benevolent paternalism of their political system and the static nature of their society. Neo-Confucianism, associated with Chu Hsi, a twelfth-century Chinese philosopher and administrator, is characterized by the addition of metaphysical speculation to the early ethical doctrines of Confucius.

Ieyasu Tokugawa's first and most important step was to establish control over the daimyo, several of whom were powerful enough to be a potential threat. The measures he put into force were continued and elaborated upon by his successors. Daimyo were required to take a written oath of loyalty to the shogun. The great daimyo of the central region who had supported the Tokugawa were designated hereditary daimyo and rewarded with high civil and military posts. They were placed in control of such strategic areas as cities on the main routes of communication and were given domains lying between those of daimyo who had submitted to the Tokugawa only after being defeated.

Later adherents to the Tokugawa, called outer daimyo, included some of the richest and most powerful men in the

Ieyasu Tokugawa, the lord of Mikawa province, was appointed shogun (military emperor) by the Japanese emperor Go-Yojo in 1603. This was the first appointment of an official shogunate in Japan. Ieyasu's reign was the founding of the Tokugawa shogunate, which lasted fifteen generations, until 1867, when feudalism was abolished in Japan.

country, and controlling them was a continuing problem. Tokugawa policies reduced their wealth by requiring contributions to public works and impaired their capability to plot by forbidding them to enter into alliances with other daimyo or to approach the imperial court. Daimyo were required to maintain residence in, and make annual visits to, Edo (modern Tokyo), the new capital of the shogunate. During their absence they were required to leave members of their families in Edo as hostages. Checkpoints were established on all important routes, among other things to look for "women leaving Edo and firearms entering Edo." Tokugawa inspectors kept the outer daimyo under close surveillance.

The fiction of imperial rule was maintained. The emperor and the court nobility in Kyōto, financially dependent on the shogun, continued their limited functions under the watchful eye of the Tokugawa.

The *bakufu* in Edo was developed into a strong administrative apparatus under a prime minister (a post, however, often left vacant), a council of state of four or five elders, a group of junior elders, and numerous administrative and judicial officers. A corps of inspectors or censors kept the shogun informed, reporting on officials of the shogunate and acting as secret police. The *bakufu* became increasingly complex and bureaucratic. The Tokugawa did not lack educated and capable men to staff the *bakufu*, however, for by the seventeenth century there was marked development of education among the upper classes.

Local government in each fief was exercised by the daimyo under restrictions imposed by the vigilant *bakufu*. Limited autonomy was permitted religious sects, merchant guilds, and some towns and villages.

Beginning in 1600, British and Dutch traders began to appear in Japan in competition with the already well-established Portuguese and Spanish. The Protestant newcomers, principally interested in trade, implied to the Japanese that their Roman Catholic competitors intended to conquer the country. Ieyasu Tokugawa, who had been initially well disposed toward Westerners, became distrustful and reverted to persecution of Christianity, and his successor ordered the expulsion or execution of all foreign missionaries. More severe persecutions followed, resulting to all intents in the destruction of the Christian community of perhaps three hundred thousand, which was centered in Kyushu. Contacts with the outside world were forbidden to the Japanese, and by 1640 all foreigners had been expelled. After 1638 only a handful of Dutch and a few Chinese were allowed to trade at Nagasaki under the closest restrictions. This policy completely halted the flourishing foreign trade of the previous centuries and cut Japan off from the rest of the world until the middle of the nineteenth century.

The early Tokugawa shogun took steps to maintain social stability as a necessary condition for the preservation of their power. They organized society by edict into a rigid hierarchy of four classes based on Confucian concepts. At the top were the samurai, whose position became unchallengeable owing to their social, administrative, and military eminence. The samurai constituted about 5 or 6 percent of the population, which probably stayed below 30 million inhabitants during the Tokugawa period. The peasants were the next class but were far below the samurai; the demarcation between samurai and peasant had been widened by a decree of Hideyoshi Toyotomi ordering peasant samurai to surrender their swords, which thereafter were the emblem of the aristocratic samurai. Artisans were in the third group. Merchants, although many were well educated, were placed in the lowest class because in Confucian terms they were thought of as unproductive. Left entirely outside the ranking system were those persons associated with occupations considered contemptible, such as tanning.

Tokugawa edicts prescribed functions and standards of behavior for each class and social relationship; the edict for the samurai was promulgated in 1615. Civil and criminal laws were set forth in edicts that typically defined the major principles involved but did not direct their application, this being left to the discretion of the magistrate. The provisions for legal liability and punishment were different for each of the social classes; there was no concept of equality of justice among classes. Civil cases rarely came before judicial officials because most were settled by negotiation between the heads of the social units involved.

Domestic peace and unity during the Tokugawa shogunate promoted the development of internal commerce and the growth of urban centers. A large market for goods and services developed in Edo, in provincial fortified towns where the samurai were concentrated, and on the heavily traveled Tōkaidō (eastern sea road) between Kyōto and Edo. Coastwise shipping was extensively used; it was, for example, the chief means of supplying rice to Edo.

The Tokugawa embarked on extensive road-building projects and such construction as their mausoleums at Nikko, which served the triple objective of draining the financial resources of potentially dangerous daimyo, of providing a road network for speedy communications and effective surveillance, and of promoting trade. Rapid courier service was instituted. The merchant class prospered and expanded, as did associations of craftsmen and tradesmen. Urban growth stimulated the gradual change to a money economy, which developed with the appearance of credit instruments. Rice exchanges were established in Osaka and Edo, the economic and financial centers of the nation.

The peasants, who had to bear almost the entire burden of supporting the government and the samurai, suffered most from the changes in the economy. Taxes increased, often by irregular exactions by the daimyo, and the value of rice declined as the money economy expanded. Although agricultural production increased as crops were diversified, fertilization and cultivation were improved, and the cultivated area was expanded through reclamation, the peasants' lot worsened to the point of impoverishment. Periodic crop failures resulted in famine. The consequences

Himeji Castle, built in 1609, is representative of the splendor of the royal estate in feudal Japan

were an increase in tenancy, migration to the cities, infanticide, and peasant rebellions—of which there were several hundred during the Tokugawa period. There was also an accompanying decline in the income of the ruling class. These conditions operated to keep the population at a constant figure estimated at below 30 million.

A popular urban culture and the rise of new intellectual currents also marked the Tokugawa period. The arts and literature blossomed in the large cities of Osaka and Edo. The new Kabuki drama and puppet plays were popular, as were *haiku* poetry, realistic novels of city life, and woodblock prints in color showing scenes of daily life. Geisha became prominent in this period. The patronage of merchants was a major reason for the flourishing state of geisha and of houses of prostitution in segregated quarters, such as Yoshiwara in Edo. Merchants were increasingly affluent but were effectively barred from social intercourse outside their own class.

There was also a change in the intellectual atmosphere of Japan. A decline in the influence of Buddhism and of the Buddhist clergy was accompanied by the development of a spirit of inquiry and criticism by the samurai. In this the chief focus of scholarship was on the Chinese classics; this was consistent with government policy. A wide range of schools of thought existed, however, because the shogunate permitted intellectual inquiry provided it did not involve Christianity or questions of government policy.

The shogunate after 1720 relaxed its restrictions on *Dutch learning*—a term applied to foreign knowledge generally—obtained from the Dutch at Nagasaki. The immediate result was an increase in knowledge of Western military techniques and such applied sciences as medicine. Another aspect of the intellectual activity of the times was the effort to revive ancient Shinto beliefs and to develop an awareness of the divine origin of the emperor. Shinto sects that appealed more to the popular mind appeared in the first half of the nineteenth century. Intellectual ferment was strongest in the southwestern fiefs among the younger samurai who administered the great domains of the daimyo there. Throughout this time, however, Tokugawa restrictions, no matter how much they may have been resented, kept the outward appearance of an unchanged order despite the growth of a spirit of inquiry, the economic growth that had produced an advanced commercial economy, and the development of a strong popular sense of national consciousness.

The successive appearance in the early nineteenth century of Russians, British, Americans, and Frenchmen demanding the opening of trade exerted new pressures on the Tokugawa structure. The superiority of Western arms was quickly recognized as a clear challenge to the policy of seclusion. The anxiety of the *bakufu* was heightened by the example of China, where the foreigners had obtained extraterritoriality and tariff rights.

In 1853 Japan's vulnerability was exposed by the arrival of United States warships under Commodore Matthew Perry, whose demands included facilities for trade. Unable to resist by force, the *bakufu* acquiesced but took the unusual step of consulting with both the emperor and daimyo. The first of Japan's modern-day treaties, however—that with the United States in 1854—was signed by the shogunate on its own authority. The demands of other Western powers then resulted in a series of treaties that marked the end of Japan's seclusion. These treaties provided for extensive commercial concessions that gave a virtual monopoly of external trade to foreigners and, like the treaties with China, granted extraterritorial status to foreign nationals in Japan, thus exempting them from Japanese jurisdiction. These "unequal treaties" outraged most samurai.

The shogunate had opened the floodgates of criticism by consulting with the court and the daimyo. This was evidence of factional division and weakness and released long-standing political, economic, and social frustrations. The onus for yielding to the foreigners was put on the shogunate, whose opponents adopted the slogan of "Revere the Emperor and Expel the Barbarians." Political initiative was seized by the young samurai bureaucrats of the outer fiefs of Satsuma, Choshu, Tosa, and Hizen. Samurai patriotism was stirred by the example of Shoin Yoshida, an antiforeign Choshu scholar executed in 1859, whose example later was the inspiration for Japanese chauvinism. Yoshida called for national unity under the emperor and for military preparedness, not only to preserve Japan's integrity but to bring Korea, Manchuria, and Formosa under Japanese hegemony.

The weapons of revolt were in the hands of the rebellious samurai, for as Tokugawa supervision relaxed, the outer daimyo in the southwest had profited from contacts with the Dutch by learning some Western industrial technology. They had established iron foundries, shipyards, and smelters; and the Choshu daimyo, in southwestern Honshū, had started to organize a peasant conscript army.

Two retaliatory attacks by Western naval forces for anti-Western acts convinced some samurai of the futility of attempting to expel the foreigners by force. The British bombarded Kagoshima in the Satsuma domain in Kyushu in 1863, and a joint United States, British, French, and Dutch force attacked Shimonoseki in Choshu in 1864. As a result, the influential samurai of these fiefs abandoned the idea of isolation in favor of strengthening Japan. They started building their own military forces—which soon proved superior to those of the shogunate—as a step toward their goal of formation of a new national regime under an emperor restored to rule. Choshu peasant troops led by samurai officers defeated forces of the shogun in 1867, and the last Tokugawa shogun voluntarily relinquished his rule of the country to the emperor.

THE MEIJI PERIOD AND MODERNIZATION, 1867–1912

INTERNAL DEVELOPMENTS

The young samurai of the southwestern fiefs, who with a few court nobles restored the emperor's rule, took over as the key figures. The new order faced formidable tasks. An effective political system and a national army had to be constructed, and material strength through industrialization had to be attained. In the next two decades there evolved the patterns for an effective centralized government and for a powerful army and navy and the foundations of a modern economy.

The emperor, whose period of reign is known as *Meiji* (enlightened government), was officially restored to rule on January 3, 1868. On April 6 of that year he took the so-called imperial charter oath. This set forth several principles of the new monarchy, notably the search for knowledge throughout the world. The first organizational steps were the temporary re-creation of the ancient bureaucratic offices of the Nara-Heian imperial state and revival of the concept that all Japanese were the loyal subjects of a divine emperor. The establishment of Shinto at this time as the state religion also fostered the growth of national patriotism centered on the throne. The Council of State, however, soon emerged as the real power in the government, performing both executive and legislative functions. In late 1868 the imperial capital was moved to Edo, which was renamed Tokyo.

Daimyo lands became the property of the throne in 1869 in return for government bonds, but the former feudal lords continued as governors until 1871 when their approximately three hundred fiefs were replaced by seventy-two prefectures. Two years later a national conscript army replaced the samurai forces of the daimyo domains. By 1873 the feudal structure had been abolished.

The Tokugawa class structure was abolished in 1871. Except for a small noble class, all Japanese became in theory socially equal after the samurai lost their special privileges in 1876. Former outcastes, however, were distinguishable by the appellation of new commoners.

The daimyo received generous compensation for their lands, which enabled them to invest in commerce and industry and thus assist in industrialization. The compensa-

Mutsuhito (Meiji), emperor of Japan from 1867 to 1912, did much to forward the establishment of Western civilization in Japan. His reign was marked by victorious wars with China and Russia. The emperor was born on November 3, 1852, the son of Emperor Komei, the 121st emperor of Japan. In the year 1867, at the age of sixteen, Mutsuhito became the 122nd emperor.

tion given most samurai, however, was small and in most cases was quickly spent. When in 1873 the general conscription law deprived the samurai of their military prerogative, they had further cause for dissatisfaction. Their discontent was potentially dangerous, and rehabilitation of impoverished former samurai was a major problem in the 1870s. Although many entered the bureaucracy, army and navy, education, business, and agriculture, enough dissidence existed among them to provide strength to rebel against the new regime. This threat remained until 1877 when the new peasant conscript army defeated an uprising led by Takamori Saigo, a samurai from Satsuma who had defected from the ruling group.

About one hundred men constituted the ruling oligarchy at this time. Differences arose among them from several causes, including personal, regional, and factional rivalries and disagreement about concentration of effort on internal reform in preference to military expansion abroad. The first phase was a conflict between the exponents of modernization and the defenders of feudal tradition and prerogative. The feudalists were defeated, but this was followed by a contest between the victors and the advocates of parliamentary government.

The first open break in the oligarchy occurred in 1873 with the rejection of the proposal of Takamori Saigo to invade Korea. The dominant Satsuma-Choshu group successfully opposed foreign adventures of this scope because they considered them to be a diversion of energy from the primary task of strengthening the country's economic and military power. After the suppression of Saigo's Satsuma Rebellion of 1877, the samurai of Tosa (in Shikoku) and Hizen (in northwestern Kyushu), who also had left the government with Saigo, turned their opposition to domestic

issues. They organized the first political parties, the Liberal party (Jiyūtō) and the Reform party (Kaishintō), in 1881.

As a result in part of the pressures of opposition to the government, the Meiji constitution, which provided for a parliament, was bestowed on the people as an imperial gift in 1889. The constitution reflected the strong influence of Germany and especially that of the chancellor of Germany, Otto von Bismarck. It vested sovereignty in the emperor, whose person was declared sacred and inviolable. The civil liberties granted his subjects were made subject to the limits of the law. The executive, centralized authority was made supreme. Despite the position given him, the emperor was a figurehead; the real effect of the constitution was to give legal sanction to the power already exercised by the bureaucracy, which with the passage of time was increasingly influenced by the military. Behind the new members of the bureaucracy the survivors of the original major figures in the restoration retained a large measure of power in their extraconstitutional role as *genrō* (elder statesmen). Japan also adopted new codes of civil, commercial, and criminal law based on French and Prussian models, although the civil code retained many traditional concepts.

There was no parallel improvement in the position of peasant cultivators, who had been given ownership of their land when the rights of the feudal classes were abolished. A 10 percent growth in population between 1880 and 1890 increased pressure on the limited area of cultivable land. Farm tenancy doubled to 40 percent between 1873 and 1887, in part owing to the requirement of paying taxes in cash. (Taxes on farmers were the main source of government revenue.)

Japanese military forces increased in size and in sophistication of equipment and organization during the early Meiji period. The leading figure in Japanese army history was Aritomo Yamagata, who was responsible for the adoption of a German style of army organization, with a general staff and a staff college and divisional organization. The new army had an effective strength of seventy-three

On April 6, 1868, Emperor Meiji issued the Five Articles of the Imperial Covenant, establishing the fundamentals of national policy. The emperor is shown listening to the covenant being read.

thousand in the 1880s. Yamagata made indoctrination of conscripts in Bushidō and Shintō a prominent feature of military service. The cost of the army and of modernizing and expanding the navy accounted for about one-third of the expenditures of the national budget in the 1880s.

In 1873 the Tokugawa edict against Christianity was repealed. American and British Protestants, Roman Catholics, and Russian Orthodox began open efforts to make converts. Progress was slow; by 1889 there were an estimated seventy-four thousand adherents to Christianity. The government tolerated Christianity but, owing to the rising nationalism of the times, Christianity on occasion was considered a subversive influence.

MEIJI JAPAN'S INTERNATIONAL RELATIONS

In the 1870s Japan secured sovereignty over nearby islands to the north and south. An agreement with czarist Russia in 1875 gave Japan the Kuril Islands while conceding Sakhalin Island (Karafuto) to Russia. The Ryukyu Islands, which had been conquered by the daimyo of Satsuma in 1609, were unilaterally annexed in 1872. In 1875 Japan's claim to the Bonin Islands (Ogasawara) was recognized by Great Britain and the United States.

The overriding foreign policy goal of the Meiji oligarchs, however, was revision of the unequal treaties forced upon Japan by the Western powers in the 1850s. A mission sent to Europe and the United States between 1871 and 1873 for this purpose returned empty-handed, convinced that Japan would have to make itself stronger before any concessions could be obtained.

The struggle for revision of the unequal treaties continued but did not meet with success until the 1890s after, at Western insistence, certain legal standards and procedures were adopted. First Great Britain in 1894 and the other powers by 1899 surrendered their extraterritorial rights. Treaty-imposed restrictions on tariffs were gradually relinquished, and by 1911 Japan resumed complete control of its tariffs.

In 1894 the issue of sovereignty over Korea precipitated war with China. In the 1895 Treaty of Shimonoseki, which

Emperor Mutsuhito opening Japan's first Diet (Congress) in 1889

followed Japan's quick victory, China recognized Korea's independence, and Japan acquired Taiwan, the Pescadores Islands (P'eng-hu), and the Liaotung Peninsula in southern Manchuria. The war demonstrated Japan's military strength and its intention to use it in competition with the Western powers for concessions and territory on the mainland. From the late Tokugawa period onward, Japanese nationalists had been preaching the divine destiny of the nation to rule Asia; its government had now decided to secure a position on the mainland and to obtain a share of the spoils.

The 1895 treaty involved Japan directly in European diplomacy concerned with privileges and territory on the Chinese mainland. Russia, seeing its ambitions for a warm water port either in Korea or on the Liaotung Peninsula blocked, took the initiative to prevent Japan from retaining this territory in Manchuria. In the same year that the Treaty of Shimonoseki was signed, Russia, France, and Germany intervened and forced Japan to renounce its claim to the peninsula. Continuing rivalry with Russia led to the conclusion of the Anglo-Japanese alliance in 1902, which marked a turning point in Japanese foreign relations and was the first time that Japan had been accepted as an equal by a major European power. It cleared the way for Japan to deal with Russia without fear of interference.

The 1895 European intervention had given a strong stimulus to Japanese nationalism. The conviction that Japan's destiny depended on its own material and spiritual strength grew stronger in 1898 when Russia took the Liaotung territory it had been instrumental in forcing Japan to renounce. Public opinion in Japan supported war with Russia in 1904 when it appeared that this was the only means of expelling Russia from Manchuria and of ensuring Japan's position as the most powerful nation in northeastern Asia.

In February 1904 the Japanese government decided that it would wait no longer for the conclusion of negotiations with Russia over their respective positions and rights in Manchuria and Korea and took military action. Without warning, the Japanese navy bombarded Port Arthur (Lushun), on the southern tip of the Liaotung Peninsula. Two days later Japan declared war, and the Japanese army advanced from Korea into Manchuria. The Russians were defeated in the major land battle for Mukden and in the

During the annual festival on November 3, the birthday of Emperor Meiji, a messenger from the emperor visits the shrine in order to pay homage to the departed emperor.

notable naval victory of the Japanese fleet over the Russian Baltic fleet in the Korea Strait off the Tsushima Islands.

Japan's victory destroyed Russian power in the Far East and raised Japan without question to the rank of a major power. The Treaty of Portsmouth (New Hampshire), signed in September 1905, which was negotiated with the assistance of the United States, gave Japan the Russian rights in the Liaotung Peninsula and sovereignty over the southern half of Sakhalin Island with fishing rights in adjacent waters. Japan also acquired control of the South Manchurian Railway, with the right to station troops along the line to protect it.

Japan's rights in Korea were recognized by the United States in 1905 and by Great Britain the same year, when a second Anglo-Japanese alliance of broader scope was signed. By an agreement in 1905 with Korea, Japan obtained a protectorate over the country. This was followed in 1910 by a treaty of annexation that made Korea an integral part of Japan. In 1908 Japan signed an agreement with the United States to maintain the territorial integrity of China and equality of commercial rights there. In 1911 the Anglo-Japanese alliance was renewed for ten years. Meanwhile, Japan continued to strengthen its military and naval forces. By the outbreak of World War I in 1914, two years after the close of the Meiji period, Japan was the dominant power in east Asia.

LIBERALISM, REACTION, AND MILITARISM, 1912–45

PARTY GOVERNMENT

The death of the Meiji emperor in 1912 and the accession of his son, whose reign period (1912–26) is known as Taisho, caused little change in government policies. (The Taisho emperor was succeeded by his son Hirohito—still the emperor in 1980—whose reign period is called Showa.) Early in the Taisho period, however, parliamentary opposition to the government's program of increasing armaments brought the ruling clique to a realization of the need for support by the political parties. Most of the original oligarchy had by that time died. The new generation in power, lacking the unchallenged position of their predecessors, found they could not attain their purposes without political support. The party organizations and the Diet proved useful machinery.

By the end of World War I in 1918, rule by a small clique had changed to struggle among diverse groups of military men, bureaucrats, businessmen, and intellectuals. In September 1918 the first party cabinet was formed under Kei Hara, president of the majority Seiyukai party. Hara was assassinated in 1921. The cabinets formed thereafter were generally short lived, but party cabinets dependent upon majority support in the Diet were the rule until 1932.

Japan's position in the Pacific Ocean area was affected in the 1920s by a series of agreements on nonaggression,

Emperor Yoshihito reigned from 1912 to 1926. He was succeeded by his son, who became Emperor Hirohito, the 124th emperor of Japan.

Emperor Hirohito at the age of five

Prince Regent Hirohito with his three younger brothers on the palace grounds shortly before his succession. Left to right: The prince regent, Prince Mikasa, Prince Takanatsu, and Prince Chichibu

Emperor Hirohito (Showa), then prince regent, was the first Japanese emperor to travel abroad. In 1921, he visited with a number of heads of state in Europe. He is shown here with King George V in London.

The emperor and empress shortly after their wedding in 1924

The young emperor Hirohito in the traditional Japanese court robes for royalty used on formal and official occasions (1928)

naval disarmament, and relations with China that resulted from the Washington Conference of 1922. The disarmament treaty of that year set a ratio of tonnage of capital ships (battleships) of five each for Great Britain and the United States to three for Japan. A similar ratio was established of 1.75 each for France and Italy. Japan agreed to the lower ratio when Great Britain and the United States undertook not to expand bases and fortifications in the Pacific other than their existing major naval installations. Japan made a conciliatory gesture toward China by announcing withdrawal of troops from Shantung province—China had refused to accept the provisions of the Treaty of Versailles. This started negotiations that led to the Sino-Japanese Treaty of 1922, in which Japan agreed to the restoration of full Chinese sovereignty in Shantung.

REACTION

By the late 1920s there were some signs of financial instability in the Japanese economy, the modern sector of which had come increasingly under *zaibatsu* (financial cliques) control. When the worldwide depression of the late 1920s reached Japan, its effects were severe; in part it was aggravated by the financial retrenchment policies of what was to be the last of the pre-World War II party cabinet governments. Unchanged taxation, drastically reduced prices for such cash crops as silk and rice, and unemployment all contributed to a gloomy situation that was accompanied by general social unrest. There was a variety of views on the best means to solve the country's problems. Some groups showed a willingness to endorse extremist military proposals, and a smaller number put credence in Marxism and communism for solutions.

During the second half of the 1920s the more extreme groups in the Japanese army were concerned about the prospect of the unification of China as the Chinese Nationalist movement extended its authority. This was especially so after the establishment of the new Nationalist capital at Nanking in 1928. Moreover, unification would eventually result in Manchuria's becoming an integral part of China.

Ultranationalist Japanese officers in the almost autonomous Kwantung (Liaotung Peninsula) army, which was assigned political and economic as well as military responsibilities, engineered the murder of Chang Tso-lin, the principal Manchurian warlord, in 1928 after he refused to cooperate in maintaining Manchuria as a separate political entity. Ultranationalism was not confined, however, to the Kwantung army nor to the military services alone. The Black Dragon Society (a name derived from the Chinese name for the Amur River), whose objective was the extension of Japan's borders to the Amur, included both military and civilians. Events as well as talk showed that some army elements were out of control of the civilian government and also of their own high command—which apparently in part condoned ultranationalist plotting and acts of insubordination.

His Majesty Emperor Hirohito was born in Tokyo on April 29, 1901. He studied at the Peers' School and later at an institute specially established for his education.

As crown prince, he traveled in Europe for six months in 1921 and became prince regent shortly after his return. In 1924, he married Princess Kuni, now Empress Nagako. He succeeded to the throne in 1926.

Emperor Hirohito, an advocate of close family ties, is seen here in the garden of the palace with the empress and their children. Pictured in this 1939 photograph are (left to right) *Princess Kazuko, the empress holding Princess Takako, the emperor, Princess Shigeko, Prince Regent Akihito, Princess Atsuko, and Prince Hitachi.*

MILITARISM

The Mukden Incident of September 18, 1931, involving an explosion in an area of the rail line guarded by Japanese troops, started a series of events that culminated in army control of Japan. As an immediate result of the Mukden incident Japanese troops occupied all of Manchuria by January 1932. The League of Nations, to which China appealed, was ineffective in the face of strong Japanese opposition. Soon afterward Japan's political position in Manchuria was secured when the new state of Manchoukuo announced its independence. The new state was ruled through the puppet emperor Hsuantung (P'u-yi), the last emperor of the Manchu Ching Dynasty of China.

The last fully party-controlled government ended with the assassination of Prime Minister Tsuyoshi Inukai by a group of young officers on May 15, 1932. The so-called national governments of the 1930s, which succeeded the Inukai cabinet, consisted of three groups: a core of professional members of the bureaucracy and party and military men who generally balanced each other.

The Diet (legislature) remained uncooperative with the national cabinets. Popular dissatisfaction was demonstrated in the February 1936 elections when the Minseito, which was more moderate than the Seiyukai on expansionism, obtained the largest bloc of seats. Ultranationalistic elements in the military reacted to this result the same month in a three-day mutiny by units of the Tokyo garrison. This was put down by troops loyal to the government. Seven leading government figures were assassinated, but the cabinet did not yield control to the extremists. The outcome, however, raised the prestige and power of the army, which subsequently found members of the bureaucracy and big businessmen more inclined to cooperate. From this position there was little effective opposition to the army from a society that had by now come under police surveillance aimed at "thought control." In any case the public generally acquiesced in the basic policy of Japanese expansion on the Asian mainland.

Japan failed to secure the degree of Chinese cooperation and the amount of economic benefit that it desired either by agreements with local Chinese authorities or from the puppet regimes that it established in parts of northern China. Nationalist Chinese authority and military forces, however, were gradually forced from that area. A minor incident near Peiping (now Peking) on July 7, 1937, since known as the Lukouch'iao (Marco Polo Bridge) Incident, provided a further pretext for direct military action. This began in northern China, from which it spread to Inner Mongolia and to central China, where Shanghai and Nanking had fallen to the Japanese by the end of the year. The Chinese government moved its capital from Nanking to Hankow and from there to Chungking in October 1938. Japanese land forces never penetrated as far as Chungking, but they did subject it to prolonged aerial attack. Japanese capture of Canton in late 1938 brought effective control of all significant routes of access to China except those overland from Southeast Asia and from the Soviet Union.

Japanese military operations in China did not attain their political objectives. The Japanese began increasingly to blame their failure to settle the "China Affair" on the European powers and the United States, whose treaty-based rights were often interfered with in China. At the time, Great Britain and France were preoccupied with Germany, the United States was confining its reactions to protests, and only the Soviet Union appeared likely to provide active opposition to Japan. Negotiations with the Soviet Union, however, in 1938 and again in 1939, after severe fighting along the Soviet-Manchoukuo border, improved Russo-Japanese relations. Relations with the United States deteriorated meanwhile. In mid-1939 the United States announced its intention to abrogate the treaty of commerce with Japan in six months. This action removed the legal barrier to the imposition by the United States of an embargo on trade with Japan.

After war started in Europe in September 1939, Japan took steps to ensure its sovereignty over European colonies in Asia should Germany and Italy defeat the European colonial powers. The Tripartite Treaty of Alliance of September 1940 resulted. Japan also undertook more effective economic planning in an effort to exploit Asian markets and materials and to coordinate domestic production and distribution. The efforts included the establishment of the Greater East Asian Co-Prosperity Sphere.

By late 1941 the military had achieved control of the Japanese economy. Dominance of domestic politics had already been attained when the political parties "voluntarily" dissolved themselves in 1940 and became part of a single ultranationalist body called the Imperial Rule Assistance Association. Until the end of World War II, this body was the only legal political organization.

Events in 1941, including Germany's invasion of the Soviet Union, a stiffening attitude against Japan on the part of the United States, and military requirements for a secure source of petroleum (prospectively available from the Netherlands East Indies), led to a decision to eliminate Western power in the western Pacific. When negotiations with the United States finally failed to produce the accommodation sought by the Japanese, the government of General Hideki Tojo ordered attacks on Hawaii, the Philippines, Wake Island, Guam, Singapore, Malaya, and Hong Kong. The attacks took place on December 7, east of the international date line and on December 8 to the west of 180° longitude. Mutual declarations of war followed.

WAR IN THE PACIFIC

Impressive successes at the beginning of the war seemed to confirm the correctness of the Japanese army's aggressive policies. The naval and air forces of the United States were largely immobilized by the attack on Honolulu, except its main aircraft carrier units. Western strongholds from Hong Kong to Burma quickly fell, and by mid-1942 Japanese might was supreme in the western Pacific.

The initial military successes evoked patriotic fervor in Japan, and the Tojo government, despite its dictatorial methods, enjoyed popular support. The military reverses that began with the loss of Guadalcanal in February 1943 made it evident that the military had miscalculated the strength of United States forces, but there appeared to be little public knowledge of this misjudgment. In November 1943, as United States military pressure increased, the Tojo government attempted further centralization of administrative and economic power by creating nine regional administrative organizations in Japan proper and the Ministry of Munitions as an overall control organization.

Japan came under steady air attack after the loss of Saipan in early July 1944. This produced a shock that forced Tojo to resign soon afterward. He was succeeded by General Kuniaki Koiso, whose government was charged with maintaining the war effort while being prepared to open negotiations for a compromise if peace appeared possible. In August 1944 another control and coordination body, the Supreme Council for the Direction of War, was established, consisting of the emperor and the chief ministers.

Heavy bombing of the Japanese islands and the landing by United States forces in Okinawa, the largest island of the Ryukyus, caused the fall of the Koiso cabinet in April 1945. Admiral Kantaro Suzuki, the new premier, was of the group that favored negotiation rather than a fight to the death. He tried to negotiate a new nonaggression pact with the Soviet Union after the Soviets made a unilateral announcement that it regarded the 1941 pact invalid. Suzuki was unsuccessful in this effort: he was also unsuccessful in obtaining Soviet good offices toward negotiating peace with the Allies.

The unconditional surrender terms of the Potsdam Declaration of July 26, 1945—in essence, occupation of Japan, laying down of arms by Japanese forces, dismantling of Japan's economic potential for war, punishment of war criminals, and democratization of the Japanese government—changed for the time being the Japanese attitude toward negotiation. There was no response from the Japanese government to the declaration. The first atomic bomb used in warfare was dropped on August 6, 1945, on Hiroshima, and the second one was dropped on Nagasaki on August 9. On August 9 the Soviet Union also declared war against Japan.

The Japanese decision to accept the terms of the Potsdam Declaration was reached on August 14 after an unsuccessful effort to modify them in order to preserve the special position of the emperor. The decision involved the active and possibly the decisive participation of the emperor, who then took an unprecedented step by himself announcing the decision to the Japanese people by radio the same day.

On September 2, 1945, the formal instrument of surrender was signed on the U.S.S. *Missouri* in Tokyo Bay. An imperial rescript was issued explaining that the surrender had been signed on the emperor's behalf and commanding obedience to government orders issued in connection with it. All authority in Japan, civil and military, became subject to General Douglas MacArthur of the United States army as Supreme Commander for the Allied powers. He was supported mainly by United States forces.

OCCUPATION AND REFORM, 1945–52

The emperor's radio broadcast stating that the Japanese must accept total surrender and "endure the unendurable" was accepted and carried out without demur. In addition to

A map of Japan at the point of its greatest conquests in 1945

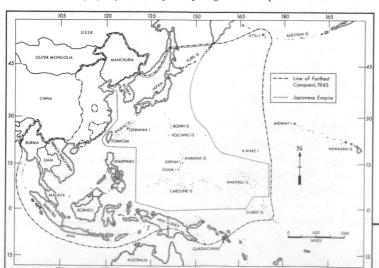

the power of the imperial utterance and the tradition of obedience to authority, psychological shock and physical weariness contributed to docile acceptance of surrender and foreign military occupation. The militant nationalist creed of the 1930s and 1940s had collapsed. The country's economy was in ruins; most major cities were heavily damaged; and the number of civilian casualties approached a million. Later the repatriation of some six million soldiers and civilians increased the demand for food and shelter, both already in short supply.

General MacArthur and his headquarters had the primary responsibility for carrying out the terms of surrender. His actions, under the policy guidance of the United States government, were more moderate and less punitive than was favored by some of the Allied powers, especially the Soviet Union. These actions were taken through the Japanese civil authorities in administrative matters. General MacArthur was under the nominal supervision of the eleven-nation Far Eastern Commission in Washington and was advised in the exercise of his authority by the Allied Council for Japan located in Tokyo, composed of representatives of the United States, Great Britain, the Republic of China, and the Soviet Union.

Demilitarization of Japan was immediately undertaken; demobilization of the former imperial army, navy, and air forces was completed by early 1946.

In October 1945 a new cabinet acceptable to occupation headquarters was formed by Baron Kijuro Shidehara, who had left public life in the 1930s because of his opposition to militarism. The government started preparation of a new constitution in late 1945. The initial draft did not satisfy occupation authorities; however, a mutually satisfactory document was promulgated on November 3, 1946, to take effect on May 3, 1947.

The Constitution of 1946 was a drastic change from the Meiji Constitution of 1889 in that the highest organization of government was the popularly elected bicameral National Diet. The emperor, who on January 1, 1946, had denied his divinity, was retained as symbol of the state, but sovereignty was transferred from him to the Japanese people. Executive power was entrusted to a cabinet responsible to the Diet. The courts were made independent of the other branches of government; the Supreme Court was given power of constitutional review. Local self-government was strengthened, and elective assemblies were created at every level of local administration.

The International Military Tribunal for the Far East, composed of representatives of the eleven Allied powers, was established in Tokyo in May 1948 to carry out the provision of the Potsdam Declaration calling for punishment of those responsible for leading the country into war. The tribunal sentenced to death or imprisonment twenty-five Japanese officials (General Tojo among them) for having planned the war in violation of international law. More than four thousand others were tried in Japan and abroad by Allied tribunals on lesser charges. Occupation authorities also excluded from public office those who had supported militant nationalism and aggression before and during the war. The latter action did not prove to be permanent; it was the first reform rescinded by the Japanese government after the occupation ended.

Whereas the initial and most important period of the occupation—from its beginning to 1948—was marked by reform, the second period was one of retrenchment, in which some reforms were modified and greater attention was given toward improvement of the Japanese economy.

The cold war between the free world and the Communist-bloc countries that developed after World War II strongly affected the policy of the United States toward Japan, whose geographic position, industrial capacity, and potential military power took on a strategic importance that did not exist when the war ended. Political instability was general in east Asia, virtually eliminating Japan's principal prewar export markets. The invasion in June 1950 of the Republic of Korea (South Korea) by the communist regime of the Democratic People's Republic of Korea (North Korea) provided further impetus for United States interest in the economic stability of Japan and the possible inclusion of Japan in regional defense arrangements.

The United States started negotiations for a treaty of peace with Japan in 1947, but no progress was made for several years because of disagreement with the Soviet Union's position. In 1950 the United States proceeded without the participation of the Soviet Union. After preliminary discussions starting early that year, the peace treaty was signed at San Francisco on September 8, 1951; it went into effect on April 28, 1952. The Soviet Union and other Communist-bloc countries refused to sign the treaty.

Under the treaty's terms, Japan regained sovereignty over the four main islands and smaller adjacent islands. It renounced claims to its former overseas possessions, including the Kuril Islands and southern Sakhalin, both of which had been occupied by the Soviet Union since 1945. Japan agreed to United States administration of the Ryukyu and Bonin islands. The treaty provided that Japan pay reparations in amounts to be fixed by bilateral agreements with claimant countries. It also provided that Japan had the right to self-defense, and it could authorize the stationing of foreign troops in the country.

A security treaty between the United States and Japan was signed the same day. This pact provided for United States bases and facilities in Japan and the stationing of United States forces there. The United States, for its part, undertook to defend Japan in case of attack. The security treaty indirectly brought Japan into the series of collective and defensive treaties that had been established by the United States in the western Pacific.

The Ryukyu Islands were administered after 1945 by the United States military authorities separate from the Allied occupation authorities in Japan proper. Beginning in 1950 the main island of Okinawa was developed into a major United States military base. The peace treaty with Japan recognized the right of the United States to administer both the Ryukyus and the Bonins. A later statement by the secretary of state of the United States that Japan had "residual sovereignty" was interpreted to mean that the islands would revert to Japan when conditions in the western Pacific permitted.

JAPAN SINCE 1952

Shigeru Yoshida, a former diplomat and leader of the major conservative party in the latter part of the occupation period, was prime minister of Japan when the peace treaty was negotiated and came into effect. He remained in office until 1954. The extreme right wing since the peace treaty has included a number of groups that represented prewar tendencies, but they remained disunited and had little practical influence. The leftist elements achieved considerable strength under the occupation until occupation headquarters purged the leadership of the Communist party in 1950, reducing it to an underground activity; in the elections of 1949 the Communists had received about 10 percent of the popular vote. After the occupation ended, the extreme left received much less popular sympathy and did not again obtain such a high percentage of the popular vote until 1972.

The Constitution of 1946 was subject to extensive study by a commission established by the government in 1956. After eight years of consideration, the commission recom-

Emperor Hirohito visits with General Douglas MacArthur, the "conqueror," in 1945 in his headquarters in Tokyo. Shortly after this, the emperor announced that it is a "false concept that the emperor is divine."

The emperor in 1946 visiting an orphanage and talking to the children

The emperor, seated, a noted marine biologist, is seen here reading to his family from a book he wrote on the subject in 1955. Standing, left to right, are: the empress, Crown Prince Akihito, Prince Yoshi, and Princess Sugu.

mended revisions strengthening central authority and modification of Article 9 renouncing force and the maintenance of armed forces.

The peace treaty did not fully restore Japan's international relations and standing in the world community. In addition to the Soviet-bloc nations, other countries such as India and Burma did not sign the original treaty; similar treaties were concluded with these two countries in 1952 and 1954, respectively. Some countries required agreement by Japan for payment of reparations for war damages as a condition for resumption of diplomatic relations. This was the case with Burma, as it was with the Philippines (1956), Indonesia (1958), and the Republic of Vietnam (South Vietnam).

In 1952 Japan signed a peace treaty with the Republic of China (Nationalist China), which since 1949 has been located on the formerly Japanese-held island of Taiwan. The agreement did not prejudice Japan's freedom to negotiate with the PRC, with which unofficial trade relations were established in 1953. In 1972 formal ties with Nationalist China were severed and normal diplomatic relations with the PRC were established. Diplomatic relations with South Korea were established in 1965 by a treaty in which Japan undertook payment of reparations and the furnishing of assistance to this southern portion of its former colony.

Japan became a member of the United Nations (UN) in December 1956 after reaching agreement with the Soviet Union terminating hostilities between them; before this agreement the Soviet Union had blocked Japan's admission, although Japan had become associated with many of the UN specialized agencies. Japan also established affiliation with the Colombo Plan, the General Agreement on Tariffs and Trade (GATT), and the Organization for Economic Cooperation and Development (OECD). The Japanese government took a major part in the foundation in 1966 of the Asian Development Bank, whose first president was a Japanese.

Changes in Japanese cultural attitudes have been observed since the 1960s especially. The new Japanese society was seen as fluid and mobile, and the degree to which it had changed was epitomized, to some, by the marriage in 1959 of Crown Prince Akihito to a commoner. Many of the intelligentsia, however, acting in the traditional role of social critics, have challenged the status quo. At the same time, they have been especially vocal in disparaging foreign, materialistic influences.

The 1946 constitution—and the governmental system it sanctions—is primarily American in its authorship and political philosophy. Major concepts and patterns contained in it are alien to the Japanese political tradition, but many of these new features proved workable—although some of the old patterns and usages still tended to show powers of survival. Foremost among the new infusions are: the concept of popular sovereignty, which replaced the theocratic sovereignty of the emperor; the supremacy of a popularly elected legislative body (instead of bureaucratic supremacy as in pre-1945 Japan); the substitution of inalienable civil rights for the time-honored duty of subservience to the absolute dictates of the emperor and the state; the decentralization of national government powers; and the formal renunciation of war as an instrument of statecraft.

In 1964 the Constitutional Inquiry Commission reported its findings and recommendations to the cabinet. The re-

Prince and Princess Hitachi in traditional court robes on the occasion of their wedding on September 30, 1964.

The Shishinden *or ceremonial hall of the Old Imperial Palace in Kyoto. For nearly eleven centuries prior to the Meiji restoration in 1868, Kyoto served as the seat of the imperial court and also as the cultural and intellectual capital of Japan.*

President Ronald Reagan (left), *during an official state visit to Japan in November 1983, toasts to Emperor Hirohito's health.* Photograph by White House photographer Pete Souza.

Visiting London in October 1971, the emperor and empress were guests of honor at a state banquet at Buckingham Palace. They are being greeted here by His Royal Highness Prince Philip, duke of Edinburgh, and Their Majesties Queen Elizabeth, the queen mother, and Queen Elizabeth II.

port, prepared by selected members of the Liberal Democratic party and by the country's major constitutional experts (the opposition Socialists had boycotted the commission), recommended some change in the 1946 document. On the controversial issue of national defense, it maintained that Japan as an independent nation had an inherent right to defend itself and that Article 9 should be revised accordingly. On the other hand, the majority of the commission members recommended the retention of the existing symbolic role of the emperor, thereby rejecting a strong argument by some of its members that the institution of the emperor be restored to its former position of authority with the appropriate powers.

THE EMPEROR

Under the 1946 constitution the emperor had no legal right to rule or to intervene in affairs of the government. He performed only those acts stipulated explicitly in the constitution. These acts were: promulgation of amendments to the constitution, laws, cabinet orders, and treaties; convocation of the Diet; dissolution of the House of Representatives; proclamation of a general election of members of the Diet; attestation of the appointment and dismissal of ministers of state and other officials as provided by law; attestation of the full powers and credentials of ambassadors and ministers; attestation of general and special amnesty, commutation of punishment, reprieve, and restoration of rights; awarding of honors; attestation of instruments of ratification and other diplomatic documents as provided by law; reception of foreign ambassadors and ministers; and performance of ceremonial functions. In contrast, under the Meiji constitution, the emperor had in effect embodied the state and been the source of the nation's sovereign powers.

None of these was of an operational or policy-making nature. They were executed only with the advice and approval of the cabinet, which was to bear responsibility for all the emperor's acts.

The affairs of the imperial household were governed by the Imperial House Law of 1947, as amended in 1949. This law restricted the imperial succession to the male line and contained a provision for a regency in the event that an emperor came to the throne in his minority. No provision was made for the abdication of the emperor.

Basic policies pertaining to the imperial household were formulated by the Imperial Household Conference, which was controlled mostly by ex officio members, including ten members of the Diet, two representatives of the imperial family, the speaker and vice-speaker of each legislative house, the prime minister, the director of the Imperial Household Agency, the chief justice, and one associate justice of the Supreme Court. The decisions of the Imperial Household Conference were executed by the Imperial Household Agency, which was responsible directly to the Office of the Prime Minister. The imperial family was supported mainly by sums that were voted annually by the Diet.

The traditions of the imperial line, extending back to the distant past, have given the throne an aura and a prestige that has not been appreciably changed by the constitutional definitions limiting its responsibilities. The respect in which the people hold the emperor continues to represent a stabilizing influence that pervades the entire political and social structure of the country.

THE ROYAL SOVEREIGNS OF THE JAPANESE EMPIRE

Reign	Title	Ruler	Birth	Death	Reign	Title	Ruler	Birth	Death
660–585 B.C.	Emperor	Jimmu (Tenno)	711 B.C.	585 B.C.	485–487	Emperor	Kenzo	440	487
					488–498	Emperor	Ninken	448	498
581–548	Emperor	Suisei	632	549	499–506	Emperor	Muretsu	489	506
548–510	Emperor	Annei	567	511	507–531	Emperor	Keitai	450	531
510–475	Emperor	Itoku	553	477	532–535	Emperor	Ankan	466	535
475–392	Emperor	Kosho	506	393	536–539	Emperor	Senkwa	467	539
392–260	Emperor	Koan	427	261	540–571	Emperor	Kimmei	510	571
260–214	Emperor	Korei	342	215	572–585	Emperor	Bidatsu	538	585
214–158	Emperor	Kogen	273	158	586–587	Emperor	Yomei	540	587
157–97	Emperor	Kaikwa	208	98	588–592	Emperor	Sujun	523	592
97–30	Emperor	Sujin	148	30	592–628	Empress	Tenno	554	628
31–70	Emperor	Suinin		A.D. 70	629–641	Emperor	Jomei	593	641
71 B.C.–A.D. 130	Emperor	Keiko	12	130	642–645	Empress	Kogyoku	594	647
					646–654	Emperor	Kotoku	596	654
A.D. 131–190	Emperor	Seimu	A.D. 83	190	655–661	Empress	Saimei	620	661
192–200	Emperor	Chuai	149	200	662–671	Emperor	Tenji	626	671
201–269	Regent (Empress)	Jingo	170	269	672–672	Emperor	Kobun	648	672
					673–686	Emperor	Temmu	622	686
201–310	Emperor	Ojin	201	310	686–696	Empress	Jito	646	703
313–399	Emperor	Nintoku	290	399	697–703	Emperor	Mommu	683	707
400–405	Emperor	Richu	336	405	708–714	Empress	Gemmei	662	722
406–411	Emperor	Hanzei	352	411	715–723	Empress	Gensho	681	748
412–453	Emperor	Inkyo	374	453	724–748	Emperor	Shomu	718	756
454–456	Emperor	Anko	401	456	749–758	Empress	Koken	718	760
457–479	Emperor	Yuryaku	418	479	757–764	Emperor	Junnin	733	765
480–484	Emperor	Seinei	444	484	765–769	Empress	Shotoku	750	769

Reign	Title	Ruler	Birth	Death	Reign	Title	Ruler	Birth	Death
770–781	Emperor	Konin	719	781	1259–1274	Emperor	Kameyama		
782–805	Emperor	Kwammu	736	805	1274–1288	Emperor	Go-Uda		
806–809	Emperor	Heijo	774	824	1288–1298	Emperor	Fushimi		
810–823	Emperor	Saga	785	842	1298–1301	Emperor	Go-Fushimi		
824–833	Emperor	Junwa	786	840	1301–1308	Emperor	Go-Nijyo		
834–850	Emperor	Nimmyo	810	850	1308–1318	Emperor	Hanazono		
851–858	Emperor	Montoku	827	858	1318–1339	Emperor	Go-Daigo		
859–876	Emperor	Seiwa	851	881	1339–1373	Emperor	Go-Murakami		
877–884	Emperor	Yozei	868	949	1373–1382	Emperor	Go-Kame-yama		
885–887	Emperor	Koko	830	887					
888–897	Emperor	Uda	867	931	1382–1414	Emperor	Go-Komatsu		
898–930	Emperor	Daigo	885	930	1414–1429	Emperor	Sholo		
931–946	Emperor	Shujaku	923	952	1429–1465	Emperor	Go-Hanazono		
947–967	Emperor	Muragami	926	967	1465–1521	Emperor	Go-Tsuchi-mikado		
968–969	Emperor	Reizei	950	1011					
970–984	Emperor	Enyu	959	991	1521–1536	Emperor	Go-Kashiwa-bara		
985–986	Emperor	Kwazan	968	1008					
987–1011	Emperor	Ichiyo	980	1011	1536–1560	Emperor	Go-Nara		
1012–1016	Emperor	Sanjo	976	1017	1560–1586	Emperor	Ogimachi		
1017–1036	Emperor	Go-Ichijo	1008	1036	1586–1611	Emperor	Go-Yozei		
1037–1045	Emperor	Go-Shujaku	1009	1045	1611–1630	Emperor	Go-Mizuo		
1046–1068	Emperor	Go-Reizei	1025	1068	1630–1643	Empress	Myosho		
1069–1072	Emperor	Go-Sanjo	1034	1073	1643–1656	Emperor	Go-Komyo		
1073–1086	Emperor	Shirakawa	1053	1129	1656–1663	Emperor	Go-Nishio		
1087–1107	Emperor	Horikawa	1078	1107	1663–1687	Emperor	Reigen		
1108–1123	Emperor	Toba	1103	1156	1687–1710	Emperor	Higashiyama		
1124–1141	Emperor	Shutoku	1119	1164	1710–1720	Emperor	Naka-mikado		
1142–1155	Emperor	Konoye	1139	1155	1720–1747	Emperor	Sakuramachi		
1156–1158	Emperor	Go-Shirakawa	1127	1192	1747–1763	Emperor	Momozono		
1159–1165	Emperor	Nijo	1143	1165	1763–1771	Empress	Go-Sakura-machi		
1166–1168	Emperor	Rokuju	1164	1176					
1169–1180	Emperor	Takakura	1161	1181	1771–1780	Emperor	Go-Momozo-no		
1181–1185	Emperor	Antoku	1178	1185					
1186–1199	Emperor	Go-Toba			1780–1817	Emperor	Kokaku		
1199–1211	Emperor	Tsuchi-mikado			1817–1847	Emperor	Jinko		
					1847–1866	Emperor	Komei	1831	1866
1211–1222	Emperor	Juntoku			1867–1912	Emperor	Meiji (Mut-suhito)	1852	1912
1222–1221	Emperor	Chukyo							
1221–1232	Emperor	Go-Horikawa			1912–1926	Emperor	Taisho (Yo-shihito)	1879	1926
1232–1242	Emperor	Yojo							
1242–1246	Emperor	Go-Saga			1926–	Emperor	Showa (Hirohito)	1901	
1246–1259	Emperor	Go-Fukakusa							

SHOGUNATES

Reign	Title	Ruler	Birth	Death	Reign	Title	Ruler	Birth	Death
MINAMOTO (Kamakura)					1443–1449	Feudal strife			
1185–1199	Shogun	Minamoto Yoritomo	1147	1199	1449–1474	Shogun	Yoshimasa	1435	1490
					1474–1489	Shogun	Yoshihisa	1465	1489
1199–1203	Shogun	Yoriie	1182	1204	1490–1493	Shogun	Yoshitane (1)	1465	1522
1203–1219	Shogun	Sanetomo	1192	1219					
1200–	Rule by the Hojo family (a family descended from Taira Saiamori, whose head, the Shikken [regent] of Kamakura, was the actual ruler of Japan from 1200 to 1333)				1493–1508	Shogun	Yoshizumi	1478	1511
					1508–1521	Shogun	Yoshitane (2)	1465	1522
					1521–1545	Shogun	Yoshiharu	1510	1550
FUJIWARA (Kamakura)					1545–1565	Shogun	Yoshiteru	1535	1565
1226–1244	Shogun	Yoritsune	1218	1256	1565–1568	Feudal strife			
1244–1252	Shogun	Yoritsugu	1239	1256	1568–1568	Shogun	Yoshihide	1564	1568
					1568–1573	Shogun	Yoshiaki	1537	1597
					1573–1603	Feudal strife			
IMPERIAL PRINCES (Kamakura)					1603–1605	Shogun	Ieyasu Tokugawa	1542	1616
1252–1256	Shogun	Munetaka	1242	1274					
1266–1289	Shogun	Koreyasu	1264	1326	1605–1623	Shogun	Hidetada	1579	1632
1289–1308	Shogun	Hisa-Akira	1274	1328	1623–1651	Shogun	Iemitsu	1604	1651
1308–1333	Shogun	Morikuni	1302	1333	1651–1680	Shogun	Ietsuna	1641	1680
1333–1334	Shogun	Morinaga	1308	1335	1680–1709	Shogun	Tsunayoshi	1646	1709
1334–1338	Shogun	Narinaga	1325	1338	1709–1712	Shogun	Ienobu	1662	1712
					1712–1716	Shogun	Ietsugu	1709	1716
					1716–1745	Shogun	Yoshimune	1684	1751
ASHIKAGA (Kyoto)					1745–1760	Shogun	Ieshige	1711	1761
1338–1358	Shogun	Takauji	1308	1358	1760–1786	Shogun	Ieharu	1737	1786
1358–1367	Shogun	Yoshiakira	1330	1368	1787–1837	Shogun	Ienari	1773	1841
1367–1395	Shogun	Yoshimitsu	1358	1408	1837–1853	Shogun	Ieyoshi	1793	1853
1395–1423	Shogun	Yoshimochi	1356	1428	1853–1858	Shogun	Iesada	1824	1858
1423–1425	Shogun	Yoshikazu	1407	1425	1858–1866	Shogun	Iemochi	1846	1866
1425–1428	Feudal strife				1866–1867	Shogun	Keiki	1837	1913
1428–1441	Shogun	Yoshinori	1394	1441	1867—Shogunates end				
1441–1443	Shogun	Yoshikatsu	1433	1443					

Appendix

A

The Sultanate of Brunei

The sultanate of Brunei is a British-protected Muslim state located in the northwest of Borneo. Since the early 1800s, once a large, important, and powerful sultanate, has become territorially insignificant, compared to the other states of Borneo. The total area of Brunei in 1980 was 2,226 square miles, with a population of nearly 150,000 people, mostly Malays. In 1888 Brunei became a British protectorate. In 1906, in a negotiated treaty, the sultanate of Brunei agreed to allow a British resident to conduct the general administration of Brunei. In 1959 the British appointed a high commissioner. Then, Brunei had its first written constitution and, in 1962, elected some members to the legislative council. In 1967 the sultan was limited in participation in the administration of the state strictly to an advisory role only.

On January 1, 1984, Brunei ended nearly a century of British rule, with a formal declaration of independence by the ruling sultan, Sir Muda Hassanal Bolkiah Mu'izzaddin Waddaulah that day. The sultan read the proclamation at midnight to 50,000 of his 200,000 subjects, who were assembled in the main square of the capital, Bandar Seri Begawan. The sultan is one of the wealthiest people on earth. His small sultanate, wedged into a tiny corner of the east Malaysian state of Sarawak, earns nearly 4 billion dollars a year from oil and natural gas sales.

Map of Brunei, showing its position surrounded by Sarawak

The ascendancy to power of Sultan Hassanal Bolkiah took place in 1967 and is commemorated on this postage stamp. Sultan Saifuddin died in 1967 and in 1970 the State capital, Brunei Town, was renamed Bandar Seri Begawan (town of the former ruler) in honor of the former ruler.

Sultan Bolkiah seated on the throne

This stamp commemorates the coronation of Sultan Bolkiah on August 1, 1968.

A postage stamp commemorating the tenth anniversary of the coronation of Sultan Hassanal Bolkiah, 1968–78.

These three Brunei stamps commemorate the wedding of Britain's Prince Charles and Princess Diana on July 29, 1981.

This Brunei stamp commemorates the wedding of the British princess Anne and Capt. Mark Phillips on November 14, 1973.

These six Brunei stamps commemorate the twenty-fifth anniversary (silver jubilee) of the coronation of Britain's Queen Elizabeth II.

ROYAL SOVEREIGNS OF BRUNEI

Reign	Title	Ruler
1796–1809	Sultan	Mohamad Tajuddin II
1809–1828	Sultan	Khanzul Alam
1828	Sultan	Mohamad Alam
1828–1852	Sultan	Omar Ali Saifuddin II
1852–1885	Sultan	Abdul Munim
1885–1906	Sultan	Hashim Jalal
1906–1924	Sultan	Jomal-ul-alam
1925–1951	Sultan	Ahmed Waddin
1951–1967	Sultan	Omar Ali Saifuddin
1967–	Sultan	Hassanal Bolkiah

B

The Kingdom of Burundi

Prior to the arrival of the Europeans, Burundi was a kingdom with a highly stratified, feudalistic social structure. The rulers were drawn from princely dynastic families *(ganwa)* from whom a king *(mwami)* was chosen. Much of the country's precolonial history was characterized by constant power struggles between the ganwa and the *mwami*. The Tutsis introduced cattle into Burundi. The animals were maintained as an indication of wealth, and over the centuries the Hutus gave up title to their lands to Tutsis in order to obtain them. This resulted in a feudal landholding system known as *ubugererwa* which was just abolished in 1977 by the Bagaza government.

Although the area was visited briefly by European explorers and missionaries as early as 1858, Burundi did not

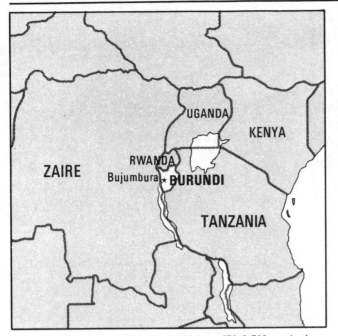

Burundi is a relatively high (2,200–8,900 feet—670–2,700 m.—in elevation) rolling country sitting astride the Nile-Congo crest. On its western border is the Ruzizi River plain and Lake Tanganyika, part of the western portion of the Great Rift Valley.

King Mwambutsa IV (left) on a visit to United Nations Headquarters in New York City in 1964 is seen here with U.N. Secretary-General U Thant.

A semi-postal stamp commemorating the assassinations of, top, *Crown Prince Louis Rwagasore who was Prime Minister, murdered in 1961 and,* bottom, *President John F. Kennedy, U.S.A. who was murdered in 1963. King Mwambutsa IV is shown on the left.*

come under European administration until the 1890s, when it became part of German East Africa. Belgian troops occupied the country in 1916 and in 1923 the League of Nations mandated it to Belgium as part of the Territory of Ruanda-Urundi, now Rwanda and Burundi. Following World War II, Ruanda-Urundi became a UN Trust Territory with Belgium as the administering authority. Burundi became independent on July 1, 1962.

Following independence the Mwami was established as a constitutional monarch. The country fell into political disorder and economic stagnation, however, and Captain Michel Micombero took charge in November 1966 with army backing and proclaimed a republic. Eventually, the Micombero government also lost control of the country, and on November 1, 1976, Lieutenant Colonel Jean-Baptiste Bagaza took control in a bloodless coup.

A special stamp commemorating the visit of the King and Queen of Belgium to Burundi, November 28, 1970. Left to right, Queen Fabiola and King Baudouin, President of Burundi, Michel Micombero and King Baudouin, and President Micombero with the coat of arms of Burundi and Belgium.

Independence Day commemorative stamps (January 7, 1962). Top to bottom, *Flag and Arms of Burundi, King Mwami Mwambutsa IV and a map of Burundi and King Mwambutsa IV and the Royal Drummers*

Postage stamps commemorating the canonization of 22 African martyrs, October 18, 1964. Top and bottom, *Pope Paul VI and King Mwambutsa IV, and* center, *the Sainted Martyrs.*

C

The Kingdom of Ceylon

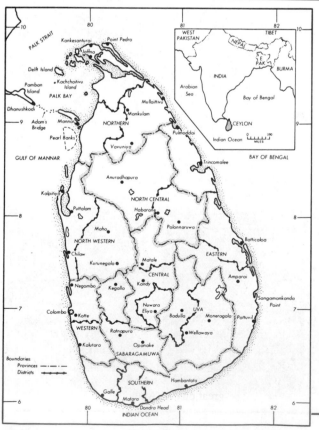

Ceylon

Figure 1. Ceylon

Both legend and linguistic evidence suggest that the Sinhalese came to Ceylon from north India about 500 B.C. According to the most popular legend, Vijaya, the grandson of a lion (and an Indian princess) was exiled from India with seven hundred followers and landed on the island the day the Buddha achieved *nirvana.* The prince married a Veddah princess but later discarded her to marry the high-caste daughter of a south Indian king. The Veddahs are thought to be descendants of the original inhabitants of Ceylon.

The legend illustrates two essential themes of the Sinhalese view of history—the Indo-Aryan colonization of the island and its associations with both Buddhism and south Indian culture. These themes were formalized in the *Mahavamsa,* a dynastic and religious history composed in Pali (Sanskritic and sacred language of Theravada Buddhism) in the sixth century A.D. Repeated clashes with south Indian Hindu Tamil kingdoms evoked a form of Sinhalese-Buddhist ethnocentrism that continues to be a significant factor in contemporary Sinhalese consciousness. In the second half of the third century B.C., a mission was sent to the island from the court of Emperor Asoka, who had secured dominance over most of India and who was a devout Buddhist. The mission was reputedly led by his son, or brother, Prince Mahinda. When the Sinhalese

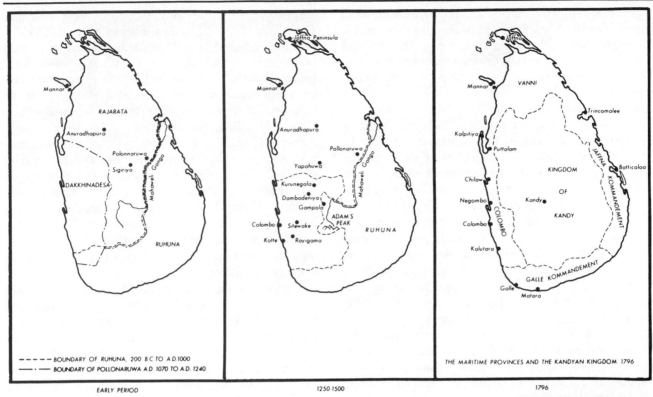

BOUNDARY OF RUHUNA, 200 B C TO A D 1000
BOUNDARY OF POLLONARUWA A D 1070 TO A D 1240

EARLY PERIOD   1250-1500   1796

THE MARITIME PROVINCES AND THE KANDYAN KINGDOM 1796

The early kingdoms of Ceylon

king, Devanampiya Tissa, converted to Buddhism, the close association between Buddhism and the state began that continued until the nineteenth century.

There is no conclusive evidence concerning the date of the first settlements in Ceylon of the other large ethnic group, the Tamils. The Tamils belong to a group of peoples speaking Dravidian languages who inhabit the peninsula of India and whose origins are in dispute. Tamil and other literary sources, however, point to flourishing urban and trading centers in south India in the third century B.C. Early trade between Ceylon and the West appears to have moved through south Indian ports.

ANURADHAPURA KINGDOM: 200 B.C.–A.D. 1000

By the first century B.C. most of the dry zone of the island was populated. Anuradhapura had become the seat of Sinhalese kings and remained the capital until the eleventh century A.D. Although King Dutthagamani is said to have unified the island under one rule in the second century B.C., the influence of Anuradhapura was little felt in the southwest, the southeast, and the central highlands.

In theory the king was an absolute ruler, but he was expected to conform to the rules of *dharma* (justice and equity) and give consideration to the counsels of the elders of the Buddhist *sangha*. Maintenance of power rested with the army, which was under the king's control.

Rajah Singah the King of Ceylon

The last reigning king of Kandy was Sri Vikrama Rajasinha. His reign was ended in 1815 when the British expelled him and his family to India.

A typical-looking king of Ceylon. They were almost all "full bearded and wore pantaloons from B.C. to A.D." This one is Raja Sinha, king of Kandy from 1629 to 1687.

The period described as the classical age of Sinhalese culture, from 200 B.C. to A.D. 1000, coinciding with the time Anuradhapura was the capital, was marked by a succession of internal dynastic struggles, wars with south Indian kingdoms, and periods of stability under a strong Sinhalese ruler. The authors of the chief sources for this period, the *Mahavamsa* and the *Culavamsa*, emphasized the role of the Sinhalese Buddhist kings, especially in the building of the great city of Anuradhapura. Special praise was accorded to those kings who repulsed invading south Indian Tamils. King Dutthagamani, who expelled the Tamil king Elara in the second century B.C., was the first of these. Another was King Dhatusena, who drove out a Tamil king in the fifth century A.D. and who is a popular cultural hero.

From its introduction into Ceylon in the third century B.C., Buddhism influenced and molded every aspect of Sinhalese life. Because the missionaries preached in the vernacular, the Sinhala language was enriched and developed. The relic of Buddha's tooth was reputedly brought to Ceylon in the fourth century A.D. Possession of the tooth was later considered essential to legitimize the rule of a Sinhalese king. During the several centuries of dynastic wars, the tooth was moved from place to place. The Kandyan kings became the final repositories of the tooth and built the Temple of the Tooth, which still stands in Kandy.

By the fifth century A.D. the island had become an important center of trade. Although trade between Ceylon and other trading centers does not appear to have taken place before the first century A.D. except through south Indian ports, the island was well known in the West for its pearls and precious stones. An early name for Ceylon, Tambapanni, is shared by a river in south India where pearls were also found.

The proximity of south India, home of the three rival Tamil dynasties of the Pandyas, Pallavas, and the Cholas, was both a threat and a source of aid for the Sinhalese. When one of these south Indian kingdoms expanded, territorial ambition often led them to extend their sway to Ceylon, especially as there were already Tamil settlements on the island. The Sinhalese usually allied with some other south Indian dynasty to drive out the invader. When internal dynastic disputes wracked the Sinahalese Kingdom, one of the claimants to the throne often called on Tamil aid. In the seventh century A.D. the Pallavas enabled a Sinhalese prince, Manavamma, to seize the throne at Anuradhapura. His dynasty continued for almost three centuries, during the early part of which the Sinhalese maintained their alliance with the Pallavas. Tamil artisans and craftsmen came to Ceylon, and their influence is especially noticeable in the architecture and sculpture of the period.

In the middle of the ninth century the Pandyas rose to power in south India, invaded the island, and sacked the city of Anuradhapura. They withdrew on the condition that the Sinhalese pay a large indemnity. Twenty years later the Sinhalese king made an alliance with a rebel Pandyan prince, invaded the mainland, and sacked the ancient capital of Madura. In the tenth century the Sinhalese again sent an expedition to the mainland, this time to aid the Pandyan king against the Cholas. The Pandyan king was defeated and fled to Ceylon, carrying with him the royal insignia. The Cholas were determined to recapture the royal insignia, and within fifty years, they had sacked Anuradhapura and attached Rajarata to the Chola Empire. Mahinda V, who ascended the throne in 982, was the last of the Sinhalese

kings to reign in Anuradhapura. The Cholas took him prisoner in 1017, and he died in south India in 1029.

Sinhalese historians note that during the earlier periods of Tamil rule in Ceylon, Tamil kings and nobles were generous toward Buddhism, although they also maintained their own Brahman priests in court. Brahman rituals, in fact, were incorporated into the ceremony of the Buddhist kings, and a Brahman was often put in charge of state administration. The seventy-five years of Chola rule marked the only time Ceylon was ruled as a province of south India. During this period Saivite Hinduism flourished and Buddhism received a serious setback. After the destruction of Anuradhapura, the Cholas made their capital at Polonnaruwa, farther to the southeast of the dry zone and near the Mahaweli River. This strategic location enabled them to control the main route to the southern Sinhalese kingdom of Ruhuna.

King Vijayabahu I, who wrested power from the Cholas in 1070, has been described as the author of Sinhalese freedom: "Had there been no Vijayabahu, there would perhaps have been no Sinhalese in Ceylon today." In order to restore Buddhist strength, Vijayabahu invited monks from Burma and rebuilt Buddhist temples and monasteries. He restored the water reservoirs and irrigation works and, himself a poet, became a patron of literature. Although Vijayabahu regained control of Anuradhapura, he made his capital at Polonnaruwa, beginning the Sinhalese retreat into the southern and central portions of the island.

Vijayabahu I and the kings Parakramabahu I and Nissamkamalla are considered the three greatest patrons of Buddhism. Parakramabahu the Great (1153–86) restored Sinhalese civilization to its former glory. He reconstructed many of the *stupas* and ancient temples at Anuradhapura and undertook extensive building in his capital at Polonnaruwa. The religious orders were purged and provided with new monasteries and shrines. He was strong enough to send a punitive expedition against the Burmese for mistreatment of a Ceylonese mission in 1164 or 1165. A few years later he invaded south India to aid a Pandyan claimant to the throne, but the expedition failed after initial success.

Nissamkamalla (1187–96), who also was a patron of the arts, reputedly regulated the caste system by the introduction of a modified Brahmanical legal system. The highest caste was the *govi,* or cultivator caste, and ownership of a piece of land conferred high status. The occupational castes were hereditary; the members lived in their own section and intermarried within the extended family. The *chandalas* corresponded roughly to the Indian untouchables. Slavery also continued to flourish, and the social structure corresponded closely to that described by the first European observers. During the Polonnaruwa period it became mandatory for the Sinhalese king to be a Buddhist.

The period 1184–1236 is referred to as that of the Kalinga kings. The Sinhalese had intermarried with the Kalinga Dynasty, whose origin is traditionally considered to be Indian. After the death of Nissamkamalla, dynastic disputes contributed to the breakup of the Polonnaruwa Kingdom and the establishment of a separate Tamil realm in the north of the island. During this troubled period, for which sources are both contradictory and fragmentary, Sinhalese claimants to the throne invited south Indian and other outside aid. The incessant wars virtually destroyed the irrigation system upon which civilization in the dry zone depended, and malaria is believed to have made its appearance at this time. The Sinhalese migrated to the malaria-free wet zones in the central highlands and the southwest and southeast coasts. Those who remained reverted to a slash-and-burn agriculture.

The destruction of the Sinhalese civilization in the dry zone has been popularly ascribed to the incursions of south Indian Tamils. This view provides the modern Sinhalese with a historic rationale for their hostility to south Indian and Ceylon Tamils. Impartial observers have pointed out, however, that disorder within the Sinhalese kingdoms themselves, as well as the depredations of malaria, which is believed to have ravaged the population at this time, were also responsible for their decline.

DECLINE OF THE SINHALESE KINGS: 1250–1500

After the rule of the Kalinga king Magha at Polonnaruwa in the thirteenth century, a rule that has been described by historians as disastrous, the next three kings ruled from Dambadeniya, and one made his royal residence at Yapahuwa. The last king to reign in Polonnaruwa was Parakramabahu III (1287–93). Subsequent kings moved to Kurunegala and later to Gampola and Kotte.

In the fifteenth century the last great Sinhalese king, Parakramabahu VI, captured and held Jaffna for seventeen years, after which it reverted to the Tamil kings of Jaffna.

The separation of the Tamil Kingdom from the Sinhalese had important psychological and cultural implications. The Tamils in the north developed a more distinct and confident Hindu culture that looked toward the rich cultural traditions of south India for its inspiration. The Sinhalese, on the other hand, restricted by circumstance to the southern and central portions of the island, developed a minority complex toward the far more numerous Tamils on the Indian mainland.

Rule over the rest of Ceylon was divided between Vikramabahu III at Gampola in the central highlands and Alakesvara at Rayigama near the west coast. Parakramabahu VI, who earned the epithet Bodhisatvavatara for his patronage of Buddhism, ruled from Kotte, a fort he established near Colombo. He had obtained the throne in 1415 with the help of the Chinese.

During the expansion of the Tamil Kingdom, the Sinhalese kings sought the aid of Arab trader-settlers. From the ninth century onward, the Arabs had developed extensive commerce and shipping on the East-West trade route.

Ceylon was invaded by the Portuguese starting in 1505. It was then captured by the Dutch in 1656. The British, in turn, captured Ceylon from the Dutch in 1795.

An agreement was signed on March 2, 1815, between the British government and the Sinhalese nobles which vested sovereignty in the British crown, guaranteed the rights and privileges of the chiefs, declared Buddhism inviolable, and placed the responsibility for its protection on the British governor. The collection of revenues was to be carried on under the supervision of British agents. Dissatisfaction with the results of the agreement, known as the Convention of 1815, soon appeared among the nobles, however, whose power was in fact curtailed, and among the Buddhist *bhikkus,* who resented rule by a Christian power. An ill-organized rebellion flared up in 1818, which the British put down with some difficulty, but was the last serious threat to British power in Kandy.

On May 22, 1972, the Ceylonese adopted a new constitution, which declared Ceylon to be the Republic of Sri Lanka. Prior to this date, Ceylon had been a completely self-governing dominion in the Commonwealth, with Queen Elizabeth II as head of state. Under the constitution, the head of state is a president appointed by the prime minister. This position is largely ceremonial, and the constitution requires the president to act upon the advice of the prime minister in most matters. Sri Lanka continues to remain within the Commonwealth in spite of the change in its constitution.

THE ROYAL SOVEREIGNS OF THE KINGDOM OF CEYLON

Reign	Title	Ruler	Reign	Title	Ruler
161–137 B.C.	King	Dutthagamani	47–47	King	Darubhatika Tissa
137–119	King	Saddhatissa	47–47	King	Niliya
119–119	King	Thulatthana	47–42	Queen	Anula
119–109	King	Lanjatissa	41–19	King	Kutakanna Tissa
109–103	King	Khallata Naga	19–A.D. 9	King	Bhatika Abhaya
103–102	King	Vattagamani	A.D. 9–21	King	Mahadathika Mahanaga
103–89—Under rule of Tamils from south India			22–31	King	Amanda-gamani Abhaya
89–77	King	Vattagamani (restored)	31–34	King	Kanirajanu Tissa
76–62	King	Mahaculi Mahatissa	34–35	King	Culabhaya
62–50	King	Coronaga	35–35	Queen	Sivali
50–47	King	Tissa	35–44	King	Ilanaga
47–47	King	Siva	44–52	King	Candamukha Siva
47–47	King	Vatuka	52–59	King	Yasalalaka Tissa

Reign	Title	Ruler	Reign	Title	Ruler
59–65	King	Sabha	815–831	King	Dappula II
65–109	King	Vasabha	831–833	King	Aggabodhi IX
109–112	King	Vankanasika Tissa	833–853	King	Sena I
112–134	King	Gajabahu I	853–887	King	Sena II
134–140	King	Mahallaka Naga	887–898	King	Udaya II
140–164	King	Bhatika Tissa	898–914	King	Kassapa IV
164–192	King	Kanittha Tissa	914–923	King	Kassapa V
192–194	King	Khujjanaga	923–924	King	Dappula III
194–195	King	Kuncanaga	924–935	King	Dappula IV
195–214	King	Sirinaga I	935–938	King	Udaya III
214–236	King	Voharika Tissa	938–946	King	Sena III
236–244	King	Abhayanaga	946–954	King	Udaya IV
244–246	King	Sirinaga II	954–956	King	Sena IV
246–247	King	Vijaya-kumara	956–972	King	Mahinda IV
247–251	King	Samghatissa I	972–982	King	Sena V
251–253	King	Sirisamghabodhi	982–1029	King	Mahinda V
253–266	King	Gothabhaya	1029–1040	King	Kassapa VI
266–276	King	Jetthatissa I	1040–1042	King	Mahalana-Kitti
276–303	King	Mahasena	1042–1043	King	Vikkama-Pandu
303–331	King	Sirimeghavanna	1043–1046	King	Jagatipala
331–340	King	Jetthatissa II	1046–1048	King	Parakkama-Pandu
340–368	King	Buddhadasa	1048–1054	King	Loka
368–410	King	Upatissa I	1054–1055	King	Kassapa VII
410–432	King	Mahanama	1055–1110	King	Vijaya Bahu I
432–432	King	Chattagahaka Jantu	1110–1111	King	Jaya Bahu I
432–433	King	Mittasena	1111–1132	King	Vikrama Bahu I
433–459—Under rule of Tamils from south India			1132–1153	King	Gaja Bahu II
459–477	King	Dhatusena	1153–1186	King	Parakrama Bahu I
477–495	King	Kasyapa I	1186–1187	King	Vijaya Bahu II
495–512	King	Moggallana I	1187–1196	King	Nissamkamalla
512–520	King	Kumara-Dhatusena	1196–1196	King	Vikrama Bahu II
520–521	King	Kittisena	1196–1197	King	Codaganga
521–521	King	Siva	1197–1200	Queen	Lilavati
522–522	King	Upatissa II	1200–1202	King	Sahassamalla
522–535	King	Silakala	1202–1208	Queen	Kalyanayati
535–535	King	Dathapabhuti	1208–1208	King	Dharmasoka
535–555	King	Moggallana II	1209–1209	King	Anikanga
555–573	King	Kittisirimegha	1209–1210	Queen	Lilavati (restored)
573–575	King	Mahanaga	1210–1211	King	Lokesvara
575–608	King	Aggabodhi I	1211–1212	Queen	Lilavati (restored)
608–618	King	Aggabodhi II	1212–1215	King	Parakrama-Pandu
618–618	King	Samghatissa II	1215–1232	King	Magha
618–623	King	Moggallana III	1232–1236	King	Vijaya Bahu III
623–632	King	Silameghavanna	1236–1270	King	Parakrama Bahu II
632–632	King	Aggabodhi III	1270–1272	King	Vijaya Bahu IV
632–632	King	Jetthatissa III	1272–1284	King	Bhuvanaika Bahu I
633–643	King	Aggabodhi III (restored)	1285–1286—Interregnum		
643–650	King	Dathopatissa I	1287–1293	King	Parakrama Bahu III
650–659	King	Kassapa II	1293–1302	King	Bhuvanaika Bahu II
659–659	King	Dappula I	1302–1326	King	Parakrama Bahu IV
659–667	King	Hatthadatha I	1326–	King	Bhuvanaika Bahu III
667–683	King	Aggabodhi IV	–1341	King	Vijaya Bahu V
683–684	King	Datta	1341–1351	King	Bhuvanaika Bahu IV
684–684	King	Hatthadatha II	1344–1357	King	Parakrama Bahu V (joint sovereign with preceding)
684–718	King	Manavamma			
718–724	King	Aggabodhi V	1357–1374	King	Vikrama Bahu III
724–730	King	Kassapa III	1372–1408	King	Bhuvanaika Bahu V (began reign as cosovereign)
730–733	King	Mahinda I			
733–772	King	Aggabodhi VI			
772–777	King	Aggabodhi VII	1408–1467	King	Parakrama Bahu VI
777–797	King	Mahinda II	1467–1469	King	Jaya Bahu II
797–801	King	Udaya I	1470–1478	King	Bhuvanaika Bahu VI*
801–804	King	Mahinda III			
804–815	King	Aggabodhi VIII			

*King Bhuvanaika Bahu VI, also, the king of Kotte, was the last king to have suzerainty over all of Ceylon.

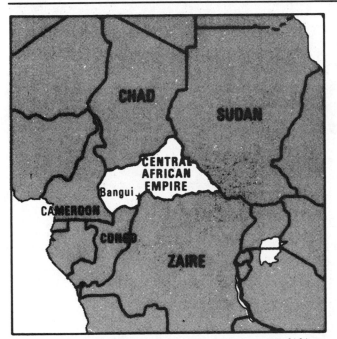

The Central African Empire is located in the approximate center of Africa.

D

The Central African Empire

The Central African Empire was located at almost the precise center of Africa, about 400 miles (640 km.) from the nearest ocean. It is bounded by Chad, Sudan, Zaïre, Congo, and Cameroon.

The precolonial history of the area now called the Central African Empire was marked by successive waves of migration, of which little is known. This period accounts for the complex ethnic and linguistic patterns today. Until 1958 the country was known as Oubangui-Chari, one of the four territories of French Equatorial Africa (AEF).

A convention concluded on April 19, 1887, with the Congo Free State granted France possession of the right bank of the Oubangui River. This convention and later international agreements established the boundaries of Oubangui-Chari.

In 1889 the French established an outpost at Bangui, located at the upper limit of the year-round navigable portion of the Oubangui River. In 1894 Oubangui-Chari became a territory; then it was placed under a High Commander and gradually given an administrative structure which began to be organized around 1900. United with Chad in 1906, it formed the Oubangui-Chari-Chad colony. In 1910 it became one of the four territories of the Federa-

tion of French Equatorial Africa, along with Chad, Congo (Brazzaville), and Gabon.

In August 1940 the territory responded, with the rest of the AEF, to call from General Charles de Gaulle to fight for Free France. After the war, the French Constitution of 1946 inaugurated the first of a series of reforms which were to lead eventually to complete independence for all the French territories in West and Equatorial Africa. The rights granted in 1946 included French citizenship for all inhabitants and establishment of local assemblies. The next major landmark was the Basic Law *(Loi Cadre)* of June 23, 1956, which eliminated all remaining voting inequalities and provided for creation of governmental organs to assure a measure of self-government to individual territories. The constitutional referendum of September 1958 led to dissolution of the AEF and further expansion of the internal powers of the former overseas territories.

The nation became an autonomous republic within the newly established French Community on December 1, 1958, and acceded to complete independence as the Central African Republic on August 13, 1960.

The first president, revered as the founder of the Central African Republic and of its mass political party Mouvement d'Evolution Sociale en Afrique Noire (ME-SAN), was Barthelemy Boganda. He died in an airplane crash in March 1959, and was succeeded by his nephew David Dacko. In January 1964 President Dacko was reelected for a seven-year term by a majority of 99.4 percent.

Following a swift and almost bloodless coup on January 1, 1966, Colonel Jean-Bédel Bokassa, chief of staff of the armed forces, assumed power as president of the Republic. He announced that he had acted to eliminate the waste and corruption of certain officials in the Dacko government; to halt the country's drift into increasing economic stagnation; and to remove the influence of Chinese Communists, who he charged with threatening the country's independence and freedom.

President Bokassa abolished the Constitution of 1959 and dissolved the National Assembly. He issued a constitutional decree which placed all legislative and executive powers in the hands of the president, maintained the independence of the judiciary and the official status of MESAN as the national movement, and stated that all previous laws and regulations remained in effect unless specifically abrogated by the government's future decrees.

On December 4, 1976, the Republic became a monarchy with the promulgation of the imperial constitution and the naming of President Bokassa as Emperor Bokassa I. The new constitution contains a Bill of Rights and provisions for the resumption of democratic institutions including the National Assembly. Bokassa I was formally crowned in an elaborate ceremony on December 4, 1977, one year after the declaration of the empire.

In late September 1979 the former president, David Dacko, in a coup, ousted the emperor Bokassa and proclaimed the country be renamed back to its old name—the Central African Republic.

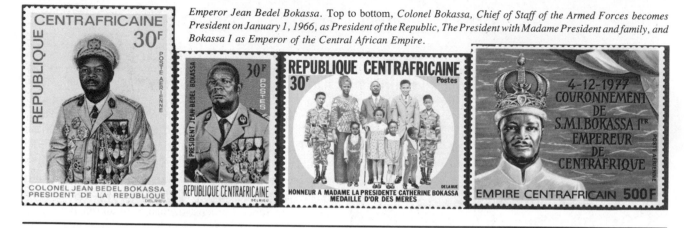

Emperor Jean Bedel Bokassa. Top to bottom, *Colonel Bokassa, Chief of Staff of the Armed Forces becomes President on January 1, 1966, as President of the Republic, The President with Madame President and family, and Bokassa I as Emperor of the Central African Empire.*

E

The Kingdom of Hawaii

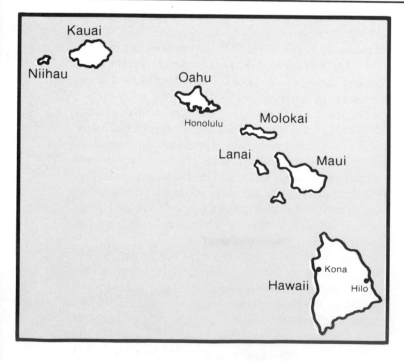

Map of Hawaii

Captain James Cook, the famous English navigator, founded the Hawaiian Islands (for the rest of the world) when he landed on Kauai on January 20, 1778. The natives who greeted him thought he was the good god Lono, but when he returned a year later, they changed their minds because he arrived with a storm that did considerable damage. They killed him.

Up until 1782 the various islands in the Hawaiians had four kingdoms. One of the kings was Kamehameha I, who reached the status of king in 1782, and set out to consolidate all of the kingdoms under his reign. By 1795 he had conquered all of the islands but Kauai and Niihau. Those two were acquired by cession in 1810.

King Kamehameha I was a very able ruler. He soon had a good central government organized, solved a bad crime situation with laws and their enforcement, and built a badly needed defense system which proved strong enough to deter the Russians in 1915 and the Spanish pirates in 1918.

In 1819, King Kamehameha II (Liholiho) ascended to the throne and in the following years of his reign (1819–24), the missionary movement took place. The missionaries brought religion, schools, books, and newspapers to the islanders; but they also exploited the Hawaiians by control-

Kamehameha the Great, the founder of the Kamehameha Dynasty. He succeeded his uncle, King Kalaniopuu, who ruled the island of Hawaii in 1782 and then conquered the other Hawaiian islands and founded the Kingdom of Hawaii.

The original statue of Kamehameha I

The official seal used by the state of Hawaii today was handed down from the Hawaiian monarchy's coat of arms with only minor changes. It bears the motto Ua Mau Ke Ea Oka Aina I Ka Pono, which translated into English from the Hawaiian means "The Life of the Land is Perpetuated by Righteousness." The two male figures on each side of the shield are Kameeiamoku and Kamanawa, the royal twins who were personal counselors to King Kamehameha I. The eight stripes represent the eight islands that make up the island chain. The second and third quarters contain the Poloulou—white balls with black staffs, which are a sign for both protection and taboo. In the center is a triangular flag (puela), over two spears (alia)—again depicting protection and taboo. The background represents the military cloak of royalty. At the sides are the supporters in feather cloaks and helmets. Kameeiamoku on the right carries a spear (ihe), while Kamanawa, his twin brother, on the left, holds a staff (Kahili), which is used only on state occasions. Above the shield is the crown, ornamented with twelve taro leaves.

ling their society and property to the degree that they were in a state of servitude. The maternal queen of Kamehameha II, Keopuolani, who was the mother of his two sons who became successors to the throne, was the first person to be converted (1823). This royal entrance into formal religion led the way for a great movement toward the church by the Hawaiians. They had a great love for Queen Keopuolani, who was also the head chief among those people of royal blood. Another important royal convert at that time was a female chief named Kaahumanu, the king's favorite queen. When King Kamehameha and Queen Keopuolani visited England in 1824, the queen died there. Their reign was then taken over by Queen Kaahumanu who had remained behind as regent.

The whaling and sugar industries began about 1826, and they brought great wealth to the islands but not to the

King Kamehameha II (Liholiho) was twenty-two years old when he came to the throne on May 20, 1819. He was considered a weak-minded king, the opposite of his father. Shortly after he was sworn in, he had a confrontation with his father's favorite wife, Kaahumanu, who announced to him in the presence of the nobles that Kamehameha the Great wanted for her to share in the throne. The king appeared to give in to her but he might have been more clever than the historians labeled him, for he made her the kuhinanui, *or premier, and not the co-ruler as she expected.*

On November 27, 1823, Kamehameha II, along with his queen, Kamamalu, sailed to England for a royal visit with King George IV. While in England, Queen Kamamalu contracted the measles, a disease for which the Hawaiians had little immunity. Queen Kamamalu died on July 8, 1824 and King Kamehameha died shortly afterward on July 14. Their bodies were returned to Hawaii for a royal burial.

King Kamehameha III

King Kamehameha IV

natives. The U.S. Navy in 1829 negotiated a treaty between the United States and Hawaii. Other nations, particularly Great Britain, were attempting to get a stronghold in the government of Hawaii so as to obtain rights to Hawaii's natural wealth.

King Kamehameha III, who had entered the throne in 1825, promulgated the Declaration of Rights, which is Hawaii's Magna Charta, on July 7, 1839. He ordered the Edict of Toleration ten days later, and on October 4, 1840, the first constitution. He is considered by modern historians to be the most able of all of Hawaii's past royal leaders. In 1849 and 1851, the French challenged the Hawaiian movement toward independence from foreign intervention, so the king, who had a preference for the United States as a protector, entered into a secret agreement that put the Hawaiian Islands under protectorate status with the United

King Lunalilo (William Charles)

The election of Kalakaua (David) to the throne by the Hawaiian legislature in 1874 resulted in widespread rioting by supporters of Queen Emma, the widow of King Kamehameha V. Once order was restored, Kalakaua moved quickly to cement relationships with the United States. Arriving in San Francisco, on his way to Washington D.C. for a state visit with President Grant, he became the first sovereign ruler to set foot on the soil of the United States. He was, also, the first monarch to address a session of the American Congress.

King Kalakaua (left) with the famous writer, Robert Louis Stevenson

King Kamehameha V

Prince Albert Edward Kauikeaouli, the son of Kamehameha and Queen Emma, was the last child born to a monarch of Hawaii. He died at the age of four.

Queen Kapiolani, the wife of King Kalakaua

In 1894, the coat of arms appeared on a postage stamp.

The statue of Kamehameha I on an 1894 stamp

King Kalakaua is depicted on this 1886 stamp as he appeared earlier in life.

King Kalakaua as he appeared later in life

Kamehameha V on an 1864 postage stamp

The royal palace at the time of Queen Lydia's reign, 1891–95

Queen Liliuokalani as she appeared on the Hawaiian throne

States government. France, made aware of this move, retreated. In 1854 the king opened negotiations with the United States for annexation, but that year Kamehameha III died, and the meetings ended. Under the king, Hawaii had become civilized and an equal member among nations.

With the next two kings, Kamehameha IV, who reigned from 1854 to 1863, and Kamehameha V, who was on the throne from 1863 to 1872, the United States played a secondary role to the British and a waiting game. King Kamehameha V promulgated a new constitution in 1864 but died in 1872 before his governmental reforms bore any fruit. With his death the Kamehameha Dynasty ended.

The Hawaiian legislature elected David Kalakaua as king of Hawaii and he took the throne on February 12, 1874. He was an able ruler and pro-American. He entered into the Reciprocity Treaty of 1876, which gave the United States exclusive rights to the Pearl Harbor section of Oahu Island as a naval base.

Toward the end of his reign, King Kalakaua promulgated a new constitution which started a series of insurrections and unrest in the Hawaiian Islands. These continued through his successor's reign. His sister Lydia (Liliuokalani) accepted the throne upon his death in 1891, and she ruled until January 17, 1893, when she was deposed. The trouble in the islands ended when the United States Congress, in a joint resolution in 1898, accepted Hawaii's annexation and the Hawaiian Islands became a territory of the United States on June 14, 1900.

A contrast in the society of Hawaiian royalty in fifty years. (Left) *King Kamehameha I with his warriors in 1815,* and (right), *King Kamehameha V with his nobles in 1870.*

Queen Liliuokalani as she appeared shortly after her abdication

Queen Liliuokalani on an 1890 stamp

THE ROYAL SOVEREIGNS OF THE KINGDOM OF HAWAII

Reign	Title	Ruler	Birth	Death
1810–1819	King	Kamehameha I	1758	1819
1819–1824	King	Kamehameha II (Liholiho)	1797	1824
1825–1854	King	Kamehameha III (Kauikeauoli)	1814	1854
1855–1863	King	Kamehameha IV (Alexander Liholiho)	1834	1863
1863–1872	King	Kamehameha V (Lot Kamehameha)	1830	1872
1872–1874	King	Lunalilo (William Charles)	1835	1874
1874–1891	King	Kalakaua (David)	1836	1891
1891–1893	Queen	Liliuokalani (Lydia)	1838	1917

F

The Kingdom of Lesotho

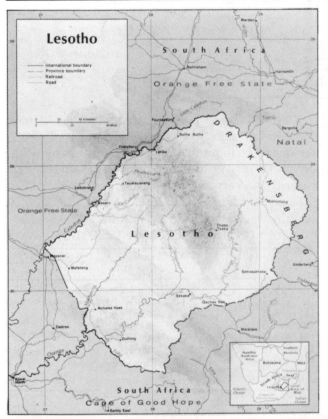

Lesotho is geographically located in the east-central part of the Republic of South Africa.

Lesotho was admitted to the United Nations on October 17, 1966. Present at the time in New York City was their leader, King Moshoeshoe II. He is seen here (left) *being congratulated by U.N. Secretary-General U Thant* (right).

Lesotho is located within the east-central part of the Republic of South Africa. About one-fourth of the western sector is lowland country, varying from five thousand to six thousand feet (1,500–1,800 m.) above sea level. This is the main agricultural zone. The rest of the country is comprised of highlands that rise to eleven thousand feet (3,350 m.) in the Drakensberg Range which forms the eastern boundary with Natal. Lesotho's mountains form part of the major watershed of the Republic of South Africa.

Basutoland (now Lesotho) apparently was sparsely populated by Bushmen until the end of the sixteenth century. Between the sixteenth and nineteenth centuries an influx of migrants (refugees from tribal wars in surrounding areas) populated the region. These new arrivals developed a fairly homogeneous cultural entity, the Basotho tribal group.

In 1818, Moshesh I, a tribal chief from the north, succeeded in uniting the Basotho people. Moshesh ruled from 1823 to 1870 and consolidated various tribes that had been scattered earlier by Zulu and Matabele warriors. During his reign, a series of wars with the Orange Free State (1856–68) resulted in the loss to South Africa of a large area now known as the Conquered Territory. Moshesh appealed to the British for help, and in 1868 the country was annexed by the United Kingdom.

For a considerable period thereafter the energies of the British administration were absorbed largely in the tasks of settling disputes, maintaining the position of the paramount chief under the system of "indirect rule," and resisting South African efforts to incorporate Basutoland into the Union of South Africa.

From 1884 to 1959 legislative and executive authority was vested in a British high commissioner. In 1910 the Basutoland Council, which came into existence on an informal basis in 1903, was formally established as a consultative body.

In 1955 the Basutoland Council asked that it be empowered to legislate on internal affairs. A new constitution in 1959 gave Basutoland its first elected legislature, a significant step in the country's political development. The British then acceded to the expressed desire of the people to achieve full independence. In April 1965 general elections with universal adult suffrage were held, following a constitutional conference at London in 1964. The Basutoland National party (BNP) won thirty-one seats in the sixty-seat

The seven past monarchs of Lesotho. 1824–1870 Morena Moshoeshoe I, 1870–1891 Morena Letsie I, 1891–1905 Morena Lerotholi, 1905–1913 Morena Letsie II, 1913–1939 Morena Griffith, 1939–1940 Morena Seeiso Griffith Lerotholi, 1960 to present—King Motlotlehi Moshoeshoe II

legislature, the Basutoland Congress party (BCP) twenty-five seats, and the Marematlou Freedom party (MFP) four seats. On October 4, 1966, Basutoland attained full independence as the kingdom of Lesotho.

The election of January 27, 1970, the first held after independence, indicated that the ruling BNP might not remain in power. Citing election irregularities, Prime Minister Leabua Jonathan nullified the elections, declared a national state of emergency, and suspended both the constitution and the Parliament.

In 1973 an appointed interim National Assembly was established. With an overwhelming progovernment majority, it is considered little more than a rubber stamp.

Under normal conditions, Lesotho is a constitutional monarchy with a bicameral parliament consisting of a National Assembly (sixty seats) and a Senate (thirty-three seats).

King Moshoeshoe II (Mo-shway-shway) is chief of state. The prime minister (head of government) is appointed by the king and is the member of the National Assembly who commands support of the majority of its members. The cabinet is also appointed by the king.

THE ROYAL SOVEREIGNS
OF THE KINGDOM OF LESOTHO

Reign	Ruler
1824–1870	Morena Moshoeshoe I
1870–1891	Morena Letsie I
1891–1905	Morena Lerotholi
1905–1913	Morena Letsie II
1913–1939	Morena Griffith
1939–1940	Morena Seeiso Griffith Lerotholi
1960 to present	King Moshoeshoe II

G

The United Kingdom of Libya

For most of its history, Libya has been subjected to foreign rule. In antiquity, various parts of it were ruled successively by the Phoenicians, Carthaginians, Greeks, Romans, Vandals, and Byzantines. Although the Greeks and Romans left impressive ruins at Cyrene, Leptis Magna, Sabratha, and elsewhere, little else remains today to testify to the presence of Libya's ancient cultures.

Libya was conquered in the seventh century by the Arabs. In the following centuries Arab language, culture,

and religion were adopted by the bulk of the indigenous population. The Ottoman Turks conquered the country in the sixteenth century, and Libya remained a part of their empire—although at times a virtually autonomous one—until it was invaded by Italy in 1911 and became an Italian colony.

In 1934 Italy adopted the name Libya (used by the Greeks for all of North Africa except Egypt) as the official name of its colony consisting of the Provinces of Cyrenaica, Tripolitania, and Fezzan. King Idris I, then emir of Cyrenaica, led Libyan resistance to Italian occupation between the two world wars. In 1947 he returned from exile in Egypt and combined forces with the Allies to liberate the country from Italian control. From 1943 to 1951 Tripolitania and Cyrenaica were under British administration, and the French controlled Fezzan. Under the terms of the 1947 peace treaty with the Allies, Italy relinquished title to Libya.

On November 21, 1949, the United Nations General Assembly passed a resolution to the effect that Libya should become independent before January 1, 1952. King Idris I represented Libya in the subsequent UN negotiations. Libya declared its independence on December 24, 1951, the first country to achieve independence through the United Nations. It was simultaneously proclaimed a constitutional and hereditary monarchy under King Idris.

King Idris ruled the kingdom of Libya until the government was overthrown by a military-led revolution on September 1, 1969. The new regime, headed by a Revolutionary Command Council, abolished the monarchy and proclaimed the new Libyan Arab Republic. Colonel Mu'ammar al-Qadhafi became the de facto chief of state. King Idris died in 1982.

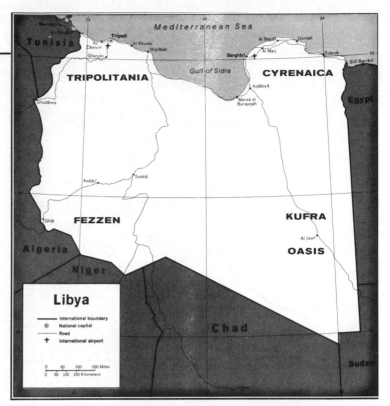

The Libyan Arab Republic is located on the north-central coast of Africa. It is bounded by the Mediterranean Sea to the north (coastline about 1,100 miles; 1,770 km.), Egypt, Sudan, Tunisia, Algeria, Niger, and Chad.

King Idris

A stamp honoring King Idris

Crown Prince Hasan Al-Rida Al-Sanusi (left), of Libya, on a visit to the United Nations Headquarters in 1962, being greeted by U.N. Secretary-General U Thant (right).

H

The Kingdom of Morocco

Morocco's strategic location has shaped its history. Beginning with the Phoenicians, invaders dominated the land. Romans, Vandals, Visigoths, and Byzantine Greeks successively ruled the area. Arab forces began occupying Morocco in the seventh century A.D. and brought with them Arab civilization and Islam. Other invasions followed. The Alaouite dynasty, which has ruled Morocco since 1649, claims descent from the Prophet Mohammed.

Because of its location and resources, Morocco was an early scene of competition among European powers in Africa. France showed a strong interest in Morocco as early as 1830. Following recognition by the United Kingdom in

Morocco as it is geographically situated today

A constitution providing for representative government under a strong monarchy was approved by referendum on December 7, 1962. Elections were held in 1963. In June 1965, following student riots and civil unrest, the King invoked article 35 of the constitution and declared a "state of exception." He assumed all legislative and executive powers and named a new government not based on political parties.

King Hassan II as he appears on Moroccan postage stamps

1904 of France's "sphere of influence" in Morocco, the Algeciras Conference (1906) formalized France's "special position" and entrusted policing of Morocco to France and Spain jointly. A Franco-Spanish treaty in 1912 made most of Morocco a protectorate of France; Spain assumed the role of protectorate over the northern and southern zones.

The first nationalist political parties based their arguments for Moroccan independence on such World War II declarations as the Atlantic Charter. A manifesto of the Istiqlal (Independence) Party in 1944 was one of the earliest public demands for independence. That party subsequently provided most of the leadership for the nationalist movement.

France's exile of the highly respected Sultan Mohammed V in 1953 and replacement of him with the unpopular Mohammed Ben Aarafa, who was perceived as illegitimate, sparked terrorist opposition to the French protectorate. France allowed Mohammed V to return to Morocco in 1955; negotiations leading to independence began the following year.

The Kingdom of Morocco recovered its political independence from France on March 2, 1956. By agreements with Spain in 1956 and 1958, control over Spanish zones of influence was restored to Morocco. On October 29, 1956, the signing of the Tangier Protocol politically reintegrated the former international zone. Spain, however, retained control over the small enclaves of Ceuta and Melilla in the north and the enclave of Sidi Ifni in the south. Sidi Ifni became part of Morocco in 1969.

After the death of his father, Mohammed V, King Hassan II succeeded to the throne on March 3, 1961. He recognized the royal charter proclaimed by his father on May 8, 1958, which outlined steps toward establishing a constitutional monarchy.

Stamp commemorating the thirtieth anniversary of the coronation of Mohammed V. The coronation was held on November 18, 1927.

Stamp honoring Sultan Moulay Ismail, who was the first of the sultans to rule a modern Morocco.

Early ruling sultans of Morocco have their lives honored on stamps. These three, top to bottom, are: al-Idrissi (1100–66), ibn Batota (1304–78), and ibn Khaldoun (1332–1406).

Sultan Moulay Hafid, who ruled Morocco from 1908 to 1912.

April 6, 1956, Sultan Sidi Mohammed ben Yusef arrives at the Madrid, Spain, Barajas airport and is greeted by Generalissimo Francisco Franco (right), head of the Spanish government. The night before the Spanish government gave independence to the Spanish part of Morocco.

King Mohammed V made a state visit to the United States in November 1957. He is seen here (above, left) on arrival with Vice President Richard M. Nixon and (below, left) with President Dwight D. Eisenhower.

In July 1970, King Hassan submitted to referendum a new constitution providing for an even stronger monarchy. Its approval and the subsequent elections formally ended the 1965 "state of exception."

The nearly successful coup on July 10, 1971, organized by senior military officers at Skhirat, was followed by Morocco's third constitution, approved by popular referendum in early 1972. The new constitution kept King Hassan's powers intact but enlarged from one-third to two-thirds the number of directly elected parliamentary representatives.

After a second coup attempt, in August 1972, by Moroccan air force dissidents and the king's powerful interior minister, General Oufkir, relations between the opposition and the crown deteriorated, and they could not agree on opposition participation in elections. The king subsequently appointed a series of nonpolitical cabinets responsible only to him.

Stemming from cooperation on the Sahara issue, a rapprochement between the king and the opposition began in mid-1974. This led to elections for local councils with opposition party participation on November 12, 1976. Parliamentary elections, deferred because of tensions over the Sahara dispute first with Spain and then with Algeria, were held in June 1977, resulting in a two-thirds majority for the government-backed Independents and allied groups, Istiqlal and the Popular Movement.

The new Parliament began its first regular session in October 1977. King Hassan formed a new government with the participation of the Istiqlal and the Popular Movement as well as the pro-royalist Independents.

A May 1980 referendum extended the parliament's four-year term to six years, changed the composition of the Regency Council, and lowered the king's majority from age eighteen to age sixteen. Crown Prince Sidi Mohammed was seventeen years old at the time of the referendum.

GOVERNMENT

The king is head of state, and his son, the crown prince, is heir apparent. Under the 1972 constitution, a prime minister appointed by the king is head of government. The members of the 264-seat unicameral Parliament are elected to six-year terms. Two-thirds of the members are chosen directly by universal adult suffrage; the remaining one-third are indirectly elected by community councils and business, labor, and farmer groups.

The highest court in the independent judicial structure is the Supreme Court, the judges of which are appointed by the king.

For administrative purposes, Morocco is divided into thirty-five provinces and six perfectures, one at Rabat-Sale and five at Casablanca. In June 1981, the city of Casablanca was subdivided into five prefectures to provide increased services and communication. Each province is headed by a governor appointed by the king. Morocco also has organized the former Spanish Sahara into four provinces.

On a later state visit to the United States, King Mohammed V is seen with President M. Nixon and the First Lady, Patricia.

King Mohammed V, formerly Sultan Sidi Mohammed ben Yusef, with his family in 1958. On the far right is the son who became King Hassan.

FOREIGN RELATIONS

Since Morocco attained independence, its foreign policy, officially attached to the principle of nonalignment, has been basically sympathetic to the West. Long-term goals are to strengthen its influence in the Arab world, Africa, and the Maghreb and to maintain its close relations with Europe.

The major issue in Morocco's foreign relations is its absorption of the Western Sahara, relinquished by Spain in February 1976. Morocco's decision to press its longstanding claim to the former Spanish Sahara when Spain withdrew has involved Morocco in a costly war against "Polisario" forces operating from a base in southern Algeria, Tindouf. King Hassan supports the OAU plan for a cease-fire, a UN peacekeeping force, and a referendum on the issue of annexation to Morocco or independence. While the United States—an arms supplier to Morocco for more than twenty years—has agreed to help the Moroccan air force defend itself from sophisticated Soviet-made surface-to-air missiles introduced into the fighting by the Polisario, the United States seeks a settlement of the war along lines advocated by the OAU and accepted by Morocco.

Morocco persistently has expressed its concern over growing Communist influence in Africa and has supported more moderate regimes in Africa—for example, in its dispatch of troops to Zaire in 1977 and 1978 to help President Mobutu repel a foreign invasion of Shaba Province. Morocco also sponsored a resolution at the 1980 Islamic Conference condemning the Soviet invasion of Afghanistan. King Hassan has been increasingly critical of the Soviets for supplying arms to the Polisario via Algeria and Libya.

Although Morocco signed a long-term development accord with the Soviet Union in 1978 for the exploitation of the Meskala phosphate deposit, which could eventually make the USSR Morocco's biggest trade partner, its relations with Moscow are cool because of Soviet arms sales to neighboring Algeria and Libya.

Morocco has sought to play a constructive role in the search for peace in the Middle East. While King Hassan was an early supporter of Egyptian president Sadat's visit to Israel, Morocco and most other Arab countries denounced the Camp David accords. Morocco has endorsed the Saudi eight-point plan for the Middle East and its call for evacua-

tion of all Arab lands occupied by Israel, including Jerusalem, and creation of a Palestinian state. King Hassan is president of the Jerusalem Committee of the Organization of the Islamic Conference, charged with lobbying in Europe and the United States for the return of Jerusalem as the capital of a Palestinian state.

Morocco enjoys excellent relations with nearly all of the Arab world (especially Saudi Arabia, but also Iraq), the only exceptions being Algeria, Libya, Syria, and the People's Democratic Republic of Yemen.

WESTERN SAHARA

The Western Sahara comprises 267,027.8 square kilometers (102,703 sq. mi.)—an area about the size of Colorado—of wasteland and desert, bordered on the north by Morocco, on the east and south by Mauritania, and for a few kilometers on the east by Algeria. From 1904 until 1975, Spain occupied the northern portion (Saguia El Hamra) as well as the southern two-thirds (Rio de Oro). Calls for the decolonization of these territories began in the 1960s, first from the surrounding nations and then from the United Nations. In 1969, Spain withdrew without incident from Sidi Ifni, a small enclave in Moroccan territory which has been peacefully integrated into Morocco.

The discovery of phosphates in Bu Craa in the Saguia El Hamra heightened demands for Spanish withdrawal from the entire territory. Spain's withdrawal in 1975 and Morocco's occupation has led to armed conflict between Morocco and the Polisario.

Morocco's claim to sovereignty over the Western Sahara is based largely on the historical argument of traditional loyalty of the Saharan tribal leaders to the Moroccan Sultan as spiritual leader and ruler. The International Court of Justice, to which the issue was referred, delivered its opinion in 1975 that while historical ties existed between the inhabitants of the Western Sahara and Morocco, they were

On March 3, 1961, King Hassan II succeeded to the throne of his father, the highly respected King Mohammed V.

King Hassan II speaking at the National Press Club during a state visit to Washington, D. C., in 1963.

King Hassan II in long white religious robes rides his royal horse through the streets of Fez, Morocco, to the Mosque of el-Sounna for a ritual Friday holiday prayer (1966).

considered an inadequate basis for Morocco's claim to sovereignty.

The Polisario claims to represent the aspirations of the Western Saharan inhabitants for independence. Algeria claims none of the territory for itself but maintains that a popular referendum on self-determination should determine the future status of the territory. In 1973, the Polisario Front (Popular Front for the Liberation of the Saguia El Hamra and Rio de Oro) was formed to combat Spanish colonization. After the Spanish left and the Moroccans and Mauritanians moved in, the Polisario turned its guerrilla operations against them.

When Spain withdrew from the Western Sahara in November 1975, 350,000 unarmed Moroccan citizens staged a march into the Western Sahara in what came to be called the "Green March." Three days after the Green March, on November 9, 1975, King Hassan requested that the marchers withdraw. They were soon replaced by Moroccan and Mauritanian troops. On November 14, Spain, Morocco, and Mauritania announced a tripartite agreement for an interim administration under which Spain agreed to share administrative authority with Morocco and Mauritania, leaving aside the question of sovereignty. With the establishment of a Moroccan and Mauritanian presence throughout the territory, however, Spain's role in the administration of the Western Sahara ceased altogether. Mauritania withdrew from the war in 1978 and signed a peace treaty with the Polisario in Algiers in 1979 renouncing all claims to the territory. Moroccan troops occupied the southern portion vacated by the Mauritanians, and tribal leaders pledged allegiance to King Hassan. Later, local elections and the election of representatives to the National Assembly took place and Morocco proclaimed the area

King Hassan II appears on the balcony of the White House with his two sons and President Carter, and the first lady, Rosalynn Carter (November 14, 1978).

reintegrated into Morocco. Morocco has built a fortification to cover the major economic and population centers, including the phosphate mine at Bu Craa.

Efforts to end the war continue. At the OAU summit in June 1981, King Hassan announced his willingness to hold a referendum in the Western Sahara. He took this decision, he explained, in deference to African and other leaders who had urged him to permit a referendum as the accepted way to settle such issues. Subsequent meetings of an OAU Implementation Committee have proposed a cease-fire, a UN peacekeeping force, and an interim administration to assist with an OAU–UN supervised referendum on the issue of independence or annexation. King Hassan's agreement to hold a referendum has evoked criticism from Morocco's Socialist party, leading to the arrest and conviction of USFP leaders for actions considered detrimental to national security and public order; they benefited from a royal pardon in March 1982.

Morocco's decision to press its longstanding claim to the Western Sahara six years ago has complicated U.S. relations with Morocco and Algeria. From 1976 to 1978, Morocco's use of American-supplied arms in the Western Saharan war brought official U.S. protests and a partial arms embargo. This injected tensions into bilateral relations, aggravated by congressional criticism of Morocco. When the Polisario launched attacks into Morocco in 1979, however, President Carter reviewed U.S. arms sales policy and a decision was reached to permit the sale of arms "that could find use in the Western Sahara." Under the Reagan administration, arms sales to Morocco have been approved

to help maintain the military balance in the region. The United States has consistently supported OAU efforts to bring the war to an end through a cease-fire and referendum. While recognizing Morocco's administrative control of the Western Sahara, the United States has not endorsed Morocco's claims of sovereignty there.

President Reagan and King Hassan confer in the Oval Room of the White House. (Official White House photograph by Michael Evans)

King Hassan II visits with Jimmy Carter, president of the United States, on November 14, 1978, at the White House in Washington, D.C.

THE ROYAL SOVEREIGNS OF THE KINGDOM OF MOROCCO

Reign	Title	Ruler		Reign	Title	Ruler
−1 B.C.—Ancient Mauretania				1634–1635	Sultan	Al-Walid
A.D. 1– 400—Under control of Roman Empire				1635–1636	Sultan	Muhammed IV
400—Under control of Vandal Empire				1636–1653		Interregnum
682—Under control of Arab Empire				1653–1664	Sultan	Ahmad II
1061–1149—Under control of Almoravide Dynasty						
1149–1269—Under control of Almohade Dynasty						
1269–1471—Under control of Marinide Dynasty				**FILALI DYNASTY**		
1471–1548—Under control of Wattasi Dynasty						
1550–1668—Under control of Saadi (Sherifian) Dynasty				**HOUSE OF SAADI**		
1668—Under control of Filali (Alaouiti) Dynasty						
1672–1727	King	Moulay Ismail		1664–1665	Sultan	Ar-Rashid ibn Muhammed ibn Ali
		b. 1646 d. 1727		1665–1672		Interregnum
				1672–1727	Sultan	Ahmad Adh-Dhababi
HASANI DYNASTY				1728–1729	Sultan	Abd Allah
				1729–1757		Interregnum
HOUSE OF SAADI				1757–1758	Sultan	Muhammed I
				1758–1789		Interregnum
				1789–1790	Sultan	Jazid
1525–1534	Sultan	Abul-Abbas Ahmad al-Araj		1791–1792	Sultan	Hisham
1534–1548	Sultan	Abu Abd Allah Muhammed I		1792–1793	Sultan	Sulaiman
1548–1557		Interregnum		1793–1822		Interregnum
1557–1570	Sultan	Abu Muhammed Abd Allah al-Ghalib		1822–1859	Sultan	Abd ur-Rahman II
1570–1574	Sultan	Abu Abd Allah Muhammed II		1859–1873	Sultan	Mohammed XVII
1575–1576	Sultan	Abu Marwan Abd al-Malik I		1873–1894	Sultan	Al-Hasan
1577–1579	Sultan	Abul-Abbas Ahmad I		1894–1908	Sultan	Abd-ul-Aziz IV
1579–1603		Interregnum		1908–1912	Sultan	Moulay Hafid
1603–1604	Sultan	Abu Abd Allah Muhammed III		1912–1927	Sultan	Moulay Yusef
1604–1607		Interregnum		1927–1957	Sultan	Sadi Mohammed ben Yusef
1607–1608	Sultan	Zaidan an-Nasir		1957–1961	King	Mohammed V (Sidi Mohammed ben Yusef)
1608–1629		Interregnum		1961–	King	Hassan II, son of Mohammed V
1629–1630	Sultan	Abu Marwan Abd al-Malik II				
1630–1634		Interregnum				

I

The Kingdom of Swaziland

Swaziland is all but surrounded by the Transvaal and Natal provinces of the Republic of South Africa; it also shares a seventy-mile (112 km.) border with Mozambique.

According to tradition, the people of the present Swazi nation migrated south before the sixteenth century to what is now Mozambique. Following a series of conflicts with people living in what is presently the area of Maputo, the Swazi settled in northern Zululand in about 1750.

Unable to match the growing Zulu strength there, the Swazi moved gradually northward in the early 1800s and established themselves in an area including what is now known as Swaziland. They consolidated their hold in this area under several extremely able leaders. The most important of these was Mswati, from whom the Swazi derive their name. Under his leadership in the 1840s, the Swazi expanded their territory to the northwest and stabilized the southern frontier with the Zulu.

The first Swazi contact with the British came early in Mswati's reign when he asked Her Majesty's agent general in South Africa for assistance against Zulu raids into Swaziland. Through the good offices of the agent general, amicable relations were established between the two nations. It was also during Mswati's reign that the first whites settled in the country.

In the years following Mswati's death, the Swazi struggled to guarantee their independence. Agreements between the British and the Transvaal (South Africa) governments in 1881 and 1884 provided that Swaziland should be independent. During this period, however, many concessions for farming, mining, and commerce were granted to whites by the Swazi ruler, Mbandzeni. A number of confusing claims stemming from these many concessions were pressed on the Swazi Government at that time. In an effort to bring some order to the chaotic situation a provisional administration for the territory was established in 1890, representative of Swazi, British, and South African (Transvaal) government interests.

In 1894, under a convention between British and South African governments, the South African Republic assumed the powers of protection and administration. Swaziland continued under this form of government until the conquest of the Transvaal during the Anglo-Boer war, when the rights and powers assumed by the South African Republic in the country passed to the British government. In 1903, Britain formally took over the administration of Swaziland.

In 1907, the British government made an effort to settle the land concession question by defining farm concession boundaries and returning about one-third of all contested land to the Swazi in return for the grant of freehold titles to the concessionaires. The boundaries of mineral concessions were also defined and all monopoly concessions were canceled. The Swazi bitterly opposed the British settlement, and the land question remains controversial to this day.

In 1921, Swaziland's first legislative body, an advisory council of elected white representatives, was established. Its purpose was to advise the high commissioner on purely non-Swazi affairs. In 1944, the high commissioner recognized the council as having official status. At the same time the high commissioner recognized the paramount chief as the native authority for the territory, empowering him to issue to the Swazi legally enforceable orders on various subjects.

The present king, Sobhuza II, became *Ngwenyama* (the Lion) or head of the Swazi nation in 1921, after twenty years of rule by a regent, the queen mother, Lobatsibeni. Before coming to the throne, the king studied for several

Swaziland is located in the southern part of Africa.

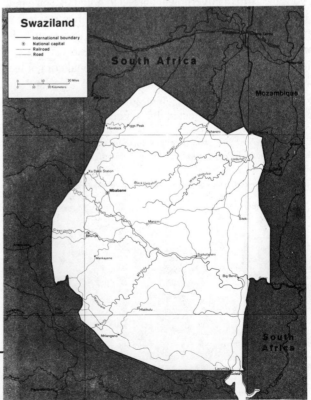

years at Lovedale in South Africa, in addition to being given special education by royal tutors. Shortly after becoming *Ngwenyama,* he traveled to London with his advisers to argue unsuccessfully the Swazi side of the land concession question before the Privy Council.

In the early years of colonial rule, the British government expected Swaziland to eventually be incorporated into South Africa. After World War II, however, South Africa's intensification of racial discrimination induced Britain to prepare Swaziland for independence. Development of educational and medical facilities and investment in agricultural projects were markedly increased.

Political activity intensified in the early 1960s. Partially in response to events elsewhere in Africa, a number of modern-style political parties were formed. These parties, which agitated for independence and economic development, were largely urban-based however, and had few ties to the rural areas where 80 percent of the Swazi live. The traditional Swazi leaders, including the king and the Swazi National Council, formed the *Imbokodvo* National movement, a political group which capitalized on its close identification with the traditional Swazi way of life. Responding to pressures for political reform, the colonial government scheduled an election in mid-1964 for the first Legislative Council in which the Swazi would participate. In the election, the Imbokodvo won all twenty-four elective seats.

Four other parties, most of them having more radical platforms, also contested the election. The largest of these, the *Ngwane* National Liberatory Congress (NNLC), received 9 percent of the vote but won no seats.

Having solidified its political base, the Imbokodvo then incorporated many of the demands of the more radical parties, especially that of immediate independence. In 1966, the British government agreed to hold talks on a new constitution. A number of conservative whites resident in the territory made an unsuccessful attempt to establish the principle of separate elections for white-reserved seats in the new national assembly. The constitutional committee, which consisted of representatives of the king and the Swazi National Council, other political parties, and the British government rejected this suggestion, however. The

King Sobhuza on three stamps commemorating his seventy-fifth birthday (left to right: as he appeared in college, in middle age, and in his later years).

These four stamps commemorate the fiftieth anniversary of King Sobhuza's reign, 1921–71.

committee agreed on a constitutional monarchy for Swaziland, with self-government to follow parliamentary elections in 1967. Swaziland became independent on September 6, 1968.

Although Dr. Ambrose Zwane's NNLC received 20 percent of the vote in the April 1967 elections, his party was weakened before then by the extensive defections of its younger and more dynamic leaders to the Imbokodvo movement. The delimitation of electoral districts and the method adopted of electing three members from each district enhanced the ability of the Imbokodvo to win all of the elective seats in Parliament.

Swaziland's first post-independence elections were held in May 1972. The Imbokodvo gained about 75 percent of the vote and carried twenty-one of the elective seats in Parliament. Dr. Zwane's NNLC received just over 20 percent of the vote and narrowly won a single constituency. His party thereby gained three seats in the House of Assembly.

On April 12, 1973, King Sobhuza repealed the 1968 constitution, suspended meetings of Parliament, and assumed all governmental powers. On March 22, 1977, he announced the expiration of parliamentary terms of office. In January 1979, a new Parliament was convened, chosen partly through indirect elections and partly through direct appointment by the king.

King Sobhuza II died in August 1982 and his senior wife, Queen Mother Dzeliwe, assumed the duties of head of state and regent. One of King Sobhuza's sons will be proclaimed his successor. If he is a minor, he will become king upon reaching majority.

J

The Kingdom of Tibet

The earliest known historical record of Tibet is a Chinese reference to the San Miao tribes. Chinese Emperor Shun, in 2255 B.C. banished the tribes from China to a southern plateau believed to be Tibet. But until the seventh century A.D. the Tibetan people were lost in history. A strong chieftain emerged at that time and led the warring tribes into a manageable army and society. This first sovereign, King Song-tsen Gam-po structured the tribes into a well-regimented society with a capital (Lhasa), a religion (Buddhism), a language (their own), an alphabet (Indian), and a legal code (Chinese). King Song-tsen Gam-po reigned from A.D. 621 to 649. A succession of kings ruled until 841.

Then, in 841, on the death of King Lang-dar-ma, his two sons inherited the land and divided it between them. On successive deaths the land was equally divided again and again among the children, until, by the eleventh century, Tibet was again reduced to many tribes run by as many chieftains.

Buddhism triumphed over the land to the extent that when eastern Tibet was conquered by China's marauding emperor Kublai Khan in the thirteenth century, the Mongol leader chose a Sakya sect member to be the governor of that part of the country, establishing the first theocratic government. But, in 1370, Prince Chang-chup Gyal-tsen set himself up as a sovereign, founding the Sitya Dynasty, which upset the Sakya lamas rule.

In the fourteenth century, a young lama sect called the Yellow Hat began replacing the Red Hat lama ruling sect. The Yellow Hat in the seventeenth century strengthened their party when the incarnation of the fourth Dalai Lama in a child of the royal family was connected with them. They then took over political as well as religious rule in Tibet.

The actual beginnings of the Dalai Lama rule were established in 1641 with the fifth Dalai Lama called the Great Fifth. From that date until 1959 when the fourteenth Dalai Lama fled to India, they maintained exclusive royal rule of Tibet.

In 1706, when the sixth Dalai Lama died, the Chinese government installed a successor to keep the Mongols from gaining control of Tibet. And, in 1720, after defeating a Mongolian army, the Chinese appointed a seventh Dalai Lama.

The Chinese gradually lost control in Tibet until 1907, when the Anglo-Russian Agreement of 1907 gave the

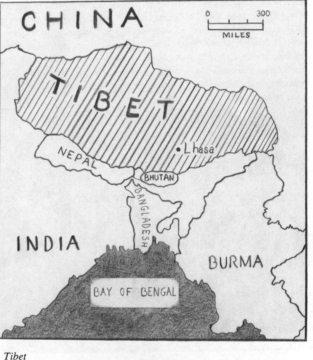

Tibet

A centuries-old sketch of the Potala, the palace of the Dalai Lamas

Chinese suzerainty over Tibet; however, this was short lived since the Tibetans expelled the Chinese in 1912. It wasn't until 1950 that the Chinese reentered Tibet, occupying Inner Tibet (eastern Tibet). Their Chinese Tibetan Agreement of 1951 gave Tibet autonomy in domestic affairs but China gained control of all military and foreign affairs.

Under the 1951 agreement, the Communist Chinese government appointed the tenth Panchen Lama, who took up official residence in Shigatse to govern that region sepa-

The first Dalai Lama was Gedun Truppa (Geden-dub), named by Chief Lama Tson-K'a-pa, who was reorganizing the Lama sect. Gedun Truppa was his nephew. It took five generations of Dalai Lamas to develop the fiction of the reincarnated by divine grant, which began with the reign of the fifth Dalai Lama. The fifth Grand Lama, as he was known to the people in Tibet at that time, connived with the Mongol emperor for full royal status. A Mongol prince, Gusri Khan, was sent to conquer Tibet. Once that was accomplished and the administrative details worked out, the Grand Lama was made the sovereign of Tibet. The year was 1650. With the package, the Mongols gave him a new title, Dalai, which means "vast as the ocean."

The thirteenth Dalai Lama, Thupten Gyatso.

An early print of the chief lamas testing a candidate for the Dalai Lama's kingship

The sixth Dalai Lama, Tsang-yang Gyatso, blessing pilgrims

rately from the rule of the Dalai Lama in western Tibet. (In 1923, the ninth Panchen Lama, who held a similar rule, was forced by the thirteenth Dalai Lama to leave Tibet for China but the Chinese cleverly "found" a reincarnation of the ninth Panchen Lama in 1947.)

In 1958 a full-scale revolt broke out in the east after the Communists started deporting the young Tibetans to China for "training" and, at the same time, moved several hundred thousand Chinese "settlers" into Tibet. The revolt reached Lhasa in March of 1959 and the Communists there made an attempt on the life of the Dalai Lama, but he was able to escape unharmed to India. The Chinese government took over Tibet with a Communist government, substituting the Panchen Lama for the Dalai Lama.

The Dalai Lamas and the Panchen Lamas are considered to be corporeal manifestations of the Buddhist gods. The Dalai Lama is believed to be the reincarnation of the Chen-re-zi, the patron deity of Tibet. And the Panchen Lama is believed to be an incarnation of Amitabha, the Buddha of Boundless Light. One of the greatest holy men in Tibetan history, Gan-den Trup-pa, who died in 1474, was believed to have had himself reincarnated in an infant two years later. That child took his place as the grand lama of Dre-pung, and ever since that event there have been reincarnations announced shortly after the death of the Dalai Lamas.

The Panchen Lama position was established in the seventeenth century by the fifth Panchen Lama, who named the head of the Tra-shi Lun-po monastery as being a reincarnation of Amitabha. The lamas believe that the Panchen Lama is of a higher order than the Dalai Lama, but in the political realm of things, the Panchen Lama had never been able to have absolute rule over the Dalai Lama until the fourteenth Dalai Lama's exile in 1959.

In reality, the lamas, Dalai or Panchen, had very little power over the sect or the politics of the country. It should be realized that they are enthroned as infants with a regent appointed until they reach age eighteen. It was rare, after age eighteen, that they were able to attain any great amount of control. The religious process in identifying the reincarnation in an infant is a due process not unlike the Catholics' selection of individuals for beatification. The infant must bear certain marks and physical attributes. When the prophets find the infant at the place and time they

Dalai Lama XIV, Tenzin Gyatso

Dalai Lama XIII (Thupten Gyatso) on his throne

The Dalai Lama's family, in a photograph taken by the lama, on the terrace rooftop of their residence near the royal palace (Potala) in Lhasa, the capital of Tibet

The fourteenth Dalai Lama reaches India in his self-imposed exile and is greeted by Nehru with a symbolic white scarf of sanctuary.

The fourteenth Dalai Lama in India with the president, Rajendra Prasad

The Potala (the Dalai Lama's palace at Lhasa)

predict, the infant is then put to tests, including one of identification with personal belongings of his predecessor.

The Tibet the Dalai Lama left in 1959 can only be a distant memory. All but a handful of the 2,100 monasteries that once shone like jewels against the mountainous landscape lie in piles of rubble today. Only a few of the 120,000 lamas who helped him run his feudal theocracy escaped persecution and still preach. The elegant manors of Tibetan noblemen have been converted into shabby state warehouses.

Although Tibet still is a troubled colony, occupied by about 100,000 Chinese civilian bosses and twice as many soldiers, it now has regained a semblance of normal life under the new, relatively liberal rule from Peking.

Tibetans once again can practice their highly ritualized form of Buddhist worship, and they are even permitted to display pictures of the Dalai Lama, as long as he is being extolled as a religious figure and not as the advocate of Tibetan statehood. Earlier any talk of him was regarded by Communist officials as treason.

The young Dalai Lama, who had fled from the Red Army in 1951 but was "allowed" to return to sign the seventeen-point agreement that ceded Tibet to China, was allowed to resume his reign for a transitional period, which ended in 1959, as noted, when his countrymen rose up against the tightening Communist hold. On the night of March 17, 1959, the Dalai Lama, disguised as a soldier, with rifle slung over his shoulder, left his summer palace and never came back.

Despite Communist prohibitions, his supporters still regard the Dalai Lama as their political as well as spiritual inspiration. A small underground of separatists distributes tape recordings of his pro-independence speeches smuggled into Tibet by religious pilgrims from India. The dissidents encourage Tibetans at least passively to resist Communist control. On the anniversary of the 1959 uprising, in 1982, they covered the bazaar with anti-Chinese pamphlets.

The separatists claim 2,500 of their confederates languish in Chinese prisons and labor camps for their political convictions.

One of the separatists' greatest fears is that the Dalai Lama will be lured back by Communist promises, put on show, and then become a captive of Peking. This, they believe, is what happened to the Panchen Lama, the second highest Buddhist reincarnation in Tibet, who now lives in the Chinese capital with a nominal job as vice chairman of the national parliament.

The present Panchen Lama had remained in Tibet until 1964, then was called to Peking, where he disappeared for fourteen years. He returned to Tibet on a government-sponsored visit last year and declared, "Only under Chinese Communist leadership can Tibet have a bright future."

Although the Panchen Lama was mobbed by tens of thousands of Tibetans during his brief return, political

The Dalai Lama on his trip to the United States in 1979 visited the Library of Congress in Washington, D.C. He is seen here, left, *examining Tibetan texts from the library's collections. Left to right: His Holiness the fourteenth Dalai Lama, Tendzin Gyatso, Venerable Doboom Tulku, and Lobsang Llalungpa*

THE ROYAL SOVEREIGNS OF THE KINGDOM OF TIBET

Reign	Title	Ruler
1481–1522	King	Donvo Dorje
1522–1550	King	Ngawang Namgye
1550–1565	King	Tondup Tseten
1565–1582	King	Karma Tseten
1582–1603	King	Lhawang Dorje
1603–1623	King	Phuntso Namgye
1623–1642	King	Karma Tsen-Kyong
1642–1655	King	Gusri
1655–1668	King	Daya Khan
1668–1697	King	Tenzin Dalai Khan
1697–1720	King	Lhabzang Khan
1720–1728—Under Chinese Control		
1728–1747	King	Phola Sonam Tobgye
1747–1750	King	Gyurme Namgyal
1750—Monarchy abolished		

DALAI LAMAS (POPES)

1391–1475	I	Gedun Truppa
1475–1543	II	Gedun Gyatso
1543–1588	III	Sonam Gyatso
1589–1617	IV	Yonten Gyatso
1617–1682	V	Nqawang Lo-zang Gyatso
1683–1706	VI	Tsang-yang Gyatso
1708–1757	VII	Kezang Gyatso
1758–1804	VIII	Jampel Gyatso
1806–1815	IX	Luntok Gyatso
1816–1837	X	Tshultrin Gyatso
1838–1856	XI	Khedrup Gyatso
1856–1875	XII	Trinle Gyatso
1876–1933	XIII	Thupten Gyatso
1935–	XIV	Tenzin Gyatso

PANCHEN LAMAS (SPIRITUAL LEADER)

1642–1662	I	Chokyi Gyaltsen
1663–1737	II	Lobzang Yishe
1738–1780	III	Lobzang Palden Yishe
1781–1854	IV	Tempe Nyima
1855–1882	V	Chokyi Trakpa
1883–1937	VI	Chokyi Nyima
1938–1947	VII	Chokyi Gyaltsen
1947—VIII, IX, X: Chinese choices of Pancher Lamas questioned		

activists view him as a Chinese puppet.

In Dharmsala, India, where the fourteenth Dalai Lama, Tenzin Gyatso, has been in exile since fleeing Tibet in 1959, he reiterated in a recent interview his desire to visit his homeland in 1985, United Press International reported, "to see with my own eyes what the situation is," but he has been vague about precise plans for a return.

He said he had not yet worked out the details of his possible visit, but said he would like to visit the provinces of Sichuan, Yunnan, and Qinghai and his birthplace, Taktser village just outside Tibet, in addition to Tibet. Asked about Tibetan fears that the Chinese might assassinate or kidnap him during his visit, the Dalai Lama said his "own judgment and wisdom" would serve as his precautions.

K

The Kingdom of Tonga

Archaeological evidence indicates that the islands of Tonga have been settled since at least 500 B.C., and local traditions have carefully preserved the names of the Tongan sovereigns for about one thousand years. The power of the Tongan monarchy reached its height in the thirteenth century. At that time Tongan power extended as far as Hawaii, three thousand miles (4,800 km.) away.

In about the fourteenth century the king of Tonga delegated much of his temporal power to a brother while keeping the spiritual authority. Sometime later, this process was repeated by the second royal line, thus resulting in three distinct lines: the Tui Tonga with spiritual authority (which is believed to have extended over much of Polynesia), and the Tui Ha'a Takalaua and the Tui Kanokupolu, both with temporal authority responsible for carrying out much of the day-to-day administration of the kingdom.

The first Europeans to sight the Tongan archipelago were Dutch navigators in 1616. The main island of Tongatapu was first visited by the Dutch explorer Abel Tasman in 1643. However, continual contact with Europeans did not begin until more than one hundred twenty-five years later. Captain James Cook visited the islands in 1773 and 1777 and gave the archipelago the name the Friendly Islands because of the gentle nature of the people he encountered. In 1789 the famous mutiny on the British ship *Bounty* took place in the waters between the Haapai and Nomuka island groups.

Tonga's peaceful state changed shortly after Captain Cook's last visit. The islands became torn by civil strife and warfare as the three lines of kings each sought dominance over the others. During this unrest, the first missionaries, attached to the London Missionary Society, arrived in 1797. A second missionary group arrived in 1822, led by Walter Lawry of the Wesleyan Missionary Society. They converted Taufa'ahau, one of the claimants to the Tui Kanokupolu line, and Christianity began to spread throughout the islands.

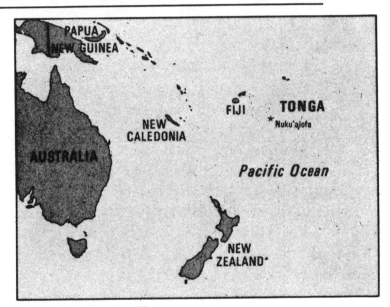

The geographical setting of Tonga

At the time of his conversion, Taufa'ahau took the name of Siaosi (George) and his consort assumed the name Salote (Charlotte), in honor of King George III and Queen Charlotte of England. In the following years he united all of the Tongan islands for the first time in recorded history. In 1845 he was formally proclaimed King George Topou I, and the present dynasty was founded. He established a constitution and a parliamentary government based in some respects on the British model. In 1862 he abolished the system of semiserfdom, which had previously existed, and established an entirely alien system of land tenure whereby every male Tongan, upon reaching the age of sixteen, was entitled to rent—for life and at a nominal fee—a plot of bush land *(api)* of eight and a quarter acres, plus a village allotment of about three-eighths of an acre for his home.

Tonga concluded a Treaty of Friendship and Protection

with the United Kingdom in 1900 and came under British protection. It retained its independence and autonomy, while the United Kingdom agreed to handle its foreign affairs and protect it from external attack.

During World War II, in close collaboration with New Zealand, Tonga formed a local defense force of about two thousand men which saw action in the Solomon Islands. In addition, New Zealand and U.S. troops were stationed on Tongatapu, which became a staging point for shipping.

A new Treaty of Friendship and Protection with the United Kingdom was signed in 1958 and ratified in May 1959. It provided for a British commissioner and consul in Tonga who were responsible to the governor of Fiji in his capacity as British chief commissioner for Tonga. In mid-1965 the British commissioner and consul became directly responsible to the U.K. secretary of state for Colonial Affairs. Tonga became a fully independent country on June 4, 1970, an event officially designated by the king as Tonga's "reentry into the comity of nations."

GOVERNMENT

Tonga's constitution, promulgated at the time of in-

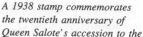
A 1938 stamp commemorates the twentieth anniversary of Queen Salote's accession to the throne.

Four Tonga stamps issued in 1951 to commemorate the fiftieth anniversary of the Treaty of Friendship between Tonga and Great Britain. Top to bottom: map of Tonga islands, the royal palace at Nukualofa, arms of Tonga and Great Britain, and Queen Salote

Queen Salote Topou III, honored on Tonga stamps that commemorated her fiftieth birthday anniversary

King Taufa'ahau Topou IV appears on many of his island's postage stamps.

King George Tupou I

Queen Salote accepting a gift in 1961 from the British chief commissioner to Tonga, left, Mr. P. D. MacDonald. To the queen's left are Mr. E. J. Coode, a British commissioner, the consul for Tonga, Rata Edward Cakobau, and Group Captain J. D. Robins.

King Taufa'ahan Tupou IV during his third visit to the United States met with Vice President George Bush on January 30, 1985. Photograph by White House photographer, Dave Valdez.

dependence, is based on the one granted in 1875 and provides for a constitutional monarchy.

The executive branch includes the monarch and the cabinet, which becomes the Privy Council when presided over by the monarch. In intervals between legislative sessions, the Privy Council makes ordinances which become law if confirmed by the legislature.

The unicameral Legislative Assembly consists of seven nobles who are elected by the thirty-three hereditary nobles of Tonga and seven people's representatives elected by universal adult suffrage for three-year terms. In addition, seven cabinet ministers, appointed by the monarch, hold office until they reach retirement age. The governors of Haapai and Vavau are appointed to their offices and serve as ex officio members of the cabinet. The Legislative Assembly sits for four or five months a year.

Tonga's court system consists of the King-in-Council, the Supreme Court, the Magistrates Court, and the Lands Court. Judges are appointed by the monarch.

PRINCIPAL GOVERNMENT OFFICIALS

Monarch—King Taufa'abau Tupou IV; Crown Prince—H. R. H. Prince Tupouto'a; Prime Minister, Minister for Foreign Affairs—H. R. H. Prince Tu'ipelehake.

THE ROYAL SOVEREIGNS OF THE KINGDOM OF TONGA

From tenth century—Sacred Kings, Tu'i Tonga
1470–1600—Tu'i Ha'a Takalaua Kings
1600–1845—The Tu'i Kanokupolu Kings

TOPOU DYNASTY

Reign	Title	Ruler
1845–1893	King	George Topou I
1893–1918	King	George Topou II
1918–1965	Queen	Salote Topou III (Charlotte)
1965–	King	Taufa'aHau Topou IV

L

The Sultanates of the Yemens

The Yemen Arab Republic, Yemen (Sana), and the People's Democratic Republic of Yemen, Yemen (Aden), though never unified under a single rule, have more in common than a name. Both evolved into republican states with a significant amount of violence, caused as much by their own tradition of divisiveness as by foreign interference in their affairs. And when the republican coup d'etat in Sana occurred, it was clear, as Harold Ingrams notes, that "the nationalists in Aden were heart and soul with them, thus stating in up-to-date terms the ancient Arab truth that all Yemen is one." An Arab proverb quoted by virtually every writer of Yemeni history, "I am against my uncle's son, but my uncle's son and I are against the stranger," explains the cooperation between the nationalists in Aden and the republicans in Sana.

In pre-Islamic times the area that encompasses both present-day states was called Arabia Felix—happy or prosperous Arabia—by the foreigners envious of such riches as frankincense, myrrh, pearls, silks, and spices that seemed to pour forth from its lands. But even then the territory was a collection of tribes constantly battling for supremacy. To Arabs the whole area was known as al-Yaman, most probably a generalization from a local place-name. After the area lost its commercial greatness, it became prey to foreign

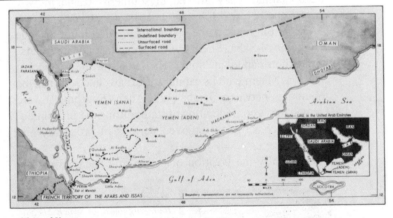

Map of Yemen

invasions but continued to be unruly even under the Islamic aegis. Various Islamic dynasties, including the Ottoman, ruled its coasts, but the forbidding terrain made foreign rule over most of the region very superficial.

PRE-ISLAMIC YEMEN

The Yemenis are very aware of their own history, and even their remotest past is preserved in folk traditions. In the late

Bronze head of a Yemen emperor from the first or second century

twentieth century, when there exist enough enmities to satisfy even the most ardent factionalist, Yemenis are able to draw from traditions over two millennia old to add further divisiveness to a society Ingrams describes as remarkable for its "genius for chaos."

Sometime in the third millennium peoples of Mesopotamia and Egypt discovered that the area of southern Arabia (the two present-day Yemens) possessed two unique and highly desirable aromatic gum resins: frankincense and myrrh.

For almost two millennia foreigners dominated and controlled this trade until descendants of Arabian migrants, attracted by the products of southern Arabia, returned from the area that is eastern Jordan and southern Iraq to their ancestral homeland. These colonists from the Fertile Crescent had benefited from the diaspora of their ancestors into Mesopotamia. They arrived in southern Arabia in two waves: one before 1400 B.C. and one about 1200 B.C.

The immigrants possessed a common culture; and the kingdoms of Saba (Sheba) with its capital at Marib, Qataban with its capital at Timna, Hadramaut with its capital at Shabwa, Maain with its capital at Qarnaw, and Ausan in the mountains between Qataban and Aden (Eudaemon) were formed into a confederation of states during the first millennium. Each kingdom enjoyed periods of prosperity and prominence.

Eventually the position of priest-king became secular-

Ancient Yemen was composed of four kingdoms, of which Sheba (Saba) was the most powerful. The others were Hadramaut, Mahrah (Tafat), and Catabania. The most famous of Sheba's sovereigns was the Queen of Sheba, named Balkis, who is well known throughout history for her visit to King Solomon's court in the tenth century B.C. to buy some of his Egyptian horses, which became the Arabian horse as it is known today. Queen Balkis is honored on this Yemen postage stamp.

ized. Under the *malik* (king) were prominent *qayls* (chieftains) who controlled the *ash'b* (sedentary tribal units).

The core of the market, frankincense and myrrh, was retained by Arabia until demand eventually evaporated when Christianity was made the religion of the Roman Empire by edict in A.D. 325 and cremations and pagan rituals, in which large amounts of frankincense had been used, were banned.

This edict created further difficulties when Christian missionaries entered Arabia in A.D. 356. Judaism, brought to southern Arabia by refugees after the destruction of Jerusalem by Titus in A.D. 70, was well-established in the south by that time. The Jews quickly made converts because the Arab's traditional enemies, Byzantium and Abyssinia, were Christian. By the fourth century there were numerous Judaized Aramaeans and Arabians, and the last Himyarite king, Dhu Naawas, was a Jew. Christianity was brought to Yemen by a monk, Theophilus Indus, at the direction of Emperor Constantius II.

The pattern of divisiveness—the hallmark of tribal chaos—and the strongly polarized geographic and religious allegiances that characterized Yemen in the twentieth century were already established in its pre-Islamic period. The ancient oligarchic kingdoms, intent only on securing wealth, had never attempted to organize or control the region further than was necessary to protect commercial interests. In preindustrial societies attitudes and values generally change little over the course of centuries, and the kingdoms of Arabia Felix (southern Arabia) left a legacy both of pride and of deep-rooted antagonisms.

Among the genealogical claims of the imams of Yemen was one that they often asserted as an argument for their legitimacy to rule over all of southern Arabia—that they were descendants of the Himyarite kings. As a symbol of the claim the imams continued to sprinkle red powder on their signatures and ciphers (*ahmar,* meaning "red," is an element in the word *Himyar*). Other customs remain from this remote period: the Grand Council of Maain, a meeting of the Banu Maain, has continued to meet for over a millennium; in Yemen (Sana) the Banu Saba and Banu Hamdan, descendants of the enemies of the Himyar, still exist in considerable numbers and remain aware of their ancient rivalry; and in Aden an important nationalist family named Luqman traces itself to Luqman ibn Ali, the king reputed to have built the well-known irrigation dam of Marib.

Popular belief held and still holds that, although all Arabs are descended from a common ancestor, Sham ibn Nuh (Shem, son of Noah), the "pure" or southern Arab (Qahtani) is descended from Qahtan ibn Abir (Joktan ben Eber), or Hud, as he is called, whereas the northern Arab (Adnani) is descended from Ismail (Ishmael) through Adnan, and many twentieth-century feuds can be traced back to it. The imams of Yemen claimed Qahtani descent as a consequence of their alleged descent from the Himyar, although they were in fact Adnanis if, as they did, they also claimed to be descendants of the Prophet Mohammed through his grandson Hassan.

THE ISLAMIC CONQUEST

Because Mohammed was aware that Yemen would not be easy to hold because the Yemeni had never been successfully united under a single rule, the Prophet chose several men to be Muslim representatives in the region. The able Khalid ibn al-Walid (Sword of God) was sent in June to quell opposition and Ali ibn Abu Talib, the son-in-law and cousin of the Prophet, in December 630. In March 632 the first *ridda*, or apostasy, in Yemen occurred. Al-Aswad, leader of a local tribe and claiming to be a prophet, murdered Badhan's son, expelled two Muslim agents, occupied Sana, and brought much of Yemen under his control. Al-Aswad was killed by one of his supporters, Qays ibn al-Mukshuh, who led the "second apostasy," which occurred after the Prophet's death and was finally put down by Abu Bakr, Mohammed's successor and the first orthodox caliph.

Uthman, the third orthodox caliph, had encountered opposition during and after his election to the caliphate. Ali had been the other contender for the caliphate, but his pietism seemed certain to dislodge vested-interest groups that perceived the more conservative Uthman as more likely to continue the policies of the previous caliph, Umar, which were in their favor.

Groups of malcontents eventually left Iraq and Egypt to seek redress at Medina. The rebels turned riotous and besieged Uthman in his home, eventually slaying him. Uthman's slayer was a Muslim and a son of the first caliph, Abu Bakr. The Muslim world was very shaken. Ali had not taken part in the siege and, therefore, was chosen caliph.

Two opponents of Ali then enlisted Aisha, a widow of the Prophet Mohammed, and together they demanded lex talionis for Uthman's death, pointing the finger at Ali. The three went to Iraq to seek support for their cause. Ali's forces engaged theirs near Basrah; Aisha's two companions were killed, and Ali was clearly victorious. Muawiyah, a kinsman of Uthman and the governor of Syria, then refused to recognize Ali and demanded the right to avenge his relative's death.

A number of leaders of the community met at Adruh in Jordan and it was announced that neither Ali nor Muawiyah should be caliph, and Abd-Allah, a son of Umar, was proposed. Both Ali and Muawiyah bided their time in their separate governorships: Muawiyah (who had been declared caliph by some of his supporters) in newly conquered Egypt and Ali in Iraq. Muawiyah contented himself with fomenting discontent among those only half committed to Ali. While praying in the mosque of Kufa, Ali was murdered by a Kharajite; Muawiyah induced Ali's son Hassan to decline any claim, and Muawiyah was declared caliph by the majority of the Islamic community. He became the first caliph of the Umayyad Dynasty.

The importance of these events for the history of Islam cannot be overemphasized. They created the greatest of the Islamic schisms, between the followers of Ali (the *shiat Ali*, known in the West as Shiites or Shias) and the upholders of Muawiyah (the Ahl al-Sunna, the Sunnis), who believe they are the followers of orthodoxy. In all Muslim countries where both sects are present, the minority tends to suffer and seldom resigns itself to the ruling power since to do so would be a matter of religious disobedience. Yemen contains both, and from the seventh through the middle of the twentieth century the events at Medina, Siffin, and Kufa would be remembered and would contribute to a state of chronic unrest among the people of the once Arabia Felix.

Ali's unnatural death ensured the future of the Shiite movement and quickened its momentum. With the single exception of the Prophet Mohammed no man has had a greater impact on Islamic history. The Shiite declaration of faith is: "There is no God but God; Mohammed is his Prophet and Ali is the Saint of God." Ali's younger son, Husain, received the title "Lord of all Martyrs" as a result of his martyrdom. Yazid I, Muawiyah's son and successor in 680, was unable to contain the opposition that his strong father had vigorously quelled. Several groups rose against him, partly out of hatred at a strong government and partly because they thought a more rigorously theocratic government would satisfy their needs. Husain refused to pay the commanded homage and fled to Mecca, where he was asked to lead the Shiites—mostly Iraqis—in a revolt against Yazid I. Ubayd Allah, governor of Kufa, discovered the plot and sent detachments to dissuade him. At Kufa Husain's band of two hundred men and women, unwilling to surrender, was finally cut down by perhaps four thousand Umayyad troops. Yazid I received Husain's head, and Husain's death on the tenth of Muharram (October 10, 680) continues to be observed as a day of mourning for all Shiites.

Husain's son escaped martyrdom, but his great-grandson Zayd ibn Ali Zain al-Abidin was to follow the family tradition. In 739 at Kufa he proclaimed himself caliph and imam (king) on the basis of hereditary succession. The

Statue of Emperor Dhamar Ali, a third century emperor

Imam Ahmad's portrait appeared on only one Yemen stamp. This issue commemorated the Universal Postal Union's first seventy-five years.

Umayyad governor dispersed the majority of Zayd's followers and engaged in battle with the remainder. Zayd was fatally wounded and his body hidden in a streambed. The governor was alerted as to the whereabouts of the gravesite and had the body disinterred and beheaded. Zayd's head was sent on a tour of Islamic realms as a warning to all potential rebels and his body was stripped naked and crucified; the cross was erected in the city garbage dump, where the corpse remained for five years.

Shortly after Zayd's death some of his followers fled to the East African coast. By 855 they were firmly established in the northern part of Yemen, which had become a haven for other Shiite sects.

The Zaydi imams of the twentieth century traced their line not from these first Zaydi immigrants but from Yahya ibn al-Husain al-Qasim al-Rassi, who arrived in 897 at Sadah from the Jabal al-Ras near Medina. Also known as al-Hadi ilal Haqq (the Guide to the Truth), Yahya firmly implanted Zaydism in the highlands of the area that is Yemen (Sana). The dynasty he founded was called Rassid after his grandfather, a sixth-generation descendant of Ali and Fatima. The kingdom itself was often referred to as the Mutawakkilite Kingdom because its imams always bore the title *al-Muta Wakil ala Allah* (he who relies on God).

By the beginning of the fourteenth century Yemen was left to its own devices and until the advent of Turkish domination was ruled mostly by Zaydi imams.

OTTOMAN DOMINATION AND THE BEGINNINGS OF YEMENI NATIONALISM

When the Ottoman Turks conquered the Mamluks in Egypt in 1517, they fell heir to areas under nominal Mamluk sovereignty on the Arabian Peninsula, including Yemen.

In 1591 al-Qasim (al-Qasim ibn Muhammad ibn Ali) was elected imam, and by the following year he had eleven provinces allied with him. By 1608, however, Qasim's tribal support was substantial enough to force the Turks to conclude a ten-year truce. Qasim decided to reside at Sana and was the first imam to do so. According to the truce terms, the imam would retain control of his provinces, the Turks would manage foreign affairs.

The British, although they had occasional tiffs with local rulers, had no political interest in the area as yet; thus they were able to pursue their commercial interests relatively unharassed, and by 1770 they controlled the largest share of the coffee trade.

Until the nineteenth century the Dutch and British had total control of Yemen's foreign trade. The imams were more than content with the arrangement. In addition to economic benefits for the imam, Europeans were becoming useful in military ways.

The situation changed abruptly in 1798 when Napoleon overthrew the Mamluk sultans of Egypt, vassals of the

The Yemen royal mansion the Palace of the Rock, Wadi Dhamar

Stamp commemorating the accession of King Ahmad to the throne of Yemen on February 18, 1948

The imam (king) of the Yemens, Yahya Mohammed ibn Hamid ad-Din, the ruler from 1904 to 1948

Ottomans. The British could not afford to allow the French to destroy their connections with India; so they quickly moved to occupy the island of Perim in the Bab al-Mandab in hopes of preventing the French from reaching the Indian Ocean. Scarcity of water compelled them to decamp to Aden, where the sultan of Lahej warmly welcomed them and even offered them Aden.

THE ESTABLISHMENT OF THE BRITISH PRESENCE

Yemen continued to be ostensibly under Ottoman rule, but it was rule characterized by benign neglect.

Aden was a small fishing port when first captured by the British in 1839, but grew to importance as a coal bunkering station with the nineteenth-century increase in steampowered ships. This growth was accelerated after the opening of the Suez Canal in 1869, when the post became important as a trading city as well. Until 1937 Aden was ruled as a part of British India, but then was transferred as a crown colony directly under the colonial office.

To protect their foothold in Aden, the British found it necessary to establish their authority in the hinterland; they eventually extended it eastward into the area known historically as the Hadramaut. The United Kingdom, influenced by the threat of the Turks occupying Yemen to the north and, following World War I, by the imams of Yemen who claimed the whole area including Aden as part of their country, began gradually to conclude treaties of protection of varying degrees of commitment with the local rulers of the hinterland. These treaties were generally short documents that gave the United Kingdom full responsibility for the conduct of the state's foreign relations and defense in return for assuming full responsibility for protecting it against other powers. From the 1930s to the early 1950s British influence increased in the area with the signing of supplementary treaties in which the rulers accepted the obligation to receive and implement British advice in matters pertaining to good government. At the same time the British signed a treaty in 1934 with the Imam of Yemen in which both sides agreed to maintain the *status quo* on the Yemen-Aden Protectorate border pending final negotiations on the location of Yemen's southern borders.

In a treaty on February 11, 1959, with six states of the Western Protectorate, the United Kingdom pledged that Aden Colony and the Aden Protectorates were to be prepared for eventual full independence. Under this treaty these six states joined together to form the Federation of Arab Amirates of the South (later changed to the Federation of South Arabia), and in the end fifteen of the sixteen states of the Western Protectorate, one of the four states of the Eastern Protectorate, and Aden Colony joined the Federation. The supplementary treaties with the individual states were canceled in 1965; the relationship of the Federation with the United Kingdom was defined by the 1959 treaty under which Britain undertook to provide financial and technical assistance and assumed full responsibility for foreign affairs and defense, although it was required to consult the Federation on foreign affairs. Aden Colony, although it acceded to the Federation on January 18, 1963

(and thereby became known as Aden State), nevertheless remained legally a crown colony with ultimate responsibility vested in the British High Commissioner.

British efforts to prepare the country for full independence by 1968 were confounded by two major factors. One was enormous difference between the busy modern port of Aden with its large foreign population and strong trade union movement and the poor, traditionally oriented, agriculturally based, small shaykhdoms and sultanates of the Protectorates. The second factor was the rising tide of Arab nationalism that opposed both British rule and the rule of the British-protected traditional rulers. This opposition developed into open terrorism in 1965 with two nationalist groups, the Front for the Liberation of Occupied South Yemen and the National Liberation Front, in competition. The British withdrew in November, 1967 from sections of Aden, from the capital of al-Ittihad, and from the Protectorate states. (Egypt, which had occupied rural areas of Yemen since 1962, withdrew on December 7, 1967.) Federal rule collapsed, with nationalist elements seizing control in the vacated areas. The British, having announced their intention of dealing with any indigenous group capable of forming a new government, met in Geneva with the National Liberation Front, which had succeeded in establishing its power at the expense of the other nationalist group. As a result of those negotiations, South Arabia, including Aden, was declared independent on November 30, 1967, and was renamed the People's Republic of Southern Yemen.

For the first time in almost two thousand years all peoples of southern Arabia were ruling themselves, without a royal family in power.

THE ROYAL SOVEREIGNS OF THE SULTANATES OF THE YEMENS

Reign	Title	Ruler
1591–1620	Imam	al-Qasim ibn Muhammad ibn Ali
1620–1644	Imam	al-Muayyad Muhammad
1644–1676	Imam	al-Mutawakkil Ismail
1676–1681	Imam	al-Mahdi Ahmad ibn al-Hasan
1681–1686	Imam	al-Hadi Muhammad
1686–1716	Imam	al-Mahdi Muhammad
1716–1726	Imam	al-Mutawakkil al-Qasim al-Husain
1726–1727	Imam	al-Mansur al-Husain
1726–1727	Imam	al-Hadi al-Majid Muhammad
1727–1728	Imam	al-Mansur al-Husain
1747–1776	Imam	al-Mandi al-Abbas
1776–1806	Imam	al-Mansur Ali
1806–1807	Imam	al-Mahdi Ahmad
1807–1841	Imam	al-Mansur Ali
1841–1845	Imam	al-Mahdi al-Qasim
1856–1862	Imam	Muhammad Yahya
1872–1890—Turkish Rule		
1891–1891	Imam	Muhammad Yahya Hamid ad-Din
1891–1904—Interregnum		
1904–1948	Imam	Yahya Muhammad ibn Muhammad (Hamid ad-Din)
1948–1962	Imam	Ahmad An-Nasir li-din Allah
1962–1970	Imam	Muhammad Mansur billah
1962—Became a republic		

The Palace of the Rock, Dar-al-Hajar, on two Yemen postage stamps

Front and side views of imam's new palace in Sana

Index